Atomic Transactions

The Morgan Kaufmann Series in Data Management Systems
Series Editor, Jim Gray

Atomic Transactions

Nancy Lynch
Michael Merritt
William Weihl
Alan Fekete

Morgan Kaufmann Publishers
San Mateo, California

Senior Editor: Bruce M. Spatz
Production Manager: Yonie Overton
Assistant Editor: Douglas Sery
Copyeditor: Barbara Ferenstein
Composition: Ed Sznyter, Babel Press
Design (Cover and Display Type): Ross Carron Design
Proofreader: Gary Morris
Printer: Courier Corporation

Morgan Kaufmann Publishers, Inc.
Editorial Office:
2929 Campus Drive, Suite 260
San Mateo, CA 94403

Library of Congress Cataloging-in-Publication Data is available for this book.
ISBN 1-55860-104-X

DEDICATION

Nancy Lynch
To Mary, Patrick and Dennis

Michael Merritt
To my grandmother, Michele Seguin

William Weihl
To Lisa

Alan Fekete
To my parents and grandmother

FOREWORD

by Jim Gray
Digital Equipment Corporation

Transaction processing gives a beautiful example of the synergy between computer science theory and practice. Sometimes theory has led practice, and sometimes the practitioners have built systems that either redefined the problem or took a new approach. Lynch, Merritt, Weihl, and Fekete put theory back in the lead with this book.

They present a fully general model for concurrent and distributed systems—the I/O automaton model. Using this model, they formalize and analyze the classical techniques and theories of transaction processing: serializability, logging, locking, nesting, timestamping, orphan handling, and replication. Each concept or technique is presented within a uniform and formal context. The technique is analyzed and then generalizations of the classic results are presented. These generalizations often derive from the more general and more precise model of concurrency offered by the I/O automaton model.

In addition to presenting the classic ideas, the book explores new areas by using I/O automata to analyze the concurrency properties of commonly used data structures, notably counters, queues, and stacks. In addition, it explores the subtleties of data replication and the corresponding issue of quorum consensus. These latter results show the power of the I/O automaton model to analyze problems that do not fit the classic models.

Concurrent and distributed systems have subtle behaviors. Understanding them requires a clear model and tools to reason about the model. This book provides such a model and, by example, shows how to reason about algorithms expressed within the model. Is all this rigor really needed? Why not just build distributed systems rather than think about them first? These questions have two answers. (1) Experienced system builders believe that a clear model and careful analysis are essential to building workable and maintainable distributed systems. Those who have hacked a distributed system together without much forethought now regret it. Hacked distributed systems have capricious behavior and are impossible to maintain or evolve. (2) This book takes extreme care to make the rigor accessible and palatable. It minimizes notation, and it is built around a set of intuitive examples drawn from the fields of database systems and data structures. Nonetheless, it presents a very general model of concurrent systems and presents techniques for decomposing the elements of a distributed system into I/O automata that can be individually analyzed.

Theory should be beautiful mathematics with simple assumptions giving rise to elegant theorems with insightful proofs. Alternatively, one wants a theory that, although fairly complex, provides a useful tool for the design and analysis of useful artifacts. Rarely is a theory both elegant and relevant. It seems to me that the theory of I/O automaton qualifies on both grounds. The model and composition rules are simple and intuitive. The I/O automaton model elegantly describes the classic algorithms used to construct concurrent and distributed systems. These algorithms took decades to discover and are still difficult to grasp. The I/O automaton model provides a useful tool to understand, analyze, and generalize these algorithms.

This book provides a very accessible introduction to the I/O automaton model and its applications. Time invested in understanding the model will be well rewarded by providing a very general model of concurrent and distributed execution. This model in turn gives rise to more powerful algorithms.

C O N T E N T S

PREFACE

What We Do

A *transaction* is a single logical operation performed on a database. The two roots of the word, trans- and action, suggest the key insight of acting *across* a boundary or interface *between* two parties. This book develops a theory for transactions, focusing on the interface between the user or application requesting them and the database that executes them.

The most important requirement for the correct execution of transactions is that they be *atomic*—that is, they appear to the user as single, indivisible units of interaction. This usage is in keeping with the original Greek philosophies, in which atoms were the indivisible elements of the universe. But much as modern atomic theories propose a detailed structure within physical atoms, we explore structures that permit transactions to be nested (much as atoms contain electrons, protons, and neutrons, which similarly contain yet smaller particles).

Atomic transactions are a useful abstraction for programming concurrent and distributed data processing systems. This book explores different ways a system can be designed to provide an atomic transaction service. It is concerned both with presenting a number of the most important algorithms used and also with showing how to prove them correct. To do this, it presents a formal model for reasoning about atomic transactions. This model allows careful statement of the correctness conditions satisfied by transaction-processing algorithms, as well as clear and concise description of such algorithms. It also serves as a framework for carrying out rigorous correctness proofs.

Distributed systems in general, and transaction systems in particular, can be very complex. Our goal in this book is to show how to manage this complexity by viewing systems at multiple levels of abstraction. At the highest level is the simple user-level view that treats transactions as atomic units of computation. At lower levels are more detailed descriptions of the system that admit the possibility of concurrency and failures, and include concurrency control and recovery algorithms. The higher levels serve as *specifications* for the lower levels; we show how to prove that the properties of the higher level follow from the details of the lower levels. We use a formal model for describing and analyzing systems because their behaviors can be subtle, and informal reasoning can easily lead one astray.

The formal model is used to describe and prove the correctness of a wide variety of important transaction-processing algorithms. These include locking algorithms, timestamp-based algorithms, hybrid algorithms that combine locking and timestamping, optimistic algorithms, algorithms for managing *orphan* transactions (those that will never be able to make lasting changes to the database), and algorithms for manipulating replicated data. The correctness proofs for these algorithms rest on a rich and general theory. The authors hope that you will be able to use this theory to understand and verify additional algorithms of interest.

Intended Audience

This book is intended for several types of readers. Of course, the authors expect you to have some interest in data processing systems, databases, or programming languages for distributed systems. The book should provide you with a better understanding both of the semantics of atomic transactions and of many of the important algorithms supporting this abstraction.

For the more pragmatically inclined reader, we hope to provide practical, intellectual tools for helping you to understand transaction-processing algorithms more clearly. You may already be familiar with transaction-processing systems, but may wish to learn techniques for expressing your knowledge precisely.

Or you may be hoping to build a transaction-processing system in which you need to combine algorithms that deal with different problems, such as concurrency control and replication. We have written this book to introduce practitioners to important tools and concepts for building systems. It is not necessary to study the proofs on the first reading as the concepts and examples in the chapters are useful in themselves. To support such a reading, the results are presented in short, digestible increments. Each expresses a useful fact about a system; for example, it may give a relationship that always holds between different variables, or it may describe conditions on each component that lead to correct functioning of the whole system. Thus, we invite you to concentrate on the *statements* of the results; the proofs can be returned to for further clarification.

For the more theoretically inclined reader, we hope to provide a means of learning about transaction processing in a setting that is based on a sound mathematical foundation and that does not require learning many details of specific computing systems.

This book is also intended as an extensive case study of the use of rigorous techniques for analyzing complex computing systems. Under the name *formal methods*, there is growing interest in the use of mathematical or logical descriptions of such systems. Where brief accounts may be unconvincing, because only trivial examples are given, we hope to demonstrate that mathematical models can *scale up* to provide understanding about systems that are large enough to be realistic.

The book is mostly self-contained and can be read without prior knowledge of transactions or of the formal framework. The only requirement is a general familiarity with basic concepts of computer systems (at the level of an undergraduate course in operating systems), and a background in the basic language and techniques of discrete mathematics (including operations on sets; the use of set theory to express relations, functions, and orders; and proof methods such as proof by contradiction, case analysis, and mathematical induction).

Courses

This book can be used as the basis for individual reading, or for a one-semester, graduate-level course on transaction processing or on formal methods.

For a course on transaction processing, this book should be supplemented with material covering topics such as performance analysis, query optimization, deadlock detection, crash recovery, and distributed commit. A reference for this purpose is the book by Gray and Reuter [42], or papers from the research literature such as those in [108]. Depending on the balance desired between theory and implementation techniques, the instructor may wish to skip many of the correctness proofs for the various algorithms, and also the whole of Section 5.6.

For a course on formal methods, it is also important to cover liveness issues and alternative models. Detailed references can be found in Section 2.10. With this emphasis, the instructor may wish to skip Chapters 7, 8, and 10, which do not present proof techniques different from those in Chapter 6.

Style

In this book, systems are presented as collections of interacting components. Each component is modeled formally as an automaton consisting of a set of states and rules for moving between states. In a real system, each component might be implemented as a process, executing a body of code compiled from a high-level programming language. The correspondence between the automaton's transition rules and the process code may not be immediately obvious, but we trust that you will see (from a few examples) how to model ideas that are familiar in common programming languages. A real system might instead be built in other ways, for example by having a single process executing code that performs in interleaved fashion the functions of all of the components. In this case, the functionality is still most easily understood by dividing it up into pieces each performing a separate task using only a part of the system state.

The correctness of each system is expressed by a mathematical theorem. To make the results more general, to aid system designers in developing new correct systems, and to make the proofs more understandable, the correctness arguments are often broken into several pieces. Specifically, mathematical definitions are stated for some properties of system components, and then a theorem is proven that says that any system is correct provided all of its components have the appropriate properties. Examples of components that satisfy the required properties are presented separately.

The proof of each main result (theorem) is presented as a collection of lemmas. Each lemma gives a small piece of information about the algorithm or system, and each is proved rather simply, either from the transition rules of the automata involved, or from previously stated lemmas. We have tried to avoid long and difficult proofs in favor of increasing the number of pieces of each proof. Although this may tend to increase the total length of proofs of some theorems, we believe that it should help your understanding by breaking the proofs up into comprehensible pieces. We do not expect that you will wish to read all the proofs of all the lemmas (many being detailed case analyses); rather, you may choose to read only the statements of the lemmas and enough of the proofs to convince yourself that the results are true.

The most important results are the *theorems*, while *propositions* are facts of less intrinsic interest. The term *lemma* is reserved for minor results, typically used in subsequent proofs or consisting of straightforward checks, and definitions have the properties suggested by the name.

The definitions, techniques, and algorithms are illustrated by examples. These are not needed for later material in the book (except perhaps for other examples) and may be skipped without loss of essential information. However, we recommend that you use the examples to check your understanding of the material in the main text. For instance, when a function is defined, an example may calculate its value in a given situation. Attempting to apply the definition to the example independently might lead you to a mistaken assumption or other weakness in your understanding.

Acknowledgements

The authors are grateful for the help of many people who have worked on this and related material, including Jim Aspnes, Ranjan Das, Ken Goldman, Nancy Griffeth, Maurice Herlihy, Tiko Kameda, John Lee, Eliot Moss, and Sharon Perl.

We also thank the many others who have contributed comments and suggestions, including Paul Barth, Adrian Colbrook, Daniel Jackson, John Keen, Dean Kuo, Dave Langworthy, Alberto Oliart, Jeff Sanders, and members of MIT's 6.852 class in Fall, 1988. We have had the benefit of careful reviews by Catriel Beeri, Jim Gray, Vassos Hadzilacos, Maurice Herlihy, Peter Lyngbaek, Gerhard Weikum, and Willy

Zwaenepoel. Our thanks also to Anna Wiseman, for translating the book from one text formatting language to another and for printing countless copies for us.

We especially acknowledge Bruce Spatz of Morgan Kaufmann, whose patience, unfailing optimism, and insightful suggestions have contributed greatly to the book, and to our enjoyment of the time spent writing it. We gratefully acknowledge production assistance from Yonie Overton and from others at Morgan Kaufmann, including Barbara Ferenstein, Ross Carron, and Ed Sznyter.

Many institutions have contributed significantly to this project, supporting both the original research and its compilation into this volume. We would like to thank AT&T, DARPA, DEC, IBM, MIT, NSF, ONR, and Sydney University.[1]

Nancy Lynch
Michael Merritt
William Weihl
Alan Fekete

---

[1]Grant support includes the following: ARO: DAAG29-84-K-0058; AT&T: LTR DTD 9/22/87, LTR DTD 9/21/92; DARPA: N00014-89-J-1988, N00014-92-J-4033, N00014-91-J-1698; DRAPER LABS: DL-H-441640; NSF: 8306854-MCS, 8302391-A02-DCR, CCR-8611442, 8915206-CCR, SUB-CONTRACT 1-G-36-63, CCR-8716884; ONR: N00014-83-K-0125, N00014-85-K-0168, N00014-91-J-1046.

1

INTRODUCTION

1.1 Distributed Systems

The early world of computing consisted of isolated uniprocessors, to which users submitted their programs for execution. Later came timeshared systems, in which a single mainframe was shared among many users, so that it appeared to each user that he or she had access to a dedicated machine. Continued evolution has produced distributed systems, in which users interact with processors that are networked together with many other processors.

Distributed systems are now commonplace. Some examples that most people have encountered are electronic mail systems, distributed databases (e.g., for airline reservations), communication networks, office systems, banking systems, point-of-sale terminals, and real-time process control systems (e.g., for controlling aircraft or factories).

There are a variety of reasons for the increasing importance of distributed computing systems. Among them are fault tolerance, expandability, and the need to merge existing facilities. Distributed systems can be more fault-tolerant than traditional architectures: a distributed system may be constructed so it continues functioning despite the failure of some of its components. For example, data might be stored redundantly on all the machines, so it remains accessible unless *every* site fails (an event much less probable than the failure of one site). By contrast, data stored on a single-site large machine is inaccessible if that single machine fails. Graceful expansion is another important characteristic of distributed computing systems. To obtain a ten percent increase in computing power in a system of many interconnected small, cheap machines, one need only buy ten percent more machines and connect them to the existing network. By contrast, if a single large mainframe is at the limits of its capacity, the only relief lies in buying a complete new system and porting all needed software and data to the new machine. Finally, distributed systems often arise when separate parts of an organization have established (single-site) computing facilities independently, and later want to connect these together, so that they can exchange data to behave as a collective computing resource.

Distributed systems are built of many machines with a combination of non-volatile (disk) and volatile (main) memories, and are subject to various kinds of failures. Processors can crash, losing the contents of their volatile memories, can proceed at erratic speeds, or can simply stop without warning. The communication media in distributed systems are also subject to failures, resulting in loss, reordering, and duplication of messages.

Distributed systems are complex: they have a large number of components, many activities can be going on concurrently, and components can fail independently. To help cope with this complexity, a variety of programming constructs have been developed over the last decade and a half, ranging from low-level network primitives that allow messages to be sent and received to high-level programming language mechanisms that mask many of the complexities caused by failures and concurrency.

This book focuses on distributed data-processing systems. This category includes, in addition to traditional database systems, any kind of distributed system that manages long-lived and valuable data: banking, airline reservations, inventory control, and payroll management systems are in this class but factory control systems, for example, are not. This book is about one particular and very important abstraction that can be used to program such systems—the notion of an *atomic transaction*.

1.2 Atomic Transactions for Distributed Systems

In order to understand the notion of atomic transactions, it is useful first to consider a distributed data-processing system from the point of view of the system's users. Later chapters consider how this view can be supported by efficient implementations.

1.2.1 Atomic Databases

Arguably the simplest kind of atomic transaction-processing system, an *atomic data-base* consists of a single monolithic component. Consider a high-level view of a distributed system, consisting of two components, the "outside world" and the "database." The outside world is composed of all the users of the system, who may be working at different locations. The users interact with the database by submitting requests to perform operations on particular objects, and getting back reports of the outcomes for those operations. There are two possible outcomes. First, an operation can complete successfully; in this case, it has *committed*. The report of the commit of an operation contains information about the results of the operation. Alternatively, an operation can fail to complete; in this case, it has *aborted*. Because the reasons for failure are generally implementation-dependent, the report of the abort of an operation is assumed to return no other information.

The users of such a system expect that, at all times, the database will reflect all the results of committed operations, and none of the effects of aborted operations; moreover, the operations that commit are executed one at a time, without interference. These properties characterize the notion of an atomic database. Note, however, that the *state of the database* is not directly observable by users. Thus, the requirement on the system design is actually that the responses users receive from the database are consistent with this expectation.

Note that there is some ambiguity in the determination of a correct response in the case of operations that are requested concurrently (more precisely, where the second request occurs before the first operation has received a response). In such cases, we say that it is acceptable for the operations to appear to occur in either order.

EXAMPLE 1.2.1 Bank Account Operations

The user's view of the database might consist of a collection of bank account objects, each account object X supporting operations **DEPOSIT**(X, k), **WITHDRAW**(X, k), and **BALANCE**(X), where k is a number of dollars. The users submit requests to perform **DEPOSIT**, **WITHDRAW**, and **BALANCE** operations. The database later responds with reports of the outcomes. In all cases, the system reports to the user whether the operations have committed or aborted. Suppose that overdrafts are not allowed, so that a **WITHDRAW** operation has the effect of updating the account balance only if the account balance is at least as great as the amount requested. Hence, when the system reports to the user that a **WITHDRAW** operation has committed, the report should notify the user whether there were sufficient funds. In the case of the commit of a **BAL-ANCE** operation, the system reports to the user the current amount of money in the designated account. Any of these operations might abort, for many reasons (the user might hit a "quit" button, there might be a communication failure, or communication delays might cause a timer to expire). Since these causes are implementation-dependent, and might also depend on concurrent activity in the system, an abort does not let the user know the reason the operation failed to complete.

For the database to be atomic, the responses given by the system to **BALANCE** operations should be the total amount of money deposited in earlier committed **DEPOSIT** operations, minus the total amount of money removed by earlier committed **WITHDRAW** operations, on the same account.

In this example, if a **BALANCE**(X) is requested just after the request for a **DEPOSIT**(X, k) operation, we do not constrain whether the **DEPOSIT** should be considered to occur before or after the **BALANCE**. That is, the reported response to the **BALANCE** operation can reflect either all previous operations plus the extra **DEPOSIT**, or just the previous operations but not the final **DEPOSIT**.

User Views and Serial Systems

The atomic database concept is a condition on the user view of the system only; it does not explicitly constrain the implementation. For example, an implementation of the banking system described above need not keep for each account a single record, containing the amount currently in that account. Rather, it is possible to replicate the contents of a single account X among several locations in a system distributed over an unreliable network. Also, the amount of money in an account might be kept as an explicit total or as the sum of several smaller amounts, or simply as a history of past **DEPOSIT** and **WITHDRAW** operations. The correctness condition we wish to preserve is simply that the system *appear to the user* as if it were an atomic database.

One way of stating the definition of an atomic database is that interactions of the users with the database should look like interactions with a particular *serial system*. A serial system is one that maintains one internal copy of all of the data. Each operation that commits is performed atomically on the internal copy of the data, *at some time between the request for that operation and the report of the commit of the operation.* The operations that abort are not performed. There can be delays between the time when an operation is requested and when it is actually performed, and between when an operation is performed and when its results are reported. Thus, if two operations are requested at approximately the same time, and later both have their commits reported at around the same time, the operations might be performed in either order.

EXAMPLE 1.2.2   Runs of the Banking Database

The following is an example of a sequence of requests and responses that is correct for the atomic database described in Example 1.2.1. Assume that each of two accounts, X and Y, starts with $100.

Each request or response is shown with several associated values in parentheses. The first item in each set of parentheses identifies the individual operation instance. Other values record account names, withdrawal amounts, balances, and notices of insufficient funds; for example, **REQUEST_DEPOSIT**$(3, Y, \$100)$ indicates a **REQUEST_DEPOSIT** action on account Y, with $100 as the amount being deposited. (Sequences run vertically on the page; indentation is used as a visual aid to help identify related actions.)

REQUEST_DEPOSIT$(1, X, \$25),$
REPORT_COMMIT_DEPOSIT$(1),$
    REQUEST_WITHDRAW$(2, X, \$5),$
        REQUEST_DEPOSIT$(3, Y, \$100),$
    REPORT_ABORT_WITHDRAW$(2),$
        REQUEST_BALANCE$(4, X),$
        REPORT_COMMIT_DEPOSIT$(3),$
            REQUEST_BALANCE$(5, Y),$
        REPORT_COMMIT_BALANCE$(4, \$125),$
            REPORT_COMMIT_BALANCE$(5, \$225)$

This reflects the apparent order of committed operations: 1, 4, 3, 5.

If, in the sequence above, the events **REPORT_COMMIT_DEPOSIT**(3) and **REQUEST_BALANCE**$(5, Y)$ were interchanged, then the final operation would be permitted to return either $125 or $225, because either response is consistent with all operations having been performed at some time during their respective intervals. That is, the following is a correct sequence:

REQUEST_DEPOSIT$(1, X, \$25),$
REPORT_COMMIT_DEPOSIT$(1),$
    REQUEST_WITHDRAW$(2, X, \$5),$
        REQUEST_DEPOSIT$(3, Y, \$100),$
    REPORT_ABORT_WITHDRAW$(2),$
        REQUEST_BALANCE$(4, X),$
            REQUEST_BALANCE$(5, Y),$
        REPORT_COMMIT_DEPOSIT$(3),$

REPORT_COMMIT_BALANCE(4, $125),
REPORT_COMMIT_BALANCE(5, $125),

reflecting the order 1, 4, 5, 3; and so is this:

REQUEST_DEPOSIT(1, X, $25),
REPORT_COMMIT_DEPOSIT(1),
REQUEST_WITHDRAW(2, X, $5),
REQUEST_DEPOSIT(3, Y, $100),
REPORT_ABORT_WITHDRAW(2),
REQUEST_BALANCE(4, X),
REQUEST_BALANCE(5, Y),
REPORT_COMMIT_DEPOSIT(3),
REPORT_COMMIT_BALANCE(4, $125),
REPORT_COMMIT_BALANCE(5, $225),

reflecting the order 1, 4, 3, 5.

In contrast, here are three sequences that are not correct. First, the sequence:

REQUEST_DEPOSIT(1, X, $25),
REPORT_COMMIT_DEPOSIT(1),
REQUEST_WITHDRAW(2, X, $5),
REQUEST_DEPOSIT(3, Y, $100),
REPORT_COMMIT_WITHDRAW(2),
REQUEST_BALANCE(4, X),
REPORT_COMMIT_DEPOSIT(3),
REPORT_COMMIT_BALANCE(4, $125)

is not correct since the response to the **BALANCE** operation does not reflect the successful **WITHDRAW** that preceded it.

Second, the sequence:

REQUEST_DEPOSIT(1, X, $25),
REPORT_COMMIT_DEPOSIT(1),
REQUEST_WITHDRAW(2, X, $5),
REQUEST_DEPOSIT(3, Y, $100),
REPORT_ABORT_WITHDRAW(2),
REQUEST_BALANCE(4, X),
REPORT_COMMIT_DEPOSIT(3),
REPORT_COMMIT_BALANCE(4, $120)

is not correct, as the response to the **BALANCE** operation reflects the **WITHDRAW** despite the fact that the **WITHDRAW** aborted.

Third, the sequence:

REQUEST_DEPOSIT$(1, X, \$20)$,
REPORT_COMMIT_DEPOSIT(1),
　　REQUEST_WITHDRAW$(2, X, \$65)$,
　　　　REQUEST_WITHDRAW$(3, X, \$60)$,
　　REPORT_COMMIT_WITHDRAW(2),
　　　　REPORT_COMMIT_WITHDRAW(3)

is not correct, since it is not possible for a total of \$125 to be successfully withdrawn from an account containing only \$120.

One of the two withdrawals must return with a report of insufficient funds, as in the following correct sequence:

REQUEST_DEPOSIT$(1, X, \$20)$,
REPORT_COMMIT_DEPOSIT(1),
　　REQUEST_WITHDRAW$(2, X, \$65)$,
　　　　REQUEST_WITHDRAW$(3, X, \$60)$,
　　REPORT_COMMIT_WITHDRAW$(2, $ *"insufficient funds"*$)$,
　　　　REPORT_COMMIT_WITHDRAW(3).

The atomic database interface is very simple for users to understand. It indicates to the users exactly which operations have been performed (that is, committed) and guarantees that all committed operations are executed in their entirety and without interference from other concurrently executing operations. Moreover, it guarantees that the order in which the operations appear to have been performed is compatible with the order of requests and reports for the operations. The task of programming a distributed system can be greatly simplified if the system presents an atomic database interface to its users.

This subsection closes with another, very simple, example of an atomic database: a *read/write register*.

EXAMPLE 1.2.3　Read/Write Register

A read/write register stores a single number; it supports operations of **READ** and **WRITE**(v), where v is an integer. The atomic database property specifies that those reads and writes that commit should appear to happen in some serial order that is compatible with the order in which the operations are requested and return. Of course, this simple type of object is a very degenerate form of atomic database, but it does fit the general definition.

The following sequence of requests and responses is correct for an atomic read/write register with an initial value of 0.

REQUEST_WRITE(1, 30),
  REQUEST_READ(2),
REPORT_COMMIT_WRITE(1),
  REPORT_COMMIT_READ(2, 30),
    REQUEST_WRITE(3, 50),
      REQUEST_READ(4),
        REQUEST_WRITE(5, 60),
        REPORT_ABORT_WRITE(5),
      REPORT_COMMIT_READ(4, 50),
    REPORT_COMMIT_WRITE(3).

Note that the **READ** operation with index 4 reports the value written by the **WRITE** operation with index 3, even though the **WRITE** operation does not report its commit until after the **READ** operation does.

A slightly more complicated atomic database can also be constructed of a collection of read/write registers, each viewed as a separate object with its own read and write operations. This is the sort of database most commonly studied in the database concurrency control literature. However, users typically do not interact with such databases directly in terms of read and write operations on individual registers; rather, users submit *transactions*, more sophisticated and complex queries or commands that represent collections of read and write operations on several objects. The users expect to observe atomicity in terms of these transactions, not in terms of the component operations. This idea is explored in the next subsection.

1.2.2 Transactions

Atomic databases typically provide a repertoire of simple operations from which more complex programs (called transactions) can be constructed. Transactions provide the interactions that users actually want. This style of system design is flexible, in that when users discover a need for additional functionality (that is, extra operations, or altered semantics for operations) this can be provided by writing new programs that use the same simple operations, rather than re-implementing the entire system.

EXAMPLE 1.2.4   Bank Transactions

As an example of building transactions from simple atomic operations, again assume that the database consists of a set of accounts with the operations listed earlier (**DEPOSIT**, **WITHDRAW**, and **BALANCE**). Suppose that the users want to use operations of the form **TRANSFER**(X, Y, k), which are supposed to move k dollars from X to Y, and also **AUDIT**, which is supposed to report the total amount of money in all the accounts. These operations can be provided by performing sequences of the basic operations already provided. One might program each **TRANSFER**(X, Y, k) operation as consisting of a **BALANCE**(X) operation to check that there is sufficient money in account X, followed (if the balance is sufficient) by **WITHDRAW**(X, k) and **DEPOSIT**(Y, k) operations, which could run concurrently. Also, we can write an **AUDIT** operation as consisting of a concurrent set of **BALANCE** operations, one for each account in the database. The decomposition of a desired database operation into a structured collection of existing simple operations is called a transaction.

Transaction Atomicity

Although a transaction consists of several lower-level operations, the meaning of a transaction is supposed to be that it is performed atomically. That is, if a transaction commits, it should appear to the outside world as if the *entire collection* of operations comprising the transaction is performed consecutively, with no intervening operations of other transactions, and without getting part way through and stopping. This consecutive ordering must respect any ordering required by the transaction itself; for instance, in the **TRANSFER** example above, the **BALANCE** operation must be ordered before the **WITHDRAW** and **DEPOSIT** operations, which may follow in either order. If a transaction aborts, the effect should be as if none of the operations comprising the transaction were performed. Moreover, the order in which the transactions appear to execute should itself be compatible with the order of transaction requests and reports. In other words, the system should be an atomic database, with the operations being the entire transactions (not the individual lower-level operations that compose them). Thinking of the atomic database as presenting the appearance of a serial system (as described earlier), it should appear to the user as if the entire sequence of operations comprising each committed transaction is performed at some particular time during the interval between the transaction's request and its report. Thus, the database system with lower-level operations (on which the transactions act) must provide to the transactions not only the atomicity of the individual lower-level operations, but also the *transaction* semantics that enable the higher-level (programmed) operations to be atomic.

EXAMPLE 1.2.5   AUDIT Transactions

Consider, for example, an **AUDIT** transaction. Looked at from the point of view of the outside world, the **AUDIT** is supposed to return the current total amount of money in the bank. Although it can be expanded into a collection of **BALANCE** operations on various accounts (followed by an internal computation to generate a report), the intended meaning is that the entire audit should be performed at a single time between its request and report. Since the data processing system under consideration includes both **TRANSFER** and **AUDIT** transactions, it is quite important that each transaction be performed as if at a single point in time, or else a wrong answer could result. Consider the following sequence of steps. (Assume there are only two accounts, X and Y, and that they both begin with $100.)

> **REQUEST_TRANSFER**(1, X, Y, $50),
>   **REQUEST_AUDIT**(2),
> **PERFORM_BALANCE**(1, X, $100),
> **PERFORM_WITHDRAW**(1, X, $50),
>   **PERFORM_BALANCE**(2, X, $50),
>   **PERFORM_BALANCE**(2, Y, $100),
> **PERFORM_DEPOSIT**(1, Y, $50),
> **REPORT_COMMIT_TRANSFER**(1),
>   **REPORT_COMMIT_AUDIT**(2, $150).

Here, the **TRANSFER** and **AUDIT** transactions are explicitly broken down into their lower-level steps. (For any lower-level operation *Op*, **PERFORM_Op** indicates the performance of operation *Op* on the database, and it records the return value, if any.) Each lower-level step is tagged with the same identifier as its parent transaction. Now the **AUDIT** transaction returns a value of $150 for the total amount of money in the bank—it has missed the $50 that is transferred between accounts during the audit. Likewise, an execution can be constructed that counts the $50 twice. The problem is that the lower-level steps that comprise the **AUDIT** and **TRANSFER** transactions are interleaved.

An example of correct behavior of this system is:

REQUEST_TRANSFER(1, X, Y, $50),
   REQUEST_AUDIT(2),
PERFORM_BALANCE(1, X, $100),
PERFORM_WITHDRAW(1, X, $50),
PERFORM_DEPOSIT(1, Y, $50),
   PERFORM_BALANCE(2, X, $50),
   PERFORM_BALANCE(2, Y, $150),
REPORT_COMMIT_TRANSFER(1),
   REPORT_COMMIT_AUDIT(2, $200).

Here, the internal steps of each transaction are performed consecutively (although steps may intervene between the request of a transaction and the performance of its steps and between the performance of its steps and the report).

Another source of potential problems is the failure of some lower-level operations. For example, consider the following sequence:

REQUEST_TRANSFER(1, X, Y, $50),
PERFORM_BALANCE(1, X, $100),
PERFORM_WITHDRAW(1, X, $50),
REPORT_ABORT_TRANSFER(1),
   REQUEST_BALANCE(2, X).

This describes the situation where the user requests a **TRANSFER**(X, Y, $50) transaction, and the **WITHDRAW**(X, $50) occurs successfully but then the transaction fails to complete (perhaps because of a machine failure, perhaps because the user cancels it, perhaps because the **DEPOSIT**(Y, $50) aborts). The **TRANSFER** must then abort, since it is not possible for it to commit and appear as if the whole sequence was correctly performed atomically. Thus, when the **BALANCE** operation occurs, it ought to return the initial value in the account ($100), so the aborted **TRANSFER** transaction seems not to have happened. However, the **WITHDRAW** operation (that forms part of the **TRANSFER**) did succeed, so the account balance has fallen to $50. Thus, the system must find a way in which the **WITHDRAW** operation can be *undone* and the account balance restored to its former value before the response to the **BALANCE** is calculated.

These examples show the difficulties faced by a system designer who wishes to provide a flexible database system, where the operations provided by the database itself will be extended by transactions to provide extra functions to the users. The main emphasis of this book is on mechanisms to guarantee to users that the operations provided by transactions will present the interface of an atomic database.

Atomicity   versus   Consistency

The historical motivation for transactions was not to provide the appearance of atomic operations, but rather to assist in maintaining the consistency of information stored in a database. A subset of the possible states of the database is designated as the set of *consistent* states: these states generally satisfy some constraints involving relationships between the values of different objects in the database. For example, in a banking system, there might be a **TOTAL** object, whose value is always supposed to be equal to the sum of the values in all the accounts. Another common consistency condition is *referential integrity*: one object should contain as its value the key (identifying value) of another object. For example, a bank database might contain for each account one value representing the Social Security number of the account's owner, used to index into a collection of customer records. Referential integrity would be violated if an account contained a Social Security number that did not have a customer record associated with it. It is considered important for the database states to remain consistent, even in the face of modifications by programs that access the data, since otherwise the database state will not be as a sensible reflection of a state of the world.

Like atomicity, maintaining consistency is difficult because the hardware can fail, programs can be interrupted, and users can access the database concurrently. But each transaction can be written to "preserve consistency." That is, each transaction expects to see a consistent state of the database, and to recreate that consistency after making its modifications, provided it runs to completion and without interference by other transactions. (The intermediate states produced by a transaction during execution of its individual operations need not necessarily be consistent, however.) If each transaction preserves consistency, then any serial execution of transactions without failures (i.e., where each transaction runs to completion) also preserves consistency. Since any behavior exhibited by an atomic database is equivalent to a serial execution without failures, any such behavior also preserves consistency.

Although much of the database literature focuses on this condition, the preservation of consistency is an inappropriate correctness condition for the general theory of transactions developed in this book. For example, it is not applicable to systems that contain multiple copies of data, or to any system in which the implementation state is more than a straightforward representation of the user view of the data. Preservation of consistency makes even less sense as a correctness condition when transactions can be *nested*; that is, when an operation that is part of a transaction is itself implemented as a transaction.

Furthermore, consistency alone is an insufficient guarantee for most applications.

Consider, for example, a trivial database system in which no transaction ever actually modifies the database. Such a database is always in a consistent state (assuming that the initial state is consistent), but it is not very useful. A useful system should also guarantee something about the relationships between different transactions, or between transactions and the database state.

A satisfactory correctness condition should apply to diverse implementations and should be adequate for any user. In place of consistency, which is concerned with only the *state* of the database, this book defines correctness in terms of the *interactions* seen by the user. The stated guarantees are entirely in terms of the request-report behavior of transactions; they say that the users only observe behavior that they could observe in a serial system.

Transactions as General Programming Primitives

In addition to their role in organizing user-database interactions, transactions have been explored as a way of organizing programs for distributed systems. Here, their purpose is not just to keep the state of the database consistent, but also to provide the programmer with mechanisms that simplify the development of correct programs. The complexity of potential interactions among concurrent activities and the multitude of failure modes that can occur in distributed systems make it harder to reason about distributed programs than centralized programs. Transactions help by allowing the programmer to view a complex piece of code as atomic: it appears to happen instantaneously, and it happens either completely or not at all. Of course, the added convenience for the applications programmer means added difficulty for the designer of the system, who must implement the transaction interface efficiently, in the face of the extra costs (e.g., communication delays) incurred by distribution.

Transactions as General Programs

Historically, transactions have often been described as just sequences of operations—essentially, straight-line programs. However, it is important to consider a more general notion of transaction that allows concurrent invocation of operations and conditional branches and other control flow statements. For example, depending on the results of some of the early lower-level operations, different later operations might be performed.

In fact, you can think of transactions as being fairly arbitrary programs, capable of using the results of previous operations to decide what to do next.

EXAMPLE 1.2.6 Overdraft Protection

Transactions having both concurrency and conditional branching have already been illustrated in Example 1.2.4. As another example, we here consider a banking system in which a user may maintain two accounts, one a checking account (called ACCT_CHK) and one a savings account (called ACCT_SVNG). In this case there might be a use for a new kind of **WITHDRAW** operation, which we will call **WITHDRAW_OD**(ACCT, k), that withdraws the money from ACCT_CHK if possible, but uses ACCT_SVNG if necessary. **WITHDRAW_OD**(ACCT, k) might be implemented by a transaction program that first performs a **BALANCE**(ACCT_CHK) operation and then, if the result *bal* returned is at least k, performs a **WITHDRAW**(ACCT_CHK, k) operation and then commits. If, however, the balance *bal* is insufficient, **WITHDRAW_OD**(ACCT, k) instead invokes **BALANCE**(ACCT_SVNG) and, if the total balance in the two accounts is adequate, concurrently performs **WITHDRAW**(ACCT_CHK, *bal*) and **WITHDRAW**(ACCT_SVNG, $k - bal$), committing when both withdrawals have succeeded. If the combined balance is too low, the program commits, returning a notification of insufficient funds.

In commercial transaction-processing systems, the transactions are usually programs written in a sequential high-level language such as COBOL or PL/1. In such a language, a transaction is limited to requesting an operation (through an embedded query language) and then blocking until that operation returns successfully, after which another operation may be requested. However, when transactions are programmed in more modern languages that allow concurrency to be expressed, it is natural to permit the transactions to request several lower-level operations concurrently; this generalization seems sensible because it often does not matter in which order the operations are performed.

Such concurrency may have significant performance advantages. For example, a banking transaction could request several operations, each designed to add five percent interest to a separate account. The order in which these interest calculations are performed does not matter. In a distributed system, if the concurrent operations are performed at different sites, then the time required to complete the transaction can be significantly reduced if the separate operations are executed in parallel. If concurrency among the operations of a single transaction is allowed, one can no longer describe the lower-level operations by single **perform** events. Rather, each such operation must be modeled in terms of a pair of events: a request for the operation and a report of its results.

User-Transaction and Transaction-Operation Interfaces

Thus, when allowing concurrent operations within a transaction, the interface between the transaction and the database looks very similar to the interface between the outside world and the entire database system—the transaction requests operations on the database and receives reports of their results, and these events may be interleaved in complicated sequences. Some correctness condition must be imposed on this lower-level interface (between the transaction and the database). A convenient way of describing this requirement is by means of the same atomic database notion that is used to describe the user interface. That is, the interaction between the transaction and the database should look as if each lower-level operation (that succeeds) is performed at some point in the interval between its request and report. In addition, no transaction should observe interleaving of operations by other transactions.

Thus, users of a database invoke (perhaps concurrently) structured collections of operations called transactions; in ensuring these transactions run atomically, the transaction-processing system supports the illusion that these transactions are primitive atomic operations. In turn, transactions invoke (perhaps concurrently) the underlying primitive operations; again, the transaction-processing system makes it appear that these operations are performed atomically. Given the similar interfaces between users and transactions and between transactions and operations, a natural generalization is to allow any transaction to invoke a child transaction, counting on the transaction-processing system to support the illusion that the child will run as an atomic primitive. This leads naturally to the notion of *nested transactions*.

1.2.3 Nested Transactions

In order for transactions to be useful for general distributed programming, it is useful to extend the notion to include *nesting*. That is, in addition to the originally provided lower-level operations on data objects, one can allow a transaction also to invoke subtransactions, which are themselves implemented by transaction programs. Thus, the transaction nesting structure can be described as a forest, that is, as a graph with a number of nodes (representing the top-level, user-invoked transactions) as roots, each with several children (representing subtransactions and operations called by the transaction) and with the subtransactions themselves having children. The nodes that represent operations that actually access the database form the leaves. The graph is a forest in that no node is a child of more than one parent, nor are there any cycles (where a node is a descendant of itself). There are in general no constraints on the structure of the transaction forest. For example, leaves may occur at any level, so that a top-level transaction might itself be a leaf representing a single operation on the data, or might request both a subtransaction and a data access.

The semantics of nested transactions generalize those of ordinary transactions as follows. Any transaction's interface with the database consists of requests and reports of its children (i.e., its subtransactions and operations). As for top-level transactions, the reports can either say that the child has committed or aborted. A transaction's committed children are supposed to execute as if they were performed sequentially,

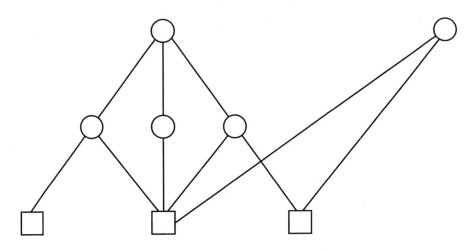

Figure 1.1: Transaction Nesting

each at a point within its interval; the transaction's aborted children should appear
not to run at all. That is, the transaction-processing system must guarantee to each
transaction, as well as to the users, the atomic database property for the operations
and subtransactions it invokes.

A parent transaction is permitted to request any number of children, either sequentially or concurrently, and can continue to request additional children and carry
out local computation while waiting for some of its children to report back. However,
the parent transaction is not allowed to complete its own activity successfully until it
has received reports from all of its requested children.

Figure 1.1 depicts the nesting structure for a set of nested transactions. The circles denote invocations of transaction and subtransaction programs, while the boxes
denote objects. An edge between circles indicates that the lower transaction is a subtransaction of the upper transaction. An edge connecting a circle and a box indicates
that the transaction represented by the circle calls an operation on the object represented by the box. Each set of sibling transactions represents transactions that can
be requested concurrently, but should appear to run serially.

EXAMPLE 1.2.7   Overdraft Protection Using Nested Transactions

Consider the **WITHDRAW_OD** operation discussed above in Example 1.2.6.
An alternative program to provide this sort of service might work in
the following way: it performs **BALANCE**(ACCT_CHK), after which it requests **WITHDRAW**(ACCT_CHK, k) to use the checking account only if the

returned balance is greater than $k +$ \$250. (This might be so that after the withdrawal, the balance will still be above \$250, thereby avoiding service charges.) Otherwise the withdrawal is made from the savings account. In addition, if the balance in ACCT_CHK is found to be \$250 or less, the program brings the balance in ACCT_CHK up to \$1000 by executing **TRANSFER**(ACCT_SVNG, ACCT_CHK, x) where x is the difference between 1000 and the balance returned for ACCT_CHK.

This example shows three levels of nesting: the **WITHDRAW_OD** transaction has children that are **BALANCE** and **WITHDRAW** operations and another child that is a **TRANSFER** subtransaction, and the **TRANSFER** subtransaction has children that are **BALANCE**, **WITHDRAW**, and **DEPOSIT** operations. The semantics of nested transactions say that a **WITHDRAW_OD** transaction runs atomically with respect to any other top-level transactions, that the **BALANCE** and **WITHDRAW** operations and **TRANSFER** subtransactions of any **WITHDRAW_OD** transaction run atomically with respect to each other, and that the **BALANCE**, **WITHDRAW**, and **DEPOSIT** operations within any **TRANSFER** subtransaction run atomically with respect to each other.

Nested transactions provide a flexible programming mechanism. They allow the programmer to describe more concurrency than would be allowed by single-level transactions, by having transactions request the creation of concurrent subtransactions. They also allow localized handling of transaction failures. That is, when a subtransaction commits or aborts, the commit or abort is reported to its parent transaction. The parent can then choose its next action based on the reported results. For example, if a subtransaction aborts, its parent can use the reported abort to trigger another subtransaction, one that implements some alternative action. This flexible mechanism for handling failures is especially useful in distributed systems, where failures are more common because of unreliable communication, and where one node can keep running while another node is down.

EXAMPLE 1.2.8 Remote Procedure Call and Replicated Data

Remote procedure call (RPC) is a common mechanism for interprocess communication. It provides programs with a mechanism that is similar to the usual procedure calls within a single program. One difficulty in making RPC seem indistinguishable from the ordinary procedure call mechanism is the behavior when failures occur. For example, RPC usually copes with lost messages by retransmitting the request. If the original request arrives but the acknowledgement is lost, it is possible for one call to result in several executions of the operation. Nested transactions can be used to implement remote procedure calls with a *zero or once* semantics. This means that the call appears to happen at most once, despite failures. This is accomplished by treating incomplete or redundant calls as aborted subtransactions of the caller, and undoing their activity without aborting the successful call.

As another example, nested transactions can simplify the construction of replicated systems. The reading and writing of individual copies of data objects can be implemented as subtransactions; even if some of the copies fail to respond (causing their subtransactions to fail), the overall transaction can still succeed if enough of the copies respond. The use of nested transactions in the construction of replicated data systems is described in Chapter 12.

Summary

Nesting of transactions is useful for two reasons:

1. It allows controlled concurrency within a transaction: one transaction can run many subtransactions in parallel, with the guarantee that they will appear to run sequentially, and each will appear to happen either completely or not at all.

2. It provides some protection against failures, by permitting checkpoints and application-specific fault management within a transaction. When a subtransaction aborts, its parent can still continue and may be able to complete its task using an alternative method.

1.3   Transaction-Processing Algorithms

A transaction-processing interface that supports atomicity helps programmers of concurrent data-processing systems to reason about their programs and helps users to understand the observed behavior. Implementing such an interface in a distributed system, however, is not an easy task. Besides guaranteeing correct atomic behavior, the implementation needs to provide fast response, and also high availability when portions of the underlying network fail. The implementation may need to be tailored to the system architecture or to the particular application. Finding implementations that satisfy all these constraints is an interesting and challenging problem.

The simplest strategy that can be used to implement an atomic database is based on a single centralized *serial scheduler* that receives all requests from transactions and decides when to run them, running siblings sequentially. Although this implementation gives the correct behavior (when no aborts occur), the response time for transactions can be quite high since no concurrency is permitted.

Allowing concurrent processing of different transactions can improve response time considerably. For example, suppose that a transaction T makes concurrent requests for subtransactions that operate on separate parts of the database. The serial scheduler would run them one at a time, but a concurrent scheduler could allow them to run concurrently. Since they do not interact, it would still appear to the outside world as if they ran serially, in some (in fact, an arbitrary) sequential order. Consider, for example, a transaction that adds five percent interest to all the accounts in the bank. The time performance of the concurrent system can be considerably faster than that of the corresponding serial system, because so much is being done concurrently; this is especially true if the separate tasks are very time-consuming.

However, it is not always possible to allow unlimited concurrency in the operation of subtransactions. In many cases, the subtransactions do not work entirely on separate parts of the data. In this case, it is still possible to allow the transactions to proceed concurrently, provided that some appropriate mechanism is supplied to prevent difficulties when the transactions collide. For example, if each transaction locks every object it touches and does not unlock them until it commits, then no two transactions can appear interleaved—each transaction that commits will appear to have been performed entirely at the time it commits.

Many different algorithms have been proposed and used for implementing non-nested atomic transactions in concurrent database systems, and also for implementing nested transactions. These algorithms make use of various techniques, including locks, timestamps, multiple versions of data objects, and multiple replicas.

1.3.1 Locking

Read/Update Locking

The most popular algorithms in practice are read/update locking algorithms, in which each transaction must acquire read locks or update locks on data objects in order to access the objects in the corresponding manner, and then must hold the locks until the whole transaction is finished. Update locks are defined to conflict with other locks on the same data object, and conflicting locks are not permitted to be held simultaneously. Because of this, update locks are sometimes called *exclusive locks*, and read locks are called *shared locks*. Thus, a transaction that updates a data object prevents or delays the operation of any other transaction that also wishes to read or update the same object.

For example, in a database consisting of a collection of read/write registers, transactions can acquire read locks on individual registers in order to read them, and update locks in order to write them. Similarly, in a database consisting of a collection of bank accounts, transactions can acquire read locks on individual accounts in order to carry out **BALANCE** operations on them, and update locks in order to perform all other operations (e.g., **DEPOSIT** and **WITHDRAW**).

Concurrency Bottlenecks for Read/Update Locking

While read/update locking is simple and widely used, it can result in poor performance in some situations. Some systems contain data items that must be accessed and updated by many transactions. If the synchronization on those data items is such that only one transaction at a time can access each item, a concurrency bottleneck or 'hot spot' can result. For example, an object in a banking database that maintains a total of the bank assets needs to be updated by all transactions that modify that total (i.e., by most transactions that update the database). If read/update locking is used, a transaction T that modifies the **TOTAL** object will prevent any other transaction from reading or updating that object until T commits or aborts and releases its lock. These conflicting transactions will be blocked for a significant period, and throughput will suffer. In general, data that summarizes other data can result in a concurrency bottleneck.

Concurrency bottlenecks also occur in cases where the data is organized into a rooted tree, where the root of the structure is likely to be updated by most of the transactions. If read/update locking is used, a transaction that modifies the root will prevent any other transaction from accessing the root until the modifying transaction releases its lock by committing or aborting. Examples of such situations arise in index structures (e.g., a B-tree) and in resource allocation problems (e.g., a free list of disk blocks).

Data-Type-Specific Algorithms

The read/update locking strategy can be generalized by taking advantage of data-type-specific properties. Notice that read/update locking itself takes advantage of special properties of read operations, namely, that they do not modify the state of the database. It follows that transactions executing read operations can be allowed to run concurrently without sacrificing atomicity. For some data types, read/update locking can be generalized to allow more concurrency. For example, operations on summary data such as the total assets of a bank often include increment, decrement, and read operations. Increment and decrement operations are executed by transactions that transfer money into or out of the bank, (e.g., **DEPOSIT** or **WITHDRAW** transactions). Using read/update locking, transactions executing increment and decrement operations on the summary data must exclude each other since each such operation updates the same summary data object, and so each transaction will need to obtain an exclusive lock. However, it is possible to design more permissive locking algorithms for this example, using the fact that increment and decrement operations commute, to allow transactions executing them to run concurrently.

1.3.2 Timestamps

Other techniques that have been suggested for implementing transactions are based on the assignment of numerical timestamps to all transactions. The assignment of timestamps may be done *a priori*, or upon submission of the transactions to the system, or at some later time during their execution. Although the assignment of timestamps may be carried out by a distributed algorithm, it is important that all the timestamps be unique. The transactions are managed so that they appear to run serially in the order of their timestamps. For example, a transaction might not be permitted to write a new value to an object if some other transaction with a higher timestamp has already read the existing value of the object. In a distributed setting, it might not be easy to determine when all conflicting transactions with smaller timestamps have finished running. Thus, it might be necessary for transactions to wait to be sure that this has happened, or to abort if they proceed too soon and later find out they have not waited long enough. Thus, timestamp-based algorithms can incur performance penalties, in the form of delays or extra aborts.

Timestamp-based algorithms can also be designed using multiple versions of data objects, with associated timestamp values. For example, suppose the operations on the data are restricted to be reads or writes, and each version carries the value and timestamp of a different completed write operation. Then read operations with time-stamps earlier than the last completed write may still proceed, by returning the value of the version with the greatest timestamp less than that of the read operation. It is also possible to design type-specific multiversion timestamp algorithms for other data types.

It is also possible to design hybrid algorithms that implement transactions using a combination of locking and timestamps. The addition of timestamp information to a locking algorithm can give each data object increased information about the order in which transactions commit; this extra information can permit extra concurrency among the operations of the object.

1.3.3 Optimistic Algorithms

Some other algorithms use optimistic strategies, where the system guesses that there will be no interference between a running transaction T and others that run concurrently with it. Thus, no checks (such as those needed to obtain locks) are made while the transaction is running. Instead, a validation procedure is used when T completes, to check that no interference took place. Such a strategy can sometimes allow the system to process the transaction very rapidly, with little overhead for concurrency control. However, if the system guesses wrong, and interfering transactions do in fact run concurrently with T, then T might be forced to abort.

1.3.4 Replication

Other algorithms for implementing an atomic database involve replicating some of the data objects at several locations of a distributed system. This strategy can lead to higher availability, in that copies of the object can be accessed from many different locations. However, replicating objects leads to the need for additional algorithms for maintaining consistency among the replicated copies.

1.3.5 Recovery

Recovery algorithms are an important part of transaction-processing systems. Recovery is typically provided for several types of failures, including transaction aborts, system crashes (in which volatile memory is lost but non-volatile memory, such as disk, remains intact), and media failures (in which some non-volatile memory is corrupted). Ideally, one would treat recovery independently from concurrency control. However, recovery and concurrency control interact in subtle ways, and it is difficult to treat them independently without making restrictive assumptions about the interface between them. In this book, we deal only with recovery from transaction aborts, and treat it together with concurrency control.

1.4 Formal Models

1.4.1 Why a Formal Model?

Although the notion of an atomic transaction is fairly intuitive, there are subtleties that can cause confusion. For example, the informal discussion above has not made completely clear under what circumstances a parent transaction is permitted to request children, or to complete its work successfully. It has not made clear exactly when transactions begin their computation, relative to the time when they are requested. It has not made clear exactly what guarantees are made for transactions that abort. In general, it is not obvious how programmers who write transactions can reason carefully about the behavior of the transactions they write. We believe that the best means of clarification is to work in terms of an underlying formal semantic model for atomic transaction systems.

A formal semantic model can also help programmers to reason carefully about the correctness of implementations of transaction-processing systems. Many of the algorithms that have been proposed for implementing transactions are complicated, and it is not easy to make convincing informal arguments about their correctness. In fact, mistakes are often made during the process of designing such algorithms. A formal model is useful for describing the implementation algorithms, for stating the precise correctness condition they are to satisfy, and also for carrying out rigorous proofs that the algorithms are correct.

As an example of the need for a formal model for reasoning about complex algorithms, consider the locking and timestamp algorithms discussed in the preceding section. Each kind of algorithm is separately correct for implementing atomic transactions. You might hope to be able to mix both kinds of algorithms in a single system, using locking for some objects and timestamp ordering for other objects. For example, you might be trying to integrate previously designed systems, of which one uses timestamps while the other uses locking. However, combining these two kinds of algorithms in the most straightforward manner leads to an incorrect system, one that does not guarantee atomicity. (See Exercise 13 in Chapter 7.) A more careful kind of combination, where there is a certain kind of compatibility between the lock and timestamp management, can be designed to operate correctly. The issues are subtle, and a formal model can help to clarify them.

1.4.2 An Operational Automaton Model

Consider the style of model that is best for the purposes described. The basic requirement is that the model must be suitable for describing both the problem to be solved (i.e., implementing an atomic database) and the algorithms that are used to solve it (e.g., locking or timestamp algorithms), both in a common framework. It should be possible to carry out rigorous mathematical proofs within the same framework, to show that an algorithm is a correct implementation. The model should support modular description of the algorithms, with separately verifiable claims about the algorithm components. It should be sufficiently expressive to describe all interesting aspects of the algorithms and their correctness conditions; many of these aspects are discussed in the previous sections of this chapter.

The style of model that we prefer is operational (rather than, say, axiomatic). It is based on a simple underlying automaton model, not necessarily finite-state, for concurrent systems. Automata generate executions, each of which describes a progression through a sequence of states by means of a sequence of actions. Correctness conditions for a concurrent system modeled as an automaton are expressed as restrictions on the sequences of actions that are part of the interface between the database and its users. Automata can be composed by identifying actions in their interfaces, thus modeling systems built from previously modeled components. Composition yields a single automaton that is a model for the whole system. One automaton can be an abstract version of another, allowing development of algorithms using a successive refinement strategy.

The structure needed to model transaction-processing systems is built upon the basic automaton model. In this framework, *all system components* are modeled as automata; this includes not only each transaction and each object in the database, but also all the users of the system![1] It also includes any other algorithm components, such as transaction schedulers or communication networks. All interesting activities of these system components are modeled as explicit actions of the corresponding automata.

1.4.3 Correct Systems Simulate Serial Systems

In order to define the basic notion of correctness of atomic transactions, it is necessary to specify the set of sequences of request and report actions that are defined to be atomic. There are several ways in which this set of sequences could be defined, for instance, using explicit mathematical statements about the sequences (such as asserting the existence of appropriate points in all the request-report intervals at which the transactions could be "deemed to occur"). Our approach is to define a hypothetical *serial system*—a system that processes each set of sibling transactions serially, and in which there are no failures. The set of correct sequences is then defined to be just those that are generated by the serial system. Thus, the goal of a correct transaction-processing algorithm is to make the system look to the user like the serial system.

Although the set of correct sequences is defined in terms of a particular hypothetical system, it is important to note that this definition only constrains the *user-visible* behavior of an implementation. There is no requirement that the implementation exhibit any of the internal state or internal activities of the serial system; it simply has to present the same behavior to the users. Thus, the specification of correct system behavior is entirely separate from the descriptions of the implementations themselves. Taking this approach allows application of a single definition of correctness to a wide range of systems, including locking systems; single-version and multi-version timestamp systems; hybrid systems; optimistic systems; and replicated data management systems.

On the other hand, it turns out to be quite useful to have the specification and the implementations all presented in the same form—as systems of automata. This means that it is possible to use a variety of techniques relating the executions of one system to those of another system, in proofs of the correctness of implementations.

---

[1]The philosophical implications of modeling users as automata are beyond the scope of this book.

This book uses an automata-theoretic model to present and prove the correctness of a number of transaction-processing algorithms, including locking, timestamp-based, hybrid, and optimistic algorithms for concurrency control; algorithms for managing orphan transactions; and algorithms for managing replicated data. One important aspect of transaction-processing that is not considered in this book is the implementation of atomic transactions in the presence of node crashes that destroy the contents of volatile memory. Modeling the interesting and complex algorithms that have been developed for this purpose is an important task that remains to be done.

1.5 Comparisons with the Classical Theory

There has been a considerable amount of work on formal modeling of transaction-processing algorithms, in frameworks somewhat different from the one in this book. A large body of this prior work is described by Bernstein, Hadzilacos, and Goodman in [12]; the theory developed in that book is referred to here as the *classical theory* of database concurrency control. The classical theory is applicable only to a subset of the situations described in this book. For example, the classical theory is primarily designed for single-level transaction systems rather than nested transaction systems, and for read and write operations rather than arbitrary database operations. Also, in much of the classical theory, it is assumed that each transaction consists of a fixed collection of operations, whereas the more general theory here allows requests that are conditional on earlier results. Nevertheless, our work has been heavily influenced by the classical theory.

1.5.1 Serializability

Much of the classical theory makes the simplifying assumption that the implementing system is organized in a very specific way: as the composition of two pieces, a *scheduler* and a *database*. All operations requested by transactions are passed from the transactions to the scheduler, which determines the order in which they are to be performed by the database. The database also handles recovery from transaction abort (as well as failure of the media on which the data is stored), in such a way that each operation that accesses a data object is performed from the state of that object resulting from the application of all previous non-aborted operations on that object.

The definition of correctness most commonly used in the classical theory is called *serializability*,[2] and is similar to the notion of atomicity for transactions. However, serializability is defined in a way that is tailored to the particular scheduler-database organization described above. Namely, serializability requires an execution of the *same* system to exist in which the committed transactions run one at a time (without interleaving of steps from different transactions) and perform the same operations on the database.

While this organization is suitable for describing single-version locking and time-stamp algorithms, it is not adequate for describing many other interesting algorithms. Multi-version timestamp algorithms and replicated data algorithms, for example, maintain state information in a form that is quite different from the (single-copy, latest-value) form used for the single-version algorithms, and the appropriate interface between the scheduler and the database is correspondingly different. The classical theory has been extended, modifying the interface between the scheduler and the database to accommodate multi-version algorithms. But this change requires a new definition of serializability, suitable for the new interface. In effect, a different definition of correctness is used for different classes of algorithms. It is more appropriate, and useful in not unduly restricting possible implementations, to state a fundamental correctness condition in a way that does not depend on the details of a particular system organization, and that does not require different definitions for different classes of algorithms.

The main weakness of serializability as a fundamental correctness condition is that it is not based on an external interface, but is given in terms of the interface between the scheduler and the database, as a condition on the order in which operations on the database are actually performed. In contrast, the theory in this book presupposes that the fundamental notions of correctness are defined in terms of the interface between the users and the system.

Also, the classical notion of serializability, stated as it is in terms of the existence of a serial execution of the *same* system, is too restrictive for our purposes here. An implementation does not serve as an adequate specification of permissible serial executions. For example, if an implementation severely restricts the orders in which it runs transactions, then an *apparent* serial order of transactions, though logically correct, might not be a possible execution of the particular implementation. In the approach taken in this book, correctness of a system is defined with respect to a *separate* specification of the permissible serial executions.

In the restricted setting for which the classical theory can be used, it provides a good basis for carrying out simple and elegant correctness proofs for concurrency control algorithms. Most of the proofs are based on a fundamental combinatorial

---

[2]That is what it is called in [12]; it is more commonly called *conflict-preserving serializability* or CPSR in the research literature.

theorem called the Serializability Theorem. This important theorem states that the serializability condition is equivalent to the absence of cycles in a graph representing dependencies among transactions; the dependencies arise from the processing of operations on the individual objects.

In this book, we prove a similar theorem, which we call the Atomicity Theorem. This is a general theorem containing a sufficient condition for proving atomicity. Because this theorem applies in a much more general setting than the classical Serializability Theorem (including arbitrary data types, transaction nesting, and a more detailed treatment of abort recovery), it is more complicated to state. However, the two theorems are similar in spirit: each asserts that the existence of a single ordering of transactions that is consistent with the processing of operations at each object is sufficient to prove correctness, correctness being formalized as serializability or atomicity, respectively.

1.5.2 Classical Treatment of Recovery

Issues of reasoning about recovery from transaction aborts are generally ignored in the classical theory. For example, an assumption is usually made that some underlying recovery mechanism ensures that aborted transactions have no effect; formally, this is captured by restricting attention to only those executions in which all transactions commit. In order to justify this restriction (i.e., in order that results about executions in which all transactions commit can have any significance for executions in which some transactions abort), strong assumptions must be made about the way the database processes operations and aborts. In the classical theory, the database is generally assumed to use an *update-in-place* strategy that maintains the latest value of each object in the database. (This is usually managed by keeping an auxiliary data structure that logs *undo* information for operations and using this to recover from transaction abort.)

However, there are useful concurrency control and recovery algorithms that are not based on update-in-place and undo logging (e.g., a deferred update strategy, using data structures known as *intentions lists* for recovery). Again, the classical assumptions are too restrictive to capture interesting implementations. Also, the interactions between concurrency control and abort recovery algorithms are subtle: for instance, there are concurrency control algorithms that work correctly when intentions lists are used for recovery but do not work with undo logs. Clearly, an understanding of these interactions requires a model that does not restrict recovery to be update-in-place.

In this book, we do not make restrictive assumptions about transaction abort recovery, but rather integrate the treatment of transaction abort recovery into the general treatment of transaction-processing algorithms.

1.5.3 Data Types and Nesting

Most of the classical theory deals with read and write operations only, although there
has been some work extending the theory to the case where more general data types
are used. In contrast, the treatment in this book focuses on general data types, with
read and write operations as only one example.

Nearly all of the classical theory deals with single-level transactions. In contrast,
we consider nested transactions throughout.

1.5.4 Operational versus Axiomatic Model

The classical model is basically an axiomatic model; it does not include an explicit
operational description of the execution of a transaction-processing system, but rather
describes transactions by means of axioms about their behavior. In contrast, this book
uses a very explicit operational model.

The distinction between axiomatic and operational approaches is more stylistic
than it is formal. Nevertheless, there are many situations in which it seems more convenient to use an operational model. For example, it is possible for a transaction in a
nested transaction system to create a subtransaction *because of the fact that an earlier
subtransaction aborted*; an operational model that explicitly includes an abort event
and describes the consequent state changes is helpful in capturing this dependency.
Also, it is sometimes interesting to describe how the same transaction would behave
in different systems. Such reasoning is facilitated by an explicit operational model for
the transaction (and the other components of the two systems).

For another example, transaction-processing algorithms typically treat transactions as black boxes, that is, as nondeterministic sources of subtransaction and operation requests, which must be scheduled, run, and the results reported to the originating
transaction. The internal structure and local computation of the transactions are ignored. A fundamental property of transactions, especially in the nested case, is that
if the environment's behavior at the transaction's external interface is the same in
two different settings, the transaction will exhibit the same range of possible behavior
in each. An operational, automaton-style model provides a natural way of describing the distinction between the internals of a transaction and its interface with its
environment.

1.5.5 A Finer Granularity of Analysis

A final distinction between this book and the classical theory is that the model used
in this book includes more kinds of events. (One might say that the operations have
finer granularity than those of the classical theory.) For example, separate events
record the request by a transaction for an operation on an object, the beginning of

the operation at the object, the completion of the operation at the object, the decision by the system that the operation is to be committed rather than aborted, and the report to the transaction of the results of the operation. In the classical theory, these five separate events are represented by a single event! The larger number of distinct events in this book is partly a consequence of the technical tools that are employed. But the introduction of nesting and abort recovery into the model requires the statement of certain properties that are difficult to state without distinguishing these different events. Finally, note that in a distributed system these events may happen at different sites, and thus at widely separated times, so that representing them as one primitive event is problematic.

The penalty paid for the extra power and expressiveness is that the resulting model is more complex (i.e., more detailed) than the classical model. We believe, however, that much of this complexity is inherent in the systems being studied. The extra detail allows the careful statement of a large number of interesting properties of nested transaction systems with abort recovery; in fact, the extra detail is also useful for understanding ordinary single-level (non-nested) transactions, particularly for transaction-processing systems embodying novel algorithms. Some of the complexity is also due to the fact that results are stated so that they apply to as broad a range of systems as possible. Finally, some complexity also results from the approach of presenting operational descriptions of the algorithms, rather than simply axioms describing their behavior.

1.6   Contents of This Book

This book presents the development of a novel theory of transaction processing systems, along with comparisons with the corresponding results of the classical theory. An automaton model for transaction-processing systems is presented, and is used to define atomicity for transaction systems (including nested transaction systems). The general Atomicity Theorem is presented and proved, as are a large number of interesting transaction-processing algorithms.

1.6.1   The Basic Theory

Chapter 2 outlines the automaton model for concurrent systems that is used for presenting all later results. Then Chapter 3 contains a description of *serial systems*, extremely constrained transaction-processing systems that are used to define *atomicity*, the basic correctness condition for more liberal systems.

Chapter 4 introduces some useful constraints on serial systems and their components, and Chapter 5 contains a description of *simple systems*, very unconstrained systems that represent the common features of most transaction-processing systems.

Chapter 5 also includes the Atomicity Theorem (stated in terms of simple systems), which contains an important sufficient condition for proving atomicity. As noted above, this theorem is similar to the classical Serializability Theorem: it shows that the existence of a single ordering of transactions that is consistent with the processing of operations at each object is sufficient to prove atomicity.

1.6.2 Fundamental Transaction-Processing Algorithms

The book presents several basic transaction-processing algorithms and verifies their correctness using the Atomicity Theorem. Chapter 6 contains a collection of descriptions and proofs for locking algorithms. This chapter begins by defining *generic systems*, systems in which each data object is represented as a separate automaton that is responsible for performing the concurrency control and recovery actions appropriate for that object. The presentation includes two algorithms that take advantage of type-specific information, specifically, the commutativity relationships among the operations on data objects, to allow a high degree of concurrency. The two algorithms differ in the way a return value is calculated, and also in the precise commutativity relation used. We also give a description of the nested transaction read/update locking algorithm, invented by Moss, that is used in the Argus and Avalon systems.

 Chapter 6 also defines a local condition for data objects, *dynamic atomicity*. The Atomicity Theorem is used to show that if all the objects in a system are dynamic atomic, then the system guarantees atomicity. An object using either of the given type-specific algorithms is shown to satisfy the dynamic atomicity condition; hence, each algorithm guarantees atomicity. The proof of the read/update algorithm involves showing that an object using it provides a subset of the behavior of an object using one general algorithm, and so also is dynamic atomic; the proof that this subset relation holds is based on exhibiting an abstraction mapping from one object to the other.

 The definition of dynamic atomicity provides modularity, in that it allows one to verify the implementations of individual objects independently. In addition, it allows the use of different implementation techniques and different algorithms in different objects. Thus, one object could use Moss's read/update locking algorithm, another could use one of the type-specific algorithms and another could use the other type-specific algorithm; since all are dynamic atomic, the entire system still guarantees atomicity.

 A similar pattern to that in Chapter 6 is followed in Chapter 7, which explores timestamp-based algorithms. More specifically, the chapter begins by defining *pseudotime systems*, systems in which timestamps known as *pseudotimes* are assigned to transactions at the time they begin running; transactions are supposed to appear to run in the order of their pseudotimes. The *static atomicity* condition (analogous to the dynamic atomicity condition) is defined for data objects, and the Atomicity Theorem is used to show that if all the objects in a pseudotime system are static atomic, then the system guarantees atomicity.

Chapter 7 then continues with a presentation and proof of a multi-version time-stamp algorithm for read/write objects designed by Reed. This algorithm is proved correct by demonstrating that the objects used in the algorithm are all static atomic. The chapter concludes with a similar presentation and proof of a timestamp-based algorithm for more general data types.

Chapter 8 develops a *hybrid* transaction-processing algorithm for general data types. It does this by defining *hybrid systems*, which can be considered to be hybrids of generic systems and pseudotime systems; in hybrid systems, timestamps are assigned to transactions at the time they commit. Analogously to the previous developments, a *hybrid atomicity* condition is defined and shown to imply that the system guarantees atomicity. The algorithm presented in this chapter is similar to a locking algorithm given in Chapter 6, but uses the commit-time timestamps to provide the objects with additional information about the serialization order; this information can sometimes lead to extra concurrency among the operations. The algorithm is proved correct by showing that its objects are all hybrid atomic.

1.6.3 More Advanced Transaction-Processing Algorithms

Chapter 9 reconsiders the relationship between the theory of this volume and the classical theory. It notes that although the proofs for locking algorithms in Chapter 6 are general and rigorous, they are not based on a simple acyclicity condition of the sort that is hypothesized in the classical Serializability Theorem.

Exploring this condition in detail, the chapter develops an appropriate generalization of the serialization graph construction used for the classical theorem and proves that *under certain circumstances*, absence of cycles in the resulting graph is sufficient to prove atomicity. The results in this chapter make clear that the classical Serializability Theorem relies on certain restrictions on concurrency control algorithms, restrictions that do not hold for all interesting transaction-processing algorithms. Thus, it clarifies the conditions for applicability of the classical theorem, extending it to handle nested transactions, and shows how it can be used to prove not only the classical serializability condition, but also atomicity. The generalized serialization graph construction is used to prove the correctness of several locking algorithms.

Chapter 10 presents several optimistic methods for concurrency control. First, a system organization is considered in which each transaction is checked as it commits, to ensure that none of its accesses are potentially incorrect because of the activity of committed siblings. Next, a very different organization is presented, in which checks are done only for transactions on a certain frontier in the nesting structure. For each

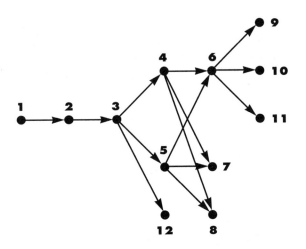

Figure 1.2: Chapter Dependencies

structure, an appropriate local atomicity condition is defined, and an algorithm is given that satisfies the local condition.

The remaining chapters explore quite different aspects of transaction-processing systems. Chapter 11 shows how mechanisms can be added to a system to prevent any transaction from discovering that it is an orphan, and is unable to commit. The proof shows that orphan management can be incorporated in a dynamic atomic system without consideration of the particular algorithms used for concurrency control. Chapter 12 shows how to manage multiple copies of a single data item, so that the appearance of a single copy is preserved. We show that any correct concurrency control mechanism may be used on the copies, considered as separate objects; the whole system will then appear to be atomic and unreplicated.

The book ends with an appendix that collects definitions from discrete mathematics. This is presented as a reminder and a reference (especially important in this subject, since terminology is not uniform between different textbooks).

The logical dependencies between chapters are indicated in Figure 1.2. For example, Chapter 7 depends on concepts from Chapter 4 and Chapter 5, but it is independent of the content of Chapter 6.

1.7 Bibliographic Notes

Each chapter of this book closes with a section discussing papers and books related to the material in the chapter. These notes are not intended to be a comprehensive survey of the entire field; they are intended to guide you in further exploring the ideas discussed in each chapter. The notes in this section provide pointers to important works on transactions in general, on alternative or related correctness conditions, and on algorithms for concurrency control and recovery. (We have kept most of the explicit citations within these sections, to aid readability of the technical content.)

1.7.1 Transactions

Bernstein *et al.*[12] motivate and describe the classical concept of transactions (without nesting) in Chapter 1 of their book on database concurrency control and recovery. A more detailed account is given by Gray and Reuter [42]. The idea of nested transactions seems to have originated in the *spheres of control* work of Davies [21]. Reed [103] developed the current notion of nesting and designed a timestamp-based implementation. Moss [91] later designed a locking implementation that serves as the basis of the implementation of the Argus programming language [75, 76]. Another system based on nested transactions is Camelot [29].

Liskov [75] and Eppinger *et al.* [29] demonstrate how transactions can be used as a way of organizing programs for distributed systems. The banking example given in [75] is a good example of the complexities caused by concurrency and failures in distributed systems, and the usefulness of nesting transactions. Recently, application domains such as design and software engineering have shown the need for still more flexible concepts of a "transaction" where cooperation is possible among concurrent users. No consensus has yet emerged on the correct constructs—a number of suggestions are surveyed in a book edited by Elmagarmid [28].

The notion of nesting studied in this book is analogous to levels of procedural abstractions. A different form of transaction nesting has been proposed to implement a notion of levels of data abstraction. (That is, subtransactions at each level are constrained to be of particular types, with the semantics of particular operations. In this restricted case, the transaction-processing system can exploit these restrictions for greater efficiency.) This concept has also been called nested transactions, but is now usually termed *open nesting* or *multi-layer* transactions. It appeared in System R [41] and has been proposed as a powerful mechanism for structuring systems (see Weikum [119] and Lomet [78]).

1.7.2 Correctness Conditions

The atomic database concept is similar to the atomic register notion introduced by Lamport [67] and studied extensively in the distributed algorithms literature. Lamport's notion is defined for read/write registers only. The notion is generalized to arbitrary data types, under the name *linearizability*, by Herlihy and Wing [53]. The notion of atomic database differs from their notion mainly in that the former considers the case in which operations abort.

The general approach taken in this book was begun by Lynch and Merritt in [80] with an analysis of an exclusive locking algorithm. The idea of using a separate specification for the allowable serial behaviors was first used by Weihl [117, 113].

The classical (conflict-preserving) serializability notion was introduced under the name *consistency* by Eswaran *et al.* [30], and is used as the principal correctness condition in [12] There are other correctness conditions for atomic transactions in the literature, different from our atomicity definition and from the definition of serializability in [12]. The definitions vary both in the way each transaction is modeled and in the sort of "equivalence" to a serial schedule that is demanded. A discussion of several correctness conditions for transactions can be found in Chapters 2 and 3 of the book by Papadimitriou [99]. For instance, the important early paper of Papadimitriou [98] only requires the final state of the database to be the same as after a serial execution in which the same transactions occur. The view serializability condition [121] insists in addition that accesses to data return the same values as in the equivalent serial execution. Also, either ordinary serializability or view serializability can be augmented by an external consistency condition, which requires that the order of transactions in the equivalent serial execution should be compatible with the order in which transaction requests and responses occur. The classical theory has been extended in order to verify multiversion and replicated algorithms, as in Chapter 5 and Chapter 8 of [12]. These definitions come closer to ours than traditional serializability, since correctness is described using a system (without versions or replicas) that is different from the implementation being examined. However, the idea that exactly the same correctness condition should be used for different system structures is not present in these variations of the classical theory.

There has been some recent work extending the definitions and proof techniques of the classical theory to encompass the multi-layer transaction model, based on system-specific levels of data abstraction rather than programmable calls to subtransactions [10, 92, 118, 119]. Definitions and proof techniques suitable for more flexible transaction models have been studied by several groups (e.g., see [20, 60]).

1.7.3 Algorithms for Concurrency Control and Recovery

The read/update algorithm described in Section 1.3.1 is due to Eswaran *et al.* [30]. Specific references to other algorithms mentioned (and many others) are provided in later chapters of this book. Also, the books by Bernstein *et al.* [12] and Gray and Reuter [42] provide excellent surveys of many of the most important transaction-processing algorithms for non-nested transactions.

Many researchers have explored the use of type-specific concurrency control algorithms to avoid concurrency bottlenecks (e.g., see [10, 58, 60, 97, 106, 115, 113, 118]). For example, in the IMS Fast Path system [36], algorithms that are more permissive than read/update locking are used for managing summary data accessed by increment and decrement operations. Another example that has attracted a great deal of attention is the *index* data type. Most commercial systems provide indices structured as a variant of B-tree, and highly concurrent access to these is crucial for good overall performance. Important papers on this topic include [9, 88, 105, 107]. A different approach is to use the semantics of the transactions, rather than that of the data, to allow more concurrency [31].

One important recovery mechanism is the *deferred update*, presented in Chapter 11 of [70]. Perhaps more common in practice are methods based on logging, as studied by Mohan *et al.* [89]. Most algorithms for recovery include many complications to deal with inconsistencies caused by caching of data in memory, since a crash destroys the information in buffers but not that on disk. Weihl [117] describes the interactions between concurrency control and abort recovery algorithms.

The classical theory has been used to verify a number of concurrency control algorithms. Some of the proofs can be found in [12]. Lynch [79] provides a complete proof of an exclusive locking algorithm for nested transactions, but the framework used there does not appear to extend easily to treat many other nested-transaction-processing algorithms.

This book presents and proves the correctness of many transaction-processing algorithms, including locking and timestamp-based algorithms for concurrency control, algorithms for managing replicated data, and algorithms for managing orphan transactions. This work is based on a series of research papers [6, 32, 33, 34, 38, 46, 72, 71, 73, 81, 100].

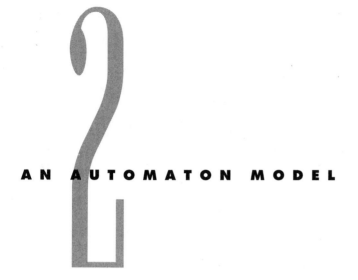

AN AUTOMATON MODEL

2.1 Introduction

In order to reason carefully about complex concurrent systems such as those that implement atomic transactions, it is important to have a simple and clearly defined formal model for concurrent computation. The model used in this book is an automaton model derived from the input/output automaton (I/O automaton) model [82, 83]. The automaton model here is simpler than the I/O automaton model, in that it omits additional structure used to deal with issues of fairness and liveness. Rather, it extracts from the I/O automaton model the features needed for discussing safety properties.

The resulting automaton model allows careful descriptions of concurrent algorithms and of their (safety) properties. The model serves as the basis for rigorous proofs that particular algorithms satisfy particular correctness conditions.

Overview of the Model: The I/O automaton model is designed to model *discrete event systems* consisting of concurrently operating components.[1] A discrete event system is an entity, either complete in itself, or a piece of a larger system, that undergoes discrete changes that may be named and observed, and through which the system interacts with its environment. The components of a discrete event system can be regarded as discrete event systems themselves. A discrete event system may be *reactive* in the sense that it interacts with its environment in an ongoing manner (rather than, say, simply accepting an input, computing a function of that input, and halting).

Each system component is modeled as an automaton, a mathematical object with states and named transitions between them.[2] The actions of an automaton are classified as either *input, output,* or *internal.* This classification is a reflection of a distinction in the system being modeled between events (such as the receipt of a message) that are caused by the environment, events (such as sending a message) that the component can perform when it chooses and that affect the environment, and events (such as changing the value of a local variable) that a component can perform when it chooses, but that are undetectable by the environment except through their effects on later output events. In the I/O automaton model, an automaton generates output and internal actions autonomously, and transmits output actions instantaneously to its environment. In contrast, the automaton's input is generated by the environment and transmitted instantaneously to the automaton. The distinction between input and other actions is fundamental, based on which component determines when the action is performed: an automaton can establish restrictions on when it will perform an output or internal action, but it is unable to block the performance of an input action.

Input Blocking: The fact that inputs cannot be blocked in the I/O automaton model is not a significant restriction on the model. There are certainly situations in which one might want to consider the behavior of a system under restrictions on the occurrence of inputs. Instead of ruling out the unwanted inputs, however, the I/O automaton model permits these inputs to occur, and handles the restrictions in other ways. For example, an automaton may be permitted to exhibit arbitrary behavior in case unwanted inputs occur. As a special case, an automaton may explicitly detect

---

[1] As discussed, the automaton model used in this book omits some features of the model in [82, 83]. However, the properties discussed in this section are shared by both the full model and its restriction. For brevity, both are referred to as "the I/O automaton model."

[2] This is similar to a nondeterministic finite-state automaton, as studied in the theory of computation (see for example [56]). However, in the I/O automaton model an automaton need not be finite-state, but can have an infinite state set.

bad inputs and respond to them with error messages. Thus, there are simple ways of describing input restrictions, without including input-blocking in the model.

Nondeterminism: An automaton can be nondeterministic, and indeed the nondeterminism is an important part of the I/O automaton model's descriptive power. Describing algorithms as nondeterministically as possible tends to make results about the algorithms quite general, since many results about nondeterministic algorithms apply *a fortiori* to all algorithms obtained by restricting the nondeterministic choices. Moreover, the use of nondeterminism helps to avoid cluttering algorithm descriptions and proofs with inessential details. Finally, the uncertainties introduced by asynchrony make nondeterminism an intrinsic property of real concurrent systems, and so an important property to capture in any formal model of such systems.

Composition: Often, a single discrete event system can also be viewed as a combination of several component systems interacting with one another. To reflect this in the I/O automaton model, a *composition* operation is defined, by which several automata can be combined to yield a single automaton. The composition operator connects each output action of a component automaton with the identically named input actions of any number (usually one) of the other component automata. In the resulting system, an output action is generated autonomously by one component and is thought of as being instantaneously transmitted to all components having the same action as an input. Each such component is a passive recipient of the input and takes that step simultaneously with the generating automaton.

Externally Visible Events: When a system is modeled by an automaton, each possible run of the system is modeled by an *execution*, an alternating sequence of states and actions. The possible activity of the system is captured by the set of all possible executions that can be generated by the automaton. However, not all the information contained in an execution is important to a user of the system, or to an environment in which the system is placed. In such contexts, what is important about the activity of a system is the externally visible events, and not the states or internal events. The externally visible events are recorded in the automaton's *behaviors*—the subsequences of its executions consisting of the external (i.e., input and output) actions. A system is suitable for a purpose if any possible sequence of externally visible events has appropriate characteristics. Thus, correctness conditions for an automaton are formulated in terms of properties of the automaton's behaviors.

This viewpoint differs from that taken in much of the algorithm specification work in the research literature, where properties of the states are often taken to be of primary concern. Although it is mostly a matter of taste, we find the behavioral approach to be more convenient for formulating properties and analyzing algorithms. See Section 2.9 for further discussion of this point.

Automata as Specifications: One convenient way to specify properties of an automaton's behaviors is in terms of another automaton. That is, one can define a particular *specification automaton B* and say that any automaton *A* is correct if it *implements B*, in the sense that each finite behavior of *A* is also a finite behavior of *B*. The model also permits description of the same system at different levels of abstraction. Abstraction mappings can be defined, which describe the relationship between automata that include implementation detail and more abstract automata that suppress some of the detail. (For example, *B* might be a simple system that is impractical as a real solution because it uses global information, while *A* might be a more realistic composition of components each of which uses only local information.) Such mappings can be used as aids in correctness proofs for algorithms: if automaton *B* is an image of automaton *A* under an appropriate abstraction mapping, then it can be shown that *A* implements *B*.

This book uses a simple language for describing automata, based on the specification of *preconditions* and *effects* for actions. Although this notation is somewhat more restrictive than most programming languages (e.g., it contains no explicit statements describing flow of control), it is sufficient for describing the large number of varied algorithms examined in this book. However, the I/O automaton model itself does not constrain the user to describe all automata using the precondition-effect language; rather, the model is general enough to serve also as a formal basis for many concurrent programming languages, including those that contain all the standard constructs for sequential flow of control.

Summary: The model allows careful description of concurrent algorithms, as well as precise statement of the correctness conditions that they are to satisfy. The correctness conditions are stated in terms of external behavior (i.e., the sequences of actions that occur at the external interface of the automaton), and are stated independently of any particular proposed solution. Finally, once both an algorithm and the correctness condition it is supposed to satisfy have been described in the model, it is then possible to use the model as a basis for a rigorous proof that the algorithm satisfies the given conditions. This book provides many examples of such proofs.

The following several sections give the definitions and basic results for the I/O automaton model. On a first reading, you may choose to read the definitions, illustrative examples, and statements of the results fairly carefully, but skip the proofs. The results are just the basic properties that show that the definitions "work properly."

2.2 Action Signatures

The actions of each automaton will be classified as either *input, output,* or *internal.* In the system being modeled, the distinctions are that input actions are not under the system's control, output actions are under the system's control and are externally observable, and internal actions are under the system's control but are not externally observable. In order to describe this classification formally, each automaton comes equipped with an *action signature.*

An **action signature** S is a triple consisting of three pairwise-disjoint sets of actions. The three components of S are written $in(S)$, $out(S)$, and $int(S)$, and the actions in these sets are referred to as the **input actions**, **output actions**, and **internal actions** of S, respectively. Let $ext(S) = in(S) \cup out(S)$ and refer to the actions in $ext(S)$ as the **external actions** of S. Also, let $local(S) = int(S) \cup out(S)$, and refer to the actions in $local(S)$ as the **locally controlled actions** of S. Finally, let $acts(S) = in(S) \cup out(S) \cup int(S)$, and refer to the actions in $acts(S)$ as the **actions** of S.

An **external action signature** is an action signature consisting entirely of external actions, that is, having no internal actions. If S is an action signature, then the **external action signature** of S is the action signature $extsig(S) = (in(S), out(S), \emptyset)$, that is, the action signature that is obtained from S by removing the internal actions.

Starting here, many detailed examples are included in this chapter to illustrate the important features of the model. If you are mainly interested in the general development and find the formal definitions easy to understand, you might wish to skip most of these examples in order to progress more quickly to Chapter 3.

EXAMPLE 2.2.1 Binary Memory Signature

Here is a very simple action signature, suitable for describing a simple binary memory. There are only four actions: two input actions, **CLEAR** and **SET**, which model the environment giving the memory a value (0 for **CLEAR** and 1 for **SET**), and two output actions, **REPORT0** and **REPORT1** by which the memory announces its current value to the environment. The signature is written as follows:

Input:
    SET
    CLEAR
Output:
    REPORT0
    REPORT1
Internal:
    none

EXAMPLE   2.2.2   Banking   Database   Signature

The following is a more complicated example of an action signature, S, having an infinite number of actions. This signature is appropriate for describing the actions of a simple banking database that maintains a collection of accounts. More accurately, what is described is actually a family of action signatures, each corresponding to a particular choice for the set of account names and for the operation identifiers that are associated with the operations on each account.

The operations available are **DEPOSIT**(X, k), **WITHDRAW**(X, k), and **BALANCE**(X), each indicating which account, X, is to be affected and also (for **DEPOSIT** and **WITHDRAW** operations) the amount of money, k, involved. As in the examples in Chapter 1, separate actions are used to model the request from a user for an operation and the response by the system reporting on the outcome of the request. The requests are modeled as input actions since they are not under the control of the banking database but rather are initiated by the environment. On the other hand, the responses are modeled as output actions since they are initiated by the banking database. There are no internal actions. For simplicity, aborts are ignored in this example, so all responses report the commit of the operation involved.

Each request action includes the name of the operation being requested, and also an integer to serve as an identifier for the operation. The operation identifier in a request must be one that is associated with the account involved. The same identifier will be used in the corresponding response. In addition, each request action includes the indicated account and amount information. Each response action for a **BALANCE** or **WITHDRAW** operation includes an amount of money as a return value. For a **WITHDRAW** operation, this return value indicates the amount actually withdrawn; this could be different from the amount requested, perhaps because of insufficient funds in the account or simply because the local branch did not have enough cash on hand.

To make the example completely specific, the set of three-digit integers is used as the set of account names, and the operation identifiers associated with account X are all the integers whose three low-order digits are given by X. Then the signature contains actions such as **REQUEST_DEPOSIT**$(5276, 276, \$100)$, which models the event in which the banking system's environment submits a request to it (with operation identifier 5276) for \$100 to be deposited in account 276. Similarly, it contains actions such as **REPORT_COMMIT_WITHDRAW**$(7310, \$20)$, which models the system delivering to its environment a report of the completion of operation 7310 (which was a withdrawal that obtained $20). The signature includes sufficiently many actions to represent the responses to a request as different actions if different values are to be returned.[3]

The action signature is written using parametric notation. For example, **REQUEST_DEPOSIT**(i, X, k) indicates the infinite collection of actions such as **REQUEST_DEPOSIT**$(5276, 276, \$100)$, **REQUEST-_DEPOSIT**$(1047, 047, \$3)$ and so on. For the formal model, however, these are simply separate actions with no more connection to one another than **SET** and **CLEAR** had in Example 2.2.1. Likewise, although the syntax suggests a connection between corresponding requests and responses, for example, between **REQUEST_DEPOSIT**$(5276, 276, \$100)$ and **REPORT_COM-MIT_DEPOSIT**(5276), this connection has no formal significance in the model. The signature is as follows:

Input:
> **REQUEST_DEPOSIT**(i, X, k), where i is an operation identifier associated with X, X is an account name, and k is a positive integer amount of money
> **REQUEST_WITHDRAW**(i, X, k), where i is an operation identifier associated with X, X is an account name, and k is a positive integer amount of money
> **REQUEST_BALANCE**(i, X), where i is an operation identifier associated with X, and X is an account name

Output:
> **REPORT_COMMIT_DEPOSIT**(i), where i is an operation identifier
> **REPORT_COMMIT_WITHDRAW**(i, k), where i is an operation identifier and k is a nonnegative integer amount of money
> **REPORT_COMMIT_BALANCE**(i, k), where i is an operation identifier and k is a nonnegative integer amount of money

Internal:
> none

That is, $in(S)$ consists of an infinite number of input actions, each a request for an operation of one of the three indicated kinds with appropriate parameters. Similarly, $out(S)$ consists of an infinite number of output actions, each a report of the commit of an operation of one of the three indicated kinds with a return value as an extra parameter in some cases. Also, $int(S)$ is empty, (i.e., there are no internal actions). Each of the sets $ext(S)$ and $acts(S)$ consists of all the actions of S, while the set $local(S)$ is identical to $out(S)$. S is an external action signature.

---

[3]The model uses the action name as the only communication between an automaton and its environment. Because of this, we must give a different name to each distinguishable action.

EXAMPLE 2.2.3   Register Signature

The following is an example of an action signature, S, with internal actions. This signature is appropriate for describing an atomic register. The operations available are **READ** and **WRITE**, but again, separate actions are used to model the request from a user for an operation and the response by the system reporting on the outcome of the request. As before, the requests are inputs and the reports are outputs. This example also includes internal **PERFORM** and **ABORT** actions. A **PERFORM** action is used to model the point between a request and the associated report at which the state of the register is actually changed or read. An **ABORT** action is used to model the point at which the designated operation is aborted.

As in Example 2.2.2, each request includes the name of the operation being requested and an integer identifier. In addition, the request for a **WRITE** operation includes an integer value to be written, and the successful response to a **READ** operation includes the value that was stored when the read was performed. For example, the action **REQUEST_WRITE**$(25, 4)$ models a user's request that the value 4 be stored in the register, with 25 as operation identifier for this request, and **REPORT_ABORT_WRITE**(63) models the response to the **WRITE** request with operation identifier 63, in which the user is told that the write did not succeed.

The action signature is as follows:

Input:
   REQUEST_READ(i), where i is an integer
   REQUEST_WRITE(i, d), where i is an integer and d is an integer
Output:
   REPORT_COMMIT_READ(i, d), where i is an integer and d is an integer
   REPORT_COMMIT_WRITE(i), where i is an integer
   REPORT_ABORT_READ(i), where i is an integer
   REPORT_ABORT_WRITE(i), where i is an integer
Internal:
   PERFORM_READ(i), where i is an integer
   PERFORM_WRITE(i), where i is an integer
   ABORT(i), where i is an integer

Thus, $in(S)$ consists of the requests for **READ** and **WRITE** operations, $out(S)$ consists of the reports, and $int(S)$ consists of actions that perform the actual **READ** and **WRITE** operations, plus actions that abort operations. The set $ext(S)$ consists of all the requests and reports, the set $acts(S)$ consists of all the actions of S, and the set $local(S)$ consists of all actions other than the requests.

2.3 Automata

This section defines *automata* and includes examples illustrating the definitions. Many of the examples are motivated by the informal banking examples discussed in Chapter 1. They also illustrate some of the notational conventions adopted throughout the remainder of the book.

An **automaton** A is a tuple that consists of four components:

- an action signature $sig(A)$,

- a set $states(A)$ of **states**,

- a nonempty set $start(A) \subseteq states(A)$ of **start states**, and

- a **transition relation** $steps(A) \subseteq states(A) \times acts(sig(A)) \times states(A)$, with the property that for every state s' and input action π there is a transition (s', π, s) in $steps(A)$.

An element (s', π, s) of $steps(A)$ is a **step** of A. The step (s', π, s) is called an **input step** of A if π is an input action, and **output steps**, **internal steps**, **external steps** and **locally controlled steps** are defined analogously. If (s', π, s) is a step of A, then π is said to be **enabled** in s'. Since every input action is enabled in every state, automata are said to be **input-enabled**. The input-enabling property means that an automaton is not able to block input actions.

Note the differences between this definition and that of ordinary nondeterministic finite-state automata. First, the set of states need not be finite. Second, more than one start state is permitted (this convention is appropriate for a nondeterministic machine). Third, the alphabet of actions is partitioned into the three categories of input, output, and internal actions, and a special enabling condition is imposed for input actions only. Fourth, no final states are specified.[4]

Note that an automaton can exhibit the usual sort of nondeterminism—the same action, applied in the same state, can lead to more than one successor state. There is also another kind of nondeterministic behavior that an automaton can exhibit, namely, that more than one locally controlled action can be enabled in the same state. Both types of nondeterminism are important to the model's descriptive power.

If A is an automaton, $acts(A)$ is sometimes used as a shorthand for $acts(sig(A))$, and likewise for $in(A)$, $out(A)$, and so on. An automaton A is said to be **closed** if all its actions are locally controlled, that is, if $in(A) = \emptyset$.

---

[4] A fifth difference will become apparent later. In this book, correctness definitions constrain every finite behavior of an automaton, whereas formal language theory requires only that some behavior lead to acceptance. The former style has been described as "don't know" nondeterminism, as distinct from "don't care" nondeterminism, and is more suitable for specifying reactive systems.

In this book, the state of an automaton will generally be determined by giving values to a collection of variables. Similarly, the transition relation of an automaton is usually not described by listing all its elements as triples; instead, we use a notation reminiscent of a programming or specification language, where an *effect* is described for each action, and a *precondition* is described for each local action. (Because of the fact that input actions are assumed to be enabled in all states, no preconditions are provided for inputs.) This notation refers to the set of all triples (s', π, s) where π is the action listed, s' is a state such that the precondition given is true in s', and the relationship between s and s' is as given in the effect.[5]

EXAMPLE 2.3.1   Binary Memory Automaton

The automaton F, modeling a simple binary memory, illustrates these definitions. The action signature is as in Example 2.2.1. There are only two states, called "*on*" and "*off*". There is one start state which is "*off*" (thus, $start(F)$ is actually the set with "*off*" as its only element). The transitions are the following six triples: ("*on*", **SET**, "*on*"), ("*off*", **SET**, "*on*"), ("*on*", **CLEAR**, "*off*"), ("*off*", **CLEAR**, "*off*"), ("*on*", **REPORT1**, "*on*"), ("*off*", **REPORT0**, "*off*"). Notice that there is a step with action **SET** starting in each possible state, as required by the model since **SET** is an input action. The following code describes the transition relation listed explicitly above:

SET
   Effect:
      $s = $ "*on*"

CLEAR
   Effect:
      $s = $ "*off*"

REPORT0
   Precondition:
      $s' = $ "*off*"
   Effect:
      $s = s'$

REPORT1
   Precondition:
      $s' = $ "*on*"
   Effect:
      $s = s'$

---

[5] If you are familiar with specification languages used for abstract data types, we stress that each precondition is an *enabling condition*; that is, the action can only take place when the condition is true, and may take place whenever it is true. In contrast, systems like VDM use the term "precondition" to refer to a limit on the implementor's responsibility: if these conditions do not hold, the operation is allowed to act arbitrarily. We also remind you that as a convention we write a prime to refer to the state before the action, rather than the state after as in Z and VDM

2.3.1 Conventions: Transition Relations

The automaton of the previous example is particularly simple. Later we will see much more complex automata, and we adopt some notational conventions that simplify the presentation of transition relations. The next example illustrates one such convention: when the effect list does not specify the value of a state component in s, that component is equal to its value in s'. This rule applies as well to compound components, such as arrays, or (as in this example) functions. When the effect of an action is to change a state component that is a function, by changing the function on only a few domain elements, only those domain elements are specified in the effect list, and the value of the function on other domain elements is equal to its value in s'. Arrays are treated similarly.

Another notational convention used here and elsewhere in this book is the omission of existential quantifiers. Thus, any variable that appears in the precondition or effect of an action but does not appear in the action itself is to be regarded as implicitly existentially quantified. For example, the code given below for the **REPORT_COMMIT-_DEPOSIT** action contains a variable X that does not appear in the action name. This indicates that $(s', \textbf{REPORT\_COMMIT\_DEPOSIT}(i), s)$ is a transition provided some value can be found for X that, when consistently applied in precondition and effect, causes both precondition and effect to have the value *true* when evaluated with the given states s' and s and the given value for X.

EXAMPLE 2.3.2 Banking Database Automaton

The next example is of an automaton that can be used to model a simple banking database with the interface described in Example 2.2.2. More accurately, a family of automata are defined, one for each choice for the set of account names and for the operation identifiers associated with each account. This example demonstrates a number of features of the model, including infinite state sets, nondeterminism, and our convention on descriptions of transition relations.

The automaton maintains a state variable giving the balance in each account, and also maintains information about requested operations. However, it only has memory for one outstanding request for an operation on each account. An operation with such a request is said to be pending. Thus, if another operation is requested while one is pending on the same account, the earlier request is overwritten. If a **DEPOSIT** or **BALANCE** operation is requested and not overwritten, the automaton performs the requested operation, and in the same action returns the appropriate results. If the user requests a **WITHDRAW** operation, however, the automaton can nondeterministically choose to deliver any amount of money between zero and the number of dollars requested (as long as there is sufficient money in the account). In any event, however, the bank debits the amount of money that it has actually delivered.

This database is modeled by the following automaton, called B (B stands for *bank*). The action signature of B, $sig(B)$, is the signature S of Example 2.2.2.

Each state s of B consists of values of the following variables, each of which is a function mapping the identifiers of accounts into the indicated set:

- *money*, a function with integer values,
- *active*, a function with Boolean values,
- *type*, a function with values in the set { "*deposit*", "*withdrawal*", "*balance*", "*null*" },
- *id*, a function with values either an operation identifier or "*null*", and
- *amount*, a function with nonnegative integer values.

There is one start state, in which *active* is the function that gives to every account name X the value *false*, *money*(X) and *amount*(X) have value 0 for each X, and the other variables all have value "*null*" on each account name X.

The transition relation of B consists of exactly those triples (s', π, s) satisfying the preconditions and yielding the effects given in Figure 2.1, where π is the indicated action.

Recall that for brevity, the description of the effect of an action only includes conditions on those components of the state s that may be changed by the action; if a component of the state is not specified in the effect, it is implicit that the value is the same in s and s'. Thus, for example, when (s', π, s) is a step of B and $\pi = $ **REQUEST_DEPOSIT**(i, X, k) then $s.money = s'.money$.

The values of the various components of state s are referenced using record notation (e.g., $s.money$).

As an example of the way to read such action descriptions, consider the action $\pi = $ **REQUEST_DEPOSIT**(i, X, k). This is an input, so no precondition appears. No matter what state s' the automaton is in, it can perform π and it will then be in a state s in which *active*(X) has value *true* (indicating that an operation on account X has been requested and is waiting for a report), and in which the other components of the state have values for X that record the various pieces of information about the requested operation. By the convention on unreferenced state components, the values of these functions on arguments other than X remain unchanged, as

REQUEST_DEPOSIT(i, X, k)
Effect:
  $s.active(X) = true$
  $s.type(X) = \text{``}deposit\text{''}$
  $s.id(X) = i$
  $s.amount(X) = k$

REQUEST_WITHDRAW(i, X, k)
Effect:
  $s.active(X) = true$
  $s.type(X) = \text{``}withdrawal\text{''}$
  $s.id(X) = i$
  $s.amount(X) = k$

REQUEST_BALANCE(i, X)
Effect:
  $s.active(X) = true$
  $s.type(X) = \text{``}balance\text{''}$
  $s.id(X) = i$
  $s.amount(X) = 0$

REPORT_COMMIT_DEPOSIT(i)
Precondition:
  $s'.active(X) = true$
  $s'.type(X) = \text{``}deposit\text{''}$
  $s'.id(X) = i$
Effect:
  $s.money(X) = s'.money(X) + s'.amount(X)$
  $s.active(X) = false$
  $s.type(X) = \text{``}null\text{''}$
  $s.id(X) = \text{``}null\text{''}$
  $s.amount(X) = 0$

REPORT_COMMIT_WITHDRAW(i, k)
Precondition:
  $s'.active(X) = true$
  $s'.type(X) = \text{``}withdrawal\text{''}$
  $s'.id(X) = i$
  $k \leq s'.amount(X)$
  $0 \leq k \leq s'.money(X)$
Effect:
  $s.money(X) = s'.money(X) - k$
  $s.active(X) = false$
  $s.type(X) = \text{``}null\text{''}$
  $s.id(X) = \text{``}null\text{''}$
  $s.amount(X) = 0$

REPORT_COMMIT_BALANCE(i, k)
Precondition:
  $s'.active(X) = true$
  $s'.type(X) = \text{``}balance\text{''}$
  $s'.id(X) = i$
  $k = s'.money(X)$
Effect:
  $s.active(X) = false$
  $s.type(X) = \text{``}null\text{''}$
  $s.id(X) = \text{``}null\text{''}$
  $s.amount(X) = 0$

Figure 2.1: Transition Relation for a Banking Database

does the value of *money* on all arguments. Without this convention, this action would take the following (much more verbose) form:

REQUEST_DEPOSIT(i, X, k)
Effect:
  $s.active(X) = true$
  $s.type(X) = \text{``}deposit\text{''}$
  $s.id(X) = i$
  $s.amount(X) = k$
  $s.money = s'.money$
  $s.active(Y) = s'.active(Y)$, for all $Y \neq X$
  $s.type(Y) = s'.type(Y)$, for all $Y \neq X$
  $s.id(Y) = s'.id(Y)$, for all $Y \neq X$
  $s.amount(Y) = s'.amount(Y)$, for all $Y \neq X$

As another example, the **REPORT_COMMIT_DEPOSIT**(i) action can only occur from a state s' in which there is some account X on which a deposit operation with identifier i is pending.[6] If this is the case, and if **REPORT-_COMMIT_DEPOSIT**(i) occurs, then the automaton is left in a state s in which there is no active operation waiting on X (i.e., $s.active(\mathrm{X}) = \textit{false}$) and the amount of money in the account is increased from its original value by the amount stored in the state s' for the active deposit operation.

Note that this automaton exhibits both of the types of nondeterminism described earlier. First, there are different locally controlled actions (for example, **REPORT_COMMIT_WITHDRAW**(i, k) operations for the same i and different k) enabled in the same state. Second, there are multiple transitions by a single report action from a single state. For example, from a state s' where $s'.active(\mathrm{X}1) = s'.active(\mathrm{X}2) = \textit{true}$, $s'.type(\mathrm{X}1) = s'.type(\mathrm{X}2) = \text{``deposit''}$, and $s'.id(\mathrm{X}1) = s'.id(\mathrm{X}2) = i$, the action **REPORT_COMMIT_DEPOSIT**(i) can lead to two states s_1 and s_2, such that $s_1.active(\mathrm{X}1) = \textit{true}$ and $s_1.active(\mathrm{X}2) = \textit{false}$ while $s_2.active(\mathrm{X}1) = \textit{false}$ and $s_2.active(\mathrm{X}2) = \textit{true}$.

Consider the specific example of B obtained when the account identifiers are 001 and 002, and as before operation identifiers are integers each associated with the account with the corresponding three low-order digits. If states are described by listing the components ($money(001)$, $active(001)$, $type(001)$, $id(001)$, $amount(001)$, $money(002)$, $active(002)$, $type(002)$, $id(002)$, $amount(002)$), then one of B's transitions is (s', π, s), where

$$s' = (100, \textit{true}, \text{``withdrawal''}, 37, 150, 200, \textit{false}, \text{``null''}, \text{``null''}, 0),$$
$$\pi = \textbf{REPORT\_COMMIT\_WITHDRAW}(37, \$85),$$
$$s = (15, \textit{false}, \text{``null''}, \text{``null''}, 0, 200, \textit{false}, \text{``null''}, \text{``null''}, 0).$$

This shows how the amount actually withdrawn can be less than what was requested and also less than the money in the account. Another transition is (t', ϕ, t) where

$$t' = (100, \textit{true}, \text{``withdrawal''}, 37, 150, 200, \textit{false}, \text{``null''}, \text{``null''}, 0),$$
$$\phi = \textbf{REQUEST\_BALANCE}(12),$$
$$t = (100, \textit{true}, \text{``withdrawal''}, 37, 150, 200, \textit{true}, \text{``balance''}, 12, 0).$$

---

[6] In fact, it is shown in Example 2.6.1 that if s' is a reachable state (one that actually occurs in any execution), then the account X involved can only be the account with which the operation identifier i is associated.

Another convention used in presentations of transition relations in later chapters is the use of *derived variables*; that is, we give a name to a particular expression involving the state variables, and we then refer to that name as if it were a variable whose value is always equal to the given expression. Of course, the value of a derived variable in s is not specified in the effect of an action; its value in s is determined by its defining expression (thus the convention of unspecified variables being unchanged does not apply to derived variables). This convention is first illustrated in the definition of the serial scheduler, in Section 3.5.3.

2.3.2 More Examples of Automata

The banking database automaton of the previous example (2.3.2) is typical for contexts in which the environment issues new requests only after receiving replies for previous requests. That is, the state records only the most recent pending request for each bank account. In contrast, the next example automaton is appropriate for more highly concurrent environments, using sets to store information about *all* outstanding requests.

EXAMPLE 2.3.3 Register Automaton

This example illustrates the use of set-valued state components and nondeterminism in the transition relation.

The automaton R models an atomic register with initial value 0. The action signature is as in Example 2.2.3. Each state s consists of values of the following variables:

- *data*, an integer, initially[7] 0,

- *requests*, a set of records, each with components *id*, holding an operation identifier; *kind*, holding the designation "*read*" or "*write*"; and *value*, holding an integer or "*null*"; initially, this set of records is empty, and

- *reports*, a set of records, each with components *id*, holding an operation identifier; *outcome*, holding the designation "*commit*" or "*abort*"; *kind*, holding the designation "*read*" or "*write*"; and *value*, holding an integer or "*null*"; initially, this set of records is also empty.

---

[7]This initialization means that in the start state or start states, the value of this component is as specified. Initializations are usually described in this way, without further explanation.

A state of R is described by listing the components in the order given above. Thus, $start(R)$ is a set containing the single state $(0, \emptyset, \emptyset)$.

The automaton R records all requests in the *requests* set.[8] It chooses nondeterministically to execute a particular internal action corresponding to performing or aborting a particular operation in the *requests* set. When R executes a **PERFORM_READ** or **PERFORM_WRITE** action, it applies the indicated operation to the data copy in *data*, updating that copy if appropriate, and putting a report of the results in the *reports* set. When R executes an **ABORT** action, it puts the appropriate report in the *reports* set, without modifying the data copy. Each report action removes the appropriate report from the *reports* set.

The transition relation is described in Figure 2.2, using the same conventions as in the previous example.

One example of a transition of R is (s', π, s) where

$$
\begin{aligned}
s' &= (3, \{(5, \text{``write''}, 4), (6, \text{``read''}, \text{``null''})\}, \emptyset), \\
\pi &= \textbf{PERFORM\_READ}(6), and \\
s &= (3, \{(5, \text{``write''}, 4)\}, \{(6, \text{``commit''}, \text{``read''}, 3)\}).
\end{aligned}
$$

Another example of a transition of R is (t', ϕ, t) where

$$
\begin{aligned}
t' &= (3, \{(5, \text{``write''}, 4), (6, \text{``read''}, \text{``null''})\}, \emptyset), \\
\phi &= \textbf{PERFORM\_WRITE}(5), and \\
t &= (4, \{(6, \text{``read''}, \text{``null''})\}, \{(5, \text{``commit''}, \text{``write''}, \text{``null''})\}).
\end{aligned}
$$

Notice that (since $t' = s'$ but $\pi \neq \phi$) this illustrates the form of nondeterminism in which different locally controlled actions are enabled in the same state. The other form of nondeterminism, in which the same action applied from the same state leads to two different states, is illustrated by the transitions (u', ψ, u_1) and (u', ψ, u_2), where

$$
\begin{aligned}
u' &= (3, \{(5, \text{``write''}, 4), (5, \text{``read''}, \text{``null''})\}, \emptyset), \\
\psi &= \textbf{ABORT}(5), \\
u_1 &= (3, \{(5, \text{``write''}, 4)\}, \{(5, \text{``abort''}, \text{``read''}, \text{``null''})\}), and \\
u_2 &= (3, \{(5, \text{``read''}, \text{``null''})\}, \{(5, \text{``abort''}, \text{``write''}, \text{``null''})\}).
\end{aligned}
$$

---

[8]One might expect the users of this automaton not to repeat in a request an operation identifier that has already been used. However, this is not something that the automaton can guarantee, because it must always be able to receive any input action. Later sections discuss *well-formedness* conditions, which provide a way of modeling expectations of reasonable user (or other environmental) activity.

REQUEST_READ(i)
Effect:
$s.requests = s'.requests \cup \{r\}$, where
$r.id = i$,
$r.kind =$ "read", and
$r.value =$ "null"

REQUEST_WRITE(i, d)
Effect:
$s.requests = s'.requests \cup \{r\}$, where
$r.id = i$,
$r.kind =$ "write", and
$r.value = d$

REPORT_COMMIT_READ(i, d)
Precondition:
$r' \in s'.reports$, where
$r'.id = i$,
$r'.outcome =$ "commit",
$r'.kind =$ "read", and
$r'.value = d.$
Effect:
$s.reports = s'.reports - \{r'\}$

REPORT_COMMIT_WRITE(i)
Precondition:
$r' \in s'.reports$, where
$r'.id = i$,
$r'.outcome =$ "commit", and
$r'.kind =$ "write"
Effect:
$s.reports = s'.reports - \{r'\}$

REPORT_ABORT_READ(i)
Precondition:
$r' \in s'.reports$, where
$r'.id = i$,
$r'.outcome =$ "abort", and
$r'.kind =$ "read"
Effect:
$s.reports = s'.reports - \{r'\}$

REPORT_ABORT_WRITE(i)
Precondition:
$r' \in s'.reports$, where
$r'.id = i$,
$r'.outcome =$ "abort", and
$r'.kind =$ "write"
Effect:
$s.reports = s'.reports - \{r'\}$

PERFORM_READ(i)
Precondition:
$r' \in s'.requests$, where
$r'.id = i$ and
$r'.kind =$ "read"
Effect:
$s.requests = s'.requests - \{r'\}$
$s.reports = s'.reports \cup \{r\}$, where
$r.id = i$,
$r.outcome =$ "commit",
$r.kind =$ "read", and
$r.value = s'.data$

PERFORM_WRITE(i)
Precondition:
$r' \in s'.requests$, where
$r'.id = i$ and
$r'.kind =$ "write"
Effect:
$s.requests = s'.requests - \{r'\}$
$s.data = r'.value$
$s.reports = s'.reports \cup \{r\}$, where
$r.id = i$,
$r.outcome =$ "commit",
$r.kind =$ "write", and
$r.value =$ "null"

ABORT(i)
Precondition:
$r' \in s'.requests$, where
$r'.id = i$
Effect:
$s.requests = s'.requests - \{r'\}$
$s.reports = s'.reports \cup \{r\}$, where
$r.id = i$,
$r.outcome =$ "abort",
$r.kind = r'.kind$, and
$r.value =$ "null"

Figure 2.2: Transition Relation for a Register

On the other hand, (s', π, s_1) with $s' = (3, \{(5, \text{``}write\text{''}, 4), (6, \text{``}read\text{''},$ $\text{``}null\text{''})\}, \emptyset)$, $\pi = \textbf{PERFORM\_READ}(6)$, and $s_1 = (3, \{(5, \text{``}write\text{''}, 4)\}, \{(6,$ $\text{``}commit\text{''}, \text{``}read\text{''}, 4)\})$), is not a transition as the effect relationship does not hold between s' and s_1. Also there is no state x for which $(s', \textbf{REPORT-}$ $\textbf{\_COMMIT\_WRITE}(6), x)$ is a transition, because s' does not satisfy the precondition given in the code of $\textbf{REPORT\_COMMIT\_WRITE}(i)$ with $i = 6$ (no record r' exists to make the precondition true).

The final example of this subsection defines an automaton which is appropriate to use as the environment of the banking database automaton in Example 2.3.2.

EXAMPLE 2.3.4   Bank User Automaton

Now consider a user of the banking database B described in Example 2.3.2. The user owns one of the accounts in the bank. He can request arbitrary operations on his own account. The user nondeterministically chooses which operation to request, and waits for each requested operation to report back before requesting another. The user keeps track of the amount of money he has in his pocket, increasing this by the amount received whenever money is withdrawn from the bank and decreasing it when a deposit is requested. (Notice that money is assumed to leave his pocket when the deposit is *requested*, but to enter it only when the withdrawal is *reported*.) One could model such a user by an automaton, $U_{X,m}$, where X is a specific account in the bank and m is the money the user starts with in his pocket. The action signature of $U_{X,m}$, $sig(U_{X,m})$, is as follows.

Input:
    REPORT_COMMIT_DEPOSIT(i), where i is an operation identifier
        associated with X
    REPORT_COMMIT_WITHDRAW(i,k), where i is an operation identifier
        associated with X and k is a nonnegative integer amount of money
    REPORT_COMMIT_BALANCE(i,k), where i is an operation identifier
        associated with X and k is a nonnegative integer amount of money
Output:
    REQUEST_DEPOSIT(i, X, k), where i is an operation identifier associated
        with X and k is a positive integer amount of money
    REQUEST_WITHDRAW(i, X, k), where i is an operation identifier associated
        with X and k is a positive integer amount of money
    REQUEST_BALANCE(i, X), where i is an operation identifier associated
        with X
Internal:
    none

REPORT_COMMIT_DEPOSIT(i)
   Effect:
      $s.waiting = false$

REPORT_COMMIT_WITHDRAW(i, k)
   Effect:
      $s.waiting = false$
      $s.cash = s'.cash + k$

REPORT_COMMIT_BALANCE(i, k)
   Effect:
      $s.waiting = false$

REQUEST_DEPOSIT(i, X, k)
   Precondition:
      $s'.waiting = false$
      $k \leq s'.cash$
   Effect:
      $s.waiting = true$
      $s.cash = s'.cash - k$

REQUEST_WITHDRAW(i, X, k)
   Precondition:
      $s'.waiting = false$
   Effect:
      $s.waiting = true$

REQUEST_BALANCE(i, X)
   Precondition:
      $s'.waiting = false$
   Effect:
      $s.waiting = true$

Figure 2.3: Transition Relation for a Bank User

Notice that for a particular user automaton (given by specific values for X and m) the letter X in the signature above is a constant, not a free variable (in contrast to the signature of the bank automaton B in Example 2.3.2).

Each state s of $U_{\mathrm{X},m}$ consists of values of the following variables: *waiting*, a Boolean, and *cash*, a nonnegative integer. There is a unique start state, in which *waiting* has value *false* and *cash* has value m.

The transition relation of $U_{\mathrm{X},m}$ is given in Figure 2.3.

For example, consider the input action **REPORT_COMMIT_WITH-DRAW**(i, k). This is an input to the user, so no precondition appears. The cash in his pocket increases by the amount mentioned in the action name; also, the fact that the user is no longer waiting for an operation is recorded. As another example, the **REQUEST_WITHDRAW**(i, X, k) action can only occur from a state in which there is no operation currently requested. Its effect is to indicate to the user that he is waiting for an operation to report back.

This automaton exhibits only one of the kinds of nondeterminism mentioned earlier: there are different locally controlled actions, namely, different request actions, enabled in the same state. However, each action applied from each state leads to a unique next state.

2.4 Executions and Behaviors

This section describes how automata perform their computations and defines *executions*, *schedules*, and *behaviors*, which record information about those computations. The essential idea is that an automaton computes by changing from a start state to another state, by a transition for some action, and then takes another step to reach another state, and so on. The sequence showing all states and actions is called an *execution*. Often the states are not important, and so we consider just the sequence of actions that happen: this is a *schedule*. When we also ignore the internal actions, and only consider the sequence of external actions, we speak of a *behavior*. All these terms are defined precisely in the rest of this section.

The basic definition is that of an *execution* of an automaton:

If A is an automaton, then an **execution fragment** of A is a finite sequence $s_0\pi_1 s_1\pi_2 \ldots \pi_n s_n$ or infinite sequence $s_0\pi_1 s_1\pi_2 \ldots \pi_n s_n \ldots$ of alternating states and actions of A such that $(s_i, \pi_{i+1}, s_{i+1})$ is a step of A for every i for which s_{i+1} exists in the sequence. An execution fragment beginning with a start state is called an **execution**. The set of executions of A is denoted by $execs(A)$. A state is said to be **reachable** in A if it is the final state of a finite execution of A.

The exposition will often want to focus attention on just the actions in an execution, rather than the states. Thus, the **schedule** of an execution fragment α of A is defined to be the subsequence of α consisting of actions and is denoted by $sched(\alpha)$. A sequence β is a **schedule** of A if β is the schedule of an execution of A. The set of schedules of A is denoted by $scheds(A)$. The **behavior** of a sequence β of actions in $acts(A)$, denoted by $beh(\beta)$, is the subsequence of β consisting of actions in $ext(A)$. We also refer to the **behavior** of an execution fragment α of A (denoted by $beh(\alpha)$) as defined to be $beh(sched(\alpha))$. Notice that this means that $beh(\alpha)$ is the subsequence of α consisting of external actions of A. A sequence β is a **behavior** of A if β is the behavior of an execution of A. The set of behaviors of A is denoted by $behs(A)$.

It is also useful to have a notion of an *extended step*, to describe a state transition that occurs as a result of a sequence of actions, not necessarily just a single action. An **extended step** of an automaton A is a triple of the form (s', β, s), where s' and s are in $states(A)$, β is a finite sequence of actions in $acts(A)$, and there is an execution fragment of A having s' as its first state, s as its last state and β as its schedule. (This execution fragment might consist of only a single state, in the case that β is the empty sequence.) If γ is a sequence of actions in $ext(A)$, then (s', γ, s) is a **move** of A if there is an extended step (s', β, s) of A such that $\gamma = beh(\beta)$.

A finite schedule β of A **can lead to** state s in A if there is some finite execution α of A with final state s and with $sched(\alpha) = \beta$. An action π is **enabled after** a finite schedule β of A if β can lead to a state s in A, such that π is enabled in s.

If β is any sequence of actions and A is an automaton, $\beta|A$ is a shorthand for $\beta|acts(A)$. (The projection operation for sequences is defined in the Appendix.)

EXAMPLE 2.4.1 **Banking Execution**

The following is an example of an execution, α, of the bank automaton B of Example 2.3.2, for the case where there are exactly two accounts, 001 and 002. As in Example 2.3.2, each state of B is described by a vector with ten components, representing, in order, the values of the variables: $(money(001),\ active(001),\ type(001),\ id(001),\ amount(001),\ money(002),$ $active(002),\ type(002),\ id(002),\ amount(002))$. As in Chapter 1, sequences run vertically on the page, with indentation to help you identify actions with a common operation identifier. Now, however, the sequences include not only actions as in Chapter 1, but also the intervening states.

$(0, false,\ \text{``}null\text{''},\ \text{``}null\text{''}, 0, 0, false,\ \text{``}null\text{''},\ \text{``}null\text{''}, 0),$
REQUEST_DEPOSIT$(1001, 001, \$100),$
$(0, true,\ \text{``}deposit\text{''}, 1, 100, 0, false,\ \text{``}null\text{''},\ \text{``}null\text{''}, 0),$
REQUEST_DEPOSIT$(2002, 002, \$150),$
$(0, true,\ \text{``}deposit\text{''}, 1, 100, 0, true,\ \text{``}deposit\text{''}, 2, 150),$
REPORT_COMMIT_DEPOSIT$(2002),$
$(0, true,\ \text{``}deposit\text{''}, 1, 100, 150, false,\ \text{``}null\text{''},\ \text{``}null\text{''}, 0),$
REQUEST_WITHDRAW$(4002, 002, \$75),$
$(0, true,\ \text{``}deposit\text{''}, 1, 100, 150, true,\ \text{``}withdrawal\text{''}, 4, 75),$
REPORT_COMMIT_WITHDRAW$(4002, \$60),$
$(0, true,\ \text{``}deposit\text{''}, 1, 100, 90, false,\ \text{``}null\text{''},\ \text{``}null\text{''}, 0),$
REPORT_COMMIT_DEPOSIT$(1001),$
$(100, false,\ \text{``}null\text{''},\ \text{``}null\text{''}, 0, 90, false,\ \text{``}null\text{''},\ \text{``}null\text{''}, 0).$

In execution α, requests and reports alternate strictly for each account; however, operations on different accounts sometimes run concurrently. There are also executions of B in which requests and reports do not alternate strictly for each account: there can be consecutive requests, as shown in the following execution, α'. (There is no execution, however, in which there are consecutive reports for one account.)

$(0, false,\ \text{``}null\text{''},\ \text{``}null\text{''}, 0, 0, false,\ \text{``}null\text{''},\ \text{``}null\text{''}, 0),$
REQUEST_DEPOSIT$(1001, 001, \$100),$
$(0, true,\ \text{``}deposit\text{''}, 1, 100, 0, false,\ \text{``}null\text{''},\ \text{``}null\text{''}, 0),$
REQUEST_DEPOSIT$(2002, 002, \$150),$
$(0, true,\ \text{``}deposit\text{''}, 1, 100, 0, true,\ \text{``}deposit\text{''}, 2, 150),$
REPORT_COMMIT_DEPOSIT$(2002),$
$(0, true,\ \text{``}deposit\text{''}, 1, 100, 150, false,\ \text{``}null\text{''},\ \text{``}null\text{''}, 0),$
REQUEST_WITHDRAW$(3001, 001, \$75),$

$(0, true, "withdrawal", 3, 75, 150, false, "null", "null", 0),$
REPORT_COMMIT_WITHDRAW$(3001, \$0),$
$(0, false, "null", "null", 0, 150, false, "null", "null", 0).$

Execution α' illustrates the fact that, in a sequence of consecutive requests for a given account, all except the last are lost. Each of the states in α and in α' is a reachable state of B. Any prefix of one of these executions ending in a state is also an execution. All of these executions just described are also execution fragments, as are all suffixes of these executions that begin with states. Although α and α' are both finite executions, it is possible to continue either indefinitely to obtain an infinite execution.

The schedule associated with execution α, $sched(\alpha)$, is as follows.

REQUEST_DEPOSIT$(1001, 001, \$100),$
   REQUEST_DEPOSIT$(2002, 002, \$150),$
      REPORT_COMMIT_DEPOSIT$(2002),$
         REQUEST_WITHDRAW$(4002, 002, \$75),$
            REPORT_COMMIT_WITHDRAW$(4002, \$60),$
REPORT_COMMIT_DEPOSIT$(1001).$

Similarly $sched(\alpha')$ is:

REQUEST_DEPOSIT$(1001, 001, \$100),$
   REQUEST_DEPOSIT$(2002, 002, \$150),$
      REPORT_COMMIT_DEPOSIT$(2002),$
         REQUEST_WITHDRAW$(3001, 001, \$75),$
            REPORT_COMMIT_WITHDRAW$(3001, \$0).$

Since all actions of B are external, these schedules are also behaviors of B.

An example of an extended step of B is the triple (s', β, s), where

$$s' = (0, true, "deposit", 1, 100, 150, false, "null", "null", 0),$$
$$\beta = \textbf{REQUEST\_WITHDRAW}(4002, 002, \$75)$$
$$\textbf{REPORT\_COMMIT\_WITHDRAW}(4002, \$60)$$
$$\textbf{REPORT\_COMMIT\_DEPOSIT}(1001),$$
$$s = (100, false, "null", "null", 0, 90, false, "null", "null", 0).$$

EXAMPLE 2.4.2   Register Execution

The following is an example of an execution, α, of the atomic register automaton of Example 2.3.3. Each state is described as a vector with three components, representing, in order, the values of the variables: (*data*, *requests*, *reports*).

$(0, \emptyset, \emptyset)$,
REQUEST_WRITE$(1, 3)$,
$(0, \{(1, \text{``write''}, 3)\}, \emptyset)$,
REQUEST_READ(2),
$(0, \{(1, \text{``write''}, 3), (2, \text{``read''}, \text{``null''})\}, \emptyset)$,
PERFORM_WRITE(1),
$(3, \{(2, \text{``read''}, \text{``null''})\}, \{(1, \text{``commit''}, \text{``write''}, \text{``null''})\})$,
PERFORM_READ(2),
$(3, \emptyset, \{(1, \text{``commit''}, \text{``write''}, \text{``null''}), (2, \text{``commit''}, \text{``read''}, 3)\})$
REPORT_COMMIT_WRITE(1),
$(3, \emptyset, \{(2, \text{``commit''}, \text{``read''}, 3)\})$,
REPORT_COMMIT_READ$(2, 3)$,
$(3, \emptyset, \emptyset)$,
REQUEST_WRITE$(3, 5)$,
$(3, \{(3, \text{``write''}, 5)\}, \emptyset)$,
REQUEST_READ(4),
$(3, \{(3, \text{``write''}, 5), (4, \text{``read''}, \text{``null''})\}, \emptyset)$,
REQUEST_WRITE$(5, 6)$,
$(3, \{(3, \text{``write''}, 5), (4, \text{``read''}, \text{``null''}), (5, \text{``write''}, 6)\}, \emptyset)$,
PERFORM_READ(4),
$(3, \{(3, \text{``write''}, 5), (5, \text{``write''}, 6)\}, \{(4, \text{``commit''}, \text{``read''}, 3)\})$,
ABORT(5)
$(3, \{(3, \text{``write''}, 5)\}, \{(4, \text{``commit''}, \text{``read''}, 3), (5, \text{``abort''}, \text{``write''}, \text{``null''})\})$,
REPORT_ABORT_WRITE(5),
$(3, \{(3, \text{``write''}, 5)\}, \{(4, \text{``commit''}, \text{``read''}, 3)\})$,
PERFORM_WRITE(3),
$(5, \emptyset, \{(3, \text{``commit''}, \text{``write''}, \text{``null''}), (4, \text{``commit''}, \text{``read''}, 3)\})$,
REPORT_COMMIT_WRITE(3),
$(5, \emptyset, \{(4, \text{``commit''}, \text{``read''}, 3)\})$,
REPORT_COMMIT_READ$(4, 3)$,
$(5, \emptyset, \emptyset)$.

Note that, unlike the bank account examples, the response of the register to consecutive requests is *not* simply to overwrite all but the last request, but rather to process (*perform*) the requests in some order. Notice in particular that even though the request for operation 3 preceded the request for operation 4, and the reports also occurred in the order 3 then 4, in fact the internal performance was in the order 4 then 3 (and the value returned reflects this). This is consistent with the idea of an atomic object, since the period between the request and the report for operation 3 overlaps the corresponding period for operation 4.

The schedule associated with this execution, $sched(\alpha)$, is:

REQUEST_WRITE(1, 3),
  REQUEST_READ(2),
PERFORM_WRITE(1),
  PERFORM_READ(2),
REPORT_COMMIT_WRITE(1),
  REPORT_COMMIT_READ(2, 3),
    REQUEST_WRITE(3, 5),
      REQUEST_READ(4),
        REQUEST_WRITE(5, 6),
      PERFORM_READ(4),
      ABORT(5),
        REPORT_ABORT_WRITE(5),
    PERFORM_WRITE(3),
    REPORT_COMMIT_WRITE(3),
      REPORT_COMMIT_READ(4, 3).

The behavior associated with this execution, $beh(\alpha)$, is the result of removing the **ABORT**, **PERFORM_READ**, and **PERFORM_WRITE** events from $sched(\alpha)$.

REQUEST_WRITE(1, 3),
  REQUEST_READ(2),
REPORT_COMMIT_WRITE(1),
  REPORT_COMMIT_READ(2, 3),
    REQUEST_WRITE(3, 5),
      REQUEST_READ(4),
        REQUEST_WRITE(5, 6),
        REPORT_ABORT_WRITE(5),
    REPORT_COMMIT_WRITE(3),
      REPORT_COMMIT_READ(4, 3).

Thus, for this example, the set of behaviors is different from the set of schedules, since the behaviors do not include the (internal) events reflecting performing or aborting previously requested operations.

2.5 Composition

This section shows how a set of automata can be *composed* to yield another automaton. The composition operator identifies output actions of one automaton with identically named input actions of any number of other automata. When a particular action occurs, all automata having that action in their signature are assumed to take steps involving that action synchronously, while other automata are assumed to take no steps.

The operator permits composition of a finite or infinite number of automata. The reason for considering infinite composition is to model systems in which some components (e.g., transactions) are created dynamically, as computation proceeds. It is convenient to model dynamically created components as if they exist from the beginning, but are not enabled to perform any steps until a special *create* action occurs. The create action will be an ordinary input action of the automaton modeling the component. Since the potential number of components that might be created during the entire collection of possible computations is infinite, it is useful to have an operator that composes infinitely many automata.

The composition of action signatures is defined first, followed by the composition of automata. Then some important basic results are given, relating the executions, schedules and behaviors of a composition of automata to the corresponding sequences for the individual components.

2.5.1 Composition of Action Signatures

Composition of action signatures is defined as a preliminary step to defining composition of automata. Informally, if each component of a system has a given action signature, the composition gives the signature applicable to the whole system. This composition is only defined in the case where the component automata satisfy some simple *compatibility* conditions.

Let I be an index set that is at most countable. A collection $\{S_i\}_{i \in I}$ of action signatures is said to be **compatible** if the following conditions hold:

1. $out(S_i) \cap out(S_j) = \emptyset$, for all $i, j \in I$ such that $i \neq j$,

2. $int(S_i) \cap acts(S_j) = \emptyset$, for all $i, j \in I$ such that $i \neq j$, and

3. no action is in $acts(S_i)$ for infinitely many i.

Thus, no action is an output of more than one signature in the collection, and internal actions of any signature do not appear in any other signature in the collection. Moreover, actions are not permitted to involve infinitely many component signatures. When we define the composition of automata, these restrictions will ensure that an action cannot be under the control of more than one component in a system, and that internal actions of one component are not detectable by other components. The final condition is technical, being needed appropriate properties to hold for compositions of automata. In this book, we rarely use actions shared between more than *two* components.

The **composition** $S = \Pi_{i \in I} S_i$ of a collection of compatible action signatures $\{S_i\}_{i \in I}$ is defined to be the action signature with

- $in(S) = \cup_{i \in I} in(S_i) - \cup_{i \in I} out(S_i)$,

- $out(S) = \cup_{i \in I} out(S_i)$, and

- $int(S) = \cup_{i \in I} int(S_i)$.

Thus, output actions are those that are outputs of any of the component signatures, and similarly for internal actions. Input actions are any actions that are inputs to any of the component signatures, but outputs of no component signature. The intuition behind these definitions is that an action is under the control of a system if it is under the control of any part of the system; conversely, an action is not under the control of a system when it is not controlled by *any* of the components. Notice that these definitions mean that interactions between components are outputs of the composition, and so are regarded as detectable by the environment of the system.

EXAMPLE 2.5.1   Composing   Signatures: Bank   Databases   and   Users

Consider the bank database B of Example 2.3.2 once again, for the specific case where there are exactly two accounts, 001 and 002, and operation identifiers are associated as before (by the three low-order digits). The signature of this database is then:

Input:
   REQUEST_DEPOSIT(i, X, k), where $X \in \{001, 002\}$,
         i is an operation identifier with X as its low-order digits,
         and k is a positive integer amount of money
   REQUEST_WITHDRAW(i, X, k), where $X \in \{001, 002\}$,
         i is an operation identifier with X as its low-order digits,
         and k is a positive integer amount of money

REQUEST_BALANCE(i, X), where $\text{X} \in \{001, 002\}$
and i is an operation identifier with X as its low-order digits
Output:
REPORT_COMMIT_DEPOSIT(i), where i is an operation identifier
REPORT_COMMIT_WITHDRAW(i, k), where i is an operation identifier
and k is a nonnegative integer amount of money
REPORT_COMMIT_BALANCE(i, k), where i is an operation identifier
and k is a nonnegative integer amount of money
Internal:
none

Now consider the user $U_{001,300}$, modeling the user who owns account 001 and starts with \$300 cash on hand. As described in Example 2.3.4, this user has the signature:

Input:
REPORT_COMMIT_DEPOSIT(i), where 001 are the low-order digits of i
REPORT_COMMIT_WITHDRAW(i, k), where 001 are the low-order digits
of i and k is a nonnegative integer amount of money
REPORT_COMMIT_BALANCE(i, k), where 001 are the low-order digits of i
and k is a nonnegative integer amount of money
Output:
REQUEST_DEPOSIT$(i, 001, k)$, where 001 are the low-order digits of i
and k is a positive integer amount of money
REQUEST_WITHDRAW$(i, 001, k)$, where 001 are the low-order digits of i
and k is a positive integer amount of money
REQUEST_BALANCE$(i, 001)$, where 001 are the low-order digits of i
Internal:
none

The composition of these two action signatures is the following action signature. (Formally, the index set for the composition can be taken to be $\{bank, a\}$, where $bank$ stands for the bank and a stands for the user with bank account 001.)

Input:
REQUEST_DEPOSIT$(i, 002, k)$, where 002 are the low-order digits of i
and k is a positive integer amount of money
REQUEST_WITHDRAW$(i, 002, k)$, where 002 are the low-order digits of i
and k is a positive integer amount of money
REQUEST_BALANCE$(i, 002)$, where 002 are the low-order digits of i
Output:
REQUEST_DEPOSIT$(i, 001, k)$, where 001 are the low-order digits of i
and k is a positive integer amount of money
REQUEST_WITHDRAW$(i, 001, k)$, where 001 are the low-order digits of i
and k is a positive integer amount of money
REQUEST_BALANCE$(i, 001)$, where 001 are the low-order digits of i
REPORT_COMMIT_DEPOSIT(i), where i is an operation identifier

REPORT_COMMIT_WITHDRAW(i, k), where i is an operation identifier
and k is a nonnegative integer amount of money
REPORT_COMMIT_BALANCE(i, k), where i is an operation identifier
and k is a nonnegative integer amount of money
Internal:
none

Note that all the requests that are outputs of $U_{001,300}$ are outputs in this composed action signature. There are also requests that are inputs to B but are not outputs of $U_{001,300}$, namely, the requests that refer to account 002. These are inputs of the composed action signature. All the responses are outputs of B and are therefore outputs of the composed action signature.

2.5.2 Composition of Automata

A collection $\{A_i\}_{i \in I}$ of automata is said to be **compatible** if their action signatures are compatible. The **composition** $A = \Pi_{i \in I} A_i$ of a compatible collection of automata $\{A_i\}_{i \in I}$ has the following components:[9]

- $sig(A) = \Pi_{i \in I} sig(A_i)$,

- $states(A) = \Pi_{i \in I} states(A_i)$,

- $start(A) = \Pi_{i \in I} start(A_i)$, and

- $steps(A)$ is the set of triples (s', π, s) such that for all $i \in I$,

    - if $\pi \in acts(A_i)$, then $(s'[i], \pi, s[i]) \in steps(A_i)$, and
    - if $\pi \notin acts(A_i)$, then $s'[i] = s[i]$.[10]

Since the automata A_i are input-enabled, so is their composition, and hence their composition is an automaton. Each step of the composition automaton consists of all the automata that have a particular action in their action signature performing that action concurrently, while the automata that do not have that action in their signature do nothing. This models the instantaneous transmission of an output of one component to all components of which that action is an input. An automaton

---

[9]Note that the second and third components listed are just ordinary Cartesian products of sets as defined in the Appendix, while the first component uses the previous definition of composition of signatures.

[10]The notation $s[i]$ denotes the ith component of the state vector s.

formed by composition is often referred to as a *system* of automata. Composition is a commutative and associative operation on automata, up to obvious isomorphisms between the state sets.

EXAMPLE 2.5.2   Composing Automata: Bank Databases and Users

Consider the composition of the bank database B with accounts 001 and 002 (as given in Example 2.3.2) and user $U_{001,300}$ (as given in Example 2.3.4). The signature of the composition is given in Example 2.5.1 above. Each state of the composition is a pair consisting of a state of the database and a state of the user (i.e., of values of all of the variables in the database and user state). There is one start state, consisting of the start state of B paired with the start state of $U_{001,300}$, namely, $((0, \textit{false}, \text{"null"}, \text{"null"}, 0, \textit{false}, \text{"null"}, \text{"null"}, 0), (\textit{false}, 300))$. (The components of the bank's state are listed in the order $(money(001), active(001), type(001), id(001), amount(001), money(002), active(002), type(002), id(002), amount(002))$, and the components of the user state are listed in the order $(\textit{waiting}, \textit{cash})$.)

An example of a step of the composition is the following: (s', π, s) where $s' = ((120, \textit{false}, \text{"null"}, \text{"null"}, 0, 145, \textit{true}, \text{"deposit"}, 12, 25), (\textit{false}, 200))$, and $\pi = \textbf{REQUEST\_DEPOSIT}(3001, 001, \$50)$, and $s = ((120, \textit{true}, \text{"deposit"}, 31, 50, 145, \textit{true}, \text{"deposit"}, 12, 25), (\textit{true}, 150))$. This step describes what happens when a **REQUEST_DEPOSIT** action occurs: it causes both the database and the user to record certain relevant information about the operation.

Another example of a step is (t', ϕ, t) where $t' = ((120, \textit{false}, \text{"null"}, \text{"null"}, 0, 145, \textit{true}, \text{"deposit"}, 12, 25), (\textit{false}, 200))$, and $\phi = \textbf{REPORT\_COMMIT\_DEPOSIT}(1002)$, and $t = ((120, \textit{false}, \text{"null"}, \text{"null"}, 0, 170, \textit{false}, \text{"null"}, \text{"null"}, 0), (\textit{false}, 200))$. Notice how **REQUEST_DEPOSIT**$(3001, 001, \$50)$ (being an action in the signature of both B and $U_{001,300}$) affects both components of the state of the composition, while **REPORT_COMMIT_DEPOSIT**(1002) as an action in the signature of B but not in the signature of $U_{001,300}$ does not change the user part of the state of the composition.

EXAMPLE 2.5.3   Composing Several Automata

The previous example illustrates the composition of a pair of automata. For an example of the composition of three automata, consider the automaton $BS_{001,300,002,250}$, which is the composition of B above with the two user automata $U_{001,300}$ and $U_{002,250}$. The action signature of this composition is:

Input:
 none
Output:
 REQUEST_DEPOSIT(i, X, k), where i is an operation identifier associated with
  X, X is either 001 or 002, and k is a positive integer amount of money
 REQUEST_WITHDRAW(i, X, k), where i is an operation identifier associated
  with X, X is either 001 or 002, and k is a positive integer amount of money
 REQUEST_BALANCE(i, X), where i is an operation identifier associated with
  X, and X is either 001 or 002
 REPORT_COMMIT_DEPOSIT(i), where i is an operation identifier
 REPORT_COMMIT_WITHDRAW(i, k), where i is an operation identifier
  and k is a nonnegative integer amount of money
 REPORT_COMMIT_BALANCE(i, k), where i is an operation identifier
  and k is a nonnegative integer amount of money
Internal:
 none

The states of $BS_{001,300,002,250}$ are now triples consisting of states of the
three components, and similarly for the start states. Each step of the
composition involves synchronized computation by one of the user automata and the database. (In general, however, in a composition, an
output action of one component need not be an input action of any
other component, or indeed it could be an input action of many oth-
ers.) For example, one step is the following: (s', π, s) where $s' = ((120,\text{-}$
$false, "null", "null", 0, 145, true, "deposit", 12, 25), (false, 200), (false, 250))$, and
$\pi = $ **REQUEST_DEPOSIT**$(3001, 001, 50)$, and $s = ((120, true, "deposit", 31,\text{-}$
$50, 145, true, "deposit", 12, 25), (true, 150), (false, 250))$.

It is also possible to extend the preceding example to accommodate a larger bank,
with any number of accounts, and a corresponding number of users. In fact, the
definitions also make sense for a hypothetical bank having infinitely many accounts,
and a corresponding infinite set of users. This makes a certain amount of informal
sense if one considers the system of automata to be modeling all the accounts that
ever get created, and all the users that ever become involved, in the course of the
indefinite (and potentially infinite) lifetime of the banking system.[11]
    Since a composition of automata is itself an automaton, the definitions for exe-
cutions, schedules, behaviors, and so on, given in Section 2.4, also make sense for
compositions of automata.

---

[11] Needless to say, one would not describe the states of such an infinite-component system by listing
the values of all variables; rather, each reachable state would be summarized in some finite fashion.

EXAMPLE 2.5.4 **Executions, Schedules, and Behaviors of Compositions**

An example of an execution of the composition of B and $U_{001,300}$ (as given in Examples 2.5.2 and 2.5.1) is

$$((0, false, ``null", ``null", 0, 0, false, ``null", ``null", 0), (false, 300))$$
REQUEST_DEPOSIT(3001, 001, $50)
$$((0, true, ``deposit", 31, 50, 0, false, ``null", ``null", 0), (true, 250))$$
REQUEST_BALANCE(1002, 002)
$$((0, true, ``deposit", 31, 50, 0, true, ``balance", 12, 0), (true, 250))$$
REPORT_COMMIT_DEPOSIT(3001)
$$((50, false, ``null", ``null", 0, 0, true, ``balance", 12, 0), (false, 250))$$
REQUEST_WITHDRAW(5001, 001, $100)
$$((50, true, ``withdrawal", 51, 100, 0, true, ``balance", 12, 0), (true, 250))$$
REPORT_COMMIT_BALANCE(1002, $0)
$$((50, true, ``withdrawal", 51, 100, 0, false, ``null", ``null", 0), (true, 250))$$
REPORT_COMMIT_WITHDRAW(5001, $20)
$$((30, false, ``null", ``null", 0, 0, false, ``null", ``null", 0), (false, 270)).$$

The corresponding schedule is

REQUEST_DEPOSIT(3001, 001, $50),
    REQUEST_BALANCE(1002, 002),
REPORT_COMMIT_DEPOSIT(3001),
    REQUEST_WITHDRAW(5001, 001, $100),
    REPORT_COMMIT_BALANCE(1002, $0),
    REPORT_COMMIT_WITHDRAW(5001, $20).

This schedule is also a behavior, because there are no internal actions.

It is useful to have a projection operator that extracts an execution of a system component from an execution of the entire system. Thus, if $A = \Pi_{i \in I} A_i$ and if $\alpha = s_0 \pi_1 s_1 \ldots$ is an execution of A, let $\alpha | A_i$ be the sequence obtained by deleting $\pi_j s_j$ when π_j is not an action of A_i, and replacing the remaining s_j by $s_j[i]$. A projection operator for action sequences is formally defined in the Appendix. The two projection operators are related as follows.

LEMMA 2.1 *Let $\{A_i\}_{i \in I}$ be a compatible collection of automata and let $A = \Pi_{i \in I} A_i$. If α is an execution of A, then $sched(\alpha | A_i) = sched(\alpha) | A_i$, and similarly for beh in place of sched.*

The following example illustrates the equation proved in Lemma 2.1.

EXAMPLE 2.5.5   Projections of Compositions

Let A be the composition of B and $U_{001,300}$ described in Example 2.5.2. Let α be the execution of this composition described in Example 2.5.4. Then $\alpha | U_{001,300}$ is the following sequence:

$$(\mathit{false}, 300)$$
$$\text{REQUEST\_DEPOSIT}(3001, 001, \$50)$$
$$(\mathit{true}, 250)$$
$$\text{REPORT\_COMMIT\_DEPOSIT}(3001)$$
$$(\mathit{false}, 250)$$
$$\text{REQUEST\_WITHDRAW}(5001, 001, \$100)$$
$$(\mathit{true}, 250)$$
$$\text{REPORT\_COMMIT\_WITHDRAW}(5001, \$20)$$
$$(\mathit{false}, 270).$$

From this it is clear that $sched(\alpha | U_{001,300})$ is the following sequence:

$$\text{REQUEST\_DEPOSIT}(3001, 001, \$50),$$
$$\text{REPORT\_COMMIT\_DEPOSIT}(3001),$$
$$\text{REQUEST\_WITHDRAW}(5001, 001, \$100),$$
$$\text{REPORT\_COMMIT\_WITHDRAW}(5001, \$20).$$

On the other hand $sched(\alpha)$ is given in Example 2.5.4:

$$\text{REQUEST\_DEPOSIT}(3001, 001, \$50),$$
$$\text{REQUEST\_BALANCE}(1002, 002),$$
$$\text{REPORT\_COMMIT\_DEPOSIT}(3001),$$
$$\text{REQUEST\_WITHDRAW}(5001, 001, \$100),$$
$$\text{REPORT\_COMMIT\_BALANCE}(1002, \$0),$$
$$\text{REPORT\_COMMIT\_WITHDRAW}(5001, \$20).$$

From this one can calculate $sched(\alpha) | U_{001,300}$ (by taking the subsequence consisting of actions that are in the signature of $U_{001,300}$) as:

$$\text{REQUEST\_DEPOSIT}(3001, 001, \$50),$$
$$\text{REPORT\_COMMIT\_DEPOSIT}(3001),$$
$$\text{REQUEST\_WITHDRAW}(5001, 001, \$100),$$
$$\text{REPORT\_COMMIT\_WITHDRAW}(5001, \$20),$$

which is the same as $sched(\alpha | U_{001,300})$.

Remarks

It is often convenient to reason about automata without specifying their internal actions. To avoid tedious arguments about compatibility, the remainder of the book follows the convention that unspecified internal actions of any automaton are unique to that automaton, and do not occur as internal or external actions of any of the other automata discussed.

All of the systems used for modeling transactions will be closed systems, as defined in Section 2.3, that is, each action is an output of some component. In addition, it will usually be the case that each output of a component is an input of at most one other component (even though the general definitions permit one output to be an input of any number of other components).

2.5.3 Properties of Systems of Automata

This subsection contains basic results relating executions, schedules and behaviors of a system of automata to those of the automata being composed. (You are encouraged to examine the statements of the results, especially Propositions 2.2 and 2.5, but may omit reading the proofs, which are quite straightforward.)

The first result says that the projections of executions of a system onto the components are executions of the components, and similarly for schedules, and so on.

PROPOSITION 2.2 *Let $\{A_i\}_{i \in I}$ be a compatible collection of automata, and let $A = \Pi_{i \in I} A_i$. If $\alpha \in execs(A)$, then $\alpha|A_i \in execs(A_i)$ for all $i \in I$. Moreover, the same result holds for scheds and behs in place of execs.*

PROOF   Suppose $\alpha \in execs(A)$. Then α is of the form $s_0 \pi_1 s_1 \pi_2 s_2 \ldots$, where each s_k is a state and each π_k is an action of A. Also, s_0 is a start state of A and each triple (s_{k-1}, π_k, s_k) is a step of A. Three facts follow from the definition of composition. First, $s_0[i]$ must be a start state of A_i, for each i. Second, if π_k is an action of A_i, then $(s_{k-1}[i], \pi_k, s_k[i])$ is a step of A_i. Third, if π_k is not an action of A_i, then $s_{k-1}[i] = s_k[i]$. Thus, if $\alpha|A_i = t_0 \phi_1 t_1 \ldots$, then t_0 is a start state of A_i, and every triple (t_{k-1}, ϕ_k, t_k) is a step of A_i. Therefore, $\alpha|A_i$ is an execution of A_i.

Now suppose $\beta \in scheds(A)$. Then $\beta = sched(\alpha)$ for some $\alpha \in execs(A)$. By the first part of the result, $\alpha|A_i \in execs(A_i)$ for all i. Then $\beta|A_i = sched(\alpha|A_i) \in scheds(A_i)$ for all i, as needed. The proof for behaviors is similar to that for schedules. □

Certain converses of the preceding proposition are also true. In particular, one can prove that schedules of component automata can be combined in a natural way to form a schedule of the composition, and similarly for behaviors. In order to prove these results, two preliminary lemmas are proven, one involving schedules and one involving behaviors, that say that executions of component automata can be combined to form an execution of the composition.

LEMMA 2.3 *Let $\{A_i\}_{i \in I}$ be a compatible collection of automata, and let $A = \Pi_{i \in I} A_i$. Let α_i be an execution of A_i, for all $i \in I$. Suppose β is a sequence of actions in $acts(A)$ such that $\beta | A_i = sched(\alpha_i)$ for every i. Then there is an execution α of A such that $\beta = sched(\alpha)$ and $\alpha_i = \alpha | A_i$ for all i.*

PROOF   Since β is a sequence of actions of A, β can be expressed in the form $\pi_1 \pi_2 \ldots$. Then for each i, there is a monotone increasing sequence, $i_1 i_2 \ldots$, of indices of events in β such that the subsequence $\beta | A_i$ is of the form $\pi_{i_1} \pi_{i_2} \ldots$. Also, define i_0 to be 0.

Since $\beta | A_i = sched(\alpha_i)$, α_i can be expressed as $s_0{}^i \pi_{i_1} s_1{}^i \pi_{i_2} s_2{}^i \ldots$, where the s components are states of A_i and the π components are actions of A_i.

Now define α to be the sequence $s_0 \pi_1 s_1 \pi_2 s_2 \ldots$, where each s_j is defined as follows: if $i_k \leq j < i_{k+1}$, then $s_j[i] = s_k{}^i$. That is, the automaton A_i remains in state $s_k{}^i$ between the performance of actions π_{i_k} and $\pi_{i_{k+1}}$, and changes state to $s_{k+1}{}^i$ upon the performance of $\pi_{i_{k+1}}$.

It remains to show that α has the required properties. It is easy to see that $\beta = sched(\alpha)$ and $\alpha_i = \alpha | A_i$ for all i. It remains to show that α is an execution of A.

First, it is argued that s_0 is a start state of A. For any i, the fact that $i_0 = 0$ implies that $s_0[i] = s_0{}^i$, which is a start state of A_i. This implies that s_0 is a start state of A.

Second, it is shown that (s_{j-1}, π_j, s_j) is a step of A for all j. Suppose $\pi_j \in acts(A_i)$. Then $\pi_j = \pi_{i_k}$ for some k. It follows that $s_{j-1}[i] = s_{k-1}{}^i$ and $s_j[i] = s_k{}^i$ since $i_{k-1} < j \leq i_k$. Thus, $(s_{j-1}[i], \pi_j, s_j[i])$ is a step of A_i. On the other hand, suppose that $\pi_j \notin acts(A_i)$. Then $i_{k-1} < j < i_k$ for some k, and it follows that $s_{j-1}[i] = s_k{}^i = s_j[i]$. Therefore, (s_{j-1}, π_j, s_j) is a step of A, as needed. $\square$

LEMMA 2.4 *Let $\{A_i\}_{i \in I}$ be a compatible collection of automata, and let $A = \Pi_{i \in I} A_i$. Let α_i be an execution of A_i, for all $i \in I$. Suppose β is a sequence of actions in $ext(A)$ such that $\beta | A_i = beh(\alpha_i)$ for every i. Then there is an execution α of A such that $\beta = beh(\alpha)$ and $\alpha_i = \alpha | A_i$ for all i.*

PROOF   Since β is a sequence of external actions of A, β can be expressed in the form $\pi_1 \pi_2 \ldots$, where each π_j is a single external action of A. For each $i \in I$, there is a natural correspondence between the external events in $sched(\alpha_i)$ and these events in β. Furthermore, by compatibility, each π_j corresponds to events in only finitely many of the schedules $sched(\alpha_i)$.

For each π_j and for all i such that π_j corresponds to an event in $sched(\alpha_i)$, let $\gamma_{i,j}$ be the finite subsequence of $sched(\alpha_i)$ consisting of internal actions of A_i that directly precede the event corresponding to π_j in $sched(\alpha_i)$. For each j, let γ_j be the concatenation, in any order, of the defined $\gamma_{i,j}$. Since each $\gamma_{i,j}$ is finite and each π_j corresponds to events in finitely many of the schedules $sched(\alpha_i)$, each γ_j is finite. Let $\beta' = \gamma_1 \pi_1 \gamma_2 \pi_2 \ldots$.

Now let $J \subseteq I$ be the set of indices i such that $sched(\alpha_i)$ ends in a sequence of internal actions of A_i. Since I is at most countable, so is J. Construct β'' by interleaving all of these sequences with β', beginning for each i after the last external action of i in β'. The resulting β'' is a sequence satisfying the conditions of Lemma 2.3, so by that lemma, there is an execution α of A such that $\beta'' = sched(\alpha)$ and $\alpha_i = \alpha|A_i$ for all i. Since $\beta = \beta''|ext(A)$, the result follows. $\square$

Now the results about patching together schedules and patching together behaviors follow easily.

PROPOSITION 2.5 *Let $\{A_i\}_{i \in I}$ be a compatible collection of automata, and let $A = \Pi_{i \in I} A_i$.*

1. *Let β be a sequence of actions in $acts(A)$. If $\beta|A_i \in scheds(A_i)$ for all $i \in I$, then $\beta \in scheds(A)$.*

2. *Let β be a sequence of actions in $ext(A)$. If $\beta|A_i \in behs(A_i)$ for all $i \in I$, then $\beta \in behs(A)$.*

PROOF Immediate from Lemmas 2.3 and 2.4. $\square$

Proposition 2.5 is useful in proving that a sequence of actions is a behavior of a composition A: it suffices to show that the sequence's projections are behaviors of the components of A and then to appeal to Proposition 2.5.

2.6 Proofs about Automata

In reasoning about a system or system component modeled as an automaton, the primary interest is in proving facts about every behavior of the automaton. Since the behaviors are simply a set of sequences, one can apply the usual techniques of mathematical proof, such as proof by contradiction or proof by case analysis. By far the most important technique used in this book is mathematical induction: proofs use the fact that each behavior is the sequence of external actions in some execution and give an induction on the length of the execution. The inductive step uses the fact that an execution of length $k + 1$ can be expressed as an execution of length k followed by a single transition of the automaton. Since the allowed transitions are determined by the state, it is often helpful to show relationships between behaviors and the states they can lead to. In addition to its usefulness in proving properties of behaviors, induction also provides a powerful proof technique for proving properties that are true of all the reachable states of an automaton.

EXAMPLE 2.6.1   Proofs about the Bank Automaton B

These techniques are demonstrated with the bank automaton B of Example 2.3.2, showing the (rather obvious) fact that no **DEPOSIT** operation is reported as having committed unless it had earlier been requested. A preliminary result shows that if a **DEPOSIT** operation i is recorded as the pending operation on account X in a reachable state of the automaton, then the behavior leading to that state must contain an event of the form **REQUEST_DEPOSIT**(i, X, k). Similar results hold, of course, for the other operations, **WITHDRAW** and **BALANCE**.

LEMMA 2.6 *Let β be a behavior of B, and s a state such that β can lead to s in B. If i is an operation identifier, X an account, and k a positive integer such that $s.type(\mathrm{X}) = $ "deposit" and $s.id(\mathrm{X}) = i$ and $s.amount(\mathrm{X}) = k$, then β contains an event **REQUEST_DEPOSIT**(i, X, k) and X is the account with which i is associated.*

PROOF   Note first, if β contains **REQUEST_DEPOSIT**(i, X, k), then X is the account with which i is associated, because the action signature of B restricts the parameters of **REQUEST_DEPOSIT** actions in this way. Thus, the final clause of the lemma holds.

The substantive part of the proof proceeds by induction on the length of β. The base case (where β is the empty sequence) is trivially true, since then s is the start state of B, so that no i, X, and k satisfy the given conditions, and therefore the implication that is given is true (since its antecedent is false).

For the inductive step, consider β of length $n + 1$. Then the sequence β can be written as $\beta'\pi$, where β' is the prefix of β whose length is n, and there is a state s' such that β' can lead to s' in B and also (s', π, s) is a step of B. Now suppose the antecedent of the implication is true for a particular choice of i, X, and k (if not, the lemma is trivially true). The argument proceeds by case analysis of the possible actions π. If $\pi = $ **REQUEST_DEPOSIT**(i, X, k), then the consequence of the implication is certainly satisfied. Otherwise, the effect of π as given in the code is either to leave $s.type(\mathrm{X}) = s'.type(\mathrm{X})$, $s.id(\mathrm{X}) = s'.id(\mathrm{X})$, and $s.amount(\mathrm{X}) = s'.amount(\mathrm{X})$, or else to set one of these variables to a value other than that given by the antecedent. In the first of these alternatives, the induction hypothesis applied to β' shows that β' contains an action **REQUEST_DEPOSIT**(i, X, k), while the second alternative is impossible by the supposition above. Thus, β' and therefore also β contains a **REQUEST_DEPOSIT**(i, X, k) action, as required. □

LEMMA 2.7 *If β is a behavior of B that contains an event **REPORT-_COMMIT_DEPOSIT**(i), where i is an operation identifier associated with account* X, *then, for some value of k, β contains an event **REQUEST-_DEPOSIT**(i, X, k).*

PROOF Since β is a behavior of B, then there is an execution α of B whose behavior is β. Thus, α contains an action **REPORT_COMMIT_DE-POSIT**(i). Let s denote the state in α immediately before this action. By the precondition of the action, $s.type(\mathrm{X}') = $ "*deposit*"; also $s.id(\mathrm{X}') = i$ and $s.amount = k$ for some[12] X' and k. Lemma 2.6 implies that $\mathrm{X}' = \mathrm{X}$ and that α contains an action **REQUEST_DEPOSIT**(i, X, k). Thus, β contains an action **REQUEST_DEPOSIT**(i, X, k). □

This book often proves facts about more complex systems using similar techniques.

EXAMPLE 2.6.2 **Proofs about a Banking System**

A second example shows that money cannot be spontaneously created in the system $BS_{001,300,002,250}$ described in Example 2.5.3.

LEMMA 2.8 *Let s be a reachable state of $BS_{001,300,002,250}$. Let the value of cash in the component of s corresponding to $U_{001,300}$ be x, and the value of money(001) in the component of s corresponding to B be y. Also let z denote the value of amount(001) in the B component of s provided type(001) = "deposit" in that component, or denote 0 otherwise. Then $x + y + z \leq 300$.*

PROOF Since s is reachable, there is a schedule β of $BS_{001,300,002,250}$ such that β can lead the system to s. The proof proceeds by induction on the length of β. The base case (where β is empty) is when s is the start

---

[12]Notice that the precondition does not immediately show that X' is the same as X, the account with which i is associated.

state of the system. Thus, $x = 300$, and $y = z = 0$, so the conclusion of the lemma is true.

For the induction step, the sequence β can be written $\beta'\pi$ where π is an action of the system. Then there is a state s' such that β' can lead the system to s' and also (s', π, s) is a step of the system. Denote by x', y', and z' the values defined as x, y, and z are, respectively, substituting the state s' instead of s. Since the length of β' is less than the length of β, the induction hypothesis says that $x' + y' + z' \leq 300$. Now consider cases depending on π.

- $\pi = $ **REQUEST_DEPOSIT**(i, X, k).

  If $\mathrm{X} = 1$, then the effect given in the code of B shows $z = k$ and $y = y'$, while the effect in the code of $U_{001,300}$ shows $x = x' - k$, ensuring that $x + y + z = x' - k + y' + k = x' + y'$, but (since z' is nonnegative, by the type of *amount*) this is at most $x' + y' + z' \leq 300$. On the other hand, if $\mathrm{X} = 2$, then the effect in the code of B shows $y = y'$ and $z = z'$, and the component of s corresponding to $U_{001,300}$ is the same as the component of s' corresponding to $U_{001,300}$, since in this case π is not in the action signature of $U_{001,300}$. This ensures that $x = x'$, so that $x + y + z = x' + y' + z' \leq 300$.

- $\pi = $ **REQUEST_WITHDRAW**(i, X, k).

  If $\mathrm{X} = 1$, then the effect given in the code of B shows $z = 0$ and $y = y'$, while the effect in the code of $U_{001,300}$ shows $x = x'$, ensuring that $x + y + z = x' + y'$, but (since z' is nonnegative, by the type of *amount*) this is at most $x' + y' + z' \leq 300$. On the other hand, if $\mathrm{X} = 2$, then the effect in the code of B shows $y = y'$ and $z = z'$, and the component of s corresponding to $U_{001,300}$ is the same as the component of s' corresponding to $U_{001,300}$, since in this case π is not in the action signature of $U_{001,300}$. This ensures that $x = x'$, so that $x + y + z = x' + y' + z' \leq 300$.

- $\pi = $ **REQUEST_BALANCE**(i, X).

  If $\mathrm{X} = 1$, then the effect given in the code of B shows $z = 0$ and $y = y'$, while the effect in the code of $U_{001,300}$ shows $x = x'$, ensuring that $x + y + z = x' + y' \leq x' + y' + z' \leq 300$. On the other hand, if $\mathrm{X} = 2$, then the effect in the code of B shows $y = y'$ and $z = z'$, and the component of s corresponding to $U_{001,300}$ is the same as the component of s' corresponding to $U_{001,300}$, so $x = x'$, whence $x + y + z = x' + y' + z' \leq 300$.

- $\pi = $ **REPORT_COMMIT_DEPOSIT**(i).

  The precondition of this action must be satisfied for some X, and (using Lemma 2.6) so X must be the account with which i is associated.

If X = 1, then the effect of this action in B shows that $y = y' + z'$ (noting that the precondition shows that $s'.type(001) = \text{``}deposit\text{''}$, so $s'.amount(001) = z'$) and $z = 0$. Also the effect of π in the code of $U_{001,300}$ shows that $x = x'$. Thus, $x + y + z = x' + (y' + z') \le 300$. On the other hand, if X = 2, then the effect in B shows $y = y'$ and $z = z'$, while the action is not in the signature of $U_{001,300}$, so that $x = x'$. Thus, in this case $x + y + z = x' + y' + z' \le 300$.

■ $\pi = \textbf{REPORT\_COMMIT\_WITHDRAW}(i, k)$.

The precondition of this action must be satisfied for some X, and (using the analog of Lemma 2.6 for the **WITHDRAW** operation) X must be the account with which i is associated. If X = 1, then the effect of this action in B shows that $y = y' - k$ and $z = 0$. Also the effect of π in the code of $U_{001,300}$ shows that $x = x' + k$. Thus, $x + y + z = x' + k + (y' - k) \le x' + y' + z' \le 300$. On the other hand, if X = 2, then the effect in B shows $y = y'$ and $z = z'$, while the action is not in the signature of $U_{001,300}$, so that $x = x'$. Thus, in this case $x + y + z = x' + y' + z' \le 300$.

■ $\pi = \textbf{REPORT\_COMMIT\_BALANCE}(i, k)$.

The precondition of this action must be satisfied for some X, and (using the analog of Lemma 2.6 for the **BALANCE** operation) X must be the account with which i is associated. If X = 1, then the effect of this action in B shows that $y = y'$ and $z = 0$. Also the effect of π in the code of $U_{001,300}$ shows that $x = x'$. Thus, $x + y + z = x' + y' \le x' + y' + z' \le 300$. On the other hand, if X = 2, then the effect in B shows $y = y'$ and $z = z'$, while the action is not in the signature of $U_{001,300}$, so that $x = x'$. Thus, in this case $x + y + z = x' + y' + z' \le 300$.

This completes the proof of the induction step. □

2.7 Relationships between Automata

This section defines the notion of one automaton *implementing* another—an implementation exhibits no finite behaviors except those that are also finite behaviors of the automaton being implemented. Thus, the implementation can replace the original, and the change will not result in unexpected behavior. Implementation is thus a useful notion in stating correctness conditions to be satisfied by automata. Also, a kind of abstraction mapping called a *possibilities mapping* is defined; this gives sufficient conditions for showing that the implementation relationship holds. Possibilities mappings will be useful in later correctness proofs.

2.7.1 Implementation

Let A and B be automata with the same external action signature; that is, with $extsig(A) = extsig(B)$. Then A is said to **implement** B if the finite behaviors of A are also behaviors of B.

One way in which these notions can be used is the following. Suppose one can show that an automaton B is *correct*, in the sense that all its finite behaviors satisfy some specified property. So if another automaton A implements B, then A is also correct.

One can also show that if A implements B, then replacing B by A in any system yields a new system in which all finite behaviors are behaviors of the original system. In fact, as the next proposition shows, one can take any collection of components of a system and replace each by an implementation and the resulting system will implement the original one.

The condition that A implements B does not require that A exhibit every possible behavior of B. Rather, B is viewed as describing the acceptable behaviors, and the behaviors of A are constrained to be acceptable.[13]

EXAMPLE 2.7.1   Implementing the Banking Database

This example defines a new banking database, B_2, which implements B (as defined in Example 2.3.2, for the case of two bank accounts, 001 and 002). B_2 is identical to B except that the bank always grants the maximum amount of money possible. That is, the signature, states, and start states of B_2 are the same as the corresponding components of B, and the steps are the same except for those associated with the **REPORT_COMMIT_WITHDRAW** actions. For these steps, B_2 has:

REPORT_COMMIT_WITHDRAW(i, k)
    Precondition:
        $s'.active(\mathrm{X}) = true$
        $s'.type(\mathrm{X}) = \text{``}withdrawal\text{''}$
        $s'.id(\mathrm{X}) = i$
        $k = min(s'.amount(\mathrm{X}), s'.money(\mathrm{X}))$

---

[13]This constraint is easy to satisfy: A could simply never produce any outputs. In other words, there is no requirement that A actually do something. Such requirements are liveness properties, which we do not address in this book.

Effect:
  $s.money(\text{X}) = s'.money(\text{X}) - k$
  $s.active(\text{X}) = false$
  $s.type(\text{X}) = \text{``null''}$
  $s.id(\text{X}) = \text{``null''}$
  $s.amount(\text{X}) = 0$

Thus, B_2 always grants the minimum of the amount requested and the actual amount in the account.

Note that B_2 does not introduce any behavior that does not already appear in B, but only imposes some extra restrictions on the behavior that are not present in B. Thus, it is not hard to argue that every behavior of B_2 is also a behavior of B. For instance, the sequence

REQUEST_DEPOSIT$(3001, 001, \$100)$,
REPORT_COMMIT_DEPOSIT(3001),
  REQUEST_WITHDRAW$(3003, 001, \$40)$,
  REPORT_COMMIT_WITHDRAW$(3003, \$40)$

is a behavior of B_2, and hence of B as well. On the other hand, there are behaviors of B that are not behaviors of B_2. For instance:

REQUEST_DEPOSIT$(3001, 001, \$100)$,
REPORT_COMMIT_DEPOSIT(3001),
  REQUEST_WITHDRAW$(3003, 001, \$40)$,
  REPORT_COMMIT_WITHDRAW$(3003, \$25)$.

Next we prove our earlier remark about replacing one component of a system by an implementation.

PROPOSITION 2.9 *Suppose that $\{A_i\}_{i \in I}$ is a compatible collection of automata, and let $A = \Pi_{i \in I} A_i$. Also suppose that $\{B_i\}_{i \in I}$ is a compatible collection of automata, and let $B = \Pi_{i \in I} B_i$. If for each index i in I, A_i implements B_i, then A implements B.*

PROOF   Suppose that β is a finite behavior of A. Proposition 2.2 implies that $\beta | A_i \in behs(A_i)$ for each index $i \in I$. Since A_i implements B_i, $\beta | A_i \in behs(B_i)$. Then Proposition 2.5 implies that $\beta \in behs(B)$.   □

EXAMPLE 2.7.2   **Compositions and Implementations**

This example illustrates Proposition 2.9. Let C_1 be the composition of
B and $U_{001,300}$ as in Example 2.5.2, and let C_2 be the composition of
B_2, the more restricted banking database of Example 2.7.1, with the user
$U_{001,260}$. Example 2.7.4, below, shows that $U_{001,260}$ implements $U_{001,300}$.
Then Proposition 2.9 implies that C_2 implements C_1.

2.7.2 Possibilities Mappings

In order to show that one automaton implements another, it is frequently helpful to
demonstrate a correspondence between states of the two automata. Such a correspondence can often be expressed in the form of a kind of abstraction mapping called a
possibilities mapping, defined in this section. Often, the possibilities mapping is used
to relate a state of a concrete algorithm to a state of a high-level or abstract algorithm,
where the same information is represented in a more general or less efficient way. The
precise definition given below allows one to construct an execution of the abstract algorithm from an execution of the concrete algorithm, by replacing each detailed state
by an abstract version, but leaving the external actions (and thus the behavior) unchanged. Once a mapping has been proposed, it is usually straightforward (although
tedious) to check by case analysis that it has the properties given in the definition. In
most simple cases, there is only a single abstract state corresponding to a state of the
detailed algorithm, but we state the definition in a general form (with a set of abstract
states for each concrete one) so that we can handle implementations that compress
unneeded information from an abstract description (see, for example, Lemma 6.32).

Suppose A and B are automata with the same external action signature, and suppose f is a function from $states(A)$ to the power set (i.e., set of subsets) of $states(B)$.
That is, if s is a state of A, $f(s)$ is a set of states of B. The function f is said to be a
possibilities mapping from A to B if the following conditions hold:

1. For every start state s_0 of A, there is a start state t_0 of B such that $t_0 \in f(s_0)$.

2. Let s' be a reachable state of A, $t' \in f(s')$ a reachable state of B, and (s', π, s)
a step of A. Then there is an extended step, (t', γ, t), of B (possibly having an
empty schedule) such that the following conditions are satisfied:

   (a) $\gamma|ext(B) = \pi|ext(A)$, and

   (b) $t \in f(s)$.

This kind of function is called a *possibilities mapping* to express the fact that there
can be many *possibilities* for states of B that correspond to a single state of A.

The following theorem expresses the important property of possibilities mappings, that they are sufficient to demonstrate implementation.

THEOREM 2.10 *Suppose that A and B are automata with the same external action signature. If there is a possibilities mapping, f, from A to B, then A implements B.*

PROOF The result follows from a proof of the following stronger statement: for every extended step, (s_0, β_A, s), of A, with s_0 a start state of A, there is an extended step, (t_0, β_B, t), of B, with t_0 a start state of B, such that $t_0 \in f(s_0), t \in f(s)$ and $\beta_A | ext(A) = \beta_B | ext(B)$. This statement is proved by induction on the length of β_A.

For the basis, assume that β_A is empty. Then $s_0 = s$. By the definition of a possibilities mapping, there is a start state t_0 of B such that $t_0 \in f(s)$. Letting β_B be the empty sequence, the extended step (t_0, β_B, t_0) satisfies the needed properties.

For the inductive step, assume that (s_0, β_A, s) is an extended step of A and β_A is of the form $\beta'_A \pi$, with π a single action. Then there exists a state s' of A such that (s_0, β'_A, s') is an extended step of A and (s', π, s) is a step of A. By inductive hypothesis, there is an extended step, (t_0, β'_B, t'), of B with t_0 a start state of B, $t_0 \in f(s_0), t' \in f(s')$, and $\beta'_A | ext(A) = \beta'_B | ext(B)$. Since (s', π, s) is a step of A, s' is a reachable state of A and $t' \in f(s')$ is a reachable state of B, the definition of a possibilities mapping implies that there is an extended step (t', γ, t) of B such that $\gamma | ext(B) = \pi | ext(A)$ and $t \in f(s)$. Then $(t_0, \beta'_B \gamma, t)$ is an extended step of B and $\beta'_B \gamma | ext(B) = (\beta'_B | ext(B))(\gamma | ext(B)) = (\beta'_A | ext(A))(\pi | ext(A)) = \beta'_A \pi | ext(A) = \beta_A | ext(A)$, and the required properties are satisfied. $\square$

EXAMPLE 2.7.3 Restricting Nondeterministic Choice

The *identity mapping* on the states, by which $f(s) = \{s\}$, is a possibilities mapping from the banking database B_2 of Example 2.7.1 to the banking database B of Example 2.3.2. (Expanding the definition of a possibilities mapping for the identity function shows that what is required is that the start states of B_2 form a subset of the start states of B, and that the steps of B_2 form a subset of the steps of B. Both hold in the present case.) This example shows how a trivial possibilities mapping can be used to show implementation for an automaton that is a simple restriction of another automaton (e.g., restricting the opportunities for nondeterministic choice).

EXAMPLE 2.7.4 A More Complex Use of Possibilities Mappings

Here is a more complicated possibilities mapping. Let n and r be two positive integers such that $n < r$. Consider the automata $U_{X,n}$ and $U_{X,r}$

given as in Example 2.3.4 by taking different values for the initial amount of cash in hand. The existence of a possibilities mapping f shows that $U_{X,n}$ implements $U_{X,r}$. The function f takes a state s of $U_{X,n}$ into the singleton set consisting of the state t of $U_{X,r}$ where $t.waiting = s.waiting$ and $t.cash = s.cash + (r - n)$.

A check of the conditions of the definitions shows that this is a possibilities mapping: the start state s_0 of $U_{X,n}$ has $s_0.waiting = false$ and $s_0.cash = n$, so that $f(s_0) = \{(false, n + (r - n))\} = \{(false, r)\}$, which is the start state of $U_{X,r}$, as required.

Also, suppose (s', π, s) is a step of $U_{X,n}$ and $t' \in f(s')$. One must prove that there is a t such that (t', π, t) is a step of $U_{X,r}$ and $t \in f(s)$.

Let t be the unique element of $f(s)$, so $t.waiting = s.waiting$ and $t.cash = s.cash + (r - n)$. It remains only to show that (t', π, t) is in the transition relation of $U_{X,r}$. The proof proceeds by case analysis on the actions π.

- ■ $\pi = $ **REPORT_COMMIT_DEPOSIT**(i).
  Since π is an input to $U_{X,r}$, t' satisfies the precondition of π. Now the effect of π requires a proof that $t.waiting = false$ and $t.cash = t'.cash$. However, $t.waiting = s.waiting$, which is *false* by the effect of π as an action of $U_{X,n}$. Also $t.cash = s.cash + (r - n)$ and $s.cash = s'.cash$ by the effect of π as an action of $U_{X,n}$. Thus, $t.cash = s'.cash + (r - n)$, but this is exactly $t'.cash$ since $t' \in f(s')$.

- ■ $\pi = $ **REPORT_COMMIT_WITHDRAW**(i, k).
  Since π is an input to $U_{X,r}$, t' satisfies the precondition of π. Now the effect of π require a proof that $t.waiting = false$ and $t.cash = t'.cash + k$. However, $t.waiting = s.waiting$, which is *false* by the effect of π as an action of $U_{X,n}$. Also, $t.cash = s.cash + (r - n)$ and $s.cash = s'.cash + k$ by the effect of π as an action of $U_{X,n}$. Thus, $t.cash = s'.cash + (r - n) + k$, but this is exactly $t'.cash + k$ since $t' \in f(s')$.

- ■ $\pi = $ **REPORT_COMMIT_BALANCE**(i, k).
  The code for this action is identical to that for **REPORT_COMMIT-_DEPOSIT**(i), so the same argument applies as in that case.

- ■ $\pi = $ **REQUEST_DEPOSIT**(i, X, k).
  The argument first shows that t' satisfies the precondition for π as an action of $U_{X,r}$, that is, that $t'.waiting = false$ and $k \leq t'.cash$. Since s' satisfies the precondition for π as an action of $U_{X,n}$, so $s'.waiting = false$ and $k \leq s'.cash$. Also, $t'.waiting = s'.waiting$ and

$t'.cash = s'.cash + (r - n)$ since $t' \in f(s')$. Combining these conditions, $t'.waiting = false$ and also $k \leq t'.cash - (r - n)$, which is less than $t'.cash$ since $r > n$. This establishes the required precondition.

It remains to show that the effect is satisfied, that is, $t.waiting = true$ and $t.cash = t'.cash - k$. Note that $s.waiting = true$ and $s.cash = s'.cash - k$, since (s', π, s) is a step of $U_{\mathrm{X},n}$. Also, note that $t'.cash = s'.cash + (r - n)$, $t.waiting = s.waiting$, and $t.cash = s.cash + (r - n)$, since $t' \in f(s')$ and $t \in f(s)$. Combining these gives exactly the needed condition.

■ π is **REQUEST_WITHDRAW**(i, X, k) or **REQUEST_BALANCE**(i, X). These cases are very similar to **REQUEST_DEPOSIT**, and are left to the reader.

EXAMPLE 2.7.5   Expanding Actions

In the examples presented so far, the second possibilities mapping condition used extended steps that involved only a single action. This example shows how more than one action could be involved.

Let R be the atomic register automaton of Example 2.3.3. Let R_1 be a variant of R that does not contain the *reports* component in the state, and in which the activity of the **PERFORM_READ**, **PERFORM_WRITE**, and **ABORT** steps is absorbed into the activity of the associated report steps. Thus, the code for R_1 is given in Figure 2.4.

Then a possibilities mapping can be constructed from R_1 to R, in which each state of R_1 is mapped to the singleton set consisting of the state of R with identical values for *requests* and *data*, and with *reports* being empty. To show this is a possibilities mapping, each **REPORT_COMMIT_READ** step of R_1 corresponds to an extended step of R in which two steps are taken, first a **PERFORM_READ** action and then the report action itself. The other reporting actions are treated similarly.

2.8   Preserving Properties

Although automata are unable to block input actions, it is often convenient to restrict attention to those behaviors of a component in which its environment provides inputs in a sensible way, that is, where the environment obeys certain *well-formedness* restrictions. In order to be sure that results proved under this assumption are relevant

REQUEST_READ(i)
 Effect:
  $s.requests = s'.requests \cup \{r\}$, where
   $r.id = i$,
   $r.kind =$ "$read$", and
   $r.value =$ "$null$"

REQUEST_WRITE(i, d)
 Effect:
  $s.requests = s'.requests \cup \{r\}$, where
   $r.id = i$,
   $r.kind =$ "$write$", and
   $r.value = d$

REPORT_COMMIT_READ(i, d)
 Precondition:
  $r' \in s'.requests$, where
   $r'.id = i$, and
   $r'.kind =$ "$read$"
  $d = r'.data$
 Effect:
  $s.requests = s'.requests - \{r'\}$

REPORT_COMMIT_WRITE(i)
 Precondition:
  $r' \in s'.requests$, where
   $r'.id = i$, and
   $r'.kind =$ "$write$"
 Effect:
  $s.requests = s'.requests - \{r'\}$
  $s.data = r'.value$

REPORT_ABORT_READ(i)
 Precondition:
  $r' \in s'.requests$, where
   $r'.id = i$, and
   $r'.kind =$ "$read$"
 Effect:
  $s.requests = s'.requests - \{r'\}$

REPORT_ABORT_WRITE(i)
 Precondition:
  $r' \in s'.requests$, where
   $r'.id = i$, and
   $r'.kind =$ "$write$"
 Effect:
  $s.requests = s'.requests - \{r'\}$

Figure 2.4: The Code for R_1 for Example 2.7.5

to the system being discussed, one needs to show that the environment does, in fact, provide only well-formed input to the component. Sometimes this can be proved from the code of the environment; more often, the input the environment provides to the component is in part determined by the input the environment has received from the component in question. This section defines a concept that can be used in such a situation, to prove properties of the behaviors of the whole system, without fallacious circular reasoning.

Accordingly, we introduce the notion that an automaton *preserves* a property of behaviors: as long as the environment does not violate the property, neither does the automaton. If the environment and automaton together are closed, induction can be used to conclude that all the finite behaviors of the composition satisfy the property. Hence, this notion is primarily interesting for safety properties.

First, let Φ be a set of actions and P be a safety property of sequences of elements of Φ, and let A be an automaton with $\Phi \cap int(A) = \emptyset$. Then A **preserves** P if whenever β is a finite sequence of actions and π is an action such that $\beta|\Phi$ has property P, $\pi \in out(A)$, and $\beta\pi|A$ is a behavior of A, then $\beta\pi|\Phi$ has property P. (Note that in the case $\Phi \cap out(A) = \emptyset$, A trivially preserves P.)

Thus, if an automaton preserves a property P, the automaton is not the *first to violate* P: as long as the environment only provides inputs such that the cumulative behavior satisfies P, the automaton will only perform outputs such that the cumulative behavior satisfies P. Note that the fact that an automaton A preserves a property P does not imply that all of A's behaviors, when projected on Φ, satisfy P; it is possible for a behavior of A to fail to satisfy P, if an input causes a violation of P.

EXAMPLE 2.8.1   Preserving a Simple Property

Consider the user $U_{001,300}$ of Example 2.3.4. Let Φ be all the actions in the action signature of $U_{001,300}$. Let P be the property that is true of all sequences of actions in Φ consisting of alternating request and report events, starting with a request and ending with either a request or a report. Then it is easy to see that $U_{001,300}$ preserves P. To do so, first use induction to show that if β is a schedule of $U_{001,300}$ that can lead the automaton to state s, then β ends with a report if and only if $s.waiting = false$. Then observe from the precondition that any output action is enabled as an output of $U_{001,300}$ in state s only if $s.waiting = false$. Thus, if a sequence β satisfies P and π is an output action such that $\beta\pi$ is a behavior, then β consists of alternating requests and reports starting with a request and ending with a report, and π (being an output) is a request. This proves that $\beta\pi$ satisfies P.

However, since

REQUEST_DEPOSIT$(3001, 001, \$20)$,
REPORT_COMMIT_DEPOSIT(3001),
   REPORT_COMMIT_WITHDRAW$(6001, \$50)$

is a behavior of $U_{001,300}$, not all of the user's behaviors satisfy P.

In contrast to the situation described in Example 2.8.1, in the case of a closed automaton A, one can show that if A preserves P, then all of A's behaviors satisfy P.

LEMMA 2.11 *Let A be a closed automaton. Let Φ be a set of actions such that $\Phi \cap int(A) = \emptyset$, and let P be a safety property of sequences of elements of Φ. If A preserves P and β is a behavior of A then $\beta|\Phi$ satisfies P.*

PROOF   For finite β this is proved by a simple induction, using the fact that every action of A that is in Φ is an output of A. (The fact that P is a safety property implies that P is true of the empty sequence, which provides the basis of the induction.)

If β is infinite, the result above shows that every finite prefix of $\beta|\Phi$ satisfies P. Since P is a safety property, $\beta|\Phi$ itself satisfies P.   □

The following proposition gives a way to deduce that all of a system's behaviors satisfy P. The proposition says that if all components of a system preserve P, then all the behaviors of the composition satisfy P.

PROPOSITION 2.12 *Let $\{A_i\}_{i \in I}$ be a compatible collection of automata, and let $A = \Pi_{i \in I} A_i$. Let Φ be a set of actions such that $\Phi \cap int(A) = \emptyset$, and let P be a safety property of sequences of elements of Φ. If every A_i preserves P, then A preserves P; if, in addition, A is closed, then for every β that is a behavior of A, $\beta|\Phi$ satisfies P.*

PROOF   Suppose β is a finite sequence of actions and π is an action such that $\beta|\Phi$ has property P, $\pi \in out(A)$ and $\beta\pi|A$ is a behavior of A. To show that A preserves P, the proof argues that $\beta\pi|\Phi$ has property P.

Since $\pi \in out(A)$, there is exactly one A_i such that $\pi \in out(A_i)$. By Proposition 2.2, $\beta\pi|A_i$ is a behavior of A_i. Since A_i preserves P, $\beta\pi|\Phi$ satisfies P. Therefore, A preserves P.

In the case that A is closed, it is immediate from Lemma 2.11 that for every behavior β of A, $\beta|\Phi$ satisfies P.   □

EXAMPLE 2.8.2   Preserving Properties in a Composition

Consider again the property P defined in Example 2.8.1, where it was stated that $U_{001,300}$ preserves P. Since no action of P is in the action signature of $U_{002,250}$, it is immediate that $U_{002,250}$ preserves P. One can also show (using Lemma 2.6 and similar results) that the bank B of Example 2.3.2 preserves P. It follows from Proposition 2.12 that any finite behavior of the composition described in Example 2.5.3 satisfies P.

2.9   Discussion

Many models have been proposed for describing and reasoning about distributed systems. This section describes several such models and indicates how they relate to the I/O automaton model. References to descriptions of specific models, and examples of their use, can be found at the end of the section.

2.9.1   Process Algebras

One class of models is based on the idea of representing each system or component as a process, and relating the processes using an algebra. Specifically, there are elementary processes, operators that build new processes by combining existing ones, and equations expressing the equality of certain combinations. These models include CCS, CSP, TCSP, and ACP. They share with our automaton model the fundamental view that a particular execution of a system is represented by a sequence of actions, and that the action of a composite system involves simultaneous actions in several components. However, the way a system is modeled is radically different. Consider the binary memory of Example 2.3.1. In the I/O automaton model, this was described by defining the internal state and showing how each action altered the state. In a process algebra model, this system would be described as the process P that solves the following simultaneous equation:[14] $P = \mathbf{REPORT0} \to P|\mathbf{CLEAR} \to P|\mathbf{SET} \to Q$, $Q = \mathbf{REPORT1} \to Q|\mathbf{CLEAR} \to P|\mathbf{SET} \to Q$. This means that P is a process that is constructed by making a three-way choice, either to perform $\mathbf{REPORT0}$ and then act like P, to perform $\mathbf{CLEAR}$ and then act like P, or else to perform $\mathbf{SET}$ and then act like Q. In general, a system that in the I/O automaton model has a number N of possible states would be described via the solution of a system of N equations among processes.

Most process algebra models do not distinguish between input and output actions, and thus they do not have a simplifying property of the I/O automaton model, where each action that might occur is controlled by a single component. As a consequence, in order to calculate the way a composition executes, the process algebra models must have the meaning of a process include information about which actions might take place after each sequence. (Thus, the meaning is more complicated than merely a set of sequences of actions, as in our model.)

For database concurrency control and recovery, the algorithms used are quite complex, and involve many states. It would be a considerable challenge to reason with, or understand, descriptions written as the solutions of huge systems of equations between processes. In addition, we believe that it is important when defining correctness to express causality, where we understand that issuing a request for an activity is the responsibility of the user and may not be prevented or even delayed by the system, but that informing the user of the outcome is the responsibility of the system and may not be prevented or delayed by the user, once the request has been made.

2.9.2 State-based Models

Another class of models uses the sequence of states rather than the sequence of actions as the important aspect of a systems activity. The description of a single system in these models looks very similar to that used in our automata: one describes a state as values for a collection of variables, and then gives the ways the state can change as

---

[14]Of course, syntax will differ between different models, but a similar equation would be written in each.

various events occur. However, the way a composite system is described can differ from our model, because the state is not required to be divided with different variables for each component. Instead, as with concurrent programming languages, there is a single address space in which all processes operate. Thus, the precondition and effect of each action may refer to all the variables of the whole system. This sometimes leads to simpler system descriptions; for example, to represent an asynchronous communication channel one could use a variable containing the message queue, which is referenced in both "send" and "receive" actions. Our model requires a separate automaton interacting with its end-stations through "send" and "receive" events. On the other hand, it is also easier in shared-state models to write descriptions that seem reasonable but in fact are unimplementable in a distributed system, by referring in a single action to variables that could not all be accessed at the same time. Thus, with these models some self-discipline is needed to ensure that each action refers only to variables of the components involved, or to variables representing attached channels.

In models where the important aspect of a system is the sequence of states through which it passes (rather than the sequence of events, as in our model or process algebra models), there are two different ways in which correctness conditions may be given. In one style the correctness condition is given by providing a state-transition system that acts as a specification, because it can pass through exactly the desired sequences of states.[15] A model that uses this sort of specification of correctness is Lamport's transition axiom method.

An alternative style of correctness condition involves writing a formula in some logic. The usual choice for logic is some variant of temporal logic. Safety conditions (which are what we discuss in this book) are usually expressed by giving a proposition (relating the values in different variables) that is to be true in every state of every execution of the system.[16] This is just like the property proved in Example 2.6.2. However, in these models the property is itself the correctness condition, rather than merely a useful step on the way to proving a result about the sequence of actions, as in our model. Models that express conditions using temporal logic include UNITY and State Transition Systems. We note that any condition on the sequence of events can be expressed as a condition on the state simply by introducing an auxiliary "history" variable, whose value is always the sequence of events that have occurred, and similarly that conditions on states can be represented as conditions on event sequences, by

---

[15] To be more precise, the actual system states are allowed to have additional variables, whose values are not constrained by the specification system. Thus, the actual system must contain variables (either explicitly, or derived from combinations of explicit variables) that pass through the sequence of states that the specification system passes through.

[16] Liveness conditions (which express that certain things must eventually happen) are not discussed in this book, but they can also be written in temporal logic, usually as a statement that in every execution there is some state in which a proposition is true.

adding a parameter to each event revealing the current state. Thus, the differences are more stylistic than intrinsic.

It is our viewpoint that state-based specification techniques have led to a significant amount of confusion in the area of database concurrency control. This is a problem domain in which there is an important interface between the database and the users of the database. We find it very natural to express correctness conditions as restrictions on the actions that cross that interface. This approach has the advantage of simplicity, while explicitly indicating (via their classification as inputs or outputs) the actions that are under the control of different components.

At the same time, since no constraints are imposed on the automata implementing the database other than their interface behavior, their states are essentially unconstrained. Our approach allows a single condition to characterize the behavior of a number of very different algorithms. In contrast, the classical theory of concurrency control has based its definitions of serializability on the state of the database and has therefore needed to provide variant definitions for separate classes of algorithms, such as those that replicate data, or those that keep out-of-date versions of data. Algorithms for these systems work perfectly, but are not serializable according to the definition used for systems with a single copy of each item. Details of the sort of algorithm employed are invisible at the user interface, and so a correctness condition stated at that interface admits these algorithms as correct, without prejudice.

Ultimately, there is little fundamental difference between the action-oriented approach we advocate, and models that focus on state predicates. The debate, as we understand it, is largely a question of taste. We simply find it more natural to express a problem as a predicate on the behavior of an automaton of a particular type (essentially, as a language) than as a predicate on states. The typing information (the automaton signature) is a convenient way of indicating the causal constraints. It is undoubtedly possible to translate the results into any of these state-based formalisms, more or less naturally.

2.9.3 Uses of Models

Different models of distributed systems can be used in many different ways, and understanding the objectives of a model can clarify the reason certain design decisions were taken. The viewpoint taken in this book is that we should be able to represent in our model various system designs, express what correctness of a design should mean, and then prove that specific designs are correct. We hope for several benefits from the proof: besides additional confidence (compared to only testing in particular circumstances), we hope that the structure of the proof will give us understanding of the principles involved in design, and thus help us generate new designs. Thus, we seek to give proofs where the lemmas we state express important facts about the system's behavior. One particular way that proofs can lead to improved understanding is that we may be able to express designs as modular combinations of various aspects (for example, different algorithms might be used at different sites, or the system might include separate components providing replication and distributed commit), and we might give conditions on each aspect that collectively provide correctness, but can be checked separately. If this is done, we can concentrate on developing an improved component in isolation, and then we can introduce it to a correct system without fear that its interaction with other aspects will destroy the correctness of the whole. In order to make the proofs as meaningful as possible, we allow ourselves in this book to use the full range of proof methods of mathematics, such as mathematical induction, proof by contradiction, case analysis, and reasoning about sets and functions.

Some researchers propose to have the correctness of a design checked automatically. The motivation for this includes the shortage of mathematically skilled people to do proofs, the length of time needed to develop a mathematical proof, avoidance of human error, and the large number of distributed systems that need proving. Clearly, automatic proof development cannot succeed with general system models (the truth of propositions will be undecidable), so these researchers operate with restricted finite-state models, and seek to verify only certain (albeit important) classes of correctness conditions, such as absence of deadlock. Even with finite-state models, the complexity of checking every reachable state is extreme for realistic sizes of system, so techniques are often developed to sample the space of executions statistically. The properties we are concerned with in this book are well beyond the scope of current automatic technology. However, some of the proofs might be verifiable by current proof *checking* systems.

One way in which some models of distributed systems can be used is by leading the design process, rather than following it. These models provide a collection of transformations that are known to preserve the properties of a system. They encourage the system designer to write a specification of correctness, and then successively "refine" it until a design is reached that is implementable with adequate efficiency on the hardware available. Because each transformation from one design to the successive refinement preserves correctness, there is no further work to prove correctness of the final design—the proof is implicit in the sequence of refinements. Refinement can be done either in a language of specifications, in a language of implementations, or most naturally in a language that includes both correctness specifications and implementable programs. Our model does not provide automatic transformations; however, the technique of proof, where a system is verified, then some component is replaced by another that is shown to implement the first (using a possibilities mapping), can be considered a form of development by refinement.

Some models concentrate on describing systems, rather than on proving correctness. For such models, features such as graphical layout and modularity of description are particularly important. Describing a system in a formal model may provide a clear method of documentation so that users can understand the functionality of the system.

It is particularly important in building components for a distributed system, when separately built components will need to interoperate. Thus, several models (LOTOS and Estelle) have been proposed as international standards for use in expressing standard communication protocols. For distributed applications, both LOTOS and Z are being considered. In contrast with these, our model is not concerned with issues of syntax. We find the style used in this book, giving preconditions and effects for actions, to be convenient, but any way of describing a set of transitions could be used without violence to the model.

A much less common use of a formal model is to prove the impossibility of certain tasks. For example, folk wisdom agrees that building a completely reliable system is impossible if any component may fail undetectably, and processor speeds are unknown so that timeouts may not be used to determine failure. In order to prove this belief, one needs a model in which one can describe both the correctness condition under discussion, and also any conceivable system. One then proves that there does not exist a system of the appropriate form that is correct under the given condition.

Finally, many researchers are interested in exploring the general properties of a model and its proof methods, rather than the description or verification of any specific system. Typical questions include whether every system that is correct can be proved to be so, and when two systems should be regarded as equivalent.

2.10 Bibliographic Notes

This section focusses on expository books or articles, rather than original research papers. These works themselves contain further references.

The I/O automaton model is defined and its properties explored by Lynch and Tuttle [82, 83]. This model has been used for describing and reasoning about several different types of systems, including distributed graph algorithms, network resource allocation algorithms, communication algorithms, shared atomic objects, and dataflow architectures. Both safety properties and liveness have been demonstrated. Examples of this work appear in [19, 82, 120]. Jonsson's model [57] is essentially the same as the I/O automaton model.

Among the process algebra models are Hoare's CSP (Communicating Sequential Processes) [54], Milner's CCS (Calculus of Communicating Systems) [87], and Baeten's ACP (Algebra of Communicating Processes) [8].

Some of the models for concurrent systems in the research literature that focus on properties of system *states* rather than behaviors, to express and prove correctness conditions, include UNITY [18], the transition axiom method, [68] and State Transition Systems [63]. The temporal logics used in many of these can be found in [84].

Work on finite state models used for automatic validation is discussed in [55]. Some

of the languages used primarily to describe systems (either at an abstract design level,
or in more detail) include Z [44], LOTOS [15], and Estelle [17]. For information
about stepwise refinement, see the articles in [22]. For an introduction to the study
of equivalence of systems and other similar issues, see [45].

A recent issue of *Distributed Computing* focuses on the application of formal methods to the specification of a simple (non-nested) database system. Lam and Shankar
use state transition systems [64], Kurki-Suonio uses an action-based model similar
to I/O automata [62], and Broy uses algebraic and functional specification techniques [16]. The issue ends with a critique by Lamport [69].

2.11   Exercises

1. Prove the following two statements about an arbitrary I/O automaton.

 a. If β is a finite schedule of A, then there exists a finite $\alpha \in execs(A)$ such
    that $\beta = sched(\alpha)$.

 b. If γ is a finite behavior of A, then there exists a finite $\beta \in scheds(A)$ such
    that $\gamma = beh(\beta)$.

2. Which of the following are behaviors of the binary memory automaton F? Why?

 a. **REPORT0**

 b. **REPORT1**

 c. **CLEAR**

 d. **SET, REPORT1**

 e. **SET, SET, REPORT1**

 f. **SET, REPORT1, CLEAR, REPORT0**

 g. **REPORT0, SET, SET, CLEAR, REPORT0**

3. Which of the following are behaviors of the banking database automaton B?
Why?

 a. **REQUEST_DEPOSIT**(5276, 276, $100)

 b. **REPORT_COMMIT_DEPOSIT**(5276)

 c. **REQUEST_DEPOSIT**(5276, 276, $100),
    REPORT_COMMIT_DEPOSIT(5276)

 d. **REQUEST_DEPOSIT**(5276, 276, $100),
    REPORT_COMMIT_WITHDRAW(5276, $25)

e.   **REQUEST_DEPOSIT**(5276, 276, $100),
     REQUEST_DEPOSIT(1276, 276, $50)

f.   **REQUEST_DEPOSIT**(5276, 276, $100),
     REPORT_COMMIT_DEPOSIT(5276),
     REQUEST_WITHDRAW(1276, 276, $50),
     REPORT_COMMIT_WITHDRAW(1276, $25)

g.   **REQUEST_DEPOSIT**(5276, 276, $100),
     REQUEST_DEPOSIT(1276, 276, $50),
     REPORT_COMMIT_DEPOSIT(1276)

h.   **REQUEST_DEPOSIT**(5276, 276, $100),
     REQUEST_WITHDRAW(1276, 276, $50),
     REPORT_COMMIT_WITHDRAW(1276, $25)

4. Consider the system that is the composition of the banking system B and the bank user automaton $U_{276,100}$. Which of the following are behaviors of the composition?

a.   **REQUEST_DEPOSIT**(5276, 276, $100)

b.   **REPORT_COMMIT_DEPOSIT**(5276)

c.   **REQUEST_DEPOSIT**(5276, 276, $50),
     REPORT_COMMIT_DEPOSIT(5276),
     REQUEST_WITHDRAW(1276, 276, $50),
     REPORT_COMMIT_WITHDRAW(1276, $25)

d.   **REQUEST_DEPOSIT**(5276, 276, $100),
     REQUEST_DEPOSIT(1276, 276, $50),
     REPORT_COMMIT_DEPOSIT(1276)

5. Complete the proof that f, the mapping from $U_{X,n}$ to $U_{X,r}$ in Example 2.7.4, is a possibilities mapping.

6. Prove that there is no possibilities mapping from the atomic register R of Example 2.3.3 to the variant R_1 described in Example 2.7.5.

SERIAL SYSTEMS AND CORRECTNESS

3.1 Introduction

This chapter develops the formal machinery needed to define *atomicity*, the fundamental correctness condition for transaction-processing systems. Unlike much of the classical work on concurrency control, which defines correctness of a transaction-processing system in terms of the existence of a serial execution of the *same* system, atomicity is defined by first giving a *separate* specification of the permissible serial executions as seen by users of the system, and then defining how executions of a transaction-processing system must relate to this specification. The permissible serial executions are specified in terms of a system of I/O automata, called a *serial system*. A serial system is a simple kind of transaction-processing system that is constrained to run transactions sequentially and that does not allow aborted transactions to access data.

Transaction-processing System Architecture: Transaction-processing systems consist of user-provided transaction code, plus transaction-processing algorithms designed to coordinate the activities of different transactions.

The transactions are written by application programmers in a suitable programming language. Transactions can invoke operations on data objects; in addition, if nesting is allowed, transactions can invoke subtransactions and receive responses from the subtransactions describing the results of their processing.

Schedulers and Databases: In a typical transaction-processing system, the transaction-processing algorithms interact with the transactions, making decisions about when to schedule subtransactions and operations on objects. In order to carry out such scheduling, the transaction-processing algorithms may manipulate locks, multiple copies of objects, and other data structures. In the system organization emphasized by the classical theory, the transaction-processing algorithms are divided into a *scheduler algorithm* and a *database* of objects. The scheduler has the power to decide when operations are to be performed on the objects in the database, but not to perform more complex manipulations on objects (such as maintaining multiple copies). Although this organization is popular, it does not encompass all useful system designs.

In this book, each component of a transaction-processing system is described as an I/O automaton. In particular, each transaction is an automaton, and all the transaction-processing algorithms together comprise another automaton. Sometimes, as when describing serial systems or explaining algorithms, a more detailed structure is used, and the transaction-processing algorithms are presented as a composition of a collection of automata, one representing each object, and one representing the rest of the system.

Modeling Nesting: It is not obvious how one ought to model the nested structure of transactions within the I/O automaton model. One might consider defining special kinds of automata that have a nested structure. However, it appears that the cleanest way to model this structure is to describe each subtransaction in the transaction nesting structure as a separate automaton. If a parent transaction T wishes to invoke a child transaction T', T will issue an output action that requests that T' be created. The transaction-processing algorithms receive this request, and at some later time might decide to issue an action that is an input to the child T' and corresponds to the *creation* of T'. Thus, the different transactions in the nesting structure comprise a forest of automata, communicating with each other indirectly through the transaction-processing automaton. The highest-level user-defined transactions (i.e., those that are not subtransactions of any other user-defined transactions), are the roots in this forest.

It is actually more convenient to model the transaction nesting structure as a tree rather than as a forest. Thus, an additional *root* automaton is added as a *dummy transaction*, located at the top of the transaction nesting structure. The highest-level user-defined transactions are considered to be children of this new root. Although formally an I/O automaton, the root can be thought of as modeling the outside world, from which invocations of top-level transactions originate and to which reports about the results of such transactions are sent; indeed, the boundary between this root transaction and the rest of the system will be regarded as the *user interface* to the system. The use of the root transaction is convenient in the formal development: in most cases, the reasoning done about this dummy root transaction is the same as the reasoning done about ordinary transactions, so that regarding the root as a transaction leads to economy in the formal arguments.

Defining Correctness: The main purpose of this chapter is to define atomicity and related correctness conditions to be satisfied by transaction-processing systems. In general, correctness conditions for systems composed of I/O automata are stated in terms of properties of sequences of external actions, and that is the convention followed in this book. Here it is most natural to define correctness conditions in terms of the actions occurring at the boundary between the transactions (including the dummy root transaction) and the transaction-processing automaton. For it is immaterial how the transaction-processing algorithms work, as long as the outside world and the transactions see *correct* behavior.

Serial Systems: It is often useful to define correct behavior for an automaton or system in terms of implementation or other relationships to another automaton or system. Here, correct behavior for a transaction-processing system is defined in terms of the behavior of a particular and heavily constrained transaction-processing system, one that processes all transactions serially. Such a system is called a *serial system.*

A serial system is the composition of a compatible set of I/O automata. The composition contains *transaction automata* (one for each transaction that might possibly run), *object automata*, and a single *serial scheduler automaton.* Transaction automata have already been mentioned above. Serial object automata serve as specifications for permissible object behavior. They describe the responses the objects should make to arbitrary sequences of operation invocations, assuming that later invocations wait for responses to previous invocations. Serial objects are much like the variables of abstract data type that occur in many sequential programming languages.

The serial scheduler handles the communication among the transactions and serial objects and thereby controls the order in which the transactions take steps. It ensures that no two sibling transactions are active concurrently—that is, it runs each set of sibling transactions serially. The serial scheduler is also responsible for deciding if a transaction commits or aborts. The serial scheduler can permit a transaction to abort only if its parent has requested its creation, but it has not actually been created. Thus, in a serial system, all sets of sibling transactions are run serially, and in such a way that no aborted transaction ever performs any steps.

It is important to understand that serial systems are introduced solely to serve as the specification of the permissible serial behaviors. Since serial systems allow no concurrency among sibling transactions and cannot cope with a transaction that fails after it has started running, they are not sufficiently general to serve directly as a model of real transaction-processing systems. However, the same simplicity that renders serial systems unusable in practice also makes them appropriate as a basis for defining the correctness of more interesting systems. Later chapters describe systems that do allow concurrency and recovery from transaction failures. (For example, they undo the effects of aborted transactions that have performed significant activity.) These systems are proven correct in the sense that certain transactions, in particular the root transaction, are unable to distinguish these systems from corresponding serial systems. In other words, it appears to these transactions as if all siblings run serially, and that aborted transactions were never created.

EXAMPLE 3.1.1   The Banking Database

Throughout this chapter, the definitions are illustrated by a simple banking database similar to those described in Chapter 1. The system we consider consists of a single user interacting with a banking database having exactly two accounts, ACCT_CHK and ACCT_SVNG, each of which can hold a nonnegative integer amount of money. Initially, both accounts hold zero money. The lowest-level operations on each account are to **DEPOSIT** an amount of money, to find the **BALANCE**, and to **WITHDRAW** an amount of money. The deposit operation returns *"OK"*, the balance operation returns the amount in the account, and the withdraw operation returns the amount actually removed; this amount is either 0 or else exactly the amount requested. These operations are similar to those considered in Example 2.3.2; however, notice that the withdrawal has less flexibility in that it may not remove a nonzero amount other than what was requested.

User X manipulates his accounts as follows. First, he deposits $2000 in ACCT_SVNG. Once this deposit has completed successfully, he requests two activities concurrently (that is, he requests each without waiting for the other to complete): a deposit of $500 to ACCT_CHK and a *flexible withdrawal* **FLEXWITHDRAW** of $200. (The activity of this subtransaction is described below; it may affect either or both accounts.) After the user receives reports of the successful completion of both concurrent activities (the **DEPOSIT** and the **FLEXWITHDRAW**), he invokes two more operations concurrently: another **DEPOSIT** of $1000 to ACCT_SVNG and a query of the **BALANCE** of ACCT_SVNG. If the user receives a response from any operation or subtransaction indicating failure (either an **ABORT** of an operation or subtransaction, or a **COMMIT** of a subtransaction returning an error indication), then he initiates no further activity.[1]

The **FLEXWITHDRAW** transaction invokes an operation to find the **BALANCE** of ACCT_CHK, and once that has succeeded, invokes either a **WITHDRAW**(ACCT_CHK, $200) or else a **WITHDRAW**(ACCT_SVNG, $200), depending on whether or not the result is greater than $450. Also, if the balance returned is under $300, a **TRANSFER** is invoked to bring the amount in ACCT_CHK up to $1000. This **TRANSFER**, in turn, invokes concurrently a **WITHDRAW** on ACCT_SVNG and a **DEPOSIT** on ACCT_CHK.

If any **BALANCE** or **WITHDRAW** subtransaction invoked by the **FLEXWITHDRAW** aborts, or if a **WITHDRAW** subaction commits but returns $0, then the **FLEXWITHDRAW** completes with an error indication telling which subtransaction failed. If **BALANCE** and then at least one **WITHDRAW** succeed, however (even if a **TRANSFER** subaction aborts), then the **FLEXWITHDRAW** completes normally, with return value indicating the amount withdrawn. (See Figure 3.1.)

Chapter Outline: The remainder of this chapter develops the necessary machinery for defining serial systems. First, it defines a type structure used to name transactions and objects. Then it describes the general structure of a serial system— the components, the actions the components perform, and the way that the components are interconnected. Next, useful concepts are developed that involve the actions of serial systems. Then the components of the serial system are described in detail, and some basic properties of serial systems are stated. Finally, serial systems are used to state the correctness conditions that are used for the remainder of the book. Some specific serial systems are described as examples.

3.2 System Types

The following definitions specify a type structure that is used to name the transactions and objects in a serial system. This captures only limited aspects of the system: names for transactions and objects, which transactions are subtransactions of others,

---

[1]This may not be a very sensible system design, since retrying the operation might well lead to success.

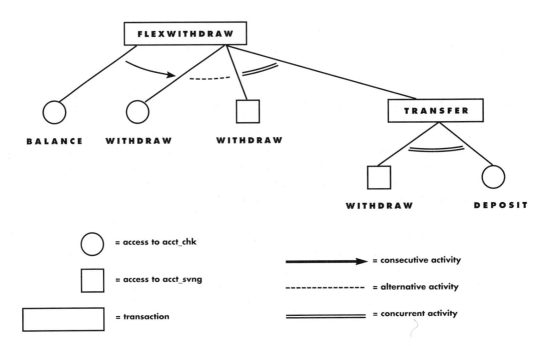

Figure 3.1: Transaction Nesting for **FLEXWITHDRAW** Transactions

and indications of which transactions act on each object. But it does not indicate the specific computations a transaction may perform, or any constraints on the order in which subtransactions are invoked.

A **system type** consists of the following:

■ a set $\mathcal{T}$ of **transaction names**,

■ a distinguished transaction name $T_0 \in \mathcal{T}$,

■ a subset **accesses** of $\mathcal{T}$ not containing T_0,

■ a function $parent : \mathcal{T} - \{T_0\} \rightarrow \mathcal{T}$, that configures the set of transaction names into a tree,[2] with T_0 as the root and the accesses as the leaves,

■ a set $\mathcal{X}$ of **object names**,

■ a function $object : accesses \rightarrow \mathcal{X}$, and

---

[2]The Appendix gives the definitions for trees and their terminology.

■ a collection (one for each transaction name T) of sets V_T of **return values for** T.

Each element of the set *accesses* is called an **access transaction name**, or simply an **access**. Also, the set of accesses T for which $object(T) = X$ is called $accesses(X)$; if $T \in accesses(X)$, say that T is an **access to** X.

The transaction tree and its components are referred to using standard tree terminology defined in the Appendix, such as *leaf node*, *child*, *ancestor*, and *descendant*. It is important to remember that each node is considered to be its own ancestor and its own descendant, that is, the *ancestor* and *descendant* relations are reflexive. The notion of the *least common ancestor* (lca) of two nodes is also used.

The transaction tree describes the nesting structure for transaction names, with T_0 as the name of the dummy *root transaction*. Each child node in this tree represents the name of a subtransaction of the transaction named by its parent. The children of T_0 represent names of the top-level user-defined transactions. The accesses represent names for the primitive transactions in the transaction nesting structure; these primitive transactions are used to model operations on data objects. Thus, the only transactions that actually access data are the leaves of the transaction tree, and these do nothing else. The other nodes model transactions whose function is to **CREATE** and manage subtransactions (including accesses), but they do not access data directly.

The tree structure should be thought of as a predefined naming scheme for all possible transactions that might ever be invoked. In any particular execution, however, only some of these transactions will actually take steps. Imagine that the tree structure is known in advance by all components of a system.[3] The tree will, in general, be an infinite structure with infinite branching.

Classical concurrency control theory, as represented, for example, in [12], considers transactions having a simple nesting structure where each user-defined transaction invokes only operations on data. As modeled in the present framework, that simple nesting structure has three levels: the top level consists of the root T_0, modeling the outside world; the next level consists of all the user-defined transactions; and the lowest level consists of the accesses to data objects.

The set $\mathcal{X}$ is the set of names for the objects used in the system. Each access transaction name is assumed to be an access to some particular object, as designated by the *object* function. The set V_T of return values for T is the set of possible values that might be returned by T to its parent, after it successfully completes. If T is an access transaction name and v is a return value for T, the pair (T, v) is called an **operation** of the given system type. Thus, an operation includes a designation of a

---

[3]This reflects the way transactions are named in Argus [75], where names are structured, so that the subtransaction's name enables one to calculate the name and location of the caller.

particular access to an object, together with a designation of the value returned by the access.

EXAMPLE 3.2.1   System Type for Banking System

For the system described informally in Example 3.1.1, the transactions are named as follows. T_0 represents the user, and the activities he invokes are T_1 (the first **DEPOSIT** access to ACCT_SVNG), T_2 (the **DEPOSIT** to ACCT_CHK), T_3 (the **FLEXWITHDRAW** transaction), T_4 (the second **DEPOSIT** to ACCT_SVNG) and T_5 (the **BALANCE** on ACCT_SVNG). The accesses invoked by the **FLEXWITHDRAW** are named $T_{3.1}$ (the **BALANCE** on ACCT_CHK), $T_{3.2}$ (the **WITHDRAW** from ACCT_CHK), $T_{3.3}$ (the alternative **WITHDRAW** from ACCT_SVNG), and $T_{3.(3+k)}$, for $k = 1, 2, 3, \ldots$ (the different possible **TRANSFER**(k) subtransactions, where k indicates the amount of money being transferred[4]). For each k, the operations invoked by $T_{3.(3+k)}$ are named $T_{3.(3+k).1}$ (the **WITHDRAW** from ACCT_SVNG) and $T_{3.(3+k).2}$ (the **DEPOSIT** to ACCT_CHK). Notice that each invocation of an activity is regarded as a separate transaction and so has its separate name, and that invoking the same code with different arguments is modeled as invoking different transactions.

Formally, $\mathcal{T} = \{T_0, T_1, T_2, T_3, T_{3.1}, T_{3.2}, T_{3.3}, T_{3.4}, T_{3.4.1}, T_{3.4.2}, T_{3.5}, T_{3.5.1}, T_{3.5.2}, T_{3.6}, \ldots, T_4, T_5\}$. The objects are ACCT_CHK and ACCT_SVNG, the accesses to ACCT_CHK are $T_2, T_{3.1}, T_{3.2}, T_{3.4.2}, T_{3.5.2}, T_{3.6.2}, \ldots$, and the accesses to ACCT_SVNG are $T_1, T_{3.3}, T_{3.4.1}, T_{3.5.1}, T_{3.6.1}, \ldots, T_4, T_5$. The tree is configured by $parent(T_1) = T_0$, $parent(T_2) = T_0$, $parent(T_3) = T_0$, $parent(T_{3.1}) = T_3, \ldots$, $parent(T_{3.4}) = T_3$, $parent(T_{3.4.1}) = T_{3.4}$, $parent(T_{3.4.2}) = T_{3.4}$, and so on. The return values are as follows: for each of T_0, T_1, T_2, and T_4 and also for each $T_{3.k.2}$ and $T_{3.k}$ (for $k = 4, 5, \ldots$) the single special value "*OK*"; for each of $T_{3.1}$ and T_5, the set of all nonnegative integers; for each $T_{3.k.1}$ (for $k = 4, 5, \ldots$) the set of two values $\{\$0, \$(k - 3)\}$; for each of $T_{3.2}$ and $T_{3.3}$ the set of two values $\{\$0, \$200\}$; and for T_3 the set containing \$200 together with the error indications "*FAIL-3.1*", "*FAIL-3.2*", and "*FAIL-3.3*".

---

[4]The description in Example 3.1.1 shows that in any **TRANSFER** that is invoked the amount of money transferred must be greater than \$700 and no more than \$1000. However, we have chosen to include a transaction in the system type for each nonnegative integer k.

3.3 General Structure of Serial Systems

The system type just described captures the naming of transactions and objects. To specify the correctness condition for a transaction-processing system, we will use a specific *serial system*, in which each transaction and object is modeled explicitly. The following sections describe the automata that will be used to model transactions, and those that will be used to model objects. Clearly, in a particular system, the automaton that models a transaction will be chosen to capture the code that governs the computations performed by that transaction.

A serial system for a given system type is a closed system consisting of a *transaction automaton* A_T for each non-access transaction name T, a *serial object automaton* $S(X)$ for each object name X, and a single *serial scheduler automaton*. Later in this chapter, a precise definition (complete automaton description) is given for the serial scheduler automaton, and conditions are specified that must be satisfied by the transaction and object automata. This section describes only the signatures of the various automata, in order to explain how the automata are interconnected.

Figure 3.2 depicts the structure of a serial system. The circles represent transaction automata, the squares represent serial object automata, and the rectangle represents the serial scheduler. The transaction nesting structure is indicated by dotted lines between transaction automata corresponding to parent and child, and between each serial object automaton and the transaction automata corresponding to parents of accesses to the object. The direct connections between automata (via shared actions) are indicated by solid lines. Thus, the transaction automata interact directly with the serial scheduler, but not directly with each other or with the object automata. The object automata also interact directly with the serial scheduler. It is important to notice here that accesses do *not* have transaction automata; instead, the activity of an access will be represented by actions of the automaton for the object involved.

Figure 3.3 shows the interface of a transaction automaton in more detail.

Transaction T has an input **CREATE**(T) action, which is generated by the serial scheduler in order to initiate $T's$ processing. No explicit arguments are passed to transactions in this model; rather, there is a different transaction for each possible set of arguments, and so any input to the transaction, including the name of the procedure to be executed, is encoded in the name of the transaction. In addition, T has **REQUEST_CREATE**(T') actions for each child T' of T in the transaction nesting structure; these are requests for creation of child transactions and are communicated directly to the serial scheduler. At some later time, the scheduler might respond to a **REQUEST_CREATE**(T') action by issuing a **CREATE**(T') action, an input to transaction T'. Transaction T also has **REPORT_COMMIT**(T',v') and **REPORT_ABORT**(T') input actions, by which the serial scheduler informs T about the fate (commit or abort) of its previously requested child T'. In the case of a commit, the report includes a return value v' that provides information about the activity of T'; in the case of an

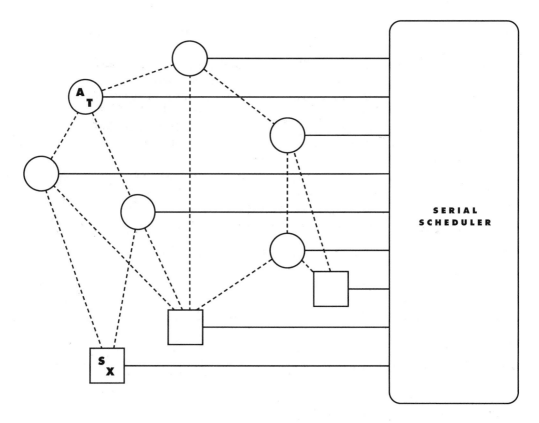

Figure 3.2: Serial System Structure

abort, no information is returned. Finally, T has a **REQUEST_COMMIT**(T, v) output action, by which it announces to the scheduler that it has completed its activity successfully, with a particular result as described by return value v.

Figure 3.4 shows the object interface. Object X has input **CREATE**(T) actions for each T that is an access to X. These actions should be thought of as invocations of operations on object X. Object X also has output actions of the form **REQUEST_COMMIT**(T, v), representing responses to the invocations. The value v in a **REQUEST_COMMIT**(T, v) action is a return value returned by the object as part of its response. (The **CREATE** and **REQUEST_COMMIT** notation is used for the object actions, rather than the more familiar *invoke* and *respond* terminology, in the interests of uniformity: there are many places in the formal arguments where access transactions can be treated uniformly with non-access transactions, and so it is useful to have a common notation for them.)

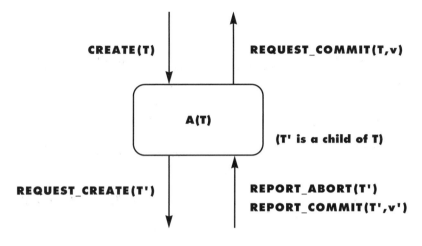

Figure 3.3: Transaction Automaton

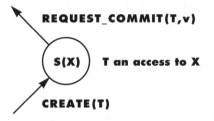

Figure 3.4: Object Automaton

Figure 3.5 shows the serial scheduler interface. The serial scheduler receives the previously mentioned **REQUEST_CREATE** and **REQUEST_COMMIT** actions as inputs from the other system components. It produces **CREATE** actions as outputs, thereby awakening transaction automata or invoking operations on objects. It also produces **COMMIT**(T) and **ABORT**(T) actions for arbitrary transactions $T \neq T_0$, representing decisions about whether the designated transactions commit or abort. These decisions are treated as separate from the transfer of information about a transaction's completion to its parent, modeled by the report events.[5] For technical convenience, the **COMMIT** and **ABORT** actions are included among the output actions of the

---

[5]This separation can be significant when discussing distributed concurrent systems, where the irrevocable decision to commit or abort may occur at a different site from that at which the parent runs.

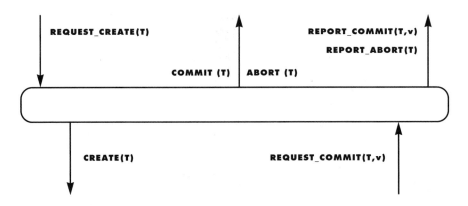

Figure 3.5: Serial Scheduler Automaton

serial scheduler, even though they are not inputs to any other system component.[6] Finally, the serial scheduler has **REPORT_COMMIT** and **REPORT_ABORT** actions as outputs, by which it communicates the fates of transactions to their parents.

As is always the case for I/O automata, the components of a system are determined statically. Even though the discussion referred earlier to the action of *creating* a child transaction, the model treats the child transaction as if it had been there all along. The **CREATE** action is treated formally as an input action to the child transaction; the child transaction will be constrained not to perform any output actions until such a **CREATE** action occurs. A consequence of this method of modeling dynamic creation of transactions is that the system must include automata for all possible transactions that might ever be created, in any execution. In most interesting cases, this means that the system will include infinitely many transaction automata.

3.4 Serial Actions and Well-Formedness

The **serial actions** for a given system type are defined to be the external actions of a serial system of that type. These are just the actions listed in the preceding section: **CREATE**(T) and **REQUEST_COMMIT**(T, v), where T is any transaction name and v is a return value for T, and **REQUEST_CREATE**(T), **COMMIT**(T), **ABORT**(T),

---

[6]Classifying actions as outputs even though they are not inputs to any other system component is permissible in the I/O automaton model. In this case, it would also be possible to classify these two actions as internal actions of the serial scheduler, but then the statements and proofs of the ensuing results would be slightly more complicated.

REPORT_COMMIT(T,v), and **REPORT_ABORT**(T) where $T \neq T_0$ is a transaction name and v is a return value for T.[7]

This section defines some basic concepts involving serial actions. All the definitions are based on the set of serial actions only, and not on the specific automata in the serial system. For this reason, they are presented before going on (in the next section) to give more information about the system components.

Introduction of some basic terminology is followed by the definition of some *well-formedness properties*, simple safety properties for sequences of external actions of transactions and objects.

3.4.1 Basic Definitions

The **COMMIT**(T) and **ABORT**(T) actions are called **completion** actions for T, while the **REPORT_COMMIT**(T,v) and **REPORT_ABORT**(T) actions are called **report** actions for T.

A transaction is associated in the natural way with each serial action π that appears in the interface of a transaction or object (that is, with any non-completion action). Formally, let T be any transaction name. If π is one of the serial actions **CREATE**(T), **REQUEST_CREATE**(T'), **REPORT_COMMIT**(T',v'), **REPORT_ABORT**(T'), or **REQUEST_COMMIT**(T,v), where T' is a child of T, then *transaction*(π) is T. If π is a completion action, then *transaction*(π) is undefined. In some contexts, transactions will need to be associated with completion actions as well as with other serial actions; since a completion action for T can be thought of as occurring *in between* T and *parent*(T), the association will sometimes be with T and sometimes with *parent*(T). Thus, the "*transaction*"(π) definition is extended in two different ways. If π is any serial action, then define *hightransaction*(π) to be *transaction*(π) if π is not a completion action, and to be *parent*(T), if π is a completion action for T. Also, if π is a serial action, define *lowtransaction*(π) to be *transaction*(π) if π is not a completion action, and to be T, if π is a completion action for T. In particular, *hightransaction*$(\pi) =$ *lowtransaction*$(\pi) =$ *transaction*(π) for all serial actions other than completion actions.

The object associated with any serial action whose transaction is an access is another important relation. If π is a serial action of the form **CREATE**(T) or **REQUEST_COMMIT**(T,v), where T is an access to X, then define *object*(π) to be X.

The preceding notation is extended to events as well as actions. (Recall from Chapter 2 that events are occurrences of actions in sequences.) For example, if π is an

---

[7]Later in the book, other kinds of systems besides serial systems are defined, such as *simple systems* and *generic systems*. These will also include the serial actions among their external actions; these actions will still be referred to as *serial actions* even though they appear in non-serial systems.

event, then we write *transaction*(π) to denote the transaction of the action of which π is an occurrence. The definitions of *hightransaction, lowtransaction,* and *object* are extended similarly. Other notation in this book is extended in the same way, without further explanation.

Next, terminology is needed to describe the status of a transaction during execution. Let β be a sequence of serial actions.[8] A transaction name T is said to be **active** in β provided that β contains a **CREATE**(T) event but no **REQUEST_COMMIT** event for T. Similarly, T is said to be **live** in β provided that β contains a **CREATE**(T) event but no completion event for T. (However, note that β may contain a **REQUEST_COMMIT** for T.) Also, T is said to be an **orphan** in β if there is an **ABORT**(U) action in β for some ancestor U of T (including possibly T itself). Note that the definition allows us to say that a transaction is an orphan in a sequence where no action of that transaction occurs, so long as an ancestor is aborted. Transactions that are not orphans in a given sequence are called **nonorphans**.

Projection operators have already been used to restrict action sequences to particular sets of actions, and to actions of particular automata. Another projection operator is introduced next, this time to sets of transaction names. That is, if β is a sequence of serial actions and $\mathcal{U}$ is a set of transaction names, then $\beta|\mathcal{U}$ is defined to be the sequence $\beta|\{\pi : transaction(\pi) \in \mathcal{U}\}$. If T is a transaction name, $\beta|T$ is sometimes written as shorthand for $\beta|\{T\}$. Similarly, if β is a sequence of serial actions and X is an object name, then $\beta|$X is used to denote $\beta|\{\pi : object(\pi) = \text{X}\}$.

Recall that an operation is a pair (T, v), consisting of an access transaction name and a return value. Operations are naturally associated with sequences of serial actions, as follows. If β is a sequence of serial actions, say that the operation (T, v) **occurs** in β if there is a **REQUEST_COMMIT**(T, v) event in β. Also, if β is a sequence of serial actions, define *operations*(β) to be the set of operations occurring in β.

Conversely, sequences of serial actions can be associated with a sequence of operations. For any operation (T, v), let *perform*(T, v) denote the two-action sequence **CREATE**(T) **REQUEST_COMMIT**(T, v), the expansion of (T, v) into its two parts. This definition is extended to sequences of operations in the natural way using an inductive definition: if ξ is the empty sequence of operations λ, *perform*(ξ) is the empty sequence of actions, while if ξ is a sequence of operations such that $\xi = \xi'(T, v)$, then *perform*(ξ) = *perform*(ξ')*perform*(T, v). Thus, the *perform* function expands a sequence of operations into a corresponding alternating sequence of **CREATE** and **REQUEST_COMMIT** actions.

Sometimes definitions from this subsection are used for sequences of actions chosen

---

[8] All these definitions are made for arbitrary sequences of serial actions, and extended below to deal with sequences of actions, some of which are not serial actions. Later in the book we will apply these definitions to behaviors of concurrent systems, as well as to behaviors of serial systems.

from some other set besides the set of serial actions—usually, a set containing the set of serial actions. The appropriate definitions of this subsection are extended to such sequences by applying them to the subsequences consisting of serial actions. Thus, if β is a sequence of actions chosen from a set Φ of actions, define $serial(\beta)$ to be the subsequence of β consisting of serial actions. A transaction name T is said to be **active** in β provided that it is active in $serial(\beta)$, and similarly for the **live** and **orphan** definitions. Also, $\beta|\mathcal{U}$ is defined to be $serial(\beta)|\mathcal{U}$, and similarly for projection on an object name. We say that operation (T, v) **occurs** in β if it occurs in $serial(\beta)$. Define $operations(\beta)$ to be $operations(serial(\beta))$.

The following properties are immediate from the definitions.

LEMMA 3.1 *Let β and γ be sequences of actions and T a transaction name. Suppose that γ is a reordering of a subsequence of β. If T is an orphan in γ, then T is an orphan in β.*

LEMMA 3.2 *Let β be a sequence of actions, and let T and T' be transaction names. If T' is an orphan in β and T' is an ancestor of T, then T is an orphan in β.*

EXAMPLE 3.4.1 Active, Live, and Orphan Transactions

This example refers to the system type introduced in Example 3.1.1 above. Let β be the sequence

CREATE(T_0)
   REQUEST_CREATE(T_1),
   CREATE(T_1),
   REQUEST_COMMIT(T_1, "*OK*"),
   COMMIT(T_1),
   REPORT_COMMIT(T_1, "*OK*"),
     REQUEST_CREATE(T_3),
     CREATE(T_3),
       REQUEST_CREATE(T_2),
         REQUEST_CREATE($T_{3.1}$),
         ABORT($T_{3.1}$),
         REPORT_ABORT($T_{3.1}$),
     REQUEST_COMMIT(T_3, "*FAIL-3.1*").

Applying the definitions, we see that T_3 is live in β, and that T_3 is not active in β.

Let β_1 be the sequence

CREATE(T_0)
  REQUEST_CREATE(T_1),
  CREATE(T_1),
  REQUEST_COMMIT(T_1, "OK"),
    REQUEST_CREATE(T_3),
      REQUEST_CREATE(T_2),
    CREATE(T_3),
        REQUEST_CREATE($T_{3.1}$),
    CREATE(T_2),
  ABORT(T_3).

Note that the activity of the siblings T_2 and T_3 are interleaved, and that T_3 is aborted after being created. This is not what one would expect in a serial system, but the definitions can still be applied. We find that T_2 and T_3 are both active in β_1, but T_1 is not. Also T_1 and T_2 are live in β_1, but T_3 is not. Finally, T_3, $T_{3.1}$, and $T_{3.2}$ are orphans in β_1, because T_3 is aborted in β.

3.4.2 Well-Formedness

Very few constraints are placed on the transaction automata and serial object automata in the definition of a serial system. However, it is convenient to assume that certain simple properties are guaranteed; for example, a transaction should not take steps until it has been created, and an object should not respond to an operation that has not been invoked. Such requirements are captured by *well-formedness conditions*, basic safety properties of sequences of external actions of the transaction and serial object components.

Later chapters will define similar well-formedness conditions for other sorts of automata. In each case, these conditions are simple characterizations of *reasonable* behavior, capturing what amount to syntactic properties and ignoring any specific properties of computations performed by individual automata. In each case, we will show that all behaviors of the system considered have these properties; thus, by considering well-formed behaviors of an automaton in isolation, we can reason about simple properties of a single automaton without worrying about bad situations that never appear in behaviors of the system as a whole.

Transaction   Well-Formedness

Let T be any transaction name. A sequence β of serial actions π (each with *transaction*$(\pi) = T$) is defined to be **transaction well-formed** for T provided the following conditions hold.

1. The first event in β, if any, is a **CREATE**(T) event, and there are no other **CREATE** events.

2. There is at most one **REQUEST_CREATE**(T') event in β for each child T' of T.

3. Any report event for a child T' of T is preceded by **REQUEST_CREATE**(T') in β.

4. There is at most one report event in β for each child T' of T.

5. If a **REQUEST_COMMIT** event for T occurs in β, then it is preceded by a report event for each child T' of T for which there is a **REQUEST_CREATE**(T') in β.

6. If a **REQUEST_COMMIT** event for T occurs in β, then it is the last event in β.

A transaction well-formed sequence is always a prefix of a sequence that starts with **CREATE**(T), ends with **REQUEST_COMMIT**(T, v), and in between has some interleaving of a collection of two-element sequences **REQUEST_CREATE**(T')**REPORT-_COMMIT**(T', v'), for various children T' of T. In particular, if T is an access transaction name, then the only sequences that are transaction well-formed for T are the prefixes of the two-event sequences of the form **CREATE**(T) **REQUEST_COMMIT**(T, v), for some v. For any T, it is easy to see that (in the language of the Appendix) the property of being transaction well-formed for T is a safety property.

It is helpful to have an equivalent form of the *transaction well-formedness* definition: This lemma expresses an inductive characterization of transaction well-formedness, suitable for use in later proofs, when we demonstrate that specific automata preserve transaction well-formedness.

LEMMA 3.3 *A sequence β of actions ϕ (each with transaction(ϕ) = T) is transaction well-formed for T if and only if for every finite prefix $\gamma\pi$ of β, where π is a single action, the following conditions hold.*

1. *If π is **CREATE**(T), then*

   *(a) there is no **CREATE**(T) event in γ.*

2. *If π is **REQUEST_CREATE**(T') for a child T' of T, then*

   *(a) there is no **REQUEST_CREATE**(T') event in γ,*

   *(b) a **CREATE**(T) event appears in γ, and*

   *(c) there is no **REQUEST_COMMIT** event for T in γ.*

3. *If π is a report event for a child T' of T, then*

   *(a) a **REQUEST_CREATE**(T') event appears in γ, and*

(b) there is no report event for T' in γ.

4. If π is **REQUEST_COMMIT**(T, v) for some value v, then

(a) there is a report event in γ for every child of T for which there is a **REQUEST_CREATE** event in γ,

(b) a **CREATE(T)** event appears in γ, and

(c) there is no **REQUEST_COMMIT** event for T in γ.

PROOF   The proof is an exercise left to the reader. (Exercise 4.)   □

EXAMPLE 3.4.2   Transaction Well-Formedness

Returning to the system of Example 3.1.1, the sequence

> **CREATE**(T_3),
>   **REQUEST_CREATE**$(T_{3.1})$,
>   **REQUEST_CREATE**$(T_{3.2})$,
>   **REPORT_COMMIT**$(T_{3.2}, \$200)$,
>   **REQUEST_CREATE**$(T_{3.5})$,
>   **REPORT_ABORT**$(T_{3.5})$,
>   **REPORT_COMMIT**$(T_{3.1}, \$400)$,
> **REQUEST_COMMIT**$(T_3, \$200)$

is transaction well-formed for T_3. Notice that while this sequence has a well-formed pattern of invocations and responses, the details do not fit the description of the **FLEXWITHDRAW** activity presented earlier (for example, creation of $T_{3.2}$ is requested before the response from $T_{3.1}$ is received).

In contrast,

> **CREATE**(T_3),
>   **REPORT_COMMIT**$(T_{3.2}, \$200)$,
>   **REQUEST_CREATE**$(T_{3.5})$,
>   **REPORT_ABORT**$(T_{3.5})$,
> **REQUEST_COMMIT**$(T_3, \$200)$

is not transaction well-formed for T_3, because there is no **REQUEST_CREATE**$(T_{3.2})$ preceding the **REPORT_COMMIT**$(T_{3.2}, \$200)$ action. Also,

CREATE(T_3),
    REQUEST_CREATE($T_{3.1}$),
    REQUEST_CREATE($T_{3.1}$),
    REPORT_COMMIT($T_{3.1}$,\$200),
REQUEST_COMMIT(T_3, \$200),
    REQUEST_CREATE($T_{3.5}$)

is not transaction well-formed for T_3, because there are two **REQUEST-_CREATE**($T_{3.1}$) actions, and also because there is an action following the **REQUEST_COMMIT**(T_3, \$200) action.

Serial Object Well-Formedness

Let X be any object name. A sequence of serial actions π with $object(\pi) = $ X is defined to be **serial object well-formed** for X if it is a prefix of a sequence of the form

CREATE(T_1)**REQUEST_COMMIT**(T_1, v_1)**CREATE**(T_2)**REQUEST_COMMIT**(T_2, v_2) $\ldots$

where $T_i \neq T_j$ when $i \neq j$. That is, β consists of an alternating sequence of **CREATE** and **REQUEST_COMMIT** actions, each for an access to X, where each **REQUEST-_COMMIT** is immediately preceded by a **CREATE** action for the same access, and where there are not two **CREATE** events for the same access in the sequence.

For any X, it is easy to see that being a serial object well-formed sequence for X is a safety property.

LEMMA 3.4 *Suppose β is a sequence of serial actions π with $object(\pi) = $ X. If β is serial object well-formed for X and T is an access to X, then $\beta|T$ is transaction well-formed for T.*

Also say that a sequence ξ of operations (T, v) with $object(T) = $ X is **serial object well-formed** for X if no two operations in ξ have the same transaction name. Clearly, if ξ is a serial object well-formed sequence of operations of X, then perform(ξ) is a serial object well-formed sequence of actions of X. Also, any serial object well-formed sequence of actions of X is a prefix of perform(ξ) for some serial object well-formed sequence of operations ξ.

As above, an equivalent form of the *serial object well-formedness* definition will be useful in later proofs.

LEMMA 3.5 *A sequence β of actions ϕ with $object(\phi) = $ X is serial object well-formed for X if and only if for every finite prefix $\gamma\pi$ of β, where π is a single action, the following conditions hold.*

1. *If* π *is* ***CREATE(T)****, then*

    (a) there is no ***CREATE(T)*** *event in* γ*, and*

    (b) there are no active accesses in γ*.*

2. *If* π *is* ***REQUEST_COMMIT****(T, v) for a return value v, then*

    (a) T *is active in* γ*.*

PROOF   The proof is an exercise left to the reader. (Exercise 5.) $\square$

EXAMPLE 3.4.3   Serial Object Well-Formedness

Once again consider the system type of Example 3.1.1. The sequence

CREATE$(T_{3.2})$,
REQUEST_COMMIT$(T_{3.2}, \$200)$,
    CREATE(T_2),
    REQUEST_COMMIT$(T_2, \text{``}OK\text{''})$

is serial object well-formed for ACCT_CHK. However, the sequence

REQUEST_COMMIT$(T_{3.2}, \$200)$,
    CREATE(T_2),
CREATE$(T_{3.2})$,
    REQUEST_COMMIT$(T_2, \text{``}OK\text{''})$

is not serial object well-formed for ACCT_CHK, because (among other reasons) the action **REQUEST_COMMIT**$(T_{3.2}, \$200)$ is not immediately preceded by the action **CREATE**$(T_{3.2})$.

3.5   Serial   Systems

A serial system is composed of transaction automata, serial object automata, and a single serial scheduler automaton. There is one transaction automaton A_T for each non-access transaction name T, and one serial object automaton $S(X)$ for each object name X. These three kinds of components are described in turn.

3.5.1 Transaction Automata

A **transaction automaton** A_T for a non-access transaction name T of a given system type is an automaton with the following external action signature, depicted in Figure 3.3. (The automaton A_T may also have an arbitrary set of internal actions.)

Input:
    CREATE(T)
    REPORT_COMMIT(T',v'), for every child T' of T, and every return value v' for T'
    REPORT_ABORT(T'), for every child T' of T
Output:
    REQUEST_CREATE(T'), for every child T' of T
    REQUEST_COMMIT(T, v), for every return value v for T

In addition, A_T is required to preserve transaction well-formedness for T. (This condition uses the technical definitions of preserving a property, which was given in Section 2.8, as well as the definition of transaction well-formedness from Section 3.4.2.) As discussed in the preceding chapter, this condition does not mean that all behaviors of A_T are transaction well-formed, but it does mean that as long as the environment of A_T does not violate transaction well-formedness, A_T will not do so. Notice that the only ways the environment can violate transaction well-formedness for T are by reporting the fate of a subtransaction that was never requested, or by generating duplicate **CREATE**(T) actions or **REPORT** actions for children of T. The only ways in which A_T can violate this condition would be to produce any output action before receiving a **CREATE**, to request the creation of a child twice, to request to commit before receiving reports on the fate of all requested children, or to produce any output action after requesting to commit.

Except for the requirement to preserve transaction well-formedness, transaction automata can be chosen arbitrarily.

Transaction automata are intended to be general enough to model the transactions defined in any reasonable programming language. Of course, there is still work required in showing how to define appropriate transaction automata for the transactions in any particular language. This correspondence depends on the special features of each language, and techniques for establishing such a correspondence are not discussed in this book. However, the examples below are intended to provide some insight.

EXAMPLE 3.5.1 Banking System Transactions

In the banking system described in Example 3.1.1, one can model the user (transaction T_0) by an automaton A_{T_0}, with the following signature:

Input:
    CREATE(T_0),
    REPORT_COMMIT(T_1,*"OK"*),
    REPORT_COMMIT(T_2,*"OK"*),
    REPORT_COMMIT(T_3,\$200),
    REPORT_COMMIT(T_3,*"FAIL-3.1"*),
    REPORT_COMMIT(T_3,*"FAIL-3.2"*),
    REPORT_COMMIT(T_3,*"FAIL-3.3"*),
    REPORT_COMMIT(T_4,*"OK"*),
    REPORT_COMMIT(T_5,*v*) for each nonnegative integer amount of money v,
    REPORT_ABORT(T_1),
    REPORT_ABORT(T_2),
    REPORT_ABORT(T_3),
    REPORT_ABORT(T_4),
    REPORT_ABORT(T_5)
Output:
    REQUEST_CREATE(T_1),
    REQUEST_CREATE(T_2),
    REQUEST_CREATE(T_3),
    REQUEST_CREATE(T_4),
    REQUEST_CREATE(T_5),
    REQUEST_COMMIT(T_0, *"OK"*)

Each state of A_{T_0} is given by the value of the following variables: a Boolean *run*, initially *false*, and an array *status*, indexed by the integers from 1 to 5, with values each being one of *"nil"*, *"requested"*, *"success"*, *"fail"*, initially all *"nil"*. For each i, *status*[i] indicates the progress of T_i as known to the user.

The transition relation for A_{T_0} is the set of steps (s', π, s) described by the preconditions and effects shown in Figure 3.6.

Notice how the well-formedness requirement that **REQUEST_CREATE**(T_4) not be issued twice, and the semantic requirement that T_4 not be requested until T_2 and T_3 have completed successfully, are both expressed in the precondition of the **REQUEST_CREATE**(T_4) action. Also notice how any report of a child transaction failing causes *run* to be set to *false*, thus preventing any further requests.

A remark is in order regarding the conditional clause in the effect of the **REPORT_COMMIT**(T_3,*v*) action, and our notational convention for unspecified state components. The *run* state component is explicitly specified when $v \neq \$2002$, but is not explicitly specified when $v = \$200$. By the convention, when $v = \$200$, then $s.run = s'.run$.

Having described a transaction automaton for T_0, we now give one that models T_3. A_{T_3} has signature

CREATE(T_0)
  Effect:
    $s.run = true$

REPORT_COMMIT(T_1,v)
  Effect:
    $s.status[1] = $ "success"

REPORT_COMMIT(T_2,v)
  Effect:
    $s.status[2] = $ "success"

REPORT_COMMIT(T_3,v)
  Effect:
    if $v = \$200$
    then $s.status[3] = $ "success"
    else $s.status[3] = $ "fail"
    $s.run = false$

REPORT_COMMIT(T_4,v)
  Effect:
    $s.status[4] = $ "success"

REPORT_COMMIT(T_5,v)
  Effect:
    $s.status[5] = $ "success"

REPORT_ABORT(T_i) for $i = 1, \ldots, 5$
  Effect:
    $s.status[i] = $ "fail"
    $s.run = false$

REQUEST_CREATE(T_1)
  Precondition:
    $s'.status[1] = $ "nil"
    $s'.run = true$
  Effect:
    $s.status[1] = $ "requested"

REQUEST_CREATE(T_2)
  Precondition:
    $s'.status[2] = $ "nil"
    $s'.status[1] = $ "success"
    $s'.run = true$
  Effect:
    $s.status[2] = $ "requested"

REQUEST_CREATE(T_3)
  Precondition:
    $s'.status[3] = $ "nil"
    $s'.status[1] = $ "success"
    $s'.run = true$
  Effect:
    $s.status[3] = $ "requested"

REQUEST_CREATE(T_4)
  Precondition:
    $s'.status[4] = $ "nil"
    $s'.status[2] = $ "success"
    $s'.status[3] = $ "success"
    $s'.run = true$
  Effect:
    $s.status[4] = $ "requested"

REQUEST_CREATE(T_5)
  Precondition:
    $s'.status[5] = $ "nil"
    $s'.status[2] = $ "success"
    $s'.status[3] = $ "success"
    $s'.run = true$
  Effect:
    $s.status[5] = $ "requested"

REQUEST_COMMIT(T_0, v)
  Precondition:
    $false$

Figure 3.6: Transition Relation for T_0

Input:
  CREATE(T_3),
  REPORT_COMMIT($T_{3.i}$,v) for $i = 1, 2 \ldots$ and v a return value for $T_{3.i}$,
  REPORT_ABORT($T_{3.i}$) for $i = 1, 2, \ldots$
Output:
  REQUEST_CREATE($T_{3.i}$) for $i = 1, 2, \ldots,$
  REQUEST_COMMIT($T_3, \$200$),
  REQUEST_COMMIT(T_3, "FAIL-3.1"),
  REQUEST_COMMIT(T_3, "FAIL-3.2"),
  REQUEST_COMMIT(T_3, "FAIL-3.3")

CREATE(T_3)
Effect:
  $s.run = true$

REPORT_COMMIT($T_{3.1}$,v)
Effect:
  $s.status[1] =$ "*success*"
  $balance = v$

REPORT_COMMIT($T_{3.2}$,v)
Effect:
  if $v = \$200$
  then $s.status[2] =$ "*success*"
  else $s.status[2] =$ "*fail*"

REPORT_COMMIT($T_{3.3}$,v)
Effect:
  if $v = \$200$
  then $s.status[3] =$ "*success*"
  else $s.status[3] =$ "*fail*"

REPORT_COMMIT($T_{3.i}$,"OK") for $i = 4, 5, \ldots$
Effect:
  $s.status[i] =$ "*success*"

REPORT_ABORT($T_{3.i}$) for $i = 1, \ldots$
Effect:
  $s.status[i] =$ "*fail*"

REQUEST_CREATE($T_{3.1}$)
Precondition:
  $s'.status[1] =$ "*nil*"
  $s'.run = true$
Effect:
  $s.status[1] =$ "*requested*"

REQUEST_CREATE($T_{3.2}$)
Precondition:
  $s'.status[2] =$ "*nil*"
  $s'.status[1] =$ "*success*"
  $s'.balance > 450$
  $s'.run = true$
Effect:
  $s.status[2] =$ "*requested*"

REQUEST_CREATE($T_{3.3}$)
Precondition:
  $s'.status[3] =$ "*nil*"
  $s'.status[1] =$ "*success*"
  $s'.balance \leq 450$
  $s'.run = true$
Effect:
  $s.status[3] =$ "*requested*"

REQUEST_CREATE($T_{3.i}$) for $i = 4, 5, \ldots$
Precondition:
  $s'.status[i] =$ "*nil*"
  $s'.status[1] =$ "*success*"
  $s'.balance < 300$
  $1000 - s'.balance = i - 3$
  $s'.run = true$
Effect:
  $s.status[i] =$ "*requested*"

REQUEST_COMMIT(T_3, $\$200$)
Precondition:
  $s'.run = true$
  $s'.status[2] =$ "*success*"
    or $s'.status[3] =$ "*success*"
  $s'.balance \geq 300$
    or $s'.status[i] \neq$ "*nil*"
      for some $i = 4, 5, \ldots$
  $s'.status[i] \neq$ "*requested*" for all i
Effect:
  $s.run = false$

Figure 3.7: Transition Relation for T_3, Part I

Each state is given by values of the variables *run* a Boolean initially *false*, *balance* an integer initially 0, and (for $i = 1, 2, \ldots$) *status[i]* with values from the set "*nil*", "*requested*", "*success*", "*fail*", initially all "*nil*". The transition relation is given in Figures 3.7 and 3.8.

REQUEST_COMMIT(T_3, *"FAIL-3.1"*)
   Precondition:
      $s'.run = true$
      $s'.status[1] = $ *"fail"*
      $s'.status[i] \neq $ *"requested"* for all i
   Effect:
      $s.run = false$

REQUEST_COMMIT(T_3, *"FAIL-3.2"*)
   Precondition:
      $s'.run = true$
      $s'.status[2] = $ *"fail"*
      $s'.status[i] \neq $ *"requested"* for all i
   Effect:
      $s.run = false$

REQUEST_COMMIT(T_3, *"FAIL-3.3"*)
   Precondition:
      $s'.run = true$
      $s'.status[3] = $ *"fail"*
      $s'.status[i] \neq $ *"requested"* for all i
   Effect:
      $s.run = false$

Figure 3.8: Transition Relation for T_3, Part II

Finally here is the description (parameterized by value $k = 4, 5, \ldots$) for a collection of automata $A_{T_{3.k}}$ to model the **TRANSFER** transactions. The signature is

Input:
   CREATE($T_{3.k}$),
   REPORT_COMMIT($T_{3.k.i}$,v) for $i = 1, 2$ and v a return value for $T_{3.k.i}$,
   REPORT_ABORT($T_{3.k.i}$) for $i = 1, 2$
Output:
   REQUEST_CREATE($T_{3.k.i}$) for $i = 1, 2$,
   REQUEST_COMMIT($T_{3.k}$, *"OK"*)

Each state is given by values of the variables *run* a Boolean initially *false*, and (for $i = 1, 2$) *status[i]* with values from the set *"nil"*, *"requested"*, *"success"*, *"fail"*, initially all *"nil"*. The transition relation is given in Figure 3.9.

Notice that here if either subactivity fails, the automaton never takes a **REQUEST_COMMIT** step.[9]

---

[9] In a serial system as discussed in this chapter, this means that the whole system will not make progress. However, in a concurrent system providing atomicity, when the transaction is eventually aborted, the system will undo the effects of any subactivity that had succeeded.

CREATE($T_{3.k}$)
    Effect:
        $s.run = true$

REPORT_COMMIT($T_{3.k.1}$,v)
    Effect:
        if $v = k - 3$
        then $s.status[1] = $ "*success*"
        else $s.status[1] = $ "*fail*"

REPORT_COMMIT($T_{3.k.2}$,"*OK*")
    Effect:
        $s.status[2] = $ "*success*"

REPORT_ABORT($T_{3.k.i}$) for $i = 1, 2$
    Effect:
        $s.status[i] = $ "*fail*"

REQUEST_CREATE($T_{3.k.i}$) for $i = 1, 2$
    Precondition:
        $s'.status[i] = $ "*nil*"
        $s'.run = true$
    Effect:
        $s.status[i] = $ "*requested*"

REQUEST_COMMIT($T_{3.k}$, "*OK*")
    Precondition:
        $s'.run = true$
        $s'.status[1] = $ "*success*"
        $s'.status[2] = $ "*success*"
    Effect:
        $s.run = false$

Figure 3.9: Transition Relation for $T_{3.k}$

3.5.2 Serial Object Automata

A **serial object automaton** $S(X)$ for an object name X of a given system type is an automaton with the following external action signature. (The automaton $S(X)$ may also have an arbitrary set of internal actions.)

Input:
    CREATE(T), for every access T to X
Output:
    REQUEST_COMMIT(T, v), for every access T to X and every return value v for T

In addition, $S(X)$ is required to preserve serial object well-formedness for X, as defined in Sections 2.8 and 3.4.2. As with transaction automata, serial object automata can be chosen arbitrarily as long as they preserve serial object well-formedness. However, as above, this does not mean that all behaviors of $S(X)$ are serial object well-formed for X, but it does mean that as long as the environment of $S(X)$ does not violate serial object well-formedness, $S(X)$ will not do so.

Serial object automata are intended to be general enough to model any of the system-provided or user-defined types found in modern programming languages, subject to the restriction that each operation involves only a single object. The *semantic information* about a data object that is used in some concurrency control algorithms is obtained from the serial object automaton.

The ability to specify the behavior of an object using a serial object automaton is essential for modeling type-specific concurrency control algorithms. As discussed earlier, concurrency can be enhanced by using information about the semantics of operations—for example, that two operations commute—in synchronizing concurrent transactions. When a system has a *hot spot*, such as an aggregate quantity (e.g., net assets for a bank, or quantity on hand for an inventory system) or a data structure representing a collection, type-specific algorithms can be essential for achieving good performance. Many examples of type-specific algorithms can be found in the literature. Later in this book, several type-specific concurrency control algorithms are described, including a locking algorithm that uses the specifications of operations to allow operations that commute to run concurrently.

EXAMPLE 3.5.2   Bank Account Serial Objects

To continue the discussion of all the automata in the system of Example 3.1.1, serial object automata are needed to model the two accounts ACCT_CHK and ACCT_SVNG. These are in fact both instances of a general class of bank account serial object automaton. A bank account serial object automaton $S(\text{X})$ has associated with it several functions that indicate for each access the essential aspects, such as the operation involved and any parameters to those.[10] The function *kind* maps each access name into one of the values "*deposit*", "*withdraw*", or "*balance*", indicating which code is to be invoked by a given access, and the function *amount* maps each access name (other than a "*balance*") into a positive integer, indicating the amount the user wished to deposit or withdraw. Thus in our example, for the object ACCT_CHK, $kind(T_2) =$ "*deposit*", $amount(T_2) = 500$ and $kind(T_{3.2}) =$ "*withdraw*" and $amount(T_{3.2}) = 200$.

The state of $S(\text{X})$ consists of two components: *active* (either "*nil*", or the name of an access to X), and *current* (a nonnegative integer). The start state s_0 has $s_0.active =$ "*nil*", and $s_0.current = 0$. The transition relation is given in Figure 3.10.

EXAMPLE 3.5.3   Read/Write Serial Objects

Another common example of a serial object is a read/write serial object. Each read/write serial object $S(\text{X})$ has an associated domain of values, D, with a distinguished initial value d_0. $S(\text{X})$ also has an associated function $kind : accesses(\text{X}) \to \{$"*read*", "*write*"$\}$, and an associated function

---

[10]Recall that the transaction name encodes all these details. The functions now discussed merely extract these details for use.

CREATE(T)
  Effect:
    $s.active = T$

REQUEST_COMMIT(T, v),
  for $kind(T) = $ "$deposit$"
  Precondition:
    $s'.active = T$
    $v = $ "OK"
  Effect:
    $s.active = $ "nil"
    $s.current = s'.current + amount(T)$

REQUEST_COMMIT(T, v),
  for $kind(T) = $ "$balance$"
  Precondition:
    $s'.active = T$
    $v = s'.current$
  Effect:
    $s.active = $ "nil"

REQUEST_COMMIT(T, v),
  for $kind(T) = $ "$withdraw$"
  Precondition:
    $s'.active = T$
    $v = amount(T)$ or $v = \$0$
  Effect:
    $s.active = $ "nil"
    $s.current = s'.current - v$

Figure 3.10: Transition Relation for Bank Account Serial Object

CREATE(T)
  Effect:
    $s.active = T$

REQUEST_COMMIT(T, v),
  for $kind(T) = $ "$write$"
  Precondition:
    $s'.active = T$
    $v = $ "OK"
  Effect:
    $s.active = $ "nil"
    $s.data = data(T)$

REQUEST_COMMIT(T, v),
  for $kind(T) = $ "$read$"
  Precondition:
    $s'.active = T$
    $s'.data = v$
  Effect:
    $s.active = $ "nil"

Figure 3.11: Transition Relation for Read/Write Serial Object

$data : T \in accesses(\mathrm{X}) : kind(T) = $ "$write$" $\rightarrow D$. The set of possible return values for each access T where $kind(T) = $ "$read$" is D, while an access T where $kind(T) = $ "$write$" has return value "OK". The state of $S(\mathrm{X})$ consists of two components: $active$ (either "nil", or the name of an access to X), and $data$ (an element of D). The start state s_0 has $s_0.active = $ "nil", and $s_0.data = d_0$. The transition relation is given in Figure 3.11.

It is useful to define the *final value* of a read/write object after a sequence of write accesses. Thus, if $S(\mathrm{X})$ is a read/write serial object with domain D, initial value d_0, and associated functions $kind$ and $data$, and if β is a sequence of serial actions, define *write-sequence*$(\beta, S(\mathrm{X}))$ to be the subsequence of β consisting of **REQUEST_COMMIT** events for transactions T such that T is an access to X with $kind(T) =$ "*write*"; then define $last\text{-}write(\beta, S(X))$ to be $transaction(\pi)$ where π is the last event in $write\text{-}sequence(\beta, S(X))$. (If $write\text{-}sequence(\beta, S(X))$ is empty, then $last\text{-}write(\beta, S(X))$ is undefined.) Finally, define $final\text{-}value(\beta, S(X))$ to be d_0 if $last\text{-}write(\beta, S(X))$ is undefined, and $data(last\text{-}write(\beta, S(X)))$, otherwise. Thus, $final\text{-}value(\beta, S(X))$ is the latest value written in β for X.

The following two lemmas formalize useful properties of the read/write serial object $S(X)$.

LEMMA 3.6 *Let β be a finite schedule of read/write serial object $S(X)$, and let s be the (unique) state of $S(X)$ after β. Then $s.data = final\text{-}value(\beta, S(X))$.*

LEMMA 3.7 *Let β be a finite behavior of $S(X)$. Then $\beta perform(T, v)$ is a behavior of $S(X)$ exactly if either $kind(T) =$ "write" and $v =$ "OK", or $kind(T) =$ "read" and $v = final value(\beta, S(X))$.*

EXAMPLE 3.5.4   Multicomponent Serial Objects

Another interesting example of a serial object is a multicomponent serial object, where each component can be read or written individually, and additionally there are accesses that read or write all the components at once. In relational databases, for example, a *tuple* consists of a number of named *fields*, and a query can refer to a single field, or to all the fields.

A multicomponent serial object $S(X)$ will be defined, for n components each from a domain[11] of values D, with a distinguished initial value d_0. $S(X)$ has associated functions $grain : accesses(X) \to \{$"*all*"$\} \cup \{1, 2, \ldots, n\}$, $kind : accesses(X) \to \{$"*read*", "*write*"$\}$, which indicate for each access which component is involved and how it is affected. There is also a function $data$, which gives a vector of n values of D (an element of D^n) to each access T for which $kind(T) =$ "*write*" and $grain(T) =$ "*all*", and which gives a single element of D to each access T for which $kind(T) =$ "*write*" and $grain(T) \neq$ "*all*". The set of possible return values for each access T where $kind(T) =$ "*read*" is either D^n (if $grain(T) =$ "*all*") or D (otherwise), while an access T where $kind(T) =$ "*write*" has return value "*OK*".

---

[11]For simplicity, the same domain and initial value are used for each component. In reality, each might have a separate domain.

CREATE(T)
  Effect:
    $s.active = T$

REQUEST_COMMIT(T, v),
  for $kind(T) = $ "*write*", $grain(T) = $ "*all*"
  Precondition:
    $s'.active = T$
    $v = $ "*OK*"
  Effect:
    $s.active = $ "*nil*"
    $s.data = data(T)$

REQUEST_COMMIT(T, v),
  for $kind(T) = $ "*write*", $grain(T) = i$
  Precondition:
    $s'.active = T$
    $v = $ "*OK*"
  Effect:
    $s.active = $ "*nil*"
    $s.data[i] = data(T)$

REQUEST_COMMIT(T, v),
  for $kind(T) = $ "*read*", $grain(T) = $ "*all*"
  Precondition:
    $s'.active = T$
    $s'.data = v$
  Effect:
    $s.active = $ "*nil*"

REQUEST_COMMIT(T, v),
  for $kind(T) = $ "*read*", $grain(T) = i$
  Precondition:
    $s'.active = T$
    $s'.data[i] = v$
  Effect:
    $s.active = $ "*nil*"

Figure 3.12: Transition Relation for Multicomponent Serial Object

The state of $S(\mathrm{X})$ consists of two components: *active* (either "*nil*", or the name of an access to X), and *data* (an element of D^n). We refer to the i-th component of *data* as *data*$[i]$. The start state s_0 has $s_0.active = $ "*nil*", and $s_0.data[i] = d_0$ for $i = 1, \ldots,$ n. The transition relation is given in Figure 3.12.

EXAMPLE 3.5.5   FIFO Queue Serial Object

As another example, we present a serial object representing a FIFO queue. The FIFO queue serial object $S(\mathrm{QUEUE})$ for object name QUEUE has an associated domain of values, $\mathcal{D}$, from which the entries are taken. $S(\mathrm{QUEUE})$ also has an associated function $kind : accesses(\mathrm{X}) \rightarrow \{$ "*insert*", "*delete*"$\}$, and an associated function $data : \{T \in accesses(\mathrm{X}) : kind(T) = $ "*insert*"$\} \rightarrow \mathcal{D}$. The set of possible return values for each access T where $kind(T) = $ "*delete*" is $\mathcal{D}$, while an access T where $kind(T) = $ "*insert*" has return value "*OK*". The state of $S(\mathrm{QUEUE})$ consists of four components: *active* (either "*nil*", or the name of an access to X), *queue* (an array of elements of $\mathcal{D}$ indexed by the positive integers), *front* (a positive integer), and *back* (another positive integer). The start state s_0 has $s_0.active = $ "*nil*", $s_0.back = 1$, and

CREATE(T)
  Effect:
    $s.active = T$

REQUEST_COMMIT(T, v),
  for $kind(T) = \text{"}insert\text{"}$
  Precondition:
    $s'.active = T$
    $v = \text{"}OK\text{"}$
  Effect:
    $s.active = \text{"}nil\text{"}$
    $s.queue[s'.back] = data(T)$
    $s.back = s'.back + 1$

REQUEST_COMMIT(T, v),
  for $kind(T) = \text{"}delete\text{"}$
  Precondition:
    $s'.active = T$
    $s'.back > s'.front$
    $s'.queue[s'.front] = v$
  Effect:
    $s.active = \text{"}nil\text{"}$
    $s.front = s'.front + 1$

Figure 3.13: Transition Relation for FIFO Queue Serial Object

$s_0.front = 1$ ($s_0.queue$ may be arbitrary). The transition relation is given in Figure 3.13.

Notice how the delete activity is blocked if the queue is empty (indicated by the condition $s'.front = s'.back$).

3.5.3 The Serial Scheduler

There is a single serial scheduler automaton for each system type. It runs transactions according to a depth-first traversal of the transaction tree, running sets of sibling transactions serially. When two or more sibling transactions are available to run (because their parent has requested their creation), the serial scheduler is free to determine the order in which they run. In addition, the serial scheduler can choose nondeterministically to abort any transaction after its parent has requested its creation, as long as the transaction has not actually been created. In the context of this scheduler, the *semantics* of an **ABORT**(T) action are that transaction T was never created. The scheduler does not permit any two sibling transactions to be live at the same time, and does not abort any transaction while any of its siblings is live. We now give a formal definition of the serial scheduler automaton.

    The action signature of the serial scheduler consists of the following actions, for every transaction name T and return value v.

Input:
  REQUEST_CREATE(T), $T \neq T_0$
  REQUEST_COMMIT(T, v)
Output:
  CREATE(T)
  COMMIT(T), $T \neq T_0$

REQUEST_CREATE(T)
    Effect:
$$s.create\_requested$$
$$= s'.create\_requested \cup \{T\}$$

REQUEST_COMMIT(T, v)
    Effect:
$$s.commit\_requested$$
$$= s'.commit\_requested \cup \{(T, v)\}$$

CREATE(T)
    Precondition:
$$T \in s'.create\_requested - s'.created$$
$$T \notin s'.aborted$$
$$siblings(T) \cap s'.created \subseteq s'.completed$$
    Effect:
$$s.created = s'.created \cup \{T\}$$

COMMIT(T)
    Precondition:
$$(T, v) \in s'.commit\_requested$$
$$T \notin s'.completed$$
    Effect:
$$s.committed = s'.committed \cup \{T\}$$

ABORT(T)
    Precondition:
$$T \in s'.create\_requested - s'.completed$$
$$T \notin s'.created$$
$$siblings(T) \cap s'.created \subseteq s'.completed$$
    Effect:
$$s.aborted = s'.aborted \cup \{T\}$$

REPORT_COMMIT(T, v)
    Precondition:
$$T \in s'.committed$$
$$(T, v) \in s'.commit\_requested$$
$$T \notin s'.reported$$
    Effect:
$$s.reported = s'.reported \cup \{T\}$$

REPORT_ABORT(T)
    Precondition:
$$T \in s'.aborted$$
$$T \notin s'.reported$$
    Effect:
$$s.reported = s'.reported \cup \{T\}$$

Figure 3.14: Transition Relation for the Serial Scheduler

ABORT(T), $T \neq T_0$
REPORT_COMMIT(T, v), $T \neq T_0$
REPORT_ABORT(T), $T \neq T_0$

Each state s of the serial scheduler consists of six sets, denoted via record notation: $s.create\_requested$, $s.created$, $s.commit\_requested$, $s.committed$, $s.aborted$, and $s.reported$. The set $s.commit\_requested$ is a set of operations. The others are sets of transactions. There is exactly one start state, in which the set $create\_requested$ is $\{T_0\}$, and the other sets are empty. The notation $s.completed$ denotes $s.committed \cup s.aborted$. Thus, $s.completed$ is not an actual variable in the state, but rather a *derived variable* whose value is determined as a function of the actual state variables.

The transition relation of the serial scheduler consists of exactly those triples (s', π, s) satisfying the preconditions and yielding the effects described in Figure 3.14. The input actions, **REQUEST_CREATE** and **REQUEST_COMMIT**, simply result in the request being recorded. The **COMMIT** and **REPORT** output actions are relatively simple: a **COMMIT** action can occur only if there has been a request (containing some return value) and no completion action has yet occurred for the indicated transaction, while the result of a transaction can be reported to its parent at any time after the **COMMIT** or **ABORT** has occurred.

The other output actions, **CREATE** and **ABORT**, are the most interesting. A **CREATE** action can occur only if a corresponding **REQUEST_CREATE** has occurred and the **CREATE** has not already occurred. Moreover, it cannot occur if the transaction was previously aborted. Similarly, an **ABORT** action can occur only if a corresponding **REQUEST_CREATE** has occurred and no completion action has yet occurred for the indicated transaction. Moreover, it cannot occur if the transaction was previously created. The third precondition on the **CREATE** action says that the serial scheduler does not **CREATE** a transaction until each of its previously created sibling transactions has completed (i.e., committed or aborted). That is, siblings are run sequentially. Similarly, the third precondition on the **ABORT** action says that the scheduler does not abort a transaction while there is activity going on on behalf of any of its siblings. That is, aborted transactions are dealt with sequentially with respect to their siblings. The combined effect of the preconditions on the **CREATE** and **ABORT** actions is that the scheduler does not consider a transaction for creation or abortion so long as a sibling is live.

Basic Properties of the Serial Scheduler

The following lemma describes simple relationships between the state of the serial scheduler and its computational history. These results show that each state component contains the set suggested by its name; for example, in any state $s.created$ is indeed the set of transactions for which **CREATE** events have occurred. The lemma also gives some simple relationships between state components, which are maintained by each action; for example, both **COMMIT** and **ABORT** actions check in the precondition that the transaction is not already in *completed* (recall that this is *committed* ∪ *aborted*) so that no transaction can be in both *committed* and *aborted*. The proof of this lemma follows the pattern of that for Lemma 2.6, and is left for the reader as Exercise 6.

LEMMA 3.8 *If β is a finite schedule of the serial scheduler that can lead to state s, then the following conditions are true.*

1. $T \in s.create\_requested$ *if and only if* $T = T_0$ *or* β *contains a* **REQUEST_CREATE**(T) *event.*

2. $T \in s.created$ *if and only if* β *contains a* **CREATE**(T) *event.*

3. $(T, v) \in s.commit\_requested$ *if and only if* β *contains a* **REQUEST_COMMIT**(T, v) *event.*

4. $T \in s.committed$ *if and only if* β *contains a* **COMMIT**(T) *event.*

5. $T \in s.aborted$ if and only if β contains an **ABORT**(T) event.

6. $T \in s.reported$ if and only if β contains a report event for T.

7. $s.committed \cap s.aborted = \emptyset$.

8. $s.reported \subseteq s.committed \cup s.aborted$.

9. $s.created \cap s.aborted = \emptyset$.

The following lemma gives simple facts about the actions appearing in an arbitrary schedule of the serial scheduler. The facts given here are proved by examining the precondition of an action in the serial scheduler, and then using Lemma 3.8 to translate that into an observation about the previous appearance of an event in the behavior. The details are left to the reader.

LEMMA 3.9 *Let β be a schedule of the serial scheduler. Then all of the following hold:*

1. *If a **CREATE**(T) event appears in β for $T \neq T_0$, then a **REQUEST_CREATE**(T) event precedes it in β.*

2. *At most one **CREATE**(T) event appears in β for each transaction T.*

3. *If a **COMMIT**(T) event appears in β, then a **REQUEST_COMMIT**(T, v) event precedes it in β for some return value v.*

4. *If an **ABORT**(T) event appears in β, then a **REQUEST_CREATE**(T) event precedes it in β.*

5. *At most one report event appears in β for each transaction.*

6. *If a **REPORT_COMMIT**(T,v) event appears in β, then a **COMMIT**(T) event and a **REQUEST_COMMIT**(T, v) event precede it in β.*

7. *If a **REPORT_ABORT**(T) event appears in β, then an **ABORT**(T) event precedes it in β.*

8. *At most one completion event appears in β for each transaction.*

9. *At most one of **ABORT**(T) and **CREATE**(T) appears in β.*

10. *If a **CREATE**(T) or **ABORT**(T) event appears in β and is preceded by a **CREATE**(T') event for a sibling T' of T, then it is also preceded by a completion event for T'.*

The final lemma of this subsection says that the serial scheduler preserves the well-formedness properties described earlier.

LEMMA 3.10

1. *Let T be any transaction name. Then the serial scheduler preserves transaction well-formedness for T.*

2. *Let X be any object name. Then the serial scheduler preserves serial object well-formedness for X.*

PROOF

1. Let Φ be the set of all serial actions ϕ with $transaction(\phi) = T$. Suppose $\beta\pi$ projected on the actions of the serial scheduler is a finite behavior of the serial scheduler, π is an output action of the serial scheduler, and $\beta|\Phi$ is transaction well-formed for T. It remains to show that $\beta\pi|\Phi$ is transaction well-formed for T. If $\pi \notin \Phi$, then the result is immediate, so assume that $\pi \in \Phi$, (i.e., that $transaction(\pi) = T$).

The proof uses Lemma 3.3. Since $\beta|\Phi$ is transaction well-formed for T, the four conditions of the lemma hold for all prefixes of $\beta|\Phi$. Thus, it remains only to prove that the four conditions of the lemma hold for $\beta\pi|\Phi$. Since π is an output of the serial scheduler, π is either a **CREATE**(T) event or a **REPORT** event for a child of T. If π is **CREATE**(T), then since $\beta\pi$ projected on the actions of the serial scheduler is a schedule of the serial scheduler, Lemma 3.9 implies that no **CREATE**(T) occurs in β. If π is a **REPORT** event for a child T' of T, then Lemma 3.9 implies that **REQUEST_CREATE**(T') occurs in β and no other **REPORT** for T' occurs in β. Then Lemma 3.3 implies that $\beta\pi|\Phi$ is transaction well-formed for T.

2. The argument for this case is similar, using Lemma 3.5.   □

3.5.4 Serial Systems, Executions, Schedules and Behaviors

A **serial system** of a given system type is the composition of a compatible set of I/O automata indexed by the union of the set of non-access transaction names, the set of object names and the singleton set $\{SS\}$ (for *serial scheduler*). Associated with each non-access transaction name T is a transaction automaton A_T for T. Associated with each object name X is a serial object automaton $S(\text{X})$ for X. Finally, associated with the name SS is the serial scheduler automaton for the given system type.

When the particular serial system is understood from context, the terms **serial executions**, **serial schedules**, and **serial behaviors** are sometimes used for the system's executions, schedules, and behaviors, respectively.

It is important to notice exactly what is meant when one says that a serial system runs sibling transactions serially. This means the serial scheduler will not issue a

CREATE(T) output action unless COMMIT actions have occurred for all previously created siblings of T. This does not mean, however, that the REQUEST_CREATE events and the REPORT events for siblings are serialized. For example, the following sequence could be a fragment of a serial behavior, where T and T' are siblings:

REQUEST_CREATE(T),
    REQUEST_CREATE(T'),
CREATE(T),
REQUEST_COMMIT(T, v),
COMMIT(T),
    CREATE(T'),
    REQUEST_COMMIT(T', v'),
    COMMIT(T'),
    REPORT_COMMIT(T', v'),
REPORT_COMMIT(T, v).

Notice that the REQUEST_CREATE and REPORT events for T and T' are interleaved, even though the CREATE and COMMIT events are serialized.

Some basic properties of serial behaviors are described next. First, serial behaviors are shown to be well-formed for each transaction and object name.

LEMMA 3.11 *If β is a serial behavior, then the following conditions hold.*

1. *For every transaction name T, $\beta|T$ is transaction well-formed for T.*

2. *For every object name X, $\beta|$X is serial object well-formed for X.*

PROOF For non-access transaction names T, or arbitrary object names X, the result is immediate by Proposition 2.12, the definitions of transaction and object automata, and Lemma 3.10.

Suppose that T is an access to X. Since $\beta|$X is serial object well-formed for X, Lemma 3.4 implies that $\beta|T$ is transaction well-formed for T. □

The next lemma shows that in a serial behavior, aborted transactions take no steps.

LEMMA 3.12 *Let β be a serial behavior. Then β does not contain an event π such that transaction(π) is an orphan in β.*

PROOF Suppose that T is a transaction such that β contains an event π with transaction(π) = T. Let U be any ancestor of T. We must show that β does not contain ABORT(U).

By Lemma 3.11, $\beta|T$ is transaction well-formed for T. Since π is in $\beta|T$, $\beta|T$ is not empty, so by the definition of transaction well-formedness, $\beta|T$ begins with **CREATE**(T). By Lemma 3.9, either $T = T_0$ or else β contains **REQUEST_CREATE**(T), which is an event ϕ with $transaction(\phi) = parent(T)$. Repeating the argument up the tree of transactions, we see that β contains an event ψ with $transaction(\psi) = U$, and hence (by transaction well-formedness for U), β contains **CREATE**(U). Thus, using Lemma 3.9, we have that β does not contain **ABORT**(U). $\square$

The next lemma shows that in a serial behavior, the set of live transactions forms a single chain from the root. The proof is left to the reader, as Exercise 7.

LEMMA 3.13 *Let β be a serial behavior.*

1. *If T is live in β and T' is an ancestor of T, then T' is live in β.*

2. *If T and T' are transaction names such that both T and T' are live in β, then either T is an ancestor of T' or T' is an ancestor of T.*

EXAMPLE 3.5.6 **The Serial Banking System**

Here is a schedule β of the serial system that models the banking system described in Example 3.1.1.

CREATE(T_0),
    REQUEST_CREATE(T_1),
    CREATE(T_1),
    REQUEST_COMMIT(T_1, "*OK*"),
    COMMIT(T_1),
    REPORT_COMMIT(T_1, "*OK*"),
      REQUEST_CREATE(T_2),
        REQUEST_CREATE(T_3),
    CREATE(T_2),
    REQUEST_COMMIT(T_2, "*OK*"),
    COMMIT(T_2),
      CREATE(T_3),
        REQUEST_CREATE($T_{3.1}$),
    REPORT_COMMIT(T_2, "*OK*"),
        CREATE($T_{3.1}$),
        REQUEST_COMMIT($T_{3.1}$, \$500),
        COMMIT($T_{3.1}$),
        REPORT_COMMIT($T_{3.1}$, \$500),
          REQUEST_CREATE($T_{3.2}$),

$$\text{CREATE}(T_{3.2}),$$
$$\text{REQUEST\_COMMIT}(T_{3.2}, \$200),$$
$$\text{COMMIT}(T_{3.2}),$$
$$\text{REPORT\_COMMIT}(T_{3.2}, \$200),$$
$$\text{REQUEST\_COMMIT}(T_3, \$200),$$
$$\text{COMMIT}(T_3),$$
$$\text{REPORT\_COMMIT}(T_3, \$200),$$
$$\text{REQUEST\_CREATE}(T_5),$$
$$\text{REQUEST\_CREATE}(T_4),$$
$$\text{CREATE}(T_4),$$
$$\text{REQUEST\_COMMIT}(T_4, \text{``}OK\text{''}),$$
$$\text{COMMIT}(T_4),$$
$$\text{CREATE}(T_5),$$
$$\text{REQUEST\_COMMIT}(T_5, \$3000),$$
$$\text{COMMIT}(T_5),$$
$$\text{REPORT\_COMMIT}(T_5, \$3000),$$
$$\text{REPORT\_COMMIT}(T_4, \text{``}OK\text{''}).$$

You should check that the projection on each component of the system is a schedule of that component, according to the transition relation given above. For example, $\beta | A_{T_3}$ is

$$\text{CREATE}(T_3),$$
$$\text{REQUEST\_CREATE}(T_{3.1}),$$
$$\text{REPORT\_COMMIT}(T_{3.1}, \$500),$$
$$\text{REQUEST\_CREATE}(T_{3.2}),$$
$$\text{REPORT\_COMMIT}(T_{3.2}, \$200),$$
$$\text{REQUEST\_COMMIT}(T_3, 200).$$

Notice that in this schedule T_5 returns \$3000, because T_2 runs before T_3, so that $T_{3.1}$ reveals enough money in ACCT_CHK that the withdrawal is made from it, and also because T_4 runs before T_5, so that the extra deposit is reflected in the balance seen by T_5. Another serial schedule is given in Exercise 1, in which T_5 returns the value \$1800, because T_3 runs before T_2 (despite the fact that these are requested concurrently) so that the withdrawal of \$200 is made from ACCT_SVNG, and also because T_4 runs after T_5. In Exercise 2, you are asked to construct another schedule, where the value returned by T_4 is \$800.

EXAMPLE 3.5.7   A Message Queue System

The banking system of Example 3.1.1 contains only serial objects of one type (bank account objects). Here is another serial system, that contains three objects with other types. The object names COPY_A and COPY_B each have an associated serial object that is a read/write object (as in Example 3.5.3) whose domain of values is the integers and whose initial value is 0. The object name QUEUE has associated serial object that is a FIFO queue (as in Example 3.5.5), whose domain of values is assumed to be the integers.

The root transaction T_0 has three infinite families of children, which it invokes arbitrarily (except for the need to preserve transaction well-formedness); that is, once T_0 has been created, it may at any time request the creation of any child that it did not previously request. One family of T_0's children (the *value generators*) is named T_{G1}, T_{G2}, ... T_{Gi}, ..., where T_{Gi} is an access to QUEUE that inserts the integer value i into the queue. Formally, $kind(T_{Gi}) =$ "*insert*" and $data(T_{Gi}) = i$.

Another family (the *value recorders*) is named T_{R1}, T_{R2}, ... T_{Rj}, ... Each transaction T_{Rj} has the same functionality: once created, it dequeues a value from QUEUE and after that access returns successfully, it concurrently stores the value returned in both COPY_A and COPY_B, and then (only after commits are reported for both writes) it requests to commit, returning the value that was dequeued. Thus T_{Rj} has the following children in the transaction tree: one, called $T_{Rj.0}$, that is an access to QUEUE with $kind(T_{Rj.0}) =$ "*dequeue*", and two infinite families $T_{Rj.Ax}$ and $T_{Rj.Bx}$ for integer values of X, where $T_{Rj.Ax}$ is an access to COPY_A with $kind(T_{Rj.Ax}) =$ "*write*" and $data(T_{Rj.Ax}) = x$, and similarly $T_{Rj.Bx}$ is an access to COPY_B with $kind(T_{Rj.Bx}) =$ "*write*" and $data(T_{Rj.Bx}) = x$.

The third family of children of T_0 is the *viewers*: T_{Vk} concurrently requests two accesses $T_{Vk.A}$ and $T_{Vk.B}$, which respectively read the value in COPY_A and COPY_B; after both have reported to T_{Vk} it requests to commit. The return value is "*BAD*" if the two values read were different; otherwise, it is the common value read.

We leave to the reader (as Exercise 10), the task of writing transaction automata to express the given descriptions of T_0, T_{Rj} and T_{Vk}. That exercise also demonstrates an important integrity constraint on this serial system: any viewer access does not return "*BAD*", since after any child of

T_0 has executed, the data values in the two read/write serial objects are equal.

3.5.5 Convention: Fixing the System Type and Serial System

Unless expressly stated, the discussion in the remainder of this book assumes an arbitrary but fixed system type and serial system, with A_T as the transaction automaton associated with non-access transaction name T, and $S(X)$ as the serial object automaton associated with object name X. The only exceptions are in Example 3.7.1 and later in Chapter 12, where we consider the relationships between several different serial systems.

3.6   Atomicity

Now that serial systems are defined, they can be used to define correctness conditions for other transaction-processing systems. It is reasonable to use serial systems in this way because of the particular constraints the serial scheduler imposes on the orders in which transactions and objects can perform steps. We contend that the given constraints correspond precisely to the way nested transaction systems ought to appear to behave; in particular, these constraints yield a natural generalization of the notion of serial execution in classical transaction systems. Serial systems can then be used to define a number of correctness conditions by considering *for which system components* this appearance must be maintained: for the external environment T_0, for all transactions, or for all nonorphan transactions.

3.6.1   Atomicity of Action Sequences

The notion of *atomicity* of a sequence of actions for a particular transaction name is defined to express these correctness conditions. A sequence β of actions is **atomic** for transaction name T provided that there is some serial behavior γ such that $\beta|T = \gamma|T$.[12]   (Recall from Section 3.4.1 that if T is a non-access, then $\beta|T = \beta|ext(A_T)$ and $\gamma|T = \gamma|ext(A_T)$). If T is a non-access transaction, the atomicity for T of a sequence β guarantees to implementors of A_T that their code has encountered only situations that could arise in serial executions.

---

[12]This condition is analogous to the *view serializability* condition of Yannakakis [121], extended to deal with operations other than reads and writes, and with subtransactions.

3.6.2 Atomicity of Systems

The intention in defining correctness for a system is to constrain its interactions with the external environment, which is modeled by the root transaction T_0. Thus, our fundamental correctness condition simply requires atomicity for T_0. In most applications of the theory, one would expect systems to contain the same transaction automaton for T_0 as in the serial system. (In other words, the external environment in the serial system will be the same as in the real transaction-processing system.) In fact, the systems described in this book have a structure that is even closer to that of the serial system: these systems contain the same automaton A_T for each transaction name T as in the serial system. However, the fundamental definition of correctness does not depend on these or other assumptions. Such constraints may seem intuitively reasonable, but they are not needed for defining correctness. Furthermore, in our experience, most such constraints rule out some interesting systems. Thus, in defining correctness, any system (modeled as an I/O automaton) may be considered as a candidate transaction-processing system. As a result, the definition of correctness does not constrain the internal structure of a transaction-processing system, or even its interface with the external environment.

A system is considered to be **atomic** for transaction name T provided all of its finite behaviors are atomic for T. Then if T is a non-access transaction, atomicity for T of a system containing A_T guarantees to implementors of A_T that their code will encounter only situations that can arise in serial executions. The principal notion of correctness for a transaction-processing system used in this book is that of atomicity for the root transaction T_0. This says that the *outside world* cannot, in a finite amount of time, distinguish between the given system and the serial system.[13]

3.6.3 Stronger Correctness Conditions

Many of the algorithms studied in this book satisfy stronger correctness conditions than atomicity for T_0. A fairly strong and interesting correctness condition is the atomicity of all finite behaviors for all non-access transaction names. Thus, neither the outside world nor any of the individual user transactions can distinguish between the given system and the serial system. Note that the definition of atomicity relative to all non-access transactions does not require that all the transactions see behavior that is part of the *same* execution of the serial system; rather, each could see behavior arising in a different serial execution.

---

[13] An interesting alternative condition would require atomicity of *all* behaviors for the root transaction name T_0, including infinite behaviors. A more detailed discussion of this point is deferred to Section 3.6.6.

Later chapters consider intermediate conditions such as atomicity for all nonorphan transaction names. This condition implies atomicity for T_0 because the serial scheduler does not have the action **ABORT**(T_0) in its signature, so T_0 cannot be an orphan. Most of the popular algorithms for concurrency control and recovery, including most of the algorithms described in this book, guarantee atomicity for all nonorphan transaction names. Intuitively, these algorithms work by simulating a serial environment for the concurrent transactions, at least until they become orphans (and hence can never commit to the root). Our Atomicity Theorem in Chapter 5 gives sufficient conditions for showing that a behavior of a transaction-processing system is atomic for an arbitrary nonorphan transaction name. This theorem is used in later chapters to prove that various algorithms guarantee this property of atomicity for all nonorphan transaction names. The usual algorithms do not guarantee atomicity for orphans, however; in order to guarantee this as well, the use of a special *orphan management* algorithm is generally required. Such algorithms are described and proved correct in Chapter 11.

3.6.4 Atomicity and Intuition

You should notice the similarity between the atomicity condition given in this section and the informally defined notion of *atomic database* given in the introduction to the book. Consider only the special case of T_0. The atomicity definition says that for all finite behaviors β, there exists a serial behavior γ such that $\beta|T_0 = \gamma|T_0$. Suppose the children of T_0 are all accesses; that is, the system type consists of just two levels. Then the serial scheduler for this system type would just process some of the requested accesses, in serial order. In particular, if the scheduler issues a **CREATE**(T), then it cannot issue any further outputs except reports until it has received a **REQUEST-_COMMIT** for T and issued a **COMMIT**(T). The effect on the data object is the same as if all three of these actions occurred consecutively, at the time of the **COM-MIT**(T). Thus, it is possible to show that every finite behavior γ of the serial system is generable by a system consisting of T_0 and a particular automaton that just performs the operations committed in γ at arbitrary times within their intervals.

EXAMPLE 3.6.1   An Atomic Schedule

For the system of Example 3.1.1, the sequence

> **CREATE**(T_0),
> **REQUEST_CREATE**(T_1),
> **REPORT_COMMIT**(T_1, *"OK"*),
> **REQUEST_CREATE**(T_2),

REQUEST_CREATE(T_3),

REPORT_COMMIT(T_2,"*OK*"),

REPORT_COMMIT(T_3,$200),

REQUEST_CREATE(T_5),

REQUEST_CREATE(T_4),

REPORT_COMMIT(T_5,$3000),

REPORT_COMMIT(T_4,"*OK*")

is atomic for T_0, because it is equal to the projection on T_0 of the serial schedule β given in Example 3.5.6. Notice that in this sequence T_5 returns the value $3000. Another atomic sequence (in which the return value of T_5 is $1800) is given in Excercise 3. However, no sequence in which T_5 has return value $1030 can be atomic; in fact, it is easy to see that in any serial execution, the amount of money in each account is always a multiple of $100. This follows from the fact that each top-level transaction preserves this property. Thus in a serial execution T_5 must return a multiple of $100, and so the same must be true in any sequence that is atomic for T_0.

3.6.5 Implications for Schedules and Executions

This subsection closes with a lemma that holds for the case where the given system and the serial system contain identical automata associated with transaction name T. Again, this will typically be the case in this book. The lemma shows that atomicity with respect to T, a notion defined in terms of similarity of behaviors, has consequences for the similarity of the schedules of T in the two systems, and also for the similarity of the executions of T in the two systems. This lemma will allow later chapters to focus on atomicity (a condition on behaviors), and avoid discussion of schedules and executions.

PROPOSITION 3.14 *Let* $\{B_i\}_{i \in I}$ *be a compatible set of I/O automata and let* $B = \Pi_{i \in I} B_i$. *Suppose that non-access transaction name* T *is in* I. *Suppose that* B_T *and* A_T *are the same automaton. Let* α *be an execution of* B. *Then the following are equivalent conditions.*

1. *$beh(\alpha)$ is atomic for T.*

2. *There is a serial execution α' such that $\alpha|B_T = \alpha'|A_T$.*

3. *There is a serial schedule β such that $sched(\alpha)|B_T = \beta|A_T$.*

4. *There is a serial behavior γ such that $beh(\alpha)|B_T = \gamma|A_T$.*

PROOF   The proof argues $1 \Rightarrow 2 \Rightarrow 3 \Rightarrow 4 \Rightarrow 1$.

The proof argues first that $1 \Rightarrow 2$. By the definition of atomicity, there is a serial behavior δ such that $beh(\alpha)|T = \delta|T$. Let α'' be a serial execution such that $\delta = beh(\alpha'')$.

Then by compatibility of the B_i and of the serial system components, $beh(\alpha|B_T) = beh(\alpha)|B_T = beh(\alpha)|ext(B_T) = beh(\alpha)|T = \delta|T = \delta|ext(A_T) = \delta|A_T = beh(\alpha'')|A_T = beh(\alpha''|A_T)$. By Proposition 2.2, $\alpha|B_T$ is an execution of B_T and hence of A_T. Let $\alpha_T = \alpha|B_T = \alpha|A_T$, for every non-access transaction name T' other than T let $\alpha_{T'} = \alpha''|A_{T'}$, for every object name X let $\alpha_X = \alpha''|S(X)$, and for the serial scheduler index SS let $\alpha_{SS} = \alpha''|SS$. Then $\delta|A_T = beh(\alpha|A_T) = beh(\alpha_T)$, and by Proposition 2.2, $\delta|S_{T'} = beh(\alpha''|S_{T'}) = beh(\alpha_{T'})$, $\delta|S(X) = beh(\alpha''|S(X)) = beh(\alpha_X)$, and $\delta|SS = beh(\alpha''|SS) = beh(\alpha_{SS})$. Then by Lemma 2.4 there is a serial execution α' such that $\alpha'|A_T = \alpha_T = \alpha|A_T = \alpha|B_T$.

Letting $\beta = sched(\alpha')$ and $\gamma = beh(\alpha')$, the second two implications follow immediately from Lemma 2.1.

To show that $4 \Rightarrow 1$, note that $beh(\alpha)|T = beh(\alpha)|B_T = beh(\alpha)|A_T$ and $\gamma|A_T = \gamma|T$; hence, $beh(\alpha)|T = \gamma|T$.   □

3.6.6   Correctness   of   Infinite   Behaviors

Recall that our definition of atomicity for T only requires that each finite behavior of the given system look to T like a serial behavior. An alternative definition would require the same for all behaviors, not just finite behaviors. However, basic transaction management systems such as those based on locking algorithms do not satisfy this stronger condition, an observation first made by Rosenkrantz et al.[104].

3.7   An   Additional   Example

In this section, we give another example to illustrate serial systems. This example describes a very simple replicated data management algorithm.

EXAMPLE   3.7.1   Simple   Data   Replication   Algorithm

We begin with an arbitrary serial system $\mathcal{A}$ in which X is one of the object names, and in which the object automaton $S(X)$ associated with the object name X is a read/write serial object with domain D and initial value d_0, as defined in Example 3.5.3.

We then consider a second serial system $\mathcal{B}$, where the object name X is replaced by a finite collection $\mathcal{Y}$ of *replicas*. The system type of $\mathcal{B}$

is obtained from that of $\mathcal{A}$ by adding a collection of children for each transaction name T that is an access to X in $\mathcal{A}$. All of these children are accesses to the new objects in $\mathcal{Y}$. The objects associated with the $\mathcal{Y}$ object names in system $\mathcal{B}$ are also read/write serial objects with domain D and initial value d_0. If T is a read access to X in $\mathcal{A}$, then all its children in $\mathcal{B}$ are read accesses to replicas, whereas if T is a write access to X in $\mathcal{A}$, then all its children in $\mathcal{B}$ are write accesses to replicas. System $\mathcal{B}$ contains all the transaction automata that are present in $\mathcal{A}$; in addition, system $\mathcal{B}$ contains a new transaction automaton A_T for each transaction name T that is an access to X in $\mathcal{A}$. These new transaction automata are defined below.

The system $\mathcal{B}$ is intended to describe an algorithm in which each read access to X in $\mathcal{A}$ is expanded into a transaction that performs a collection of read accesses to the individual replicas in $\mathcal{Y}$, and likewise for write accesses. In order to simulate a read to X, the corresponding read transaction in $\mathcal{B}$ attempts to obtain a data value from any one of the replicas. On the other hand, in order to simulate a write access to X, the corresponding write transaction in $\mathcal{B}$ must succeed in writing the new value to *all* of the replicas. This strategy may be useful, for example, in a distributed system in which read operations are frequent and writes are rare: the reads could be done quickly at a local copy of the data, whereas only the writes need to incur the penalty of a global operation.

If T is a read access to X in $\mathcal{A}$, then the state of A_T consists of four components: *active*, a Boolean, initially *false*; *requested*, a set of names of children of T, initially empty; *reported*, a set of names of children of T, initially empty; and *data*, an element of D or *nil*, initially *nil*. The transition relation is given in Figure 3.15.

That is, after T is created, it is allowed to spawn any number of children (which are read accesses to replicas). It keeps track of all that it has requested, in its *requested* component. It also keeps track of which accesses have reported back, either successfully or unsuccessfully (i.e., via a **REPORT_COMMIT** or a **REPORT_ABORT**). In addition, the value carried by the first **REPORT_COMMIT** is recorded in the data component, as the eventual return value. Transaction T requests to commit if it ever reaches a state in which all of its requested children have reported, either successfully or unsuccessfully, and in which *some* child has reported its commit (and provided it with a data value).

Analogously, if T is a write access to X in $\mathcal{A}$, then the state of A_T consists of four components: *active*, a Boolean, initially *false*; *requested*, a set of names of children of T, initially empty; *reported*, a set of names of children

CREATE(*T*)
  Effect:
    s.active = true

REQUEST_CREATE(*T′*), *T′* a child of *T*
  Precondition:
    s′.active = true
    T′ ∉ s′.requested
  Effect:
    s.requested = s′.requested ∪ {T′}

REPORT_COMMIT(*T′,v*), *T′* a child of *T*
  Effect:
    s.reported = s′.reported ∪ {T′}
    if *s′.data = nil*
    then *s.data = v*

REPORT_ABORT(*T′*), *T′* a child of *T*
  Effect:
    s.reported = s′.reported ∪ {T′}

REQUEST_COMMIT(*T,v*)
  Precondition:
    s′.active = true
    s′.data = v ≠ nil
    s′.reported = s′.requested
  Effect:
    s.active = false

Figure 3.15: Transition Relation for Logical Read

CREATE(*T*)
  Effect:
    s.active = true

REQUEST_CREATE(*T′*), *T′* a child of *T*
  Precondition:
    s′.active = true
    T′ ∉ s′.requested
  Effect:
    s.requested = s′.requested ∪ {T′}

REPORT_COMMIT(*T′,v*), *T′* a child of *T*
  Effect:
    s.reported = s′.reported ∪ {T′}
    s′.written-replicas
      = s′.written-replicas ∪ {object(T′)}

REPORT_ABORT(*T′*), *T′* a child of *T*
  Effect:
    s.reported = s′.reported ∪ {T′}

REQUEST_COMMIT(*T,v*)
  Precondition:
    s′.active = true
    s′.written-replicas = 𝒴
    s′.reported = s′.requested
  Effect:
    s.active = false

Figure 3.16: Transition Relation for Logical Write

of *T*, initially empty; and *written-replicas*, a subset of *𝒴*, initially empty. The transition relation is given in Figure 3.16.

That is, after *T* is created, it is allowed to spawn any number of children (which are write accesses to replicas). It keeps track of all that it has requested and all that have reported back. In addition, it keeps track of which replicas have had a write access commit. Transaction *T* requests to commit if it ever reaches a state in which all of its requested children have reported and in which write accesses to all replicas have succeeded. Notice that T can deal with the **ABORT** of some child by requesting the creation of another child that accesses the same replica as the aborted one. Indeed, T *could* request the creation of multiple accesses to each replica initially, or it could request a second only after the first aborted. The nondeterminism in the automaton allows many different behaviors.

The following proposition describes the relationship between systems $\mathcal{A}$ and $\mathcal{B}$.

PROPOSITION 3.15 *Let β be a behavior of $\mathcal{B}$. Then there exists a behavior, γ, of $\mathcal{A}$, such that $\gamma|T = \beta|T$ for all transaction names T that appear in the type of $\mathcal{A}$ and are not accesses to* X.

Because all sibling transactions execute serially in systems $\mathcal{A}$ and $\mathcal{B}$, it is not hard to see that Proposition 3.15 is true. All of the replica accesses involved in each single read or write operation of $\mathcal{A}$ complete without interference from those involved in other such operations. The writes succeed in writing to all replicas, and the reads read from one of the replicas, which ensures that they get the latest value written.

In later chapters, we will present algorithms that allow the transactions of serial systems such as $\mathcal{B}$ to execute concurrently, and yet preserve the appearance that the system is serial. Such a system will therefore preserve the appearance that the user is interacting with system $\mathcal{A}$. Also, in Chapter 12, we will present some additional, more complicated and more efficient, replication algorithms.

3.8 Bibliographic Notes

The idea of defining correctness of a transaction system relative to a separately specified serial system was first proposed by Weihl [117, 113]. In particular, the serial objects described in this chapter serve the same purpose as the *serial specifications* for data objects used by Weihl. However, Weihl's model is based only on traces of systems (analogous to the behaviors of the automata used in this book); he does not provide the underlying operational semantics of systems. In addition, he uses different notations for serial and concurrent systems and deals only with single-level transaction systems. The work described here generalizes Weihl's work to nested transaction systems and provides a rigorous foundation based on an automaton model.

The basic ideas underlying the model of nesting used here were first developed by Lynch and Merritt in [80].

Other references to work on models and correctness conditions in the database literature are discussed in Section 1.7.

3.9   Exercises

1 . Show that the following is a serial schedule for the system described in Example 3.1.1.

CREATE(T_0),
  REQUEST_CREATE(T_1),
  CREATE(T_1),
  REQUEST_COMMIT(T_1, "*OK*"),
  COMMIT(T_1),
  REPORT_COMMIT(T_1, "*OK*"),
   REQUEST_CREATE(T_2),
    REQUEST_CREATE(T_3),
    CREATE(T_3),
     REQUEST_CREATE($T_{3.1}$),
     CREATE($T_{3.1}$),
     REQUEST_COMMIT($T_{3.1}$, 0),
     COMMIT($T_{3.1}$),
     REPORT_COMMIT($T_{3.1}$, 0),
      REQUEST_CREATE($T_{3.3}$),
      CREATE($T_{3.3}$),
       REQUEST_CREATE($T_{3.1003}$),
      REQUEST_COMMIT($T_{3.3}$, **\$200**),
      COMMIT($T_{3.3}$),
       ABORT($T_{3.1003}$),
      REPORT_COMMIT($T_{3.3}$, **\$200**),
       REPORT_ABORT($T_{3.1003}$),
    REQUEST_COMMIT(T_3, **\$200**),
    COMMIT(T_3),
   CREATE(T_2),
   REQUEST_COMMIT(T_2, "*OK*"),
   COMMIT(T_2),
   REPORT_COMMIT(T_2, "*OK*"),
    REPORT_COMMIT(T_3, **\$200**),
      REQUEST_CREATE(T_5),
      CREATE(T_5),
      REQUEST_COMMIT(T_5, **\$1800**),

> **REQUEST_CREATE**(T_4),
> **COMMIT**(T_5),
> **REPORT_COMMIT**(T_5,\$1800),
> **CREATE**(T_4),
> **REQUEST_COMMIT**(T_4, "*OK*"),
> **COMMIT**(T_4),
> **REPORT_COMMIT**(T_4,"*OK*").

2. Find a schedule of the serial system of Example 3.1.1, in which the return value of T_4 is \$800.

3. Show that the following sequence is atomic for T_0, with respect to the serial system of Example 3.1.1:

> **CREATE**(T_0),
> **REQUEST_CREATE**(T_1),
> **REPORT_COMMIT**(T_1,"*OK*"),
> **REQUEST_CREATE**(T_2),
> **REQUEST_CREATE**(T_3),
> **REPORT_COMMIT**(T_2,"*OK*"),
> **REPORT_COMMIT**(T_3,\$200),
> **REQUEST_CREATE**(T_5),
> **REQUEST_CREATE**(T_4),
> **REPORT_COMMIT**(T_5,\$2000),
> **REPORT_COMMIT**(T_4,"*OK*").

4. Prove Lemma 3.3.

5. Prove Lemma 3.5.

6. Prove Lemma 3.8.

7. Prove Lemma 3.13.

8. If β is a serial behavior and T is a transaction name such that **REQUEST-_CREATE**(T) appears in β and neither **CREATE**(T) nor **ABORT**(T) appears, show that $parent(T)$ is live in β.

9. Let us say that two sequences of serial operations β and β' are *equivalent* when $\beta|T = \beta'|T$ for every transaction name T and also $\beta|\mathrm{X} = \beta'|\mathrm{X}$ for every object name X. Prove that if β_1 and β_2 are equivalent serial behaviors, and γ is a sequence of serial actions so that $\beta_1\gamma$ is a serial behavior, then $\beta_2\gamma$ is a serial behavior that is equivalent to $\beta_1\gamma$.

10. Write (using precondition and effect notation) transaction automata to be associated with the transaction names T_0, T_{Rj} and T_{Vk} in the system described in Example 3.5.7. Give a serial schedule for the the serial system constructed from these transaction automata and the serial object automata described in the example. Show that in *every* such schedule, the return value for any transaction T_{Vk} is *not* "BAD".

11. Discuss different serial schedulers and/or systems, their impact on correctness conditions, and whether the algorithms continue to be correct under the different conditions. For example, what if the report order does correspond to the serial order? Or what if transactions other than the root never request the creation of concurrent children, but always wait for one child to complete before requesting another?

12. Develop a serial system S like the banking system developed throughout this chapter, with serial objects each of Bank Account type introduced in Example 3.5.2. Include **TRANSFER** transactions that transfer money between accounts by executing a **WITHDRAW** on one account and a **DEPOSIT** on another, and **AUDIT** transactions that execute **BALANCE** on all the accounts and return the sum. Do *not* include any **DEPOSIT** or **WITHDRAW** accesses except as children of the **TRANSFER** and **AUDIT** transactions. Suppose that the total of all the money initially in the accounts is k dollars.

(a) Sketch a proof that the answer returned by any **AUDIT** transaction is k.

(b) Suppose another system S' is atomic for T_0, with respect to the serial system S. Prove that the answer returned by any **AUDIT** transaction in S' is also k.

This latter problem demonstrates an analogy to the classical idea of *consistency constraints*.

13. Construct a serial system for which there is a sequence of serial behaviors, each of which is an extension of the previous ones, whose limit (the infinite sequence that has each given behavior as a prefix) is not a serial behavior.

SPECIAL CLASSES OF SERIAL SYSTEMS

4.1 Introduction

This chapter introduces some general conditions on serial objects and serial systems that will be useful later in the book. The correctness of some of the algorithms studied in later chapters depends on semantic information about the types of serial object automata used in the underlying serial system. For example, Moss's algorithm for concurrency control using read/write locking, which is presented in Chapter 6, provides special treatment for *read accesses* (accesses that do not modify the state of the object). The timestamp-based algorithm of Reed, which is presented in Chapter 7, provides special treatment not only for read accesses but also for *write accesses* (accesses that do not depend on the state of the object). Also, the locking algorithms presented in Chapter 6 use information about particular pairs of operations in order to determine the orders in which these operations are permitted to occur. This section provides the appropriate definitions for these concepts.

The important concept of *equieffectiveness* of two sequences of external actions of a serial object is introduced first. Roughly speaking, two sequences are *equieffective* if they lead the automaton to states that are indistinguishable by the outside world. This concept is instrumental in defining some general notions, expressing insensitivity in an object to the order of operations performed on it. These are *forward commutativity*, and *backward commutativity*. Next, the essential properties of read and write accesses are defined, respectively, as *transparent* and *obliterating* operations. Finally, *serial dependency relations*, used in Chapters 7 and 8, are defined.

4.2 Equieffectiveness

The notion of *equieffectiveness* is a generalization of the notion of the *same state*. This generalization is important: it is used because a serial object automaton is not always presented in the simplest, most abstract form. It is reasonable for a serial object automaton to collect information in its state on every action; for example, recording the set of accesses for which a **CREATE** has occurred. As long as such information cannot affect the values returned by accesses, it should not be considered an *essential* part of the state. The definitions are chosen so that a state is equieffective to any other state that differs only in such inessential information. Usually one thinks of a read as an access that does not modify the state of the serial object, but an access that only modified *inessential* data ought still to be considered a read access. That is, instead of requiring read accesses to leave the state of the automaton unchanged, one need only require that they result in a state that is equieffective to the original.

Equieffectiveness is defined for finite sequences of external actions of a particular serial object automaton $S(X)$. Roughly speaking, the definition says that the two sequences lead $S(X)$ to states that cannot be distinguished by any environment in which $S(X)$ can appear. Formally, this indistinguishability is defined by requiring that $S(X)$ exhibit the same behaviors as continuations for each of the two given sequences.

Let X be an object name, and recall that $S(X)$ is a particular serial object automaton for X. Let β and β' be finite sequences of actions in $ext(S(X))$. Then β is **equieffective** to β' (with respect to $S(X)$) if for every sequence γ of actions in $ext(S(X))$ such that both $\beta\gamma$ and $\beta'\gamma$ are serial object well-formed for X, $\beta\gamma \in behs(S(X))$ if and only if $\beta'\gamma \in behs(S(X))$.

An immediate consequence of the definition (considering the extension γ as the empty sequence) is that if β and β' are serial object well-formed sequences for X and β is equieffective to β', then if β is in $behs(S(X))$, β' must also be in $behs(S(X))$. On the other hand, as trivial cases of the definition, any sequence that is not serial object well-formed for X is equieffective to all sequences; also, any sequence of actions in $ext(S(X))$ that is not a finite behavior of $S(X)$ is equieffective to any other sequence that is not a finite behavior.

One might expect being indistinguishable to be an equivalence relation.[1] This is not quite true, because of the restriction to consider only extensions that are serial object well-formed. However, we have some useful properties.

Obviously, equieffectiveness is reflexive: β is equieffective to β. Also, equieffectiveness is a symmetric relation, so that if β is equieffective to β', β and β' are often said to be **equieffective**. In the sense of semantic theory, equieffective sequences pass the same tests, where a test involves determining if a given sequence of external actions can occur after the sequence being tested. The tests are limited to sequences that do not violate well-formedness, because objects are not required to behave sensibly if the inputs violate well-formedness.

Equieffectiveness is not transitive, but does satisfy a restricted transitivity property:

LEMMA 4.1 *Let* X *be an object name, and let* ξ, η, *and* ζ *be three finite sequences of operations of* X *that are serial object well-formed for* X, *such that every operation in* η *appears in either* ξ *or* ζ. *If perform*(ξ) *is equieffective to perform*(η), *and perform*(η) *is equieffective to perform*(ζ), *then perform*(ξ) *is equieffective to perform*(ζ).

PROOF Suppose *perform*(ξ) and *perform*(η) are equieffective, and that *perform*(η) and *perform*(ζ) are equieffective. Let γ be a sequence of external actions of $S(X)$ such that *perform*(ξ)γ and *perform*(ζ)γ are serial object well-formed for X, and suppose that *perform*(ξ)γ is a behavior of $S(X)$. The proof shows that *perform*(ζ)γ is a behavior of $S(X)$.

The crucial observation is that *perform*(η)γ is serial object well-formed. To see this, note that by the definition of serial object well-formedness, γ must be either of the form *perform*(τ) or *perform*(τ) **CREATE**(T), where the transaction names that are the first components of the operations in τ (and T as well, if appropriate) are distinct from the first components of all the operations in ξ and ζ. By the condition on the operations in η, the first components of all the operations in τ (and T as well, if appropriate) are distinct from the first components of the operations in η. Thus, *perform*(η)γ is serial object well-formed.

Since *perform*(ξ) and *perform*(η) are equieffective, the definition of equieffectiveness then implies that *perform*(η)γ is a behavior of $S(X)$. From this and the fact that *perform*(η) and *perform*(ζ) are equieffective we find that *perform*(ζ)γ is a behavior of $S(X)$, as needed. □

The following proposition says that identical extensions of equieffective sequences are also equieffective. The proof is left as a simple exercise.

---

[1]The definitions for equivalence relation and related terms are given in the Appendix.

PROPOSITION 4.2 *Let* X *be an object name. Let* β *and* β' *be equieffective sequences of actions in* $ext(S(X))$. *Let* γ *be a finite sequence of actions in* $ext(S(X))$. *Then* $\beta\gamma$ *is equieffective to* $\beta'\gamma$.

A special case of equieffectiveness occurs when the final states of two finite executions are identical:

LEMMA 4.3 *Let* X *be an object name and let* β *and* β' *be two finite behaviors of* $S(X)$. *Let* U *be the set of states of* $S(X)$ *to which* β *can lead, and let* U' *be the set of states of* $S(X)$ *to which* β' *can lead. If* $U = U'$, *then* β *is equieffective to* β'.

PROOF   This is immediate from the definition, and the fact that $\beta\gamma$ is a behavior of $S(X)$ exactly if for some element s of U, there is an execution fragment of $S(X)$ beginning with state s and with behavior γ.   □

The classical notion of serializability uses this special case, in requiring concurrent executions to lead to a state of the database that is also led to by some serial execution of the same transactions. However, this property is too restrictive for reasoning about an implementation in which details of the system state may be different, following a concurrent execution, than after any serial one. (Relations may be stored on different pages, or data structures such as B-trees may be configured differently.) Generally, these details are irrelevant to the perceived future behavior of the database. The notion of equieffectiveness formalizes this indistinguishability of different implementation states.

EXAMPLE 4.2.1   FIFO Queue Object

We now give an example where sequences may be equieffective without leading to the same state. Consider the serial object $S(\text{QUEUE})$ from Example 3.5.5, representing a FIFO queue. The "abstract state" of the queue depends only on the sequence of values stored in locations with indices from *front* to *back* $- 1$ inclusive, and not on other values, nor on the position of this sequence within the array; this fact is made precise by the following claim: two states s and t of $S(\text{QUEUE})$ are equieffective provided $s.active = t.active$, $s.back - s.front = t.back - t.front$, and $s.queue[s.front + i] = t.queue[t.front + i]$ for all i such that $0 \le i < (s.back - s.front)$.

4.3 Commutativity

Many concurrency control algorithms are based on a simple intuition: if the order in which two operations take place does not affect the result, then a transaction-processing system should be able to allow different transactions to perform those operations concurrently. Chapter 6 presents some algorithms that do this. This section provides precise definitions of which operations are allowed to run concurrently.

Mathematical operations *commute* provided the same result is obtained regardless of the order in which the operations are performed. The commutativity definitions here are somewhat more complicated, because operations on objects may have more than one result, and sometimes may not have a result at all.[2] In addition to returning a value, operations may affect the *apparent* future behavior of the object. The exact definitions given are determined by the needs of the algorithms presented in Chapter 6.

4.3.1 Forward Commutativity

Now one notion of commutativity can be defined that is appropriate for operations of a particular serial object $S(X)$. This definition will be used in Section 6.3, to control which accesses are allowed to run concurrently. Informally, this notion is appropriate for concurrent algorithms that compute a return value for each access, based on the previous accesses that have committed, but not on those that are not committed yet.

We say that operations (T, v) and (T', v') **commute forward**, where T and T' are accesses to X, if for any finite sequence of operations ξ such that both $perform(\xi(T, v))$ and $perform(\xi(T', v'))$ are serial object well-formed behaviors of $S(X)$, then $perform(\xi(T, v)(T', v'))$ and $perform(\xi(T', v')(T, v))$ are equieffective serial object well-formed behaviors of $S(X)$.

That is, consider for any operation (T, v) the test that determines if a behavior of $S(X)$ can be extended by $perform(T, v)$. Then (T, v) and (T', v') commute forward if whenever a behavior passes each test, it passes both in any order, and furthermore, no later test can determine which order was used.

The definition is illustrated in Figure 4.1, where the solid lines indicate sequences of operations assumed to be legal, and the dashed lines indicate extensions whose existence is required as a consequence. Parallel lines represent the same operation.

A consequence of the definition of forward commutativity is the following extension to sequences of operations.

---

[2]For example, an attempt to delete from an empty queue may not return at all, as in Example 3.5.5.

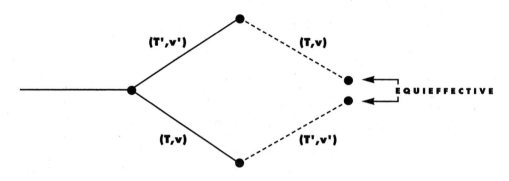

Figure 4.1: Forward Commutativity

PROPOSITION 4.4 *Suppose that ζ and ζ' are finite sequences of operations of* X *such that each operation in ζ commutes forward with each operation in ζ'. If ξ is a finite sequence of operations of $S(X)$ such that perform$(\xi\zeta)$ and perform$(\xi\zeta')$ are serial object well-formed behaviors of $S(X)$, then perform$(\xi\zeta\zeta')$ and perform$(\xi\zeta'\zeta)$ are equieffective serial object well-formed behaviors of $S(X)$.*

EXAMPLE 4.3.1   Read/Write Object

For the read/write serial object $S(X)$ of Example 3.5.3, the operations (T, v) and (T', v') commute forward if $T \neq T'$, $kind(T) =$ "*read*", and $kind(T') =$ "*read*".

In order to see this, the proof must consider an arbitrary sequence of operations ξ such that both $perform(\xi(T, v))$ and $perform(\xi(T', v'))$ are serial object well-formed behaviors of $S(X)$. If no such ξ exists, then the operations commute trivially; otherwise, let s' be the (unique) state of the serial object led to by $perform(\xi)$. From the code see that $s'.active =$ "*nil*". Let s_1 be the unique state led to by $perform(\xi(T, v))$; thus, $(s', perform((T, v)), s_1)$ is an extended step of $S(X)$. Examining the code of $S(X)$, see that $s'.data = v$ (from the effect of **CREATE**(T) and the precondition of **REQUEST-_COMMIT**(T, v)) and that $s_1.data = s'.data$ and $s_1.active =$ "*nil*" (from the effect of **REQUEST_COMMIT**(T, v)). Thus, $s' = s_1$. Similarly, since $perform(\xi(T', v'))$ is a behavior of $S(X)$, $s'.data = v'$ and $(s', perform((T', v')), s')$ is an extended step of $S(X)$.

Therefore, $perform(\xi(T, v)(T', v'))$ and $perform(\xi(T', v')(T, v))$ are both behaviors of $S(X)$, and both lead to the same (unique) state s, and they are thus equieffective by Lemma 4.3. Finally, notice that since $T \neq T'$, and

	(T', v')	
(T, v)	$(read, v')$	$(write, \text{``}OK\text{''})$
$(read, v)$	true	$v = data(T')$
$(write, \text{``}OK\text{''})$	$data(T) = v'$	$data(T) = data(T')$

Figure 4.2: Forward commutativity for read/write serial object. Operations (T, v) and (T', v') commute forward if $T \neq T'$ and the indicated conditions hold.

$perform(\xi(T, v))$ and $perform(\xi(T', v'))$ are both serial object well-formed, the collection consisting of the transaction components of the operations in ξ together with T and T' are all distinct, so that $perform(\xi(T, v)(T', v'))$ and $perform(\xi(T', v')(T, v))$ are both serial object well-formed.

Thus $perform(\xi(T, v)(T', v'))$ and $perform(\xi(T', v')(T, v))$ are equieffective serial object well-formed behaviors of $S(X)$, as required to show that (T, v) and (T', v') commute forward.

On the other hand suppose $U \neq U'$, $kind(U) = \text{``}read\text{''}$, $kind(U') = \text{``}write\text{''}$, and $u \neq data(U')$. Then in general (U, u) and $(U', \text{``}OK\text{''})$ do not commute forward.[3] For if $V$ is an access with $kind(V) = \text{``}write\text{''}$ and $data(V) = u$, then $perform((V, \text{``}OK\text{''})(U, u))$ and $perform((V, \text{``}OK\text{''})(U', u'))$ are both serial object well-formed behaviors of $S(X)$, but $perform((V, \text{``}OK\text{''})(U', u') (U, u))$ is not a behavior.

However, the operations (U, u) and $(U', \text{``}OK\text{''})$ commute forward if $U \neq U'$, $kind(U) = \text{``}read\text{''}$, $kind(U') = \text{``}write\text{''}$, and $u = data(U')$. The proof is left to the reader.

Figure 4.2 describes the forward commutativity relation for the read/write serial object.[4]

---

[3]In some particular serial systems, with restricted system types, these operations may commute forward. This could be due to the absence from the system of any write access to serve as V in the argument given.

[4]The conditions listed in this table and later tables in this chapter are sufficient, but *not* necessary and sufficient, conditions for the listed operations to commute. In some systems, the conditions are also necessary; however, in certain special systems (e.g., if there are only two access transactions, and both are writes) the conditions may fail to hold yet the operations may still commute.

EXAMPLE 4.3.2   Bank Account Object

For the bank account serial object $S(\mathrm{X})$ described in Example 3.5.2, the operations (T, v) and (T', v') commute forward if $T \neq T'$ and $kind(T) = kind(T') = $ "*balance*". The proof is left to the reader, being essentially the same as the proof in Example 4.3.1 that operations of distinct read accesses commute.

To provide an example where operations of two accesses commute even though the accesses do modify the state in important ways, we show that the operations (T, v) and (T', v') commute forward if $T \neq T'$ and $kind(T) = kind(T') = $ "*deposit*". The system type shows that the return values v and v' must both be "*OK*". (See Section 3.2.1.)

In order to see that these operations commute forward, the proof must consider an arbitrary sequence of operations ξ such that both $perform(\xi(T, v))$ and $perform(\xi(T', v'))$ are serial object well-formed behaviors of $S(\mathrm{X})$. If no such ξ exists, then the operations commute trivially; otherwise let s' be the (unique) state of the serial object led to by $perform(\xi)$. From the code see that $s'.active = $ "*nil*". Let s_1 be the unique state led to by $perform(\xi(T, v))$; thus $(s', perform((T, v)), s_1)$ is an extended step of $S(\mathrm{X})$. Examining the code of $S(\mathrm{X})$, see that $s_1.current = s'.current + amount(T)$ and that $s_1.active = $ "*nil*" (from the effect of **REQUEST_COMMIT**(T, v)). Similarly, letting s_2 denote the unique state led to by $perform(\xi(T', v'))$, it must be that $s_2.current = s'.current + amount(T')$ and that $s_2.active = $ "*nil*".

Now the code shows that $(s_1, perform((T', v')), s)$ is an extended step of $S(\mathrm{X})$, where $s.current = s_1.current + amount(T')$ and that $s.active = $ "*nil*". That is, $perform(\xi(T, v)(T', v'))$ is a behavior of $S(\mathrm{X})$, and s is the unique state of $S(\mathrm{X})$ it leads to. Also, since $s.current = s'.current + amount(T) + amount(T') = s_2.current + amount(T)$, $(s_2, perform((T, v)), s)$ is also an extended step of $S(\mathrm{X})$, so that $perform(\xi(T', v')(T, v))$ is a behavior of $S(\mathrm{X})$, and s is the unique state of $S(\mathrm{X})$ it leads to. Thus by Lemma 4.3, $perform(\xi(T, v)(T', v'))$ and $perform(\xi(T', v')(T, v))$ are equieffective. Finally, notice that since $T \neq T'$, and $perform(\xi(T, v))$ and $perform(\xi(T', v'))$ are both serial object well-formed, the collection consisting of the transaction components of the operations in ξ together with T and T' are all distinct, so that $perform(\xi(T, v)(T', v'))$ and $perform(\xi(T', v')(T, v))$ are both serial object well-formed.

Thus $perform(\xi(T, v)(T', v'))$ and $perform(\xi(T', v')(T, v))$ are equieffective serial object well-formed behaviors of $S(\mathrm{X})$, as required to show that (T, v) and (T', v') commute forward.

(T,v)	(T',v')			
	$(balance,v')$	$(withdraw,0)$	$(deposit,\text{``}OK\text{''})$	$(withdraw,v')$
$(balance,v)$	true	true	false	false
$(withdraw,0)$	true	true	true	true
$(deposit,\text{``}OK\text{''})$	false	true	true	true
$(withdraw,v)$	false	true	true	false

Figure 4.3: Forward commutativity for bank account serial object. Operations (T,v) and (T',v') commute forward if $T \neq T'$ and the indicated conditions hold.

You must be careful, however: you might expect that just like two deposits, two withdraw operations would commute forward. This is not in general the case. Consider the accesses T and T' where $T \neq T'$ and $kind(T) = kind(T') = \text{``}withdraw\text{''}$. Then take an access $U$ such that $kind(U) = \text{``}deposit\text{''}$, $amount(T) + amount(T') > amount(U) > max(amount(T), amount(T'))$. Examining the code shows that $perform((U, \text{``}OK\text{''})(T, amount(T)))$ and $perform((U, \text{``}OK\text{''})(T', amount(T')))$ are behaviors of $S(\mathrm{X})$, but that $perform((U, \text{``}OK\text{''})(T, amount(T))\text{-}(T', amount(T')))$ is not a behavior of $S(\mathrm{X})$.

Figure 4.3 describes the forward commutativity relation for the bank account serial object.

EXAMPLE 4.3.3   FIFO Queue Object

For the FIFO queue serial object $S(\text{QUEUE})$ defined in Example 3.5.5, the operations (T,v) and (T',v') commute forward if $T \neq T'$, $kind(T) = kind(T') = \text{``}insert\text{''}$ and $data(T) = data(T')$. The system type shows that the return values $v$ and $v'$ must both be "$OK$". Also, we observe that $(T,v)$ and $(T',v')$ commute forward if $T \neq T'$, $kind(T) = \text{``}insert\text{''}$, $kind(T') = \text{``}delete\text{''}$. By symmetry, $(T,v)$ and $(T',v')$ commute forward if $T \neq T'$, $kind(T) = \text{``}delete\text{''}$, $kind(T') = \text{``}insert\text{''}$. Finally, $(T,v)$ and $(T',v')$ commute forward if $T \neq T'$, $kind(T) = kind(T') = \text{``}delete\text{''}$ and $v \neq v'$, since there will be no sequence β such that $\beta(perform(T,v))$ and $\beta(perform(T',v'))$ are both finite behaviors of $S(\text{QUEUE})$.

Figure 4.4 gives the forward commutativity table for the FIFO queue serial object.

(T, v)	(T', v')	
	$(insert, \text{``}OK\text{''})$	$(delete, v')$
$(insert, \text{``}OK\text{''})$	$data(T) = data(T')$	true
$(delete, v)$	true	true

Figure 4.4: Forward commutativity for FIFO queue serial object. Operations (T, v) and (T', v') commute forward if $T \neq T'$ and the indicated conditions hold.

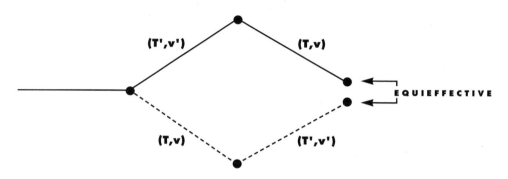

Figure 4.5: Backward Commutativity

4.3.2 Backward Commutativity

Here is a slightly different definition that is appropriate for concurrent algorithms like the one in Section 6.5, where each access returns a value based on previous accesses, including those not yet known to have committed. Backward and forward commutativity are incomparable: there are pairs of operations that commute forward but not backward, and other pairs that commute backward and not forward.

Let $S(\text{X})$ be a serial object for object name X, and let (T, v) and (T', v') be operations, where T and T' are accesses to X. Then we say that (T', v') **commutes backward through** (T, v) provided that for all finite sequences of operations ξ the following holds. If $perform(\xi(T, v)(T', v'))$ is a finite behavior of $S(\text{X})$ and both $perform(\xi(T, v)(T', v'))$ and $perform(\xi(T', v')(T, v))$ are serial object well-formed then $perform(\xi(T', v')(T, v))$ is a behavior of $S(\text{X})$, which is equieffective to $perform(\xi(T, v)(T', v'))$. (Note that there is redundancy in this definition, since if $perform(\xi(T, v)(T', v'))$ is serial object well-formed, then so is $perform(\xi(T', v')(T, v))$.)

Figure 4.5 illustrates this definition, using the same conventions as in Figure 4.1.

We say that two operations **commute backward** if each commutes backward through the other. We say that two operations (T, v) and (T', v') **conflict** provided that they fail to commute backward. Ane we say that two accesses T and T' **conflict** provided that there exist v and v' such that (T, v) and (T', v') conflict.

PROPOSITION 4.5 *Suppose that ξ is a finite sequence of operations of X such that perform(ξ) is a serial object well-formed behavior of $S(X)$. Suppose that η is a re-ordering of ξ such that all pairs of conflicting operations occur in the same order in η and in ξ. Then perform(η) is a behavior of $S(X)$.*

PROOF The sequence η can be obtained from ξ by a finite sequence of reordering steps, in each of which two consecutive non-conflicting operations are interchanged. The proof proceeds by induction on the number of such reordering steps. If there are no such steps, then $\eta = \xi$ and the result is immediate. So suppose the result is true for any number of reordering steps up to $k \geq 1$, and suppose that η is obtained from ξ by k+1 reordering steps. Then there exists another finite sequence η' such that η' is obtained from ξ in k reordering steps and η is obtained from η' in one reordering step. The inductive hypothesis implies that *perform*(η') is a behavior of $S(X)$.

Then there exist operations (T, v) and (T', v') and sequences ν and ν' of operations such that (T, v) and (T', v') commute backward, $\eta' = \nu(T, v)(T', v')\nu'$, and $\eta = \nu(T', v')(T, v)\nu'$. Then *perform*($\nu(T, v)(T', v')$) is a behavior of $S(X)$, and both *perform*($\nu(T, v)(T', v')$) and *perform*($\nu(T', v')(T, v)$) are serial object well-formed. Since (T, v) and (T', v') commute backward, *perform*($\nu(T', v')(T, v)$) is also a behavior of $S(X)$, and it is equieffective to *perform*($\nu(T, v)(T', v')$). Since *perform*($\nu(T, v)(T', v')\nu'$) is a behavior of $S(X)$, the definition of equieffectiveness implies that *perform*($\nu(T', v')(T, v)\nu'$) is also a behavior of $S(X)$. □

LEMMA 4.6 *Suppose ξ is a finite sequence of operations such that perform(ξ) is a serial object well-formed behavior of $S(X)$, and let η be a subsequence of ξ such that the following is true: if (T, v) precedes (T', v') in ξ, where (T, v) is not in η and (T', v') is in η, then (T, v) commutes backward with (T', v'). Then perform(η) is a behavior of $S(X)$.*

PROOF Define $\xi' = \eta(\xi - \eta)$; that is, the result of moving all operations not in η to follow those in η, but preserving the order among operations in $\xi - \eta$. Then ξ' is a reordering of ξ such that all pairs of conflicting operations occur in the same order in ξ' and in ξ. Proposition 4.5 implies that *perform*(ξ') is a behavior of $S(X)$. Then *perform*(η), which is a prefix of *perform*(ξ'), is also a behavior of $S(X)$. □

EXAMPLE 4.3.4 Bank Account Object

For the bank account serial object $S(X)$ described in Example 3.5.2, the operations (T, v) and (T', v') commute backward if $T \neq T'$ and $kind(T) =$

(T, v)	(T', v')			
	$(balance, v')$	$(withdraw, 0)$	$(deposit, \text{``}OK\text{''})$	$(withdraw, v')$
$(balance, v)$	true	true	false	false
$(withdraw, 0)$	true	true	true	true
$(deposit, \text{``}OK\text{''})$	false	true	true	false
$(withdraw, v)$	false	true	true	true

Figure 4.6: Backward commutativity for bank account serial object. Operations (T', v') commutes backward through (T, v) if $T \neq T'$ and the indicated conditions hold. (Note: this table is not symmetric.)

$kind(T') = \text{``}withdraw\text{''}$. The case in which $v \neq 0$ and $v' \neq 0$ is argued below; the other cases are left to the reader.

Let ξ be a sequence of operations for which $perform(\xi(T, v)(T', v'))$ is a finite serial object well-formed behavior of $S(X)$. The proof must show that $perform(\xi(T', v')(T, v))$ is also a finite behavior and that it is equieffective to $perform(\xi(T, v)(T', v'))$. Let s' be the (unique) state led to by $perform(\xi)$, and s the state led to by $perform(\xi(T, v)(T', v'))$. The code of $S(X)$ shows that $v = amount(T)$, $v' = amount(T')$, $s.active = \text{``}nil\text{''}$, $s'.current \geq v + v'$, and $s.current = s'.current - v - v'$.

The code then shows that, defining $s_1.active = \text{``}nil\text{''}$ and $s_1.current = s'.current - v'$, then $(s', perform((T', v')), s_1)$ and $(s_1, perform((T, v)), s)$ are extended steps of $S(X)$. That is, $perform(\xi(T', v')(T, v))$ is a finite behavior of $S(X)$ and s is the (unique) state it leads to. By Lemma 4.3, $perform(\xi(T', v')(T, v))$ is equieffective to $perform(\xi(T, v)(T', v'))$. Thus, (T, v) and (T', v') commute backward.

Figure 4.6 gives the backward commutativity table for the bank account serial object.

Notice that this example (together with Example 4.3.2) shows that commuting forward and commuting backward are different relations between operations.

We also remark that if (T, v) and (T', v') are operations of $S(X)$ such that $T \neq T'$, $kind(T) = \text{``}withdraw\text{''}$, and $v \neq 0$, $kind(T') = \text{``}deposit\text{''}$, and $v' = \text{``}OK\text{''}$, then (T', v') commutes backward through (T, v), but (T, v) does not commute backward through (T', v'). Thus, (T, v) and (T', v') conflict. The proof is left to the reader, as Exercise 10.

4.4 Special Classes of Operations

4.4.1 Transparent Operations

Transparency is the essential property of read accesses, reflecting the fact that the state of the serial object is not altered in any essential way. The algorithm of Section 6.4 treats transparent operations differently from other operations. Say that an operation (T, v) at X is **transparent** if for any finite sequence of operations ξ of $S(X)$ such that $perform(\xi(T, v))$ is a serial object well-formed behavior of $S(X)$, $perform(\xi(T, v))$ and $perform(\xi)$ are equieffective behaviors of $S(X)$. Thus, a transparent operation does not affect the later behavior of the object automaton. (Notice that this definition applies to *operations*. Access transactions may only sometimes modify the (apparent) object state—specific return values indicate that no change was made. For example, a withdrawal from a bank account can modify the amount, but a return value of $0 in a withdrawal indicates that no money was removed.)

The following simple proposition shows that any subsequence consisting of transparent operations can be removed from a behavior, resulting in a behavior equieffective to the original one.

PROPOSITION 4.7 *Let η be a finite serial object well-formed sequence of operations of X such that $perform(\eta)$ is a behavior of $S(X)$, and let ξ be a subsequence of η such that every operation in $\eta - \xi$ is transparent. Then $perform(\eta)$ and $perform(\xi)$ are equieffective serial object well-formed behaviors of $S(X)$.*

LEMMA 4.8 *Let X be an object name and let (T, v) be an operation of $S(X)$. If $s = s'$ for every extended step $(s', perform((T, v)), s)$ of $S(X)$, then (T, v) is transparent.*

EXAMPLE 4.4.1   Read/Write and Bank Account Objects

Lemma 4.8 shows that if $S(X)$ is a read/write serial object described in Example 3.5.3 and T is an access to X with $kind(T) = $ "*read*", then any operation of the form (T, v) is transparent. Similarly, if $S(X)$ is a bank account serial object described in Example 3.5.2 and T is an access to X with $kind(T) = $ "*balance*", then any operation of the form (T, v) is transparent. As a final example, if $S(X)$ is a bank account serial object described in Example 3.5.2, T is an access to X with $kind(T) = $ "*withdraw*" and $v = 0$, then the operation (T, v) is transparent.

It is easy to see that distinct transparent operations commute forward.

PROPOSITION 4.9 *Let (T, v) and (T', v') be transparent operations of X such that $T \neq T'$. Then (T, v) commutes forward with (T', v').*

PROOF   Suppose ξ is a finite sequence of operations of X such that $perform(\xi(T, v))$ and $perform(\xi(T', v'))$ are serial object well-formed behaviors of $S(X)$. Then no operation in ξ has T or T' as first component, and all the operations in ξ have distinct first components. Therefore, $perform(\xi(T, v)(T', v'))$ and $perform(\xi(T', v')(T, v))$ are serial object well-formed sequences of external actions of $S(X)$. Now $perform(\xi(T, v))$ and $perform(\xi)$ are equieffective, since (T, v) is transparent. Since $perform(\xi)perform(T', v')$ is a behavior of $S(X)$, the definition of equieffectiveness implies that $perform(\xi(T, v)) \times perform(T', v') = perform(\xi(T, v)(T', v'))$ is also a behavior of $S(X)$. Similarly, the fact that (T', v') is transparent implies that $perform(\xi(T', v')(T, v))$ is a behavior of $S(X)$. By Proposition 4.7, each of $perform(\xi(T, v)(T', v'))$ and $perform(\xi(T', v')(T, v))$ is equieffective to $perform(\xi)$. Lemma 4.1 now shows that they are equieffective to each other, as required.   □

4.4.2 Obliterating Operations

Similarly, equieffectiveness is used to define the essential properties of write accesses; that is, those that prevent the detection of any preceding accesses.

Let (T, v) be an operation of X. Then (T, v) is **obliterating** if, for any finite sequence of operations ξ of $S(X)$ such that $perform(\xi)$ is a behavior of $S(X)$ and $perform(\xi(T, v))$ is serial object well-formed for X, $perform(\xi(T, v))$ and $perform(T, v)$ are equieffective.

Note that it is possible that $perform(T, v) \notin behs(S(X))$ for an obliterating operation (T, v); in this case, $perform(\xi(T, v))$ is also not in $behs(S(X))$. However, if $perform(T, v) \in behs(S(X))$ for obliterating operation (T, v), then $perform(\xi(T, v))$ is in $behs(S(X))$ whenever it is serial object well-formed and $perform(\xi)$ is a behavior of $S(X)$. Thus, whether an obliterating operation is possible is independent of any preceding actions, so long as serial object well-formedness is preserved. Furthermore, any future behavior of the object is independent of any preceding actions.

Of course, it would be remarkable for an operation to obliterate all previous activity on the data base as a whole; however, the division of the preserved state into separate objects means that it is reasonable for an operation to prevent detection of any earlier activity on the same object, by overwriting the state of that object. It is important to note that an operation may be neither transparent nor obliterating, if the new state that results is different from the old but retains information from it (for example, a deposit to a bank account, which adds the deposited amount to the previous balance).

EXAMPLE 4.4.2   Read/Write Object

For the read/write serial object $S(X)$ of Example 3.5.3, if T is an access to X with $kind(T) = $ "$write$", then the operation $(T, $ "OK") is obliterating, since for any finite behavior $perform(\xi)$, the (unique) state s led to by $perform(\xi(T, \text{“}OK\text{”}))$ has $s.active = \text{“}nil\text{”}$ and $s.data = data(T)$, and so s is equal to the unique state led to by $perform((T, \text{“}OK\text{”}))$ in $S(X)$.

4.5   Serial Dependency Relations

This section defines the notion of a *serial dependency relation*. The intuition underlying this is that two operations should be related whenever the possibility of the second occurring is influenced by the presence or absence of the first. However, there are many subtleties, and the precise definition that we give is chosen to be what is needed in the algorithms of Sections 7.5 and 8.3.

Recall from the Appendix that when R is a binary relation on operations of serial object $S(X)$, ξ is a serial object well-formed sequence of operations of $S(X)$, and η is a subsequence of ξ, we say that η is R-closed in ξ provided that whenever η contains an operation (T, v), it also contains all preceding operations (T', v') of ξ such that $((T', v'), (T, v)) \in R$.

We say that R is a **serial dependency relation** for $S(X)$ provided that the following holds. Whenever ξ is a finite serial object well-formed sequence of operations of $S(X)$ such that for each (T, v) in ξ, there is an R-closed subsequence η of ξ where η contains (T, v) and $perform(\eta)$ is a behavior of $S(X)$, then $perform(\xi)$ is a behavior of $S(X)$.

Note in particular that every serial object $S(X)$ has at least the trivial serial dependency relation that relates all operations of $S(X)$. Also note that if a relation R is a serial dependency relation, then any relation that is a superset of R is also a serial dependency relation.

The following proposition gives the crucial property needed to show that the type-specific timestamp-based algorithm described in Chapter 7 is correct.

PROPOSITION 4.10 *Suppose R is a serial dependency relation for $S(X)$. Let η be a serial object well-formed sequence of operations of $S(X)$ and let η' and η'' be subsequences of η such that each operation of η is in at least one of η' and η''. Suppose that $perform(\eta')$ and $perform(\eta'')$ are both in $behs(S(X))$. Moreover, suppose that the following hold.*

1. *If $\pi_1 \in \eta' - \eta''$ and $\pi_2 \in \eta'' - \eta'$ and π_1 precedes π_2 in η, then $(\pi_1, \pi_2) \notin R$.*

2. *If $\pi_1 \in \eta'' - \eta'$ and $\pi_2 \in \eta' - \eta''$ and π_1 precedes π_2 in η, then $(\pi_1, \pi_2) \notin R$.*

Then $perform(\eta) \in behs(S(X))$.

PROOF   Note that by the two numbered conditions, η' and η'' are R-closed subsequences of η. Since every operation π in η occurs either in η' or η'', it follows from the definition of serial dependency relation that $perform(\eta) \in behs(S(\mathrm{X}))$. $\square$

EXAMPLE 4.5.1   Read/Write Object

For the read/write serial object $S(\mathrm{X})$ of Example 3.5.3, consider the relation R containing $((T, v), (T', v'))$ whenever $kind(T) = \text{``write''}$ and $kind(T') = \text{``read''}$. This is a serial dependency relation. To see this, consider a finite sequence ξ of operations, with the property that for each π in ξ, there is an R-closed subsequence η of ξ containing π such that $perform(\eta)$ is a behavior of $S(\mathrm{X})$. The proof must show that $perform(\xi)$ is a behavior of $S(\mathrm{X})$. This is done by induction on the length of prefixes of ξ. Thus suppose ξ' is a prefix of ξ, $perform(\xi')$ is a finite behavior of $S(\mathrm{X})$, and (T, v) is the operation in ξ after ξ'. If $kind(T) = \text{``write''}$, then the only return value allowed by the system type is $v = \text{``}OK\text{''}$, and Lemma 3.7 shows that $perform(\xi'(T, v))$ is a behavior of $S(\mathrm{X})$. However, if $kind(T) = \text{``read''}$, then consider the R-closed sequence η that contains (T, v) and for which $perform(\eta)$ is a behavior of $S(\mathrm{X})$. Let η' denote the prefix of η preceding (T, v). By Lemma 3.7, $v = final\text{-}value(\eta', S(\mathrm{X}))$. However, since η is R-closed and contains (T, v), η contains every operation (T', v') in ξ that precedes (T, v) for which $kind(T') = \text{``write''}$. That is, $last\text{-}write(\eta', S(\mathrm{X})) = last\text{-}write(\xi', S(\mathrm{X}))$. Deduce $v = final\text{-}value(\xi', S(\mathrm{X}))$, so that by Lemma 3.7, $perform(\xi'(T, v))$ is a behavior of $S(\mathrm{X})$, as required.

One serial dependency relation for any object is the relation containing all pairs of operations that do not commute forward.

PROPOSITION 4.11   *Let C denote a binary relation on operations of $S(\mathrm{X})$ such that the pair $((T, v), (T', v'))$ is in C if $T \neq T'$ and (T, v) and (T', v') do not commute forward. Then C is a serial dependency relation.*

PROOF   Suppose not. Then there must exist ξ a finite serial object well-formed sequence of operations of $S(\mathrm{X})$, such that $perform(\xi)$ is not a behavior of $S(\mathrm{X})$ and for each (T, v) in ξ there is a C-closed subsequence η of ξ containing (T, v) such that $perform(\eta)$ is a behavior of $S(\mathrm{X})$. Let ξ' denote the longest prefix of ξ for which $perform(\xi')$ is a behavior of $S(\mathrm{X})$, and let (U, u) be the operation in ξ immediately following ξ'.

Using the property of ξ (followed by truncating the C-closed sequence containing (U, u)), there is a subsequence η of ξ' such that $\eta(U, u)$ is C-closed in ξ and

$perform(\eta(U, u))$ is a behavior of $S(X)$. Let η' denote a subsequence with these properties such that there is no sequence that has these properties and also contains η' as a proper subsequence. That is, η' is a maximal subsequence with these properties. Since $perform(\xi'(U, u))$ is not a behavior of $S(X)$ (by the choice of ξ') we deduce that $\eta' \neq \xi'$, and so there is at least one operation in ξ' that is not in η'. Let (U', u') be the first such operation, and let ζ denote the prefix of ξ' preceding (U', u'). Now define ξ_1 so that $\xi' = \zeta(U', u')\xi_1$. By the choice of (U', u'), we must have that ζ is also a prefix of η', so we may define η_1 so that $\eta' = \zeta\eta_1$.

Because $\zeta\eta_1(U, u)$ is C-closed, and (U', u') precedes $\eta_1(U, u)$ in ξ without being in $\zeta\eta_1(U, u)$, we must have $((U', u'), (U'', u'')) \notin C$, for every operation (U'', u'') in $\eta_1(U, u)$. That is, (U', u') commutes forward with every operation in $\eta_1(U, u)$. Now $perform(\zeta\eta_1(U, u))$ and $perform(\zeta(U', u'))$ are both behaviors of $S(X)$, so by Proposition 4.4, $perform(\zeta(U', u')\eta_1(U, u))$ is a behavior of $S(X)$.

Let $\eta'' = \zeta(U', u')\eta_1$, that is, η'' consists of η' with an extra operation (U', u') inserted. This is a subsequence of ξ'; we have shown that $perform(\eta''(U, u))$ is a behavior of $S(X)$, and also $\eta''(U, u)$ is C-closed in ξ (this follows from the C-closure of $\eta'(U, u)$ and the fact that η'' includes every operation in ξ preceding the inserted (U', u')). Since η' is a proper subsequence of η'', this contradicts the maximality of η' with these properties. The contradiction establishes the falsity of our assumption that C was not a serial dependency relation. $\square$

EXAMPLE 4.5.2 FIFO Queue Object

For the FIFO queue serial object $S(\text{QUEUE})$ of Example 3.5.5, Proposition 4.11 and Example 4.3.3 show that there is a serial dependency relation R_1, containing pairs $((T, v), (T', v'))$ where $T \neq T'$ and either of the following holds: $kind(T) = kind(T') = \text{``insert''}$ and $data(T) \neq data(T')$; or $kind(T) = kind(T') = \text{``delete''}$ and $v = v'$.

There is another serial dependency relation for $S(\text{QUEUE})$. This is R_2 that contains pairs $((T, v), (T', v'))$ where $T \neq T'$, $kind(T') = \text{``delete''}$, and either of the following holds: $kind(T) = \text{``insert''}$ and $data(T) \neq v'$; or $kind(T) = \text{``delete''}$ and $v = v'$.

Since the intersection of R_1 and R_2 is not a serial dependency relation for this serial object, we see that it is not always the case that each serial object has a single minimal serial dependency relation of which every other serial dependency relation is a superset.

4.6 Bibliographic Notes

Many concurrency control algorithms are based on some notion of commutativity, and allow transactions whose accesses commute to run concurrently. The two kinds of commutativity defined in this chapter are generalizations of the notions defined by Weihl [115], adapted to the formal framework used in this book. These commutativity concepts are related to similar notions defined in the database literature dealing with type-specific locking (e.g., see [7, 10, 20, 43, 58, 92]); Weihl extended the definition of commutativity in several ways: to handle nondeterministic and partial operations— that is, accesses whose return values may be undefined or multiply defined from a given state—and to take into account the results of accesses as well as their types and arguments. In contrast, much earlier work used a model in which accesses are viewed as total functions, and did not allow the results of an access to be used in testing for commutativity.

It is possible to define even more permissive notions of commutativity, which can be used to permit even more concurrency. One extension is based on a one-sided version of equieffectiveness (which Weihl [116] calls "looks like"). Exercise 3 below explores this issue. Another possible extension considers the current state of the object, when determining whether the order of occurrence of operations is important.

As shown in the algorithms in Chapter 6, and discussed in detail by Weihl in [116], backward commutativity is appropriate for concurrency control algorithms that use update-in-place recovery mechanisms; forward commutativity is necessary for algorithms that use deferred update.

The definition of *serial dependency relation* is a variation of a definition originally given by Herlihy in [47], adapted to the formal framework used in this book. More examples of serial dependency relations can be found in the paper by Herlihy and Weihl [52].

4.7 Exercises

1. Prove Propositions 4.2 and 4.4.

2. Show that it is possible for a serial object to have a pair of behaviors β and β' that are not equieffective but where the following is true for every single operation (T, v): $\beta perform(T, v)$ is a behavior of $S(X)$ if and only if $\beta' perform(T, v)$ is a behavior of $S(X)$. Hint: consider the FIFO queue.

3. Define a one-sided version of equieffectiveness, where β' must pass the tests that β passes, but the converse is not required. Also, use your definition to define variants of commutativity, and prove properties of these relationships.

As a research problem, try to develop algorithms similar to (but allowing more concurrency than) those of Chapter 6.

4. For the read/write serial object of Example 3.5.3, show that the operations (T, v) and (T', v') commute forward if $T \neq T'$, $kind(T) =$ "$write$", $kind(T') =$ "$write$", $data(T) = data(T')$, and $v = v' =$ "OK". Show that in general the operations (T, v) and (T', v') do not commute forward if $T \neq T'$, $kind(T) =$ "$write$", $kind(T') =$ "$write$", $data(T) \neq data(T')$, and $v = v' =$ "OK".

5. For the bank account serial object $S(X)$ described in Example 3.5.2, show that the operations (T, v) and (T', v') commute forward if $T \neq T'$, $kind(T) =$ "$balance$", $kind(T') =$ "$withdraw$", and $v = 0$. On the other hand, show that the operations do not in general commute forward if $T \neq T'$, $kind(T) =$ "$balance$", $kind(T') =$ "$withdraw$", and $v \neq 0$.

Also, show that the operations (T, v) and (T', v') commute forward if $T \neq T'$, $kind(T) =$ "$deposit$", and $kind(T') =$ "$withdraw$".

Also, show that the operations (T, v) and (T', v') do not commute forward if $T \neq T'$, $kind(T) =$ "$deposit$", and $kind(T') =$ "$balance$".

6. For the multicomponent serial object $S(X)$ described in Example 3.5.4, show that the operations (T, v) and (T', v') commute forward if $T \neq T'$, $kind(T) =$ "$read$" and $kind(T') =$ "$read$". Also, show that the operations (T, v) and (T', v') commute forward if $T \neq T'$, $grain(T) = i$, $grain(T') = j$, $i \neq$ "all", $j \neq$ "all", and $i \neq j$.

7. For the read/write serial object of Example 3.5.3, show that the operations (T, v) and (T', v') commute backward if $T \neq T'$, $kind(T) =$ "$write$", $kind(T') =$ "$write$", $data(T) = data(T')$, and $v = v' =$ "OK". Show that in general the operations (T, v) and (T', v') do not commute backward if $T \neq T'$, $kind(T) =$ "$write$", $kind(T') =$ "$write$", $data(T) \neq data(T')$, and $v = v' =$ "OK".

8. For the bank account serial object $S(X)$ described in Example 3.5.2, show that the operations (T, v) and (T', v') commute backward if $T \neq T'$, $kind(T) =$ "$balance$", $kind(T) =$ "$withdraw$", and $v = 0$. On the other hand, so that the operations do not in general commute backward if $T \neq T'$, $kind(T) =$ "$balance$", $kind(T) =$ "$withdraw$", and $v \neq 0$.

9. Determine which operations commute backward for the FIFO queue serial object of Example 3.5.5.

10. For the bank account serial object $S(X)$ described in Example 3.5.2, suppose that (T, v) and (T', v') are operations of $S(X)$ such that $T \neq T'$, $kind(T) =$ "$withdraw$", $v \neq 0$, $kind(T') =$ "$deposit$", and $v' =$ "OK". Show that (T', v')

commutes backward through (T, v), but (T, v) does not commute backward through (T', v').

11. Construct a serial object $S(X)$ with an operation that is both transparent and obliterating.

12. For the bank account serial object $S(X)$ described in Example 3.5.2, consider the relation R that contains $((T, v), (T', v'))$ in the following cases

(a) $kind(T) = $ "*deposit*" and $kind(T') = $ "*balance*"

(b) $kind(T) \doteq $ "*withdraw*", $v \neq 0$, and $kind(T') = $ "*balance*"

(c) $kind(T) = $ "*withdraw*", $v \neq 0$, $kind(T') = $ "*withdraw*", and $v' \neq 0$

Show that R is a serial dependency relation.

13. Provide a serial object automaton that represents a Stack, where each access is either a "*push*" or a "*pop*", and where an attempt to pop from an empty stack returns a special exception called "*empty*". Give the forward commutativity and backward commutativity relations for this object.

14. Let $S(X)$ be a serial object automaton. We say that an operation (T, v) of X is **blind** provided that $perform(\xi(T, v))$ is a finite behavior of $S(X)$ whenever $perform(\xi)$ is a behavior of $S(X)$ and $\xi(T, v)$ is a serial object well-formed sequence of operations. Thus a blind operation does not reveal anything about the state of the serial object when it occurs. However, it may affect the state. Let R denote the relation on operations of $S(X)$ where $((T, v), (T', v')) \in R$ whenever $T \neq T'$ and (T', v') is not blind. Show that R is a serial dependency relation for $S(X)$.

15. Provide a serial object automaton that represents a Semaphore containing a value *count*. Each access is either a "*signal*" that increases *count* by 1, or a "*wait*" that decreases *count* by one if the new value would be nonnegative, and blocks otherwise. Each access has return value of "*OK*". Give a minimal serial dependency relation for this object.

THE ATOMICITY THEOREM

5.1 Introduction

This chapter presents the Atomicity Theorem, which embodies a fairly general method for proving that a concurrency control algorithm guarantees atomicity. This theorem expresses the following intuition: a behavior of a system is atomic provided that there is a way to order the transactions so that, when the operations at each object are arranged in the corresponding order, the result is a behavior of the corresponding serial object. The correctness of many different concurrency control algorithms can be proved using this theorem; in later chapters, it is used to prove correctness of both locking and timestamp algorithms.

You can model any particular transaction-processing system by a composition of automata, and then directly prove that the resulting composition has atomic behaviors. Our experience has been that different proofs done this way involve a large amount of similar reasoning. The result of this chapter encapsulates common work from the verification of many systems.

The Atomicity Theorem is in many ways an analog for the classical Serializability Theorem presented in [12]. Both theorems hypothesize that there is some ordering on transactions consistent with the behavior at each object. In both cases, this hypothesis is used to show atomicity. The Atomicity Theorem is somewhat more complicated, however, because it deals with nesting and aborts, and with objects whose operations are more complex than simple reads and updates, and also because it makes fewer assumptions about the structure of the transaction-processing system.[1]

The chapter begins with some additional definitions that are needed to accommodate these complications. In an attempt to be as general as possible, the theorem talks about sequences of actions and not about particular system organizations. However, not all sequences of actions are reasonable; the theorem applies to those sequences that could be behaviors of systems containing the transaction automata A_T. In other words, the projection of the sequence on each transaction must be a behavior of that transaction's automaton. In addition, certain other constraints, such as that a **CREATE**(T) action does not occur without a preceding **REQUEST_CREATE**(T) action, must also be satisfied. To capture these constraints on sequences of actions, *simple systems* are defined in Section 5.3. Next, various orders on events and transactions are defined that are used to reorder behaviors of real transaction-processing systems to show the existence of appropriate serial behaviors. The chapter closes with the statement and proof of the Atomicity Theorem.

5.2   Visibility

One difference between the Atomicity Theorem and the classical Serializability Theorem is that the conclusion of the former result is atomicity for an arbitrary transaction T, whereas the classical result essentially considers only atomicity for T_0. Thus, the Atomicity Theorem does not deal with all the operations at each object, but only with those that are in some sense *visible* to the particular transaction T. This subsection defines a notion of *visibility* of one transaction to another. This notion is a technical one, but one that is natural and convenient in the formal statements of results and in their proofs. Visibility is defined so that, in the usual transaction-processing systems, only a transaction T' that is visible to another transaction T can affect the behavior of T.

A transaction T' can affect another transaction T in several ways. First, if T' is an ancestor of T, then T' can affect T by passing information down the transaction tree via invocations. Second, a transaction T' that is not an ancestor of T can affect

---

[1]Chapter 9 presents a detailed account of the connection between our theorem and the classical one.

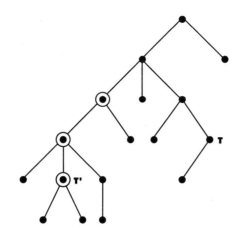

Figure 5.1: Visibility

T through **COMMIT** actions for T' and all ancestors of T' up to the level of the least common ancestor with T; information can be propagated from T' up to the least common ancestor via **REPORT_COMMIT** actions (and the associated return values), and from there down to T via invocations. Third, a transaction T' that is not an ancestor of T can affect T by accessing an object that is later accessed by T; in most of the usual transaction-processing algorithms, this is only allowed to occur if there are intervening **COMMIT** actions for all ancestors of T' up to the level of the least common ancestor with T.

Thus, *visibility* is defined as follows. Let β be any sequence of actions. If T and T' are transaction names, say that T' is **visible** to T in β if there is a **COMMIT**(U) action in β for every U in *ancestors*(T') − *ancestors*(T). Thus, every ancestor of T' up to (but not necessarily including) the least common ancestor of T and T' has committed in β. It follows from the definition that T is visible to itself in any sequence; that is, visibility is a reflexive relationship. Notice though that visibility is not in general a symmetric relation; T can be visible to T' in β while T' is not visible to T. In Lemma 5.1, we see that visibility is transitive.

The definition of visibility has been chosen for ease of argument. Note, however, that it says that T' is visible to T even in some situations where T' cannot affect the behavior of T; for example, when T' follows T in β. Intuitively, the definition includes all transactions that, as far as T can *see*, participate in the computation, either before or after T.

Figure 5.1 depicts two transactions, T and T', neither an ancestor of the other. If the transactions represented by all of the circled nodes have committed in some sequence of serial actions, then the definition implies that T' is visible to T.

EXAMPLE 5.2.1   Visibility in the Banking System

Throughout this chapter, we will refer to the following sequence β of serial actions of the banking system described in Example 3.1.1.

CREATE(T_0),
  REQUEST_CREATE(T_1),
  CREATE(T_1),
  REQUEST_COMMIT$(T_1, "OK")$,
  COMMIT(T_1),
  REPORT_COMMIT$(T_1, "OK")$,
    REQUEST_CREATE(T_2),
      REQUEST_CREATE(T_3),
      CREATE(T_3),
        REQUEST_CREATE$(T_{3.1})$,
    CREATE(T_2),
        CREATE$(T_{3.1})$,
        REQUEST_COMMIT$(T_{3.1}, \$0)$,
    REQUEST_COMMIT$(T_2, "OK")$,
        COMMIT$(T_{3.1})$,
        REPORT_COMMIT$(T_{3.1}, \$0)$,
          REQUEST_CREATE$(T_{3.3})$,
          CREATE$(T_{3.3})$,
            REQUEST_CREATE$(T_{3.1003})$,
            CREATE$(T_{3.1003})$,
              REQUEST_CREATE$(T_{3.1003.1})$,
              CREATE$(T_{3.1003.1})$,
          REQUEST_COMMIT$(T_{3.3}, \$200)$,
          COMMIT$(T_{3.3})$,
                REQUEST_CREATE$(T_{3.1003.2})$,
              REQUEST_COMMIT$(T_{3.1003.1}, \$1000)$,
              COMMIT$(T_{3.1003.1})$,
              REPORT_COMMIT$(T_{3.1003.1}, \$1000)$,
          REPORT_COMMIT$(T_{3.3}, \$200)$,
            ABORT$(T_{3.1003})$,
            REPORT_ABORT$(T_{3.1003})$,
      REQUEST_COMMIT$(T_3, \$200)$,
      COMMIT(T_3),
    COMMIT(T_2),
  REPORT_COMMIT$(T_2, "OK")$,
    REPORT_COMMIT$(T_3, \$200)$,

$$\text{REQUEST\_CREATE}(T_5),$$
$$\text{REQUEST\_CREATE}(T_4),$$
$$\text{CREATE}(T_{3.1003.2}),$$
$$\text{CREATE}(T_4),$$
$$\text{REQUEST\_COMMIT}(T_4, ``OK"),$$
$$\text{REQUEST\_COMMIT}(T_{3.1003.2}, ``OK"),$$
$$\text{COMMIT}(T_{3.1003.2}),$$
$$\text{CREATE}(T_5),$$
$$\text{REQUEST\_COMMIT}(T_5, \$1800),$$
$$\text{COMMIT}(T_5),$$
$$\text{REPORT\_COMMIT}(T_5, \$1800).$$

In β, the transaction $T_{3.3}$ is visible to T_5 because β contains $\text{COMMIT}(T_{3.3})$ and $\text{COMMIT}(T_3)$ events. Also $T_{3.1003.1}$ is visible in β to $T_{3.1003.2}$ because β contains $\text{COMMIT}(T_{3.1002.1})$. However, T_4 is not visible in β to $T_{3.3}$, since $\text{COMMIT}(T_4)$ does not appear, and $T_{3.1003.1}$ is not visible to $T_{3.1}$ because (while $\text{COMMIT}(T_{3.1003.1})$ does occur) $\text{COMMIT}(T_{3.1003})$ is not present.

Here is the complete list of transactions visible in β to T_0: T_0, T_1, T_2, T_3, $T_{3.1}$, $T_{3.3}$, and T_5. The transactions visible to T_4 are all of the above and also T_4. The transactions visible in β to $T_{3.1003}$ are those visible to T_0 and also $T_{3.1003}$ and $T_{3.1003.1}$.

The notion of visibility is used to pick, out of a sequence of actions, a subsequence consisting of the actions corresponding to transactions that are visible to a given transaction T. More precisely, if β is any sequence of actions and T is a transaction name, then $visible(\beta, T)$ denotes the subsequence of β consisting of serial actions π with $hightransaction(\pi)$ visible to T in β. Note that every action occurring in $visible(\beta, T)$ is a serial action, even if β itself contains other actions. Note also that the use of $hightransaction$ in the definition implies that if T' is visible to T in β and T'' is a child of T' that has an $\text{ABORT}(T'')$ in β, then any $\text{REQUEST\_CREATE}(T'')$, $\text{ABORT}(T'')$, and $\text{REPORT\_ABORT}(T'')$ actions in β are included in $visible(\beta, T)$, but actions of T'' are not.

EXAMPLE 5.2.2   Banking System

For the sequence β given in Example 5.2.1, $visible(\beta, T_0)$ is

$$\text{CREATE}(T_0),$$
$$\text{REQUEST\_CREATE}(T_1),$$
$$\text{CREATE}(T_1),$$

REQUEST_COMMIT(T_1, "*OK*"),
COMMIT(T_1),
REPORT_COMMIT(T_1,"*OK*"),
  REQUEST_CREATE(T_2),
    REQUEST_CREATE(T_3),
    CREATE(T_3),
      REQUEST_CREATE($T_{3.1}$),
  CREATE(T_2),
      CREATE($T_{3.1}$),
      REQUEST_COMMIT($T_{3.1}$, \$0),
  REQUEST_COMMIT(T_2, "*OK*"),
      COMMIT($T_{3.1}$),
      REPORT_COMMIT($T_{3.1}$,\$0),
        REQUEST_CREATE($T_{3.3}$),
        CREATE($T_{3.3}$),
          REQUEST_CREATE($T_{3.1003}$),
        REQUEST_COMMIT($T_{3.3}$, \$200),
        COMMIT($T_{3.3}$),
        REPORT_COMMIT($T_{3.3}$,\$200),
          ABORT($T_{3.1003}$),
          REPORT_ABORT($T_{3.1003}$),
    REQUEST_COMMIT(T_3, \$200),
    COMMIT(T_3),
  COMMIT(T_2),
  REPORT_COMMIT(T_2,"*OK*"),
    REPORT_COMMIT(T_3,\$200),
                REQUEST_CREATE(T_5),
                CREATE(T_5),
                REQUEST_COMMIT(T_5, \$1800),
                COMMIT(T_5),
                REPORT_COMMIT(T_5,\$1800).

Notice how the activity of $T_{3.1003}$ and its subtransactions has been removed, but the **REQUEST_CREATE**($T_{3.1003}$), **ABORT**($T_{3.1003}$), and **REPORT_ABORT**($T_{3.1003}$) events are retained. Similarly the activity of T_4 has been removed.

The following lemmas describe elementary properties of *visibility*.

LEMMA 5.1 *Let β be a sequence of actions, and let T, T', and T'' be transaction names.*

1. If T' is an ancestor of T, then T' is visible to T in β.

2. T' is visible to T in β if and only if T' is visible to $lca(T, T')$ in β.

3. If T'' is visible to T' in β and T' is visible to T in β, then T'' is visible to T in β.

4. If T' is a proper descendant of T, T'' is visible to T' in β, but T'' is not visible to T in β, then T'' is a descendant of the child of T that is an ancestor of T'.

5. If T'' is visible to T' and to T in β, then T'' is visible to T' in $visible(\beta, T)$.

LEMMA 5.2 Let β and γ be sequences of actions such that γ is a reordering of a subsequence of β. Let T and T' be transaction names.

1. If T' is visible to T in γ, then T' is visible to T in β.

2. $visible(\gamma, T)$ is a reordering of a subsequence of $visible(\beta, T)$.

The following easy lemma says that the *visible* operator on sequences picks out either all or none of the actions having a particular transaction.

LEMMA 5.3 Let β be a sequence of actions, and let T and T' be transaction names. Then $visible(\beta, T)|T'$ is equal to $\beta|T'$ if T' is visible to T in β, and is equal to the empty sequence otherwise.

LEMMA 5.4 Let β be a sequence of actions.

1. If T' is live in β and T' is visible to T in β, then T is a descendant of T'.

2. If T' is an orphan in β and T' is visible to T in β, then T is an orphan in β.

5.3 Simple Systems

It is desirable to state the Atomicity Theorem in such a way that it can be used for proving correctness of many different kinds of transaction-processing systems, with radically different architectures. To this purpose, *simple systems* are defined, which embody the common features of most transaction-processing systems, independent of their concurrency control and recovery algorithms, and even of their division into modules to handle different aspects of transaction-processing. A *simple system* consists of the transaction automata together with a special automaton called the *simple database.* That is, simple systems only distinguish architecturally between the user-specified components (the transactions) and the rest of the transaction-processing system, modeled by the simple database.

In addition to this trivial architectural assumption, simple databases are required to preserve trivial syntactic properties, including the following:

- A transaction is not created without first being requested.

- A transaction does not both commit and abort.

- A transaction does not commit without first requesting to commit.

- A **REPORT** event does not occur for a transaction unless it is preceded by a corresponding completion event.

However, the simple database does not include any constraints based on the semantics of the objects as specified by the serial system. In other words, the simple database is allowed to return arbitrary responses to accesses.

In practice, a real transaction-processing system will obey all the constraints imposed by a simple system, and will also impose additional constraints on the responses to accesses that guarantee atomicity. The Atomicity Theorem is stated in terms of simple systems; it can be applied to any system that *implements* the simple system in the sense that each of its behaviors is a simple behavior. In our experience, many complicated transaction-processing algorithms can be modeled as implementations of the simple system. For example, a system containing separate objects that manage locks and a *controller* that passes information among transactions and objects can be represented in this way, and so the Atomicity Theorem can be used to prove its correctness. The same strategy works for a system containing objects that manage timestamped versions and a controller that issues timestamps to transactions.

5.3.1 Simple Database

There is a single simple database for each system type. The action signature of the simple database is that of the composition of the serial scheduler with the serial objects:

Input:
    REQUEST_CREATE(T), $T \neq T_0$
    REQUEST_COMMIT(T, v), T a non-access, v a return value for T
Output:
    CREATE(T)
    COMMIT(T), $T \neq T_0$
    ABORT(T), $T \neq T_0$
    REPORT_COMMIT(T, v), $T \neq T_0$, v a return value for T

REPORT_ABORT(T), $T \neq T_0$
REQUEST_COMMIT(T, v), T an access, v a return value for T

Note that this signature distinguishes the **REQUEST_COMMIT** events, based on whether their first arguments are accesses. Recall (from Section 3.5.1) that the **REQUEST_COMMIT**(T, v) actions, when T is a non-access, are outputs of the corresponding transaction automaton A_T specified by the users. In addition, the action **REQUEST_COMMIT**(T, v), when T *is* an access, is an operation of the corresponding object (or its implementation), supported by the transaction-processing system.

States of the simple database are the same as for the serial scheduler, and the start states are also the same. In particular, although the signature of the serial scheduler has been extended by adding the actions of the serial objects, no additional state information about the objects occurs in the simple database. Intuitively, the behaviors of the simple database are *syntactically well-formed*, but are not constrained to satisfy any substantive *semantic* constraints, particularly as to the serial object actions. Semantic constraints are added in the statement of the Atomicity Theorem, which specifies general sufficient conditions for the atomicity of behaviors of the simple system.

The transition relation of the simple database is given in Figure 5.2.

EXAMPLE 5.3.1   Banking System

The sequence β given in Example 5.2.1 is a schedule of the simple database.

Basic Properties of the Simple Database

The next two lemmas are analogous to those previously given for the serial scheduler in Lemmas 3.8 and 3.9. Notice, however, that we do not have results corresponding to Part 9 of Lemma 3.8 or to Parts 9 and 10 of Lemma 3.9. Instead we have two extra results about access, as Parts 9 and 10 of Lemma 5.6.

LEMMA 5.5 *If β is a finite schedule of the simple database that can lead to state s, then the following conditions are true.*

1. *$T \in s.create\_requested$ if and only if $T = T_0$ or β contains a **REQUEST_CREATE**(T) event.*

2. *$T \in s.created$ if and only if β contains a **CREATE(T)** event.*

3. *$(T, v) \in s.commit\_requested$ if and only if β contains a **REQUEST_COMMIT**(T, v) event.*

4. *$T \in s.committed$ if and only if β contains a **COMMIT(T)** event.*

REQUEST_CREATE(T)
  Effect:
    $s.create\_requested$
      $= s'.create\_requested \cup \{T\}$

REQUEST_COMMIT(T, v), T a non-access
  Effect:
    $s.commit\_requested$
      $= s'.commit\_requested \cup \{(T, v)\}$

CREATE(T)
  Precondition:
    $T \in s'.create\_requested - s'.created$
  Effect:
    $s.created = s'.created \cup \{T\}$

COMMIT(T)
  Precondition:
    $(T, v) \in s'.commit\_requested$
    $T \notin s'.completed$
  Effect:
    $s.committed = s'.committed \cup T$

ABORT(T)
  Precondition:
    $T \in s'.create\_requested - s'.completed$
  Effect:
    $s.aborted = s'.aborted \cup \{T\}$

REPORT_COMMIT(T, v)
  Precondition:
    $T \in s'.committed$
    $(T, v) \in s'.commit\_requested$
    $T \notin s'.reported$
  Effect:
    $s.reported = s'.reported \cup \{T\}$

REPORT_ABORT(T)
  Precondition:
    $T \in s'.aborted$
    $T \notin s'.reported$
  Effect:
    $s.reported = s'.reported \cup \{T\}$

REQUEST_COMMIT(T, v), T an access
  Precondition:
    $T \in s'.created$
    $(T, v') \notin s'.commit\_requested$ for all v'
  Effect:
    $s.commit\_requested$
      $= s'.commit\_requested \cup \{(T, v)\}$

Figure 5.2: Transition Relation for the Simple Database

5. $T \in s.aborted$ if and only if β contains an **ABORT(T)** event.

6. $T \in s.reported$ if and only if β contains a report event for T.

7. $s.committed \cap s.aborted = \emptyset$.

8. $s.reported \subseteq s.committed \cup s.aborted$.

LEMMA 5.6 *Let β be a schedule of the simple database. Then all of the following hold:*

1. *If a **CREATE(T)** event appears in β for $T \neq T_0$, then a **REQUEST_CREATE**(T) event precedes it in β.*

2. *At most one **CREATE(T)** event appears in β for each transaction T.*

3. If a **COMMIT**(T) event appears in β, then a **REQUEST_COMMIT**(T,v) event precedes it in β for some return value v.

4. If an **ABORT**(T) event appears in β, then a **REQUEST_CREATE**(T) event precedes it in β.

5. At most one completion event appears in β for each transaction.

6. At most one report event appears in β for each transaction.

7. If a **REPORT_COMMIT**(T,v) event appears in β, then a **COMMIT**(T) event and a **REQUEST_COMMIT**(T,v) event precede it in β.

8. If a **REPORT_ABORT**(T) event appears in β, then an **ABORT**(T) event precedes it in β.

9. If T is an access and a **REQUEST_COMMIT**(T,v) event occurs in β, then a **CREATE**(T) event precedes it in β.

10. If T is an access, then at most one **REQUEST_COMMIT** event for T occurs in β.

Thus, the simple database embodies those constraints that one would expect any reasonable transaction-processing system to satisfy—that is, well-formedness and control-flow (communication) requirements. The simple database does not allow **CREATE**, **ABORT**, or **COMMIT** actions without an appropriate preceding request, does not allow any transaction to have two creation or completion events, and does not report completion events that never happened. Also, it does not produce responses to accesses that were not invoked, nor does it produce multiple responses to accesses. On the other hand, the simple database allows almost any ordering of transactions, allows concurrent execution of sibling transactions, and allows arbitrary responses to accesses.

It is not claimed that the simple database produces only atomic behaviors; rather, the simple database is used to model features common to more sophisticated systems. Such systems will usually include a controller (perhaps with constraints of its own) and complicated objects with concurrency control and recovery built into them. Such a system will have additional actions for communication between these objects and the controller. The Atomicity Theorem states a condition that ensures that a behavior of the simple database is atomic for a particular transaction. Later chapters show that behaviors of sophisticated transaction-processing systems satisfy this condition and hence are atomic for many or all of the transactions.

The next technical lemma shows that the simple database preserves transaction well-formedness.

LEMMA 5.7 *Let T be any transaction name. Then the simple database preserves transaction well-formedness for T.*

PROOF   Let Φ be the set of all serial actions ϕ with $transaction(\phi) = T$. Suppose β is a sequence of actions and π is an action, such that $\beta\pi$ projected on the actions of the simple database is a finite behavior of the simple database, π is an output action of the simple database, and $\beta|\Phi$ is transaction well-formed for T. The proof must show that $\beta\pi|\Phi$ is transaction well-formed for T. If $\pi \notin \Phi$, then the result is immediate, so assume that $\pi \in \Phi$, that is, that $transaction(\pi) = T$.

Use Lemma 3.3. Since $\beta|\Phi$ is transaction well-formed for T, the four conditions of that lemma hold for all prefixes of $\beta|\Phi$. Thus, it remains only to prove the four conditions of that lemma hold for $\beta\pi|\Phi$. Since π is an output of the simple database, π is either a **CREATE**(T) event for an arbitrary transaction T, a **REPORT** event for a child of an arbitrary transaction T, or a **REQUEST_COMMIT** for T, where T is an access. If π is **CREATE**(T), then since $\beta\pi$ projected on the actions of the simple database is a schedule of the simple database, Lemma 5.6 implies that no **CREATE**(T) occurs in β. If π is a **REPORT** event for a child T' of T, then Lemma 5.6 implies that **REQUEST_CREATE**(T') occurs in β and no other **REPORT** for T' occurs in β. If π is **REQUEST_COMMIT**(T,v) and T is an access, then Lemma 5.6 implies that **CREATE**(T) occurs in β, and no **REQUEST_COMMIT** for T occurs in β. Then Lemma 3.3 implies that $\beta\pi|\Phi$ is transaction well-formed for T. $\square$

5.3.2 Simple Systems, Executions, Schedules, and Behaviors

A **simple system** is the composition of a compatible set of automata indexed by the union of the set of non-access transaction names and the singleton set $\{SD\}$ (for *simple database*). Associated with each non-access transaction name T is the transaction automaton A_T for T, and associated with the name $\{SD\}$ is the simple database automaton for the given system type.

When the particular simple system is understood from context, the terms **simple executions**, **simple schedules**, and **simple behaviors** are used for the system's executions, schedules, and behaviors, respectively.

EXAMPLE 5.3.2   Banking System

The sequence β given in Example 5.2.1 is a simple behavior.

The following are immediate.

PROPOSITION 5.8 *If β is a simple behavior and T is a transaction name, then $\beta|T$ is transaction well-formed for T.*

PROOF By Lemma 5.7 and the definition of transaction automata, all the components of the simple system preserve transaction well-formedness for T. The result is immediate from Proposition 2.12. □

The following is a basic fact about simple behaviors.

LEMMA 5.9 *Let β be a simple behavior. Let T and T' be transaction names, where T' is an ancestor of T. If T is live in β and not an orphan in β then T' is live in β.*

5.4 Event and Transaction Orders

The general approach to showing that a system is correct is to extract a subsequence of each behavior of the system, reorder the subsequence in certain ways, and then show that the resulting sequence is a behavior of the serial system. Two constraints are placed on the reordering: first, it must preserve the order of certain events from the original behavior, and second, it must order all the activity done on behalf of a transaction (including all the actions of its descendants) either before or after all the activity done on behalf of any sibling transaction. The first constraint is sometimes described as *external consistency*, because it means that the apparent order of events is consistent with what is known about the true order.[2] The second constraint corresponds to giving the apparent order in which the siblings seem to execute. The first constraint is captured by the notion of an *affects order*, while the second is captured by a *sibling order*. This section defines these orders precisely and proves some simple facts about them.

5.4.1 SD-Affects Order

The affects order we define here is a partial order on the events in a sequence of actions. This order relates two events when the occurrence of one might have caused the later occurrence of the other.[3] This possible influence is transmitted in two different ways: through the simple database, as when a request influences the later fulfillment of that request, or through the transactions, as when a request is issued because a previous

---

[2] As an example, when one subtransaction U is invoked because an earlier one T returned a special value, the apparent order should also have the actions of U before those of T.

[3] Recall from the Appendix we define partial orders to be irreflexive.

response was returned. For technical reasons we present the affects order in two stages; first, we define the SD-affects order, which reflects the influence transmitted in the database. In Section 5.4.2 we extend this relation to also reflect influences transmitted by transactions.

The relation SD-$affects(\beta)$ is defined on the events of a sequence β of serial actions. This relation describes basic dependencies between events in behaviors of the simple database; any appropriate reordering of β will be required to be consistent with these dependencies.

The relation SD-$affects(\beta)$ is defined by first defining a subrelation, *directly-SD-affects(β)*, and then taking its transitive closure. This decomposition is useful later in proofs about the relation SD-$affects(\beta)$, since it is often easy to reason about *directly-SD-affects(β)*. For a sequence β of serial actions, and events ϕ and π in β, say that ϕ **directly SD-affects** π in β (and that $(\phi, \pi) \in$ *directly-SD-affects(β)*) if at least one of the following is true.

- $\phi = \textbf{REQUEST\_CREATE}(T)$ and $\pi = \textbf{CREATE}(T)$

- $\phi = \textbf{CREATE}(T)$ and $\pi = \textbf{REQUEST\_COMMIT}(T, v)$

- $\phi = \textbf{REQUEST\_COMMIT}(T, v)$ and $\pi = \textbf{COMMIT}(T)$

- $\phi = \textbf{REQUEST\_CREATE}(T)$ and $\pi = \textbf{ABORT}(T)$

- $\phi = \textbf{COMMIT}(T)$ and $\pi = \textbf{REPORT\_COMMIT}(T, v)$

- $\phi = \textbf{ABORT}(T)$ and $\pi = \textbf{REPORT\_ABORT}(T)$

LEMMA 5.10 *If β is a transaction well-formed behavior of the simple database and $(\phi, \pi) \in$ directly-SD-affects(β), then ϕ precedes π in β.*

PROOF   Note first that the actions of the simple database are exactly the serial actions: hence β is a sequence of serial actions and *directly-SD-affects(β)* is defined.

Transaction well-formedness implies that there cannot be two **REQUEST-_CREATE**(T) events in β for the same T, and that there cannot be two **REQUEST-_COMMIT** events for the same transaction. Also, Lemma 5.6 says that β does not contain two completion events for the same T. Hence, in each case ϕ is the only occurrence of the appropriate action in β. In each case, π is an output of the simple database, and the simple database preconditions test for the presence of the appropriate preceding action. □

For a sequence β of serial actions, define the relation SD-$affects(\beta)$ to be the transitive closure of the relation *directly-SD-affects(β)*. If the pair (ϕ, π) is in the relation SD-$affects(\beta)$, say that ϕ **SD-affects** π in β. The following are immediate.

LEMMA 5.11 *Let β be a sequence of events and β' a subsequence of β. Then SD-affects(β) contains SD-affects(β').*

LEMMA 5.12 *Let β be a transaction well-formed behavior of the simple database. Then SD-affects(β) is a partial order on the events in β.*

PROOF By Lemma 5.10, ϕ directly SD-affects π in β only if ϕ precedes π in β. Therefore ϕ SD-affects π in β only if ϕ precedes π in β. Thus, *SD-affects*(β) is irreflexive and antisymmetric. Since *SD-affects*(β) is constructed as a transitive closure, the result follows. $\square$

EXAMPLE 5.4.1 Banking System

For the simple behavior β given in Example 5.2.1, we have
REQUEST_CREATE$(T_{3.1003})$ SD-affects **REPORT_ABORT**$(T_{3.1003})$, and
REQUEST_COMMIT$(T_{3.3}, \$200)$ SD-affects **REPORT_COMMIT**$(T_{3.3}, \$200)$.
However, **CREATE**$(T_{3.1003})$ does not SD-affect **REQUEST_CREATE**$(T_{3.1003.1})$.

Recall from the Appendix the definition of a subsequence being R-closed in a sequence, for a binary relation R on the events of the sequence.

LEMMA 5.13 *Let β be a finite behavior of the simple database, let β' be an SD-affects(β)-closed subsequence of β, and let γ be any reordering of β' that is consistent with SD-affects(β). Then γ is a finite behavior of the simple database.*

PROOF The proof is by induction on the prefixes of γ. Let $\gamma'\pi$ be a prefix of γ with π a single event, and assume that γ' is a behavior of the simple database. If π is an input to the simple database (a **REQUEST_CREATE** or **REQUEST_COMMIT** for a non-access transaction), the fact that inputs are always enabled implies that $\gamma'\pi$ is a behavior of the simple database. So assume that π is an output. Let s' be the state of the simple database after γ'. The proof considers the different output actions and shows in each case that π is enabled in the simple database automaton in state s'.

1. π is **CREATE**(T'). The proof must show that $T' \in s'.create\_requested - s'.created$.
By the preconditions of the simple database and Lemma 5.5, there is a **REQUEST_CREATE**(T') event ϕ preceding π in β. Then $(\phi, \pi) \in SD\text{-}affects(\beta)$, so ϕ precedes π in γ, that is, ϕ occurs in γ', and again by Lemma 5.5, $T' \in s'.create\_requested$. By Lemma 5.6, π is the only **CREATE**(T') event in β, hence no **CREATE**(T') event occurs in γ', and finally by Lemma 5.5, $T' \notin s'.created$.

2. π is **REQUEST_COMMIT**(T', v), for access T'. The proof must show that $T' \in s'.created$ and $(T', v') \notin s'.commit\_requested$ for all v'.

By the preconditions of the simple database and Lemma 5.5, there is a **CREATE**(T') event ϕ preceding π in β. Then $(\phi, \pi) \in SD\text{-}affects(\beta)$, so ϕ precedes π in γ, that is, ϕ occurs in γ', and again by Lemma 5.5, $T' \in s'.created$. By Lemma 5.6, π is the only **REQUEST_COMMIT** event in β for T', hence no **REQUEST_COMMIT** event for T' occurs in γ', and finally by Lemma 5.5, $(T', v') \notin s'.commit\_requested$ for all v'.

3. π is **COMMIT**(T'). The proof must show that $(T', v) \in s'.commit\_requested$ for some v, and that $T' \notin s'.completed$.

By the preconditions of the simple database, and Lemma 5.5, there is a value v such that a **REQUEST_COMMIT**(T', v) event ϕ appears in β. Then $(\phi, \pi) \in SD\text{-}affects(\beta)$, so ϕ is in γ'. Thus $(T', v) \in s'.commit\_requested$.

By Lemma 5.6, there is only one completion event for T' in β and hence only one in γ. Hence, $T' \notin s'.completed$.

4. π is **ABORT**(T'). The proof must show that $T' \in s'.create\_requested - s'.completed$.

By the preconditions of the simple database, a **REQUEST_CREATE**(T') event ϕ appears in β. Then $(\phi, \pi) \in SD\text{-}affects(\beta)$, so ϕ is in γ'. Thus, $T' \in s'.create\_requested$.

Since by Lemma 5.6 there is at most one completion event in β, there can be no completion event in γ'. Thus, $T' \notin s'.completed$.

5. π is **REPORT_COMMIT**(T',v). The proof must show that $T' \in s'.committed$, that $(T', v) \in s'.commit\_requested$, and that $T' \notin s'.reported$.

By the preconditions of the simple database and Lemma 5.5, a **COMMIT**(T') event ϕ appears in β. Then $(\phi, \pi) \in SD\text{-}affects(\beta)$, so ϕ is in γ'. Similarly, there is a value v such that a **REQUEST_COMMIT**(T', v) event ψ appears in β. Then $(\psi, \phi) \in SD\text{-}affects(\beta)$, so ψ is in γ'. Thus $(T', v) \in s'.commit\_requested$. Also, by Lemma 5.6 there is at most one report event in β, so there can be no report event in γ'. Thus, $T' \notin s'.reported$.

6. π is **REPORT_ABORT**(T'). The proof must show that $T' \in s'.aborted$ and that $T' \notin s'.reported$.

By the preconditions of the simple database and Lemma 5.5, an **ABORT**(T') event ϕ appears in β. Then $(\phi, \pi) \in SD\text{-}affects(\beta)$, so ϕ is in γ'. Also, by Lemma 5.6 there is at most one report event in β, so there can be no report event in γ'. Thus, $T' \notin s'.reported$.

Thus, π is enabled in the simple database in state s'. $\square$

LEMMA 5.14 *Let β be a behavior of the simple database and let T be a transaction name. Then visible(β, T) is an SD-affects(β)-closed subsequence of β.*

PROOF   It suffices to show that if π is in $visible(\beta, T)$ and ϕ directly SD-affects π in β, then ϕ is in $visible(\beta, T)$. A simple case analysis using the definition of $directly\text{-}SD\text{-}affects(\beta)$ shows that when ϕ directly SD-affects π in β, then $hightransaction(\phi)$ is visible to T whenever $hightransaction(\pi)$ is. $\square$

5.4.2 Affects Order

Next, a second partial order, $affects(\beta)$, is defined on the events of a sequence β of serial actions. This partial order extends $SD\text{-}affects(\beta)$ to include dependencies that arise at transactions. This will be used to describe basic dependencies between events in a simple behavior; any appropriate reordering of β will be required to be consistent with these dependencies.

As before, the affects relation is defined by first defining a subrelation, the *directly affects* relation, and then taking its transitive closure. For a sequence β of serial actions, and events ϕ and π in β, say that ϕ **directly affects** π in β (and that $(\phi, \pi) \in directly\text{-}affects(\beta)$) if at least one of the following is true.

- $transaction(\phi) = transaction(\pi)$ and ϕ precedes π in β.[4]

- ϕ directly SD-affects π in β.

The next lemma is immediate from Lemma 5.10.

LEMMA 5.15 *If β is a simple behavior and $(\phi, \pi) \in directly\text{-}affects(\beta)$, then ϕ precedes π in β.*

For a sequence β of serial actions, define the relation $affects(\beta)$ to be the transitive closure of the relation $directly\text{-}affects(\beta)$. If the pair (ϕ, π) is in the relation $affects(\beta)$, also say that ϕ *affects* π in β. The following is immediate.

LEMMA 5.16 *Let β be a simple behavior. Then $affects(\beta)$ is a partial order on the events in β.*

The conditions listed in the definition of "*directly-affects*" should seem a reasonable collection of dependencies among the events in a simple behavior. At a technical level, the justification for them is that the affects relation is used to extract serial behaviors from a simple behavior. The order of the events in the serial behavior will be consistent

---

[4]This includes accesses as well as non-accesses.

with the affects ordering. Thus, if β is a simple behavior and $(\phi, \pi) \in \text{affects}(\beta)$, all the serial behaviors constructed that contain π will also contain ϕ, and ϕ will precede π in each such behavior. The first case of the *directly-affects* definition is necessary because there is no assumption of special knowledge of transaction behavior; if π and not ϕ were included in the candidate serial behavior, there would be no way of proving that the result included correct behaviors of the transaction automata. The remaining cases (when the definition of *directly-SD-affects* is expanded into cases) naturally parallel the preconditions of the serial scheduler; in each case, the precondition of π as an action of the serial scheduler include a test for a previous occurrence of ϕ, so a sequence of actions with π not preceded by ϕ could not possibly be a serial behavior.

EXAMPLE 5.4.2   Simple Behaviors

Recall (from Chapter 3) that a serial system only constrains the **CREATE** and completion actions of siblings, not the **REQUEST_CREATE** and **REPORT** actions. For example, consider the following fragment of a simple behavior, where T and T' are siblings:

REQUEST_CREATE(T),
   REQUEST_CREATE(T'),
CREATE(T),
   CREATE(T'),
   REQUEST_COMMIT(T', v'),
REQUEST_COMMIT(T, v),
COMMIT(T),
   COMMIT(T'),
   REPORT_COMMIT(T', v'),
REPORT_COMMIT(T, v).

Notice that T and T' are not run serially. However, the events of T do not affect the events of T', or vice-versa. Thus, the following reordering of the sequence above is consistent with the affects relation for the sequence:

REQUEST_CREATE(T),
   REQUEST_CREATE(T'),
CREATE(T),
REQUEST_COMMIT(T, v),
COMMIT(T),
   CREATE(T'),
   REQUEST_COMMIT(T', v'),
   COMMIT(T'),

REPORT_COMMIT(T',v'),
REPORT_COMMIT(T,v).

In addition, this reordering is a schedule of the serial scheduler, and it illustrates how one can reorder a simple behavior into a serial one without violating the affects ordering.

EXAMPLE 5.4.3 Banking System

For the simple behavior β given in Example 5.2.1, the event CREATE($T_{3.1003}$) *affects* REQUEST_CREATE($T_{3.1003.1}$), because both are actions with transaction $T_{3.1003}$ and they occur in this order in β. Notice the contrast to Example 5.4.1.

Also CREATE(T_1) affects CREATE($T_{3.1003}$) through the chain (where each action directly affects the one following):

CREATE(T_1),
REQUEST_COMMIT(T_1, "*OK*"),
COMMIT(T_1),
REPORT_COMMIT(T_1,"*OK*"),
   REQUEST_CREATE(T_3),
   CREATE(T_3),
   REQUEST_CREATE($T_{3.1003}$),
   CREATE($T_{3.1003}$).

However, CREATE(T_2) does not affect CREATE(T_3).

The following lemmas contain some constraints on the kinds of events that can affect other events in a simple behavior. The first lemma shows that events of transactions in the subtree rooted at T can only affect events of transactions outside the subtree if they first affect a REPORT event for T.

LEMMA 5.17 *Let β be a simple behavior and T a transaction name. Let ϕ and π be events of β such that ϕ affects π in β, lowtransaction(ϕ) is a descendant of T and lowtransaction(π) is not a descendant of T. Then β contains a REPORT event ψ for T, ϕ affects ψ, and either $\pi = \psi$ or ψ affects π. Furthermore, if ψ is a REPORT_ABORT event then $\phi = ABORT(T)$.*

PROOF Since ϕ affects π in β, there is a sequence $\pi_0\pi_1 \ldots \pi_k$ where π_0 is ϕ, π_k is π, and for each $0 \leq i \leq k-1$, π_i *directly affects* π_{i+1} in β. Let j be the least index such that $lowtransaction(\pi_j)$ is not a descendant of T. That is, $lowtransaction(\pi_{j-1})$ is a descendant of T, $lowtransaction(\pi_j)$ is not a descendant of U, and π_{j-1} *directly   affects* π_j in β. Examining the definition of *directly affects*, see that when ϕ *directly affects* ϕ' then $lowtransaction(\phi')$ is a descendant of $lowtransaction(\phi)$ except when ϕ' is a **REPORT** event for $lowtransaction(\phi)$ (and ϕ is a completion event). Thus, π_j is a **REPORT** event for U that occurs in β. Take π_j as ψ.

The final property follows from the observation that no event of a descendant of T directly affects an **ABORT** event for T. $\square$

The next lemma shows that events of transactions outside the subtree rooted at T can only affect events of descendants of T if they first affect a **REQUEST_CREATE**(T) event. Its proof is similar to that of the previous lemma.

LEMMA 5.18 *Let β be a simple behavior and T a transaction name. Let ϕ and π be events of β such that ϕ affects π in β, $lowtransaction(\phi)$ is not a descendant of T, and $lowtransaction(\pi)$ is a descendant of T. Then either ϕ is a **REQUEST_CREATE**(T) event, or ϕ affects a **REQUEST_CREATE**(T) event for T that affects π.*

Together, Lemmas 5.17 and 5.18 describe conditions under which the effects of events can "leave" or "enter" subtrees of the transaction tree. An immediate consequence of the two previous lemmas is the following. This will be useful in later proofs, whenever we want to show that a certain order is consistent with $affects(\beta)$.

LEMMA 5.19 *Let β be a simple behavior and T a transaction name, and let U and U' be distinct children of T. Suppose π affects π' in β, where $lowtransaction(\pi)$ and $lowtransaction(\pi')$ are descendants of U and U', respectively. Then a report for U and a **REQUEST_CREATE**(U') occur in β, in that order.*

As before, the *affects* definition is extended to sequences β of arbitrary actions by saying that ϕ affects π in β if and only if ϕ affects π in $serial(\beta)$.

5.4.3 Sibling Orders

The essential feature of any concurrency control mechanism is the choice of a consistent serialization order throughout the system. Because children run concurrently with their parents in a nested system, the serialization ordering needed for a nested transaction system is more complicated than that used in the classical theory. In place of the classical total orderings on transactions, a relation is used that only orders transactions that are siblings in the nesting tree. Such an ordering is a *sibling order*. Interesting examples of sibling orders are the order of completion of transactions or an order determined by assigned timestamps. Sibling orders are defined in this subsection.

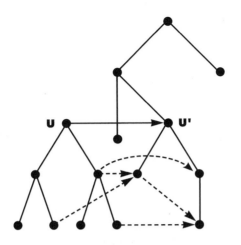

Figure 5.3: The Relation R_{trans}

Let **SIB** be the (irreflexive) sibling relation among transaction names, for a particular system type.[5] If $R \subseteq SIB$ is a partial order then call R a **sibling order**. Sibling orders are the analog for nested transaction systems of serialization orders in single-level transaction systems. Note that sibling orders are not necessarily total, in general; totality is not always appropriate for our results.

A sibling order can be extended in two natural ways. First, if R is a binary relation on the set of transaction names (such as a sibling order), then let R_{trans} be the extension of R to descendants, that is, the binary relation on transaction names containing (T, T') exactly when there exist transaction names U and U' such that T and T' are descendants of U and U' respectively, and $(U, U') \in R$. If R is a sibling order, R_{trans} echoes the manner in which the serial scheduler runs transactions when it runs siblings with no concurrency, in the order specified by R. Second, if β is any sequence of actions, then $R_{event}(\beta)$ is the extension of R to serial events in β, that is, the binary relation on events in β containing (ϕ, π) exactly when ϕ and π are distinct serial events in β with *lowtransactions* T and T' respectively, where $(T, T') \in R_{trans}$. (The function *lowtransaction* is used in this definition to ensure that completion actions are ordered along with the actions of the completing transaction.)

Figure 5.3 illustrates the definition of R_{trans}. The solid arrow shows how R or-

---

[5]Recall from the Appendix that this means $(T, T') \in SIB$ if and only if $T \neq T'$ and $parent(T) = parent(T')$.

ders two siblings, and the dashed arrows represent some of the orderings that R_{trans} contains.

EXAMPLE 5.4.4   Banking System

For the banking system of Example 3.1.1, a sibling order is the relation R containing exactly the following pairs: (T_1, T_3), (T_3, T_2), (T_2, T_5), (T_5, T_4), (T_1, T_2), (T_1, T_5), (T_1, T_4), (T_3, T_5), (T_3, T_4), (T_2, T_4), $(T_{3.1}, T_{3.3})$, $(T_{3.3}, T_{3.1003})$, and $(T_{3.1}, T_{3.1003})$.

For this order, and the sequence β given in Example 5.2.1, the relation $R_{event}(\beta)$ contains (among others) the pairs (**COMMIT**(T_5),**CREATE**(T_4)) (since the *lowtransactions* involved are T_5 and T_4); (**CREATE**$(T_{3.3})$,**CREATE**(T_2)) (where the *lowtransactions* are $T_{3.3}$ and T_2, descendants of the siblings T_3 and T_2 that are ordered by R); and (**REQUEST_COMMIT**$(T_{3.3}200,,)$**CREATE**$(T_{3.1003.1})$).

However, $R_{event}(\beta)$ does not contain the pair (**REQUEST_CREATE**(T_3), **REQUEST_COMMIT**$(T_2, \text{``}OK\text{''})$) (since the *lowtransactions* involved are T_0 and T_2, which are not descendants of a pair of siblings in R); (**CREATE**$(T_{3.1003.1})$,**CREATE**$(T_{3.1003.2})$) (since the *lowtransactions* are $T_{3.1003.1}$ and $T_{3.1003.2}$); nor (**REPORT_COMMIT**$(T_{3.1},0)$,**CREATE**$(T_{3.3})$).

The following are straightforward.

LEMMA 5.20 *Let R be a sibling order. Then R_{trans} is a partial order on transaction names, and for any sequence β of actions, $R_{event}(\beta)$ is a partial order on events in β. Furthermore, if β' is a subsequence of β, then the subrelation of $R_{event}(\beta)$ containing only events in β' is exactly $R_{event}(\beta')$.*

LEMMA 5.21 *Let β be a sequence of actions and R a sibling order. Let π and π' be serial events of β with lowtransactions U and U' respectively. Let ψ and ψ' be distinct serial events of β with lowtransactions T and T' respectively, where T is a descendant of U and T' is a descendant of U'. If $(\pi, \pi') \in R_{event}(\beta)$ then $(\psi, \psi') \in R_{event}(\beta)$.*

The concept of a *suitable sibling order* describes two basic conditions that will be required of the sibling orders to be used in our theorem. Given T, the goal is to find a serial behavior that includes the actions of transactions visible to T (i.e., that can be *seen* by T). Each set of siblings that appears in this serial behavior must be totally ordered, motivating the first condition below.[6] The second condition asserts that R does not contradict the dependencies described by the affects relation.

Formally, let β be a sequence of actions and T a transaction name. A sibling order R is **suitable** for β and T if the following conditions are met:

1. R orders all pairs of siblings T' and T'' that are *lowtransactions* of actions in $visible(\beta, T)$.

2. $R_{event}(\beta)$ and $affects(\beta)$ are consistent partial orders on the events in $visible(\beta, T)$.

The use of *lowtransaction* in this definition ensures that **ABORT** events in $visible(\beta, T)$ are included in the events ordered by R_{event}.

The following is an extension of the first property above.

LEMMA 5.22 *Let β be a simple behavior and T a transaction name. If the sibling order R is suitable for β and T, then R orders all pairs of siblings T' and T'' such that some descendant of each is the lowtransaction of an action in $visible(\beta, T)$.*

PROOF The lemma follows from the following fact about simple behaviors: if a descendant of T is the *lowtransaction* of an action in a simple behavior β, then T is the *lowtransaction* of some action in β. □

EXAMPLE 5.4.5 Banking System

The relation R given in Example 5.4.4 is suitable for β and T_0, where β is the sequence given in Example 5.2.1.

The next technical lemma will be useful for proving that particular sibling orders are suitable.

LEMMA 5.23 *Let β be a sequence of serial events and let A be a partial order on the events in β. Let R be a sibling order satisfying the following condition: if π and π' are events in β such that $(\pi, \pi') \in A$ and $lowtransaction(\pi)$ is neither an ancestor nor a descendant of $lowtransaction(\pi')$, then $(\pi, \pi') \in R_{event}(\beta)$. Then $R_{event}(\beta)$ and A are consistent partial orders on the events of β.*

---

[6]This condition is easily achieved, since one can consider orders that are total on each set of siblings. However, the natural orders that we will use in Chapters 6, 7, and 8 do not determine the relative order of transactions that are not created. Thus we want to use orders that do not relate every pair of siblings. This condition controls which siblings must be related by any order we use.

PROOF   The proof is by contradiction. If $R_{event}(\beta)$ and A are not consistent partial orders on the events of β, then there is a cycle in the relation $R_{event}(\beta) \cup A$, and thus there must be some shortest cycle. Let $\pi_0, \pi_1, \pi_2, \ldots, \pi_{n-1}, \pi_n = \pi_0$ be such a shortest cycle, where for each $i, (\pi_i, \pi_{i+1}) \in R_{event}(\beta) \cup A$. The following discussion uses arithmetic modulo n for subscripts, so that if $i = n$, π_{i+1} is to be interpreted as π_1. Note that $n > 1$, since both $R_{event}(\beta)$ and A are irreflexive.

Since the relation $R_{event}(\beta)$ is acyclic, there must be at least one index i such that $(\pi_i, \pi_{i+1}) \notin R_{event}(\beta)$, and hence $(\pi_i, \pi_{i+1}) \in A$. Let T and T' be the *lowtransactions* of π_i and π_{i+1} respectively. By hypothesis, T is either an ancestor or a descendant of T'. There are two cases.

1. T is an ancestor of T'.

> If the pair (π_{i-1}, π_i) is in A, then by the transitivity of A, $(\pi_{i-1}, \pi_{i+1}) \in A$. On the other hand, if $(\pi_{i-1}, \pi_i) \in R_{event}(\beta)$, then by Lemma 5.21, $(\pi_{i-1}, \pi_{i+1}) \in R_{event}(\beta)$. In either situation, there is a shorter cycle in the relation $R_{event}(\beta) \cup A$, obtained by omitting π_i. This contradicts the assumption that the cycle chosen is as short as possible.

2. T is a descendant of T'.

> If the pair (π_{i+1}, π_{i+2}) is in A, then by the transitivity of A, $(\pi_i, \pi_{i+2}) \in A$. On the other hand, if $(\pi_{i+1}, \pi_{i+2}) \in R_{event}(\beta)$, then by Lemma 5.21, $(\pi_i, \pi_{i+2}) \in R_{event}(\beta)$. In either situation, there is a shorter cycle in the relation $R_{event}(\beta) \cup A$, obtained by omitting π_{i+1}. This contradicts the assumption that the cycle chosen is as short as possible.

In both cases, there is a contradiction; thus, the assumption that the relation $R_{event}(\beta) \cup A$ contains a cycle must be wrong.   □

5.5   Atomicity Theorem

The main result, presented in this section, says that a simple behavior β is atomic for a nonorphan transaction name T provided that there is a suitable sibling order R for which a certain "view condition" holds for each object name X. The view condition says that the portion of β occurring at X that is visible to T, reordered according to R, is a behavior of the serial object $S(X)$. In essence, the theorem expresses the idea that if each object delivers responses to accesses in a way reflecting a particular apparent order of activity, then the whole behavior reflects this order. To make all of this precise, suppose β is a finite simple behavior,[7] T a transaction name, R a sibling order that is suitable for β and T, and X an object name. Let ξ be the sequence consisting of those operations occurring in β whose transaction components are accesses to X and are visible to T in β, ordered according to R_{trans} on the transaction components. (Lemma 5.22 implies that this ordering is uniquely determined.) Define $view(\beta, T, R, X)$ to be $perform(\xi)$.

Informally, $view(\beta, T, R, X)$ represents the portion of the behavior β occurring at X that is visible to T, reordered according to R. Stated in other words, this definition extracts from β the **REQUEST_COMMIT** actions for accesses to X that are visible to T; it then reorders those **REQUEST_COMMIT** actions according to R, and then inserts an appropriate **CREATE** action just prior to each **REQUEST_COMMIT** action. The theorem uses a hypothesis that each $view(\beta, T, R, X)$ is a behavior of the serial object $S(X)$ to conclude that β is atomic for T.

EXAMPLE 5.5.1 Banking System

The sequence $view(\beta, T_0, R, \text{ACCT\_SVNG})$ is calculated for the sequence β given in Example 5.2.1 and the sibling order R given in Example 5.4.4,

The accesses to ACCT_SVNG that are visible to T_0 are T_1, $T_{3.3}$ and T_5. The operations that occur in β with these as their transaction are $(T_1, \text{``}OK\text{''})$, $(T_{3.3}, \$200)$ and $(T_5, \$1800)$, and the order R_{trans} has T_1 before $T_{3.3}$ before T_5. Thus $view(\beta, T_0, R, \text{ACCT\_SVNG})$ is

CREATE(T_1),
REQUEST_COMMIT$(T_1, \text{``}OK\text{''})$,
    CREATE$(T_{3.3})$,
    REQUEST_COMMIT$(T_{3.3}, \$200)$,
        CREATE(T_5),
        REQUEST_COMMIT$(T_5, \$1800)$.

Similarly $view(\beta, T_0, R, \text{ACCT\_CHK})$ is

---

[7]We remark here that the theorem is stated as a condition on a single sequence β, order R, and transaction name T. In general, one wants to show that *every* finite behavior of a system is atomic. This can be done by applying the Atomicity Theorem to each behavior. We have stated the theorem for a single behavior for two reasons. First, the apparent order of transactions (expressed in the theorem as the sibling order) will clearly vary from one behavior to another, so if all behaviors β were considered, we would need not a single order but a function from behaviors to sibling orders. Second, the common concurrency control algorithms give atomicity for all nonorphan transactions, and again whether a transaction is an orphan depends on the behavior considered.

CREATE($T_{3.1}$),
REQUEST_COMMIT($T_{3.1}, 0$),
   CREATE(T_2),
   REQUEST_COMMIT(T_2, "*OK*").

As a final example, $view(\beta, T_4, R, \text{ACCT\_SVNG})$ is

CREATE(T_1),
REQUEST_COMMIT(T_1, "*OK*"),
   CREATE($T_{3.3}$),
   REQUEST_COMMIT($T_{3.3}, \$200$),
      CREATE(T_5),
      REQUEST_COMMIT($T_5, \$1800$),
         CREATE(T_4),
         REQUEST_COMMIT(T_4, "*OK*").

5.5.1 Theorem and Proof Sketch

THEOREM 5.24 *(Atomicity Theorem) Let β be a finite simple behavior, T a transaction name such that T is not an orphan in β, and R a sibling order suitable for β and T. Suppose that for each object name* X, $view(\beta, T, R, \text{X})$ *is a behavior of $S(\text{X})$. Then β is atomic for T.*

EXAMPLE 5.5.2   Banking System

The Atomicity Theorem applies to the sequence β given in Example 5.2.1, the transaction T_0, and the sibling order R given in Example 5.4.4. Example 5.3.2 noted that β was a simple behavior, the suitability of R was checked in Example 5.4.5, and the views (which were calculated in Example 5.5.1) are easily checked to be behaviors of the serial objects involved. Thus one can deduce that the sequence β is atomic for T_0. An explicit serial behavior with the same projection on T_0 as β can be found by considering the sequence given in Exercise 1 and deleting the last four actions.

The following is a rough sketch of the proof of the Atomicity Theorem. A completely detailed proof appears in the next section.

PROOF   (Sketch) Given appropriate β, T, and R, the needed serial behavior is constructed explicitly. The construction is done in several steps. First, $visible(\beta, T)$, the portion of β visible to T, is extracted from β. This sequence is then reordered according to R and $affects(\beta)$. (There may be many ways of doing this.) The reordered sequence is then truncated at an appropriate place, just after the last action involving T or any of its descendants. The resulting sequence γ is seen to be a serial behavior by showing separately that its projections are behaviors of the transaction automata, of the serial object automata, and of the serial scheduler, and then applying Proposition 2.5.

If T' is a nonaccess transaction name, Proposition 2.2 implies that $\beta|T'$ is a behavior of $A(T')$. Lemma 5.3 and the fact that the reordering is consistent with $affects(\beta)$ ensure that $\gamma|T'$ is a prefix of $\beta|T'$ and so is a behavior of $A(T')$. Thus, the projection of γ on each of the transaction automata is a behavior of that automaton.

For each object name X, unwinding the definitions shows that $\gamma|\mathrm{X}$ is a prefix of $view(\beta, T, R, \mathrm{X})$ (perhaps followed by a single **CREATE**(T)). The view condition hypothesis of the theorem, that $view(\beta, T, R, \mathrm{X})$ is a behavior of $S(\mathrm{X})$, together with the fact that **CREATE**(T) is an input to $S(\mathrm{X})$, implies that $\gamma|\mathrm{X}$ is a behavior of $S(\mathrm{X})$. Thus, the projection of γ on each of the serial object automata is a behavior of that automaton.

Finally, the proof argues that γ is a behavior of the serial scheduler. □

The theorem has a straightforward corollary that applies to other systems besides simple systems—in particular, to systems that have additional, non-serial actions in their signature.

COROLLARY 5.25 *Let* $\{B_i\}_{i\in I}$ *be a compatible set of automata and let* $B = \Pi_{i\in I}B_i$. *Suppose that all non-access transaction names* T *are in the index set* I *and that* A_T *and* B_T *are identical automata for all such* T.

Let β *be a finite behavior of* B, T *a transaction name that is not an orphan in* β, *and* R *a sibling order suitable for* $serial(\beta)$ *and* T. *Suppose that the following conditions hold.*

1. *$serial(\beta)$ is a simple behavior.*

2. *For each object name* X, *$view(serial(\beta), T, R, \mathrm{X})$ is a behavior of* $S(\mathrm{X})$.

Then β *is atomic for* T.

Using the Atomicity Theorem to Verify Concurrency Control Algorithms

Specific applications of Theorem 5.24 are the subject of Chapters 6, 7, 8 and 10. In outline, these applications proceed as follows. A system is modeled as a collection of automata, including transaction automata, object automata that each encapsulate the information about one serial object (such as locks, a log of previous activity, perhaps several versions), and a *controller* that passes information around (this includes the requests for invocation and responses but also facts about timestamps or the completion of transactions). The system must be shown to generate behaviors that (projected to the serial actions) are simple behaviors. Understanding such a system involves identifying the apparent order of transactions: this order is determined and proved to be suitable. The Atomicity Theorem then shows that atomicity of system behaviors can be proved by checking the view condition for the chosen order at each object. Since the view condition depends on facts (such as which transactions are orphans) that depend on global facts (such as what has aborted), a similar condition is presented that implies the view condition but uses only local facts (such as which transactions are known to have aborted). The result is a modular proof obligation: the system is correct if each object has behaviors that satisfy the local sufficient condition. Now the algorithm used by each object is checked, to see that this is indeed the case.

The rest of this chapter contains a careful (and somewhat technical) proof of the Atomicity Theorem. If you are more interested in the applications of the theorem than in its proof, you may wish to go on to later chapters without reading the rest of this chapter. Nothing after this point in the chapter is necessary for understanding the material in the rest of the book.

5.6 Proof of the Atomicity Theorem

This section is devoted to a proof of the Atomicity Theorem. Several technical terms are defined, such as *ordered-visible* and *pictures*, to use in the proof. These definitions are not used elsewhere in the book.

The general strategy is as follows. Given a finite simple behavior β, a nonorphan transaction T, and a suitable sibling order R, produce a serial behavior γ that looks the same as β to T (i.e., such that $\beta|T = \gamma|T$). The construction of γ is done in three steps. First, $visible(\beta, T)$, the portion of β visible to T, is extracted from β. Second, this sequence is reordered consistent with R and $affects(\beta)$. (There may be many ways of doing this.) The set of all acceptable reorderings is called $ordered\text{-}visible(\beta, T, R)$. Third, a prefix γ is taken of a sequence in $ordered\text{-}visible(\beta, T, R)$ that includes all events of T. The set of all acceptable such prefixes is called $pictures(\beta, T, R)$. Argue that each element of $pictures(\beta, T, R)$ is a serial behavior by showing separately that its projections are behaviors of the transaction automata, of the serial object automata, and of the serial scheduler, and then apply Proposition 2.5; since the projection of an element of $pictures(\beta, T, R)$ on T is the same as $\beta|T$, the desired result follows.

5.6.1 Pictures

If β is a finite simple behavior, T a transaction name, and R a suitable sibling order for β and T, then define $ordered\text{-}visible(\beta, T, R)$ to be the set of reorderings of $visible(\beta, T)$ that are consistent with $affects(\beta) \cup R_{event}(\beta)$. Also, define $pictures(\beta, T, R)$ to be the set of all sequences γ obtained as follows. If no actions π with $transaction(\pi) = T$ appear in $visible(\beta, T)$ then γ is the empty sequence. Otherwise, take a sequence δ in $ordered\text{-}visible(\beta, T, R)$. Then γ is the prefix of δ ending with π, where π is the last event in δ such that $hightransaction(\pi)$ is a descendant of T.

LEMMA 5.26 *Let β be a finite simple behavior, T a transaction name, and R a suitable sibling order for β and T. Then $ordered\text{-}visible(\beta, T, R)$ and $pictures(\beta, T, R)$ are nonempty sets of sequences.*

PROOF By the fact that R is suitable for β and T. $\qquad\square$

LEMMA 5.27 *Let β be a finite simple behavior, T a transaction name, and R a sibling order that is suitable for β and T. Let $\gamma \in pictures(\beta, T, R)$. If ϕ and π are events of β, ϕ affects π in β, and π is an event of γ, then ϕ is an event in γ, and ϕ precedes π in γ.*

PROOF Since $affects(\beta)$ is the transitive closure of the finite relation $directly\text{-}affects(\beta)$, it suffices to prove the lemma in the case that ϕ directly affects π in β. Since π is in $visible(\beta, T)$, examination of the six cases of the definition of $directly\text{-}affects(\beta)$ shows that ϕ is also in $visible(\beta, T)$. By definition, γ is a prefix of a sequence δ in $ordered\text{-}visible(\beta, T, R)$. Since δ is ordered consistently with $affects(\beta)$, ϕ precedes π in δ. Therefore, ϕ is in γ. $\qquad\square$

5.6.2 Behavior of Transactions

This subsection shows that any sequence in $pictures(\beta, T, R)$ projects to yield a finite behavior of each transaction automaton. Also, for T itself, each sequence in $pictures(\beta, T, R)$ projects to yield $\beta|T$.

LEMMA 5.28 *Let β be a finite simple behavior, T a transaction name, and R a sibling order that is suitable for β and T. Suppose $\gamma \in pictures(\beta, T, R)$. Then $\gamma|T = \beta|T$, and $\gamma|T'$ is a prefix of $\beta|T'$ for all transaction names T'.*

PROOF By the definition of pictures, using Lemma 5.3 and the fact that the directly affects relation orders all events in β with the same transaction. $\qquad\square$

LEMMA 5.29 *Let β be a finite simple behavior, T a transaction name, and R a sibling order that is suitable for β and T. Suppose $\gamma \in pictures(\beta, T, R)$. Then $\gamma|T'$ is a finite behavior of $A_{T'}$ for every non-access transaction name T'.*

PROOF By Lemma 5.28 and Proposition 2.2. $\qquad\square$

5.6.3 Behavior of Serial Objects

Next, the view condition is used to show that any sequence in $pictures(\beta, T, R)$ projects to yield a finite behavior of each serial object automaton. Thus, this subsection begins by relating the definitions of *view* and *pictures*.

LEMMA 5.30 *Let β be a finite simple behavior, T a transaction name, and R a sibling order suitable for β and T. Let $\delta \in$ ordered-visible(β, T, R). Let X be an object name. Then one of the following two possibilities holds:*

1 . *$\delta|X$ is identical to view(β, T, R, X).*

2 . *T is an access to X and $\delta|X$ is the result of inserting a single **CREATE(T)** event somewhere in the sequence view(β, T, R, X).*

PROOF   The two constructions imply that $\delta|X$ and $view(\beta, T, R, X)$ have identical subsequences of **REQUEST_COMMIT** actions. The sequence $view(\beta, T, R, X)$ contains exactly one **CREATE(U)** immediately preceding each **REQUEST_COMMIT** for U. Each such **CREATE(U)** also appears in $\delta|X$, by the preconditions for the simple database and the definition of visibility; moreover, the definition of ordered-visible implies that each such **CREATE(U)** also appears immediately preceding the corresponding **REQUEST_COMMIT** for U. Thus, the only possible difference between $\delta|X$ and $view(\beta, T, R, X)$ is that $\delta|X$ might contain some extra **CREATE(U)** events, without matching **REQUEST_COMMIT** events for U.

Since δ is a reordering of a subsequence of $visible(\beta, T)$, any such unmatched **CREATE(U)** event must have U visible to T in β. Since no **REQUEST_COMMIT** for U appears in $\delta|X$, none appears in $visible(\beta, T)$ and hence none appears in β. Simple database preconditions imply that no **COMMIT**(U) appears in β. Therefore, it must be that $U = T$, and that T is an access to X.   □

LEMMA 5.31 *Let β be a finite simple behavior, T a transaction name such that T is not an orphan in β, and R a sibling order suitable for β and T. Let $\gamma \in$ pictures(β, T, R). Let X be an object name. Then $\gamma|X$ is either a prefix of view(β, T, R, X) or else is a prefix of view(β, T, R, X) followed by a single **CREATE(T)** event.*

PROOF   By definition of $pictures(\beta, T, R)$, γ is obtained as a prefix of a sequence $\delta \in$ $ordered\text{-}visible(\beta, T, R)$. The previous lemma implies that $\delta|X$ and $view(\beta, T, R, X)$ are identical except that an extra **CREATE(T)** event might appear in $\delta|X$, and this can only occur in case T is an access to X.

If $\delta|X$ contains no extra **CREATE** events not present in $view(\beta, T, R, X)$, then it is immediate by the construction of γ as a prefix of δ that $\gamma|X$ is a prefix of $view(\beta, T, R, X)$, as needed. So suppose that $\delta|X$ is the same as $view(\beta, T, R, X)$

except that $\delta|\mathrm{X}$ contains an extra **CREATE**(T) event. Then the definition of pictures implies that $\gamma|\mathrm{X}$ is the prefix of $\delta|\mathrm{X}$ ending with the **CREATE**(T) event. Then $\gamma|\mathrm{X}$ is a prefix of $view(\beta, T, R, \mathrm{X})$ followed by a single **CREATE**(T) event.   □

LEMMA 5.32 *Let β be a simple behavior, T a transaction name, R a sibling order that is suitable for β and T, and X an object name. Suppose that $view(\beta, T, R, \mathrm{X})$ is a finite behavior of $S(\mathrm{X})$. Suppose $\gamma \in pictures(\beta, T, R)$. Then $\gamma|\mathrm{X}$ is a finite behavior of $S(\mathrm{X})$.*

PROOF   By Lemma 5.31 and the fact that inputs to $S(\mathrm{X})$, as with any automaton, are always enabled.   □

5.6.4 Behavior of the Serial Scheduler

This subsection shows that any sequence in $pictures(\beta, T, R)$ is a behavior of the serial scheduler.

The following lemma gives a sufficient condition for a behavior of the simple database to also be a behavior of the serial scheduler. The condition is based on the existence of a sibling order R with appropriate properties.

LEMMA 5.33 *Let β be a finite behavior of the simple database, T a transaction name, and R a sibling order such that the following are true:*

- *R orders all pairs of siblings T' and T'' that are lowtransactions of events in β.*

- *The event ordering in β is consistent with $R_{event}(\beta)$.*

- *β contains no events π such that hightransaction(π) is an orphan in β.*

- *The only live transactions in β are ancestors of T.*

- *For every ancestor T' of T, R orders T' after any sibling of T' that is the lowtransaction of an event in β.*

Then β is a behavior of the serial scheduler.

PROOF   The proof is by induction on prefixes of β, with a trivial basis. Let $\beta'\pi$ be a prefix of β with π a single event, and assume that β' is a behavior of the serial scheduler. If π is an input action of the serial scheduler, then the fact that inputs are always enabled implies that $\beta'\pi$ is a behavior of the serial scheduler. So assume that π is an output action of the serial scheduler. Let s' be the state of the serial scheduler after β'. The proof must show that π is enabled in the serial scheduler automaton in state s'. Let t' be the state of the simple database after β'. It is clear that π is enabled in t'. The proof will use a case analysis, in each case using the precondition of π as an action of the simple database to deduce something about t', and then using Lemmas 5.5 and 3.8 to deduce a similar condition on s'.

1. π is **CREATE**(T'). The proof must show that $T' \in s'.create\_requested - s'.created$, that $T' \notin s'.aborted$, and that $siblings(T') \cap s'.created \subseteq s'.completed$.

Since π is enabled in t', then $T' \in t'.create\_requested - t'.created$. By Lemma 5.5, β' contains **REQUEST_CREATE**(T') and β' does not contain **CREATE**(T'). Thus by 3.8, $T' \in s'.create\_requested - s'.created$.

By assumption, as $T' = hightransaction(\pi)$, T' is not an orphan in β; hence no **ABORT**(T') occurs in β, so by Lemma 3.8, $T' \notin s'.aborted$.

Suppose T'' is a sibling of T' that is in $s'.created$. Then **CREATE**(T'') occurs in β', by Lemma 5.5. Since the order of events in β is consistent with $R_{event}(\beta)$, and by assumption R orders T' and T'', $(T'',T') \in R$. Since T' is ordered after T'' by R and is the *lowtransaction* of an action in β, by assumption T'' is not an ancestor of T. Because of this, two other assumptions imply that T'' is neither live nor an orphan in β. Hence, a **COMMIT**(T'') event occurs in β and (by the consistency of order of occurrence with the $R_{event}(\beta)$ ordering) precedes π. Then by Lemma 3.8, $T'' \in s'.completed$.

2. π is **ABORT**(T'). The proof must show that $T' \in s'.create\_requested - s'.completed$, that $T' \notin s'.created$, and that $siblings(T') \cap s'.created \subseteq s'.completed$.

Since π is enabled in t', by the transition relation for the simple database and by Lemmas 5.5 and 3.8, $T' \in s'.create\_requested - s'.completed$.

By assumption, no **CREATE**(T') event occurs in β; so by Lemma 3.8, $T' \notin s'.created$.

The remainder of this case is identical to the first case above, when π is **CREATE** (T').

3. π is **COMMIT** a **REPORT_COMMIT**, or **REPORT_ABORT** event for T'.

Since π is enabled in t', in each case the transition relation for the simple database and Lemmas 5.5 and 3.8 imply that π is enabled in s'.

Thus, π is enabled in the serial scheduler in state s'. □

LEMMA 5.34 *Let β be a finite simple behavior, T a transaction name such that T is not an orphan in β, and R a sibling order that is suitable for β and T. If $\gamma \in pictures(\beta, T, R)$, then γ is a behavior of the serial scheduler.*

PROOF The proof uses Lemma 5.33, showing first that γ is a behavior of the simple database, and that each of the conditions of the Lemma hold. By Lemma 5.14, $visible(\beta, T)$ is an $SD\text{-}affects(\beta)$-closed subsequence of β, so Lemma 5.13 implies that the sequences in *ordered-visible*(β, T, R) are behaviors of the simple database. As a prefix of such a sequence, it follows that γ is a behavior of the simple database.

The five conditions of the lemma are considered in turn.

1. R orders all pairs of siblings T' and T'' that are *lowtransactions* of events in γ. This follows immediately from the definition of a suitable sibling order, and the fact that any action in γ is an action in *visible*(β, T).

2. The event ordering in γ is consistent with $R_{event}(\gamma)$. This follows from the definition of *ordered-visible*(β, T, R) and the observation that $R_{event}(\gamma)$ is a subrelation of $R_{event}(visible(\beta, T))$.

3. γ contains no events π such that *hightransaction*(π) is an orphan in γ. This follows from the fact that any action π in γ is an action in *visible*(β, T) (and thus *hightransaction*(π) is visible to T in β), the assumption that T is not an orphan in β, and Lemma 5.4.

4. The only live transactions in γ are ancestors of T. By Lemma 5.4, the only live transactions in *visible*(β, T) are ancestors of T. This property remains true in any reordering of *visible*(β, T), and so holds for every sequence in *ordered-visible*(β, T, R). The sequence γ is either empty (and the property holds trivially) or is a prefix of a sequence $\delta \in$ *ordered-visible*(β, T), specifically, the prefix of δ ending with the last event π in δ with *hightransaction*(π) a descendant of T. Let T' be a transaction that is live in γ. We need to show that T' is an ancestor of T. If T' is live in δ, then T' is an ancestor of T, as noted above.

On the other hand, suppose that T' is not live in δ. Since T' is live in the prefix γ, a **CREATE**(T') event precedes π in δ and a **COMMIT**(T') event follows π in δ. If T' is neither an ancestor nor descendant of T, then there are siblings U and U' such that U in *ancestors*(T) − *ancestors*(T') and U' in *ancestors*(T') − *ancestors*(T). Moreover, since *visible*(T, β) contains actions π and **CREATE**(T') whose *lowtransactions* are descendants of T and T' respectively, Lemma 5.22 implies that either (U, U') or (U', U) is in R. But it would follow that the **CREATE**(T') and the **COMMIT**(T') should be ordered either both before or both after π. This is a contradiction with the fact that π occurs between them. Thus, T' is either an ancestor or descendant of T. Since the **COMMIT**(T') is not included in γ, *hightransaction*(**COMMIT**(T')) = *parent*(T') is not a descendant of T, and therefore T' is not a descendant of T. Hence, T' is an ancestor of T.

5. For every ancestor T' of T, R orders T' after any sibling of T' that is the *lowtransaction* of an event in γ. If γ is empty this is trivially true. Otherwise, let T' be an ancestor of T, let T'' be a sibling of T', and suppose γ contains an event ϕ with *lowtransaction* T''. Lemma 5.22 implies that either (T', T'') or

(T'', T') is in R. Since γ ends with an action π that has $lowtransaction(\pi)$ a descendant of T (and thus also a descendant of T'), and γ is ordered according to $R_{event}(visible(\beta, T))$, it follows that $(T'', T') \in R$.   □

5.6.5 Proof of the Main Result

It is straightforward to tie the pieces together to prove Theorem 5.24, the Atomicity Theorem.

PROOF   Let $\gamma \in pictures(\beta, T, R)$. (Lemma 5.26 implies that this set is nonempty.) Lemma 5.29 shows that $\gamma|T'$ is a finite behavior of $A_{T'}$ for all non-access transaction names T'. Lemma 5.32 shows that $\gamma|X$ is a finite behavior of $S(X)$ for all object names X. Lemma 5.34 implies that γ is a finite behavior of the serial scheduler. Proposition 2.5 implies that γ is a finite serial behavior. Lemma 5.28 implies that $\gamma|T = \beta|T$.   □

It is easy to see that the serial behavior γ constructed to show atomicity for T_0 also has the property that $\gamma|T = \beta|T$ for all T visible to T_0 in β. Thus, if the view condition holds for a suitable sibling order for T_0, then there exists a single serial schedule (namely, γ) that looks like β to all the transactions that commit to the top level.

5.7 Discussion

The Atomicity Theorem is used in subsequent chapters to reason about the correctness of a wide variety of algorithms for implementing atomic transactions. In particular, it is used in constructing correctness proofs for several algorithms that use locking (see Chapter 6), for timestamp-based algorithms (see Chapter 7), hybrid methods (see Chapter 8), and optimistic systems (see Chapter 10).

The Atomicity Theorem is somewhat more complicated than the classical Serializability Theorem. The classical theorem is stated in simple combinatorial terms, while the Atomicity Theorem involves a complicated fine-grained treatment of individual actions. Chapter 9 shows how to obtain simpler results than those in this chapter, by making restrictive assumptions about the system structure, as is done in the classical theorem.

5.8 Bibliographic Notes

The notion of visibility defined in this chapter is natural for nested transaction systems. Essentially the same concept has been used informally in other work on nested transactions, including Moss's original work on locking algorithms [91], a number of papers on the Argus system (e.g., [76, 77]), and papers on Avalon [23]. For example, the Argus implementation passes a lock from one transaction to another when the first is "committed up to the least common ancestor" with the second; this is essentially the same as saying that the first is visible to the second.

Simpler notions of visibility have appeared elsewhere in the literature on concurrency control. For example, if $T = T_0$, $visible(\beta, T)$ corresponds to the *committed projection* of β as defined in [12]. For single-level transaction systems, it suffices to consider only the committed projection; for nested transaction systems, it is necessary to consider what may be visible to many different transactions.

Sibling orders are fundamental to studying nested transactions. Relations similar to R_{trans} are defined by Beeri *et al.* [11], by Hadzilacos and Hadzilacos [43], and by Lynch [79].

Weihl used a result that is similar to but much simpler than the Atomicity Theorem, to prove the correctness of a variety of concurrency control methods [117, 113]. His result says that an execution is serializable in a given order if its projection on each object is serializable locally in that order. However, Weihl's result is proved based on a few simple axioms about the behavior of systems, and does not rest on a precise operational model. In addition, the setting considered by Weihl is much simpler than that considered in this book, allowing only single-level transactions with no internal concurrency.

The theory presented in this chapter is taken from [33]. A preliminary version appeared in [81].

5.9 Exercises

1. Prove Lemma 5.1, about the properties of *visibility*.

2. Let β be a sequence of actions, and let $\pi = \textbf{COMMIT}(U)$, where $parent(U)$ is not visible to T in β. Show that $visible(\beta\pi, T)$ is equal to $visible(\beta, T)$.

3. Show that the serial system implements the simple system (constructed using the same transaction automata). This means that any serial behavior is a simple behavior. (Of course, there are in general simple behaviors that are not serial behaviors.)

4. Let β be a serial behavior, and let π be an event in β. Show that there exists a transaction T such that $hightransaction(\pi)$ is visible to T in β, and T is live in β. Give an example to show that this does not hold for simple behaviors in general.

5. Let β be a simple behavior and let T be a transaction name. Show that $visible(\beta, T)$ is a simple behavior. If β is a serial behavior, show that $visible(\beta, T)$ is a serial behavior.

6. Calculate $visible(\beta, T_4)$, where β is the sequence given in Example 5.2.1. Show directly from the transition relations that $visible(\beta, T_4)$ is a simple behavior. Find a reordering of $visible(\beta, T_4)$ that is a serial behavior.

7. Prove the following result.

LEMMA 5.35 *Let β be a finite simple behavior, T a transaction name, and R a sibling order that is suitable for β and T. Let X be an object name. If γ and γ' are both in $pictures(\beta, T, R)$, then $\gamma|X = \gamma'|X$.*

8. Prove the following well-formedness result.

LEMMA 5.36 *Let β be a finite simple behavior, T a transaction name, and R a sibling order that is suitable for β and T. Let $\gamma \in pictures(\beta, T, R)$. Then $\gamma|X$ is serial object well-formed for X.*

9. Construct an example to show that the following lemma is NOT true.

LEMMA 5.37 *Let β be a finite simple behavior, T a transaction name, and R a sibling order that is suitable for β and T. Let $\gamma \in ordered\text{-}visible(\beta, T, R)$. Then $\gamma|X$ is serial object well-formed for X.*

This and the previous exercise explain why the definition of *pictures* requires that γ be chosen to be a certain prefix of δ, rather than all of δ, and why this "chopping" is needed in the proof of the Atomicity Theorem.

10. Show that the serial behavior γ produced in the proof of the Atomicity Theorem has the property that $\gamma|T' = \beta|T'$ for all transaction names T' that are visible to T in β.

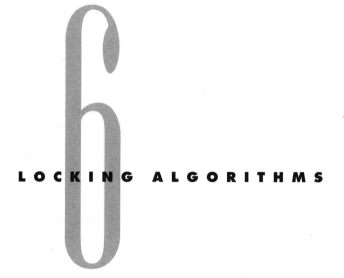

LOCKING ALGORITHMS

6.1 Introduction

The Atomicity Theorem of Chapter 5 gives a general sufficient condition for proving the correctness of transaction-processing algorithms. This chapter specializes these ideas to the particular case of locking algorithms. Typical locking algorithms serialize transactions according to a particular sibling order, the order in which transactions complete. *Dynamic atomicity* is a property of objects that captures this aspect of locking algorithms. The definition of dynamic atomicity is phrased in terms of a system organization consisting of transaction automata, a *generic object* automaton for each object name, which handles the concurrency control and recovery for that object, and a single *generic controller* automaton that handles communication among the other components. The Dynamic Atomicity Theorem is presented, which shows that a *generic system* in which all generic objects are dynamic atomic, is itself atomic.

Proving that an algorithm is dynamic atomic gives more than just the correctness of a single system. In particular, one can derive as immediate corollaries the correctness of any system in which each object is dynamic atomic. This affords useful modularity. For example, one can initially implement each object in a system using a simple concurrency control and recovery algorithm that provides relatively little concurrency. If some objects are *hot spots* or *concurrency bottlenecks*, these objects can be reimplemented using sophisticated algorithms that provide more concurrency. In implementing a particular object, however, one does not need to be concerned with the other objects in the system; instead, one simply needs to show that the particular object ensures dynamic atomicity.

Local Dynamic Atomicity: The definition of dynamic atomicity for an object is phrased in terms of the behaviors of all possible systems in which the object could be placed. To simplify subsequent proofs, another local condition is defined on objects, called *local dynamic atomicity*, which is stated solely in terms of the behavior of an individual object and suffices to ensure dynamic atomicity.

This chapter presents a number of algorithms that provide local dynamic atomicity; they can therefore be combined freely in a generic system.[1] Each algorithm is given by describing a construction that takes an arbitrary serial object automaton and produces a generic object automaton. The generic object automaton models the activity of the algorithm in an abstract way. For example, state components include functions whose values can be long lists of operations, and action preconditions are given declaratively, testing for existence or non-existence of members of certain sets. When designing an implementation for an object, a system builder will generally be more concrete; for example, the state might include a table of locks held, and a precondition might be simply that a variable has a particular value. The philosophy of this chapter is that you should see the automaton that describes this concrete construction as an implementation (in the technical sense of Section 2.7.1) of the automaton that gives the abstract algorithm, and prove this relationship by (for example) showing a possibilities mapping between the two automata.

Three Algorithms: The third section of this chapter presents a general commutativity-based locking algorithm and its correctness proof. This algorithm specifies a particular generic object automaton, the locking object $L(X)$, in terms of the serial object automaton $S(X)$, and the forward commutativity of its operations. It is shown that each locking object $L(X)$ is locally dynamic atomic, hence dynamic atomic.

The fourth section presents Moss's algorithm for read/update locking and its correctness proof. This algorithm is provided as the system default in the Argus system

---

[1] You should note that these algorithms do not in any way exhaust the possible ways to provide local dynamic atomicity. They are offered as important examples that include as special cases a number of algorithms that have been proposed by researchers.

[75]. Once again, the algorithm is given as a particular generic object automaton, the *Moss object* $M(X)$, in terms of a classification of the accesses to the serial object $S(X)$ as either *reads* or *updates*. In this case we do not verify the algorithm directly from the definition of local dynamic atomicity; instead, it is shown that each Moss object $M(X)$ implements the corresponding locking object $L(X)$, and hence is dynamic atomic.

The fifth section develops a quite different concurrency control algorithm, based on an *undo log* recovery mechanism. For this, backward commutativity is the important condition for concurrent accesses. This algorithm also provides dynamic atomicity.

By the Dynamic Atomicity Theorem,, a generic system is atomic for T_0 provided each object uses one of the algorithms described here.

6.2   Dynamic   Atomicity

This section tailors the concepts of the preceding chapter to typical locking algorithms. In such algorithms, a transaction obtains locks on data objects as it runs, releasing them when it commits. Concurrent transactions are prevented from obtaining conflicting locks until they are released. Transactions with conflicting accesses to objects are thus serialized in the order in which they obtain conflicting locks, which is indicated by the order in which they commit (since locks are held until they commit). Hence, the sibling order appropriate for locking algorithms is derived from the order in which completion actions occur. This order is determined dynamically, at the end of each transaction's execution, so we use the term *dynamic* atomicity.

6.2.1   Completion   Order

The key property of typical locking algorithms is that they serialize transactions according to their completion (commit or abort) order. To apply the Atomicity Theorem, we need to define a sibling order that formalizes this fact. If β is a sequence of actions, then define *completion-order*(β) to be the binary relation on transaction names containing (T, T') if and only if T and T' are siblings and one of the following holds:

1. There are completion events for both T and T' in β, and a completion event for T precedes a completion event for T'.

2. There is a completion event for T in β, but there is no completion event for T' in β.

The first condition in this definition is a natural expression of the idea of one transaction completing before another. The second condition is based on the idea that if one transaction has completed, and a second has not, then once the second does complete, its completion will be later than the first transaction's completion. It is needed so that the resulting order relates enough transactions to be *suitable*.

The following is an easy consequence of the definition.

LEMMA 6.1 *If β is a simple behavior, then completion-order(β) is a sibling order.*

You should notice two (possibly unexpected) aspects of the definition. First, *completion-order(β)* may relate two transaction names even in cases where β contains no event at all of the second transaction. Second, the extension to descendants,[2] *completion-order$(\beta)_{trans}$*, relates two transactions according to the order in which their sibling ancestors completed; this may not be the same as the order in which the completion events occur for the transactions themselves.

EXAMPLE 6.2.1   Completion Order for the Banking System

Consider the simple behavior β given in Example 5.2.1. Then *completion-order(β)* contains the following pairs of transactions: (T_1, T_3), (T_3, T_2), (T_2, T_5), (T_5, T_4), (T_1, T_2), (T_1, T_5), (T_1, T_4), (T_3, T_5), (T_3, T_4), $(T_{3.1}, T_{3.3})$, $(T_{3.3}, T_{3.1003})$, $(T_{3.j}, T_{3.k})$ for $j = 1, 3, 1003$ and $k = 2, 4,$ 5,..., 1002, 1004, 1005, ..., $(T_{3.1}, T_{3.1003})$, and $(T_{3.1003.1}, T_{3.1003.2})$.

The next few lemmas show that the completion order is suitable, which allows application of the Atomicity Theorem. The first shows that events of one transaction T can affect events of an unrelated transaction T' only if the events are related by the extension of the completion order to events. We use *affect* in the technical sense of the *affects(β)* relation defined in Section 5.4.2. To prove this lemma, we show that the chain in the directly affects relation must involve the completion event for T.

LEMMA 6.2 *Let β be a simple behavior and let $R = $ completion-order(β). Let π and π' be distinct events in β with lowtransactions T and T' respectively. If T is neither an ancestor nor a descendant of T', and $(\pi, \pi') \in $ affects(β), then $(\pi, \pi') \in R_{event}(\beta)$.*

PROOF   Since T is neither an ancestor nor a descendant of T', $lca(T, T')$ is neither T nor T'. Therefore, there are siblings U and U' (which are children of $lca(T, T')$) such that T is a descendant of U and T' is a descendant of U'. Since π affects π' in β, by Lemmas 5.17 and 5.18, there must be events ϕ and ϕ' in β such that ϕ is a **REPORT** event for U; ϕ' is **REQUEST_CREATE**(U'); and (π, ϕ), (ϕ, ϕ'), and (ϕ', π') are all in *affects(β)*. Furthermore, the events π, ϕ, ϕ', and π' occur in β in the indicated order.

---

[2]This extension is defined in Section 5.4.3.

The simple database preconditions and transaction well-formedness imply that any completion event for U' in β must occur after the unique **REQUEST_CREATE**(U') event. Similarly, by Lemma 5.6, ϕ is preceded in β by a unique completion event for U. Thus, β contains a completion event for U, which precedes ϕ, which precedes ϕ', which in turn precedes any completion event for U'. Thus, $(U, U') \in R = $ *completion-order*(β), and therefore $(\pi, \pi') \in R_{event}(\beta)$. $\qquad\qquad\square$

The two partial orders defined on the events of β are consistent:

LEMMA 6.3 *Let β be a simple behavior and let $R = $ completion-order(β). Then $R_{event}(\beta)$ and affects(β) are consistent partial orders on the events of β.*

PROOF   Immediate by Lemmas 6.2 and 5.23. $\qquad\qquad\square$

LEMMA 6.4 *Let β be a simple behavior and T a transaction name. If T' and T'' are siblings that are lowtransactions of actions in visible(β, T), then either (T', T'') or $(T'', T') \in $ completion-order(β).*

PROOF   Since T' and T'' are distinct siblings, T is not a descendant of both T' and T''. Without loss of generality, assume that T is not a descendant of T'. Note that therefore the least common ancestor of T and T' must be an ancestor of *parent*(T'). There is an event π in *visible*(β, T) such that *lowtransaction*$(\pi) = T'$. Thus, either π is a completion event for T' or *hightransaction*(π) must be T'. In the case where *hightransaction*$(\pi) = T'$, it follows that T' is visible to T in β, and thus (since T' is not an ancestor of T), that β contains a **COMMIT**(T') event. Thus, in either case β contains a completion event for T', and so *completion-order*(β) orders T' and T''. $\qquad\square$

Now one can conclude that the completion order is suitable.

LEMMA 6.5 *Let β be a simple behavior and T a transaction name. Then completion-order(β) is suitable for β and T.*

PROOF   Let $R = $ *completion-order*(β). By Lemma 6.4, R orders all pairs of siblings T' and T'' that are *lowtransactions* of actions in *visible*(β, T). By Lemma 6.3, $R_{event}(\beta)$ and *affects*(β) are consistent partial orders on the events of β. Since *visible*(β, T) is a subsequence of β, these relations are also consistent partial orders on the events of *visible*(β, T). $\qquad\qquad\square$

We can now apply the Atomicity Theorem to the situation where the sibling order used is the completion order.

PROPOSITION 6.6 *Let β be a finite simple behavior, T a transaction name such that T is not an orphan in β, and let $R = $ completion-order(β). Suppose that for each object name X, view(β, T, R, X) is a behavior of $S(X)$. Then β is atomic for T.*

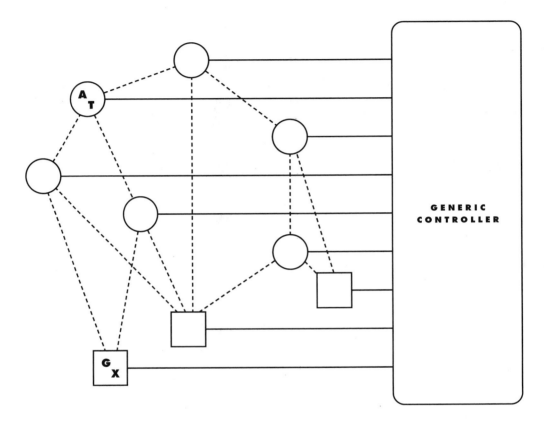

Figure 6.1: Generic System Structure

PROOF   Lemma 6.5 implies that R is suitable for β and T. The result is immediate from Corollary 5.25.   □

6.2.2 Generic Systems

This subsection defines the system decomposition appropriate for describing locking algorithms. Such algorithms are formulated as instances of *generic systems*, which are composed of transaction automata, *generic object automata* and a *generic controller*. The general structure of the system is illustrated in Figure 6.1. Notice that it is very much like the structure shown in Figure 3.2 for serial system,, except that generic object automata replace serial object automata, and the generic controller replaces the serial scheduler.

The object signature for a generic object contains more actions than that for serial objects. Unlike the serial object for X, the corresponding generic object is responsible for carrying out the concurrency control and recovery algorithms for X, for example, by maintaining lock tables. In order to do this, the automaton requires information about the completion of some of the transactions, in particular, those that have accessed that object. Thus, a generic object automaton has in its signature special **INFORM- _COMMIT** and **INFORM_ABORT** input actions to inform it about the completion of transactions. These **INFORM** actions are not restricted to mention only accesses to X, since the automaton will also need information about the completion of ancestors of the accesses.

The generic controller is similar to the serial scheduler, in that it passes messages between pairs of transaction automata, and between transaction and generic object automata. Like the simple database, and unlike the serial scheduler, it allows concurrent activity among siblings and aborts of created transactions. It also transmits information about completion of transactions to the generic objects.

Generic Object Automata

A **generic object** $G(X)$ for an object name X of a given system type is an automaton with the following external action signature.

Input:
    CREATE(T), for T an access to X
    INFORM_COMMIT_AT(X)**OF**(T), for $T \neq T_0$
    INFORM_ABORT_AT(X)**OF**(T), for $T \neq T_0$
Output:
    REQUEST_COMMIT(T, v), for T an access to X and v a value for T

In addition, $G(X)$ may have an arbitrary set of internal actions.

The actions **CREATE**(T) and **REQUEST_COMMIT**(T, v) correspond to invocations of accesses and responses to accesses, just as for a serial object $S(X)$. In addition, a generic object has input actions that correspond to the receipt of information about the commit or abort of transactions.[3]

As for serial objects, we collect (as *generic object well-formedness*) a number of properties that one would expect to hold for the sequence of actions of a generic object in a sensible environment. By considering only behaviors that satisfy these properties, we simplify the reasoning about individual generic objects.

---

[3]In systems like Argus [75], an object may send *queries* about the outcome of a transaction if information does not arrive within a reasonable time. We abstract away from such details, and only model the eventual arrival of the information.

A generic object automaton $G(X)$ is required to preserve *generic object well-formedness*, defined as follows. A sequence β of actions π in the external signature of $G(X)$ is said to be **generic object well-formed** for X provided that the following conditions hold.

1. There is at most one **CREATE**(T) event in β for any access T.

2. There is at most one **REQUEST_COMMIT** event in β for any access T.

3. If there is a **REQUEST_COMMIT** event for an access T in β, then there is a preceding **CREATE**(T) event in β.

4. There is no transaction T for which both an **INFORM_COMMIT_AT**(X)**OF**(T) event and an **INFORM_ABORT_AT**(X)**OF**(T) event occur in β.

5. If an **INFORM_COMMIT_AT**(X)**OF**(T) event occurs in β and T is an access to X, then there is a preceding **REQUEST_COMMIT** event for T.

Generic object well-formedness is significantly less restrictive than serial object well-formedness. Serial object well-formedness requires the **CREATE** and **REQUEST_COMMIT** actions to alternate, so that only one access is active at a time. Generic object well-formedness allows multiple simultaneously active accesses. The only constraints are that **CREATE**'s and **REQUEST_COMMIT**'s not be repeated, that a **REQUEST_COMMIT** be generated only if the access has already been invoked by a **CREATE**, that conflicting information about the completion of transactions not be received by the object, and that no access commit until after it has run. Note that we do not prevent repeated information about the completion of transactions, and do not constrain the order of arrival of that information except in the case of **INFORM_COMMIT** for an access to X.

As with previous well-formedness properties, there is an alternative form of the definition.

LEMMA 6.7 *A sequence β of actions in the external signature of a generic object for object name X is generic object well-formed for X exactly if for every finite prefix $\gamma\pi$ of β, where π is a single action, the following conditions hold.*

1. *If π is CREATE(T), then*

　　(a) *there is no CREATE event for T in γ.*

2. *If π is INFORM_COMMIT_AT(X)OF(T), then*

　　(a) *if T is an access to X, then there is a REQUEST_COMMIT for T in γ, and*

　　(b) *there is no INFORM_ABORT_AT(X)OF(T) in γ.*

3 . *If π is* ***INFORM_ABORT_AT(X)OF(T)****, then*

    (a) *there is no* ***INFORM_COMMIT_AT(X)OF(T)*** *in γ.*

4 . *If π is* ***REQUEST_COMMIT****(T, v), then*

    (a) *there is a* ***CREATE(T)*** *in γ, and*

    (b) *there is no* ***REQUEST_COMMIT*** *for T in γ.*

Generic Controller

There is a single generic controller for each system type. It passes requests for the creation of subtransactions to the appropriate recipient, makes decisions about the commit or abort of transactions, passes reports about the completion of children back to their parents, and informs objects of the fate of transactions. Unlike the serial scheduler, it does not prevent sibling transactions from being live simultaneously, nor does it prevent the same transaction from being both created and aborted. Rather, it leaves the task of coping with concurrency and recovery to the generic objects. Indeed, the generic controller is almost identical to the simple database, which guarantees only simple syntactic conditions. The difference is that **REQUEST_COMMIT** actions for access transactions are *outputs* of the simple database, and are *inputs* to the generic controller. Otherwise, the actions and states of the two automata are identical. In the simple database, **REQUEST_COMMIT** actions for access transaction T is enabled whenever a corresponding **CREATE**(T) and no other **REQUEST_COMMIT** for T has occurred. In generic systems, these **REQUEST_COMMIT** actions are under the control of the generic objects—which enforce concurrency control and recovery conditions by imposing conditions on when these actions can occur.

The generic controller should not be confused with the *scheduler* component of some classical database architectures. In the formal system decomposition in this book, the classical scheduler has been decomposed into the controller and the generic objects. Again, the important scheduling events are controlled by the objects, and the generic controller acts as a communication system, merely informing transaction and object automata of the occurrence of relevant events.

The generic controller is very nondeterministic. It may delay passing requests or reports or making decisions for arbitrary lengths of time, and may decide at any time to abort a transaction whose creation has been requested (but that has not yet completed). Each specific implementation of a system will make particular choices from among the many nondeterministic possibilities. For instance, Moss [91] devotes considerable effort to describing a particular distributed implementation of the controller that copes with node and communication failures yet still commits a subtransaction whenever possible. Our results apply *a fortiori* to all implementations of the generic controller obtained by restricting its nondeterminism. (A simple example implementation is the subject of Exercise 12.)

The generic controller has the following action signature.

Input:
    REQUEST_CREATE(T), $T \neq T_0$
    REQUEST_COMMIT(T, v), v a return value for T
Output:
    CREATE(T)
    COMMIT(T), $T \neq T_0$
    ABORT(T), $T \neq T_0$
    REPORT_COMMIT(T,v), $T \neq T_0$, v a return value for T
    REPORT_ABORT(T), $T \neq T_0$
    INFORM_COMMIT_AT(X)**OF**(T), $T \neq T_0$
    INFORM_ABORT_AT(X)**OF**(T), $T \neq T_0$

All the actions except the **INFORM** actions play the same roles as in the simple database. The **INFORM_COMMIT** and **INFORM_ABORT** actions pass information about the fate of transactions to the generic objects.

Like the serial scheduler of Chapter 3 and the simple database of Chapter 5, each state s of the generic controller consists of six sets: $s.create\_requested$, $s.created$, $s.commit\_requested$, $s.committed$, $s.aborted$, and $s.reported$. The set $s.commit\_requested$ is a set of operations, and the others are sets of transactions. All are empty in the start state except for $create\_requested$, which is $\{T_0\}$. Define $s.completed = s.committed \cup s.aborted$.

As discussed above, with the exception of **REQUEST_COMMIT** actions for access transactions, the transition relation is identical to that of the simple database. The transition relation is given in Figure 6.2.

Note that **INFORM** events may occur any number of times, once they are enabled. This simplifies the description of some of the algorithms implemented in the generic objects, which otherwise would have to store information about the fates of completed transactions.

Basic Properties of the Generic Controller

The following simple lemmas follow the pattern of Lemmas 5.5 and 5.6 for the simple database. The first relates a schedule of the generic controller to the resulting states, and gives simple invariants. The second gives some simple properties of schedules of the generic controller. Notice that we do not have results analogous to parts 9 and 10 of Lemma 5.6. Instead, we have extra facts about the **INFORM_COMMIT** and **INFORM_ABORT** actions.

LEMMA 6.8 *If β is a finite schedule of the generic controller that can lead to state s, then the following conditions are true.*

REQUEST_CREATE(T)
 Effect:
  $s.create\_requested$
   $= s'.create\_requested \cup \{T\}$

REQUEST_COMMIT(T, v)
 Effect:
  $s.commit\_requested$
   $= s'.commit\_requested \cup \{(T, v)\}$

CREATE(T)
 Precondition:
  $T \in s'.create\_requested - s'.created$
 Effect:
  $s.created = s'.created \cup \{T\}$

COMMIT(T)
 Precondition:
  $(T, v) \in s'.commit\_requested$
  $T \notin s'.completed$
 Effect:
  $s.committed = s'.committed \cup \{T\}$

ABORT(T)
 Precondition:
  $T \in s'.create\_requested - s'.completed$
 Effect:
  $s.aborted = s'.aborted \cup \{T\}$

REPORT_COMMIT(T, v)
 Precondition:
  $T \in s'.committed$
  $(T, v) \in s'.commit\_requested$
  $T \notin s'.reported$
 Effect:
  $s.reported = s'.reported \cup \{T\}$

REPORT_ABORT(T)
 Precondition:
  $T \in s'.aborted$
  $T \notin s'.reported$
 Effect:
  $s.reported = s'.reported \cup \{T\}$

INFORM_COMMIT_AT(X)**OF**(T)
 Precondition:
  $T \in s'.committed$

INFORM_ABORT_AT(X)**OF**(T)
 Precondition:
  $T \in s'.aborted$

Figure 6.2: Transition Relation for the Generic Controller

1. T is in $s.create\_requested$ if and only if either $T = T_0$ or β contains a **REQUEST_CREATE**(T) event.

2. T is in $s.created$ if and only if β contains a **CREATE(T)** event.

3. (T, v) is in $s.commit\_requested$ if and only if β contains a **REQUEST_COMMIT**(T, v) event.

4. T is in $s.committed$ if and only if β contains a **COMMIT(T)** event.

5. T is in $s.aborted$ if and only if β contains an **ABORT(T)** event.

6. T is in $s.reported$ if and only if β contains a report event for T.

7. $s.committed \cap s.aborted = \emptyset$.

8. $s.reported \subseteq s.committed \cup s.aborted.$

LEMMA 6.9 *Let β be a schedule of the generic controller. Then all of the following hold:*

1. *If a* ***CREATE(T)*** *event appears in β for $T \neq T_0$, then a* ***REQUEST_CREATE**(T)* *event precedes it in β.*

2. *At most one* ***CREATE(T)*** *event appears in β for each transaction T.*

3. *If a* ***COMMIT(T)*** *event appears in β, then a* ***REQUEST_COMMIT**(T, v)* *event precedes it in β for some return value v.*

4. *If an* ***ABORT(T)*** *event appears in β, then a* ***REQUEST_CREATE**(T)* *event precedes it in β.*

5. *At most one completion event appears in β for each transaction.*

6. *At most one report event appears in β for each transaction.*

7. *If a* ***REPORT_COMMIT**(T,v)* *event appears in β, then a* ***COMMIT(T)*** *event and a* ***REQUEST_COMMIT**(T, v)* *event precede it in β.*

8. *If a* ***REPORT_ABORT(T)*** *event appears in β, then an* ***ABORT(T)*** *event precedes it in β.*

9. *If an* ***INFORM_COMMIT_AT**(X)**OF(T)* *event appears in β, then a* ***COMMIT(T)*** *event and a* ***REQUEST_COMMIT*** *event for T precede it in β.*

10. *If an* ***INFORM_ABORT_AT**(X)**OF(T)* *event appears in β, then an* ***ABORT(T)*** *event precedes it in β.*

Generic Systems

A **generic system** of a given system type is the composition of a compatible set of automata indexed by the union of the set of non-access transaction names, the set of object names, and the singleton set $\{GC\}$ (for *generic controller*). Associated with each non-access transaction name T is a transaction automaton A_T for T, the same automaton as in the serial system. Associated with each object name X is a generic object automaton $G(X)$ for X. Finally, associated with the name GC is the generic controller automaton for the system type.

The external actions of a generic system are called **generic actions**, and the executions, schedules, and behaviors of a generic system are called **generic executions**, **generic schedules**, and **generic behaviors**, respectively.

The following proposition says that generic behaviors have the appropriate well-formedness properties. Its proof is analogous to that of Lemma 3.11, the similar result for serial behaviors.

PROPOSITION 6.10 *If β is a generic behavior, then the following conditions hold.*

1. *For every transaction name T, $\beta|T$ is transaction well-formed for T.*

2. *For every object name X, $\beta|G(X)$ is generic object well-formed for X.*

The following result says that if the **INFORM** events are removed from any generic behavior, the result is a simple behavior. (This is in part the justification for our remarks, in Section 5.3.1, that the simple database captures common features of sophisticated systems.)

PROPOSITION 6.11 *If β is a generic behavior then $serial(\beta)$ is a simple behavior and $serial(\beta)|T = \beta|T$ for all transaction names T.*

PROOF By a straightforward induction on the length of prefixes of β.[4]   □

The following variant of Corollary 5.25 to the Atomicity Theorem applies to the special case where R is the completion order and the system is a generic system.

PROPOSITION 6.12 *Let β be a finite generic behavior and T a transaction name that is not an orphan in β, and let $R = completion\text{-}order(\beta)$. Suppose that for each object name X, $view(serial(\beta), T, R, X)$ is a behavior of $S(X)$. Then β is atomic for T.*

PROOF Immediate from Proposition 6.6, using Proposition 6.11 and the observation that $completion\text{-}order(\beta) = completion\text{-}order(serial(\beta))$.   □

6.2.3 Dynamic Atomicity

Now *dynamic atomicity* (for a generic object automaton) is defined; roughly speaking, it says that the object satisfies the condition on the *view* of nonorphan transactions given in the Atomicity Theorem, using the completion order as the sibling order R. This restatement of the view condition as a property of a generic object is convenient for decomposing correctness proofs for locking algorithms: the Atomicity Theorem implies that if all the generic objects in a generic system are dynamic atomic, then

---

[4]An alternative proof can be formulated in terms of the notion of implementation, using a possibilities mapping.

the system guarantees atomicity for all nonorphan transaction names. All that remains is to show that the generic objects that model the locking algorithms of interest are dynamic atomic.

Let $G(X)$ be a generic object automaton for object name X. Say that $G(X)$ is **dynamic atomicity** for a given system type if for all generic systems $\mathcal{S}$ of the given type in which $G(X)$ is associated with X, the following is true. Let β be a finite behavior of $\mathcal{S}$, $R = completion\text{-}order(\beta)$, and T a transaction name that is not an orphan in β. Then $view(serial(\beta), T, R, X)$ is a behavior of $S(X)$.

THEOREM 6.13 *(Dynamic Atomicity Theorem) Let $\mathcal{S}$ be a generic system in which all generic objects are dynamic atomic. Let β be a finite behavior of $\mathcal{S}$. Then β is atomic for every nonorphan transaction name.*

PROOF   Immediate from Proposition 6.12 and the definition of dynamic atomicity.   □

As discussed earlier, this proof structure can be used to yield much stronger results than just the correctness of the locking algorithms in this book. As long as each object is dynamic atomic, the whole system will guarantee that any finite behavior is atomic for all nonorphan transaction names. Thus, one is free to use an arbitrary implementation for each object, independent of the choice of implementation for each other object, as long as dynamic atomicity is satisfied. For example, a simple algorithm such as Moss's can be used for most objects, while a more sophisticated algorithm permitting extra concurrency by using type-specific information can be used for objects that are very frequently accessed (these are called *hot spots*).

6.2.4   Local Dynamic Atomicity

The previous subsection showed that to prove that a generic system guarantees atomicity for nonorphan transactions, it is enough to check that each generic object automaton is dynamic atomic. This subsection defines another property of generic object automata called *local dynamic atomicity*, which is a convenient sufficient condition for showing dynamic atomicity. For each generic object automaton G, dynamic atomicity is a local condition in that it only depends on G. However, the form in which the condition is stated may be difficult to check directly: one must be able to verify a condition involving $view(serial(\beta), T, completion\text{-}order(\beta), X)$ for all finite behaviors β of all generic systems containing G. Local dynamic atomicity is defined more directly in terms of the behaviors of G, without any consideration of other automata.

First some terms are introduced to describe information about the status of transactions that is deducible from the behavior of a particular generic object. Let $G(X)$ be a generic object automaton for X, β a sequence of external actions of $G(X)$, and T

and T' transaction names. Then T is **locally visible at** X to T' in β if β contains an **INFORM_COMMIT_AT**(X)**OF**(U) event for every U in $ancestors(T) - ancestors(T')$. (Thus, local visibility is defined just like visibility, except in referring to **INFORM-_COMMIT** actions instead of **COMMIT** actions.) Also, T is a **local orphan at** X in β if an **INFORM_ABORT_AT**(X)**OF**(U) event occurs in β for some ancestor U of T.

These definitions are safe, in the sense (made precise in Lemma 6.16) that the global property is implied by the local one. However, it is not the case that everything about the global situation is captured in the local definition. For example, it is easy to find a generic behavior β and a transaction T where T is an orphan in β and *not* a local orphan in $\beta|G(X)$: one simply considers a behavior in which there is only one **ABORT** for an ancestor of T, and that is the last action of the behavior (recall that **INFORM_ABORT_AT**(X)**OF**(U) must not appear unless preceded by **ABORT**(U); since the last step in the behavior is the **ABORT**, there can be no **INFORM_ABORT**). In this example, the local information does not enable one to *know* that T is an orphan; this is shown by the fact that there are other generic behaviors with the same projection on $G(X)$ (that is, the same local information) in which T is not an orphan. For example, the prefix of β excluding the last action is such a generic behavior.

While some facts about the global behavior cannot be inferred from local information, these definitions do not capture all the global properties that *can* be inferred locally. That is, there may be some conclusions that are implied by the local information, but are deduced from the behavior of $G(X)$ in more complex ways than those used in the definitions above.[5] For example, Exercise 1 asks you to show that there may be a transaction that is not a local orphan in β by our definition, but is an orphan in every behavior of a generic system with projection to $G(X)$ equal to β.

The following are obvious facts about local visibility and local orphans.

LEMMA 6.14 *Let $G(X)$ be a generic object automaton for X. Let β be a sequence of external actions of $G(X)$, and let T, T', and T'' be transaction names. If T is locally visible at X to T' in β, and T' is locally visible at X to T'' in β, then T is locally visible at X to T'' in β.*

LEMMA 6.15 *Let $G(X)$ be a generic object automaton for X. Let β be a generic object well-formed sequence of external actions of $G(X)$. If T' is a local orphan in β and T' is locally visible to T in β, then T is a local orphan in β.*

---

[5] These additional deductions could have been included in defining local properties; if this were done one would have a more powerful proof technique, which could be used to show that more algorithms are dynamic atomic. The simple definitions used here are adequate for the algorithms we consider.

The names introduced above are justified by the relationships between the local properties defined above and the corresponding global properties:

LEMMA 6.16 *Let β be a behavior of a generic system in which generic object automaton $G(X)$ is associated with X. If T is locally visible at X to T' in $\beta|G(X)$ then T is visible to T' in β. Similarly, if T is a local orphan at X in $\beta|G(X)$ then T is an orphan in β.*

PROOF   These are immediate consequences of the generic controller preconditions, which imply that any **INFORM_COMMIT_AT**(X)**OF**(T) event in β must be preceded by a **COMMIT**(T) event and that any **INFORM_ABORT_AT**(X)**OF**(T) is preceded by **ABORT**(T).   □

Next, a relation on accesses to X is defined to describe some information about the completion order that is deducible from the behavior of $G(X)$. Given a sequence β of external actions of $G(X)$, define a binary relation *local-completion-order*(β) on accesses to X. Namely, $(U, U') \in$ *local-completion-order*(β) if and only if $U \neq U'$, β contains **REQUEST_COMMIT** events for both U and U', and U is locally visible at X to U' in β', where β' is the longest prefix of β not containing the given **REQUEST_COMMIT** event for U'. (Note that the local completion order is a binary relation on accesses to X, in contrast to the completion order, which relates sibling transactions.)

The intuition underlying this definition is that when (U, U') is in *local-completion-order*(β), then in any generic behavior γ such that $\gamma|G(X) = \beta$, the ancestors of U and U' that are siblings, say T and T' respectively, complete in this order (i.e., T before T'). However, this is not precisely correct (orphan transactions violate this intuition), and the exact statement is given by Lemma 6.18 below. The justification for the lemma is that when the **REQUEST_COMMIT** occurs for U', U is locally visible to U', so all the ancestors of U up to and including T have committed before this point in the behavior. On the other hand, U' cannot commit until after its **REQUEST_COMMIT**, and similarly each ancestor of U' including T' cannot commit until after its children have completed. Thus, unless one of these transactions aborts, T' cannot commit before the **REQUEST_COMMIT** for U'.

LEMMA 6.17 *If β is a generic object well-formed sequence of external actions of a generic object automaton for X, then local-completion-order(β) is a partial order on accesses to X.*

PROOF   The proof must show that *local-completion-order*(β) is irreflexive, antisymmetric and transitive. Irreflexivity follows immediately from the definition.

Suppose that (T, T') and (T', T) are both in *local-completion-order*(β). Then β contains a **REQUEST_COMMIT** event for each of T and T', and generic object well-formedness implies that there is only one of each. Since $(T, T') \in$ *local-completion-*

$order(\beta)$, T is locally visible at X to T' in the longest prefix β' of β not containing the **REQUEST_COMMIT** for T'. Therefore, an **INFORM_COMMIT** for T occurs in β', and generic object well-formedness implies that the **REQUEST_COMMIT** for T precedes the **REQUEST_COMMIT** for T' in β. But the same reasoning implies that the **REQUEST_COMMIT** for T' precedes the **REQUEST_COMMIT** for T in β, a contradiction. Therefore, $local\text{-}completion\text{-}order(\beta)$ is antisymmetric.

Now suppose (T, T') and (T', T'') are both in $local\text{-}completion\text{-}order(\beta)$. Let β' and β'' be the longest prefixes of β not containing a **REQUEST_COMMIT** for T' and not containing a **REQUEST_COMMIT** for T'', respectively. As in the argument above, the **REQUEST_COMMIT** for T' must precede the **REQUEST_COMMIT** for T'' in β, so β' is a prefix of β''. Since T is locally visible at X to T' in β', T is locally visible at X to T' in β'', and since T' is locally visible at X to T'' in β'', Lemma 6.14 implies that T is locally visible at X to T'' in β''. Thus, $(T, T'') \in local\text{-}completion\text{-}order(\beta)$. □

The relationship between the local completion order and the true completion order in a generic system is as follows.

LEMMA 6.18 *Let β be a behavior of a generic system in which generic object automaton $G(X)$ is associated with X, and let $R = completion\text{-}order(\beta)$. Let T and T' be accesses to X. If $(T, T') \in local\text{-}completion\text{-}order(\beta|G(X))$, and T' is not an orphan in β, then $(T, T') \in R_{trans}$.*

PROOF   By definition of $local\text{-}completion\text{-}order(\beta)$, $\beta|G(X)$ contains a **REQUEST_COMMIT** event for T', and T is locally visible at X to T' in $\beta'|G(X)$, where β' is the longest prefix of β not containing the **REQUEST_COMMIT** for T'. Lemma 6.16 implies that T is visible to T' in β'.

Since β is transaction well-formed for T', it contains at most one **REQUEST_COMMIT** event for T', and so β' does not contain a **REQUEST_COMMIT** event for T'. By the controller preconditions, and Lemma 6.9, β' does not contain a **COMMIT**(T') event.   Since $\beta|G(X)$ is generic object well-formed, β' contains a **CREATE**(T') event. Since T' is not an orphan in β, β' does not contain an **ABORT**(T') event. Therefore, T' is live in β'.

Let U and U' denote the siblings such that T is a descendant of U, and T' is a descendant of U'. Since T is visible to T' in β', β' contains a **COMMIT**(U) event. By Proposition 6.11 and Lemma 5.9, U' must be live in β'. Since β' contains a return for U, and no return for U', it follows that $(U, U') \in R$. Therefore, $(T, T') \in R_{trans}$.   □

Notice that the completion order is a total order on siblings that actually complete. The local completion order, however, might be partial, since two siblings might run descendant accesses before either sibling completes. In such a situation, the object does not know which order the siblings completed in.

One might expect *local-completion-order*$(\beta|G(X))$ to be a subset of *completion-order*$(\beta)_{trans}$. Lemma 6.18 shows that many pairs (T, T') in *local-completion-order*$(\beta|G(X))$ are also in *completion-order*$(\beta)_{trans}$, but only if T' is not an orphan. The following example shows why this assumption is necessary. Suppose T and T' are accesses to X with parents U and U', respectively, and that U and U' are siblings. Consider the following fragment of a generic behavior (for brevity, most of the **REQUEST** actions have been omitted):

CREATE(U'),
   REQUEST_CREATE(T'),
ABORT(U'),
     CREATE(U),
        CREATE(T),
        COMMIT(T),
        INFORM_COMMIT_AT(X)**OF**(T),
      COMMIT(U),
      INFORM_COMMIT_AT(X)**OF**(U),
    CREATE(T'),
    REQUEST_COMMIT(T', v').

The generic controller allows an orphan transaction such as T' to continue running, so even after U' has been aborted T' can be created. (In fact, the **REQUEST_CREATE**(T') action could occur after the **ABORT**(U') action, since U' can also keep running after **ABORT**(U') occurs.) The fragment of this behavior involving $G(X)$ consists of the following sequence of actions:

CREATE(T),
INFORM_COMMIT_AT(X)**OF**(T),
   INFORM_COMMIT_AT(X)**OF**(U),
     CREATE(T'),
     REQUEST_COMMIT(T', v').

The definition of the local completion order implies that (T, T') is in the local completion ordering. However, notice that U' aborted before U committed, so (U', U) is in the completion order. Hence, (T', T) is in *completion-order*$_{trans}$.

The next definition describes how to reorder the external actions of a generic object automaton according to a given local completion order. This definition is analogous to the definition of $view(\beta, T, completion\text{-}order(\beta), \mathrm{X})$ except that local information is used, rather than global information. However, because the **INFORM_COMMIT** actions do not necessarily convey to $G(\mathrm{X})$ all the facts about relative completion order, there may be accesses whose relative order is not determined by *local-completion-order*. Thus, the local definition below gives a set of sequences, rather than a single sequence.

Suppose β is a finite generic object well-formed sequence of external actions of $G(\mathrm{X})$ and T is a transaction name. Let *local-views*(β, T) be the set of sequences defined as follows. Let Z be the set of operations occurring in β whose transactions are locally visible at X to T in β. Then the elements of *local-views*(β, T) are the sequences of the form $perform(\xi)$, where ξ is a total ordering of Z in an order consistent with the partial order *local-completion-order*(β) on the transaction components. The following is straightforward from the definitions.

LEMMA 6.19 *If β is a finite generic object well-formed sequence of external actions of $G(\mathrm{X})$ and T is a transaction name, then every element of local-views(β, T) is serial object well-formed.*

Finally, *local dynamic atomicity* can be defined. This is analogous to the definition of dynamic atomicity, but using local views and transactions that are local orphans, instead of the corresponding global terms. Say that generic object automaton $G(\mathrm{X})$ for object name X is **locally dynamic atomic** if whenever β is a finite generic object well-formed behavior of $G(\mathrm{X})$ and T is a transaction name that is not a local orphan at X in β, then every sequence in *local-views*(β, T) is a finite behavior of $S(\mathrm{X})$. That is, any result of reordering a behavior of $G(\mathrm{X})$ according to the given local completion order is a finite behavior of the corresponding serial object automaton. The main result of this subsection says that local dynamic atomicity is a sufficient condition for dynamic atomicity. Arguing loosely, this result follows because the sequence (given in the view condition) that must be a serial behavior for dynamic atomicity to hold, should be one among the sequences in the set *local-views*(β, T).[6]

THEOREM 6.20 *If $G(\mathrm{X})$ is a generic object automaton for object name X that is locally dynamic atomic then $G(\mathrm{X})$ is dynamic atomic.*

PROOF Let $\mathcal{S}$ be a generic system in which $G(\mathrm{X})$ is associated with X. Let β be a finite behavior of $\mathcal{S}$, $R = completion\text{-}order(\beta)$, and T a transaction name that is not

---

[6]You should note that the definition of *local-views* is a simple analog of the definition used in the view condition. A more powerful definition is possible, capturing more facts deducible about the sequence that occurs in the global view condition. This would result in an alternative notion corresponding to local dynamic atomicity, which would require fewer sequences to be behaviors of the serial object, but would still satisfy the analog to Theorem 6.20. In this way, more algorithms might be proved correct. See Chapter 8 for an example of such a more powerful definition.

an orphan in β. The proof must establish that $view(serial(\beta), T, R, \mathrm{X})$ is a behavior of $S(\mathrm{X})$. By definition, $view(serial(\beta), T, R, \mathrm{X}) = perform(\xi)$, where ξ is the sequence of operations occurring in β whose transactions are visible to T in β, arranged in the order given by R_{trans} on the transaction components.

Let γ be a finite sequence of actions consisting of exactly one **INFORM_COMMIT-_AT(X)OF**(U) for each **COMMIT**(U) that occurs in β. Then $\beta\gamma$ is a behavior of the system $\mathcal{S}$, since each action in γ is an enabled output action of the generic controller, by Lemma 6.8. Then $\beta\gamma|G(\mathrm{X})$ is a behavior of $G(\mathrm{X})$, and Proposition 6.10 implies that it is generic object well-formed.

Since **INFORM_COMMIT_AT(X)OF**(U) occurs in $\beta\gamma|G(\mathrm{X})$ if and only if **COMMIT**(U) occurs in β, an access T' to X is visible to T in β if and only if it is locally visible at X to T in $\beta\gamma|G(\mathrm{X})$. Therefore, the same operations occur in $view(serial(\beta), T, R, \mathrm{X})$ and in any sequence in $local\text{-}views(\beta\gamma|G(\mathrm{X}), T)$. To show that $view(serial(\beta), T, R, \mathrm{X}) \in local\text{-}views(\beta\gamma|G(\mathrm{X}), T)$, the proof must show that the order of operations in the first sequence is among the orders considered in the latter set of sequences.

If T' is any access that is locally visible at X to T in $\beta\gamma|G(\mathrm{X})$, then T' is visible to T in β, so Lemma 5.1 implies that T' is not an orphan in β, and hence not an orphan in $\beta\gamma$. Also, note that $completion\text{-}order(\beta\gamma) = completion\text{-}order(\beta) = R$. Then Lemma 6.18 implies that if accesses that are locally visible at X to T in $\beta\gamma|G(\mathrm{X})$ are ordered by $local\text{-}completion\text{-}order(\beta\gamma|G(\mathrm{X}))$, they are also ordered in the same way by R_{trans}.

Thus, the sequence ξ can be obtained by taking those operations (T', v') such that **REQUEST_COMMIT**(T', v') occurs in $\beta\gamma|G(\mathrm{X})$ and T' is locally visible at X to T in $\beta\gamma|G(\mathrm{X})$, and arranging them in an order that is consistent with $local\text{-}completion\text{-}order(\beta\gamma|G(\mathrm{X}))$ on the transaction component. Thus, $perform(\xi)$ is an element of $local\text{-}views(\beta\gamma|G(\mathrm{X}), T)$. Since $G(\mathrm{X})$ is locally dynamic atomic, $perform(\xi)$ is a finite behavior of $S(\mathrm{X})$, as required. $\square$

This proof uses an interesting general technique: it introduces a behavior in which extra information reaches $G(\mathrm{X})$, causing the local calculations to be accurate reflections of the global concepts. Similar techniques will be used in Chapters 7 and 8.

6.3 General Commutativity-based Locking

This section presents a general commutativity-based locking algorithm and its correctness proof. The algorithm is described as a generic object automaton in a generic system. The system type and the transaction automata are assumed to be fixed, and are the same as those of the given serial system. The generic controller automaton has already been defined. Thus, all that remains is to define the generic object and show that it is dynamic atomic.

6.3.1 Locking Objects

This subsection describes, for each object name X, a generic object automaton $L(X)$ (a *locking object*). The object automaton uses the forward commutativity relation[7] between operations to decide when to allow operations to be performed. Recovery is handled using intentions lists.

We first sketch the algorithm's principles in the non-nested situation, where each top-level transaction invokes a sequence of accesses, but no subtransactions. The state of each object can be thought of as consisting of two parts: a *base state*, which reflects the effects of the committed transactions (in the order in which they committed), and a set of *intentions lists*, one for each active top-level transaction. The intentions list for a top-level transaction T contains the sequence of operations performed by T (the accesses invoked, each with its return value).[8] Transactions running concurrently with T receive results based on the base state and their own activity (that is, they do not reveal the effects of T's activity). Only when T commits (i.e., when an **INFORM-_COMMIT** action occurs for the transaction) are all its operations installed in the base state, so that other transactions will observe their influence. If T aborts, the object can simply discard the list of activity done on its behalf.

In order to provide dynamic atomicity, a transaction is sometimes *blocked*, that is, an operation is prevented from occurring until a certain condition is met (i.e., this condition is part of the precondition of the **REQUEST_COMMIT** action). The condition is as follows: an operation is blocked if there is any operation, in the intentions list of a concurrently executing transaction, that does not commute forward with the one being blocked.

The following example illustrates why forward commutativity is the relationship used in this algorithm. Consider the simple case of three transactions T_1, T_2, and T_3, each of which performs a sequence of accesses to objects, including to a particular object X. Suppose that T_1 runs and commits, and that X is informed of the commit. Suppose that T_2 and T_3 then run concurrently, performing accesses to X, and that after both have finished all their accesses, both commit. Let σ_i be the sequence of operations performed by T_i on X. Because of the use of intentions lists, the return values for T_2's accesses are determined so that $perform(\sigma_1\sigma_2)$ is a behavior of the serial object X; that is, the return values for T_2's accesses are based on activity done

---

[7]Forward commutativity is defined in Section 4.3.

[8]The name reflects the idea that these are the changes T intends to make to the object, but that the changes are not actually installed until T commits.

by T_1 and T_2, but they are independent of the accesses done by T_3. Similarly, the return values for T_3's accesses are independent of the accesses done by T_2. Since T_2's accesses are not visible to T_3's when they are performed (or vice-versa), the test for forward commutativity ensures that $perform(\sigma_1\sigma_2\sigma_3)$ is a behavior of the serial object X and that $perform(\sigma_1\sigma_3\sigma_2)$ is a behavior of the serial object X. This means that the transactions can be serialized in all orders consistent with the local completion order.

Extending the above ideas to a nested transaction system, we obtain the following algorithm. For uniformity, the effective state of the object (the effect of all the top-level transactions that have committed) is represented as an intentions list[9] of T_0. When a transaction executes an operation (i.e., when a response is returned for an access), the operation is recorded in the transaction's intentions list. When a transaction commits, the transaction's intentions list is appended to its parent's. When a transaction aborts, its intentions list is discarded. The response for an access is constrained so that the resulting operation can be performed by the serial object from a state resulting from executing the intentions lists of the access's ancestors. There is an additional constraint for responses to accesses: a response is given only if all the operations in the intentions list of any non-ancestral transaction commute forward with the one representing the response.

The algorithm is illustrated in Figure 6.3, which shows a transaction tree, with the intentions list next to each node.

To express this algorithm in our model, we define a generic object automaton $L(\mathrm{X})$. Automaton $L(\mathrm{X})$ has the usual external action signature of a generic object automaton for X, and there are no internal actions. A state s of $L(\mathrm{X})$ has components $s.created$, $s.commit\_requested$ and $s.intentions$. Of these, $created$ and $commit\_requested$ are sets of transactions, initially empty; the set difference of these is just the collection of active accesses. The component $intentions$ is a function from transactions to sequences of operations of X, initially mapping every transaction to the empty sequence λ. In any state, $intentions(U)$ should be thought of as the activity that was performed by descendants of U that are known to have "committed up" to U. When (T, v) is a member of $s.intentions(U)$, say that U **holds** a (T, v)-lock, because in this situation operations that do not commute forward with (T, v) may not be performed (except if they are descendants of U).

Given a state s and a transaction name T also define the sequence $s.total(T)$ of operations by the recursive definition $s.total(T_0) = s.intentions(T_0)$, and $s.total(T) = s.total(parent(T))s.intentions(T)$ for $T \neq T_0$. Thus, $s.total(T)$ is the sequence of operations obtained by concatenating the values of intentions along the chain from T_0 to T, in order. (Here, $total$ is a $derived$ $variable$; that is, its value is used in

---

[9]Exercise 6 shows how a realistic system could compress this into a single state of $S(\mathrm{X})$.

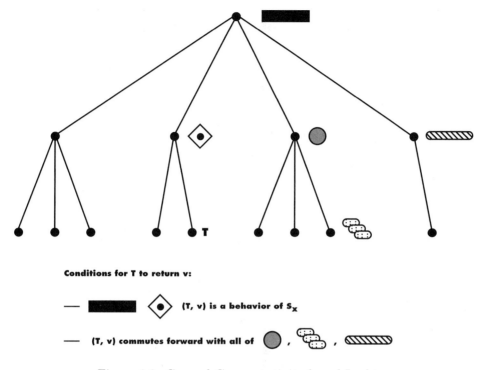

Figure 6.3: General Commutativity-based Locking

preconditions, but is not mentioned in any effect clause, since the value is always determined by the values of the genuine state variables.)

The precondition for **REQUEST_COMMIT**(T, v), where T is an access, explicitly references semantic properties of serial object $S(X)$.

Two fundamental properties of the algorithm may help your intuition.[10] Both hold in any state led to by generic object well-formed behaviors of $L(X)$; $perform(s.total(T))$ is a behavior of $S(X)$ for any transaction T, and for any transactions T and T' where neither is an ancestor of the other, every operation in $s.intentions(T)$ commutes forward with every operation in $s.intentions(T')$. The proof of these facts is left to the reader as Exercise 2; the main point is that these are established for an access T when its response is returned (notice the explicit test in the precondition for **REQUEST_COMMIT**(T, v), which ensures that $perform(s.total(T))$ is a behavior of $S(X)$, and

---

[10]These facts are not used in this form later in the book. In Section 6.3.2, we state (and prove) more complicated results than these, in order to give a direct proof of dynamic atomicity.

CREATE(T)
  Effect:
    $s.created = s'.created \cup \{T\}$

INFORM_COMMIT_AT(X)**OF**(T)
  Effect:
    $s.intentions(T) = \lambda$
    $s.intentions(parent(T))$
      $= s'.intentions(parent(T))$
        $s'.intentions(T)$

INFORM_ABORT_AT(X)**OF**(T)
  Effect:
    $s.intentions(U) = \lambda,$
      $U \in descendants(T)$

REQUEST_COMMIT(T, v)
  Precondition:
    $T \in s'.created - s'.commit\_requested$
    there do not exist U, T', and v' such that
      (T, v) does not commute forward
        with (T', v')
      (T', v') is an element of $s'.intentions(U)$
      $U \notin ancestors(T)$
    $perform(s'.total(T)(T, v))$ is a behavior of $S(X)$
  Effect:
    $s.commit\_requested$
      $= s'.commit\_requested \cup \{T\}$
    $s.intentions(T) = (T, v)$

Figure 6.4: Transition Relation for General Commutativity-based Locking

that every operation in the intentions list of a non-ancestor commutes forward with (T, v)) and their truth is maintained by later actions.

The transition relation of $L(X)$ is given in Figure 6.4.

Thus, when an access transaction is created, it is simply added to the set created. When $L(X)$ is informed of a commit, it passes any locks held by the transaction to the parent, appending them at the end of the parent's intentions list. When $L(X)$ is informed of an abort, it discards all locks held by descendants of the transaction. A response containing return value v to an access T can be returned only if the access has been created but not yet responded to, every holder of an *incompatible* (that is, non-forward-commuting) lock is an ancestor of T, and $perform(T, v)$ can occur in a move of $S(X)$ from a state following the behavior $perform(s'.total(T))$. When this response is given, T is added to *commit_requested* and the operation (T, v) is appended to *intentions*(T) to indicate that the (T, v)-lock was granted.

EXAMPLE 6.3.1   A Bank Account Locking Object

Consider the bank account serial object $S(X)$ defined in Example 3.5.2 for the banking database of Example 3.1.1. Let $L(X)$ be constructed as above based on this serial object automaton and its forward commutativity relation given in Example 4.3.2 and Exercise 5 of Chapter 4.

Consider the following behavior β of $L(X)$:

CREATE(T_1),
REQUEST_COMMIT(T_1, "*OK*"),
INFORM_COMMIT_AT(X)**OF**(T_1),
    CREATE($T_{3.3}$),
        CREATE($T_{3.1003.1}$),
            REQUEST_COMMIT($T_{3.1003.1}$, $1000),
            INFORM_COMMIT_AT(X)**OF**($T_{3.1003.1}$),
            INFORM_COMMIT_AT(X)**OF**($T_{3.1003}$),
    REQUEST_COMMIT($T_{3.3}$, $200),
            CREATE(T_4),
                CREATE(T_5).

This behavior can lead to a state s of $L(\mathrm{X})$ in which

> $s.created = \{T_1, T_{3.3}, T_{3.1003.1}, T_4, T_5\}$
> $s.commit\_requested = \{T_1, T_{3.1003.1}, T_{3.3}\}$,
> $s.intentions(T_0) = (T_1, \text{"}OK\text{"})$,
> $s.intentions(T_3) = (T_{3.1003.1}, \$1000)$,
> $s.intentions(T_{3.3}) = (T_{3.3}, \$200)$,
> and for every other transaction T, $s.intentions(T)$ is the
>   empty sequence.

We claim that the action **REQUEST_COMMIT**(T_4, "*OK*") is enabled in state s. Checking the clauses of the precondition we see that T_4 is active, that the operation $(T_4, \text{"}OK\text{"})$ commutes forward with both $(T_{3.1003.1}, \$1000)$ and $(T_{3.3}, \$200)$ (recall that $kind(T_4) = \text{"}deposit\text{"}$, while $kind(T_{3.1003.1}) = kind(T_{3.3}) = \text{"}withdraw\text{"}$), and that $perform((T_1, \text{"}OK\text{"})(T_4, \text{"}OK\text{"}))$ is a behavior of $S(\mathrm{X})$. However, in state s the action **REQUEST_COMMIT**(T_5, v) is not enabled for any value of v, since (T_5, v) does not commute forward with either $(T_{3.1003.1}, \$1000)$ or $(T_{3.3}, \$200)$.

Notice that the response value to $T_{3.1003.1}$ was chosen so that $perform((T_1, \text{"}OK\text{"})(T_{3.1003.1}, \$1000))$ is a behavior of the serial object automaton. Let β_1 denote the behavior consisting of β followed by the sequence

> **REQUEST_COMMIT**(T_4, "*OK*"),
>   **INFORM_COMMIT_AT**(X)**OF**(T_4),
> **INFORM_COMMIT_AT**(X)**OF**(T_3),
> **INFORM_ABORT_AT**(X)**OF**($T_{3.3}$).

Then the accesses locally visible to T_0 in β_1 are T_1, $T_{3.1003.1}$, and T_4. The order *local-completion-order*(β_1) contains the pairs $(T_1, T_{3.1003.1})$, $(T_1, T_{3.3})$, and (T_1, T_4). It does not, however, relate $T_{3.1003.1}$ and T_4, since when T_4 ran, $T_{3.1003.1}$ was not locally visible to it, and *vice versa*. Thus, the set *local-views*(β_1, T_0) contains two sequences

$$perform((T_1, \text{``}OK\text{''})(T_{3.1003.1}, \$1000)(T_4, \text{``}OK\text{''}))$$

and

$$perform((T_1, \text{``}OK\text{''})(T_4, \text{``}OK\text{''})(T_{3.1003.1}, \$1000)).$$

You can check directly that both of these are behaviors of the bank account object; the same conclusion follows from the facts that $perform((T_1, \text{``}OK\text{''})(T_{3.1003.1}, \$1000))$ and $perform((T_1, \text{``}OK\text{''})$ $(T_4, \text{``}OK\text{''}))$ are behaviors and that $(T_4, \text{``}OK\text{''})$ commutes forward with $(T_{3.1003.1}, \$1000)$. Indeed this example illustrates why commuting forward is the relationship used to determine when locks are compatible.

The sequence β_1 can lead to a state s_1 of $L(X)$, where $s_1.created = \{T_1, T_{3.3}, T_{3.1003.1}, T_4, T_5\}$ $s_1.commit\_requested = \{T_1, T_{3.1003.1}, T_{3.3}, T_4\}$, $s_1.intentions(T_0) = (T_1, \text{``}OK\text{''})(T_4, \text{``}OK\text{''})(T_{3.1003.1}, \$1000)$, and for every other transaction T, $s_1.intentions(T)$ is the empty sequence. In state s_1, the action $\pi = $ **REQUEST_COMMIT**$(T_5, \$2000)$ is enabled. Notice that the incompatible withdrawal operations $(T_{3.1003.1}, \$1000)$ and $(T_{3.3}, \$200)$, which blocked the occurrence of π in state s, do not block it in s_1. This is because the $(T_{3.3}, \$200)$-lock is discarded since $T_{3.3}$ aborted, and the $(T_{3.1003.1}, \$1000)$-lock is passed to T_0 after $T_{3.1003}$ and T_3 commit. Thus, the balance access T_5 has its response value based on the deposit T_1 of $\$2000$, the deposit T_4 of $\$1000$, and the successful withdrawal $T_{3.1003.1}$ of $\$1000$, since the completion order must place T_1, T_4, and $T_{3.1003.1}$ before T_5 (unless T_5 aborts, in which case it could be earlier in the completion order, but anyway the value it returns would not matter).

LEMMA 6.21 $L(X)$ *is a generic object for* X.

PROOF It is easy to see that $L(X)$ has the correct external signature. The fact that it preserves generic object well-formedness follows by Lemma 6.7. $\square$

The locking object $L(X)$ is quite nondeterministic; implementations[11] of $L(X)$ can be designed that restrict the nondeterminism in various ways, and correctness of such

---

[11]Recall that *implementation* has a formal definition, given in Section 2.7.1. The *implementation* relation only relates external behaviors, but allows complete freedom in the choice of automaton states.

algorithms follows immediately from the correctness of $L(X)$, once the implementation relationship has been proved, for example, by using a possibilities mapping.

EXAMPLE 6.3.2 Some Example Implementations

As a trivial example, consider an algorithm expressed by a generic object that is just like $L(X)$ except that a stronger precondition is placed on the **REQUEST_COMMIT**(T, v) action, say requiring (in conjunction with the precondition in $L(X)$) that no lock at all is held by any non-ancestor of T. (This corresponds to exclusive locking.) Every behavior of this generic object is necessarily a behavior of $L(X)$ (although the converse need not be true). That is, this object implements $L(X)$ and so is dynamic atomic (since, as shown below, $L(X)$ is dynamic atomic).

For another example, note that the general locking algorithm models both choosing a return value and testing that no incompatible locks are held by non-ancestors of the access in question. These are part of the precondition on the single **REQUEST_COMMIT** event for the access. This means that whether an operation is allowed to take place may depend on the return value, as well as on the access. For example, if the general locking algorithm is used for an object name, where the serial object automaton (that is, the type specification) is the Bank Account of Example 3.5.2, then an access with $kind =$ "$withdraw$" may be allowed to occur with return value 0, even if a balance access has occurred but not been committed. However, the withdraw could not be allowed to occur with a non-zero return value.

Traditional database management systems have used an architecture in which a lock manager first determines whether an access is to proceed or be delayed, and then another component determines the response later. In such an architecture, it is infeasible to use the return value in determining which activities are incompatible. One can model such an algorithm by an automaton in which the granting of locks by the lock manager is an internal event whose precondition tests for incompatible locks using a *conflict table*,[12] where the conflict table requires a lock for access T to be incompatible with a lock for access T' whenever there are any return values v and v' such that (T, v) does not commute forward with (T', v'). (For read/write serial objects, the lock table is the negation of the entries in the forward commutativity table, Figure 4.2.) Then one would have

---

[12]Note that despite the name, the relationship used is not that of operations conflicting, that is, failing to commute backward.

a **REQUEST_COMMIT** action whose precondition included the condition that the return value is appropriate and that a lock had previously been granted for the access. Doing this, one obtains an object that can be shown to be an implementation of $L(X)$, and therefore its correctness follows from that of $L(X)$.

Many slight variations on these algorithms can be considered, in which locks are obtained at different times, recorded in different ways, and tested for compatibility using different relations; so long as the resulting algorithm treats non-forward-commuting operations as incompatible, it should not be hard to prove that these algorithms implement $L(X)$, and so are correct. Such implementations could exhibit much less concurrency than $L(X)$, because they use a coarser test for deciding when an access may proceed. In many cases the loss of potential concurrency might be justified by the simpler computations needed in each indivisible step.

Another aspect of our algorithm that one might wish to change in an implementation is the complicated data structure maintaining the *intentions*, and the corresponding need to replay all the operations recorded there when determining the response to an access. The next section considers an algorithm that is able to summarize all these lists of operations in a stack of versions of the serial object, at the cost of reducing available concurrency by using a compatibility relation in which all updates exclude one another.

The ideas of this subsection are explored in Exercises 6, 7, and 8 of this chapter.

6.3.2 Correctness Proof

This subsection proves several lemmas about $L(X)$, leading to the theorem that $L(X)$ is dynamic atomic.

The next lemma says that the ordering of operations in the *total* sequences does not change during execution of $L(X)$.

LEMMA 6.22 *Let $\beta_1\beta_2$ be a finite generic object well-formed schedule of $L(X)$, such that β_1 can lead $L(X)$ to state s' and (s', β_2, s) is an extended step of $L(X)$. Let T_1, T_2, U and V be transaction names. Suppose (T_1, v_1) precedes (T_2, v_2) in $s'.total(U)$ and (T_2, v_2) occurs in $s.total(V)$. Then (T_1, v_1) occurs in $s.total(V)$ and precedes (T_2, v_2) in $s.total(V)$.*

PROOF   By a straightforward induction on the length of β_2.   □

A definition is next introduced to describe the information $L(\mathrm{X})$ uses about visibility. If β is a sequence of actions of $L(\mathrm{X})$ and T and T' are transaction names, say that T is **lock visible** at X to T' in β if β contains a subsequence β' consisting of an **INFORM_COMMIT_AT(X)OF**(U) event for every $U \in ancestors(T) - ancestors(T')$, arranged in ascending order (so the **INFORM_COMMIT** for $parent(U)$ is preceded by that for U). Lock visibility is similar to local visibility, with the added constraint that the **INFORM** actions occur in leaf-to-root order. This reflects the way locks are transferred during the execution of the algorithm.

The following lemma characterizes the contents of the various intentions lists in terms of lock visibility.

LEMMA 6.23 *Let β be a finite generic object well-formed schedule of $L(\mathrm{X})$. Suppose that β can lead $L(\mathrm{X})$ to state s.*

1. *Let T be an access to X such that $\textbf{REQUEST\_COMMIT}(T, v)$ occurs in β and T is not a local orphan at X in β, and let T' be the highest ancestor of T such that T is lock visible to T' at X in β. Then (T, v) is a member of $s.intentions(T')$.*

2. *If (T, v) is an element of $s.intentions(T')$ then T is a descendant of T', $\textbf{REQUEST\_COMMIT}(T, v)$ occurs in β, and T' is the highest ancestor of T to which T is lock visible at X in β.*

3. *If T' is not a local orphan at X in β, then $s.intentions(T')$ consists of exactly the operations (T, v) such that T is a descendant of T', $\textbf{REQUEST\_COMMIT}(T, v)$ occurs in β, and T' is the highest ancestor of T to which T is lock visible at X in β.*

PROOF By a straightforward induction on the length of β. □

Also define a binary relation $lock$-$completion$-$order(\beta)$ on accesses to X, where $(U, U') \in lock$-$completion$-$order(\beta)$ if and only if $U \neq U'$, β contains **REQUEST_COMMIT** events for both U and U', and U is lock visible to U' at X in β', where β' is the longest prefix of β not containing the given **REQUEST_COMMIT** event for U'. (The lock completion order is identical to the local completion order, except that it uses lock visibility instead of local visibility.)

The following simple lemmas relate lock visibility and the lock completion order to local visibility and the local completion order. They follow immediately from the definitions.

LEMMA 6.24 *Let β be a generic object well-formed sequence of actions of $L(\mathrm{X})$. Then $lock$-$completion$-$order(\beta)$ is a partial order.*

LEMMA 6.25 *Let β be a sequence of actions of $L(X)$ and T and T' transaction names. If T is lock visible at X to T' in β then T is locally visible at X to T' in β. Also lock-completion-order(β) is a subrelation of local-completion-order(β).*

The next lemmas relate the contents of the intentions lists to the lock-completion order Lemma 6.26 characterizes the operations in an intentions list, while Lemma 6.27 characterizes the order in which the operations appear in an intentions list.

LEMMA 6.26 *Let β be a finite generic object well-formed behavior of $L(X)$, and suppose that a **REQUEST_COMMIT**(T, v) event π occurs in β, where T is not a local orphan at X in β. Let β' be the prefix of β ending with π, and let s be the (unique) state of $L(X)$ led to by β'.*

1. *The operations in $s.total(T)$ are exactly (T, v) plus the operations (T', v') that occur in β such that $(T', T) \in$ lock-completion-order(β).*

2. *Also perform$(s.total(T))$ is a finite behavior of $S(X)$.*

PROOF   Lemma 6.23 implies that the operations in $s'.total(T)$ are exactly those (T', v') that occur in β' such that T' is lock visible to an ancestor of T in β'. By the definition of *lock-completion-order*(β) and the generic object well-formedness of β, $(T', T) \in$ *lock-completion-order*(β).

Let us denote by β'' the longest prefix of β not including the event π, and let s' be the state of $L(X)$ led to by β''. Then (s', π, s) is a step of $L(X)$. The effect of π is to ensure $s.total(T)$ is $s'.total(T)$ followed by (T, v), so the precondition of π ensures that *perform*$(s.total(T))$ is a finite behavior of $S(X)$.   □

LEMMA 6.27 *Let β be a generic object well-formed finite behavior of $L(X)$ that leads $L(X)$ to state s, and let T be any transaction name. Then the order of operations in $s.total(T)$ is consistent with lock-completion-order(β).*

PROOF   Suppose (T_1, v_1) and (T_2, v_2) are two operations in $s.total(T)$ such that $(T_1, T_2) \in$ *lock-completion-order*(β). By the definition of the lock-completion order, T_1 is lock visible to T_2 at X in the longest prefix, β_1, of β that does not include **REQUEST_COMMIT**(T_2, v_2). Then Lemma 6.23, applied to β_1, implies that (T_1, v_1) is in the intentions list of an ancestor of T_2 in the state s_1 reached by β_1, and by the effect of **REQUEST_COMMIT**(T_2, v_2), (T_1, v_1) precedes (T_2, v_2) in $s_2.total(T_2)$, where s_2 is the state reached by β_1 **REQUEST_COMMIT**(T_2, v_2). By Lemma 6.22, (T_1, v_1) precedes (T_2, v_2) in $s.total(T)$. Thus, the order of operations in $s.total(T)$ is consistent with *lock-completion-order*(β).   □

The key lemma is next, which shows that certain sequences of actions, extracted from a generic object well-formed behavior of $L(X)$, are serial object well-formed behaviors of $S(X)$. The second conclusion, that certain such sequences are equieffective, is needed to carry out the induction step of the proof of this lemma.

It is helpful to have an auxiliary definition. Suppose β is a generic object well-formed finite behavior of $L(X)$. Then a set Z of operations of X is said to be **allowable** for β provided that for each operation (T, v) that occurs in Z, the following conditions hold.

1. (T, v) occurs in β.

2. T is not a local orphan at X in β.

3. If (T', v') is an operation that occurs in β such that $(T', T) \in$ *lock-completion-order*(β), then $(T', v') \in Z$.

An allowable set of operations corresponds roughly to a set of operations whose accesses either are or could become visible to some nonorphan transaction U. Thus, each operation in the set must occur in β and must not be a local orphan (since otherwise it could never be visible to a nonorphan). In addition, if T' is visible to T and T becomes visible to U, T' also becomes visible to U, so if (T, v) is in the set and T' is visible to T, (T', v') should also be in the set. The third condition only requires (T', v') to be in the set if T' precedes T in the lock-completion order; thus, it considers more sets of operations than just those whose accesses could become visible to U. This only strengthens the next lemma, since it shows that all allowable sets of operations for β, when ordered consistently with *lock-completion-order*(β), correspond to behaviors of $S(X)$.

LEMMA 6.28 *Let β be a generic object well-formed finite behavior of $L(X)$ and let Z be an allowable set of operations for β. Let $R = $ lock-completion-order(β).*

1. *If ξ is a total ordering of Z that is consistent with R on the transaction components, then perform(ξ) is a behavior of $S(X)$.*

2. *If ξ and η are both total orderings of Z such that each is consistent with R on the transaction components, then perform(ξ) and perform(η) are equieffective.*

PROOF   Use induction on the size of the set Z. The basis, when Z is empty, is trivial. So let $k \geq 1$ and suppose that Z contains k operations and the lemma holds for all allowable sets of $k - 1$ operations. Let ξ be a total ordering of Z that is consistent with R on the transaction component. Let (T, v) be the last operation in ξ, and let $Z' = Z - (T, v)$. Let ξ' be the sequence of operations such that $\xi = \xi'(T, v)$. Then Z' is an allowable set of $k - 1$ operations, since Z is, and there is no operation (T', v') in Z such that $(T, T') \in R$. Also, ξ' is a total ordering of Z' consistent with R.

Let β' be the longest prefix of β not containing $\textbf{REQUEST\_COMMIT}(T, v)$, and let s' be the (unique) state of $L(X)$ led to by β'. Let $\zeta_1 = s'.total(T)$, and let ζ_2 be some total ordering that is consistent with R of the operations in $Z' - \zeta_1$. Lemma 6.26 implies that the operations in ζ_1 are exactly those (T', v') that occur in β such that $(T', T) \in R$, and Lemma 6.27 implies that the order of operations in ζ_1 is consistent with R.

The proof shows that (T, v) commutes forward with every operation (T'', v'') in ζ_2. There are two cases.

1. $\textbf{REQUEST\_COMMIT}(T'', v'')$ precedes $\textbf{REQUEST\_COMMIT}(T, v)$ in β.

Then let U denote the highest ancestor of T'' to which T'' is lock visible at X in β'. By Lemma 6.23, $(T'', v'') \in s'.intentions(U)$. By definition of ζ_2, U is not an ancestor of T. Therefore, by the precondition for $\textbf{REQUEST\_COMMIT}(T, v)$, which is enabled in state s', (T, v) commutes forward with (T'', v'').

2. $\textbf{REQUEST\_COMMIT}(T, v)$ precedes $\textbf{REQUEST\_COMMIT}(T'', v'')$ in β.

Then let β'' be the longest prefix of β not containing $\textbf{REQUEST\_COMMIT}(T'', v'')$, and let t be the state of $L(X)$ led to by β''. Also let U denote the highest ancestor of T to which T is lock visible at X in β'', so that $(T, v) \in t.intentions(U)$. U is not an ancestor of T'', since if it were, then the definition of the lock-completion order implies that $(T, T'') \in R$, contradicting the assumption that (T, v) is the last operation in ξ. Therefore, by the precondition for $\textbf{REQUEST\_COMMIT}(T'', v'')$, which is enabled in state t, (T'', v'') commutes forward with (T, v).

Next, the proof claims that if (T', v') and (T'', v'') are operations in ζ_1 and ζ_2 respectively, then $(T'', T') \notin R$. For if $(T'', T') \in R$, then since $(T', T) \in R$, by Lemma 6.24, we have also $(T'', T) \in R$. Then the characterization of ζ_1 above implies that (T'', v'') occurs in ζ_1, a contradiction.

This claim implies that $\zeta_1 \zeta_2$ is also a total ordering of Z' consistent with R. The inductive hypothesis then implies that $perform(\xi')$ and $perform(\zeta_1 \zeta_2)$ are equieffective serial object well-formed behaviors of $S(X)$.

By the precondition for $\textbf{REQUEST\_COMMIT}(T, v)$, which is enabled in state s', the sequence $perform(s'.total(T)(T, v)) = perform(\zeta_1(T, v))$ is a finite behavior of $S(X)$, and it is clearly serial object well-formed, since β is generic object well-formed. The proof also showed above that $perform(\zeta_1 \zeta_2)$ is a serial object well-formed behavior of $S(X)$. Since (T, v) commutes forward with every operation in ζ_2, Proposition 4.4 implies that $perform(\zeta_1 \zeta_2 (T, v))$ is a serial object well-formed behavior of $S(X)$. Since $perform(\zeta_1 \zeta_2)$ is equieffective to $perform(\xi')$, and since $perform(\xi) = perform(\xi'(T, v))$ is clearly serial object well-formed, the definition of equieffectiveness implies that $perform(\xi)$ is a behavior of $S(X)$. This completes the proof that $perform(\xi)$ is a serial object well-formed behavior of $S(X)$.

Now let η be any other total ordering of Z that is consistent with R on the transaction component. Let η_1 and η_2 be the sequences of operations such that $\eta = \eta_1(T, v)\eta_2$. Then $\eta_1\eta_2$ is a total ordering of Z' consistent with R. The inductive hypothesis shows that $perform(\eta_1\eta_2)$ is a serial object well-formed behavior of $S(\mathrm{X})$ and that it is equieffective to $perform(\xi')$. Therefore, by Proposition 4.2, $perform(\eta_1\eta_2(T, v))$ is equieffective to $perform(\xi)$.

Part 1 applied to η implies that $perform(\eta)$ is a serial object well-formed behavior of $S(\mathrm{X})$; therefore, its prefix $perform(\eta_1(T, v))$ is also a serial object well-formed behavior of $S(\mathrm{X})$.

By the characterization above for ζ_1, every operation in ζ_1 has its transaction component preceding T in R. Thus, since η is consistent with R, every operation in ζ_1 is contained in η_1. Thus, every operation in η_2 is contained in ζ_2, and so (T, v) commutes forward with every operation in η_2. Therefore, $perform(\eta) = perform(\eta_1(T, v)\eta_2)$ is equieffective to $perform(\eta_1\eta_2(T, v))$, by Proposition 4.4.

Since $perform(\eta)$ is equieffective to $perform(\eta_1\eta_2(T, v))$ and $perform(\eta_1\eta_2(T, v))$ is equieffective to $perform(\xi)$, Lemma 4.1 implies that $perform(\eta)$ is equieffective to $perform(\xi)$, completing the proof. □

Now one can prove that locking objects are locally dynamic atomic.

PROPOSITION 6.29 $L(\mathrm{X})$ *is locally dynamic atomic.*

PROOF Let β be a finite generic object well-formed behavior of $L(\mathrm{X})$ and let T be a transaction name that is not a local orphan at X in β. The proof must show that every sequence in $local\text{-}views(\beta, T)$ is a behavior of $S(\mathrm{X})$. So let Z be the set of operations occurring in β whose transactions are locally visible to T at X in β. Let ξ be a total ordering of Z consistent with $local\text{-}completion\text{-}order(\beta)$ on the transaction components. The proof must show that $perform(\xi)$ is a behavior of $S(\mathrm{X})$.

The proof argues first that Z is allowable for β. To see this, suppose that (T', v') is an operation that occurs in Z. Then (T', v') occurs in β. Since T' is locally visible at X to T in β and T is not a local orphan at X in β, Lemma 6.15 implies that T' is not a local orphan at X in β. Now suppose that (T'', v'') is an operation that occurs in β and $(T'', T') \in lock\text{-}completion\text{-}order(\beta)$. Then T'' is lock visible at X to T' in β, and hence, by Lemma 6.25, is locally visible at X to T' in β. Therefore, (T'', v'') is in Z.

The proof argues next that the ordering of ξ is consistent with $lock\text{-}completion\text{-}order(\beta)$ on the transaction components. This is because the total ordering of ξ is consistent with $local\text{-}completion\text{-}order(\beta)$, and Lemma 6.25 implies that $lock\text{-}completion\text{-}order(\beta)$ is a subrelation of $local\text{-}completion\text{-}order(\beta)$.

Lemma 6.28 then implies that $perform(\xi)$ is a behavior of $S(\mathrm{X})$, as needed. □

Finally, one can show the main result of this section.

THEOREM 6.30 $L(\mathrm{X})$ *is dynamic atomic.*

PROOF   By Proposition 6.29 and Theorem 6.20.   □

An immediate consequence of Theorem 6.30 and the Dynamic Atomicity Theorem is that if $\mathcal{S}$ is a generic system in which each generic object is a locking object, then $\mathcal{S}$ is atomic for all nonorphan transaction names.

6.4 Moss's Algorithm

This section presents Moss's algorithm for read/update locking and its correctness proof. Once again, the algorithm is described as a generic system, and all that needs to be defined is the generic objects. The appropriate objects are defined here, and shown to implement locking objects. It follows that they are dynamic atomic.

6.4.1 Moss Objects

A generic object automaton $M(\mathrm{X})$ (a *Moss object*) is described, for each object name X. The automaton $M(\mathrm{X})$ maintains a stack of *versions* of the corresponding serial object $S(\mathrm{X})$ and manages *read locks* and *update locks*. The construction of $M(\mathrm{X})$ is based on a classification of all the accesses to X as either **read accesses** or **update accesses**. Assume that this classification satisfies the property that every operation (T, v) of a read access T is transparent, as defined in Section 4.4. If ξ is a sequence of operations of X, let *update*(ξ) denote the subsequence of ξ consisting of those operations whose first components are update accesses. Proposition 4.7 implies that if *perform*(ξ) is a serial object well-formed behavior of $S(\mathrm{X})$, then *perform*(*update*(ξ)) is also a serial object well-formed behavior of $S(\mathrm{X})$, and *perform*(*update*(ξ)) is equieffective to *perform*(ξ).

The algorithm maintains multiple copies of the serial object automaton, each representing the version created by a different access that has run. Each version is labeled with the name of the transaction whose activity produced it and whose abort would result in it being unneeded (the label is the name of the access itself when the version is first produced, but as the access and its ancestors commit, the version's label is changed). One complication occurs when a version is labeled with a transaction whose parent already labels a version; when the transaction commits, *its* version is relabeled with its parent's name, and the version previously labeled with the parent is discarded. When a transaction aborts, any versions labeled with its name (or the name of any descendant) are discarded.

The algorithm ensures (using the locking rules described below) that at any time, two versions are not labeled with unrelated transactions. Thus, the collection of labels forms a chain within the transaction naming tree; the collection of versions can be kept as a list organized according to this chain. Because the version accessed is generally the most recently created (called the *current* version), the list is sometimes implemented as a stack.

When a transaction is the label of a version, a concurrent unrelated transaction is prevented from reading existing versions or producing new ones, so we say that the version's label holds an update lock on the object. In addition, the algorithm keeps a set of transactions on whose behalf some version of the object has been read; these transactions are said to hold read locks on the object. Read locks may be held simultaneously by unrelated transactions.[13] The response value to an access (and the value of the new version, if the access is an update) is determined by considering the access as performed on the current version.

Figure 6.5 illustrates the algorithm. It shows the transaction tree, with transactions holding read locks indicated by being circled. Each version is indicated by a square next to the transaction that labels it. In the state depicted, if access T is a read, it can return a value based on the current version, which is B. However, if access T' is a read it cannot return any value, since U has an update lock but is not an ancestor of T'.

We now model the algorithm as a generic object automaton $M(X)$. $M(X)$ has the usual external action signature for a generic object automaton for X, without internal actions. A state s of $M(X)$ has components *s.created, s.commit_requested, s.update-lockholders,* and *s.read-lockholders,* all sets of transactions, and *s.map,* which is a function from *s.update-lockholders* to states of the serial object automaton $S(X)$. We remark here that *map* represents the collection of versions, but is expressed as a function from label to the value of the version.[14] We say that a transaction in *update-lockholders* **holds an update-lock**, and similarly that a transaction in *read-lockholders* **holds a read lock**. The start states of $M(X)$ are those in which *update-lockholders* = $\{T_0\}$ and $map(T_0)$ is a start state of the serial object $S(X)$, and the other components are empty.

If $\mathcal{U}$ is a finite nonempty set of transactions such that for all T and T' in $\mathcal{U}$, either T is an ancestor of T' or vice-versa (that is, $\mathcal{U}$ forms a chain in the transaction naming tree), then define $least(\mathcal{U})$ to be the unique transaction in $\mathcal{U}$ that is a descendant of all transactions in $\mathcal{U}$. Some of the following actions contain precondi-

---

[13]Read locks are sometimes called *shared* locks, and update locks are described as *exclusive*.

[14]This method of modeling the label-version association is possible, since at any time at most one version is labeled with a given transaction. It is convenient, since the most common use of the versions is to find which version has a given transaction as label.

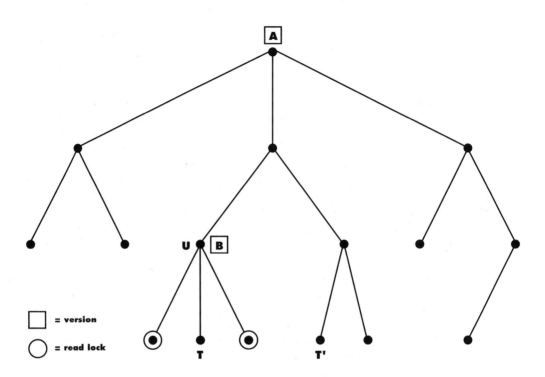

Figure 6.5: Moss's Algorithm

tions in which the function *least* is applied to the set *s'.update-lockholders*. In case *least(s'.update-lockholders)* is undefined,[15] the precondition is assumed to be false.[16]

The transition relation of $M(\mathrm{X})$ is given in Figure 6.6. (Recall that the state component *map* is a function whose domain is given by another state component, *update-lockholders*. Thus, any transition in which *update-lockholders* is altered must necessarily involve altering *map*. Elsewhere in the book, a function's value is explicitly specified in the effect list only for arguments where the value is changed. For clarity, in this instance we diverge from that convention and describe the entire partial function *map*. For example, the effect given for **INFORM_ABORT_AT**(X)**OF**(T) shows that all versions present after the action are unchanged; the alteration to *map* only involves

---

[15]This might be because *s'.update-lockholders* is empty, or not a chain in the transaction tree.

[16]In fact, in all states s' that arise in executions having generic object well-formed behaviors, *least(s'.update-lockholders)* is defined.

CREATE(T)
    Effect:
        $s.created = s'.created \cup \{T\}$

INFORM_COMMIT_AT(X)**OF**(T)
    Effect:
        if $T \in s'.update\text{-}lockholders$
        then $s.update\text{-}lockholders =$
            $(s'.update\text{-}lockholders - \{T\})$
                $\cup \{parent(T)\}$
            $s.map(parent(T)) = s'.map(T)$
            $s.map(U) = s'.map(U)$ for
                $U \in s.update\text{-}lockholders$
                  $- \{parent(T)\}$
        if $T \in s'.read\text{-}lockholders$
        then $s.read\text{-}lockholders$
            $= (s'.read\text{-}lockholders - \{T\})$
                $\cup \{parent(T)\}$

INFORM_ABORT_AT(X)**OF**(T)
    Effect:
        $s.update\text{-}lockholders$
            $= s'.update\text{-}lockholders$
                $- descendants(T)$
        $s.read\text{-}lockholders$
            $= s'.read\text{-}lockholders$
                $- descendants(T)$
        $s.map(U) = s'.map(U)$
            for all $U \in s.update\text{-}lockholders$

REQUEST_COMMIT(T, v),
    for T a read access to X
    Precondition:
        $T \in s'.created - s'.commit\_requested$
        $s'.update\text{-}lockholders \subseteq ancestors(T)$
        there is a state t of S(X) such that
            $(s'.map(least(s'.update\text{-}lockholders)),$
                $perform(T, v), t)$ is a move of S(X)
    Effect:
        $s.commit\_requested$
            $= s'.commit\_requested \cup \{T\}$
        $s.read\text{-}lockholders$
            $= s'.read\text{-}lockholders \cup \{T\}$

REQUEST_COMMIT(T, v),
    for T an update access to X
    Precondition:
        $T \in s'.created - s'.commit\_requested$
        $s'.update\text{-}lockholders \cup s'.read\text{-}lockholders$
            $\subseteq ancestors(T)$
        there is a state t of S(X) such that
            $(s'.map(least(s'.update\text{-}lockholders)),$
                $perform(T, v), t)$ is a move of S(X)
    Effect:
        $s.commit\_requested$
            $= s'.commit\_requested \cup \{T\}$
        $s.update\text{-}lockholders$
            $= s'.update\text{-}lockholders \cup \{T\}$
        $s.map(T) = t$
        $s.map(U) = s'.map(U)$
            for all $U \in s.update\text{-}lockholders - \{T\}$

Figure 6.6: Transition Relation for Moss's Algorithm

removing some elements from its domain. This models the algorithm discarding those versions that were previously labeled with any descendant of T.)

When an access transaction is created, it is added to the set *created*. When M(X) is informed of a commit, it passes any locks held by the transaction to the parent, and also passes any serial object state stored in *map*. When M(X) is informed of an abort, it discards all locks and versions held by descendants of the transaction. Notice that the function $s.map$ agrees with $s'.map$ for all transactions in the domain of $s.map$, but the functions differ, in that the domain of $s.map$ (which is $s.update\text{-}lockholders$) excludes any descendants of T in the domain of $s'.map$.

A response containing return value v to an access T can be returned only if the access has been created but not yet responded to, every holder of an incompatible lock is an ancestor of T, and $perform(T, v)$ can occur in a move of $S(\mathrm{X})$ from the state that is the value of map at $least(update\text{-}lockholders)$. When this response is given, T is added to $commit\_requested$ and granted the appropriate lock. Also, if T is an update access, the resulting state is stored as $map(T)$, while if T is a read access, no change is made to map.

It is easy to see that $M(\mathrm{X})$ is a generic object (i.e, that it has the correct external signature and preserves generic object well-formedness). Note that it is permissible to classify all accesses as update accesses. The Moss object constructed from such a classification implements exclusive locking. Thus, the results obtained about Moss objects also apply to exclusive locking as a special case.

EXAMPLE 6.4.1   A Bank Account Moss Object

Consider the bank account serial object $S(\mathrm{X})$ defined in Example 3.5.2 for the banking database of Example 3.1.1. In Example 6.3.1 we examined a sequence β of actions. This sequence is also a behavior of $M(\mathrm{X})$, the object obtained using Moss's algorithm with the classification where *balance* accesses are classified as reads, and *deposit* and *withdrawal* accesses are classified as updates.

The behavior β can lead $M(\mathrm{X})$ to the state s where $s.created = \{T_1, T_{3.3},$ $T_{3.1003.1}, T_4, T_5\}$, $s.commit\_requested = \{T_1, T_{3.1003.1}, T_{3.3}\}$, $s.update\text{-}lock\text{-}$ $holders = \{T_0, T_3, T_{3.3}\}$, $s.read\text{-}lockholders = \emptyset$, $s.map(T_0) = u$ where u is the state of $S(\mathrm{X})$ with $u.active = ``nil"$ and $u.current = 2000$, $s.map(T_3) =$ $u'$ where $u'.active = ``nil"$ and $u'.current = 1000$, and $s.map(T_{3.3}) = u''$ where $u''.active = ``nil"$ and $u''.current = 800$.

The action **REQUEST_COMMIT**$(T_4, ``OK")$ is *not* enabled in s, because T_4 is classified as an update, and both T_3 and $T_{3.3}$ hold locks. This shows how Moss's algorithm provides less concurrency than the general commutativity based locking, which does allow the deposit acess T_4 to run concurrently with the withdrawals $T_{3.1003.1}$ and $T_{3.3}$.

6.4.2 Correctness Proof

This subsection shows that $M(\mathrm{X})$ is dynamic atomic. In order to show this, a possibilities mapping (as defined in Section 2.7.2) is produced from $M(\mathrm{X})$ to $L(\mathrm{X})$, thereby showing that $M(\mathrm{X})$ implements $L(\mathrm{X})$. Note that $M(\mathrm{X})$ is not describable as a simple special case of $L(\mathrm{X})$: the two algorithms maintain significantly different data structures. Nevertheless, a possibilities mapping can be defined.

To begin, the following is easy to prove, using induction of the length of a schedule. It expresses the fact that the versions are labeled by a chain in the transaction tree, and that read locks are held only by descendants of the lowest element of that chain. This is illustrated in Figure 6.5 above.

LEMMA 6.31 *Let β be a finite schedule of $M(X)$. Suppose that β can lead $M(X)$ to state s. Suppose $T \in s.update\text{-}lockholders$ and $T' \in s.read\text{-}lockholders \cup s.update\text{-}lockholders$. Then either T is an ancestor of T' or else T' is an ancestor of T.*

Now the possibilities mapping f is defined: let f map a state s of $M(X)$ to the set of states t of $L(X)$ that satisfy the following conditions.

1. $s.created = t.created$.

2. $s.commit\_requested = t.commit\_requested$.

3. $s.read\text{-}lockholders$ is the set of transaction names T such that $t.intentions(T)$ contains a read operation.

4. $s.update\text{-}lockholders$ is the set of transaction names T such that $t.intentions(T)$ contains an update operation, together with T_0.

5. For every transaction name T, $perform(update(t.total(T)))$ is a finite behavior of $S(X)$ that can lead $S(X)$ to the state $s.map(T')$, where T' is the least ancestor of T such that $T' \in s.update\text{-}lockholders$.

LEMMA 6.32 *f is a possibilities mapping from $M(X)$ to $L(X)$.*

PROOF The proof involves checking the conditions in the definition of a possibilities mapping. These checks are completely straightforward, but numerous and tedious. As this is the first substantive proof using possibilities mappings, we give the full details. You may choose to skip them.

It is easy to see that $T_0 \in f(s_0)$, where s_0 and T_0 are start states of $M(X)$ and $L(X)$, respectively. Let s' and t' be reachable states of $M(X)$ and $L(X)$, respectively, such that $t' \in f(s')$. Suppose (s', π, s) is a step of $M(X)$. The proof must produce t such that (t', π, t) is a step of $L(X)$ and $t \in f(s)$. It proceeds by cases.

1. $\pi = \textbf{CREATE}(T)$, T an access to X.

Since π is an input of $L(X)$, π is enabled in state t'. Choose t so that (t', π, t) is a step of $L(X)$. The proof must show that $t \in f(s)$.

The effects of π as an action of $M(X)$ and $L(X)$ imply that $s.created = s'.created \cup \{T\}$ and $t.created = t'.created \cup \{T\}$. Moreover, all of the other components of s or t are identical to the corresponding components of s' or t', respectively. Since $t' \in f(s')$, then $s'.created = t'.created$, so that $s.created = t.created$, thus showing the first condition in the definition of f. The other conditions hold in s and t because they hold in s' and t' and none of the relevant components are modified by π.

2. $\pi = \textbf{INFORM\_COMMIT\_AT}(\text{X})\textbf{OF}(U)$.

Since π is an input of $L(\text{X})$, π is enabled in state t'. Choose t so that (t', π, t) is a step of $L(\text{X})$. The proof must show that $t \in f(s)$.

The first and second conditions hold in s and t because they hold in s' and t' and none of the relevant components are modified by π.

The effect of π as an action of $L(\text{X})$ implies that $t.intentions(W) = t'.inten\text{-} tions(W)$ unless $W \in \{U, parent(U)\}$, $t.intentions(parent(U)) = t'.intentions(parent(U))$ $t'.intentions(U)$, and $t.intentions(U) = \lambda$. Consider two cases.

(a) $t'.intentions(U)$ contains a read operation.

Then the set of transaction names T such that $t.intentions(T)$ contains a read operation is exactly the set of T such that $t'.intentions(T)$ contains a read operation, with U removed and $parent(U)$ added. Since $t' \in f(s')$, $s'.read\text{-}lockholders$ is the set of transaction names T such that $t'.intentions(T)$ contains a read operation; in particular, $U \in s'.read\text{-}lockholders$. The effect of π as an action of $M(\text{X})$ implies that $s.read\text{-}lockholders = s'.read\text{-}lockholders - \{U\} \cup \{parent(U)\}$. Thus, $s.read\text{-}lockholders$ is exactly the set of T such that $t.intentions(T)$ contains a read operation.

(b) $t'.intentions(U)$ does not contain a read operation.

Then the set of transaction names T such that $t.intentions(T)$ contains a read operation is exactly the set of T such that $t'.intentions(T)$ contains a read operation. Since $t' \in f(s')$, $s'.read\text{-}lockholders$ is the set of transaction names T such that $t'.intentions(T)$ contains a read operation; in particular, $U \notin s'.read\text{-}lockholders$. The effect of π as an action of $M(\text{X})$ implies that $s.read\text{-}lockholders = s'.read\text{-}lockholders$. Thus, $s.read\text{-}lockholders$ is exactly the set of T such that $t.intentions(T)$ contains a read operation.

This shows the third condition. The proof of the fourth condition is analogous to that for the third condition.

Finally, fix some transaction T and let T' be the least ancestor of T such that $T' \in s.update\text{-}lockholders$. The discussion is divided into subcases, depending on the relation between T and U in the transaction tree.

(a) U is an ancestor of T.

Then $t.total(T) = t'.total(T)$. Let T'' be the least ancestor of T that is in $s'.update\text{-}lockholders$. Since $t' \in f(s')$, $perform(update(t'.total(T)))$ is a finite behavior of $S(\mathrm{X})$ that can lead $S(\mathrm{X})$ to the state $s'.map(T'')$.

If $U = T''$, then the effect of π as an action of $M(\mathrm{X})$ implies that $s.update\text{-}lockholders = s'.update\text{-}lockholders - \{T''\} \cup \{parent(T'')\}$, so $T' = parent(T'')$. Then $s.map(T') = s.map(parent(T'')) = s'.map(T'')$.

If $U \neq T''$ and $U \in s'.update\text{-}lockholders$, then by definition of T'', U is a strict ancestor of T''. Then $s.map(T'') = s'.map(T'')$ and $T'' = T'$, so again $s.map(T') = s'.map(T'')$.

If $U \neq T''$ and U is not in $s'.update\text{-}lockholders$, then $s.update\text{-}lockholders = s'.update\text{-}lockholders$ and $s.map = s'.map$; thus, $T'' = T'$ and so $s.map(T') = s'.map(T'')$.

In each case, the proof has shown that $s.map(T') = s'.map(T'')$; therefore, $perform(update(t.total(T)))$ is a finite behavior of $S(\mathrm{X})$ that can lead $S(\mathrm{X})$ to the state $s.map(T')$.

(b) U is not an ancestor of T, but $parent(U)$ is an ancestor of T. If $U \in s'.update\text{-}lockholders$ then Lemma 6.31 implies that no transaction in $ancestors(T) - ancestors(parent(U))$ can be in $s'.update\text{-}lockholders \cup s'.read\text{-}lockholders$. The effect of π as an action of $M(\mathrm{X})$ therefore shows that $T' = parent(U)$. This effect also shows that $s.map(parent(U)) = s'.map(U)$. Since $t' \in f(s')$, $t'.intentions(W)$ must be empty for all $W \in ancestors(T) - ancestors(parent(U))$. By the effect of π as an action of $L(\mathrm{X})$, $t.intentions(W) = t'.intentions(W)$ unless W equals U or $parent(U)$, so $t.intentions(W)$ is empty for all $W \in ancestors(T) - ancestors(parent(U))$. Thus, $t.total(T) = t.total(parent(U))$. The effect of π as an action of $L(\mathrm{X})$ also shows that $t.total(parent(U)) = t'.total(U)$, so that $t.total(T) = t'.total(U)$. Since $t' \in f(s')$ and U is the least ancestor of U in $s'.update\text{-}lockholders$, $perform(update(t'.total(U)))$ is a finite behavior of $S(\mathrm{X})$ that can lead $S(\mathrm{X})$ to state $s'.map(U)$. The equalities proven show that $perform(update(t.total(T)))$ is a finite behavior of $S(\mathrm{X})$ that can lead $S(\mathrm{X})$ to state $s.map(T')$.

If U is not in the set $s'.update\text{-}lockholders$ then $s.update\text{-}lockholders = s'.update\text{-}lockholders$ and $s.map = s'.map$. Thus, T' is the least ancestor of T in $s'.update\text{-}lockholders$, and $s.map(T') = s'.map(T')$. Since $t' \in f(s')$, there are no update operations in $t'.intentions(U)$. Then the effect of π as an action of $L(\mathrm{X})$ implies that $update(t.total(T)) = update(t'.total(T))$. Thus, $perform(update(t.total(T))) = perform(update(t'.total(T)))$, which is, by the fact that $t' \in f(s')$, a finite behavior of $S(\mathrm{X})$ that can lead $S(\mathrm{X})$ to state $s'.map(T') = s.map(T')$.

(c) $parent(U)$ is not an ancestor of T.

The effect of π ensures that T' is the least ancestor of T in $s'.update\text{-}lockholders$, $s.map(T') = s'.map(T')$, and $t.total(T) = t'.total(T)$. The result follows immediately from the fact that $t' \in f(s')$.

This completes the demonstration of the fifth condition.

3. $\pi = \textbf{INFORM\_ABORT\_AT}(X)\textbf{OF}(U)$.

Since π is an input of $L(X)$, π is enabled in state t'. Choose t so that (t', π, t) is a step of $L(X)$. The proof must show that $t \in f(s)$.

The first and second conditions hold in s and t because they hold in s' and t' and none of the relevant components are modified by π.

The effect of π as an action of $L(X)$ implies that $t.intentions(W) = t'.intentions(W)$ unless W is a descendant of U, and $t.intentions(W) = \lambda$ if W is a descendant of U. Thus, the set of transaction names T such that $t.intentions(T)$ contains a read operation is equal to the set of T such that $t'.intentions(T)$ contains a read operation with the descendants of U removed. Similarly the effect of π as an action of $M(X)$ shows that $s.read\text{-}lockholders$ equals $s'.read\text{-}lockholders$ with the descendants of U removed. Since $t' \in f(s')$, the set of transaction names T such that $t'.intentions(T)$ contains a read operation equals $s'.update\text{-}lockholders$. Thus, the set of T such that $t.intentions(T)$ contains a read operation equals $s.update\text{-}lockholders$, as required. This shows the third condition. The proof of the fourth condition is analogous to that for the third condition.

Finally, fix some transaction T and let T' be the least ancestor of T such that $T' \in s.update\text{-}lockholders$. The discussion is divided into subcases, depending on the relation between T and U.

(a) U is an ancestor of T.

Then $t.total(T) = t'.total(parent(U))$. The effect of π as an action of $M(X)$ implies that $s.update\text{-}lockholders = s'.update\text{-}lockholders - descendants(U)$ and $s.map(W) = s'.map(W)$ if W is not a descendant of U. Thus, T' is an ancestor of $parent(U)$, and in fact must be the least ancestor of $parent(U)$ in $s'.update\text{-}lockholders$. Since $t' = f(s')$, $perform(update(t'.total(parent(U))))$ is a finite behavior of $S(X)$ that can lead $S(X)$ to state $s'.map(T')$. Thus, $perform(update(t.total(T)))$ is a finite behavior of $S(X)$ that can lead $S(X)$ to state $s.map(T')$.

(b) U is not an ancestor of T.

The effect of π ensures that T' is the least ancestor of T in $s'.update\text{-}lockholders$, $s.map(T') = s'.map(T')$, and $t.total(T) = t'.total(T)$. The result follows immediately from the fact that $t' \in f(s')$.

This completes the demonstration of the fifth condition.

4. $\pi = $ **REQUEST_COMMIT**(U, u), U a read access to X.

The proof first shows that π is enabled as an action of $L(\mathrm{X})$ in state t'. That is, the proof must show that $U \in t'.created - t'.commit\_requested$, that (U, u) commutes forward with every (V, v) in $t'.intentions(U')$, where $U' \notin ancestors(U)$, and that $perform(t'.total(U)(U, u))$ is a behavior of $S(\mathrm{X})$.

Since $t' \in f(s')$, it follows that $t'.created = s'.created$ and $t'.commit\_requested = s'.commit\_requested$. Since π is enabled as an action of $M(\mathrm{X})$ in state s', then $U \in s'.created - s'.commit\_requested$. Therefore, $U \in t'.created - t'.commit\_requested$.

Suppose (in order to obtain a contradiction) that there exist U', V, and v such that $U' \notin ancestors(U)$, (V, v) is in $t'.intentions(U')$, and (U, u) does not commute forward with (V, v). Since U is a read access and read accesses are transparent, Proposition 4.9 implies that either $U = V$ or else V is an update access. Lemma 6.23 implies that U' is an ancestor of V, so that it cannot be that $V = U$. Therefore, V is an update access. Since V is an update access and (V, v) is in $t'.intentions(U')$, the fact that $t' \in f(s')$ shows that $U' \in s'.update\text{-}lockholders$. Thus, since π is enabled in state s', U' is an ancestor of U. This is a contradiction; thus, the proof has shown that if U' is not an ancestor of U and (V, v) is in $t'.intentions(U')$, then (U, u) and (V, v) commute forward.

Finally, let $U' = least(s'.update\text{-}lockholders)$. Since π is enabled in s', U' must be an ancestor of U and is thus the least ancestor of U in $s'.update\text{-}lockholders$. Therefore, the fact that $t' \in f(s')$ implies that $perform(update(t'.total(U)))$ is a finite behavior of $S(\mathrm{X})$ that can lead $S(\mathrm{X})$ to state $s'.map(U')$. Since π is enabled in s', there is a move of $S(\mathrm{X})$ with behavior $perform(U, u)$ starting from state $s'.map(U')$. Thus, $perform(update(t'.total(U)))perform(U, u)$ is a behavior of $S(\mathrm{X})$. Since $perform(update(t'.total(U)))$ is equieffective to $perform(t'.total(U))$, $perform(t'.total(U))perform(U, u) = perform(t'.total(U)(U, u))$ is a behavior of $S(\mathrm{X})$, since it is serial object well-formed.

Thus, π is enabled as an action of $L(\mathrm{X})$ in state t'. Choose t such that (t', π, t) is a step of $L(\mathrm{X})$. The proof must show that $t \in f(s)$.

The effect of π implies that $s.created = s'.created$, $t.created = t'.created$, $s.commit\_requested = s'.commit\_requested \cup \{U\}$, and $t.commit\_requested = t'.commit\_requested \cup \{U\}$. Since $t' \in f(s')$, then $t'.created = s'.created$ and $t'.commit\_requested = s'.commit\_requested$. Thus, $s.created = t.created$ and $s.commit\_requested = t.commit\_requested$, so the first and second conditions hold.

The effect of π implies that $s.read\text{-}lockholders = s'.read\text{-}lockholders \cup \{U\}$, $t.intentions(U) = t'.intentions(U)(U, u)$, and $t.intentions(W) = t'.intentions(W)$ for $W \neq U$. Since $t' \in f(s')$, $s'.read\text{-}lockholders$ is the set of transaction names T such that $t'.intentions(T)$ contains a read operation. Then $s.read\text{-}lockholders = s'.read\text{-}lockholders \cup \{U\}$, which is exactly the set of transaction names T such that $t.intentions(T)$ contains a read operation, so the third condition holds.

It is easy to see that the fourth condition holds in s and t, because it holds in s' and t' and the only relevant component that is modified is that $t.intentions(U) = t'.intentions(U)(U, u)$, and (U, u) is a read operation.

For the final condition, consider any transaction T. Note that $perform(update\text{-}(t.total(T))) = perform(update(t'.total(T)))$ and $s.map = s'.map$. Since the fifth condition holds in s' and t', it is easy to see that it holds in s and t.

5. $\pi = \textbf{REQUEST\_COMMIT}(U, u)$, U an update access to X.

The proof first shows that π is enabled as an action of $L(X)$ in state t'. The proofs that $U \in t'.created - t'.commit\_requested$ and that $perform(t'.total(U)(U, u))$ is a behavior of $S(X)$ are identical to the corresponding proofs for the read update case. The proof must show that (U, u) commutes forward with every (V, v) in $t'.intentions(U')$, where $U' \notin ancestors(U)$. The proof will show the stronger statement that if $t'.intentions(U')$ is not the empty sequence, then $U' \in ancestors(U)$. Since $t' \in f(s')$, if $t'.intentions(U')$ is nonempty, then $U' \in s'.read\text{-}lockholders \cup s'.update\text{-}lockholders$. Thus, since π is enabled as an action of $M(X)$ in state s', $U' \in ancestors(U)$.

Thus, π is enabled as an action of $L(X)$ in state t'. Choose t such that (t', π, t) is a step of $L(X)$. The proof must show that $t \in f(s)$. The first two conditions follow as for the read access case. The third condition holds in s and t because it holds in s' and t' and the only relevant component that is modified is that $t.intentions(U) = t'.intentions(U)(U, u)$, and (U, u) is an update operation.

The effect of π implies that $s.update\text{-}lockholders = s'.update\text{-}lockholders \cup \{U\}$, $t.intentions(U) = t'.intentions(U)(U, u)$, and $t.intentions(W) = t'.intentions(W)$ for $W \neq U$. Since $t' \in f(s')$, $s'.update\text{-}lockholders$ is the set of transaction names T such that $t'.intentions(T)$ contains an update operation, together with T_0. Thus, $s.update\text{-}lockholders = s'.update\text{-}lockholders \cup \{U\}$, which is exactly the set of T such that $t.intentions(T)$ contains an update operation, together with T_0. Thus, the fourth condition is satisfied.

Finally, the proof must show the fifth condition. Fix any transaction name T. If $T \neq U$, then since U is an access, T is not a descendant of U; then the fifth condition holds in s and t because it holds in s' and t' and none of the relevant components are modified. So suppose that $T = U$.

The effect of π as an action of $M(\text{X})$ implies that $s.map(U)$ is equal to some state r of $S(\text{X})$ such that $(s'.map(U'), perform(U, u), r)$ is a move of $S(\text{X})$, where $U' = least(s'.update\text{-}lockholders)$; also, $s.map(W) = s'.map(W)$ for all $W \neq U$. Since all members of $s'.update\text{-}lockholders$ must be ancestors of U by the pre-condition of π in $M(\text{X})$, U' is the least ancestor of U in $s'.update\text{-}lockholders$, so the fact that $t' \in f(s')$ implies that $perform(update(t'.total(U)))$ is a finite behavior of $S(\text{X})$ that can lead $S(\text{X})$ to state $s'.map(U')$. Thus, $perform(update(t'.total(U)))\ perform(U, u)$ is a finite behavior of $S(\text{X})$ that can lead $S(\text{X})$ to state $s.map(U)$. But $perform\ (update(t'.total(U)))perform(U, u) = perform(update(t'.total(U)(U, u))) = perform(update(t.total(U)))$. Thus, $perform(update(t.total(U)))$ is a finite behavior of $S(\text{X})$ that can lead $S(\text{X})$ to state $s.map(U)$, as required. □

PROPOSITION 6.33 $M(\text{X})$ *implements* $L(\text{X})$.

PROOF By Lemma 6.32 and Theorem 2.10. □

THEOREM 6.34 $M(\text{X})$ *is dynamic atomic.*

PROOF By Proposition 6.33 and Theorem 6.30. □

An immediate consequence of Theorems 6.34, 6.30, and the Dynamic Atomicity Theorem is that if $\mathcal{S}$ is a generic system in which each generic object is either a Moss object or a locking object, then $\mathcal{S}$ is atomic for all nonorphan transaction names.

6.4.3 Read/Write Locking Algorithm
Read/Write Locking Objects

Suppose that $S(\text{X})$ is a read/write serial object as defined in Example 3.5.3. This subsection describes a generic object automaton $M1(\text{X})$. $M1(\text{X})$ is closely related to the Moss object $M(\text{X})$ defined above (in fact, it will turn out to implement $M(\text{X})$). The code is somewhat simpler for the read/write case because of the special properties of reads and writes. The object $M1(\text{X})$ maintains a stack of *values* and manages *read locks* and *write locks*. It is simpler than $M(\text{X})$, in that it keeps only return values rather than states of $S(\text{X})$ (which include both an active transaction and a data value). The code also looks more direct because the return value for an access is given explicitly, instead of being constrained in a clause of the precondition that in turn refers to the behaviors of $S(\text{X})$.

$M1(\text{X})$ has the usual action signature for a generic object automaton for X. A state s of $M1(\text{X})$ has components $s.created,\ s.commit\_requested,\ s.write\text{-}lockholders,$

CREATE(T)
  Effect:
    $s.created = s'.created \cup \{T\}$

INFORM_COMMIT_AT(X)**OF**(T)
  Effect:
    if $T \in s'.write\text{-}lockholders$
    then $s.write\text{-}lockholders$
        $= (s'.write\text{-}lockholders - \{T\})$
          $\cup \{parent(T)\}$
      $s.value(parent(T)) = s'.value(T)$
      $s.value(U) = s'.value(U)$
        for $U \in s.write\text{-}lockholders$
           $- \{parent(T)\}$
    if $T \in s'.read\text{-}lockholders$
    then $s.read\text{-}lockholders$
      $= (s'.read\text{-}lockholders - \{T\})$
          $\cup \{parent(T)\}$

INFORM_ABORT_AT(X)**OF**(T)
  Effect:
    $s.write\text{-}lockholders$
      $= s'.write\text{-}lockholders - descendants(T)$
    $s.read\text{-}lockholders$
      $= s'.read\text{-}lockholders - descendants(T)$
    $s.value(U) = s'.value(U)$
      for all $U \in s.write\text{-}lockholders$

REQUEST_COMMIT(T, v),
  for $kind(T) = $ "read"
  Precondition:
    $T \in s'.created - s'.commit\_requested$
    $s'.write\text{-}lockholders \subseteq ancestors(T)$
    $v = s'.value(least(s'.write\text{-}lockholders))$
  Effect:
    $s.commit\_requested$
      $= s'.commit\_requested \cup \{T\}$
    $s.read\text{-}lockholders$
      $= s'.read\text{-}lockholders \cup \{T\}$

REQUEST_COMMIT(T, v),
  for $kind(T) = $ "write"
  Precondition:
    $T \in s'.created - s'.commit\_requested$
    $s'.write\text{-}lockholders \cup s'.read\text{-}lockholders$
      $\subseteq ancestors(T)$
    $v = $ "OK"
  Effect:
    $s.commit\_requested$
      $= s'.commit\_requested \cup \{T\}$
    $s.write\text{-}lockholders$
      $= s'.write\text{-}lockholders \cup \{T\}$
    $s.value(T) = data(T)$
    $s.value(U) = s'.value(U)$
      for all $U \in s.write\text{-}lockholders - \{T\}$

Figure 6.7: Transition Relation for Read/Write Locking

and *s.read-lockholders*, all sets of transactions, and *s.value*, which is a function from *s.write-lockholders* to $\mathcal{D}$ the domain of basic values. Say that a transaction in write-lockholders **holds a write-lock**, and similarly that a transaction in read-lockholders **holds a read-lock**. The start states of $M1(X)$ are those in which *write-lockholders* = $\{T_0\}$, *value*(T_0) is the initial value for $S(X)$, and the other components are empty.

The transition relation of $M1(X)$ is given in Figure 6.7.

When an access transaction is created, it is added to the set *created*. When $M1(X)$ is informed of a commit, it passes any locks held by the transaction to the parent and also passes any stored value to the parent. When $M1(X)$ is informed of an abort, it discards all locks and values held by descendants of the transaction. A response to an access T can be returned only if the access has been created but not yet responded to, every holder of an incompatible lock is an ancestor of T, and the return value is appropriate, being *OK* for a write access and the value corresponding to the least holder of a write lock if the access is a read. When this response is given, T is added to *commit_requested* and granted the appropriate lock. Also, if T is a write access, the new value is stored as *value*(T), while if T is a read access, no change is made to *value*.

Basic Properties of M1(X)

A number of simple properties of the generic object $M1(\mathrm{X})$ are given in Exercise 4. They can be proved by induction.

The following two lemmas characterize the value component of the state, relating the state component *s.value*(T) to the events that are lock visible to T or to ancestors of T in *s.write-lockholders*, using the definition of *final-value*($\delta, S(\mathrm{X})$), from Section 3.5.2. (Briefly, *final-value*($\delta, S(\mathrm{X})$) is the latest value written in δ for X. The lock visible events are defined in Section 6.3.2.)

These lemmas are not used until Section 9.4, and the proofs are left as an exercise in that chapter. The statements are included here because they may help you to verify your intuition about the $M1(\mathrm{X})$ objects.

LEMMA 6.35 *Let β be a finite generic object well-formed schedule of $M1(\mathrm{X})$. Suppose that β can lead $M1(\mathrm{X})$ to state s. Let T be a transaction name that is not a local orphan in β such that $T \in s.write\text{-}lockholders$. Then $s.value(T) = final\text{-}value(\delta, S(\mathrm{X}))$, where δ is the subsequence of β consisting of events π such that transaction(π) is lock visible to T in β.*

LEMMA 6.36 *Let β be a finite generic object well-formed schedule of $M1(\mathrm{X})$. Suppose that β can lead $M1(\mathrm{X})$ to state s. Let T be a transaction name that is not a local orphan in β. Let U denote the least ancestor of T such that $U \in s.write\text{-}lockholders$. Then $s.value(U) = final\text{-}value(\gamma, S(\mathrm{X}))$, where γ is the subsequence of β consisting of events π such that transaction(π) is lock visible to T in β.*

Proof of the Implementation

This subsection shows formally that $M1(\mathrm{X})$ is dynamic atomic, by showing that it implements $M(\mathrm{X})$, which was shown to be dynamic atomic in Theorem 6.34.

LEMMA 6.37 *For any object name X such that $S(\mathrm{X})$ is a read/write object, the generic object automaton $M1(\mathrm{X})$ implements $M(\mathrm{X})$.*

PROOF   Assume $S(\mathrm{X})$ is a read/write object. Classify the accesses of $S(\mathrm{X})$ as read and update accesses, where the write accesses are exactly those that classified as updates. Note that the read accesses are all transparent, as needed for the read/update classification.

Now say that a state u of $M(\text{X})$ is in $f(s)$, where s is a state of $M1(\text{X})$, provided that the following conditions hold.

1. $s.created = u.created$

2. $s.commit\_requested = u.commit\_requested$

3. $s.read\text{-}lockholders = u.read\text{-}lockholders$

4. $s.write\text{-}lockholders = u.update\text{-}lockholders$

5. $s.value(U) = u.map(U).data$ for $U \in s.write\text{-}lockholders$

We leave to the reader (as Exercise 5) the details of checking that f is a possibilities mapping from $M1(\text{X})$ to $M(\text{X})$.   □

6.5 General Undo Logging Algorithm

6.5.1 General Undo Logging Objects

This section describes another algorithm suitable for arbitrary serial objects $S(\text{X})$. Here, each access returns a value based on the *current state*, the result of all previously performed operations (except those that are known to be orphans), rather than on the *base state* which reflects only on the operations that are committed, as in the algorithm of Section 6.3. A consequence of this is that concurrent access by operations must be prevented unless they commute *backward*, as defined in Section 4.3. Because the backward and forward commutativity relations are sometimes incomparable, neither the undo logging nor the commutativity-based locking algorithm allows intrinsically more concurrency than the other.[17]

The following example illustrates why backward commutativity is the relationship used in this algorithm. Consider the simple case of three transactions T_1, T_2, and T_3, each of which performs a sequence of accesses to objects, including one access to X. Suppose that T_1 runs and commits, and that X is informed of the commit. Suppose that T_2 and T_3 then run concurrently, but T_2 has its access to X performed before T_3's access. After both have finished running, they both commit, but T_3 commits first. Let v_i be the return value of the access to X by T_i. Now v_2 is determined based on the effect of T_1; that is, so that $perform((T_1, v_1)(T_2, v_2))$ is a behavior of the serial object. However, v_3 is based on the activity of both T_1 and T_3, so that $perform((T_1, v_1)(T_2, v_2)(T_3, v_3))$ is a behavior of the serial object. However, dynamic atomicity requires that the operations be serializable in the completion order (i.e.,

---

[17]In particular, neither is an implementation of the other.

CREATE(T)
    Effect:
        $s.created = s'.created \cup \{T\}$

INFORM_COMMIT_AT(X)**OF**(T)
    Effect:
        $s.committed = s'.committed \cup \{T\}$

INFORM_ABORT_AT(X)**OF**(T)
    Effect:
        $s.operations = s'.operations$
           $- \{(T', v') | T' \text{ is a descendant of } T \}$

REQUEST_COMMIT(T, v)
    Precondition:
        $T \in s'.created - s'.commit\_requested$
        there do not exist U, T', and v' such that
          (T, v) does not commute backward
           with (T', v')
          (T', v') is in $s'.operations$
          $U \in ancestors(T') - ancestors(T)$
          $U \notin s'.committed$
          $perform(s'.operations\ (T, v))$
          is a behavior of $S(X)$
    Effect:
        $s.operations = s'.operations(T, v)$
        $s.commit\_requested$
          $= s'.commit\_requested \cup \{T\}$

Figure 6.8: Transition Relation for Undo Logging Algorithm

that $perform((T_1, v_1)(T_3, v_3)(T_2, v_2))$ be a behavior of the serial object). That (T_2, v_2) and (T_3, v_3) commute backward is what is needed to deduce this.

The algorithm is described very abstractly in this section; for example, the current state is kept simply as a log of operations, rather than in some more compact form. This makes it easy to restore the previous state after learning of an **ABORT**, but is inefficient in space and time, since computing a return value involves "replaying the history" recorded in the log. Practical implementations would need to compact the information in the operations log, and restrict the nondeterminism in choosing which active invocation to respond to. They would also need to give efficient ways of using the compacted information to compute return values and to restore state after receiving **INFORM_ABORT** actions. Our results can be applied to verify implementations of the algorithm in which the state is compacted, and in which the nondeterminism is restricted. See for example Exercise 10.

An undo logging algorithm for X is described by a generic object $UL(X)$, with definition based on the serial object automaton $S(X)$ and its backward commutativity relation. The external action signature of $UL(X)$ is the usual one for a generic object automaton for X, and there are no internal actions.

A state s of $UL(X)$ consists of four components: $s.created$, $s.commit\_requested$, $s.committed$, and $s.operations$. The first three are sets of transactions, initially empty, and the last is a sequence of operations of X, initially the empty sequence.

The transition relation of $UL(X)$ is given in Figure 6.8.

Informally, the algorithm works as follows. When an operation is executed (i.e., a **REQUEST_COMMIT** occurs for an access), the operation is appended to $s.operations$. A **REQUEST_COMMIT**(T, v) is allowed to occur only if it commutes backward with all operations executed by transactions that are not visible to T. The commit of a transaction is simply recorded in $s.committed$; this component is used in the precondition for **REQUEST_COMMIT**(T, v) to determine which transactions are visible to T. When a transaction aborts, all operations executed by its descendants are removed from the log; this has the effect of *undoing* all the effects of the transaction.

EXAMPLE 6.5.1   A Bank Account Undo Logging Object

Consider the bank account serial object $S(\mathrm{X})$, defined in Example 3.5.2 for the banking database of Example 3.1.1. Let $UL(\mathrm{X})$ be constructed as above based on this serial object automaton and its backward commutativity relation given in Example 4.3.4 and Exercise 8 of Chapter 4.

Consider the following behavior γ of $UL(\mathrm{X})$:

CREATE(T_1),
REQUEST_COMMIT$(T_1, \text{``}OK\text{''})$,
INFORM_COMMIT_AT(X)**OF**(T_1),
   CREATE$(T_{3.3})$,
      CREATE$(T_{3.1003.1})$,
   REQUEST_COMMIT$(T_{3.3}, \$200)$.

This behavior can lead $UL(\mathrm{X})$ to the state s where $s.created = \{T_1, T_{3.3}, T_{3.1003.1}\}$, $s.commit\_requested = \{T_1, T_{3.3}\}$, $s.committed = \{T_1\}$, and $s.operations = (T_1, \text{``}OK\text{''})(T_{3.3}, \$200)$.

We claim that the action **REQUEST_COMMIT**$(T_{3.1003.1}, \$1000)$ is enabled in state s. Checking the clauses of the precondition we see that $T_{3.1003.1}$ is active, that the operation $(T_{3.1003.1}, \$1000)$ commutes backward with $(T_{3.3}, \$200)$ (recall that both $T_{3.3}$ and $T_{3.1003.1}$ are withdrawals), and that $perform((T_1, \text{``}OK\text{''})(T_{3.3}, \$200)(T_{3.1003.1}, \$1000))$ is a behavior of $S(\mathrm{X})$.

Let γ_1 denote the behavior consisting of γ followed by the sequence

     REQUEST_COMMIT$(T_{3.1003.1}, \$1000)$,
   INFORM_ABORT_AT(X)**OF**$(T_{3.3})$,
      CREATE(T_4).

The sequence γ_1 can lead $UL(\mathrm{X})$ to the state s_1, where $s.created = \{T_1, T_{3.3}, T_{3.1003.1}, T_4\}$ $s.commit\_requested = \{T_1, T_{3.1003.1}, T_{3.3}\}$, $s.committed = \{T_1\}$, and $s.operations = (T_1, \text{``}OK\text{''})(T_{3.1003.1}, \$1000)$. Notice how the aborted access $T_{3.3}$ has been removed from the *operations* sequence.

The action **REQUEST_COMMIT**$(T_4, \text{``}OK\text{''})$ is not enabled in $s_1$, since $(T_4, \text{``}OK\text{''})$ and $(T_{3.1003.1}, \$1000)$ do not commute backward.[18]

6.5.2 Correctness Proof

Basic Properties of UL(X)

LEMMA 6.38 *Let β be a finite generic object well-formed schedule of $UL(\mathrm{X})$ that can lead to state s. Then $s.operations$ is exactly the subsequence of $operations(\beta)$ obtained by removing all operations (T, v) such that an **INFORM_ABORT_AT(X)OF(U)** for some ancestor U of T occurs after the **REQUEST_COMMIT**(T, v) in β.*

PROOF   Straightforward by induction.   □

LEMMA 6.39 *Let β be a finite generic object well-formed schedule of $UL(\mathrm{X})$ that can lead to state s. Let $\mathcal{T}$ be any set of transaction names such that $\mathcal{T} \cap s.committed = \emptyset$.*

1. *If (T', v') precedes (T'', v'') is $s.operations$, T' is a descendant of a transaction in $\mathcal{T}$ and T'' is not, then (T', v') commutes backward with (T'', v'').*

2. *If ξ is the sequence of operations obtained by removing the descendants of all transactions in $\mathcal{T}$ from $s.operations$, then $perform(\xi)$ is a behavior of $S(\mathrm{X})$.*

PROOF   By induction on the length of β. The basis, length 0, is trivial. Suppose that $\beta = \beta'\pi$, where π is a single event and the property holds for β'. Let s' be the unique state such that β' can lead to s'. Consider cases.

1. $\pi = \textbf{CREATE}(T)$.

Then the properties for s' immediately imply the properties for s.

2. $\pi = \textbf{INFORM\_COMMIT\_AT}(\mathrm{X})\textbf{OF}(T)$.

Let $\mathcal{T}$ be any set of transactions such that $\mathcal{T} \cap s.committed = \emptyset$. Since $s'.committed \subseteq s.committed$, it follows that $\mathcal{T} \cap s'.committed = \emptyset$. Since $s.operations = s'.operations$, the properties for s' immediately imply the properties for s.

3. $\pi = \textbf{INFORM\_ABORT\_AT}(\mathrm{X})\textbf{OF}(T)$.

Let $\mathcal{T}$ be any set of transactions such that $\mathcal{T} \cap s.committed = \emptyset$. Let $\mathcal{T}' = \mathcal{T} \cup \{T\}$; since $s.committed = s'.committed$, generic object well-formedness implies that $\mathcal{T}' \cap s'.committed = \emptyset$. The inductive hypothesis implies that

---

[18]In fact, allowing this action to occur would not violate dynamic atomicity. This is explored in Exercise 9.

(a) If (T', v') precedes (T'', v'') in $s'.operations$, T' is a descendant of a transaction in $\mathcal{T}'$ and T'' is not, then (T', v') commutes backward with (T'', v'').

(b) If ξ' is the sequence of operations obtained by removing the descendants of all transactions in $\mathcal{T}'$ from $s'.operations$, then $perform(\xi')$ is a behavior of $S(\mathrm{X})$.

Now, $s.operations$ is the result of removing the descendants of T from $s'.operations$. Suppose (T', v') precedes (T'', v'') in $s.operations$, T' is a descendant of a transaction in $\mathcal{T}$, and T'' is not. Then also (T', v') precedes (T'', v'') in $s'.operations$, T' is a descendant of a transaction in $\mathcal{T}'$, and T'' is not (since T'' is not a descendant of a transaction in $\mathcal{T}$, and also not a descendant of T since (T'', v'') is in $s.operations$). Then (T', v') commutes backward with (T'', v''), showing the first property. Now let ξ be the sequence of operations obtained by removing the descendants of all transactions in $\mathcal{T}$ from $s.operations$; then $\xi = \xi'$, so $perform(\xi)$ is a behavior of $S(\mathrm{X})$, showing the second property.

4. $\pi = \mathbf{REQUEST\_COMMIT}(T, v)$.

Then $s.operations = s'.operations(T, v)$ and $s.committed = s'.committed$. Let $\mathcal{T}$ be any set of transactions such that $\mathcal{T} \cap s.committed = \emptyset$. Then $\mathcal{T} \cap s'.committed = \emptyset$. Let ξ and ξ' be the results of removing the descendants of all transactions in $\mathcal{T}$ from $s.operations$ and $s'.operations$, respectively. Consider two cases.

(a) There is an ancestor of T that is in T.

Then $\xi = \xi'$ and the second property follows immediately by induction. Now suppose (T', v') precedes (T'', v'') in $s.operations$, T' is a descendant of a transaction in $\mathcal{T}$ and T'' is not. Then (T'', v'') is not (T, v), by the defining assumption for this case. Thus, also (T', v') precedes (T'', v'') in $s'.operations$. The inductive hypothesis implies that (T', v') commutes backward with (T'', v''), showing the first property.

(b) There is no ancestor of T in $\mathcal{T}$.

Suppose that (T', v') precedes (T'', v'') in $s.operations$, T' is a descendant of a transaction in $\mathcal{T}$ and T'' is not. If $T'' \neq T$ then also (T', v') precedes (T'', v'') in $s'.operations$, and the inductive hypothesis implies that (T', v') commutes backward with (T'', v''). On the other hand, suppose that $T'' = T$. Then by generic object well-formedness, $(T'', v'') = \pi$, the last event in β. Now, (T', v') is in $s'.operations$ and has an ancestor U in $\mathcal{T}$; it must be that U is in $ancestors(T') - ancestors(T)$, and also U is not in $s'.committed$. Therefore, the precondition of $\mathbf{REQUEST\_COMMIT}(T, v)$ implies that (T, v) commutes backward with (T', v'). This shows property 1.

It remains to show that $perform(\xi)$ is a behavior of $S(X)$. The precondition and effect of **REQUEST_COMMIT**(T, v) imply that $perform(s.operations)$ is a behavior of $S(X)$. Property 1 proved above implies that if (T', v') precedes (T'', v'') in $s.operations$, where (T', v') is not in ξ and (T'', v'') is in ξ, then (T', v') commutes backward with (T'', v''). Then Lemma 4.6 implies that $perform(\xi)$ is a behavior of $S(X)$. □

LEMMA 6.40 *Let β be a generic object well-formed schedule of $UL(X)$. Suppose distinct events $\pi = $ **REQUEST_COMMIT**(T, v) and $\pi' = $ **REQUEST_COMMIT**(T', v') occur in β, where (T, v) and (T', v') conflict. If π precedes π' in β then either T is a local orphan in β' or T is locally visible to T' in β', where β' is the prefix of β preceding π'.*

PROOF Straightforward from the description of the algorithm. □

Proving Local Dynamic Atomicity

This subsection gives a correctness proof for undo logging, using local dynamic atomicity.

THEOREM 6.41 $UL(X)$ *is locally dynamic atomic.*

PROOF Let β be a finite generic object well-formed behavior of $UL(X)$ and let T be a transaction name that is not a local orphan in β. The proof must show that every sequence in $local\text{-}views(\beta, T)$ is a behavior of $S(X)$. So let $perform(\xi)$ be an element of $local\text{-}views(\beta, T)$; that is, let Z be the set of operations occurring in β whose transactions are locally visible to T at X in β, and let ξ be a total ordering of Z in an order consistent with the partial order $local\text{-}completion\text{-}order(\beta)$ on the transaction components.

The proof must show that $perform(\xi)$ is a behavior of $S(X)$.

Let s be the unique state of $UL(X)$ such that β can lead to s; then a transaction name T' is locally visible to T in β exactly if $ancestors(T') - ancestors(T) \subseteq s.committed$. Let $\mathcal{T}$ be the set of transaction names that are not ancestors of T and are not in $s.committed$.

CLAIM 6.42 *Z is exactly the set of operations in β whose transactions are not descendants of transactions in $\mathcal{T}$.*

PROOF First suppose that $(T', v') \in Z$. Then T' is locally visible to T at X in β, so that $ancestors(T') - ancestors(T) \subseteq s.committed$. Then T' cannot have an ancestor in $\mathcal{T}$, since such an ancestor U would be in $ancestors(T') - ancestors(T)$ and not in $s.committed$.

Conversely, suppose that (T', v') is an operation in β such that T' is not a descendant of any transaction in $\mathcal{T}$. Then any ancestor of T' that is not an ancestor of T must be in $s.committed$. Therefore, T' is locally visible to T at X in β and so $(T', v') \in Z$. $\square$

Now let η be subsequence of $operations(\beta)$ that results by removing the operations whose transactions are descendants of transactions in $\mathcal{T}$. Claim 6.42 implies that the set of operations in η is exactly Z, the same as those in ξ. By Lemma 6.39, $perform(\eta)$ is a behavior of $S(\mathrm{X})$.

The proof must show that all pairs of conflicting operations occur in the same order in η and ξ. Suppose that (T', v') and (T'', v'') are two conflicting operations in η, occurring in that order. Let s' be the unique state to which β' can lead, where β' is the prefix of β preceding **REQUEST_COMMIT**(T'', v'').

The proof must show that $(T', v') \in s'.operations$. Since (T', v') occurs in η, T' does not have an ancestor in $\mathcal{T}$. That is, every ancestor of T' that is not an ancestor of T is in $s.committed$, so that **INFORM_COMMIT_AT**(X)**OF**(U) events occur in β for every $U \in ancestors(T') - ancestors(T)$. By generic object well-formedness, no **INFORM_ABORT_AT**(X)**OF**(U) occurs in β for any element of $ancestors(T') - ancestors(T)$.

Also, no **INFORM_ABORT_AT**(X)**OF**(U) occur in β for any ancestor U of T, because T is not a local orphan in β; thus, no **INFORM_ABORT** occurs in β for any ancestor of T'. Since (T', v') occurs in β' and there is no **INFORM_ABORT** in β' for any ancestor of T', it follows that $(T', v') \in s'.operations$.

Then the precondition of **REQUEST_COMMIT**(T'', v'') and the fact that (T', v') and (T'', v'') conflict imply that $ancestors(T') - ancestors(T'') \subset s'.committed$, which in turn implies that $(T', T'') \in local\text{-}completion\text{-}order(\beta)$. Since the ordering of operations in ξ is consistent with $local\text{-}completion\text{-}order(\beta)$, (T', v') must also precede (T'', v'') in ξ. Thus, all pairs of conflicting operations occur in the same order in η and ξ.

By Proposition 4.5, $perform(\xi)$ is a behavior of $S(\mathrm{X})$, as needed. $\square$

By Theorems 6.41, 6.20, and 6.13, systems containing undo logging objects are atomic for every nonorphan transaction name. Chapter 9 revisits undo logging using a more classical proof technique to prove a weaker result, that such systems are atomic for T_0. See Theorem 9.14.

6.6   Discussion

This chapter has focused the ideas developed in the previous chapter by applying them to the case of locking algorithms. It defined a local correctness property, dynamic atomicity, that affords useful modularity, both in decomposing proofs and in building systems. Using this modularity, correctness proofs of particular algorithms are split into two parts: one showing that dynamic atomicity is sufficient to ensure global atomicity, and another showing that particular algorithms ensure dynamic atomicity. (The algorithms considered in this chapter actually satisfy a sufficient condition for dynamic atomicity, called local dynamic atomicity.) The first part of the proof need be done only once; the second part must be done for each separate algorithm. In building systems, this decomposition allows us to use different algorithms at different objects, as long as each ensures dynamic atomicity.

A different form of modularity is displayed in the hierarchical proofs of correctness. Here, an algorithm is presented that uses relatively abstract data structures (for example, sets of functions) and preconditions (such as the nonexistence of values satisfying a condition). The high level of abstraction allows for proofs of local dynamic atomicity that are not complicated by pragmatic details. A number of other, more practical, algorithms can be shown to be implementations of the abstract one, with more compact or concrete data structures and preconditions. The possibilities mapping is a powerful proof technique in such cases.

There are many other algorithms that use some sort of locks held till transactions commit. The next section lists some references. Many of these algorithms might provide dynamic atomicity, if generalized to nested transaction systems. Perhaps some would be implementations of the abstract algorithms given here; others may need to be verified directly.

6.7 Bibliographic Notes

The use of locking to prevent data inconsistency was introduced to database systems by Eswaran *et al.* [30]. Since then, these techniques have provided the concurrency control in almost every database management system with support for concurrent users.

The idea of a condition on objects that guarantees atomicity was introduced by Weihl [113, 117] for systems without transaction nesting. Such local properties provide useful modularity, allowing different parts of a system to be built independently once the local property used throughout the system has been chosen. This issue is particularly relevant to heterogeneous database systems, in which databases constructed by different vendors are interconnected. A number of authors in recent years have explored how to achieve atomicity (and whether it can be achieved) in heterogeneous systems (e.g., [86, 101]). In addition, defining the properties required of each local database for them to work together properly has been the subject of several standards efforts. The framework presented here provides a rigorous foundation for work on these problems.

Weihl [113] defined three local properties, dynamic atomicity, static atomicity, and hybrid atomicity, that characterize the non-local interactions among objects for three important classes of algorithms. In this chapter we have extended and generalized

Weihl's notion of dynamic atomicity to accommodate nested transactions, and used it to prove the correctness of several algorithms; in later chapters we do the same for the two other local properties.

The notion of dynamic atomicity defined by Weihl is closest to the definition of local dynamic atomicity given here. However, dynamic atomicity as defined here is more fundamental, and should be viewed as the correctness condition; local dynamic atomicity is an important sufficient condition for achieving it. Weihl's definition of dynamic atomicity is based on a partial order on transactions that he calls the "precedes" order; this partial order is essentially equivalent to the local completion order used here. His requirement that a behavior be serializable in all orders consistent with the precedes order corresponds to the requirement here for local dynamic atomicity that says that all elements of *local-views* must be behaviors of the appropriate serial object.

Weihl also proves that under appropriate conditions, there is no local property strictly weaker than his notion of dynamic atomicity that also guarantees global atomicity. This proof relies on the fact that the precedes order captures precisely an object's local information about the global commit order. It would be interesting to explore similar optimality issues for the local dynamic atomicity property defined here.

The first commutativity-based locking algorithm described in this chapter is a generalization of an algorithm due to Weihl [113, 115], to accommodate nested transactions. That algorithm also uses intentions lists and forward commutativity. Intentions lists were first suggested by Lampson and Sturgis in a famous unpublished paper; they were later described by Lampson in [70]. Intentions lists are similar to shadow page techniques used for recovery in System R [41] and to the private workspace technique used in many optimistic concurrency control algorithms (e.g., [61]). The algorithm of Section 6.4 is used in the Argus [75] and Avalon [29] nested transaction systems. It was first presented by Moss [91]. Undo logging, as modeled in Section 6.5 is one of the most common techniques used for recovery, both from crashes and from aborts. It is provided by many systems (as described in [89]). The algorithm presented in this chapter is based on one given by Weihl in [115]. In this algorithm the recovery was presented abstractly; in practice it is important to have efficient ways to calculate the current state after a transaction aborts. Of particular importance is support for "logical logging", which involves logging a compensating operation to be used if the transaction doing the operation aborts. (See, e.g., [59]).

In our presentation of locking algorithms, an access is prevented from occurring except when it can obtain an appropriate lock. In practice, if the lock is initially not available, the system could either block the transaction until the lock is available, or it could abort the transaction immediately (in such a case the assumption is that the transaction would be restarted later). The performance of these alternatives has been studied through simulations (see, e.g., [4]), and also through analysis (see, e.g., [109]). One important problem for performance in locking algorithms is the possibility of deadlock (which has been neglected here because it does not affect atomicity). A survey of mechanisms for dealing with this is given in Chapter 3 of [12].

Many of the results of this chapter appeared in [33]. The results of Exercise 8 are taken from [71]. The algorithm is based on one for systems without nesting from [40]. The methods of this chapter have also been applied in [73] to a *predicate locking* algorithm generalizing one in [30]. Other papers describing important algorithms that (suitably extended to nested transaction systems) might provide dynamic atomicity include [9, 27, 88, 105, 107].

6.8 Exercises

1. Find a transaction T and a generic object well-formed behavior β of a generic object $G(\text{X})$, such that T is not a local orphan in β, but T is an orphan in any generic behavior γ such that $\gamma|G(\text{X}) = \beta$.

Define a more inclusive notion of local orphan than the one used in this chapter. The new definition should allow the object to make more sophisticated deductions to conclude that a transaction is an orphan. However, note that the deductions should be valid, that is, the relevant part of Lemma 6.16 should still be true. Show how your more inclusive notion could be used as the basis for a more inclusive definition of a locally dynamic atomic object, which still suffices for proving dynamic atomicity.

2. Prove the following:

LEMMA 6.43 *Let β be a finite generic object well-formed schedule of $L(\text{X})$. Suppose that β can lead $L(\text{X})$ to state s. Then the following are true about s.*

(a) No two intentions lists contain operations for the same transaction.

(b) For any transaction T, perform$(s.total(T))$ is the behavior of a schedule of $S(\text{X})$.

(c) If (T, v) and (T', v') are two operations appearing in intentions lists of incomparable transactions, then (T, v) and (T', v') commute forward.

3. Show that there is a system type such that Moss's read/update locking algorithm for that system type exhibits the following anomaly. There is an (infinite) behavior β of the algorithm and a transaction name T such that T is not an orphan in β and β is not atomic for T.

4. Prove the following facts about the object $M1(\text{X})$:

(a) Let $\beta = \beta'\pi$ be a finite sequence of actions of $M1(X)$, and let T and T' be transaction names. If T' is lock visible to T in β then either T' is lock visible to T in β' or else $\pi = \mathbf{INFORM\_COMMIT\_AT}(X)\mathbf{OF}(U)$ and T' is lock visible to U in β', where U is an ancestor of T' such that $parent(U) = lca(U, T)$. (That is, U is a child of an ancestor of T but is not itself an ancestor of T.)

(b) Let β be a finite schedule of $M1(X)$. Suppose β can lead $M1(X)$ to state s. Suppose $T \in s.write\text{-}lockholders$ and $T' \in s.read\text{-}lockholders \cup s.write\text{-}lockholders$. Then either T is an ancestor of T' or else T' is an ancestor of T.

(c) Let β be a finite schedule of $M1(X)$. Suppose that β can lead $M1(X)$ to state s. Let T be an access to X such that $\mathbf{REQUEST\_COMMIT}(T, v)$ occurs in β and T is not a local orphan in β, and let T' be the highest ancestor of T such that T is lock visible to T' in β. If $kind(T) =$ "$write$" then $T' \in s.write\text{-}lockholders$. If $kind(T) =$ "$read$" then $T' \in s.read\text{-}lockholders$.

(d) Let β be a generic object well-formed schedule of $M1(X)$. Suppose distinct events $\pi = \mathbf{REQUEST\_COMMIT}(T, v)$ and $\pi' = \mathbf{REQUEST\_COMMIT}(T', v')$ occur in β, where at least one of T and T' is a write access. If π precedes π' in β then either T is a local orphan in β' or T is lock visible to T' in β', where β' is the prefix of β preceding π'.

5. Complete the proof of Lemma 6.37.

6. Consider the following generic object automaton $L1(X)$, which models an algorithm similar to $L(X)$, except that the (continually growing) list of intentions of transactions that are "committed to the top" is compressed into a single state of $S(X)$. Automaton $L1(X)$ has the usual signature of a generic object automaton for X. A state s of $L1(X)$ has components $s.created$, $s.commit\_requested$, $s.intentions$, and $s.compress$. Of these, $created$ and $commit\_requested$ are sets of transactions, initially empty,; $intentions$ is a function from transactions to sequences of operations of X, initially mapping every transaction to the empty sequence λ; and $compress$ is a state of $S(X)$, initially any start state of the serial object. Given a state s and a transaction name T also define the sequence $sum(s, T)$ of operations by the recursive definition $sum(s, T_0) = \lambda$, $sum(s, T) = sum(s, parent(T))s.intentions(T)$. Thus, $sum(s, T)$ is the sequence of operations obtained by concatenating the values of intentions along the chain from a child of T_0 to T, in order.

The transition relation of $L1(X)$ is given in Figure 6.9.

Show that for every reachable state s of $L1(X)$, $s.intentions(T_0) = \lambda$. Show that $L1(X)$ implements $L(X)$ by checking that the function f is a possibilities mapping from $L1(X)$ to $L(X)$, where $f(s)$ is the set of all states t of

CREATE(T)
  Effect:
    $s.created = s'.created \cup \{T\}$

INFORM_COMMIT_AT(X)**OF**(T),
  for $parent(T) \neq T_0$
  Effect:
    $s.intentions(T) = \lambda$
    $s.intentions(parent(T))$
      $= s'.intentions(parent(T))$
        $s'.intentions(T)$

INFORM_COMMIT_AT(X)**OF**(T),
  for $parent(T) = T_0$
  Effect:
    $s.intentions(T) = \lambda$
    $s.compress = t$ where
      $(s'.compress, s'.intentions(T), t)$
      is an extended step of S(X)

INFORM_ABORT_AT(X)**OF**(T)
  Effect:
    $s.intentions(U) = \lambda$,
      $U \in descendants(T)$

REQUEST_COMMIT(T, v)
  Precondition:
    $T \in s'.created - s'.commit\_requested$
    there do not exist U, T', and v' such that
      (T, v) does not commute forward
        with (T', v')
      (T', v') is an element of $s'.intentions(U)$
      $U \notin ancestors(T)$
    there is an execution fragment of S(X)
      with starting state $s'.compress$ and
      behavior $perform(sum(s', T)(T, v))$
  Effect:
    $s.commit\_requested$
      $= s'.commit\_requested \cup \{T\}$
    $s.intentions(T) = (T, v)$

Figure 6.9: Transition Relation for Locking with Compression

L(X) such that $t.created = s.created$, $t.commit\_requested = s.commit\_requested$, $t.intentions(T) = s.intentions(T)$ for all $T \neq T_0$, and $t.intentions(T_0)$ is a finite behavior of S(X) that can lead S(X) to state $s.compress$.

7. Consider the following generic object $M2$(X), which models an algorithm that is similar to Moss's, except that two separate actions are used for obtaining a lock and computing a return value. Thus, $M2$(X) has an internal action **OBTAIN_LOCK_FOR**(T) for each access T to X. A state s of $M2$(X) has components $s.created$, $s.commit\_requested$, $s.update\text{-}lockholders$, $s.version\text{-}holders$, and $s.read\text{-}lockholders$, all sets of transactions, and $s.map$, which is a function from $s.version\text{-}holders$ to states of the serial object automaton S(X). Say that a transaction in update-lockholders **holds an update-lock**, and similarly that a transaction in read-lockholders **holds a read-lock**. The start states of M(X) are those in which $update\text{-}lockholders = version\text{-}holders = \{T_0\}$ and $map(T_0)$ is a start state of the serial object S(X), and the other components are empty.

The transition relation of $M2$(X) is given in Figure 6.10.

When an access transaction is created, it is added to the set $created$. When $M2$(X) is informed of a commit, it passes any locks held by the transaction to the parent, and also passes any version stored in map. When $M2$(X) is informed of an abort, it discards all locks and versions held by descendants of the transaction. A lock can be obtained for an access when every incompatible lock is held by

CREATE(T)
    Effect:
        $s.created = s'.created \cup \{T\}$

INFORM_COMMIT_AT(X)**OF**(T)
    Effect:
        if $T \in s'.version\text{-}holders$
        then $s.version\text{-}holders =$
            $(s'.version\text{-}holders - \{T\})$
                $\cup \{parent(T)\}$
            $s.map(parent(T)) = s'.map(T)$
            $s.map(U) = s'.map(U)$ for
                $U \in s.version\text{-}holders$
                   $- \{parent(T)\}$
        if $T \in s'.update\text{-}lockholders$
        then $s.update\text{-}lockholders =$
            $(s'.update\text{-}lockholders - \{T\})$
                $\cup \{parent(T)\}$
        if $T \in s'.read\text{-}lockholders$
        then $s.read\text{-}lockholders$
            $= (s'.read\text{-}lockholders - \{T\})$
                $\cup \{parent(T)\}$

INFORM_ABORT_AT(X)**OF**(T)
    Effect:
        $s.update\text{-}lockholders$
            $= s'.update\text{-}lockholders$
                $- descendants(T)$
        $s.read\text{-}lockholders$
            $= s'.read\text{-}lockholders$
                $- descendants(T)$
        $s.version\text{-}holders$
            $= s'.version\text{-}holders$
                $- descendants(T)$
        $s.map(U) = s'.map(U)$
            for all $U \in s.version\text{-}holders$

OBTAIN_INTENT_LOCK_FOR(T),
    for T a read access to X
    Precondition:
        $s'.update\text{-}lockholders \subseteq ancestors(T)$
    Effect:
        $s.read\text{-}lockholders$
            $= s'.read\text{-}lockholders \cup \{T\}$

OBTAIN_INTENT_LOCK_FOR(T),
    for T an update access to X
    Precondition:
        $s'.update\text{-}lockholders \cup s'.read\text{-}lockholders$
            $\subseteq ancestors(T)$
    Effect:
        $s.update\text{-}lockholders$
            $= s'.update\text{-}lockholders \cup \{T\}$

REQUEST_COMMIT(T, v),
    for T a read access to X
    Precondition:
        $T \in s'.created - s'.commit\_requested$
        $T \in s'.read\text{-}lockholders$
        there is a state t of $S(X)$ such that
            $(s'.map(least(s'.version\text{-}holders)),$
                $perform(T, v), t)$ is a move of $S(X)$
    Effect:
        $s.commit\_requested$
            $= s'.commit\_requested \cup \{T\}$

REQUEST_COMMIT(T, v),
    for T an update access to X
    Precondition:
        $T \in s'.created - s'.commit\_requested$
        $T \in s'.update\text{-}lockholders$
        there is a state t of $S(X)$ such that
            $(s'.map(least(s'.version\text{-}holders)),$
                $perform(T, v), t)$ is a move of $S(X)$
    Effect:
        $s.commit\_requested$
            $= s'.commit\_requested \cup \{T\}$
        $s.version\text{-}holders$
            $= s'.version\text{-}holders \cup \{T\}$
        $s.map(T) = t$
        $s.map(U) = s'.map(U)$
            for all $U \in s.version\text{-}holders - \{T\}$

Figure 6.10: Transition Relation with Separate Obtaining of Lockings

an ancestor of the transaction seeking a lock. A response containing return value v to an access T can be returned only if the access has been created but not responded to, T holds an appropriate lock, and the response is appropriate, based on the version currently held by the least transaction in the set version-holders. When this response is given, T is added to commit_requested. Also, if T is an update access, a new version is created for it.

Prove the following invariants of any reachable state s of $M2(X)$: if $T \in s.update\text{-}lockholders$ and $T' \in s.read\text{-}lockholders \cup s.update\text{-}lockholders$ then either T is an ancestor of T' or T' is an ancestor of T; and also $s.version\text{-}holders \subseteq s.update\text{-}lockholders$.

Using these, show that the function f is a possibilities mapping from $M2(X)$ to $M(X)$, where $f(s)$ is the set of all states t of $M(X)$ such that $t.created = s.created$, $t.commit\_requested = s.commit\_requested$, $t.read\text{-}lockholders \subseteq s.read\text{-}lockholders$, $t.update\text{-}lockholders = s.version\text{-}holders$, and $t.map(T) = s.map(T)$ for all $T \in t.update\text{-}lockholders$.

8. Consider the following generic object $M3(X)$, representing a concurrent form of the multicomponent serial object of Example 3.5.4. In this algorithm, each access must obtain an appropriate lock, either on the single component that it accesses, or on the whole structure. In order to prevent erroneous concurrent access to the same component by accesses of different granularities, two extra classes of *intention* locks are introduced. Before a lock is obtained on a component, a corresponding intention lock must be obtained on the whole structure. The lock compatibility rules state that any two intention locks may be held concurrently, but that intention and ordinary locks are not compatible unless both are for reading.

Thus, $M3(X)$ has internal actions **OBTAIN_LOCK_FOR**(T) and **OBTAIN_INTENT_LOCK_FOR**(T) for each access T to X. A state s of $M3(X)$ has components $s.created$, $s.commit\_requested$. Also for each possible grain i in $\{\text{``all''}\} \cup \{1, 2, \ldots, n\}$, there are components $s.write\text{-}lockholders[i]$, $s.read\text{-}lockholders[i]$, both sets of transactions. There are also $s.write\text{-}intent\text{-}lockholders$, and $s.read\text{-}intent\text{-}lockholders$, both sets of transactions. Finally for each i in $\{1, \ldots, n\}$ (representing one component of the serial object) there are $s.version\text{-}holders[i]$, a set of transactions, and $s.map[i]$, which is a function from $s.version\text{-}holders[i]$ to values in the domain D used in the definition of $S(X)$. The start state of $M(X)$ is that in which $write\text{-}lockholders[\text{``all''}] = \{T_0\}$, and for $i \in \{1, \ldots, n\}$ $version\text{-}holders[i] = \{T_0\}$, and $map[i](T_0) = d_0$. All other components are empty in the start state of $M3(X)$.

The transition relation of $M3(X)$ is given in Figures 6.11 and 6.12.

CREATE(T)
  Effect:
    $s.created = s'.created \cup \{T\}$

INFORM_COMMIT_AT(X)**OF**(T)
  Effect:
    for each i where $T \in s'.version\text{-}holders[i]$
      $s.version\text{-}holders[i] =$
        $(s'.version\text{-}holders[i] - \{T\})$
          $\cup \{parent(T)\}$
      $s.map[i](parent(T)) = s'.map[i](T)$
      $s.map[i](U) = s'.map[i](U)$ for
        $U \in s.version\text{-}holders[i]$
          $- \{parent(T)\}$
    for each i where $T \in s'.write\text{-}lockholders[i]$
      $s.write\text{-}lockholders[i] =$
        $(s'.write\text{-}lockholders[i] - \{T\})$
          $\cup \{parent(T)\}$
    for each i where $T \in s'.read\text{-}lockholders[i]$
      $s.read\text{-}lockholders[i]$
        $= (s'.read\text{-}lockholders[i] - \{T\})$
          $\cup \{parent(T)\}$
    if $T \in s'.write\text{-}intent\text{-}lockholders$
      then
        $s.write\text{-}intent\text{-}lockholders =$
          $(s'.write\text{-}intent\text{-}lockholders - \{T\})$
            $\cup \{parent(T)\}$
    if $T \in s'.read\text{-}intent\text{-}lockholders$
      then $s.read\text{-}intent\text{-}lockholders$
        $= (s'.read\text{-}intent\text{-}lockholders - \{T\})$
          $\cup \{parent(T)\}$

OBTAIN_INTENT_LOCK_FOR(T),
  for $kind(T) = $ "read", $grain(T) = $ "all"
  Precondition:
    $s'.write\text{-}lockholders[$"all"$] \subseteq ancestors(T)$
    $s'.write\text{-}intent\text{-}lockholders \subseteq ancestors(T)$
  Effect:
    $s.read\text{-}lockholders[$"all"$]$
      $= s'.read\text{-}lockholders[$"all"$] \cup \{T\}$

INFORM_ABORT_AT(X)**OF**(T)
  Effect:
    $s.write\text{-}lockholders[i]$
      $= s'.write\text{-}lockholders[i]$
        $- descendants(T)$
          for all $i \in \{1, \ldots, n\} \cup \{$"all"$\}$
    $s.read\text{-}lockholders[i]$
      $= s'.read\text{-}lockholders[i]$
        $- descendants(T)$
          for all $i \in \{1, \ldots, n\} \cup \{$"all"$\}$
    $s.write\text{-}intent\text{-}lockholders$
      $= s'.write\text{-}intent\text{-}lockholders$
        $- descendants(T)$
    $s.read\text{-}intent\text{-}lockholders$
      $= s'.read\text{-}intent\text{-}lockholders$
        $- descendants(T)$
    $s.version\text{-}holders[i]$
      $= s'.version\text{-}holders[i]$
        $- descendants(T)$
          for all $i \in \{1, \ldots, n\}$
    $s.map[i](U) = s'.map[i](U)$
      for all $U \in s.version\text{-}holders[i]$
        for all $i \in \{1, \ldots, n\}$

OBTAIN_INTENT_LOCK_FOR(T),
  for $kind(T) = $ "read", $grain(T) \neq $ "all"
  Precondition:
    $s'.write\text{-}lockholders[grain(T)]$
      $\subseteq ancestors(T)$
    $T \in s'.read\text{-}intent\text{-}lockholders$
  Effect:
    $s.read\text{-}lockholders[grain(T)]$
      $= s'.read\text{-}lockholders[grain(T)] \cup \{T\}$

OBTAIN_INTENT_LOCK_FOR(T),
  for $kind(T) = $ "write", $grain(T) = $ "all"
  Precondition:
    $s'.write\text{-}lockholders[$"all"$]$
      $\cup s'.read\text{-}lockholders[$"all"$]$
        $\subseteq ancestors(T)$
    $s'.write\text{-}intent\text{-}lockholders$
      $\cup s'.read\text{-}intent\text{-}lockholders$
        $\subseteq ancestors(T)$
  Effect:
    $s.read\text{-}lockholders[$"all"$]$
      $= s'.read\text{-}lockholders[$"all"$] \cup \{T\}$

Figure 6.11: Transition Relation for Multi-Granularity Locking, Part I

OBTAIN_INTENT_LOCK_FOR(T),
    for $kind(T) = $ "$write$", $grain(T) \neq $ "all"
    Precondition:
        $s'.write\text{-}lockholders[grain(T)]$
        $\cup\ s'.read\text{-}lockholders[grain(T)]$
        $\subseteq ancestors(T)$
        $s'.write\text{-}intent\text{-}lockholders$
        $T \in s'.write\text{-}intent\text{-}lockholders$
    Effect:
        $s.read\text{-}lockholders[grain(T)]$
        $= s'.read\text{-}lockholders[grain(T)] \cup \{T\}$

OBTAIN_INTENT_LOCK_FOR(T),
    for $kind(T) = $ "$read$"
    Precondition:
        $s'.write\text{-}lockholders[\text{"}all\text{"}] \subseteq ancestors(T)$
    Effect:
        $s.read\text{-}intent\text{-}lockholders$
        $= s'.read\text{-}intent\text{-}lockholders \cup \{T\}$

OBTAIN_INTENT_LOCK_FOR(T),
    for $kind(T) = $ "$write$"
    Precondition:
        $s'.write\text{-}lockholders[\text{"}all\text{"}]$
        $\cup\ s'.read\text{-}lockholders[\text{"}all\text{"}]$
        $\subseteq ancestors(T)$
    Effect:
        $s.write\text{-}intent\text{-}lockholders$
        $= s'.write\text{-}intent\text{-}lockholders \cup \{T\}$

REQUEST_COMMIT(T, v),
    for $kind(T) = $ "$read$", $grain(T) = $ "all"
    Precondition:
        $T \in s'.created - s'.commit\_requested$
        $T \in s'.read\text{-}lockholders[\text{"}all\text{"}]$
        $s'.map[j](least(s'.version\text{-}holders[j]))$
        $= v[j]$ for all j
    Effect:
        $s.commit\_requested$
        $= s'.commit\_requested \cup \{T\}$

REQUEST_COMMIT(T, v),
    for $kind(T) = $ "$read$", $grain(T) \neq $ "all"
    Precondition:
        $T \in s'.created - s'.commit\_requested$
        $T \in s'.read\text{-}lockholders[grain(T)]$
        $s'.map[grain(T)](least$
            $(s'.version\text{-}holders[grain(T)])) = v$
    Effect:
        $s.commit\_requested$
        $= s'.commit\_requested \cup \{T\}$

REQUEST_COMMIT(T, v),
    for $kind(T) = $ "$write$", $grain(T) = $ "all"
    Precondition:
        $T \in s'.created - s'.commit\_requested$
        $T \in s'.write\text{-}lockholders[\text{"}all\text{"}]$
        $v = $ "OK"
    Effect:
        $s.commit\_requested$
        $= s'.commit\_requested \cup \{T\}$
        for all $i \in \{1, \ldots, n\}$
          $s.version\text{-}holders[i]$
          $= s'.version\text{-}holders[i] \cup \{T\}$
          $s.map[i](T) = data(T)[i]$
          $s.map[i](U) = s'.map[i](U)$
            for all $U \in s.version\text{-}holders[i] - \{T\}$

REQUEST_COMMIT(T, v),
    for $kind(T) = $ "$write$", $grain(T) \neq $ "all"
    Precondition:
        $T \in s'.created - s'.commit\_requested$
        $T \in s'.write\text{-}lockholders[grain(T)]$
        $v = $ "OK"
    Effect:
        $s.commit\_requested$
        $= s'.commit\_requested \cup \{T\}$
        $s.version\text{-}holders[grain(T)]$
        $= s'.version\text{-}holders[grain(T)] \cup \{T\}$
        $s.map[grain(T)](T) = data(T)[grain(T)]$
        $s.map[grain(T)](U) = s'.map[grain(T)](U)$,
          for all $U \in s.version\text{-}holders[grain(T)]$
           $- \{T\}$

Figure 6.12: Transition Relation for Multi-Granularity Locking, Part II

Prove that $M3(X)$ is locally dynamic atomic, by finding a possibilities mapping to the general locking object for $S(X)$, using the facts about forward commutativity given in Exercise 6 in Chapter 4.

9. The undo logging algorithm actually only needs to check for a new operation *commuting backward through* other operations rather than *commuting backward with* the other operations as in the code. Modify the object $UL(X)$ so that it only uses this unidirectional version of the definition, and modify the correctness proofs accordingly.

10. Develop a generic object automaton that is a more space-efficient version of $UL(X)$, in which a summary state of $S(X)$ is maintained instead of the prefix of the operation sequence up to the first operation that has not committed to the top. (Of course, the rest of the operation sequence is still kept as a sequence.) Prove that your algorithm is correct by finding a possibilities mapping to $UL(X)$.

11. This question shows that read/write locking is sufficiently restrictive, in the concurrency it allows and the way it does recovery, that it can be viewed as a concrete form of both the algorithm based on intentions lists (and forward commutativity) and the algorithm based on undo logs (and backward commutativity).

Here are the main ideas. First, the read/write locking algorithm restricts concurrency sufficiently that transactions are allowed to execute operations concurrently only if both are reads, so that the operations commute both forward and backward. Second, the two recovery algorithms for general operations differ in the *view* of the serial object each uses to choose the response for an operation. The algorithm based on intentions lists uses a view formed by executing the operations of the committed transactions, followed by the operations of the transaction itself (technically, the ones lock visible to it, in the order they became lock visible). The algorithm based on undo logs uses a view formed by executing all operations whose transactions are not local orphans (in the actual execution order). These *views* contain the same write accesses, when concurrency is as restricted as in the read/write locking case. Any operation that passes the test for conflicts will get a view consisting of the operations that are lock visible to it, in which the write accesses are those that are lock visible to it, which are exactly the write accesses that are not local orphans, and the order in which these writes became lock visible is in fact the execution order.

Suppose X is an object name such that $S(X)$ is a read/write serial object. Show that any generic object well-formed[19] behavior of $M1(X)$ is a behavior of $UL(X)$.

---

[19] We remark that there are differences between $M1(X)$ and $UL(X)$ in their responses after behaviors

1 2. This exercise explores one way to provide the functionality of the generic controller, replacing a single global entity with a collection of entities, each located at a single site, together with a collection of point-to-point links between pairs of sites. In order to talk about multiple sites, assume that the system type (which represents naming, arguments to procedures, calling pattern, etc.) is extended to include a set of names for *sites*, and a function *site* that takes a non-access transaction name or object name and indicates the site at which that transaction or object is permanently located. We abuse notation and extend the function to access transactions, by letting $site(T)$ be the site of the object to which T is an access.

In a distributed system acting as a controller, we can model the activity of the protocol at a single site n by a *local manager automaton L_n*. Clearly, the interface of L_n must include all the actions shared between the controller and those among the transaction automata and crashing object automata that are located at site n. The interface also must include actions that represent the sending and receipt of messages. This determines most of the interface, but a choice must be made as to which site's local manager executes the completion action for a transaction. It is natural to restrict each completion action to occur only at the site that is the location of the transaction involved. Thus, the actions of L_n are

Input:
    REQUEST_CREATE(T), $T \neq T_0$, $n = site(parent(T))$
    REQUEST_COMMIT(T, v), v a return value for T, $n = site(T)$
    RECV(m)**AT**(n)**FROM**(p), m a message, $p \neq n$
Output:
    CREATE(T), $n = site(T)$
    COMMIT(T), $T \neq T_0$, $n = site(T)$
    ABORT(T), $T \neq T_0$, $n = site(T)$
    REPORT_COMMIT(T,v), $T \neq T_0$, v a return value for T, $n = site(parent(T))$
    REPORT_ABORT(T), $T \neq T_0$, $n = site(parent(T))$
    INFORM_COMMIT_AT(X)**OF**(T), $T \neq T_0$, $n = site(X)$
    INFORM_ABORT_AT(X)**OF**(T), $T \neq T_0$, $n = site(X)$
    SEND(m)**AT**(n)**TO**(p), m a message, $p \neq n$

The state components of state s of the local manager L_n are exactly all the components of a state of the generic controller, with the same types and initial values. Each component represents what is known at the site n about transaction status, and so forth, corresponding to the variable of the same name in

---

in which **INFORM_ABORT** occurs for a transaction after **INFORM_COMMIT**. Of course such behaviors are not generic object well-formed.

the generic controller. Use the usual derived state component $s.completed = s.committed \cup s.aborted$.

In this system, we will use the following format for the messages sent between local managers: a *message* is a record whose components are those of a state of a local manager. Thus, a message indicating that T has committed could be modeled as a record m in which $m.committed = \{T\}$, and the other components are empty. By using this general notation, we allow ourselves to model piggybacking multiple information into a single message, and also make the code easy to write. In fact, some of the components are not actually useful: one site never needs information about which transactions were created or reported at other sites. For uniformity, however, all components can exist in a message. The description is highly nondeterministic; it allows information to be sent anywhere in the system, and it allows unlimited retransmission. In realistic implementations, one would send information only where and when it is needed. For example, the fact that a transaction T is in *create_requested* should be sent only to $site(T)$. The correctness of implementations that restrict nondeterminism follows immediately.

The transition relation of a local manager automaton is given in Figure 6.13.

Each communication channel is represented as a simple unreliable buffer. It can receive messages; each is remembered and may be delivered at any time. Notice that the channels may not preserve message order; they also allow messages to be duplicated. A channel that is FIFO, or one that does not duplicate messages, would implement the channel described here.

The action signature of the automaton for the channel from n to p is as follows:

Input:
  SEND(m)**AT**(n)**TO**(p), m a message
Output:
  RECV(m)**AT**(p)**FROM**(n), m a message

Each state s of the channel automaton consists of just one component: $s.messages$, which is a set of messages, initially empty.

The transition relation of the channel automaton is as follows:

SEND(m)**AT**(n)**TO**(p) **RECV**(m)**AT**(p)**FROM**(n)
  Effect: Precondition:
    $s.messages = s'.messages \cup \{m\}$ $m \in s'.messages$

Let DC, the *distributed controller*, be the composition of all local manager automata, together with all the link automata. The correctness of the distributed

REQUEST_CREATE(T)
Effect:
$s.create\_requested$
$= s'.create\_requested \cup \{T\}$

REQUEST_COMMIT(T, v)
Effect:
$s.commit\_requested$
$= s'.commit\_requested \cup \{(T, v)\}$

RECV(m)**AT**(n)**FROM**(p)
Effect:
$s.create\_requested$
$= s'.create\_requested$
$\cup\, m.create\_requested$
$s.created = s'.created \cup m.created$
$s.commit\_requested$
$= s'.commit\_requested$
$\cup\, m.commit\_requested$
$s.committed$
$= s'.committed \cup m.committed$
$s.aborted = s'.aborted \cup m.aborted$
$s.reported = s'.reported \cup m.reported$

COMMIT(T)
Precondition:
$(T, v) \in s'.commit\_requested$
$T \notin s'.completed$
Effect:
$s.committed = s'.committed \cup \{T\}$

REPORT_COMMIT(T, v)
Precondition:
$T \in s'.committed$
$(T, v) \in s'.commit\_requested$
$T \notin s'.reported$
Effect:
$s.reported = s'.reported \cup \{T\}$

REPORT_ABORT(T)
Precondition:
$T \in s'.aborted$
$T \notin s'.reported$
Effect:
$s.reported = s'.reported \cup \{T\}$

CREATE(T)
Precondition:
$T \in s'.create\_requested - s'.created$
Effect:
$s.created = s'.created \cup \{T\}$

ABORT(T)
Precondition:
$T \in s'.create\_requested - s'.completed$
Effect:
$s.aborted = s'.aborted \cup \{T\}$

INFORM_COMMIT_AT(X)**OF**(T)
Precondition:
$T \in s'.committed$

INFORM_ABORT_AT(X)**OF**(T)
Precondition:
$T \in s'.aborted$

SEND(m)**AT**(n)**TO**(p)
Precondition:
$m.create\_requested \subseteq s'.create\_requested$
$m.created \subseteq s'.created$
$m.commit\_requested \subseteq s'.commit\_requested$
$m.committed \subseteq s'.committed$
$m.aborted \subseteq s'.aborted$
$m.reported \subseteq s'.reported$

Figure 6.13: Local Manager Transition Relation

controller is expressed formally by saying: given any behavior of DC, the subsequence of that behavior consisting of crash actions is a behavior of the generic controller. (This subsequence is exactly the subsequence formed by hiding all **SEND** and **RECV** actions.) Prove this correctness claim.

TIMESTAMP ALGORITHMS

7.1 Introduction

Most database management systems implement transactions using locking algorithms like those described in Chapter 6. However, the research prototype SDD-1 [13] used a different technique, where each transaction is given a timestamp, and the serial execution that the concurrent execution simulates is ordered according to the timestamps. In this algorithm, each object maintains the highest timestamp of the accesses that have read it, and also the timestamp of the transaction that wrote the current version. Accesses are disallowed if their timestamps are not appropriate (for example, attempting to read with a timestamp less than that of the writer of the current version). A number of similar algorithms have been suggested. Practical experience and simulation studies have cast doubt on the performance of timestamp algorithms, but the ideas have undoubted appeal, especially because in many variants deadlocks are not possible (so the expense of deadlock detection can be avoided).

The first implementation of a nested transaction system (by Reed in 1978 [103]) did not use an algorithm based on locks. Instead it used an algorithm where each transaction is assigned an *effective interval* of *pseudotime*. You can think of this as being a time period within which the transaction *appears* to execute. That is, the correctness condition (atomicity) requires that there be a serial execution that looks the same as the actual execution. If you were to record time passing in the serial execution, each transaction would be active during a particular interval. Since the serial execution is only *apparent* (it does not actually occur), the intervals are referred to as being periods of *pseudotime*. We remark that the structure of a serial execution means that these pseudotime intervals will satisfy some constraints: for example, the effective interval in which a subtransaction appears to be active must lie within the interval in which its parent appears to be active, and it must be disjoint from the period in which any sibling appears to be active.

In Reed's system, the assignment of an effective interval to a transaction takes place at the transaction's initiation. The concurrency control mechanism uses these intervals to control the responses given to accesses, in a way that provides atomicity; it ensures that the serial system has an execution that could be observed with the times assigned. Reed's algorithm is a *multiversion* algorithm, based on the realization that since recovery from transaction abort requires the system to maintain information about earlier versions of the object, read accesses can be allowed to see those versions, and thus read transactions can run even with pseudotimes earlier than other transactions concurrently in the system.

This chapter applies the Atomicity Theorem to prove correctness of some algorithms that are based on the use of pseudotime intervals. Each algorithm serializes transactions in the order given by these intervals. As in Chapter 6, different algorithms that use the same serialization order can coexist in a single system without atomicity being endangered, and our correctness proofs are structured to allow modular verification of a system.

Syntactic Constraints: Simple-Pseudotime Systems: In the development of Chapter 5, *simple systems* were defined: these consisted of the (user-defined) transaction automata composed with a *simple database* automaton. The latter imposed only simple syntactic constraints on the behaviors of simple systems. The Atomicity Theorem then stated specific semantic conditions on simple behaviors that are sufficient to maintain atomicity.

To apply this theory to algorithms like Reed's, it is convenient to "expose" the assignment of transactions' effective pseudotime intervals at the external interface of the system. This is done by defining a new class of systems, *simple-pseudotime systems*, in which the simple database automaton has been replaced by a *simple-pseudotime database automaton*. This automaton extends the simple database by adding events that assign intervals to transactions. The simple-pseudotime database provides enough information to define and reason about the sibling order used by the algorithms in this chapter. It is also general enough that it applies to other system organizations as well, such as one presented in Chapter 10. As with the simple database, the simple-pseudotime database imposes only syntactic restrictions on behaviors of simple-pseudotime systems. In particular, when the extra events are removed, behaviors of pseudotime systems are also simple behaviors. This relationship allows us to apply the Atomicity Theorem, which refers to simple behaviors, to behaviors of simple-pseudotime systems.

Sufficient Conditions: Static Atomicity and Local Static Atomicity: Just as generic systems decompose simple systems by replacing the simple database with a generic controller and generic objects, *pseudotime systems* decompose the simple-pseudotime database into a *pseudotime controller* and *pseudotime objects*. The pseudotime controller is an automaton similar to the generic controller, with additional actions that assign pseudotime intervals to transactions. The substantive concurrency control and recovery algorithms are implemented in the pseudotime objects, just as locking algorithms are implemented in generic objects. *Static atomicity*, a condition on pseudotime objects, guarantees atomicity. This condition corresponds to the dynamic atomicity condition on generic objects, except that the serialization order is that of the pseudotime intervals and not the completion order.

Finally, corresponding to the local dynamic atomicity condition, which is sufficient for dynamic atomicity, *local static atomicity* is a sufficient condition for static atomicity. Like local dynamic atomicity, this local condition affords modularity: different concurrency control and recovery algorithms can be used at different objects, as long as each object ensures local static atomicity. Note that one cannot in general combine correct algorithms and be certain of retaining correctness; for example, using Moss's algorithm described in Chapter 6 for some objects and Reed's algorithm for others can lead to behavior that is not atomic (see Exercise 13).

Two Algorithms: Next, two timestamp-based concurrency control algorithms are studied, both of which ensure local static atomicity. The results of this chapter imply that one of the algorithms could be used at some objects in a system, and the other at other objects, and global correctness would still be guaranteed. Such modularity is essential in distributed or object-oriented databases, in which different objects are implemented independently. Specifically, formal descriptions and correctness proofs are given for two algorithms: a multiversion timestamp-based algorithm based on Reed's [103], and a type-specific timestamp-based algorithm that is a generalization to nested transactions of an algorithm of Herlihy [49]. The latter algorithm uses the semantics of operations to permit a higher level of concurrency than can be achieved when the operations are simply reads and writes. In both cases, the algorithms are described in a general fashion that permits a high level of concurrency and requires relatively few aborts by maintaining precise information about what transpires during an execution.

Parallels to Earlier Material: The theory developed in the early sections of this chapter parallels material found earlier in the book. Section 7.2, introducing simple-pseudotime systems, is identical in outline to Section 5.3, where simple systems are introduced. Section 7.3, introducing pseudotime systems, static atomicity, and local static atomicity, has the same organization as Section 6.2, where generic systems, dynamic atomicity, and local dynamic atomicity are developed. Differences between the latter two sections can be attributed to the total ordering information available to objects in the context of timestamp algorithms, while only partial ordering information is available to objects in locking algorithms. (Contrast Lemma 7.21 with Lemma 6.17, and Lemma 7.22 with 6.18.)

Timestamps: Pseudotime Intervals: The essential feature of the systems considered in this chapter is the explicit construction of a sibling order representing the intended serialization of an execution. This order is represented in terms of intervals of **pseudotime**, an arbitrarily chosen totally ordered set. Formally, let $\mathcal{P}$ be the set of pseudotimes, ordered by $<$. Pseudotime intervals, represented as half-open intervals [p,q) in $\mathcal{P}$, are referred to by capital letters. If $P = $ [p,q), then write P_{min} for p and P_{max} for q. If P and Q are intervals of pseudotime, write $P < Q$ if $P_{max} \leq Q_{min}$. Clearly, if $P < Q$, then P and Q are disjoint.

One obvious choice for pseudotimes is the set of positive real numbers. This set has the advantage that it is dense, so that one can always find a subinterval within a given interval (as might be required if the transaction tree is arbitrarily deep). Due to the finite precision of computer representations, an alternative might be to use integers as pseudotimes. In this case both the depth of nesting and the number of children invoked by any transaction would need to be restricted, or in some execution it would not be possible to assign a satisfactory interval to a transaction that had been invoked.

A more complex choice for pseudotimes, which is actually particularly suitable for distributed systems, is the set of all finite sequences of positive integers ordered lexicographically. Thus if $p = 2, 4, 1, 2, 5, 3$ and $q = 2, 4, 1, 4, 3$, then $p < q$ (since the first entry that is different is the fourth, which is 2 in p and 4 in q). In this case, some pseudotime intervals are particularly easy to specify: those that consist of all sequences with a given prefix. We introduce the notation $p, \star$ to represent the set consisting of those sequences with p as prefix. For example, when $p = 2, 4, 1, 2, 5, 3$, then $p, \star$ is a set that contains pseudotimes such as $2, 4, 1, 2, 5, 3, 6$ and $2, 4, 1, 2, 5, 3, 3, 1$; you can check that in this case $p, \star = [p, p')$ where $p' = 2, 4, 1, 2, 5, 4$, showing that $p, \star$ is indeed a pseudotime interval.

It is fairly easy to design a system that gives each transaction a *timestamp* that is a positive integer greater than any timestamp already given to a sibling. The pseudotime interval assigned to a transaction can be the interval of all pseudotimes that have as prefix the sequence of timestamps given to the transaction's ancestors (in order from T_0 to the transaction itself). Assigning pseudotime intervals in this way ensures that each transaction's pseudotime interval is contained within its parent's pseudotime interval and is disjoint from any sibling's pseudotime interval.

7.2 Simple-Pseudotime Systems

This section describes the interval generation mechanism, as an extension to the simple database introduced in Section 5.3.1. In addition to the simple syntactic properties guaranteed by the simple database, the *simple-pseudotime database* guarantees that siblings are assigned disjoint intervals of pseudotime, and that each transaction's interval is a subset of that of its parent. The serialization order for the system will be the comparative order of pseudotime intervals.

7.2.1 Simple-Pseudotime Database

The **simple-pseudotime database** for a given system type, like the simple database, is a specific automaton. This automaton generates pseudotime intervals for transactions in the way suggested by Reed; that is, each transaction after creation is assigned an **effective interval** of values from a domain of pseudotimes, chosen so as to be a subinterval of the parent transaction's interval and disjoint from (and following) the intervals of previously assigned sibling transactions. These restrictions reflect the way the actions of the transaction must appear in a schedule of a serial system: they must all be during the period in which the parent is active, but in a period disjoint from that when any sibling is active. The simple-pseudotime database has the actions of the simple database together with an extra class of output actions **ASSIGN_PSEUDOTIME**(T, P) for $T \neq T_0$ and P a pseudotime interval. A state s of the simple-pseudotime database has the same components as a state of the simple database, together with an additional component $s.interval$, which is a partial function from $\mathcal{T}$ to the set of pseudotime intervals. This component records the pseudotime interval that has been assigned to each transaction.[1]

---

[1] Recall that a partial function may be thought of as a total function that evaluates to a special "*undefined*" value on some elements. The domain of this function is the set of elements that do

In the initial state of the simple-pseudotime database, $interval(T_0) = P_0$, for some pseudotime interval P_0, and $interval$ is undefined elsewhere. All other components are as in the initial state of the simple database.

The transition relation is the same as that for the simple database, except in the following ways:

- the actions **CREATE**(T) and **ABORT**(T) have an additional precondition: $T \in domain(s'.interval)$,

- and the additional **ASSIGN_PSEUDOTIME** actions are determined as follows:

> **ASSIGN_PSEUDOTIME**(T, P)
>   Precondition:
> $T \in s'.create\_requested$
> $T \notin domain(s'.interval)$
> $parent(T) \in domain(s'.interval)$
> $P \subseteq s'.interval(parent(T))$
> $P > s'.interval(T')$
>   for all T' in $siblings(T) \cap domain(s'.interval)$
>   Effect:
> $s.interval(T) = P$

This ensures that before being created or aborted, any transaction has been assigned a pseudotime interval, and that the intervals are related in the way needed to represent a serialization order. Also, the order of the intervals among a group of siblings is the same as the order of a set of events (the **ASSIGN_PSEUDOTIME** events) that occur each after the corresponding **REQUEST_CREATE**; this is needed for the sibling order defined to be suitable. In essence, this is what ensures *external consistency*; that is, that the serial order is consistent with the observed order (for example, when one subtransaction's **CREATE** follows another's **REPORT_COMMIT**, the parent knows the relative order).

EXAMPLE 7.2.1   A Message Queue System

Consider the message queue system of Example 3.5.7. We will use as the set of pseudotimes, the set of finite sequences of positive integers, ordered lexicographically, as discussed in Section 7.1. Here is a schedule

---

not evaluate to "*undefined*". In transition relation descriptions that refer to partial functions, the convention on unspecified state components is extended to partial functions: if the value of the partial function on some element is unspecified in an effect, that value is unchanged by the action. In particular if the partial function was undefined, it remains undefined.

of the simple-pseudotime database constructed for that system type and pseudotime domain.

CREATE(T_0),
  REQUEST_CREATE(T_{G3}),
    REQUEST_CREATE(T_{G2}),
      REQUEST_CREATE(T_{R1}),
    ASSIGN_PSEUDOTIME(T_{G2}, 1, $\star$),
      ASSIGN_PSEUDOTIME(T_{R1}, 2, $\star$),
  ASSIGN_PSEUDOTIME(T_{G3}, 3, $\star$),
  CREATE(T_{G3}),
  REQUEST_COMMIT(T_{G3}, "*OK*"),
        REQUEST_CREATE(T_{R2}),
  CREATE(T_{G2}),
COMMIT(T_{G3}),
  REQUEST_COMMIT(T_{G2}, "*OK*"),
    CREATE(T_{R1}),
      REQUEST_CREATE($T_{R1.0}$),
      ASSIGN_PSEUDOTIME($T_{R1.0}$, 2, 1, $\star$),
      CREATE($T_{R1.0}$),
        ASSIGN_PSEUDOTIME(T_{R2}, 4, $\star$),
      CREATE(T_{R2}),
        REQUEST_CREATE($T_{R2.0}$),
        ASSIGN_PSEUDOTIME($T_{R2.0}$, 4, 1, $\star$),
        CREATE($T_{R2.0}$),
        REQUEST_COMMIT($T_{R2.0}$, 3),
      REQUEST_COMMIT($T_{R1.0}$, 2),
        COMMIT($T_{R2.0}$),
        REPORT_COMMIT($T_{R2.0}$, 3),
          REQUEST_CREATE($T_{R2.A3}$),
            REQUEST_CREATE($T_{R2.B3}$),
            ASSIGN_PSEUDOTIME($T_{R2.B3}$, 4, 2, $\star$),
          ASSIGN_PSEUDOTIME($T_{R2.A3}$, 4, 3, $\star$),
          CREATE($T_{R2.A3}$),
          REQUEST_COMMIT($T_{R2.A3}$, "*OK*"),
          COMMIT($T_{R2.A3}$),
             CREATE($T_{R2.B3}$),
          REPORT_COMMIT($T_{R2.A3}$, "*OK*"),
             REQUEST_COMMIT($T_{R2.B3}$, "*OK*"),
             COMMIT($T_{R2.B3}$),
             REPORT_COMMIT($T_{R2.B3}$, "*OK*"),

$$\textbf{REQUEST\_COMMIT}(T_{R2}, ``OK"),$$
$$\textbf{COMMIT}(T_{R2}).$$

This schedule can lead the simple-pseudotime database to a state s where $s.interval(T_{G3}) = 1, \star$, $s.interval(T_{R1}) = 2, \star$, $s.interval(T_{R1.0}) = 2, 1, \star$, $s.interval(T_{G2}) = 3, \star$, $s.interval(T_{R2}) = 4, \star$, $s.interval(T_{R2.0}) = 4, 1, \star$, $s.interval(T_{R2.A3}) = 4, 3, \star$, $s.interval(T_{R2.B3}) = 4, 2, \star$, and $s.interval(T)$ is undefined for other values of T.

You should notice some features of this schedule. First, the pseudotime intervals assigned to the siblings $T_{R2.0}$, $T_{R2.A3}$, and $T_{R2.B3}$ are related (by the order induced by the lexicographic order on pseudotimes) in the same order as the occurrence of the **ASSIGN_PSEUDOTIME** events for those siblings, which is different from the order of **REQUEST_CREATE** events or **CREATE** events. Second, the pseudotime interval assigned to $T_{R1.0}$ is less than the pseudotime interval assigned to T_{G3} because of the order in which the **ASSIGN_PSEUDOTIME** events occurred for their sibling ancestors T_{R1} and T_{G3}, despite the fact that the **ASSIGN_PSEUDOTIME** events for the accesses themselves occurred in the reverse order.

Basic Properties of the Simple-Pseudotime Database

The following simple lemma follows the pattern of Lemma 5.5 for the simple database. It relates a schedule of the simple-pseudotime database to the resulting states, and gives simple invariants. The extra facts (parts 3, 10, and 11) relate to the additional actions and state component, compared to the simple database.

LEMMA 7.1 *If β is a finite schedule of the simple-pseudotime database that can lead to state s, then the following conditions are true.*

1. *T is in $s.create\_requested$ if and only if either $T = T_0$ or β contains a **REQUEST-_CREATE**(T) event.*

2. *T is in $s.created$ if and only if β contains a **CREATE(T)** event.*

3. *The transaction T is in $domain(s.interval)$ and $s.interval(T) = P$ if and only if either $T = T_0$ and $P = P_0$, or β contains an **ASSIGN_PSEUDOTIME(T, P)** event.*

4. *(T, v) is in $s.commit\_requested$ if and only if β contains a **REQUEST_COMMIT**(T, v) event.*

5. T is in s.committed if and only if β contains a **COMMIT**(T) event.

6. T is in s.aborted if and only if β contains an **ABORT**(T) event.

7. T is in s.reported if and only if β contains a report event for T.

8. s.committed $\cap$ s.aborted $= \emptyset$.

9. s.reported $\subseteq$ s.committed $\cup$ s.aborted.

10. If T and T' are sibling transactions in domain(s.interval), then s.interval(T) is disjoint from s.interval(T').

11. If T is in domain(s.interval), then parent(T) is in domain(s.interval), and s.interval$(T) \subseteq$ s.interval(parent(T)).

We next give some immediate consequences of the previous lemma and the preconditions of the actions of the simple-pseudotime database.

LEMMA 7.2 *Let β be a schedule of the simple-pseudotime database. Then all of the following hold:*

1. *If an **ASSIGN_PSEUDOTIME**(T, P) event appears in β for $T \neq T_0$, then a **REQUEST_CREATE** event for T precedes it in β.*

2. *If a **CREATE**(T) event appears in β for $T \neq T_0$, then an **ASSIGN_PSEUDOTIME** event for T precedes it in β.*

3. *If an **ABORT**(T) event appears in β, then an **ASSIGN_PSEUDOTIME** event for T precedes it in β.*

4. *If an **ASSIGN_PSEUDOTIME** event for T appears in β, and parent$(T) \neq T_0$, then an **ASSIGN_PSEUDOTIME** event for parent(T) precedes it in β.*

5. *At most one **ASSIGN_PSEUDOTIME** event appears in β for each transaction.*

6. *If T and T' are sibling transactions, and **ASSIGN_PSEUDOTIME**(T, P) precedes **ASSIGN_PSEUDOTIME**(T', P') in β, then $P < P'$.*

7. *$T \in$ domain(s.interval) if and only if $T = T_0$ or if an **ASSIGN_PSEUDOTIME** event for T appears in β.*

8. *If $T \in$ domain(s.interval) and T is a descendant of T', then $T' \in$ domain(s.interval) and s.interval$(T) \subseteq$ s.interval(T').*

7.2.2 Simple-Pseudotime Systems, Executions, Schedules, and Behaviors

A **simple-pseudotime system** is the composition of a set of automata indexed by the set of non-access transaction names and the single name *SPD* (for *simple-pseudotime database*). Associated with each non-access transaction name T is a transaction automaton A_T for T. Also, associated with the name *SPD* is the simple-pseudotime database automaton for the given system type.

When the particular simple-pseudotime system is understood from context, the terms **simple-pseudotime executions**, **simple-pseudotime schedules**, and **simple-pseudotime behaviors** are used for the system's executions, schedules, and behaviors, respectively.

The following is immediate.[2]

PROPOSITION 7.3 *If β is a simple-pseudotime behavior, then $serial(\beta)$ is a simple behavior and $serial(\beta)|T = \beta|T$ for all transaction names T.*

We also have the following straightforward result, whose proof is left as Exercise 1.

LEMMA 7.4 *Let β be a simple-pseudotime behavior, and let T be a transaction name such that $serial(\beta)$ contains an event π with lowtransaction a descendant of T. Then an **ASSIGN_PSEUDOTIME** event for T precedes π in β.*

EXAMPLE 7.2.2   Simple-Pseudotime Behavior in a Message Queue System

Consider the serial system described in Example 3.5.7. The schedule given in Example 7.2.1 is a simple-pseudotime behavior.

7.3 Static Atomicity

This section tailors the concepts of Chapter 5 to algorithms like Reed's. In these algorithms, siblings are ordered by explicitly assigned pseudotimes. Transactions with conflicting accesses to objects are serialized by those objects in the order of the transactions' pseudotimes. Hence, we define the appropriate sibling order, and then model the system containing objects that use this order.

---

[2]Recall from Section 3.4.1 that $serial(\beta)$ denotes the subsequence of β obtained by removing those actions that are not serial actions. In this case, the actions removed are the **ASSIGN_PSEUDO-TIME** actions.

7.3.1 Pseudotime Order

The purpose of the **ASSIGN_PSEUDOTIME** actions is to construct, at run-time, a sibling order that specifies the apparent serial ordering of transactions. If β is a sequence of events, then define the relation *pseudotime-order*(β) as follows. Say that $(T, T') \in pseudotime\text{-}order(\beta)$ exactly if T and T' are siblings, and **ASSIGN_PSEU-DOTIME**(T, P) and **ASSIGN_PSEUDOTIME**(T', P') occur in β with $P < P'$. (We emphasize that the pseudotime order only relates siblings.)

The following is immediate.

LEMMA 7.5 *If β be a simple-pseudotime behavior, then pseudotime-order(β) is a sibling order.*

The next few lemmas show that the pseudotime order is suitable, which allows application of the Atomicity Theorem. The first shows that events of one transaction T can affect (in the technical sense of the *affects*(*serial*(β)) relation, defined in Section 5.4.2) events of an unrelated transaction T' only if T is ordered before T' by the descendant closure of the pseudotime order. In essence, this is because the least common ancestor must receive the report of the completion of the ancestor of T before requesting the creation of the ancestor of T'; since the **ASSIGN_PSEUDOTIME** event for one transaction must precede its completion, and the **ASSIGN_PSEUDO-TIME** event for the other must follow the request to create it, we see that the sibling ancestors of T and T' have their **ASSIGN_PSEUDOTIME** events in that order. Since pseudotime intervals are assigned among siblings in increasing order, the pseudotime intervals of the ancestors of T and T' are in that order. And since the intervals of T and T' are subintervals of those of their respective ancestors, the result follows.

LEMMA 7.6 *Let β be a simple-pseudotime behavior and let $R = pseudotime\text{-}order(\beta)$. Let π and π' be distinct events in serial(β) with lowtransactions T and T' respectively. If T is neither an ancestor nor a descendant of T', and $(\pi, \pi') \in affects(serial(\beta))$, then $(\pi, \pi') \in R_{event}(serial(\beta))$.*

PROOF Since T is neither an ancestor nor a descendant of T', there must be siblings U and U' such that T is a descendant of U, and T' is a descendant of U'. Let U'' denote $parent(U) = parent(U') = lca(T, T')$. By Lemma 7.4, β contains events **ASSIGN_PSEUDOTIME**(U, P) and **ASSIGN_PSEUDOTIME**(U', P').

By Lemmas 5.17 and 5.18, there must be events ϕ and ϕ' in *serial*(β) such that ϕ is a report event for U, ϕ' is **REQUEST_CREATE**(U'), and $(\pi, \phi), (\phi, \phi')$, and (ϕ', π') are all in *affects*(*serial*(β)). Thus, ϕ occurs before ϕ' in β. The preconditions of the simple-pseudotime database ensure that ϕ is preceded by a completion event for

U, and Lemma 7.4 shows that this is preceded by an **ASSIGN_PSEUDOTIME**(U, P) event. The simple-pseudotime database preconditions ensure that **ASSIGN_PSEUDO-TIME**(U', P') follows ϕ'. Thus the **ASSIGN_PSEUDOTIME**(U, P) event precedes the **ASSIGN_PSEUDOTIME**(U', P') event. By Lemma 7.2, $P < P'$. Thus $(U, U') \in R$. The result follows.   □

We now show that the two partial orders defined on the events of $serial(\beta)$ are consistent.

LEMMA 7.7 *Let β be a simple-pseudotime behavior, and let $R = pseudotime\text{-}order(\beta)$. Then $R_{event}(serial(\beta))$ and affects$(serial(\beta))$ are consistent partial orders on the events in $serial(\beta)$.*

PROOF   This is immediate by Lemmas 7.6 and 5.23.   □

LEMMA 7.8 *Let β be a simple-pseudotime behavior and T a transaction name. If T and T' are siblings that are lowtransactions of actions in $serial(\beta)$, then either (T, T') or $(T', T) \in pseudotime\text{-}order(\beta)$.*

PROOF   By Lemmas 7.4 and 7.2.   □

Now one can conclude that the pseudotime order is suitable.

LEMMA 7.9 *Let β be a simple-pseudotime behavior and T a transaction name. Then $pseudotime\text{-}order(\beta)$ is suitable for $serial(\beta)$ and T.*

PROOF   By Lemmas 7.8 and 7.7.   □

The following variant of Corollary 5.25 to the Atomicity Theorem applies to the special case where R is the pseudotime order and the system is a simple-pseudotime system.

PROPOSITION 7.10 *Let β be a finite simple-pseudotime behavior, T a transaction name such that T is not an orphan in β, and let $R = pseudotime\text{-}order(\beta)$. Suppose that for each object name X, $view(serial(\beta), T, R, X)$ is a behavior of $S(X)$. Then β is atomic for T.*

PROOF Proposition 7.3 implies that $serial(\beta)$ is a simple behavior, and Lemma 7.9 implies that R is suitable for $serial(\beta)$ and T. The result is immediate from Corollary 5.25. □

EXAMPLE 7.3.1   Atomicity In A Message Queue System

Let β be the sequence given in Example 7.2.1. The calculation of $view(serial(\beta), T_0, R, X)$, where $R = pseudotime\text{-}order(\beta)$, is left as Exercise 2. You are invited to check that β is atomic for T_0.

7.3.2 Pseudotime Systems

This subsection defines the system decomposition appropriate for describing many timestamp-based algorithms. Analogous to the *generic systems* used for modeling locking algorithms, these algorithms are formulated as objects in *pseudotime systems*. These systems are composed of transaction automata, *pseudotime object automata*, and a *pseudotime controller*. The general structure of the system is the same as that given in Figure 3.2 for serial systems.

A separate *pseudotime object* automaton for each object name handles the concurrency control and data for that object in an as yet unspecified way, using information about pseudotimes of accesses and the fates of transactions. The *pseudotime controller* assigns pseudotime intervals and passes requests and information around the system.

Pseudotime Object Automata

A **pseudotime object automaton** $P(X)$ for an object name X of a given system type is an automaton with the following external action signature.

Input:
    CREATE(T), for T an access to X
    INFORM_COMMIT_AT(X)**OF**(T), for $T \neq T_0$
    INFORM_ABORT_AT(X)**OF**(T), for $T \neq T_0$
    INFORM_TIME_AT(X)**OF**(T, p), for $T \in accesses(\mathrm{X}), p \in \mathcal{P}$
Output:
    REQUEST_COMMIT(T, v), for T and access to X and v a value for T

In addition, $P(X)$ may have an arbitrary set of internal actions.

The actions **CREATE**(T) and **REQUEST_COMMIT**(T, v) correspond to invocations of accesses and responses to accesses, just as for a serial object $S(X)$. In addition, a pseudotime object has input actions that correspond to the receipt of information about the commit or abort of a transaction, and about the pseudotimes[3] assigned to an access transaction.

A pseudotime object automaton $P(X)$ is required to preserve *pseudotime object well-formedness*, defined as follows. A sequence β of actions π in the external signature of $P(X)$ is said to be **pseudotime object well-formed** for X provided that the following conditions hold. These conditions are similar to those used to define generic object well-formedness, in Section 6.2.2. The additional conditions constrain the object not to respond to an access until the pseudotime is known, and also constrain the environment not to provide contradictory information about pseudotimes.[4]

1. There is at most one **CREATE**(T) event in β for any access T.

2. There is at most one **REQUEST_COMMIT** event in β for any access T.

3. If there is a **REQUEST_COMMIT** event for an access T in β, then there is a preceding **CREATE**(T) in β and also a preceding **INFORM_TIME_AT**(X)**OF**(T, p) event, for some pseudotime p.

4. There is no access T for which there are two different pseudotimes, p and p', such that **INFORM_TIME_AT**(X)**OF**(T, p) and **INFORM_TIME_AT**(X)**OF**(T, p') both occur in β.

5. There is no pseudotime p for which there are two different accesses, T and T', such that **INFORM_TIME_AT**(X)**OF**(T, p) and **INFORM_TIME_AT**(X)**OF**(T', p) both occur in β.

6. There is no transaction T for which both an **INFORM_COMMIT_AT**(X)**OF**(T) and an **INFORM_ABORT_AT**(X)**OF**(T) event occur in β.

7. If an **INFORM_COMMIT_AT**(X)**OF**(T) event occurs in β and T is an access to X, then there is a preceding **REQUEST_COMMIT** event for T.

As with previous well-formedness properties, there is an alternative form of the definition.

----

[3]We have made the decision to transfer to an object only a single pseudotime for each access, rather than an entire interval. Similarly, our model does not include any transfer of information about the intervals assigned to non-access transactions, except what can be inferred from the pseudotimes of their descendant accesses. Enriching the object interface with more information would require minor changes to the proofs and development of this chapter.

[4]We remark that there are other conditions that will be true in every behavior in a pseudotime system; for example, that for any transaction, the pseudotimes known for its descendants will not be separated from one another by the pseudotime known for an access that is not a descendant. The conditions listed here are a straightforward collection that are adequate for the purpose of simplifying local reasoning for the algorithms chosen.

LEMMA 7.11 *A sequence β of actions in the external signature of a pseudotime object for object name* X *is pseudotime object well-formed for* X *exactly if for every finite prefix $\gamma\pi$ of β, where π is a single action, the following conditions hold.*

1. *If π is **CREATE(T)**, then*

    *(a) there is no **CREATE** event for T in γ.*

2. *If π is **INFORM_COMMIT_AT(X)OF(T)**, then*

    (a) If T is an access to X*, then there is a **REQUEST_COMMIT** for T in γ, and*

    *(b) there is no **INFORM_ABORT_AT(X)OF(T)** in γ.*

3. *If π is **INFORM_ABORT_AT(X)OF(T)**, then*

    *(a) there is no **INFORM_COMMIT_AT(X)OF(T)** in γ.*

4. *If π is **INFORM_TIME_AT(X)OF(T,p)**, then*

    *(a) there is no **INFORM_TIME_AT(X)OF(T',p)** event in γ, where $T \neq T'$, and*

    *(b) there is no **INFORM_TIME_AT(X)OF(T,p')** event in γ, where $p \neq p'$.*

5. *If π is **REQUEST_COMMIT**(T,v), then*

    *(a) there is a **CREATE(T)** in γ,*

    *(b) there is no **REQUEST_COMMIT** for T in γ, and*

    *(c) there is an **INFORM_TIME_AT(X)OF(T,p)** in γ for some p.*

Pseudotime Controller

There is a single pseudotime controller for each system type. As with the generic controller of Chapter 6, the pseudotime controller passes requests for the creation of subtransactions to the appropriate recipient, makes decisions about the commit or abort of transactions, passes reports about the completion of children back to their parents, and informs objects of the fate of transactions. In addition to these functions of the generic controller, the pseudotime controller assigns pseudotime intervals to transactions and informs objects of the pseudotimes of relevant accesses. Again like the generic controller, and unlike the serial scheduler, it does not prevent sibling transactions from being live simultaneously, nor does it prevent the same transaction from being both created and aborted. Rather, it leaves the task of coping with concurrency and recovery to the pseudotime objects.

The pseudotime controller has the following action signature.

Input:
   REQUEST_CREATE(T), $T \neq T_0$
   REQUEST_COMMIT(T, v), v a value for T
Output:
   ASSIGN_PSEUDOTIME(T, P), P a pseudotime interval, $T \neq T_0$
   CREATE(T)
   COMMIT(T), $T \neq T_0$
   ABORT(T), $T \neq T_0$
   REPORT_COMMIT(T,v), $T \neq T_0$, v a value for T
   REPORT_ABORT(T), $T \neq T_0$
   INFORM_COMMIT_AT(X)**OF**(T), $T \neq T_0$
   INFORM_ABORT_AT(X)**OF**(T), $T \neq T_0$
   INFORM_TIME_AT(X)**OF**(T, p), T an access to X

A state s of the pseudotime controller has the same components as that of the simple-pseudotime database, with the same initialization. The actions of the pseudotime controller are the same as the corresponding actions of the pseudotime database, except for **REQUEST_COMMIT** and **INFORM** actions.[5] For those actions, the transition relation is as follows.

REQUEST_COMMIT(T, v)
   Effect:
      $s.commit\_requested$
         $= s'.commit\_requested \cup \{(T, v)\}$

INFORM_COMMIT_AT(X)**OF**(T)
   Precondition:
      $T \in s'.committed$

INFORM_ABORT_AT(X)**OF**(T)
   Precondition:
      $T \in s'.aborted$

INFORM_TIME_AT(X)**OF**(T, p)
   Precondition:
      $T \in domain(s'.interval)$
      $s'.interval(T) = P$
      $p = P_{min}$

Except for the new **INFORM_TIME** action, the actions are also the same as the corresponding actions of the generic controller. Notice that the **INFORM_TIME** events only provide the lowest pseudotime within the assigned interval, and this information is only given to the object to which the transaction is an access.

Basic Properties of the Pseudotime Controller

The following simple lemmas are analogous to those given for the generic controller and the simple-pseudotime database. The first relates a schedule of the pseudotime controller to the resulting states, and the second gives some simple properties of schedules of the pseudotime controller.

---

[5] Notice that for accesses, **REQUEST_COMMIT** actions are *outputs* of the pseudotime database, but they are *inputs* to the pseudotime controller, just as they are outputs of the simple database, but inputs to the generic controller. These actions are outputs of the object automata.

LEMMA 7.12 *If β is a finite schedule of the pseudotime controller that can lead to state s, then the following conditions are true.*

1. *T is in $s.create\_requested$ if and only if either $T = T_0$ or β contains a **REQUEST-_CREATE**(T) event.*

2. *T is in $s.created$ if and only if β contains a **CREATE**(T) event.*

3. *The transaction T is in $domain(s.interval)$ and $s.interval(T) = P$ if and only if either $T = T_0$ and $P = P_0$, or β contains an **ASSIGN_PSEUDOTIME**(T, P) event.*

4. *(T, v) is in $s.commit\_requested$ if and only if β contains a **REQUEST_COMMIT** (T, v) event.*

5. *T is in $s.committed$ if and only if β contains a **COMMIT**(T) event.*

6. *T is in $s.aborted$ if and only if β contains an **ABORT**(T) event.*

7. *T is in $s.reported$ if and only if β contains a report event for T.*

8. *$s.committed \cap s.aborted = \emptyset$.*

9. *$s.reported \subseteq s.committed \cup s.aborted$.*

10. *If T and T' are sibling transactions in $domain(s.interval)$, then $s.interval(T)$ is disjoint from $s.interval(T')$.*

11. *If T is in $domain(s.interval)$, then $parent(T) \in domain(s.interval)$, and $s.interval(T) \subseteq s.interval(parent(T))$.*

LEMMA 7.13 *Let β be a schedule of the pseudotime controller. Then all of the following hold:*

1. *If an **ASSIGN_PSEUDOTIME**(T, P) event appears in β, for any $T \neq T_0$, then a **REQUEST_CREATE** event for T precedes it in β.*

2. *If a **CREATE**(T) event appears in β, for any $T \neq T_0$, then an **ASSIGN_PSEU-DOTIME** event for T precedes it in β.*

3. *If an **ABORT**(T) event appears in β, then an **ASSIGN_PSEUDOTIME** event for T precedes it in β.*

4. *If an **ASSIGN_PSEUDOTIME** event for T appears in β, and $parent(T) \neq T_0$, then an **ASSIGN_PSEUDOTIME** event for $parent(T)$ precedes it in β.*

5. *At most one **ASSIGN_PSEUDOTIME** event appears in β for each transaction.*

6. If *ASSIGN_PSEUDOTIME*(T, P) *precedes* *ASSIGN_PSEUDOTIME*(T', P') *in* β, *for sibling transactions* T *and* T', *then* $P < P'$.

7. $T \in domain(s.interval)$ *if and only if* $T = T_0$ *or if an* *ASSIGN_PSEUDOTIME* *event for* T *appears in* β.

8. *If* $T \in domain(s.interval)$ *and* T *is a descendant of* T', *then* $T' \in domain(s.interval)$ *and* $s.interval(T) \subseteq s.interval(T')$.

9. *If an* *INFORM_COMMIT_AT*(X)*OF*(T) *event appears in* β, *then a* *COMMIT* *event for* T *precedes it in* β.

10. *If an* *INFORM_ABORT_AT*(X)*OF*(T) *event appears in* β, *then an* *ABORT* *event for* T *precedes it in* β.

11. *If an* *INFORM_TIME_AT*(X)*OF*(T,p) *event appears in* β, *then an* *ASSIGN_PSEUDOTIME*(T, P) *event appears in* β *with* $p = P_{min}$.

Pseudotime Systems

A **pseudotime system** is the composition of a set of automata indexed by the union of the set of non-access transaction names, the set of object names, and the singleton set PC (for *pseudotime controller*). Associated with each non-access transaction name T is a transaction automaton A_T for T. Associated with each object name X is a pseudotime object automaton $P(\text{X})$. Also, associated with the name PC is the pseudotime controller for the given system type.

The external actions of a pseudotime system are called **pseudotime actions**, and the executions, schedules, and behaviors of a pseudotime system are called **pseudotime executions**, **pseudotime schedules**, and **pseudotime behaviors**, respectively.

If β is a sequence of external actions of a pseudotime system, then define $pseudo(\beta)$ by removing from β all **INFORM** actions.

Since the pseudotime controller, the transaction automata, and each pseudotime object automaton all preserve transaction and pseudotime object well-formedness, we have the following result.

PROPOSITION 7.14 *If* β *is a pseudotime behavior, then the following conditions hold.*

1. *For every transaction name* T, $\beta | T$ *is transaction well-formed for* T.

2. *For every object name* X, $\beta | P(\text{X})$ *is pseudotime object well-formed for* X.

The following captures the relationship between a pseudotime system and the simple-pseudotime system.

PROPOSITION 7.15 *If β is a pseudotime behavior, then $pseudo(\beta)$ is a pseudotime behavior and $pseudo(\beta)|T = \beta|T$ for all transaction names T.*

The earlier results on simple-pseudotime behaviors can now be applied to obtain a sufficient condition for proving the atomicity of a pseudotime behavior.

PROPOSITION 7.16 *Let β be a finite pseudotime behavior, T a transaction name such that T is not an orphan in β, and let $R = pseudotime\text{-}order(\beta)$. Suppose that for each object name X, $view(serial(\beta), T, R, X)$ is a behavior of $S(X)$. Then β is atomic for T.*

PROOF By Propositions 7.10 and 7.15.   □

7.3.3 Static Atomicity

When designing a distributed database management system, the choice of concurrency control and recovery algorithms should guarantee the atomicity of all the finite behaviors of the system. Also, it is advantageous to consider the algorithm used in implementing one object without reasoning about the implementations of all the other objects. Thus, one is lead to define the local property of *static atomicity*. Like dynamic atomicity, this is a property that can be checked for each object separately. A static atomic object is one that uses the order of accesses' pseudotimes to serialize them.[6]

Let $P(X)$ be a pseudotime object automaton for object name X. Say that $P(X)$ is **static atomic** for a given system type if for all pseudotime systems S of the given type in which $P(X)$ is associated with X, the following is true. Let β be a finite behavior of S, $R = pseudotime\text{-}order(\beta)$, and T a transaction name that is not an orphan in β. Then $view(serial(\beta), T, R, X)$ is a behavior of $S(X)$.

THEOREM 7.17 *(Static Atomicity Theorem) Let S be a pseudotime system in which all pseudotime objects are static atomic. Let β be a finite behavior of S. Then β is atomic for every nonorphan transaction name.*

PROOF Immediate from Proposition 7.16 and the definition of static atomicity.   □

---

[6]The name reflects the idea that the position of a transaction in the serialization order is that of the pseudotime interval, and this is determined earlier in an execution than the completion order used in dynamic atomicity; in particular, it is not influenced by the activity of the transaction itself.

7.3.4 Local Static Atomicity

This subsection defines another property of pseudotime object automata called *local static atomicity*, which is a convenient sufficient condition for showing static atomicity. For each pseudotime object automaton P, static atomicity is a local condition in that it only depends on P. However, the form in which the condition is stated may be difficult to check directly: one must be able to verify a condition involving $view(serial(\beta), T, pseudotime\text{-}order(\beta), X)$ for all finite behaviors β of all pseudotime systems containing P. Local static atomicity is defined more directly in terms of the behaviors of P. (This parallels the development in Chapter 6, where local dynamic atomicity is used to prove dynamic atomicity.)

First some terms are introduced to describe information about the status of transactions that is deducible from the behavior of a particular pseudotime object. Let $P(X)$ be a pseudotime object automaton for X, β a sequence of external actions of $P(X)$, and T and T' transaction names. Then T is **locally visible at** X **to** T' in β if β contains an **INFORM_COMMIT_AT**(X)**OF**(U) event for every U in $ancestors(T) - ancestors(T')$. Also, T is a **local orphan at** X in β if β contains an **INFORM_ABORT_AT**(X)**OF**(U) event for some ancestor U of T. These definitions are essentially the same as the corresponding definitions in Section 6.2.4.[7]

The next results are analogous to those in Section 6.2.4.

LEMMA 7.18 *Let $P(X)$ be a pseudotime object automaton for X. Let β be a sequence of external actions of $P(X)$, and let T, T', and T'' be transaction names. If T is locally visible at X to T' in β, and T' is locally visible at X to T'' in β, then T is locally visible at X to T'' in β.*

LEMMA 7.19 *Let $P(X)$ be a pseudotime object automaton for X. Let β be a pseudotime object well-formed sequence of external actions of $P(X)$, and let T and T' be transaction names. If T is locally visible at X to T' in β, and T is a local orphan at X in β, then T' is a local orphan at X in β.*

The names introduced above are justified by the relationships between the local properties defined above and the corresponding global properties. This shows that the definitions express safe deductions from local information.

LEMMA 7.20 *Let β be a behavior of a pseudotime system in which pseudotime object automaton $P(X)$ is associated with X. If T is locally visible at X to T' in $\beta|P(X)$,*

---

[7]The only difference is in the signatures of the objects, and therefore in the types of actions that appear in the sequences considered.

then T *is visible to* T' *in* β. *Similarly, if* T *is a local orphan at* X *in* $\beta|P(X)$, *then* T *is an orphan in* β.

PROOF   These are immediate consequences of the pseudotime controller preconditions, which imply that any **INFORM_COMMIT_AT**(X)**OF**(T) event in β must be preceded by a **COMMIT**(T) event and that any **INFORM_ABORT_AT**(X)**OF**(T) is preceded by **ABORT**(T). □

Next, a relation on accesses to X is defined to describe information about the pseudotime order that is deducible from the behavior of $P(X)$. Given a sequence β of external actions of $P(X)$, define a binary relation *local-pseudotime-order*(β) on accesses to X, where $(U, U') \in$ *local-pseudotime-order*(β) exactly when β contains both **INFORM_TIME_AT**(X)**OF**(U, p) and **INFORM_TIME_AT**(X)**OF**(U', p') events for some p and p' with $p < p'$. You should note that unlike *pseudotime-order*, this definition relates accesses to X, rather than just siblings. Also, unlike the *local-completion-order* of Section 6.2.4, the local pseudotime order relates every pair of distinct accesses for which operations occur.

LEMMA 7.21 *If* β *is a pseudotime object well-formed sequence of external actions of pseudotime object automaton for* X, *then local-pseudotime-order*(β) *is a total order on accesses to* X *having* **REQUEST_COMMIT** *actions in* β.

The relationship between the local-pseudotime order and the global pseudotime order in a pseudotime system is as follows. You should notice that this result is much stronger than the corresponding Lemma 6.18. In particular, the local information is a correct reflection of the global pseudotime order, even for orphans.

LEMMA 7.22 *Let* β *be a behavior of a pseudotime system in which pseudotime object automaton* $P(X)$ *is associated with* X. *Let* $R =$ *pseudotime-order*(β) *and* $R' =$ *local-pseudotime-order*($\beta|P(X)$). *Then the following are true.*

1. $R' = R'_{trans} \subseteq R_{trans}$.

2. $R'_{event}(\beta|P(X)) \subseteq R_{event}(\beta)$.

PROOF   The equality $R' = R'_{trans}$ is immediate, since R' is a relation on accesses. To show the inclusion $R' \subseteq R_{trans}$, suppose $(T, T') \in R'$. Then β contains **INFORM_TIME_AT**(X)**OF**(T, p) and **INFORM_TIME_AT**(X)**OF**(T', p') events with $p < p'$. By the pseudotime controller preconditions, there are pseudotime intervals P and P' such that β contains **ASSIGN_PSEUDOTIME**(T, P) and **ASSIGN_PSEUDOTIME**(T', P'), and $p = P_{min}$ and $p' = P'_{min}$. Now let U and U' be siblings that are ancestors of T and T' respectively. Lemma 7.13 shows that β contains **ASSIGN_PSEUDOTIME**(U, Q) and **ASSIGN_PSEUDOTIME**(U', Q') events, with Q and Q' such that $P \subseteq Q$ and $P' \subseteq Q'$.

Since Q and Q' are disjoint and $p < p'$ with $p \in Q$ and $p' \in Q'$, it follows that $Q < Q'$. Thus $(U, U') \in R$ and so $(T, T') \in R_{trans}$.

The inclusion of $R'_{event}(\beta | P(X))$ in $R_{event}(\beta)$ follows immediately.   □

Now we give a definition to describe how to reorder the external actions of a pseudotime object automaton according to a given local pseudotime order. This definition is similar to that used to define the view condition that is given in Proposition 7.16, except that it uses local approximations rather than global concepts such as visibility and the pseudotime order.

Suppose β is a finite pseudotime object well-formed sequence of external actions of a pseudotime object automaton for X and T is a transaction name. Let $local\text{-}view(\beta, T)$ be the unique sequence defined as follows. Let Z be the set of operations occurring in β whose transactions are locally visible at X to T in β. Then $local\text{-}view(\beta, T) = perform(\xi)$, where ξ is the result of reordering Z according to the order $local\text{-}pseudotime\text{-}order(\beta)$ on the transaction components. (Note that Lemma 7.21 implies that this reordering is unique.[8]) The following is straightforward from the definitions.

LEMMA 7.23 *If β is a finite pseudotime object well-formed sequence of external actions of pseudotime object automaton $P(X)$, and T is a transaction name, then $local\text{-}view(\beta, T)$ is serial object well-formed.*

Finally, *local static atomicity* can be defined. This is similar to static atomicity, but using the local approximations to visibility, the pseudotime order, and so on. Say that pseudotime object automaton $P(X)$ for object name X is **locally static atomic** if whenever β is a finite pseudotime object well-formed behavior of $P(X)$, and T is a transaction name that is not a local orphan at X in β, then $local\text{-}view(\beta, T)$ is a behavior of $S(X)$. That is, the result of reordering a behavior of $P(X)$ according to the given local-pseudotime order is a finite behavior of the corresponding serial object automaton.

The main result of this subsection says that local static atomicity is a sufficient condition for static atomicity.

THEOREM 7.24 *If $P(X)$ is a pseudotime object automaton for object name X that is locally static atomic then $P(X)$ is static atomic.*

PROOF   Let $\mathcal{S}$ be a pseudotime system in which $P(X)$ is associated with X. Let β be a finite behavior of $\mathcal{S}$, $R = pseudotime\text{-}order(\beta)$, and T a transaction name that is not

---

[8]The *local-view* function is similar to the *local-views* function defined in Chapter 6, which reorders according to the (total) local pseudotime order, in place of the partial local completion order used by *local-views*.

an orphan in β. The proof must establish that $view(serial(\beta), T, R, \mathrm{X})$ is a behavior of $S(\mathrm{X})$. By definition, $view(serial(\beta), T, R, \mathrm{X}) = perform(\xi)$, where ξ is the sequence of operations occurring in β whose transactions are visible to T in β, arranged in the order given by R_{trans} on the transaction component.

Let γ be a finite sequence of actions consisting of exactly one **INFORM_COMMIT-_AT**(X)**OF**(U) for each **COMMIT**(U) that occurs in β. Then $\beta\gamma$ is a behavior of the system $\mathcal{S}$, since each action in γ is an enabled output of the pseudotime controller, by Lemma 7.12. Then $\beta\gamma|P(\mathrm{X})$ is a behavior of $P(\mathrm{X})$, and Proposition 7.14 implies that it is pseudotime object well-formed.

Since **INFORM_COMMIT_AT**(X)**OF**(U) occurs in $\beta\gamma|P(\mathrm{X})$ if and only if **COMMIT**(U) occurs in β, an access T' to X is visible to T in β if and only if it is locally visible at X to T in $\beta\gamma|P(\mathrm{X})$. Also, $R = pseudotime\text{-}order(\beta) = pseudotime\text{-}order(\beta\gamma)$. Moreover, Lemma 7.22 implies that if accesses are ordered by $local\text{-}pseudotime\text{-}order(\beta\gamma|P(\mathrm{X}))$ they are also ordered in the same way by R_{trans}.

Comparing the definitions of $view(serial(\beta), T, R, \mathrm{X})$ and $local\text{-}view(\beta\gamma|P(\mathrm{X}), T)$, one sees the correspondences given above imply that they are the same. Since T is not an orphan in β, it is not an orphan in $\beta\gamma$, and thus not a local orphan in $\beta\gamma|P(\mathrm{X})$. Since $P(\mathrm{X})$ is locally static atomic, $local\text{-}view(\beta\gamma|P(\mathrm{X}), T)$ is a behavior of $S(\mathrm{X})$. That is, $view(serial(\beta), T, R, \mathrm{X})$ is a behavior of $S(\mathrm{X})$, as required to satisfy the definition of static atomicity. $\qquad\square$

7.4   Reed's Algorithm

This section formally describes a multiversion timestamp-based algorithm that is based on one proposed by Reed [103]. The algorithm works for object names where the serial specification is a read/write serial object, as defined in Example 3.5.3.

We begin with an informal sketch of Reed's algorithm: the system keeps a separate *version* (containing the value written) for each write access that has occurred. Each version whose writer is not an orphan is regarded as being the *effective* version for an interval of pseudotime, starting at the pseudotime assigned to the write access that produced the version, and extending to the highest pseudotime assigned to any nonorphan read access that returned the version.[9] The effective intervals of different versions must be disjoint, and each read access must return the version that is effective at the pseudotime assigned to the reader. To ensure that these key properties are maintained, a write access is prevented from occurring if there is already an effective

---

[9]If no read has yet returned the value from a version written by a nonorphan, that version is effective at a single pseudotime—the one assigned to the writer.

version at the pseudotime assigned to the writer. A read access returns the version written by the nonorphan write access whose pseudotime most closely precedes the time assigned to the reader; however, the read must not return unless the writer involved is visible to it.[10]

Below, we present an abstract form of the algorithm as a pseudotime object automaton; this is shown to be a locally static atomic object. Then correctness of a more concrete algorithm, closer to Reed's original proposal, is discussed.

7.4.1   Reed   Objects

A pseudotime object automaton $R(X)$ (a *Reed object*) is described, for any object name X where $S(X)$ is a read/write serial object. The automaton $R(X)$ maintains multiple versions of data, the names of the readers and writers of each version, and their corresponding timestamps.

Recall from Example 3.5.3 that for a read/write serial object there is a domain D of values; an initial value d_0; a function *kind*, which indicates whether an access is reading or writing; and a function *data*, which indicates the value to which each write access sets the serial object.

Let T_X be a *dummy* transaction name (a name not in $\mathcal{T}$), regarded as the writer of the initial version. Also let $-\infty$ be a *dummy* pseudotime (not in $\mathcal{P}$) that is regarded as being less than any pseudotime in $\mathcal{P}$ and is used to represent the time at which the initial version of $S(X)$ is written.

Each state s of $R(X)$ has the following components: *s.created*, *s.committed*, *s.aborted*, *s.commit_requested*, *s.time*, *s.version*, and *s.reads-from*. The components *s.created* and *s.commit_requested*, which are sets of accesses to X, record the occurrence of the appropriate actions. Thus the active accesses in any state s are those in *s.created* − *s.commit_requested*. The components *s.committed* and *s.aborted* are sets of transactions that record the information received about the outcome of transactions; this information is kept for all transactions, not only for accesses. The component *s.time* is a partial function from $accesses(X) \cup \{T_X\}$ to $\mathcal{P} \cup \{-\infty\}$. The fact that $s.time(T) = p$ reflects the knowledge at the object that the pseudotime assigned to the access T is p; we will see that $s.time(T_X) = -\infty$ since the initial version is regarded as written by T_X before any genuine pseudotime. The component *s.version* is a partial function from $\{T : T \text{ is a write accesses to X}\} \cup \{T_X\}$ to D, the domain of values of $S(X)$. The fact that $s.version(T) = d$ represents the maintenance of a version with value d that was written by access T; we will see that $s.version(T_X) = d_0$ since d_0 is the initial version. The component *s.reads-from* is a partial function from $\{T : T \text{ is a write}$

---

[10]This ensures that the writer cannot become an orphan unless the reader also becomes an orphan.

access to X$\} \cup \{T_{\mathrm{X}}\}$ to the set of sets of read accesses to X. The set $s.reads\text{-}from(T)$ records the collection of read accesses that have returned the version written by T; we will see that $domain(s.reads\text{-}from) = domain(s.reads\text{-}from)$.

An initial state s_0 of $R(\mathrm{X})$ is one where $s_0.time(T_{\mathrm{X}}) = -\infty$, $s_0.reads\text{-}from(T_{\mathrm{X}}) = \emptyset$, $s_0.version(T_{\mathrm{X}}) = d_0$ (recall that d_0 is the initial value from the domain D), all three partial functions are undefined elsewhere, and all other components of s_0 are empty.

In a state s, the components $s.created$, $s.committed$, and $s.aborted$ keep track of those transactions for which the object has received either a **CREATE**, an **INFORM-_COMMIT**, or an **INFORM_ABORT**, respectively. In addition, the component $s.time$ keeps track of the pseudotime associated with each access transaction for which an **INFORM_TIME** has been received. The component $s.commit\_requested$ records all transactions for which the object has sent out a **REQUEST_COMMIT**. The $s.version$ component keeps track of the versions produced by different write accesses, while the $s.reads\text{-}from$ component records, for each write access and the version it creates, the set of read accesses which read that version.

In describing the pseudotime object algorithm, it will be useful to use some shorthand. Given a state s, define $s.nonorphans = \{T : ancestors(T) \cap s.aborted = \emptyset\}$. If T_1 and T_2 are accesses of X, say T_1 is **visible in** s to T_2 if $ancestors(T_1) - ancestors(T_2) \subseteq s.committed$.

The transition relation is given in Figure 7.1.

The principle that underlies the action of $R(\mathrm{X})$ is straightforward. The versions and reads-from relationships give partial information about an execution of $S(\mathrm{X})$, viewed as taking place in pseudotime order rather than real time order. If s is a state of $R(\mathrm{X})$, the facts that $s.version(T') = r$ and $T \in s.reads\text{-}from(T')$ mean that (provided the accesses involved are not aborted) r is the effective version during the interval of pseudotime $[s.time(T'), s.time(T))$.

Regions of $\mathcal{P}$ that are not covered by any interval $[s.time(T'), s.time(T''))$, for nonorphan write T' and nonorphan read T'' with T'' in $s.reads\text{-}from(T')$, represent those regions in which no particular state must hold; thus write accesses can safely occur only in those regions. Thus a **REQUEST_COMMIT**(T, v) action for a write access has a precondition that checks that the pseudotime associated with the write does not lie in any interval $[s.time(T'), s.time(T''))$, for nonorphan write T' and nonorphan read T'' with T'' in $s.reads\text{-}from(T')$. The effect of the action is to record a new version, $s.version(T)$, whose value is $data(T)$.

If T is a read access, it should return the value produced by the nonorphan write access T' whose pseudotime is closest to (but preceding) the pseudotime associated with T. To preclude the write from aborting after the read has committed (an event that could violate atomicity for T, since the writer's actions would then not be in the view of T) the read access must be blocked until T' is visible to T. The code for the **REQUEST_COMMIT** for a read mentions a variable T' (representing the writer whose

CREATE(T)
　Effect:
　　$s.created = s'.created \cup \{T\}$

INFORM_COMMIT_AT(X)**OF**(T)
　Effect:
　　$s.committed = s.committed \cup \{T\}$

REQUEST_COMMIT(T, "OK"),
　for $kind(T) =$ "$write$"
　Precondition:
　　$T \in s'.created$
　　$T \notin s'.commit\_requested$
　　$T \in domain(s'.time)$
　　there do not exist T' and T'' such that
　　　$T' \in domain(s'.time)$
　　　$T' \in domain(s'.reads\text{-}from)$
　　　$T'' \in domain(s'.time)$
　　　$T'' \in s'.reads\text{-}from(T')$
　　　$T'' \in s'.nonorphans$
　　　$s'.time(T') < s'.time(T) < s'.time(T'')$
　Effect:
　　$s.commit\_requested$
　　　$= s'.commit\_requested \cup \{T\}$
　　$s.version(T) = data(T)$
　　$s.reads\text{-}from(T) = \emptyset$

INFORM_ABORT_AT(X)**OF**(T)
　Effect:
　　$s.aborted = s'.aborted \cup \{T\}$

INFORM_TIME_AT(X)**OF**(T, p)
　Effect:
　　$s.time(T) = p$

REQUEST_COMMIT(T, v),
　for $kind(T) =$ "$read$"
　Precondition:
　　$T \in s'.created$
　　$T \notin s'.commit\_requested$
　　$T \in domain(s'.time)$
　　$T' \in domain(s'.time)$
　　$T' \in domain(s'.version)$
　　$s'.time(T') < s'.time(T)$
　　there does not exist T'' such that
　　　$T'' \in domain(s'.version)$
　　　$T'' \in domain(s'.time)$
　　　$T'' \in s'.nonorphans$
　　　$s'.time(T') < s'.time(T'') < s'.time(T)$
　　either $T' = T_X$ or T' is visible to T in s'
　　$v = s'.version(T')$
　Effect:
　　$s.commit\_requested$
　　　$= s'.commit\_requested \cup \{T\}$
　　$s.reads\text{-}from(T') = s'.reads\text{-}from(T') \cup \{T\}$

Figure 7.1: Transition Relation for Reed's Algorithm

version is returned) in both precondition and effect, but no quantification is given for T'. Recall that this usage is a convention; the action can occur when some transaction name T' can be found satisfying the clauses listed in the precondition, and the effect then refers to the value of T' which made the precondition true.

EXAMPLE 7.4.1　Reed's Algorithm in a Message Queue System

Consider the message queue system of Example 3.5.7. This system contains a read/write serial object COPY_A, which is accessed by transaction names $T_{Rj.Ax}$, the value recorders (with $kind(T_{Rj.Ax}) =$ "$write$" and $data(T_{Rj.Ax}) = x$) and $T_{Vk.A}$, the viewers (with $kind(T_{Vk.A}) =$ "$read$"). When we use the set of finite sequences of positive integers, ordered lexicographically, as pseudotimes, we can construct the pseudotime object automaton $R(\text{COPY\_A})$ using Reed's algorithm for this serial object. The following sequence β is a schedule of $R(\text{COPY\_A})$.

INFORM_TIME_AT(COPY_A)**OF**($T_{R1.A3}, 2, 2$),
CREATE($T_{R1.A3}$),
$\quad$**CREATE**($T_{V1.A}$),
REQUEST_COMMIT($T_{R1.A3}$, "OK"),
$\quad$**INFORM_TIME_AT**(COPY_A)**OF**($T_{V1.A}, 8, 3$),
$\quad\quad$**CREATE**($T_{V3.A}$),
$\quad\quad$**INFORM_TIME_AT**(COPY_A)**OF**($T_{V3.A}, 3, 5$),
INFORM_COMMIT_AT(COPY_A)**OF**($T_{R1.A3}$),
INFORM_COMMIT_AT(COPY_A)**OF**(T_{R1}),
$\quad\quad$**REQUEST_COMMIT**($T_{V3.A}, 3$),
$\quad$**REQUEST_COMMIT**($T_{V1.A}, 3$),
$\quad\quad$**INFORM_COMMIT_AT**(COPY_A)**OF**($T_{V3.A}$),
$\quad\quad$**CREATE**($T_{R2.A1}$),
$\quad\quad\quad$**INFORM_TIME_AT**(COPY_A)**OF**($T_{V6.A}, 6, 1$),
$\quad\quad$**CREATE**($T_{V6.A}$),
$\quad\quad\quad$**CREATE**($T_{V5.A}$),
$\quad\quad\quad\quad$**INFORM_TIME_AT**(COPY_A)**OF**($T_{R4.A9}, 7, 2$),
$\quad\quad\quad$**INFORM_TIME_AT**(COPY_A)**OF**($T_{V5.A}, 4, 3$),
$\quad\quad\quad$**CREATE**($T_{R4.A9}$),
INFORM_ABORT_AT(COPY_A)**OF**(T_{V1}),
$\quad\quad$**INFORM_TIME_AT**(COPY_A)**OF**($T_{R2.A1}, 5, 2$),
$\quad\quad$**REQUEST_COMMIT**($T_{R2.A1}$, "OK").

The schedule β can lead $R(\text{COPY\_A})$ to a state s where:
$s.created = \{T_{R1.A3}, T_{V1.A}, T_{V3.A}, T_{R2.A1}, T_{V6.A}, T_{V5.A}, T_{R4.A9}\}$,
$s.committed = \{T_{R1.A3}, T_{R1}, T_{V3.A}\}$, $s.aborted = \{T_{V1}\}$,
$s.commit\_requested = \{T_{R1.A3}, T_{V3.A}, T_{V1.A}, T_{R2.A1}\}$, $s.time(T_{\text{COPY\_A}}) = -\infty$,
$s.time(T_{R1.A3}) = 2, 2$, $s.time(T_{V1.A}) = 8, 3$,
$s.time(T_{V3.A}) = 3, 5$, $s.time(T_{V6.A}) = 6, 1$,
$s.time(T_{R4.A9}) = 7, 2$, $s.time(T_{V5.A}) = 4, 3$,
$s.time(T_{R2.A1}) = 5, 2$, $s.version(T_{\text{COPY\_A}}) = 0$,
$s.version(T_{R1.A3}) = 3$, $s.version(R2.A1) = 1$,
$s.reads\text{-}from(T_{\text{COPY\_A}}) = \emptyset$, $s.reads\text{-}from(T_{R1.A3}) = \{T_{V3.A}, T_{V1.A}\}$, and
$s.reads\text{-}from(T_{R2.A1}) = \emptyset$.

Figure 7.2 illustrates the state s of $R(\text{X})$. The timeline of pseudotime is shown, and versions are represented as boxes, each placed above the writer's *time* and labeled with the value written. Readers are represented

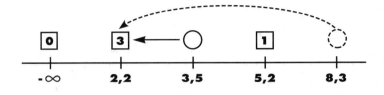

Figure 7.2: State s of $R(X)$

as circles above the reader's *time*, and each is linked by an arrow to the version it read from. In the case that the reader has aborted, the circle and arrow are dashed. An effective version exists in any region of pseudotime above which lies a solid arrow or a solid square.

In the state s, the action **REQUEST_COMMIT**($T_{V5.A}, 3$) is enabled, returning the value of the version written by $T_{R1.A3}$, since the pseudotime recorded for that transaction $(2,2)$ is the highest that is less than the pseudotime recorded for $T_{V5.A}$ among those recorded for write accesses that are in $s.nonorphans$. Notice that since $T_{R1.A3}$ and T_{R1} are in $s.committed$, the writer of the version is visible in s to $T_{V5.A}$.

In the state s, the action **REQUEST_COMMIT**($T_{R4.A9},$ "*OK*") is enabled. Notice that although the pseudotime recorded for $T_{R4.A9}$ lies in between the times recorded for the write access $T_{R1.A3}$ and the access $T_{V1.A}$ that read from that version, the precondition is satisfied because $T_{V1.A}$ is not in $s.nonorphans$.

By contrast, in the state s there is no value v for which **REQUEST-_COMMIT**($T_{V6.A}, v$) is enabled, since the version written by a nonorphan with the highest recorded pseudotime less than $6,1$ (the pseudotime of $T_{V6.A}$) is the version written by $T_{R2.A1}$, which is *not* visible in s to $T_{V6.A}$. As more information arrives about the fate of transactions, the correct return value can be determined. For example, the sequence β**INFORM_ABORT_AT**(COPY_A)**OF**($T_{R2.A1}$) can lead the automaton to a state where **REQUEST_COMMIT**($T_{V6.A}, 3$) is enabled; on the other hand the sequence β**INFORM_COMMIT_AT**(COPY_A)**OF**($T_{R2.A1}$)**INFORM-_COMMIT_AT**(COPY_A)**OF**(T_{R2}) can lead the automaton to a state where **REQUEST_COMMIT**($T_{V6.A}, 1$) is enabled.

Let β' denote the sequence:

INFORM_COMMIT_AT(COPY_A)**OF**($T_{R2.A1}$),
INFORM_COMMIT_AT(COPY_A)**OF**(T_{R2}),

REQUEST_COMMIT$(T_{V6.A}, 1)$,
REQUEST_COMMIT$(T_{V5.A}, 3)$,
INFORM_COMMIT_AT(COPY_A)**OF**$(T_{V5.A})$,
INFORM_COMMIT_AT(COPY_A)**OF**(T_{V5}).

We leave the reader to check (as Exercise 4) that $local\text{-}view(\beta\beta', T_{V6.A}) = perform(\xi)$ where $\xi = (T_{R1.A3}, "OK")(T_{V5.A}, 3)(T_{R2.A1}, "OK")(T_{V6.A}, 1)$. The order[11] of operations in ξ is given by $local\text{-}pseudotime\text{-}order(\beta\beta')$.

7.4.2 Correctness Proof

Basic Properties of R(X)

We have the following straightforward lemmas. The first gives connections between a schedule and the record kept in the state. The second gives the main invariants of the state.

LEMMA 7.25 *Let β be a finite pseudotime object well-formed schedule of $R(X)$. Suppose that β can lead $R(X)$ to state s. Then the following conditions hold.*

1. $T \in s.created$ *if and only if* **CREATE(**T**)** *appears in β.*

2. $T \in s.committed$ *if and only if* **INFORM_COMMIT_AT(**X**)OF(**T**)** *appears in β.*

3. $T \in s.aborted$ *if and only if* **INFORM_ABORT_AT(**X**)OF(**T**)** *appears in β.*

4. $s.time(T) = p$ *if and only if either $T = T_X$ and $p = -\infty$ or else* **INFORM_TIME_AT(**X**)OF(**T,p**)** *appears in β.*

5. $T \in s.commit\_requested$ *if and only if a* **REQUEST_COMMIT** *for T appears in β.*

PROOF By induction on the length of β. □

LEMMA 7.26 *Let β be a finite pseudotime object well-formed schedule of $R(X)$. Suppose that β can lead $R(X)$ to state s. Then the following conditions hold.*

1. *If $s.time(T) = s.time(T')$, then $T = T'$.*

---

[11]You should note that this order is not consistent with what can be deduced about the completion order in the system; for example, T_{R2} must commit before the **INFORM_COMMIT** for it occurs, which is before the **REQUEST_COMMIT** for T_{V5}, which must be before T_{V5} commits. This reflects the distinction between static atomicity and dynamic atomicity.

2. $s.commit\_requested \subseteq domain(s.time)$.

3. $T_X \in domain(s.version)$ and $s.version(T_X) = d_0$.

4. If $T \in domain(s.version)$ and $T \neq T_X$ then

    (a) T is a write access to X, and

    (b) A **REQUEST_COMMIT**$(T, \text{``OK''})$ occurs in β and $s.version(T) = data(T)$.

5. If T is a write access to X and $T \in s.commit\_requested$ then $T \in domain(s.version)$.

6. $domain(s.reads\text{-}from) = domain(s.version)$.

7. If $T \in s.reads\text{-}from(T')$, then

    (a) T is a read access,

    (b) either $T' = T_X$ or T' is visible to T in s,

    (c) $s.time(T') < s.time(T)$.

    (d) If $T'' \in domain(s.version)$, $T \in s.nonorphans$ and $s.time(T') < s.time(T'') < s.time(T)$ then $T'' \notin s.nonorphans$, and

    (e) a **REQUEST_COMMIT**(T, v) occurs in β where $v = s.version(T')$.

8. Suppose T is a read access to X and $T \in s.commit\_requested$. Then $T \in s.reads\text{-}from(T')$ for some T'.

9. Suppose T and T' are write accesses to X in $s.commit\_requested$. Then $s.reads\text{-}from(T) \cap s.reads\text{-}from(T') = \emptyset$.

10. Suppose $T \in s.nonorphans$, and $T \in s.reads\text{-}from(T')$. Then either $T' = T_X$ or else $T' \in s.nonorphans$.

PROOF   By induction on the length of β.   □

We can use these facts to see that $R(X)$ preserves pseudotime object well-formedness. The details are left as Exercise 3.

LEMMA 7.27 $R(X)$ is a pseudotime object for X.

Proving Local Static Atomicity

The following results demonstrate that this algorithm is satisfactory for use in a system that uses timestamp order for serialization.

First a technical notion is defined, reflecting the intuition of a mutually consistent collection of nonorphan accesses, that is, a set of accesses that might comprise those visible to a particular transaction.[12] Recall that a read access was blocked until the writer whose value it returns is visible to it; this implies that the writer will be visible to a transaction if the reader is visible to it. This motivates the third condition in the following definition.

If s is a state of $R(\mathrm{X})$, then define $\mathcal{U}$ to be an **allowable** set of accesses to X for s provided that the following conditions hold.

- All accesses in $\mathcal{U}$ are in $s.nonorphans$.

- All accesses in $\mathcal{U}$ are in $s.commit\_requested$.

- If $T' \in s.reads\text{-}from(T)$ and $T' \in \mathcal{U}$, then either $T = T_{\mathrm{X}}$ or $T \in \mathcal{U}$.

EXAMPLE 7.4.2   Allowable Set of Accesses

Consider the pseudotime object $R(\mathrm{COPY\_A})$ and its schedule β, discussed in Example 7.4.1. Let s_1 denote the state to which the schedule β**REQUEST-_COMMIT**$(T_{V5.A}, 3)$ can lead the automaton. For s_1, an allowable set of accesses is $\{T_{R1.A3}, T_{V5.A}, T_{R2.A1}\}$. Another allowable set is $\{T_{R1.A3}, T_{V5.A}, T_{V3.A}\}$. However, the set $\{T_{R1.A3}, T_{V5.A}, T_{V1.A}\}$ is not allowable, because $T_{V1.A}$ is is not in $s_1.nonorphans$. Also, $\{T_{R2.A1}, T_{V5.A}\}$ is not allowable because the write access $T_{R2.A3}$ (whose version $T_{V5.A}$ read) is absent.

The value of variable $s.time$ can be used to define a derived partial order $s.timeorder$ on accesses to X, as follows. If T and T' are distinct accesses to X, $s.time(T)$ and $s.time(T')$ are both defined, and $s.time(T) < s.time(T')$, then (T, T') is included in $s.timeorder$. This is a reflection of *local-pseudotime-order*, except that it uses the time recorded in the state rather than the time information in **INFORM_TIME** events in the schedule. This alternative order makes it easier to reason inductively using the state of the automaton.

---

[12]The definition given is somewhat more permissive than one that would exactly capture this intuition. However, it is safe, in the sense that the collection visible to a given transaction will be *allowable*

The following lemma shows that the operations of an allowable set of accesses, arranged in the order of the recorded pseudotimes, provide a behavior of $S(X)$. This is the key to the proof that the algorithm provides static atomicity.

LEMMA 7.28 *Let β be any finite schedule of $R(X)$ that is pseudotime object well-formed for X, and suppose β can lead to state s. Let $\mathcal{U}$ be an allowable set of accesses to X for s. Let Z be the set of operations occurring in β whose transaction components are in $\mathcal{U}$. Let ξ be the sequence that results when Z is arranged in an order consistent with that determined by s.timeorder on the transaction components. Let $\gamma = perform(\xi)$. Then γ is a behavior of $S(X)$.*

PROOF   By pseudotime object well-formedness, no transaction can have more than one **REQUEST_COMMIT** in β, and thus all operations in S have distinct transaction components. Thus, $perform(\xi)$ is serial object well-formed.

Proceed by induction on the length of prefixes ζ of ξ, showing that for each such ζ, $perform(\zeta)$ is a behavior of $S(X)$. The basis is trivial, so suppose that $\zeta = \zeta'(T, v)$, where ζ is a prefix of ξ, $perform(\zeta')$ is a behavior of $S(X)$, and (T, v) is an operation in S. There are two cases.

1. T is a write access.

By the precondition of **REQUEST_COMMIT**(T, v) in $R(X)$, $v = \text{``}OK\text{''}$. In Example 4.4.2 we showed that (T, v) is an obliterating operation of $S(X)$. That is, $perform(\zeta) = perform(\zeta'(T, v))$ is equieffective to $perform(T, v)$. By the code of $S(X)$, $perform(T, v)$ is a behavior of $S(X)$. Since $perform(\zeta)$ is equieffective to $perform(T, v)$, $perform(\zeta)$ is also a behavior of $S(X)$.

2. T is a read access.

Since $\mathcal{U}$ is allowable for s, T is in $s.reads\text{-}from(T')$ for some T' that is either T_X or else is a write access in $\mathcal{U}$.

If $T' = T_X$, then $s.time(T') = -\infty$, so by Part 7 of Lemma 7.26, ζ' is a sequence of operations of the form (T'', v'') where each T'' is a read access. By Example 4.4.1, each operation in ζ' is transparent. Thus, Proposition 4.7 implies that $perform(\zeta')$ is equieffective to the empty sequence. By Proposition 4.2, $perform(\zeta) = perform(\zeta'(T, v))$ is equieffective to $perform(T, v)$. Since $T \in s.reads\text{-}from(T_X)$, Parts 3 and 7 of Lemma 7.26 imply that $v = s.version(T_X) = d_0$. By the code of $S(X)$, $perform(T, v) \in behs(S(X))$. Since $perform(\zeta)$ is equieffective to $perform(T, v)$, $perform(\zeta) \in behs(S(X))$.

If on the other hand $T' \neq T_X$, then $T' \in \mathcal{U}$. Then Parts 4 and 7 of Lemma 7.26 imply that β contains a **REQUEST_COMMIT**(T', v') where $v' = \text{``}OK\text{''}$ action, and $s.time(T') < s.time(T)$. Thus, ζ' also contains the operation (T', v'), that is, ζ' is of the form $\eta(T', v')\eta'$. By Part 7 of Lemma 7.26, η' is a sequence of operations of the form (T'', v''), where each T'' is a read access. By Example 4.4.1, each operation in η' is transparent. Thus, Proposition 4.7 implies that $perform(\zeta') = perform(\eta(T', v')\eta')$ is equieffective to $perform(\eta(T', v'))$; this in turn is equieffective to $perform(T', v')$ since (T', v') is obliterating by Example 4.4.2. Thus, $perform(\zeta')$ is equieffective to $perform(T', v')$. Then Proposition 4.2 implies that $perform(\zeta)$ is equieffective to $perform(T', v')perform(T, v)$.

Since $T \in s.reads\text{-}from(T')$, Part 7 of Lemma 7.26 implies that $v = s.version(T')$. Also, since $T' \in domain(s.version)$, Part 4 of Lemma 7.26 implies that $s.version(T) = data(T)$. Thus by the code of $S(\mathrm{X})$, $perform(T', v')perform(T, v)$ is in $behs(S(\mathrm{X}))$. Since $perform(\zeta)$ is equieffective to $perform(T', v')perform(T, v)$, $perform(\zeta) \in behs(S(\mathrm{X}))$. $\qquad\square$

Now one can prove that a data object is locally static atomic if it is implemented using the algorithm described in this section.

PROPOSITION 7.29 $R(\mathrm{X})$ *is locally static atomic.*

PROOF   Let β be a finite pseudotime object well-formed behavior of $R(\mathrm{X})$, and T a transaction name that is not a local orphan in β. Let Z be the set of operations occurring in β whose transactions are locally visible to T in β. Then $local\text{-}view(\beta, T) = perform(\xi)$, where ξ is the result of ordering Z according to the order $local\text{-}pseudotime\text{-}order(\beta)$ on the transaction components. The proof must show that $local\text{-}view(\beta, T)$ is a behavior of $S(\mathrm{X})$.

Since $R(\mathrm{X})$ has no internal actions, β is also a schedule of $R(\mathrm{X})$. Choose state s of $R(\mathrm{X})$ such that β can lead to s. Let $\mathcal{U}$ be the set of transaction components of operations in Z. The proof shows that $\mathcal{U}$ is an allowable set of accesses to X for s.

Let T' be an access in $\mathcal{U}$. If $T' \notin s.nonorphans$, then T' is a local orphan at X in β by Lemma 7.25. Since T' is locally visible at X to T in β, Lemma 7.19 implies that T is a local orphan in β, a contradiction. Thus, $T' \in s.nonorphans$.

Since a **REQUEST_COMMIT** for T' occurs in β, $T' \in s.commit\_requested$.

Now suppose $T' \in s.reads\text{-}from(T'')$ and $T'' \neq T_{\mathrm{X}}$. Then Part 7 of Lemma 7.26 implies that T'' is visible to T' in s, so that T'' is locally visible at X to T' in β, by Lemma 7.25. Thus, T'' is locally visible at X to T in β, by Lemma 7.18. Also by Part 7 of Lemma 7.26, there is a **REQUEST_COMMIT** for T'' in β, that is, $T'' \in \mathcal{U}$. It follows that $\mathcal{U}$ is an allowable set of accesses to X, for s.

Now let Z' be the set of operations occurring in β whose transaction components are in $\mathcal{U}$. Let ξ' be the result of ordering Z' consistent with $s.timeorder$ on the transaction components. Let $\gamma' = perform(\xi')$. Then Lemma 7.28 implies that γ' is a behavior of $S(X)$.

However, observe that pseudotime object well-formedness implies that each access in $\mathcal{U}$ has at most one **REQUEST_COMMIT** in β. Thus, $Z = Z'$. Furthermore, *local--pseudotime-order*(β) is the same as *s.timeorder*. Therefore, $\xi = \xi'$ and hence $\gamma = \gamma'$. Therefore, γ is a behavior of $S(X)$, as required.   □

7.4.3   A   Concrete   Implementation

The algorithm described by Reed in [103] differs from the abstract algorithm in the Section 7.4.1 primarily in the way in which the reads-from component of the state is maintained. $R(X)$ maintains, for each version of the object written by a write access, the entire set of read accesses that read that version. Reed's concrete algorithm maintains instead simply the maximum timestamp of all accesses that read a given version, and hence may be much more space-efficient. We will see that Reed's concrete algorithm is essentially an implementation of the abstract algorithm, in the sense that behavior permitted by Reed's is permitted by the other, provided both are in the context of pseudotime systems. (See Section 7.4.4.) However, there are behaviors permitted by the abstract algorithm that are not permitted by Reed's implementation. For example, if a read access T returns a version written by T' and then aborts, $R(X)$ permits a later writer T'' whose timestamp falls between the timestamps for T' and T to create a new version. Reed's implementation would force T'' to abort in this situation, since the maximum timestamp of readers for a given version is not decreased when a reader aborts. If aborts are rare, then Reed's implementation is probably adequate. If aborts are more frequent, however, then one might prefer an implementation closer to the abstract algorithm given above, which kept more precise information about the set of readers for each version, and thus could avoid some unnecessary aborts. Another way in which this concrete implementation is more space-efficient is that it removes versions created by write accesses that are orphaned, rather than keeping them in the state and merely not checking them in preconditions.

Reed's implementation is modeled using an automaton $R1(X)$ The external action signature of $R1(X)$ is the same as that of any pseudotime object for X. In addition, $R1(X)$ has the following internal actions, each representing the discarding of a version created by an orphan writer.

Internal:
   DISCARD(T), T an access to X, $kind(T) = \text{``write''}$

The state of $R1(X)$ has components *s.created*, *s.committed*, *s.aborted*, *s.commit_re-quested*, *s.time*, and *s.version*, with the same types as before. Instead of *s.reads-from*, there is *s.max-reads-from*, which is a partial function from $\{T : T$ is a write access to

CREATE(T)
 Effect:
  $s.created = s'.created \cup \{T\}$

INFORM_COMMIT_AT(X)**OF**(T)
 Effect:
  $s.committed = s.committed \cup \{T\}$

INFORM_ABORT_AT(X)**OF**(T)
 Effect:
  $s.aborted = s'.aborted \cup \{T\}$

INFORM_TIME_AT(X)**OF**(T, p)
 Effect:
  $s.time(T) = p$

REQUEST_COMMIT$(T, \text{``}OK\text{''})$,
 for $kind(T) = \text{``}write\text{''}$
 Precondition:
  $T \in s'.created$
  $T \notin s'.commit\_requested$
  $T \in domain(s'.time)$
  there does not exist T' such that
   $T' \in domain(s'.max\text{-}reads\text{-}from)$
   $T' \in domain(s'.time)$
   $s'.time(T') < s'.time(T)$
    $< s'.max\text{-}reads\text{-}from(T')$
 Effect:
  $s.commit\_requested$
   $= s'.commit\_requested \cup \{T\}$
  $s.version(T) = data(T)$
  $s.max\text{-}reads\text{-}from(T) = s'.time(T)$

REQUEST_COMMIT(T, v),
 for $kind(T) = \text{``}read\text{''}$
 Precondition:
  $T \in s'.created$
  $T \notin s'.commit\_requested$
  $T \in domain(s'.time)$
  $T' \in domain(s'.time)$
  $T' \in domain(s'.version)$
  $s'.time(T') < s'.time(T)$
  there does not exist T'' such that
   $T'' \in domain(s'.version)$
   $T'' \in domain(s'.time)$
   $s'.time(T') < s'.time(T'') < s'.time(T)$
  either $T' = T_X$ or T' is visible to T in s'
  $v = s'.version(T')$
 Effect:
  $s.commit\_requested$
   $= s'.commit\_requested \cup \{T\}$
  $s.max\text{-}reads\text{-}from(T')$
   $= max(s'.max\text{-}reads\text{-}from(T'), s'.time(T))$

DISCARD(T)
 Precondition:
  $T \in domain(s'.version)$
  $T \notin s'.nonorphans$
 Effect:
  $s.version(T) = \text{``}undefined\text{''}$
  $s.max\text{-}reads\text{-}from(T) = \text{``}undefined\text{''}$

Figure 7.3: Transition Relation for a Concrete Implementation of Reed's Algorithm

$X\} \cup \{T_X\}$ to $\mathcal{P} \cup \{-\infty\}$. It represents the maximum timestamp for any read access that has read a particular version. (If no access has read the version written by T, $max\text{-}reads\text{-}from(T)$ is just $time(T)$.) Given a state s, define $s.nonorphans$ and "T_1 is visible in s to T_2" exactly as for $R(X)$.

In the initial state s_0 of $R1(X)$, $s_0.time(T_X) = -\infty$, $s_0.version(T_X) = d_0$, where d_0 is the initial value from the domain D, and $s_0.max\text{-}reads\text{-}from(T_X) = -\infty$. Furthermore, $s_0.time$, $s_0.version$, and $s_0.max\text{-}reads\text{-}from$ are otherwise undefined, and all other components of s_0 are empty.

The transition relation is given in Figure 7.3.

7.4.4 Correctness Proof

Basic Properties of $R1(X)$

LEMMA 7.30 *Let β be a finite schedule of $R1(X)$ that can lead to state s such that $\beta|ext(R1(X))$ is pseudotime object well-formed for* X. *Then the following conditions hold.*

1. $domain(s.version) = domain(s.max\text{-}reads\text{-}from)$.

2. *If $T \in domain(s.max\text{-}reads\text{-}from)$, then $s.time(T)$ is defined and either $T = T_X$ or $T \in s.commit\_requested$.*

3. *If $T \in domain(s.max\text{-}reads\text{-}from)$ and $s.max\text{-}reads\text{-}from(T) \neq s.time(T)$, then there is a read access T' to X such that $s.time(T') = s.max\text{-}reads\text{-}from(T)$.*

4. *If $s.max\text{-}reads\text{-}from(T) = s.time(T')$ and $T' \neq T$, then $T' \in s.commit\_requested$.*

Proving Implementation

It is interesting to note that the automaton $R1(X)$ *does not* implement $R(X)$ in the technical sense defined in Section 2.7.1, which requires *every* finite behavior of $R1(X)$ to also be a behavior of $R(X)$; rather, it is in the context of a pseudotime system that their behaviors are indistinguishable. Thus the proof of correctness uses a possibilities mapping between entire pseudotime systems, rather than between single pseudotime objects.[13]

First we mention the following invariant.

LEMMA 7.31 *Let $\mathcal{S}$ be a pseudotime system in which $R1(X)$ is associated with* X. *If s is a reachable state of $\mathcal{S}$, $T \in domain(s[X].time)$ and **INFORM_TIME_AT(X)OF**(T, p) is enabled in s, then $p = s[X].time$.*

Now we prove the correctness of $R1(X)$.

---

[13]For an example in which the behavior of $R1(X)$ can differ from that of $R(X)$, suppose in both $R(X)$ and $R1(X)$ a read access T_2 reads from an earlier T_1. Suppose also that a write access T_3 with a later timestamp than T_2's is pending. Now suppose a second **INFORM_TIME_AT(X)OF**(T_2, p) changes T_2's timestamp to a time p later than that of T_3. Because $max\text{-}reads\text{-}from(T_1)$ is unchanged, $R1(X)$ will still permit a **REQUEST_COMMIT** for T_3. But $R(X)$ will not, because the precondition for **REQUEST_COMMIT** depends on the new value of $time(T_2)$. But in a pseudotime system, the second **INFORM_TIME_AT(X)OF**(T_2, p) cannot occur, no change to T_2's timestamp can occur, and this difference in behavior cannot arise.

THEOREM 7.32 *Let S be a pseudotime system in which $R1(X)$ is associated with X, and $\mathcal{T}$ be the same system with $R(X)$ associated with X. Then $\mathcal{T}$ implements S.*

PROOF The proof uses a possibilities mapping f from states of S to the power set of states of $\mathcal{T}$. If s is a state of $\mathcal{T}$, define $f(s)$ to be the set of states t of $\mathcal{T}$ such that:

1. For all component names i except X, $s[i] = t[i]$.

2. $s[X].created = t[X].created$, and similarly for *committed, aborted, time* and *commit-requested*.

3. $domain(s[X].version) \subseteq domain(t[X].version) \subseteq \{domain(s[X].version) \cup (s[X].orphans)\}$.

4. If $T \in domain(s[X].version)$, then $t[X].version(T) = s[X].version(T)$.

5. If $T \in domain(s[X].max\text{-}reads\text{-}from)$, then

(a) If $s[X].max\text{-}reads\text{-}from(T) = s[X].time(T)$, then $t[X].reads\text{-}from(T) = \emptyset$,

(b) If $s[X].max\text{-}reads\text{-}from(T) = s[X].time(T')$, where $T' \neq T$, then $T' \in t[X].reads\text{-}from(T)$, and

(c) If $T' \in t[X].reads\text{-}from(T)$, then $s[X].time(T') \leq s[X].max\text{-}reads\text{-}from(T)$.

The proof now shows that f is a possibilities mapping.

First suppose that s is a start state of S. Define t so that $t[i] = s[i]$ for all $i \neq X$. Also, $t[X].created, t[X].committed, t[X].aborted, t[X].time$, and $t[X].commit\_requested$ are all empty. Define $t[X].version$ to be $\{(T_X, r_0)\}$ and $t[X].reads\text{-}from$ to be $\{(T_X, \emptyset)\}$. Clearly, t is a start state of $\mathcal{T}$ and s and t are related as required by the definition of f.

Now consider a reachable state s' of S, a step (s', π, s) of S, and a reachable state $t' \in f(s')$ of $\mathcal{T}$. The proof must show that there is an extended step (t', γ, t) of $\mathcal{T}$ such that $T \in f(s)$.

The proof now proceeds by case analysis, examining the different actions of S of which π could be an instance. Checking the necessary conditions is straightforward, and is left as Exercise 5.

One case is examined in detail: $\pi = \mathbf{INFORM\_TIME\_AT(X)OF}(T, p)$. This case is interesting because it relies on the global system invariant summarized in the previous lemma.

Since π is an output of the pseudotime controller that is enabled in s' and the pseudotime controller states are the same in s' and t', π is also enabled in t'. Choose T so that (t', π, t) is a step of $\mathcal{T}$. Again, $T' \in f(s')$. Now T is the same as T' except that $(T, p) \in t.time$, and s is the same as s' except that $(T, p) \in s.time$. In checking that $T \in f(s)$, all properties are immediate except for the last. So suppose that $U \in domain(s[X].max\text{-}reads\text{-}from)$. Then $U \in domain(s'[X].max\text{-}reads\text{-}from)$ and $s[X].max\text{-}reads\text{-}from(U) = s'[X].max\text{-}reads\text{-}from(U)$. Lemma 7.30 implies that $s'[X].time(U)$ is defined.

Suppose that $s[X].time(U) = s[X].max\text{-}reads\text{-}from(U)$. If $U = T$, then $s[X].time(U) = p, = s'[X].time(U)$ by Lemma 7.31. Thus, $s'[X].time(U) = s[X].max\text{-}reads\text{-}from(U) = s'[X].max\text{-}reads\text{-}from(U)$. On the other hand, if $U \neq T$, then it is immediate that $s'[X].time(U) = s'[X].max\text{-}reads\text{-}from(U)$, Thus in either case, $s'[X].time(U) = s'[X].max\text{-}reads\text{-}from(U)$, so that $t'.reads\text{-}from(U) = \emptyset$, so $t.reads\text{-}from(U) = \emptyset$.

Now suppose that $s[X].max\text{-}reads\text{-}from(U) = s[X].time(U')$, where $U' \neq U$. Then $s'[X].max\text{-}reads\text{-}from(U) = s.[X].max\text{-}reads\text{-}from(U) = s[X].time(U') \neq s'[X].time(U)$, by Lemma 7.26, $= s[X].time(U')$. Then Lemma 7.30 implies that there is a read access U'' to X such that $s'[X].time(U'') = s'[X].max\text{-}reads\text{-}from(U)$. Then $s[X].time(U'') = s'[X].time(U'') = s'[X].max\text{-}reads\text{-}from(U) = s[X].max\text{-}reads\text{-}from(U) = s[X].time(U')$, so that $U' = U''$. Thus, $s'[X].max\text{-}reads\text{-}from(U) = s'[X].time(U')$. So $U' \in t'[X].reads\text{-}from(U)$, so $U' \in t.reads\text{-}from(U)$.

Finally, suppose that $U' \in t[X].reads\text{-}from(U)$. Then $U' \in t'[X].reads\text{-}from(U)$, so $s'[X].time(U') \leq s'[X].max\text{-}reads\text{-}from(U)$. Thus, $s[X].time(U') \leq s[X].max\text{-}reads\text{-}from(U)$. □

The previous theorem implies that $R1(X)$ is static atomic.

COROLLARY 7.33 $R1(X)$ *is static atomic.*

7.5 Type-specific Concurrency Control

The previous section described an algorithm that could be used for an object whose serial specification (its type) was given as a read/write serial object. This section describes an algorithm due to Herlihy that applies to any object and that uses more information about the semantics of the operations of the object [49]. In fact, what is discussed here is a family of algorithms, one for each possible choice of serial dependency relation among the accesses.[14]

Unlike Reed's algorithm described earlier, this algorithm does not keep explicit versions of the serial object; instead it keeps track of all the operations that have occurred. A version is given implicitly, as the result on the serial object of applying in timestamp sequence all the operations of nonorphan accesses whose pseudotime is less than a given value. The algorithm is based on the following idea: an access T receives a return value based on all the nonorphan accesses that are visible to it and have pseudotimes less than that of T. The access T is blocked until every nonorphan

---

[14]See Section 4.5 for the definition and examples of serial dependency relations.

access which has pseudotime less than that of T and on which T depends is visible to T. This prevents T receiving a result that will lead to a failure of the view condition in the Atomicity Theorem.[15] In addition, the response to an access T cannot be given if any previous operation has occurred for a transaction with a pseudotime greater than T's, unless the response to T does not interfere with the appropriateness of that previous operation.[16]

7.5.1 Herlihy Objects

Let X be any object name, and let R be a serial dependency relation for serial object automaton $S(\mathrm{X})$, as defined in Section 4.5. A particular pseudotime object automaton $H(\mathrm{X}, R)$ (a **Herlihy**) is described, as a pseudotime object automaton.

Each state s of $H(\mathrm{X}, R)$ has the following components: $s.created$, $s.committed$, $s.aborted$, which are sets of transactions; $s.commit\_requested$, which is a set of operations; and $s.time$, which is a partial function from $accesses(\mathrm{X})$ to $\mathcal{P}$. Notice that unlike Reed objects, here $commit\_requested$ stores operations, that is, return values as well as accesses are retained.

Initially, all sets are empty and $s.time$ is undefined everywhere.

As for $R(\mathrm{X})$, some shorthand is useful, to correspond to the concepts of local orphan and local visibility, but using the information recorded in the state of $H(\mathrm{X}, R)$ rather than the actions in the schedule. Given a state s, define $s.nonorphans = \{T : ancestors(T) \cap s.aborted = \emptyset\}$. If T_1 and T_2 are accesses of X, say T_1 is **visible in s** to T_2 if $ancestors(T_1) - ancestors(T_2) \subseteq s.committed$. The transition relation is given in Figure 7.4.

The precondition for **REQUEST_COMMIT**(T, v) deserves some explanation. The first three conditions simply require that T is active and its pseudotime is known to the object. The next condition requires that no nonorphan access with a later pseudotime depend on T; this is called the *ratchet lock* condition, since it prevents an access from

---

[15] Recall that the view condition refers to the arrangement (in pseudotime order) of operations visible to some transaction. The operation of T will be placed in that sequence after those operations used to compute it, and also after operations with lower pseudotimes that are not visible to T at the time of the response, but become visible to the given transaction. Since T does not depend on such an operation, the definition of serial dependency relation ensures that the sequence in the view condition is a serial behavior.

[16] Suppose a response is given for T. Recall that the previous operation includes a return value, computed using a collection of operations. When the accesses are serialized in pseudotime order, the resulting sequence will place the previous operation after a collection that includes those used to compute it, but also includes the operation of T (since the serialization uses pseudotime order rather than the order of occurrence in the pseudotime system). Thus inserting the operation of T in a sequence must not change the legality of the sequence as a behavior of $S(\mathrm{X})$. This is what the serial dependency relation expresses.

CREATE(T)
    Effect:
        $s.created = s'.created \cup \{T\}$

INFORM_COMMIT_AT(X)**OF**(T)
    Effect:
        $s.committed = s'.committed \cup \{T\}$

INFORM_ABORT_AT(X)**OF**(T)
    Effect:
        $s.aborted = s'.aborted \cup \{T\}$

INFORM_TIME_AT(X)**OF**(T, p)
    Effect:
        $s.time(T) = p$

REQUEST_COMMIT(T, v)
    Precondition:
        $T \in s'.created$
        $(T, w) \notin s'.commit\_requested$ for any w
        $T \in domain(s'.time)$
        there do not exist T' and v' such that
            $(T', v') \in s'.commit\_requested$,
            $T' \in domain(s'.time)$
            $T' \in s'.nonorphans$,
            $s'.time(T) \leq s'.time(T')$
            $((T, v), (T', v')) \in R$,
        there do not exist T' and v' such that
            $(T', v') \in s'.commit\_requested$
            $T' \in domain(s'.time)$
            $T' \in s'.nonorphans$
            $s'.time(T') < s'.time(T)$
            $((T', v'), (T, v)) \in R$,
            T' is not visible to T in s'
        $perform(\xi(T, v))$ is a behavior of $S(X)$
            where ξ is the result of ordering,
                in $s'.time$ order,
                the set of operations (T', v') such that
                    $(T', v') \in s'.commit\_requested$
                    $T' \in domain(s'.time)$
                    $T' \in s'.nonorphans$
                    T' is visible to T in s'
                    $s'.time(T') < s'.time(T)$
    Effect:
        $s.commit\_requested$
            $= s'.commit\_requested \cup \{(T, v)\}$

Figure 7.4: Transition Relation for Herlihy's Algorithm

occurring unless its pseudotime is sufficiently advanced.[17] The fifth condition requires that T not depend on any operation of a nonorphan access with an earlier pseudotime, unless that access is visible to T. This is called the *no dirty data* condition. The final condition requires that the return value be appropriate for the version of $S(X)$ based on applying all the the operations of accesses that are visible to T and have earlier pseudotimes.

---

[17]The term is taken from the algorithm described in [49], where the corresponding limit on pseudotime never decreases during an execution, in the same way that a ratchet turns only one way. See Exercise 11.

EXAMPLE 7.5.1   A FIFO Queue Object

Consider the message queue system of Example 3.5.7. This system contains a FIFO queue serial object QUEUE, which is accessed by transaction names T_{Gx}, the value generators (with $kind(T_{Gx}) =$ "*insert*" and $data(T_{Gx}) = x$) and $T_{Ri.0}$, the value recorders (with $kind(T_{Ri.0}) =$ "*delete*"). Let R_2 denote the serial dependency relation for this object given in Example 4.5.2, so that R_2 contains all pairs $((T, v), (T', v'))$ where $T \neq T'$, $kind(T') =$ "*delete*", and either of the following holds: $kind(T) =$ "*insert*" and $data(T) \neq v'$; or $kind(T) =$ "*delete*" and $v = v'$. When we use the set of finite sequences of positive integers, ordered lexicographically, as pseudo-times, we can construct the pseudotime object automaton $H(\text{QUEUE}, R_2)$ using Herlihy's algorithm for this serial object. The following sequence β is a schedule of $H(\text{QUEUE}, R_2)$.

CREATE(T_{G3}),
INFORM_TIME_AT(QUEUE)**OF**$(T_{G3}, 1)$,
    INFORM_TIME_AT(QUEUE)**OF**$(T_{G6}, 2)$,
    CREATE(T_{G6}),
        CREATE$(T_{R2.0})$,
    REQUEST_COMMIT$(T_{G6}, \text{"}OK\text{"})$,
REQUEST_COMMIT$(T_{G3}, \text{"}OK\text{"})$,
INFORM_COMMIT_AT(QUEUE)**OF**(T_{G3}),
        INFORM_TIME_AT(QUEUE)**OF**$(T_{R2.0}, 3, 1)$,
    INFORM_COMMIT_AT(QUEUE)**OF**(T_{G6}),
        REQUEST_COMMIT$(T_{R2.0}, 3)$,
    INFORM_ABORT_AT(QUEUE)**OF**$(T_{R2.0})$,
        CREATE$(T_{R1.0})$,
        INFORM_TIME_AT(QUEUE)**OF**$(T_{R1.0}, 5, 1)$,
        REQUEST_COMMIT$(T_{R1.0}, 3)$,
            CREATE$(T_{R3.0})$,
            INFORM_TIME_AT(QUEUE)**OF**$(T_{R3.0}, 11, 1)$,
        INFORM_COMMIT_AT(QUEUE)**OF**$(T_{R1.0})$,
        INFORM_COMMIT_AT(QUEUE)**OF**(T_{R1}),
            REQUEST_COMMIT$(T_{R3.0}, 6)$,
            INFORM_ABORT_AT(QUEUE)**OF**(T_{R3}),
                CREATE(T_{G4}),
                    CREATE(T_{G1}),
                    INFORM_TIME_AT(QUEUE)**OF**$(T_{G1}, 7)$,
                INFORM_TIME_AT(QUEUE)**OF**$(T_{G4}, 8)$,
                REQUEST_COMMIT$(T_{G4}, \text{"}OK\text{"})$,

$$\textbf{CREATE}(T_{G2}),$$
$$\textbf{INFORM\_TIME\_AT}(\text{QUEUE})\textbf{OF}(T_{G2}, 4),$$
$$\textbf{CREATE}(T_{G9}),$$
$$\textbf{INFORM\_TIME\_AT}(\text{QUEUE})\textbf{OF}(T_{G9}, 10),$$
$$\textbf{CREATE}(T_{R6.0}),$$
$$\textbf{INFORM\_TIME\_AT}(\text{QUEUE})\textbf{OF}(T_{R6.0}, 6, 1),$$
$$\textbf{CREATE}(T_{R4.0}),$$
$$\textbf{INFORM\_TIME\_AT}(\text{QUEUE})\textbf{OF}(T_{R4.0}, 9, 1).$$

The schedule β can lead $H(\text{QUEUE}, R_2)$ to state s where $s.created = \{T_{G3}, T_{G6}, T_{R2.0}, T_{R1.0}, T_{R3.0}, T_{G4}, T_{G1}, T_{G2}, T_{G9}, T_{R6.0}, T_{R4.0}\}$, $s.committed = \{T_{G3}, T_{G6}, T_{R1.0}, T_{R1}\}$, $s.aborted = \{T_{R2.0}, T_{R3}\}$, $s.commit\_requested = \{(T_{G6}, \text{``}OK\text{''}), (T_{G3}, \text{``}OK\text{''}), (T_{R2.0}, 3), (T_{R1.0}, 3), (T_{R3.0}, 6), (T_{G4}, \text{``}OK\text{''})\}$, $s.time(T_{G3}) = 1$, $s.time(T_{G6}) = 2$, $s.time(T_{R2.0}) = 3, 1$, $s.time(T_{R1.0}) = 5, 1$, $s.time(T_{R3.0}) = 11, 1$, $s.time(T_{G1}) = 7$, $s.time(T_{G4}) = 8$, $s.time(T_{G2}) = 4$, $s.time(T_{G9}) = 10$, $s.time(T_{R6.0}) = 6, 1$, $s.time(T_{R4.0}) = 9, 1$, and $s.time(T)$ is undefined for other access names T.

In the state s, the action **REQUEST_COMMIT**$(T_{G9}, \text{``}OK\text{''})$ is enabled. This is because the only operation that is in $s.commit\_requested$ for a nonorphan access that is not visible in $s$ to $T_{G9}$ and has recorded pseudotime less than 10 is $(T_{G4}, \text{``}OK\text{''})$ and $((T_{G4}, \text{``}OK\text{''}), (T_{G9}, \text{``}OK\text{''})) \notin R_2$ (as both accesses are inserts), and also there is no operation in $s.commit\_requested$ for a nonorphan access whose recorded pseudotime is greater than 10. Notice that the return value is calculated using all operations with timestamps lower than 10, that are visible in s to T_{G9}, that is, it is "OK" because the sequence $perform(\xi)$ be a finite behavior of $S(queue)$, where $\xi = (T_{G3}, \text{``}OK\text{''})(T_{G6}, \text{``}OK\text{''})(T_{R1.0}, 3)(T_{G9}, \text{``}OK\text{''})$. Notice also that the order of operations in ξ is that given by the recorded pseudotimes, rather than the order in which the **REQUEST_COMMIT** actions occur.

Similarly **REQUEST_COMMIT**$(T_{G1}, \text{``}OK\text{''})$ is enabled in s. This is because there is no operation that is in $s.commit\_requested$ for a nonorphan access that is not visible in s to T_{G9} and has recorded pseudotime than 10, and also the only operation in $s.commit\_requested$ for a nonorphan access whose recorded pseudotime is greater than 10 is $(T_{G4}, \text{``}OK\text{''})$ but $((T_{G1}, \text{``}OK\text{''}), (T_{G4}, \text{``}OK\text{''}))$ is not in R_2.

By contrast, **REQUEST_COMMIT**$(T_{G2}, \text{``}OK\text{''})$ is not enabled in $s$, because of the existence of $(T_{R1.0}, 3)$ in $s.commit\_requested$. Notice that $((T_{G2}, \text{``}OK\text{''}), (T_{R1.0}, 3))$ is an element of the serial dependency relation R_2.

We leave as Exercise 10 the determination that in s, **REQUEST-_COMMIT**$(T_{R6.0}, 6)$ is enabled, but there is no value v for which **REQUEST-_COMMIT**$(T_{R4.0}, v)$ is enabled.

7.5.2 Correctness Proof

Basic Properties of H(X,R)

We begin by stating immediate connections between the actions in a schedule of $H(X, R)$ and the state to which it can lead. The proof of this lemma is a simple induction.

LEMMA 7.34 *Let β be a finite pseudotime object well-formed schedule of $H(X, R)$. Suppose that β can lead to state s. Then the following conditions hold.*

1. $T \in s.created$ *if and only if CREATE(T) appears in β.*

2. $T \in s.committed$ *if and only if INFORM_COMMIT_AT(X)OF(T) appears in β.*

3. $T \in s.aborted$ *if and only if INFORM_ABORT_AT(X)OF(T) appears in β.*

4. $s.time(T) = p$ *if and only if INFORM_TIME_AT(X)OF(T,p) appears in β.*

5. $(T, v) \in s.commit\_requested$ *if and only if REQUEST_COMMIT(T,v) appears in β.*

By using the previous lemma and the preconditions of the actions, it is easy to see that $H(X, R)$ preserves pseudotime object well-formedness.

LEMMA 7.35 $H(X, R)$ *is a pseudotime object for* X.

Proving Local Static Atomicity

The next two lemmas give the main properties of the algorithm that are used to prove its correctness. The first lemma shows that the conditions checked in the precondition of a **REQUEST_COMMIT**(T, v) action remain true as long as T is not an orphan.

LEMMA 7.36 *Let β be a finite pseudotime object well-formed schedule of $H(X, R)$. Suppose that β can lead to state s. Then the following conditions hold.*

1. *If T and T' are both in $domain(s.time)$ and $s.time(T) = s.time(T')$ then $T = T'$.*

2. $\{T : (T, v) \in s.commit\_requested \text{ for some } v\} \subseteq domain(s.time)$.

3. *Suppose that the following hold: $(T, v) \in s.commit\_requested$, $T \in s.nonorphans$, $(T', v') \in s.commit\_requested$, $T' \in s.nonorphans$, $s.time(T') < s.time(T)$, and, finally, $((T', v'), (T, v)) \in R$. Then T' is visible to T in s.*

4. *Suppose $(T, v) \in s.commit\_requested$ and $T \in s.nonorphans$. Let $S = \{(T', v') \in s.commit\_requested$: T' is visible to T in s and $s.time(T') \leq s.time(T)\}$. Let ζ be the result of ordering the operations in S in $s.time$ order. Then $perform(\zeta) \in behs(S(\mathrm{X}))$.*

PROOF The proof is by induction on the length of β. The base is obvious, so consider the inductive step. Let $\beta = \beta'\pi$, where π is a single action, where β' can lead to state s', and where (s', π, s) is a step of $H(\mathrm{X}, R)$. The first two claims are straightforward.

Let (T, v) and (T', v') satisfy the hypothesis of Claim 3. Since T and T' are in $s.nonorphans$, they are in $s'.nonorphans$ also. By well-formedness and the fact that T and T' are in $s.commit\_requested$, it follows that T and T' are in $domain(s'.time)$, and that $s'.time(T) = s.time(T)$ and $s'.time(T') = s.time(T')$. There are three cases.

1. (T, v) and (T', v') are both in $s'.commit\_requested$.

Then the inductive hypothesis implies that T' is visible to T in s' and therefore in s.

2. $(T, v) \in s'.commit\_requested$ and π is **REQUEST_COMMIT**(T', v').

This contradicts the *ratchet lock* clause in the precondition of π.

3. $(T', v') \in s'.commit\_requested$ and π is **REQUEST_COMMIT**(T, v).

Then the *no dirty data* clause in the precondition of π ensures that T' is visible to T in s' and hence in s.

Claim 3 follows.

Now let (T, v), S, and ζ satisfy the hypothesis of Claim 4. Let $S' = \{(T', v') \in s'.commit\_requested$: T' is visible to T in s' and $s'.time(T') \leq s'.time(T)\}$. Let ζ' be the result of ordering the operations in S' in $s'.time$ order. (Thus, S' and ζ' are defined just like S and ζ but using s' rather than s.)

If π is **REQUEST_COMMIT**(T, v), then $S = S' \cup \{(T, v)\}$, $\zeta = \zeta'(T, v)$, and the operation sequence called β in the precondition of π is equal to ζ'. Thus the claim is guaranteed by the precondition of π. So assume that π is not **REQUEST_COMMIT**(T, v). Then $(T, v) \in s'.commit\_requested$. Since $T \in s'.nonorphans$, the inductive hypothesis ensures that $perform(\zeta')$ is in $behs(S(\mathrm{X}))$.

Now consider cases.

1. π is neither a **REQUEST_COMMIT**(T', v') action nor an **INFORM_COMMIT _AT**(X)**OF**(U) for U a child of an ancestor of T.

Then $S' = S$ and $\zeta' = \zeta$, so the result follows.

2. $\pi = $ **REQUEST_COMMIT**(T', v'), where $T' \neq T$.

Then pseudotime object well-formedness implies that $S = S'$ and $\zeta = \zeta'$, so again the result follows. (T' cannot become visible to T as a result of this action, since **INFORM_COMMIT_AT**(X)**OF**(T') cannot precede **REQUEST_COMMIT**(T', v') in a pseudotime object well-formed sequence.)

3. $\pi = $ **INFORM_COMMIT_AT**(X)**OF**(U) for U a child of an ancestor of T.

Then consider the operations in $S - S'$. Let T'' be the access with the largest value of $s'.time$ among those that appear as first component in $S - S'$. Clearly, $(T'', v'') \in s'.commit\_requested$ for some v'' and $T'' \in s'.nonorphans$. Let $S'' = \{(T', v') \in s'.commit\_requested : T'$ is visible to T'' in s' and $s'.time(T') \leq s'.time(T'')\}$. Let ζ'' be the result of ordering the operations in S'' in $s'.time$ order. (Thus, S'' and ζ'' are defined just like S and ζ but using s' rather than s and T'' instead of T.) The inductive hypothesis ensures that $perform(\zeta'')$ is in $behs(S(X))$. Also note that $S = S' \cup S''$; since T'' is visible to T in s, T'' is visible to U in s', and an access is visible to U in s' if and only if it is visible to T'' in s'. Thus, ζ' and ζ'' are both subsequences of ζ, and each operation in ζ is in at least one of the two subsequences.

If $(T_1, v_1) \in \zeta'' - \zeta', (T_2, v_2) \in \zeta' - \zeta''$, and $s'.time(T_1) < s'.time(T_2)$, then Claim 3 implies that $((T_1, v_1), (T_2, v_2)) \notin R$. Likewise, if $(T_1, v_1) \in \zeta' - \zeta'', (T_2, v_2) \in \zeta' - \zeta''$, and $s'.time(T_1) < s'.time(T_2)$, then $((T_1, v_1), (T_2, v_2)) \notin R$.

Then Proposition 4.10 implies that $perform(\zeta) \in behs(S(X))$. $\qquad\square$

One can use the preceding lemma to obtain the following corollary, proving a property very similar to local static atomicity, but stated using components of the object's state rather than properties of the behavior when determining which accesses are visible and nonorphans, and the order to use in arranging operations.

LEMMA 7.37 *Let β be a finite schedule of $H(X, R)$ such that the behavior of β is pseudotime object well-formed. Suppose that β can lead to state s. Let T be in $s.nonorphans$. Let ξ be the result of ordering the operations (T', v') in $s.commit\_requested$ such that T' is visible to T in s in $s.time$ order. Then $perform(\xi)$ is a behavior of $S(X)$.*

PROOF Consider any operation (T', v') in ξ. By Claim 4 of Lemma 7.36, $perform(\eta)$ is a behavior of $S(X)$, where η is the result of ordering the operations $(T'', v'') \in s.commit\_requested$ with T'' visible to T' in s and $s.time(T'') \leq s.time(T')$, in $s.time$ order. Since (by Claim 3 of Lemma 7.36), η is an R-closed subsequence of ξ containing (T', v'), the fact that R is a serial dependency relation implies that $perform(\xi)$ is a behavior of $S(X)$. $\qquad\square$

Now one can prove that a data object is locally static atomic if it is implemented using the algorithm described in this section.

PROPOSITION 7.38 $H(X, R)$ *is locally static atomic.*

PROOF   Let β be a finite pseudotime object well-formed behavior of $H(X, R)$, and T a transaction name that is not a local orphan in β. Let S be the set of operations occurring in β whose transactions are locally visible to T in β. Then $local\text{-}view(\beta, T) = perform(\xi)$, where ξ is the result of ordering S according to the order $R = local\text{-}pseudotime\text{-}order(\beta)$ on the transaction components. The proof must show that $local\text{-}view(\beta, T)$ is a behavior of $S(X)$.

Since $H(X, R)$ has no internal actions, β is a schedule of $H(X, R)$. Choose a state s of $H(X, R)$ such that β can lead to s. Since T is not a local orphan in β, T is not in $s.nonorphans$, by Lemma 7.34. Furthermore any transaction is locally visible to T in β if and only if it is visible to T in s, and the order defined by $s.time$ is the same as R.

Now the result is immediate from Lemma 7.37.   □

As a consequence, using Theorem 7.24, one sees that $H(X, R)$ is static atomic.

7.6   Discussion

This chapter dealt with timestamp-based algorithms in the same way the previous chapter covered locking algorithms. An appropriate system decomposition was given, and a local property defined, which, applying to each object, ensures the correctness of the whole system. A number of abstract algorithms were shown to have this property; other more concrete implementations were also given. The results of this chapter show that any of these algorithms may be combined in a single system, and atomicity will not be violated for nonorphan transactions.

7.7   Bibliographic Notes

The idea of issuing timestamps and using their order to determine serialization order was introduced in [110]. The local static atomicity condition generalizes work of Weihl for transaction systems without nesting [117, 113]. In contrast to the approach taken here, in which pseudotimes are assigned to transactions when they start, Weihl assumed that the pseudotime order was represented by a total order on the transactions' names. While the two approaches are formally different, for all practical purposes they are really equivalent, since one can easily view the assignment of a pseudotime as the point at which a transaction's name is chosen when the transaction is created. As with dynamic atomicity, Weihl also showed his static atomicity condition to be optimal, in the sense that no strictly weaker local condition suffices to ensure global atomicity.

The pseudotimes discussed in Section 7.1 (based on finite sequences of integers, ordered lexicographically) were proposed by Reed in his original work on pseudotime systems [103]. The Avalon system uses the same kinds of pseudotimes, but in a slightly different way [29]. (The pseudotimes are assigned when transactions commit, rather than when they start.) The approach taken in Avalon is the subject of Chapter 8.

Reed's algorithm is presented in [102, 103]. Herlihy's algorithm was originally described for single-level transaction systems [49]. It is extended here to encompass nested transactions, and generalized slightly, by testing for conflicts on *ratchet locks* only for nonorphan transactions. Herlihy's original algorithm does not release ratchet locks when a transaction aborts, so conflicts on ratchet locks are tested against all transactions, aborted or not. This is similar to the way Reed's algorithm maintains only the maximum timestamp for the set of readers of a given version, regardless of whether the readers have committed or aborted.

A complicated algorithm based on timestamps was implemented by Bernstein *et al.* in the SDD-1 prototype system [13].

A simulation study of the performance of timestamp-based algorithms is provided by Lin and Nolte [74].

A preliminary version of some of the material in the chapter is in [6].

7.8   Exercises

1. Prove Lemma 7.4.

2. Show that for the sequence β given in Example 7.2.1, and for each object name X in the system, $view(serial(\beta), T_0, R, X)$ is a behavior of $S(X)$, where $R = pseudo\text{-}time\text{-}order(\beta)$.

3. Prove Lemma 7.27.

4. For the pseudotime object $R(\text{COPY\_A})$ of Example 7.4.1, and the sequences β and β' given there, show that $local\text{-}view(\beta\beta', T_{V6.A})$ has the value given. Also calculate $local\text{-}view(\beta\beta', T_{V5.A})$. Show that both are finite behaviors of the read/write serial object automaton $S(\text{COPY\_A})$.

5. Complete the details of the proof of Theorem 7.32.

6. Consider the read/write object COPY_A in the message queue system of Example 3.5.7, and let $R1(\text{COPY\_A})$ be the pseudotime object automaton corresponding to COPY_A, using the concrete version of Reed's algorithm presented in Section 7.4.3. Show that the sequence β of Example 7.4.1 is *not* a schedule of $R1(\text{COPY\_A})$. This implies that $R(\text{COPY\_A})$ does not implement $R1(\text{COPY\_A})$, since β is a schedule of $R(\text{COPY\_A})$.

7. Design and verify a more space-efficient but restrictive variant of Reed's concrete implementation $R1(X)$, where the maximum time of a reading transaction is kept only for the *current* version (that whose writer has the highest timestamp among nonorphan writers) and all other versions are presumed to exist in the pseudotime interval from their writer until the timestamp of the writer with the closest higher timestamp.

8. Design and verify an algorithm similar to Reed's for a general serial object. Accesses that are obliterating should be treated like writes (they cause a new version to be produced), accesses that are transparent like reads (they return a value based on the closest preceding version in timestamp order), and other accesses, that are neither transparent nor obliterating, are treated as a combination of read and write.

9. Suppose X is an object name where the serial object $S(X)$ is a read/write object. Let R be the serial dependency relation described in Example 4.5.1, and $H(X, R)$ be the object constructed using Herlihy's algorithm with the relation. Show that $R(X)$ is not an implementation of $H(X, R)$, that is, Reed's algorithm allows some behaviors not allowed by Herlihy's.

10. Consider the pseudotime object $H(\text{QUEUE}, R_2)$ and its schedule β that leads to state s, as given in Example 7.5.1. Show that in s **REQUEST_COMMIT**$(T_{R6.0}, 6)$ is enabled, but there is no value v for which **REQUEST_COMMIT**$(T_{R4.0}, v)$ is enabled.

11. Design a space-efficient implementation of a Herlihy object, using ideas similar to those for Reed's implementation $R1(X)$. The algorithm should group operations together (for example, an object based on a bank account serial object might treat all deposit accesses as one group, all withdrawals with non-zero return value as another, and so on). The object should maintain pseudotime information for active accesses; for those that have requested to commit, it should keep a single pseudotime for each group, representing the largest pseudotime of an access belonging to the group. Prove the implementation correct using a possibilities mapping.

12. Consider the pseudotime system that uses the system type and transaction automata of the message queue system of Example 3.5.7, with pseudotime objects

$R(\text{COPY\_A})$ (as given in Example 7.4.1), $H(\text{QUEUE}, R_2)$ (as given in Example 7.5.1), and $R(\text{COPY\_B})$ (using Reed's algorithm). Let β_1 denote the sequence

CREATE$(T_{R1.A3})$,
INFORM_TIME_AT(COPY_A)**OF**$(T_{R1.A3}, 4, 3)$,
    INFORM_TIME_AT(COPY_A)**OF**$(T_{V1.A}, 3, 3)$,
    CREATE$(T_{V1.A})$,
REQUEST_COMMIT$(T_{R1.A3}, \text{``OK''})$,
INFORM_COMMIT_AT(COPY_A)**OF**$(T_{R1.A3})$,
    REQUEST_COMMIT$(T_{V1.A}, 0)$,
    INFORM_COMMIT_AT(COPY_A)**OF**$(T_{V1.B})$.

Let β_2 denote

INFORM_TIME_AT(QUEUE)**OF**$(T_{G6}, 2)$,
    INFORM_TIME_AT(QUEUE)**OF**$(T_{R1.0}, 4, 1)$,
CREATE(T_{G6}),
REQUEST_COMMIT$(T_{G6}, \text{``OK''})$,
INFORM_COMMIT_AT(QUEUE)**OF**(T_{G6}),
    REQUEST_COMMIT$(T_{R1.0}, 6)$,
        INFORM_COMMIT_AT(QUEUE)**OF**(T_{V1}),
    INFORM_COMMIT_AT(QUEUE)**OF**$(T_{R1.0})$,
        INFORM_COMMIT_AT(QUEUE)**OF**$(T_{V1.A})$,

and let β_3 denote

CREATE$(T_{R1.B3})$,
INFORM_TIME_AT(COPY_B)**OF**$(T_{R1.B3}, 4, 2)$,
    INFORM_TIME_AT(COPY_B)**OF**$(T_{V1.B}, 3, 1)$,
    CREATE$(T_{V1.B})$,
REQUEST_COMMIT$(T_{R1.B3}, \text{``OK''})$,
INFORM_COMMIT_AT(COPY_B)**OF**$(T_{R1.B3})$,
INFORM_COMMIT_AT(COPY_B)**OF**(T_{R1}),
    REQUEST_COMMIT$(T_{V1.B}, 0)$,
    INFORM_COMMIT_AT(COPY_B)**OF**$(T_{V1.A})$.

Show that each β_i is a behavior of the appropriate pseudotime object. Construct a behavior β of the system, so that $\beta|R(\text{COPY\_A}) = \beta_1$, $\beta|H(\text{QUEUE}, R_2) = \beta_2$, and $\beta|R(\text{COPY\_B}) = \beta_3$. Show that β is atomic for T_0 by giving a serial behavior with the same projection as β on T_0.

1 3 . Develop a pseudotime object for a read/write serial object $S(\mathrm{X})$ using Moss's algorithm as described in Section 6.4.3. The object should be almost identical to $M1(\mathrm{X})$ presented there, except that there should be extra **INFORM_TIME** actions that have no effect on the state. Show that this object is *not* locally static atomic. Consider the pseudotime system like that in Exercise 12, except that (for the object name COPY_B) Moss's algorithm is used instead of $R(\text{COPY\_B})$. Find an execution of this system that is not atomic for T_0. Hint: use the same β_1 and β_2 as in exercise 12, and use for COPY_B a sequence just like β_3 except with a different return value for $T_{V1.B}$.

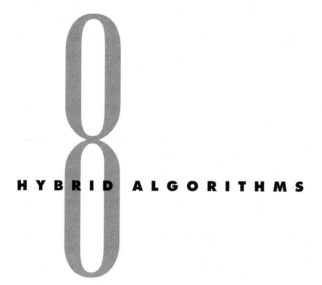

HYBRID ALGORITHMS

8.1 Introduction

In Chapter 6, a number of locking algorithms were presented. The concept of dynamic atomicity was defined in order to show why these algorithms work correctly. A dynamic atomic object has a particular interface with the rest of the system by which it obtains explicit notification about the completion of transactions; these notifications constrain the set of possible orders for transaction completion. A dynamic atomic object is defined to be one for which reordering the events at that object according to any possible completion order (as deduced from these explicit notifications) yields a correct serial behavior of the corresponding serial object.

The information about transaction completion order that is provided to the dynamic atomic objects used in Chapter 6 is somewhat limited: a dynamic atomic object simply learns that particular transactions have committed or aborted. The relative times at which the object learns about the commits and aborts can be used by the object to make some deductions about the completion order, but the object might not always be able to determine that order completely. For instance, an object might learn that two particular sibling transactions, T and T', have committed, and yet not know the order in which the commits occurred. In this case, the dynamic atomicity condition requires that the object issue responses that are compatible with either completion order. This requirement can limit the allowed responses; in particular, it can limit the concurrent activities of different transactions that can be permitted by the object.

Hybrid Atomic Objects: In this chapter, we consider augmenting the information that an object receives about completion order. More specifically, we define a new type of object, which we call a "hybrid atomic" object. (The name "hybrid" is chosen because the algorithms combine ideas from dynamic and static atomicity.) The interface of a hybrid atomic object is similar to that of a dynamic atomic object; the only difference is that notifications of commits of transactions for hybrid atomic objects include specific "timestamp" information indicating the order in which these commits took place.

The Avalon system, built on top of Camelot, provides exactly this information to the objects [29]. In Avalon, the **tid**, or transaction identifier, generated by the system has a comparison operation that indicates which of two transactions committed first.

Using the timestamps in commit notifications, a hybrid atomic object can deduce more about the transaction completion order than can a corresponding dynamic atomic object. A hybrid atomic object, like a dynamic atomic object, is required to give responses that are compatible with any possible completion order that is consistent with the object's local knowledge; however, since there are fewer such possible orders for a hybrid atomic object than for a dynamic atomic object, there are fewer constraints on its responses. In some cases, this extra freedom can permit more concurrent activity among transactions.

For example, a concurrent FIFO queue implemented using commutativity-based locking does not allow concurrent enqueue accesses to occur. In essence, the reason is that if these were permitted, the queue would not know which value to return for a later dequeue operation, since the item dequeued should be whichever is enqueued by the access that comes first in the serialization order. If the queue can learn about the eventual serialization order of concurrent enqueue accesses, then it can permit such concurrent accesses to proceed, and still be able to determine the appropriate return values for later dequeues.

Parallels to Earlier Material: This chapter shows how to reason about a system containing hybrid atomic objects. The development is parallel to that in Chapters 6 and 7, and is based on the Atomicity Theorem using the completion order as the serialization order. We introduce a system decomposition, with a hybrid system consisting of a hybrid controller and hybrid object automata as well as transaction automata. Each object may use a different concurrency control algorithm, and we define hybrid atomicity so that the system as a whole is correct provided each hybrid object is hybrid atomic. We define local hybrid atomicity, a property of an object that is easily checked and is sufficient to ensure hybrid atomicity. We then present an algorithm for implementing an object that uses the semantics of operations (as expressed in a commutative serial dependency relation—see Section 4.5) and ensures that the object is hybrid atomic.

Chapter Outline: The rest of this chapter is organized as follows. Section 8.2 presents the definitions of a hybrid system and of hybrid atomic objects, and proves the correctness of a hybrid system in which each object is hybrid atomic. Then Section 8.3 presents one hybrid atomic algorithm, together with its correctness proof.

8.2 Hybrid Atomicity

The development in this section closely parallels that in Chapters 6 and 7. For that reason, we provide less commentary than before, concentrating on those aspects that are different from the previous chapters.

8.2.1 Hybrid Systems

This subsection defines the system decomposition appropriate for describing algorithms using information about the completion order. Specifically, *hybrid systems* are introduced. Hybrid systems are composed of transaction automata, *hybrid object automata*, and a *hybrid controller*.

Timestamps

We use a totally ordered set $\mathcal{P}$ of *timestamps*. The development will not actually need the set $\mathcal{P}$ to be totally ordered—it will be enough that the timestamps assigned to sibling transactions be ordered with respect to each other. However, for simplicity we assume the total ordering, and leave the (minor) generalization as an exercise. A natural choice for $\mathcal{P}$ is the set of positive integers, or more realistically, the integers less than some (extremely large) maximum.

Hybrid Object Automata

A **hybrid object automaton** $HY(\mathrm{X})$ for an object name X of a given system type is an automaton with the following external action signature.

Input:
    CREATE(T), for T an access to X
    INFORM_COMMIT_AT(X)**OF**(T, p), for $T \neq T_0, p \in \mathcal{P}$
    INFORM_ABORT_AT(X)**OF**(T), for $T \neq T_0$
Output:
    REQUEST_COMMIT(T, v), for T an access to X and v a value for T

In addition, $HY(\mathrm{X})$ may have an arbitrary set of internal actions.

The signature of a hybrid object automaton $HY(\mathrm{X})$ is similar to that of a generic object $G(\mathrm{X})$, as defined in Section 6.2.2. It differs in that explicit timestamp information is included in all **INFORM_COMMIT** actions. It is also similar to that of a pseudotime object, as defined in Section 7.3.2, in that the object receives timestamp information for transactions. However, hybrid objects differ from pseudotime objects in that the timestamp information is included in the **INFORM_COMMIT** actions rather than in separate **INFORM_TIME** actions; thus, timestamp information only arrives for transactions that have committed. Also, hybrid objects receive timestamp information for arbitrary transactions, not just for accesses to X. (Unlike pseudotimes, the relative order of timestamps assigned to siblings cannot be inferred from timestamps assigned to descendants.)

A hybrid object automaton $HY(\mathrm{X})$ is required to preserve *hybrid object well-formedness*, defined as follows. A sequence β of actions π in the external signature of $HY(\mathrm{X})$ is said to be **hybrid object well-formed** for X provided that the following conditions hold.

1. There is at most one **CREATE**(T) event in β for any access T.

2. There is at most one **REQUEST_COMMIT** event in β for any access T.

3. If there is a **REQUEST_COMMIT** event for access T in β, then there is a preceding **CREATE**(T) event in β.

4. There is no transaction T for which there are two different timestamps, p and p', such that **INFORM_COMMIT_AT**(X)**OF**(T, p) and **INFORM_COMMIT_AT**(X)**OF**(T, p') both occur in β.

5. There is no timestamp p for which there are two different transactions, T and T', such that T and T' are siblings and **INFORM_COMMIT_AT**(X)**OF**(T, p) and **INFORM_COMMIT_AT**(X)**OF**(T', p) both occur in β.

6. There is no transaction T for which both an **INFORM_COMMIT** event and an **INFORM_ABORT** event at X for T occur in β.

7. If an **INFORM_COMMIT** event occurs at X for T in β and T is an access to X, then there is a preceding **REQUEST_COMMIT** event for T in β.

This definition includes all the constraints corresponding to those in the definition of generic object well-formedness. In addition, there are restrictions on the timestamps supplied, similar to those in the definition of pseudotime object well-formedness. However, notice that the same timestamp may be assigned to different transactions, so long as they are not siblings.[1]

Hybrid Controller

There is a single hybrid controller for each system type. It behaves much the same as the generic controller of the same type. The main difference is that, when it commits a transaction, it simultaneously assigns a timestamp to that transaction; subsequently, it passes that timestamp to the hybrid objects in **INFORM_COMMIT** actions. The only constraint on the assignment of timestamps is that they get assigned to siblings in increasing order, as they commit.

The assignment of timestamps is somewhat different from the assignment of pseudotimes that occurs in the pseudotime controller of Chapter 7. In a hybrid system, individual timestamps are assigned to transactions, whereas in a pseudotime system, intervals of pseudotime are assigned. Also, in a hybrid system, the timestamp for a transaction is chosen when the transaction commits, whereas in a pseudotime system, the pseudotime interval for a transaction is chosen when the transaction starts executing.

The automaton given below is highly nondeterministic, in particular because each timestamp can be chosen arbitrarily, subject to the constraint that it is greater than the timestamps of all previously committed siblings. Actual implementations will restrict the nondeterminism by choosing timestamps in a controlled way. One simple method in a centralized system is to assign to each transaction the value of the clock at the instant the transaction commits. In this case, each transaction's timestamp is greater than that of *all* previously committed transactions, instead of merely the committed siblings as required. In a distributed system, one might use the value on the clock at the machine where the commit occurs: if each transaction's commit occurs at the same machine as the commits of all its siblings,[2] this provides an implementation of the hybrid controller without requiring complex clock synchronization algorithms. Another implementation can be obtained by assigning the timestamp i to a transaction if it is the i-th child of its parent that commits.

The hybrid controller has the following action signature.

---

[1]In contrast, recall that pseudotime object well-formedness requires all accesses to have different pseudotimes.

[2]Usually, this is the machine where the siblings' common parent runs.

Input:
    REQUEST_CREATE(T), $T \neq T_0$
    REQUEST_COMMIT(T, v), v a value for T
Output:
    CREATE(T)
    COMMIT(T), $T \neq T_0$
    ABORT(T), $T \neq T_0$
    REPORT_COMMIT(T,v), $T \neq T_0$
    REPORT_ABORT(T), $T \neq T_0$
    INFORM_COMMIT_AT(X)**OF**(T, p), $T \neq T_0$, $p \in \mathcal{P}$
    INFORM_ABORT_AT(X)**OF**(T), $T \neq T_0$

Each state s of the hybrid controller consists of the same six components as in the generic controller: $s.create\_requested$, $s.created$, $s.commit\_requested$, $s.committed$, $s.aborted$, and $s.reported$, plus an additional component $s.time$. The set $s.commit\text{-}requested$ is a set of operations, $s.time$ is a partial function from $\mathcal{T}$ to $\mathcal{P}$, and the others are sets of transactions. All the sets are empty in the start state except for $create\_requested$, which is $\{T_0\}$. Initially, $time$ is undefined everywhere. As before, we write $s.completed = s.committed \cup s.aborted$.

The transitions of the hybrid controller are given in Figure 8.1. Notice that they are identical to those of the generic controller, except that the **COMMIT**(T) action chooses a timestamp p and records it as $s.time(T)$, and the **INFORM_COMMIT** action includes the appropriate timestamp.

We use the usual convention on unspecified state components in the transition relation: if the value of a partial function (in this case $time$) on some element is unspecified in an effect, that value is unchanged by the action. In particular, if the partial function was undefined, it remains undefined. Recall also the convention on free variables in preconditions and effects (such as p in the code for **COMMIT**): such a variable is existentially quantified in the precondition, and in the effect, it takes any value making the precondition true.

We leave it to the reader (as Exercise 1) to show from the transition relation in Figure 8.1 that in fact the set where $time$ is defined is exactly $committed$.

Hybrid Systems

A **hybrid system** of a given system type is the composition of a compatible set of automata indexed by the union of the set of non-access transaction names, the set of object names and the singleton set $\{HC\}$ (for *hybrid controller*). Associated with each non-access transaction name T is a transaction automaton A_T for T, the same automaton as in the serial system. Associated with each object name X is a hybrid object automaton $HY(X)$ for X. Finally, associated with the name HC is the hybrid controller automaton for the system type. The external actions of a hybrid system are called **hybrid actions**, and the behaviors of a hybrid system are called **hybrid**

REQUEST_CREATE(T)
  Effect:
    $s.create\_requested$
      $= s'.create\_requested \cup \{T\}$

REQUEST_COMMIT(T, v)
  Effect:
    $s.commit\_requested$
      $= s'.commit\_requested \cup \{(T, v)\}$

CREATE(T)
  Precondition:
    $T \in s'.create\_requested - s'.created$
  Effect:
    $s.created = s'.created \cup \{T\}$

COMMIT(T)
  Precondition:
    $(T, v) \in s'.commit\_requested$
    $T \notin s'.completed$
    $p > s'.time(T')$
      for every $T' \in siblings(T) \cap s'.committed$
  Effect:
    $s.committed = s'.committed \cup \{T\}$
    $s.time(T) = p$

ABORT(T)
  Precondition:
    $T \in s'.create\_requested - s'.completed$
  Effect:
    $s.aborted = s'.aborted \cup \{T\}$

REPORT_COMMIT(T, v)
  Precondition:
    $T \in s'.committed$
    $(T, v) \in s'.commit\_requested$
    $T \notin s'.reported$
  Effect:
    $s.reported = s'.reported \cup \{T\}$

REPORT_ABORT(T)
  Precondition:
    $T \in s'.aborted$
    $T \notin s'.reported$
  Effect:
    $s.reported = s'.reported \cup \{T\}$

INFORM_COMMIT_AT(X)**OF**(T, p)
  Precondition:
    $T \in s'.committed$
    $T \in domain(s'.time)$
    $s'.time(T) = p$

INFORM_ABORT_AT(X)**OF**(T)
  Precondition:
    $T \in s'.aborted$

Figure 8.1: Transition Relation for the Hybrid Controller

behaviors. We have the following results, exactly parallel to Propositions 6.10 and 6.11.

PROPOSITION 8.1 *If β is a hybrid behavior, then the following conditions hold.*

1. *For every transaction name T, $\beta|T$ is transaction well-formed for T.*

2. *For every object name* X, *$\beta|HY$(X) is hybrid object well-formed for* X.

PROPOSITION 8.2 *If β is a hybrid behavior, then $serial(\beta)$ is a simple behavior and $serial(\beta)|T = \beta|T$ for all transaction names T.*

8.2.2 Hybrid Atomicity

Now *hybrid atomicity* is defined. The definition is analogous to the definition of dynamic atomicity or static atomicity, but it is based on hybrid systems instead of generic systems or pseudotime systems.

Let $HY(X)$ be a hybrid object automaton for object name X. Say that $HY(X)$ is **hybrid atomic** for a given system type if for all hybrid systems S of the given type in which $HY(X)$ is associated with X, the following is true: let β be a finite behavior of S, $R = completion\text{-}order(\beta)$, and T a transaction name that is not an orphan in β. Then $view(serial(\beta), T, R, X)$ is a behavior of $S(X)$.

The following theorem is a direct consequence of the Atomicity Theorem (Theorem 5.24), Proposition 8.2, and Lemma 6.5.

THEOREM 8.3 *(Hybrid Atomicity Theorem) Let S be a hybrid system in which all hybrid objects are hybrid atomic. Let β be a finite behavior of S. Then β is atomic for every nonorphan transaction name.*

8.2.3 Local Hybrid Atomicity

We now give a local version of hybrid atomicity. The development is analogous to that for local dynamic atomicity in Section 6.2.4, but includes some significant technical changes. We begin by defining *local visibility* and the *local completion order* exactly as in Chapter 6. That is, if $HY(X)$ is a hybrid object automaton for object name X, and β is a sequence of external actions of $HY(X)$, then T is **locally visible at** X to T' in β if β contains an **INFORM_COMMIT_AT(X)OF**(U, p) event for every U in $ancestors(T) - ancestors(T')$. Also, $local\text{-}completion\text{-}order(\beta)$ is the binary relation on accesses to X where $(U, U') \in local\text{-}completion\text{-}order(\beta)$ if and only if $U \neq U'$, β contains **REQUEST_COMMIT** events for both U and U', and U is locally visible at X to U' in β', where β' is the longest prefix of β not containing the given **REQUEST-_COMMIT** event for U'.

In this chapter we will use a different notion of *local orphans* from that in Section 6.2.4. Recall that the prior definition designated a transaction T as a local orphan exactly if an **INFORM_ABORT** appears for an ancestor of T. The new definition includes additional conditions that imply that a transaction is an orphan. For example, it can be deduced that an access T' to object X is an orphan provided that T' is created and that an **INFORM_COMMIT** event occurs for an ancestor of T' without any preceding **REQUEST_COMMIT** for T'. Moreover, if such an access T' is locally visible to any transaction T, then it can also be deduced that T is an orphan.

More formally, if β is a sequence of external actions of $HY(X)$, then we define an access T' to object X to be **excluded** in β provided that β contains **CREATE**(T'), and also contains an **INFORM_COMMIT** event for an ancestor of T' with no preceding

REQUEST_COMMIT event for T'. Then we define a transaction name T to be a **local orphan** in β provided that at least one of the following holds:

1. An **INFORM_ABORT** event occurs in β for some ancestor of T, or

2. there is some excluded access to X that is locally visible to T.

The relationship between these local definitions and their corresponding global versions is expressed in the following result.

LEMMA 8.4 *Let β be a behavior of a hybrid system in which hybrid object automaton $HY(\mathrm{X})$ is associated with X. If T is locally visible at X to T' in $\beta|HY(\mathrm{X})$ then T is visible to T' in β. Similarly, if T is a local orphan at X in $\beta|HY(\mathrm{X})$ then T is an orphan in β.*

The following lemma follows easily by considering the two cases of the definition of a local orphan.

LEMMA 8.5 *Let $HY(\mathrm{X})$ be a hybrid object automaton for X. Let β be a hybrid object well-formed sequence of external actions of $HY(\mathrm{X})$. If T' is a local orphan in β and T' is locally visible to T in β, then T is a local orphan in β.*

EXAMPLE 8.2.1   A Bank Account Object

Let us consider the savings account object named ACCT_SVNG, in the banking database of Example 3.1.1. Suppose $HY(\mathrm{X})$ is a hybrid object automaton for X. Consider the following sequence β of actions of $HY(\mathrm{X})$.

CREATE(T_1),
REQUEST_COMMIT(T_1, "*OK*"),
INFORM_COMMIT_AT(ACCT_SVNG)**OF**(T_1, 1),
    CREATE($T_{3.3}$),
        CREATE($T_{3.1003.1}$),
    REQUEST_COMMIT($T_{3.3}$, \$200),
        INFORM_COMMIT_AT(ACCT_SVNG)**OF**(T_3, 3),
        REQUEST_COMMIT($T_{3.1003.1}$, \$1000),
        INFORM_COMMIT_AT(ACCT_SVNG)**OF**($T_{3.1003.1}$, 5).

In β the access $T_{3.1003.1}$ is excluded and is a local orphan at X, since the **INFORM_COMMIT** for T_3 occurs before the **REQUEST_COMMIT** for $T_{3.1003.1}$.

We define another binary relation, *local-timestamp-order*(β), on accesses to X. Namely, $(T, T') \in$ *local-timestamp-order*(β) if and only if T and T' are distinct accesses to X, U and U' are sibling transactions that are ancestors of T and T', respectively, β contains an **INFORM_COMMIT_AT**(X)**OF**(U, p) event, and β contains an **INFORM-_COMMIT_AT**(X)**OF**(U', p') event, where $p < p'$. Notice the difference between the local timestamp order and the local pseudotime order, defined in Section 7.3, where the order was based on the timestamps of the accesses, rather than on the timestamps of the sibling ancestors of the accesses.

LEMMA 8.6 *Suppose β is a hybrid object well-formed sequence of external actions of $HY(X)$. Then local-timestamp-order(β) is a partial order.*

Before giving our definition of local hybrid atomicity, one additional technical notion is needed. Namely, define a sequence ξ of operations of X to be **transaction-respecting** provided that for every transaction name T, all the operations for descendants of T appear consecutively in ξ. Notice that if a sequence of operations is totally ordered by R_{trans} for any sibling order R, then the sequence is transaction-respecting. In particular, if β is a hybrid behavior, T is a transaction name that is not an orphan in β, $R = completion\text{-}order(\beta)$, and X is an object name, then $view(\beta, T, R, X)$ is $perform(\xi)$ where ξ is transaction-respecting, since it is totally ordered by R_{trans}. Thus, by only considering transaction-respecting orderings in the definition of local-views below, rather than all orderings consistent with local information, as we did in Section 6.2.4, we ensure that the concept of local hybrid atomicity is a closer approximation to the concept of hybrid atomicity. Thus, a wider class of correct algorithms can be verified using the definitions of this section than would have been the case if the definition of local-views did not include the restriction to transaction-respecting orderings. In particular, the algorithm that we present in Section 8.3 can be proved to be local hybrid atomic using the definition as given in this section.

Suppose that β is a finite hybrid object well-formed sequence of external actions of $HY(X)$ and T is a transaction name. Let *local-views*(β, T) be the set of sequences defined as follows. Let Z be the set of operations occurring in β whose transactions are locally visible at X to T in β. Then the elements of *local-views*(β, T) are the sequences of the form $perform(\xi)$, where ξ is a transaction-respecting total ordering of Z in an order consistent with both the partial orders *local-completion-order*(β) and *local-timestamp-order*(β), on the transaction components. (Compare with the definition of *local-views* in Chapter 6.)

We say that hybrid object automaton $HY(X)$ for object name X is **locally hybrid atomic** if whenever β is a finite hybrid object well-formed behavior of $HY(X)$, and T is a transaction name that is not a local orphan at X in β, then every sequence that is an element of the set *local-views*(β, T) is a finite behavior of $S(X)$.

The main result of this section, Theorem 8.8, says that local hybrid atomicity is a sufficient condition for hybrid atomicity. The proof of this theorem is analogous to that of Theorem 6.20. We extract a lemma giving the relationship between the local-completion and local-timestamp orders and the true completion order in a hybrid system.

LEMMA 8.7 *Let β be a behavior of a hybrid system in which hybrid object automaton $HY(X)$ is associated with* X, *and let* $R = completion\text{-}order(\beta)$. *Let* T *and* T' *be accesses to* X. *If* $(T, T') \in local\text{-}completion\text{-}order(\beta|HY(X))$ *and* T' *is not an orphan in* β, *then* $(T, T') \in R_{trans}$. *If* $(T, T') \in local\text{-}timestamp\text{-}order(\beta|HY(X))$, *then* $(T, T') \in R_{trans}$.

PROOF The first of these is argued as in the proof of Lemma 6.18, while the latter follows from the fact that the hybrid controller assigns timestamps in completion order. □

THEOREM 8.8 *If* $HY(X)$ *is a hybrid object automaton for object name* X *that is locally hybrid atomic then* $HY(X)$ *is hybrid atomic.*

PROOF The proof is analogous to that of Theorem 6.20. The main new point to note is the following. In the earlier proof, it is shown that $view(serial(\beta), T, R, X) \in local\text{-}views(\beta\gamma|G(X, T))$. In order to show the corresponding condition $view(serial(\beta), T, R, X) \in local\text{-}views(\beta\gamma|HY(X), T)$, it must be shown not only that ξ is consistent with the *local-completion-order* order as before, but also that it is consistent with the *local-timestamp-order* order and that it is transaction-respecting. The consistency with the *local-completion* and *local-timestamp* orders follows from Lemma 8.7. The fact that ξ is transaction-respecting follows from the definition of *view*, which arranges operations in an order induced by a sibling order. □

EXAMPLE 8.2.2   A Bank Account Object

Let us consider the savings account object named ACCT_SVNG, in the banking database of Example 3.1.1. Recall that in Example 3.5.2 we gave the serial object automaton for this object; it was a bank account object. Suppose $HY(X)$ is a hybrid object automaton for X. Consider the following sequence β of actions of $HY(X)$.

CREATE(T_1),
REQUEST_COMMIT(T_1, *"OK"*),
INFORM_COMMIT_AT(ACCT_SVNG)**OF**(T_1, 1),
    CREATE($T_{3.3}$),
        CREATE($T_{3.1003.1}$),

$$\textbf{REQUEST\_COMMIT}(T_{3.1003.1}, \$1000),$$
$$\textbf{REQUEST\_COMMIT}(T_{3.3}, \$200),$$
$$\textbf{INFORM\_COMMIT\_AT}(\text{ACCT\_SVNG})\textbf{OF}(T_{3.1003.1}, 5),$$
$$\textbf{INFORM\_COMMIT\_AT}(\text{ACCT\_SVNG})\textbf{OF}(T_{3.1003}, 2),$$
$$\textbf{CREATE}(T_4),$$
$$\textbf{REQUEST\_COMMIT}(T_4, \text{``}OK\text{''}),$$
$$\textbf{INFORM\_COMMIT\_AT}(\text{ACCT\_SVNG})\textbf{OF}(T_{3.3}, 3),$$
$$\textbf{INFORM\_COMMIT\_AT}(\text{ACCT\_SVNG})\textbf{OF}(T_3, 3),$$
$$\textbf{CREATE}(T_5).$$

In β, the accesses that are locally visible at X to T_4 are T_1, $T_{3.3}$, $T_{3.1003.1}$, and T_4. No accesses are local orphans at X in β. The partial order *local-completion-order*(β) consists of the pairs $(T_1, T_{3.1003.1})$, $(T_1, T_{3.3})$, and (T_1, T_4). The partial order *local-timestamp-order*(β) includes the pair $(T_{3.1003.1}, T_{3.3})$ since the timestamp of $T_{3.1003}$ is less than that for $T_{3.3}$. (Notice that the timestamp for $T_{3.1003.1}$ is not involved in determining the local timestamp order between these two accesses.) Other elements of *local-timestamp-order*(β) include $(T_1, T_{3.1003.1})$ and $(T_1, T_{3.3})$.

The set *local-views*(β, T_4) has two elements: the sequence

$$perform((T_1, \text{``}OK\text{''})(T_{3.1003.1}, \$1000)(T_{3.3}, \$200)(T_4, \text{``}OK\text{''}))$$

and the sequence

$$perform((T_1, \text{``}OK\text{''})(T_4, \text{``}OK\text{''})(T_{3.1003.1}, \$1000)(T_{3.3}, \$200)).$$

You can check that these are both finite behaviors of $S(\text{X})$. Notice that the sequence

$$perform((T_1, \text{``}OK\text{''})(T_{3.1003.1}, \$1000)(T_4, \text{``}OK\text{''})(T_{3.3}, \$200))$$

is not an element of *local-views*(β, T_4), despite the fact that its operations are ordered consistently with both *local-completion-order*(β) and *local-timestamp-order*(β), because their order is not transaction-respecting, having the operation of T_4 in between two operations of descendants of T_3.

You should notice that the information in the *local-completion* and *local-timestamp* orders does not determine whether the serialization order will have the descendants of T_3 ahead of, or following, T_4. Thus, *local-views* must include both possibilities. In this case our knowledge of the semantics of the transaction T_0 allows us to deduce that the completion order must have T_3 before T_4, since T_4 is not invoked until T_3 has completed. (See

Example 3.1.1.) Such knowledge of the code of individual transactions
is not used in any of the algorithms in this book, which provide atomic
transaction processing regardless of the transactions the user writes.

8.3 Dependency-Based Hybrid Locking

This section presents a hybrid algorithm and its correctness proof. It is based on a
serial dependency relation, as defined in Section 4.5. The algorithm is described as a
hybrid object automaton in a hybrid system.

8.3.1 Dependency Objects

This subsection describes, for each object name X and binary relation C between
operations of X, a hybrid object automaton $D(X, C)$ (a *dependency object*). Later, we
will show that a sufficient condition for $D(X, C)$ to be locally hybrid atomic is that C
be a symmetric serial dependency relation.

The algorithm is closely related to the commutativity-based locking algorithm of
Section 6.3. The main difference is that the *intentions* of concurrent transactions
are not applied to the base state in the order in which **INFORM_COMMIT** events
arrive, but rather in the order given by timestamps. Thus when the object learns
of the commit of a subtransaction, the intentions will be transferred to the parent,
but rather than being appended at the end of the parent's previous intentions, they
may be inserted into the sequence in an earlier place. To reflect this behavior in the
automaton, we no longer keep the intentions list explicitly; instead, we keep a set of
descendant accesses (in the state component *intset*), and keep track of the timestamps
provided by the system (in the component *time*). The intentions sequence is then
obtained as a derived variable whose value is computed from these components. As
in commutativity-based locking, the response to an access is constrained so that the
resulting operation can be performed by the serial object from a state resulting from
executing the intentions sequences of the access's ancestors.

The other change from $L(X)$ is in the condition under which an access is enabled.
The condition here is that every other access that is related to it by C is locally
visible to it, whereas in $L(X)$ the enabling condition is that every other access that
does not commute forward with it is locally visible to it. The reason that we need C
to be a symmetric serial dependency relation is that if an access T completes when
another access T' has occurred but is not locally visible to T, then the object does not
yet have sufficient information to know whether T or T' will be ordered first by the
completion order. Since the return value of T is computed using only the intentions
list of ancestors of T, this return value is computed without using T'; therefore, the

object must be sure that even if T' commits and is serialized before T, the return value is appropriate. That is, the operation of T should not be affected by T'. Also, it is possible that T will be serialized before T', so the object must ensure that T does not make the previously given response to T' inappropriate. That is, T' should not be affected by T.

Note also that the discussion in the previous paragraph illustrates why C does not need to contain all pairs of operations that do not commute forward (and why the precondition for accesses is correspondingly weaker). In hybrid systems, the greater information available at each object means that, once concurrent accesses become locally visible to each other, their actual commit order will be known by the object, and later accesses only need to return responses consistent with that commit order. In generic systems, the actual commit order will never become known to the object, and later accesses need to return responses consistent with both possible commit orders for the concurrent accesses. Since the later accesses choose responses based on one of those orders, the commutativity constraint is needed to guarantee that those responses are also acceptable for the other commit orders.

The state components of $D(X, C)$ are $s.created$, $s.commit\_requested$, $s.intset$, and $s.time$. Here, $s.created$ and $s.commit\_requested$ are sets of transactions, both initially empty. Also $s.intset$ is a total function from transactions to sets of operations, initially mapping every transaction to the empty set $\emptyset$, and $s.time$ is a partial function from transactions to timestamps, initially everywhere undefined.

We would like to define the derived variable $total(T)$, which serves the same purpose here as in Section 6.3, that is, it is a sequence of operations of $S(X)$ which when performed gives the effective state produced by a transaction T. The cleanest presentation of this variable is by an expression that is not meaningful in arbitrary states of $D(X, C)$; however, it is meaningful in any state that is reachable by hybrid object well-formed executions of $D(X, C)$. We identify three properties of these states.[3] First, there is at most one operation for each access transaction name in the union of all the *intset*s. Second, if $(T', v') \in s.intset(T)$, then T' is a descendant of T, and $s.time(T'')$ is defined for all $T'' \in s.ancestors(T') - s.ancestors(T)$. Third, whenever U and U' are siblings such that $s.time(U)$ and $s.time(U')$ are both defined, then $s.time(U) \neq s.time(U')$.

In any state s that satisfies the properties above, we can use the value of the variable $s.time$ to define a binary relation R on accesses to X, as follows. If T and

---

[3]To be precise, and to avoid circular reasoning, one should define the transition relation so that **REQUEST_COMMIT** is not enabled in states that do not satisfy the properties given here, while in states that do satisfy these properties it is enabled if the precondition as listed below (which is then well-defined) is true. One can then prove that each state reachable in a hybrid object well-formed execution satisfies these properties, so that in these states the transition relation is just as listed.

CREATE(T)
    Effect:
        $s.created = s'.created \cup \{T\}$

INFORM_COMMIT_AT(X)**OF**(T, p)
    Effect:
        $s.intset(T) = \emptyset$
        $s.intset(parent(T))$
            $= s'.intset(parent(T)) \cup s'.intset(T)$
        $s.time(T) = p$

INFORM_ABORT_AT(X)**OF**(T)
    Effect:
        $s.intset(U) = \emptyset$,
          for all $U \in descendants(T)$

REQUEST_COMMIT(T, v)
    Precondition:
        $T \in s'.created - s'.commit\_requested$
        there do not exist U, T', and v' such that
           $((T, v), (T', v')) \in C$
           (T', v') is an element of $s'.intset(U)$
           $U \notin ancestors(T)$
           $perform(s'.total(T)(T, v))$
           is a behavior of $S(X)$
    Effect:
        $s.commit\_requested$
           $= s'.commit\_requested \cup \{T\}$
        $s.intset(T) = \{(T, v)\}$

Figure 8.2: Transition Relation for Dependency Locking

T' are distinct accesses to X, then we define $(T, T') \in R$ exactly if $s.time(U)$ and $s.time(U')$ are both defined and $s.time(U) < s.time(U')$, where U and U' are the sibling transactions that are ancestors of T and T', respectively. Note that if β is a hybrid object well-formed schedule of $D(X, C)$ that can lead to state s, then R coincides with the relation *local-timestamp-order*(β).

The three properties above ensure that R is a partial order that totally orders the operations in $s.intset(T)$, for any transaction name T. Thus, in a state s that satisfies the properties, we define a derived variable $s.intentions$, which is a mapping from transaction names to sequences of operations. Namely, if T is any transaction name, then the operations in the sequence $s.intentions(T)$ are exactly those in $s.intset(T)$. The order in which these operations occur is determined by the relation R defined from $s.time$, as described just above.

Finally, we let $s.total(T)$ be the sequence of operations defined recursively as follows: $s.total(T_0) = s.intentions(T_0)$, and $s.total(T) = s.total(parent(T)) \times s.intentions(T)$ for $T \neq T_0$. Notice that this definition is just the same as in Section 6.3.

The transition relation of $D(X, C)$ is given in Figure 8.2.

LEMMA 8.9 $D(X, C)$ *is a hybrid object for* X.

EXAMPLE 8.3.1   Dependency-based Locking for a FIFO Queue Object

Consider the message queue system of Example 3.5.7. This system contains a FIFO queue serial object QUEUE, which is accessed by transaction names T_{Gx} (the value generators, with $kind(T_{Gx}) = $ "*insert*" and $data(T_{Gx}) = x$) and $T_{Ri.0}$ (the value recorders, with $kind(T_{Ri.0}) = $ "*delete*"). When we use the set of positive integers as timestamps, we can construct the hybrid object automaton $D(\text{QUEUE}, C)$ where C contains all pairs of operations $((T, v), (T', v'))$ where $T \neq T'$ and either $kind(T) = $ "*delete*" or $kind(T') = $ "*delete*" (or both). This is clearly a symmetric relation, and it is a serial dependency relation because it contains as a subset the serial dependency relation R_2 given in Example 4.5.2.

The following sequence β is a schedule of $D(\text{QUEUE}, C)$.

CREATE(T_{G3}),
    CREATE(T_{G6}),
        CREATE($T_{R2.0}$),
            CREATE($T_{R1.0}$),
        REQUEST_COMMIT(T_{G6}, "*OK*"),
    REQUEST_COMMIT(T_{G3}, "*OK*"),
INFORM_COMMIT_AT(QUEUE)**OF**(T_{G3}, 2).

Notice that this schedule involves concurrent insertions into the queue, since the response to T_{G3} occurs before the fate of T_{G6} is known.

The schedule β leads $D(\text{QUEUE}, C)$ to a state s where $s.created = \{T_{G3}, T_{G6}, T_{R2.0}, T_{R1.0}\}$, $s.commit\_requested = \{T_{G3}, T_{G6}\}$, $s.intset(T_0) = \{(T_{G3}, "OK")\}$, $s.intset(T_{G6}) = \{(T_{G6}, "OK")\}$, $s.intset(T)$ is the empty set for all other transaction names T, and $s.time(T_{G3}) = 2$. The derived variable $s.total(T_{R1.0})$ is just the sequence of a single operation $(T_{G3}, "OK")$.

In the state s there is no value v for which either action **REQUEST_COMMIT**($T_{R1.0}, v$) or **REQUEST_COMMIT**($T_{R2.0}, v$) is enabled, because of the operation $(T_{G6}, "OK")$ in $s.intset(T_{G6})$. In essence, a delete access can't proceed at this point because the value to be returned ought to be 3 if T_{G6} has a timestamp after that for T_{G3}, or if T_{G6} aborts, but if T_{G6} commits before T_{G3}, then the delete should return the value 6.

Let β_1 be the sequence consisting of β followed by:

    INFORM_COMMIT_AT(QUEUE)**OF**(T_{G6}, 1),
        REQUEST_COMMIT($T_{R2.0}$, 6),
            INFORM_COMMIT_AT(QUEUE)**OF**($T_{R2.0}$, 1).

You can check that β_1 is a schedule of $D(\text{X}, C)$ that can lead $D(\text{X}, C)$ to a state s_1 where $s_1.created = \{T_{G3}, T_{G6}, T_{R2.0}, T_{R1.0}\}$,

$s_1.commit\_requested = \{T_{G3}, T_{G6}, T_{R2.0}\}$, $s_1.intset(T_0) = \{(T_{G3}, \text{``}OK\text{''}),$ $(T_{G6}, \text{``}OK\text{''})\}$, $s_1.intset(T_{R2.0}) = \{(T_{R2.0}, 1)\}$, $s_1.time(T_{G3}) = 2$, and $s_1.time(T_{G6}) = 1$. The derived variable $s_1.total(T_{R1.0})$ is just the sequence $(T_{G6}, \text{``}OK\text{''})(T_{G3}, \text{``}OK\text{''})$. There is no value v such that **REQUEST-_COMMIT**$(T_{R1.0}, v)$ is enabled[4] in s_1. This is because of the operation $(T_{R2.0}, 6)$ in $s_1.intset(T_{R2})$. The return value for a delete should be 3 if the delete is serialized after $T_{R2.0}$, but the value 6 should be returned if T_{R2} is aborted. Until the outcome of T_{R2} is resolved, the second delete must be blocked.

8.3.2 Correctness Proof

The correctness proof roughly follows the corresponding one in Section 6.3. We define lock visibility and the lock completion order exactly as in that section. That is, we say that T is **lock visible** at X to T' in β if β contains a subsequence β' consisting of an **INFORM_COMMIT_AT**(X)**OF**(U, p_U) event for every $U \in ancestors(T) - ancestors(T')$, arranged in ascending order (so the **INFORM_COMMIT** for $parent(U)$ is preceded by that for U). Also we say that $(U, U') \in lock\text{-}completion\text{-}order(\beta)$ if and only if $U \neq U'$, β contains **REQUEST_COMMIT** events for both U and U', and U is lock visible to U' at X in β', where β' is the longest prefix of β not containing the given **REQUEST_COMMIT** event for U'.

We have basic lemmas similar to those in Section 6.3.

LEMMA 8.10 *Let β be a hybrid object well-formed sequence of actions of $D(X, C)$. Then lock-completion-order(β) is a partial order.*

LEMMA 8.11 *Let β be a sequence of actions of $D(X, C)$ and T and T' transaction names. If T is lock visible at X to T' in β then T is locally visible at X to T' in β. Also lock-completion-order(β) is a subrelation of local-completion-order(β).*

The following lemmas relate the *intsets* to lock visibility and the lock completion order.

LEMMA 8.12 *Let β be a finite hybrid object well-formed behavior of $D(X, C)$. Suppose that β can lead to a state s, in $D(X, C)$. If $(T, v) \in s.intset(T')$ then T is a descendant of T', **REQUEST_COMMIT**(T, v) occurs in β, and T' is the highest ancestor of T to which T is lock visible at X in β.*

---

[4]Notice that **REQUEST_COMMIT**$(T_{R1.0}, 6)$ was enabled during the period after the **INFORM_COMMIT_AT**(QUEUE)**OF**$(T_{G6}, 1)$ and before **REQUEST_COMMIT**$(T_{R2.0}, 6)$.

LEMMA 8.13 *Let β be a finite hybrid object well-formed behavior of $D(X, C)$, and suppose that a **REQUEST_COMMIT**(T, v) event π occurs in β, where T is not a local orphan at X in β. Let β' be the prefix of β ending with π, and let s be the (unique) state led to by β', in $D(X, C)$. Then the following are true.*

1. *The operations in $s.total(T)$ are exactly (T, v) plus the operations (T', v') that occur in β such that $(T', T) \in lock\text{-}completion\text{-}order(\beta)$.*

2. *perform$(s.total(T))$ is a finite behavior of $S(X)$.*

The key lemma is next, which shows that certain sequences of actions, extracted from a hybrid object well-formed behavior of $D(X, C)$, are serial object well-formed behaviors of $S(X)$. This lemma is similar to Lemma 6.28. As in that lemma, we need an extra definition. Suppose β is a hybrid object well-formed finite behavior of $D(X, C)$. Then a set Z of operations of X is said to be **allowable** for β provided that for each operation (T, v) that occurs in Z, the following conditions hold.

1. (T, v) occurs in β.

2. T is not a local orphan at X in β.

3. If (T', v') is an operation that occurs in β such that $(T', T) \in lock\text{-}completion\text{-}order(\beta)$, then $(T', v') \in Z$.

Notice that this definition uses the same words as the one in Section 6.3; however, recall that in this case the term *local orphan* has a new (extended) meaning.

LEMMA 8.14 *Suppose that C is a symmetric serial dependency relation. Let β be a finite hybrid object well-formed behavior of $D(X, C)$ and let Z be an allowable set of operations for β. If ξ is a transaction-respecting total ordering of Z that is consistent with both lock-completion-order(β) and local-timestamp-order(β) on the transaction components, then perform(ξ) is a finite behavior of $S(X)$.*

PROOF   We use the definition of a serial dependency relation. Since no two operations in Z have the same transaction name, ξ is a serial object well-formed sequence of operations of $S(X)$. Let (T, v) be any operation in ξ. We will produce a C-closed subsequence η of ξ containing (T, v) such that perform(η) is a behavior of $S(X)$. Since C is a serial dependency relation, it will follow that perform(ξ) is a finite behavior of $S(X)$, as needed.

Let β_1 be the prefix of β strictly preceding **REQUEST_COMMIT**(T, v), and let s_1 be the state resulting from β_1; also let β_2 be β_1**REQUEST_COMMIT**(T, v), and let s_2 be the state resulting from β_2. Let η be the sequence $s_2.total(T)$, and let Z' be the set of operations occurring in η. By Lemma 8.13, Z' consists exactly of

(T, v), together with the set of operations (T', v') occurring in β such that $(T', T) \in$ *lock-completion-order*(β).

The precondition and effect of the **REQUEST_COMMIT**(T, v) action immediately imply that *perform*(η) is a finite behavior of $S(X)$.

We show that η is a subsequence of ξ. First, we show that $Z' \subseteq Z$. As noted above, Z' consists exactly of (T, v), together with the set of operations (T', v') occurring in β such that $(T', T) \in$ *lock-completion-order*(β). By assumption, $(T, v) \in Z$. If $(T', v') \in Z'$ and $(T', T) \in$ *lock-completion-order*(β), then since $(T, v) \in Z$ and Z is allowable, it follows that $(T', v') \in Z$. Therefore, $Z' \subseteq Z$.

Now we show that the order of operations in η is the same as that in ξ. Suppose (T_1, v_1) and (T_2, v_2) are two distinct operations in η, where (T_1, v_1) precedes (T_2, v_2) in η. We show that (T_1, v_1) precedes (T_2, v_2) in ξ. There are two cases to consider. (These are exhaustive.)

1. (T_1, v_1) precedes (T_2, v_2) in $s_2.intentions(U)$ for the same transaction U.

Then none of T_1, T_2, or U is equal to T, since the effect of the **REQUEST_COMMIT** event is to place an operation of T alone in *intset*(T). Since $s_2.intset(U) = s_1.intset(U)$ for $U \neq T$, we see that (T_1, v_1) precedes (T_2, v_2) in $s_1.intentions(U)$, and Lemma 8.12 implies that T_1 and T_2 are both descendants of U and are *lock visible* to U in β_1. Then both are locally visible to U in β_1, by Lemma 8.11. Let U_1 and U_2 be the children of $lca(T_1, T_2)$ that are ancestors of T_1 and T_2, respectively. By definition of local visibility, it must be that **INFORM_COMMIT** events occur in β_1 for both U_1 and U_2. Since (T_1, v_1) precedes (T_2, v_2) in $s_1.intentions(U)$, it must be that $s_1.time(U_1) < s_1.time(U_2)$. Since *time* records the timestamps from the **INFORM_COMMIT** events in β, it follows that $(T_1, T_2) \in$ *local-timestamp-order*(β). Since ξ is consistent with *local-timestamp-order*(β), it follows that (T_1, v_1) precedes (T_2, v_2) in ξ.

2. $(T_1, v_1) \in s_2.intset(U)$ and $(T_2, v_2) \in s_2.intset(V)$, for some transactions U and V, where U is a proper ancestor of V.

Then let U' be the ancestor of V that is a child of U. Then T and T_2 are both descendants of V, and hence of U'. However, we claim that T_1 is not a descendant of U'. Suppose it is; then, there must be an **INFORM_COMMIT** event for U' in β_2, since (as T_1 is lock visible in β_2 to U by Lemma 8.13) there is an **INFORM_COMMIT** event in β_2 for each ancestor of T_1 that is a proper descendant of U. As $\beta_2 = \beta_1$**REQUEST_COMMIT**(T, v), we deduce that there is an **INFORM_COMMIT** event for U' in β_1, where U' is an ancestor of T. That is, T is an excluded access in β, which implies that T is a local orphan in β, by the new definition of this chapter. This contradicts the fact that Z is an allowable set. This contradiction establishes the claim that T_1 is not a descendant of U'.

Also, $(T_1, T) \in$ *lock-completion-order*(β), by the characterization of Z' given above. (Note that (T_1, v_1) is not (T, v), because (T_1, v_1) appears in $s_2.intset(U)$

and U is not an access, as it has a proper descendant.) Since ξ is consistent with *lock-completion-order*(β), it must be that (T_1, v_1) precedes (T, v) in ξ. Since ξ is transaction-respecting, it must also be that (T_1, v_1) precedes (T_2, v_2) in ξ.

Thus, in either case, (T_1, v_1) precedes (T_2, v_2) in ξ, which implies that η is a subsequence of ξ. Now we show that η is C-closed in ξ. Suppose that (T_1, v_1) appears in η, (T_2, v_2) precedes (T_1, v_1) in ξ, and $((T_2, v_2), (T_1, v_1)) \in C$. We must show that (T_2, v_2) appears in η. There are two cases.

1. **REQUEST_COMMIT**(T_1, v_1) precedes **REQUEST_COMMIT**(T_2, v_2) in β.

Then let β_3 be the prefix of β ending with **REQUEST_COMMIT**(T_2, v_2), and s_3 the state after β_3. Then since $((T_2, v_2), (T_1, v_1)) \in C$, the definition of **REQUEST-COMMIT**(T_2, v_2) implies that $(T_1, v_1) \in s_3.intset(U)$ for some ancestor U of T_2. Therefore, by Lemma 8.13 and the fact that T_2 is not a local orphan since Z is allowable, $(T_1, T_2) \in$ *lock-completion-order*(β). Since ξ is consistent with *lock-completion-order*(β), it follows that (T_1, v_1) precedes (T_2, v_2) in ξ. This is a contradiction.

2. **REQUEST_COMMIT**(T_2, v_2) precedes **REQUEST_COMMIT**(T_1, v_1) in β.

Then let β_3 be the prefix of β ending with **REQUEST_COMMIT**(T_1, v_1), and s_3 the state after β_3. Then since $((T_2, v_2), (T_1, v_1)) \in C$ and C is symmetric, the definition of **REQUEST_COMMIT**(T_1, v_1) implies that $(T_2, v_2) \in s_3.intset(U)$ for some ancestor U of T_1. Then by Lemma 8.13 and the fact that T_1 is not a local orphan, $(T_2, T_1) \in$ *lock-completion-order*(β).

Since (T_1, v_1) is in η, either $(T_1, v_1) = (T, v)$ or $(T_1, T) \in$ *lock-completion-order*(β), by the characterization of Z'. Then transitivity of *lock-completion-order*(β) (Lemma 6.24) implies that $(T_2, T) \in$ *lock-completion-order*(β). The characterization of Z' then implies that (T_2, v_2) appears in η.

Thus, we have shown that (T_2, v_2) appears in η, which implies that η is C-closed in ξ. The definition of a serial dependency relation then implies that *perform*(ξ) is a finite behavior of $S(\mathrm{X})$, as needed to complete the proof of the lemma. $\square$

Now we prove that the objects $D(\mathrm{X}, C)$ are locally hybrid atomic.

PROPOSITION 8.15 *If C is a symmetric serial dependency relation, then $D(\mathrm{X}, C)$ is locally hybrid atomic.*

PROOF   Let β be a finite hybrid object well-formed behavior of $D(\mathrm{X}, C)$ and let T be a transaction name that is not a local orphan at X in β. We must show that *local-views*(β, T) is a subset of the set of finite behaviors of $S(\mathrm{X})$. So let Z be the set of operations occurring in β whose transactions are locally visible to T at X in β. Let ξ be a transaction-respecting total ordering of Z consistent with *local-completion-order*(β)

and *local-timestamp-order*(β) on the transaction components. We must show that *perform*(ξ) is a behavior of $S(\mathrm{X})$.

We argue first that Z is allowable for β. To see this, suppose that (T', v') is an operation that occurs in Z. Then (T', v') occurs in β. Since T' is locally visible at X to T in β and T is not a local orphan at X in β, Lemma 8.5 implies that T' is not a local orphan at X in β.

Now suppose that (T'', v'') is an operation that occurs in β and $(T'', T') \in$ *lock-completion*(β). Then T'' is lock visible at X to T' in β, and hence, by Lemma 8.11, is locally visible at X to T' in β. So T'' is locally visible to T in β, by transitivity of local visibility. Therefore, (T'', v'') is in Z.

We argue next that the ordering of ξ is consistent with *lock-completion-order*(β) on the transaction components. This is because the ordering of ξ is consistent with *local-completion-order*(β), and Lemma 8.11 implies that *lock-completion-order*(β) is a subrelation of *local-completion-order*(β).

Lemma 8.14 then implies that *perform*(ξ) is a behavior of $S(\mathrm{X})$, as needed. $\square$

Finally, we show the main result of this section.

THEOREM 8.16 *If C is a symmetric serial dependency relation, then $D(\mathrm{X}, C)$ is hybrid atomic.*

PROOF By Proposition 8.15 and Theorem 8.8. $\square$

An immediate consequence of Theorem 8.16 and the Hybrid Atomicity Theorem is that if $\mathcal{S}$ is a hybrid system in which each hybrid object is of the form $D(\mathrm{X}, C)$, where C is a symmetric serial dependency relation, then every finite behavior of $\mathcal{S}$ is atomic for all nonorphan transaction names.

8.4 Discussion

This chapter has shown how the Atomicity Theorem can be applied to systems like Avalon, where information about the order in which siblings complete is made available. Just as in Chapters 6 and 7, a local correctness property was presented, with a proof that it is sufficient to ensure global atomicity. An algorithm was also described.

There are several directions in which this work can be extended. One is to find and verify further algorithms that provide hybrid atomicity for particular data types. These might keep information in more compact forms, rather than as sets of operations as used in $D(\mathrm{X}, C)$. Another is to consider the possibility that timestamps do not give exactly the order of completion, but rather another order consistent with Lamport causality [65] between siblings. Both the modular atomic property and the algorithm should carry over to this situation.

8.5   Bibliographic Notes

The notion of local hybrid atomicity given here is related to Weihl's original definition of hybrid atomicity [113, 117], extended to accommodate nested transactions. Weihl's definition is in one way significantly more general than the definition given here; he assumes that each transaction is characterized as either a read-only or an update transaction. Read-only transactions can be given timestamps when they start, rather than when they commit. This can eliminate interference between read-only and update transactions, by admitting algorithms that maintain multiple versions and allow read-only transactions to read old versions while update transactions are changing the current version. Algorithms based on this idea can be found in [3, 90, 114].

The algorithm described in this chapter is based on an algorithm presented by Herlihy and Weihl [52], generalized to accommodate nested transactions. That paper also describes ways to compact the information used in the algorithm.

8.6   Exercises

1. Show that in any reachable state s of the hybrid controller, $domain(s.time) = s.committed$.

2. The development in this chapter does not really require a totally ordered set of timestamps. A partially ordered set would suffice, as long as the timestamps assigned to each set of siblings in any particular execution are totally ordered with respect to each other. Describe the changes to the definitions, algorithm, and proofs that are needed to accommodate this modification.

3. Give a careful proof of Theorem 8.8, following the outline provided by the proof of Theorem 6.20.

4. Can the definition of a local orphan be generalized any further, while still maintaining the truth of Theorem 8.8?

5. Prove the preliminary lemmas in Section 8.3.2.

6. Show that an analog of Lemma 6.22 fails for the objects $D(X, C)$, that is, that the ordering established by the derived variable $s.total$ can change during an execution.

7. Show that the symmetry hypothesis is needed for Lemma 8.14, by finding an execution where the conclusion fails for $D(X, R)$ where X is the read/write serial object of Example 3.5.3 and R is the particular (non-symmetric) serial dependency relation given in Example 4.5.1.

8. Develop carefully a way of mixing hybrid and locking algorithms in a single system. That is, design a controller that interacts with a combination of generic objects and hybrid objects, in such a way that if the generic objects are all dynamic atomic and the hybrid objects are all hybrid atomic, then the entire system is serially correct. Prove the correctness of your design.

Hint: The fact that there are slightly different interfaces at different objects should not matter very much. Essentially, modulo suppression of some unneeded timestamp information, dynamic atomic objects *are* hybrid atomic, so are usable with an ordinary hybrid controller. A mixed controller that withholds the unneeded information from the generic objects should then work in the same way. A mapping proof can be used to demonstrate the correspondence.

9. (Research) The proof of Lemma 8.14 seems considerably simpler than that of the corresponding lemma in Chapter 6, Lemma 6.28. Is it possible to simplify the proof of Lemma 6.28 using similar ideas to those in this chapter? In particular, can the fact that non-forward-commutativity is a serial dependency relation (Lemma 4.11) be exploited?

10. In a distributed hybrid system, it might not be convenient to ensure that timestamps for siblings are assigned in exactly the same order as the transactions commit; this is because it might be convenient to allow commits to occur at widely dispersed locations in a distributed network. Modify the development to permit weaker constraints on the timestamp order for siblings.

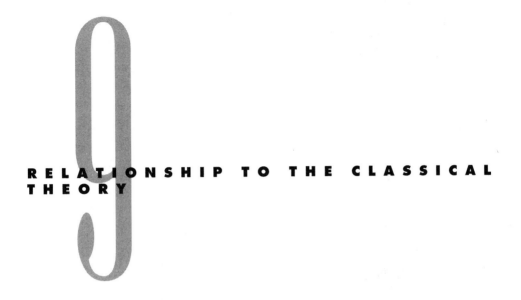

RELATIONSHIP TO THE CLASSICAL THEORY

9.1 Introduction

This chapter describes a connection between the theory presented in the earlier chapters and classical serializability theory. More specifically, it presents a proof technique that offers system designers the same ease of reasoning about nested transaction systems as is given by the classical theory for systems without nesting, and yet can be used to verify that a system satisfies the stronger *user view* definition of correctness. As applications of the technique, two of the algorithms described in Chapter 6 are verified: the read/write implementation of Moss's read/update locking algorithm and the undo logging algorithm. The assumptions used for this proof technique are made explicit, assumptions that are usually made *implicitly* in the classical theory. This clarifies the type of system for which the classical theory itself can reliably be used.

Atomicity: In this book, the notion of correctness is *atomicity*, which is defined in terms of the *user view* of the transaction system: the users should only be able to observe behavior that they could observe when interacting with a system in which their transactions were run without concurrency and without failure after partial activity. The definition of atomicity embodies not only the serializability condition of the classical theory, but also the *external consistency* condition, (i.e., that the apparent serial execution must not reverse the order of any pair of transactions for which one completed before the other was invoked). Unlike the classical correctness conditions, the definition of atomicity is explicitly formulated to apply to systems in which transactions can abort; in the classical theory, aborts are handled by considering only executions in which all transactions commit.

Serializability: In contrast, the classical theory uses a system model and correctness definition that are somewhat more restrictive than necessary; for example, the original correctness definition assumes that the concurrent transaction-processing system stores a value for each serial object, and that write accesses change this while read accesses return its value. The classical model and definition work very well for a number of update-in-place algorithms that fit this framework, but a different *definition* of correctness is needed to cope with multiversion algorithms, and yet another for replication management. The classical theory is also restricted in that it deals almost exclusively with data objects allowing only read and write operations. Our definitions avoid these assumptions, and (as shown in the various chapters of this book) we can use the same correctness condition for a wide range of systems.

An advantage of the classical theory is that for the simplest concurrency control algorithms such as two-phase locking or single-version timestamps, it yields extremely simple and intuition-supporting proofs. These proofs are based on the absence of cycles in a *serialization graph*, a graph whose nodes are the transactions and whose edges record conflicts between activity of the transactions. These proofs are much simpler than those we have given in the earlier chapters of this book.

Combining Both Theories: It would be advantageous to combine the best features of both theories. In particular, we wish to use serialization graph proof techniques similar to those of the classical theory to reason about nested transaction systems, wherever this is possible. It would be especially advantageous to use such techniques to prove that such systems satisfy the *user view* atomicity condition, also to extend the applicability of serialization graph techniques to data objects that admit other kinds of operations besides reads and writes. This chapter shows how to combine the two theories in these ways.

More specifically, it develops a proof technique for nested transaction systems in which proofs have the same simple form as in the classical theory, namely, one must show that a graph (having transactions for nodes, and edges representing necessary ordering between transactions) is acyclic. Thus, a new kind of serialization graph is defined, and it is proven that, under certain assumptions, the absence of cycles in this graph is a sufficient condition to ensure the atomicity of a system. The first part of the chapter restricts attention to systems in which each data object admits only read and write operations. For such systems, it is assumed that (once aborted transactions' activity is ignored) a read operation always returns the value written by the most recent write operation. This assumption is true of systems in which each data object is stored in a single location that is overwritten by any write access, and where an underlying recovery system restores the appropriate old value when an ancestor of the most recent write is aborted.

In much of the classical work on database concurrency control, these restrictions and assumptions are made early on, and in fact the definition of correctness often includes them. Systems satisfying these assumptions are very common, and while we feel that it is inappropriate to make these assumptions when defining the correctness condition to be satisfied, it is clearly useful to find a simple sufficient condition that guarantees correctness when the system does satisfy them.

Note that in contrast to the classical theory, the acyclicity of the graphs constructed here is merely a sufficient condition for atomicity, rather than necessary and sufficient. This is primarily because the notion of atomicity, based as it is on the user's view of the system, is not as restrictive as the one used in the classical theory.

Chapter Outline: After presenting the results for reads and writes, the theory is generalized to arbitrary data types. That is, serialization graphs are defined for systems with objects of arbitrary data type, and it is proven once again that absence of cycles implies atomicity. Once again, the values returned by accesses to objects are assumed to satisfy special restrictions.

These serialization graphs are used to prove correctness of two locking algorithms described in Chapter 6.

The specific organization of this chapter is as follows. First, Section 9.2 gives the assumptions made for systems based on read/write objects; that is, such systems are defined and the condition is stated that all reads return the latest value. Section 9.3, presents the serialization graph construction and the theorem that says that acyclicity of the serialization graph implies atomicity. Then Section 9.4 gives a proof of the read/write algorithm using serialization graphs, and Section 9.5 indicates how to extend the work to other data types besides read/write objects; this section includes a proof of the general undo logging algorithm. The chapter concludes with a discussion.

9.2 Assumptions

This section presents two main assumptions. First, for all of this chapter except Section 9.5 we assume that the fixed serial system (with respect to which atomicity is

defined) contains only read/write serial objects. This assumption reflects the reality
at the lowest level of many database management systems, since these are the only
accesses possible to a disk. While many systems do contain more complicated data
types at a higher level of abstraction (for example, in a relational database the accesses at the conceptual level include joins, selections, etc.) the assumption that all
the objects have this simple type is usually made in the classical development of serializability theory, and it is made here to show the relationships between our results
and the classical theory.

Second, assume that the concurrent system under study has the property that (if
one ignores the activity of aborted transactions) a read operation always returns the
value written by the most recent write operation.

In Section 9.5 these assumptions are relaxed.

9.2.1 Read/Write Serial Objects

The first assumption is that the fixed serial system contains only read/write serial
objects. Thus, there is a fixed serial object automaton $S(X)$ for each object name X,
and for each X there is a domain of values $\mathcal{D}$, a function $kind : accesses \rightarrow \{$ "$read$",
"$write$" $\}$, a function $data : \{T : kind(T) = $ "$write$" $\} \rightarrow \mathcal{D}$, and an initial value d.
The state and transition relation for the serial object $S(X)$ are as defined in Example
3.5.3. The definition of the automaton $S(X)$ ensures that, in the given serial system,
each read access returns the most recent value written. (This can be seen from the
effect of a **REQUEST_COMMIT** for a write access, which stores the value written by
the access in the state component $data$, and from the precondition for a **REQUEST-
_COMMIT** for a read access, which ensure that the value returned is the value of the
state component $data$.)

Some definitions introduced in Example 3.5.3 will be useful—we repeat them here.
First, a definition is needed for the $final\ value$ of a read/write serial object after a
sequence of write accesses. Thus, if $S(X)$ is a read/write serial object with domain
D, initial value d_0, and associated functions $kind$ and $data$, and if β is a sequence
of serial actions, define $write\text{-}sequence(\beta, S(X))$ to be the subsequence of β consisting of **REQUEST_COMMIT** events for transactions T such that T is an access to X
with $kind(T) = $ "$write$"; then define $last\text{-}write(\beta, S(X))$ to be $transaction(\pi)$ where
π is the last event in $write\text{-}sequence(\beta, S(X))$. (If $write\text{-}sequence(\beta, S(X))$ is empty,
then $last\text{-}write(\beta, S(X))$ is undefined.) Finally, define $final\text{-}value(\beta, S(X))$ to be d_0
if $last\text{-}write(\beta, S(X))$ is undefined, and $data(last\text{-}write(\beta, S(X)))$ otherwise. Thus,
$final\text{-}value(\beta, S(X))$ is the latest value written in β for X. The following lemmas
characterize the state and behaviors of the read/write serial object $S(X)$ in terms of
$final\text{-}value$:

LEMMA 9.1 *Let β be a finite schedule of read/write serial object $S(\mathrm{X})$, and let s be the (unique) state of $S(\mathrm{X})$ after β. Then $s.data = final\text{-}value(\beta, S(\mathrm{X}))$.*

LEMMA 9.2 *Let β be a finite behavior of $S(\mathrm{X})$. Then $\beta perform(T, v)$ is a behavior of $S(\mathrm{X})$ if and only if either T is a write access to X and $v = OK$, or T is a read access to X and $v = final\text{-}value(\beta, S(\mathrm{X}))$.*

9.2.2 Appropriate Return Values

In a real transaction-processing system, different transactions can access an object concurrently. Concurrency control and recovery algorithms are needed to ensure that the effect of a concurrent execution is the same as that of some execution of the serial system, as far as the users of the system can observe. Rather than developing a complex model of a real transaction-processing system, this chapter proves results about behaviors of simple systems (as defined in Section 5.3) satisfying certain restrictions; it then shows that a particular real transaction-processing system implements the simple system (so each of its behaviors is also a simple behavior) and that its behaviors satisfy the necessary restrictions. One advantage of this approach is that it makes very few assumptions about the *structure* of a transaction-processing system; instead, assumptions are made about its behaviors, represented as simple behaviors.

In defining these assumptions, and in the remainder of the chapter, the definitions above of *write-sequence*, *last-write*, and *final-value* are applied to behaviors of simple systems. Notice that each of these was defined in terms of general sequences of serial actions and so can be applied to simple behaviors.

The first assumption described above, namely that each serial object is a read/write object, applies to serial systems. The second assumption applies to behaviors of simple systems. Informally, it assumes the existence of some underlying recovery system that ensures that descendants of aborted and uncommitted transactions appear never to have happened; once the actions of these transactions have been removed from consideration, the return value for an access is what one would expect from a simplistic model of the simple system, where each object's value is stored in a location, being overwritten with a new value by write accesses and unaffected by read accesses. Much of the classical work on concurrency control has used this simplistic model without comment.

A definition is needed to make this formal: if β is a simple behavior, then say that β **has appropriate return values** provided that whenever π is a **REQUEST_COMMIT**(T, v) event occurring in $visible(\beta, T_0)$ and T is an access to an object X, then either T is a write access and $v = OK$, or T is a read access and $v = final\text{-}value(\delta, S(\mathrm{X}))$, where δ is the prefix of $visible(\beta, T_0)$ preceding π. Notice that here attention is restricted to the part of the sequence β that is visible to T_0. This restriction corresponds to the classical theory's focus on the *permanent* part of the computation (called the *committed projection* in [12])—the part that has committed to the outside world.

The following is a convenient characterization of appropriate return values for systems in which all serial objects are read/write objects.

LEMMA 9.3 *Let β be a finite simple behavior. Then β has appropriate return values if and only if perform(operations(visible(β, T_0))|X) is a behavior of S(X) for all X.*[1]

PROOF Suppose β has appropriate return values and X is an object name. The proof must show that $perform(operations(visible(\beta, T_0)|X))$ is a behavior of S(X). The proof shows the equivalent statement that for any prefix ξ of $operations(visible(\beta, T_0)|X)$, $perform(\xi)$ is a behavior of S(X), by induction on the number of operations in ξ. The base case, when there are no operations, is trivial. Otherwise $\xi = \xi'(T, v)$. By the induction hypothesis, $perform(\xi')$ is a behavior of S(X). Now since (T, v) is in $operations(visible(\beta, T_0)|X)$, see that T is an access to X and there is an event $\pi =$ **REQUEST_COMMIT**(T, v) in $visible(\beta, T_0)$. Since β has appropriate return values, either T is a write access and $v = OK$, or T is a read access and $v = final\text{-}value(\delta, S(X))$, where δ is the prefix of $visible(\beta, T_0)$ preceding π. In the case where T is a read access, then note that $write\text{-}sequence(\delta, S(X)) = write\text{-}sequence(perform(\xi'), S(X))$ and so $final\text{-}value(\delta, S(X)) = final\text{-}value(perform(\xi'), S(X))$. Thus, $perform(\xi(T, v))$ is a behavior of S(X) by Lemma 9.2.

Conversely, suppose $perform(operations(visible(\beta, T_0)|X))$ is a behavior of S(X) for all X. Consider π, a **REQUEST_COMMIT**(T, v) event occurring in $visible(\beta, T_0)|$X where T is an access. Then (T, v) in $operations(visible(\beta, T_0)|X)$, where $object(T) =$ X. Let ξ' be the prefix of $operations(visible(\beta, T_0)|X)$ preceding (T, v). Since $perform(\xi'(T, v))$ is a behavior of S(X), by Lemma 9.2 conclude that either T is a write access and $v = OK$, or T is a read access and $v = final\text{-}value(perform(\xi'), S(X))$. However, note that if δ is the prefix of $visible(\beta, T_0)$ preceding π, then $write\text{-}sequence(\delta, S(X)) = write\text{-}sequence(perform(\xi'), S(X))$ and so $final\text{-}value(\delta, S(X)) = final\text{-}value(perform(\xi'), S(X))$. Thus, either T is a write access and $v = OK$, or T is a read access and $v = final\text{-}value(\delta, S(X))$. Since π was arbitrary, β has appropriate return values. □

9.2.3 A Sufficient Condition for Appropriate Return Values

The hypothesis that a system's behaviors have appropriate return values is commonly made, and in the classical development of serializability theory it is usually regarded

---

[1] Recall that an *operation* is a pair (T, v); the operator *operations* extracts the sequence of operations corresponding to the **REQUEST_COMMIT** events in an event sequence.

as axiomatic. However when one studies or designs a real system one must consider how particular algorithms lead to this hypothesis being met. For write accesses it is certainly easy to ensure that the return value is *OK*. However the situation with read accesses is very different. This section defines simple conditions that are sufficient to ensure appropriate return values. While these conditions are only sufficient and not necessary, they do apply to many algorithms.

The property needed is as follows: for every **REQUEST_COMMIT**(T, v) event π in $visible(\beta, T_0)$, where T is a read access to X, the return value v is equal to $final\text{-}value(\delta, S(X))$, where δ is the prefix of visible(β, T_0) preceding π. Now, at the time π occurs, the sequence δ is not yet determined, since it depends on all the **COMMIT** events in β, including those that follow π. That is, there might be an access T' whose response precedes π in β, where T' is visible to T in β but not in the prefix of β ending in π. It is useful to have conditions that can be checked when π occurs and that are sufficient to ensure appropriate return values. Two conditions are defined. The first requires that the return value for a **REQUEST_COMMIT** event be *current*, using the sequence of events that occur before the **REQUEST_COMMIT** event. Informally, a **REQUEST_COMMIT** event for a read access is current if the return value provides the appearance of accessing a variable that is overwritten when each new write access requests to commit and is restored when a transaction **ABORT** occurs in order to remove all trace of the descendants of the aborted transaction. The second condition requires that the return value be *safe*, in the sense that all the needed **COMMIT** events are already present in the sequence before the **REQUEST_COMMIT**. Informally, a **REQUEST_COMMIT** event for a read access is safe if the writer of the current value (under the assumption that there is a current value that is overwritten and restored) is visible to the reader. This ensures that any ancestor of the writer that is not yet committed is also an ancestor of the reader. Thus, the writer cannot be aborted (by aborting one of its ancestors) without also aborting the reader. A read access that is not safe is sometimes described as reading *dirty data*.

More formally, if β is any sequence of serial actions, define $clean(\beta)$ to be the subsequence of β containing all events whose *hightransactions* are not orphans in β. Then if β is a sequence of serial actions and X is an object name, define $clean\text{-}write\text{-}sequence(\beta, S(X))$ to be $write\text{-}sequence(clean(\beta), S(X))$. Also, define $clean\text{-}last\text{-}write(\beta, S(X))$ to be $last\text{-}write(clean(\beta), S(X))$. Similarly, define $clean\text{-}final\text{-}value(\beta, S(X))$ to be $final\text{-}value(clean(\beta), S(X))$.

Now, if β is a sequence of serial actions and π is a **REQUEST_COMMIT**(T, v) event that appears in β, where T is a read access to X, then say that π is **current** in β if $v = clean\text{-}final\text{-}value(\beta', S(X))$, where β' is the longest prefix of β that does not include the event π. In addition, if β is a sequence of serial actions and π is a **REQUEST_COMMIT**(T, v) event that appears in β, where T is a read access to X, then say that π is **safe** in β if $clean\text{-}last\text{-}write(\beta', S(X))$ is either undefined or visible to T in β', where β' is the longest prefix of β that does not include the event π.

A key lemma follows.

LEMMA 9.4 *Let β be a simple behavior such that the following hold.*

1. *If π is a REQUEST_COMMIT(T, v) event that occurs in visible(β, T_0) where T is a write access to X, then $v = OK$.*

2. *If π is a REQUEST_COMMIT(T, v) event that occurs in visible(β, T_0) where T is a read access to X, then π is current and safe in β.*

Then β has appropriate return values.

PROOF   Condition (1) above is the first condition needed to argue that β has appropriate return values. It remains to show that if π is a REQUEST_COMMIT(T, v) event that occurs in *visible*(β, T_0) where T is a read access to X, and π is current in β and safe in β, then $v = \textit{final-value}(\delta, S(\mathrm{X}))$ where δ is the prefix of *visible*(β, T_0) preceding π.

Now, if π is current in β, then by definition $v = \textit{clean-final-value}(\beta', S(\mathrm{X}))$ where β' is the prefix of β preceding π. Thus, the proof need only show that *clean-last-write*$(\beta', S(\mathrm{X})) = \textit{last-write}(\delta, S(\mathrm{X}))$. Since β is a simple behavior (and so does not contain both a **COMMIT** and an **ABORT** for any transaction), any transaction that is visible to T_0 in β is not an orphan in β, and hence is not an orphan in β'. Thus *write-sequence*$(\delta, S(\mathrm{X}))$ is a subsequence of *clean-write-sequence*$(\beta', S(\mathrm{X}))$.

The proof will show that the last event in *clean-write-sequence*$(\beta', S(\mathrm{X}))$, if any, does occur in δ. Note that this last event is a **REQUEST_COMMIT** for *clean-last-write*$(\beta', S(\mathrm{X}))$. By the hypothesis that π is safe, see that *clean-last-write*$(\beta', S(\mathrm{X}))$ is visible to T in β', and hence in β. Since π occurs in *visible*(β, T_0), it follows that T is visible to T_0 in β. Then deduce that *clean-last-write*$(\beta', S(\mathrm{X}))$ is visible to T_0 in β, and so the last event in *clean-write-sequence*$(\beta', S(\mathrm{X}))$ occurs in *visible*$(\beta, S(\mathrm{X}))$. Since it precedes π, it occurs in δ as claimed. Now (as it is a **REQUEST_COMMIT** for a write access to X) one can deduce it will occur in *write-sequence*$(\delta, S(\mathrm{X}))$. Further, since the order of events in *write-sequence*$(\delta, S(\mathrm{X}))$ is the same as the order of those events in *clean-write-sequence*$(\beta', S(\mathrm{X}))$ (each order is just the order in β), it must be the last event as required. $\square$

9.3 The Serialization Graph Construction

This section presents a serialization graph construction. Recall that the definition of atomicity embodies not only the serializability condition of the classical theory, but also the external consistency condition. Therefore, the serialization graphs will have two kinds of edges, *conflict edges* and *precedence edges*. The former are similar to those used in the classical theory, and serve to fix the order of conflicting operations. The latter are added to capture restrictions required for external consistency.

Define a *conflict* relation between accesses so that two write accesses to the same object conflict, as do a write and a read access to the same object, but not two read accesses or two accesses to different objects. More formally, let $S(X)$ be a serial object for object name X, and let T and T' be accesses to X. Then say that T and T' **conflict** if either T or T' is a write access.

Extend the preceding definition to a conflict relation on *operations*: if $S(X)$ is a serial object for object name X, (T, v) and (T', v') are operations where T and T' are accesses to X, then we say that (T, v) and (T', v') **conflict** if and only if T and T' conflict. The following proposition shows that non-conflicting operations can be reordered in serial behaviors:

PROPOSITION 9.5 *Suppose that ξ is a sequence of operations of* X *such that* $perform(\xi)$ *is a serial object well-formed behavior of $S(X)$. Suppose that η is a reordering of ξ such that all pairs of conflicting operations occur in the same order in η and in ξ. Then $perform(\eta)$ is a behavior of $S(X)$.*

Next, a conflict relation between sibling transactions is derived, based on conflicts between descendant operations. Formally, if β is a sequence of serial actions, define $conflict(\beta)$ to be the relation such that $(T, T') \in conflict(\beta)$ if and only if T and T' are siblings and the following holds: there are events ϕ and ϕ' in $visible(\beta, T_0)$ such that $\phi = $ **REQUEST_COMMIT**(U, v) where U is a descendant of T, $\phi' = $ **REQUEST-_COMMIT**(U', v') where U' is a descendant of T', (U, v) conflicts with (U', v'), and ϕ precedes ϕ' in $visible(\beta, T_0)$. Informally, T conflicts with T' if a descendant of T' accesses some object X after a descendant of T accesses X in a conflicting manner (i.e., at least one access is a write). Note that if two siblings are related by $conflict(\beta)$ then they (and thus, their common parent) are visible to T_0 in β.

If β is a sequence of serial actions, define $precedes(\beta)$ to be the relation such that $(T, T') \in precedes(\beta)$ if and only if T and T' are siblings whose common parent is visible to T_0 in β, and a report event for T and a **REQUEST_CREATE**(T') occur in β, in that order. Informally, T precedes T' if their parent knows that T finished before it requests the creation of T'.

If β is a sequence of serial actions, the information in the relations $conflict(\beta)$ and $precedes(\beta)$ are incorporated into a graph, as follows. Define the serialization graph $SG(\beta)$ to be the union of a collection of disjoint directed graphs $SG(\beta, T)$, one for each transaction T that is visible to T_0 in β. The graph $SG(\beta, T)$ has nodes labeled by the children of T, and a directed edge from the node labeled T' to the node labeled

T'' if and only if T' and T'' are children of T and $(T', T'') \in precedes(\beta) \cup conflict(\beta)$.

The following theorem gives a sufficient condition for a sequence β of serial actions to be atomic for T_0. It relies on our Atomicity Theorem (Theorem 5.24).

THEOREM 9.6 *Let β be a finite simple behavior that has appropriate return values. Suppose that $SG(\beta)$ is acyclic. Then β is atomic for T_0.*

PROOF   For each transaction T that is visible to T_0 in β, one can choose some total order on the children of T that is a topological sort of the directed graph $SG(\beta, T)$, since that graph is acyclic. Let R denote the sibling order given by the union of the chosen total orders. The proof claims that R is suitable for β (as defined in Section 5.4) and that for every object name X, $view(\beta, T_0, R, X)$ is a behavior of $S(X)$. Once the truth of these claims are shown, Theorem 5.24 (the Atomicity Theorem in Section 5.5) completes the proof.

To show that R is suitable means to check that R orders all pairs of siblings T and T' that are *lowtransactions* of events in $visible(\beta, T_0)$, and that $R_{event}(\beta)$ and $affects(\beta)$ are consistent partial orders on the events in $visible(\beta, T_0)$.

By construction, R orders all pairs of siblings whose common parent is visible to T_0 in β. The proof argues that this includes all pairs of siblings that are *lowtransactions* of actions in $visible(\beta, T_0)$ as follows: the *hightransaction* of an action in $visible(\beta, T_0)$ is visible to T_0 in β, and the parent of an action's *lowtransaction* is either the action's *hightransaction* (for completion actions) or the parent of the action's *hightransaction* (for other actions). Since the action's *hightransaction* is visible to T_0 in β, so is the parent of the action's *hightransaction*. Thus, R orders all pairs of siblings T and T' that are *lowtransactions* of events in $visible(\beta, T_0)$.

Suppose that π and π' are events in $visible(\beta, T_0)$ such that π affects π' in β and $lowtransaction(\pi)$ is neither an ancestor nor a descendant of $lowtransaction(\pi')$. It is easy to show that there must be a common ancestor T of $lowtransaction(\pi)$ and $lowtransaction(\pi')$ such that a report event for T_1 precedes a **REQUEST_CREATE**(T_2) event in β, where T_1 and T_2 are the children of T that are ancestors of $lowtransaction(\pi)$ and $lowtransaction(\pi')$, respectively. It follows that $(T_1, T_2) \in precedes(\beta)$. Since R was chosen using a topological sort of the graphs $SG(\beta, T)$, $precedes(\beta) \subseteq R$. Thus, $(T_1, T_2) \in R$, and so $(\pi, \pi') \in R_{event}(\beta)$. Then Lemma 5.20 implies that $(\pi, \pi') \in R_{event}(visible(\beta, T_0))$. It follows from Lemma 5.23 that $R_{event}(\beta)$ and $affects(\beta)$ are consistent partial orders on the events in $visible(\beta, T_0)$. Thus, R is suitable for β.

Now let X be an object name. The proof must show that $\gamma = view(\beta, T_0, R, X)$ is a behavior of $S(X)$. Lemma 9.3 implies that $perform(operations(visible(\beta, T_0)|X))$ is a behavior of $S(X)$. Now γ is of the form $perform((T_1, v_1)(T_2, v_2)\ldots(T_n, v_n))$, where the (T_i, v_i) are the operations of X that occur in $visible(\beta, T_0)$, and $(T_i, T_{i+1}) \in R_{trans}$

for every i from 1 to $n-1$ inclusive. The proof makes the claim: if T_i conflicts with T_j and $i < j$, then **REQUEST_COMMIT**(T_i, v_i) precedes **REQUEST_COMMIT**(T_j, v_j) in $visible(\beta, T_0)$. In other words, γ can be obtained from $perform(operations(visible(\beta, T_0)|X))$ simply by reordering non-conflicting operations.

The claim is proved as follows: since **REQUEST_COMMIT**(T_i, v_i) and **REQUEST_-COMMIT**(T_j, v_j) both occur in $visible(\beta, T_0)$ it is enough to show that **REQUEST_-COMMIT**(T_i, v_i) does not precede **REQUEST_COMMIT**(T_j, v_j) in $visible(\beta, T_0)$. Suppose it did. Then letting U and U' denote the children of $lca(T_i, T_j)$ that are ancestors of T_i and T_j respectively, one would have $(U', U) \in conflict(\beta)$, and so $(U', U) \in SG(\beta, lca(T_i, T_j))$ and therefore $(U', U) \in R$. Thus, $(T_j, T_i) \in R_{trans}$, contradicting $(T_i, T_j) \in R_{trans}$ (which follows from the fact that $i < j$). Thus, the claim is established.

By definition, the operations in $operations(visible(\beta, T_0)|X)$ are exactly the same as those in the sequence $(T_1, v_1)(T_2, v_2) \ldots (T_n, v_n)$. Moreover, as the claim above asserts, conflicting operations occur in the same order. Therefore, by Proposition 9.5 and the fact that $perform(operations(visible(\beta, T_0)|X))$ is a behavior of $S(X)$, it follows that γ is a finite behavior of $S(X)$.

Theorem 5.24 then implies the result. □

9.4 Moss's Algorithm

This section uses the serialization graph described above to prove the correctness of the read/write implementation of Moss's read/update algorithm, as described in Chapter 6.

Consider a generic system (as defined in Section 6.2.2) in which the generic object automaton for each object name X is $M1(X)$, the read/write object defined in Section 6.4.3. This section uses Theorem 9.6 to prove that every behavior of this system is atomic for T_0. The proof relies on first establishing that the system's behaviors have appropriate return values and then showing that the serialization graph is acyclic. The system's behaviors are shown to have appropriate return values by showing that **REQUEST_COMMIT** events for read accesses are current and safe.

LEMMA 9.7 *Let S be a generic system where for each object name X, $M1(X)$ is used as the corresponding generic object automaton. Let β be a finite behavior of S. If π is a **REQUEST_COMMIT**(T, v) event that occurs in $visible(\beta, T_0)$ where T is a read access to X, then π is current and safe in $serial(\beta)$.*

PROOF Let β' be the prefix of β preceding π and let $\beta'' = \beta'|M1(X)$. The precondition of π and Lemma 6.36 imply that $v = final\text{-}value(\gamma, S(X))$ where γ is the subsequence of β'' consisting of events whose transaction is lock-visible to T in β''. Thus, to show that π is current in β, it suffices to show that $write\text{-}sequence(\gamma, S(X)) = clean\text{-}write\text{-}sequence(serial(\beta'), S(X))$.

Since T is not an orphan in β, any transaction lock-visible to T in β'' (and hence visible to T in β) is not an orphan in $serial(\beta')$. Therefore, $write\text{-}sequence(\gamma, S(X))$ is a subsequence of $clean\text{-}write\text{-}sequence(serial(\beta'), S(X))$. On the other hand, consider any **REQUEST_COMMIT**(T', v') event in $clean\text{-}write\text{-}sequence(serial(\beta'), S(X))$. Then T' is a write access and T' is not an orphan in $serial(\beta')$; thus, T' is not a local orphan in $\beta''\pi$. Since T' conflicts with T, Exercise 4d of Chapter 6 applied to $\beta''\pi$ implies that T' is lock-visible to T in $\beta''\pi$ and hence in β''. Therefore, **REQUEST_COMMIT**(T', v') occurs in $write\text{-}sequence(\gamma, S(X))$. Thus, $clean\text{-}write\text{-}sequence(serial(\beta'), S(X))$ is a subsequence of $write\text{-}sequence(\gamma, S(X))$, so in fact $clean\text{-}write\text{-}sequence(serial(\beta'), S(X)) = write\text{-}sequence(\gamma, S(X))$. Therefore, π is current in $serial(\beta)$.

If $clean\text{-}last\text{-}write(serial(\beta'), S(X))$ is defined, then Exercise 4d of Chapter 6 applied to $\beta''\pi$ implies that $clean\text{-}last\text{-}write(serial(\beta'), S(X))$ is lock-visible to T in $\beta''\pi$. Therefore, it is visible to T in $serial(\beta')$. It follows that π is safe in $serial(\beta)$. ☐

PROPOSITION 9.8 *Let $\mathcal{S}$ be a generic system where for each object name X, $M1(X)$ is used as the corresponding generic object automaton. Let β be a finite behavior of $\mathcal{S}$. Then $serial(\beta)$ has appropriate return values.*

PROOF The following is claimed:

1. If π is a **REQUEST_COMMIT**(T, v) event occurring in $visible(\beta, T_0)$, and T is a write access to X, then $v = OK$.

2. If π is a **REQUEST_COMMIT**(T, v) event occurring in $visible(\beta, T_0)$, and T is a read access to X, then π is current and safe in $serial(\beta)$.

The first of these is immediate, since in the transition relation for each object $M1(X)$, $v = OK$ is a precondition on each **REQUEST_COMMIT**(T, v) action where T is a write access to X. The second follows from Lemma 9.7. Then the conclusion follows from Lemma 9.4. ☐

The following proposition shows that $M1(X)$ ensures that the serialization graph is acyclic. The serialization graph consists of two parts, $conflict(serial(\beta))$ and $precedes(serial(\beta))$. The proof shows that each of these is consistent with the completion order; that is, that if $(U, U') \in conflict(serial(\beta))$, the U completes before U' (and similarly for $precedes$).

PROPOSITION 9.9 *Let $\mathcal{S}$ be a generic system where for each object name X, $M1(X)$ is used as the corresponding generic object automaton. Let β be a finite behavior of $\mathcal{S}$. Then $SG(serial(\beta))$ is acyclic.*

PROOF   Let T be visible to T_0 in β. The proof shows that $SG(serial(\beta), T)$ is acyclic by showing that both $conflict(serial(\beta))$ and $precedes(serial(\beta))$ are subrelations of the partial order $completion\text{-}order(\beta)$, where $(U, U') \in completion\text{-}order(\beta)$ if U and U' are siblings such that either β contains a completion event for U preceding a completion event for U' or β contains a completion event for U and no completion event for U'.

Suppose $(T, T') \in precedes(serial(\beta))$. Then a report event for T and a **REQUEST_CREATE**(T') occur in $serial(\beta)$, in that order. But there must be a completion event for T preceding the report event; moreover, any completion event for T' must follow the **REQUEST_CREATE**(T'). It follows that $(T, T') \in completion\text{-}order(\beta)$.

Now suppose that $(T, T') \in conflict(serial(\beta))$. Then there are events ϕ and ϕ' in $visible(\beta, T_0)$ such that $\phi = $ **REQUEST_COMMIT**(U, v) where U is a descendant of T, $\phi' = $ **REQUEST_COMMIT**(U', v') where U' is a descendant of T', U conflicts with U', and ϕ precedes ϕ' in $visible(\beta, T_0)$. Since U and U' conflict, there is some object name X such that U and U' are both accesses to X. Then $\beta | M1(X)$ is a generic object well-formed behavior of $M1(X)$ that contains both ϕ and ϕ'. Since $U = transaction(\phi)$ is visible to T_0 in β, it follows that U is not a local orphan in $\beta | M1(X)$. Exercise 4d of Chapter 6 implies that U is lock-visible to U' in the prefix of $\beta | M1(X)$ preceding ϕ'. Since $lca(U, U') = parent(T)$, see that β contains an **INFORM_COMMIT_AT**(X)**OF**(T) event preceding ϕ', and thus, (since β is a generic behavior), that a **COMMIT**(T) event occurs in β preceding ϕ'. On the other hand, U' is live in the prefix of β ending in ϕ', and U' is not an orphan in β (since **REQUEST_COMMIT**(U', v') occurs in $visible(\beta, T_0)$). Thus, T' is live in the prefix of β ending in ϕ' so any completion event for T' in β must follow ϕ' and thus, follow the completion event for T. That is, $(T, T') \in completion\text{-}order(\beta)$.   □

Now one can prove the main correctness theorem for the read/write algorithm.

THEOREM 9.10 *Let $\mathcal{S}$ be a generic system where for each object name X, $M1(X)$ is used as the corresponding generic object automaton. Let β be a finite behavior of $\mathcal{S}$. Then β is atomic for T_0.*

PROOF   Proposition 9.8 implies that $serial(\beta)$ has appropriate return values. Proposition 9.9 implies that the graph $SG(serial(\beta))$ is acyclic. Then Theorem 9.6 implies that β is atomic for T_0.   □

9.5 Extension to General Data Types

This section extends some of the previous results to arbitrary data types. Thus, serial objects are allowed to have arbitrary operations, rather than being restricted to being read/write objects.

9.5.1 Serialization Graphs

In order to define a serialization graph analogous to the previous definition, one must know how to define *conflict edges*, which in turn requires a definition of conflicts between operations of an arbitrary data type. The definitions of *backward commutativity* and *conflicts* from Section 4.3.2 are used.

Given the resulting notion of conflict relation and the same notion of precedes used earlier, serialization graphs are defined exactly as before. However, one cannot use the same definition of appropriate return values, since it relies on the properties of read/write objects. It is generalized as follows: if β is a simple behavior, say that β **has appropriate return values** provided that for all object names X, the following is true: $perform(operations(\gamma))$ is a behavior of $S(X)$, where $\gamma = visible(\beta, T_0)|X$. Notice that Lemma 9.3 shows that this is indeed a generalization of the more concrete definition given for systems where every serial object is a read/write object.

Now one can prove the main theorem for arbitrary data types.

THEOREM 9.11 *Let β be a finite simple behavior that has appropriate return values. Suppose that $SG(\beta)$ is acyclic. Then β is atomic for T_0.*

PROOF   The proof is essentially identical to the earlier proof for the read/write case (Theorem 9.6) this time using Proposition 4.5.   □

9.5.2 An Undo Logging Algorithm

Now serialization graphs can be used to give a proof of correctness of a system in which the general *undo logging algorithm* algorithm (from Section 6.5) is used everywhere. This algorithm works for objects of arbitrary data type. Specifically, consider a generic system in which the generic object automaton for each object name X is the *undo logging object automaton* $UL(X)$ described in Section 6.5. The correctness argument begins by showing that the condition on appropriate return values is satisfied.

PROPOSITION 9.12 *Let S be a generic system where for each object name X, $UL(X)$ is used as the corresponding generic object automaton. Let β be a finite behavior of S. Then $serial(\beta)$ has appropriate return values.*

PROOF   Fix a particular object name X.   The proof must show that $perform(operations(visible(\beta, T_0)|X))$ is a behavior of $S(X)$. Let s be the unique state of $UL(X)$ such that β can lead to s. Define $\mathcal{T}$ to be the set of all transactions other than T_0 that are not committed in β. It follows that no transaction in $\mathcal{T}$ can be in $s.committed$.

Lemma 6.38 implies that $s.operations$ is exactly the subsequence of $operations(\beta)$ obtained by removing all operations (T, v) such that an **INFORM_ABORT_AT**(X)**OF**(T) for some ancestor U of T occurs after the **REQUEST_COMMIT**(T, v) in β. Let ξ be the sequence of operations that results by removing descendants of transactions in $\mathcal{T}$ from $s.operations$. It is claimed that $operations(visible(\beta, T_0)|\mathrm{X}) = \xi$.

The claim is proved as follows: both sequences are subsequences of $operations(\beta)$, and so common operations occur in the same order. The proof must show that the same operations appear in both sequences.

Suppose that (T, v) appears in $operations(visible(\beta, T_0)|\mathrm{X})$. Then no **ABORT**($U$) appears in β for any ancestor U of T, and hence no **INFORM_ABORT_AT**(X)**OF**(U) appears in β. Therefore, (T, v) is in $s.operations$. Also, T cannot be a descendant of any transaction in $\mathcal{T}$, since T is visible to T_0 in β. Therefore, (T, v) appears in ξ.

Now suppose (T, v) appears in ξ. Then T is not a descendant of any transaction in $\mathcal{T}$, so that all ancestors of T except for T_0 are committed in β. Therefore, T is visible to T_0 in β, and so (T, v) appears in $operations(visible(\beta, T_0)|\mathrm{X})$. This establishes the claim.

Now Lemma 6.39 implies that $operations(visible(\beta, T_0)|\mathrm{X})$ is a behavior of $S(\mathrm{X})$, as needed.   □

Next, the correctness argument shows that the serialization graphs are acyclic; the proof of this result is quite similar to that of Proposition 9.9.

PROPOSITION 9.13 *Let S be a generic system where for each object name* X, $UL(\mathrm{X})$ *is used as the corresponding generic object automaton. Let β be a finite behavior of S. Then $SG(serial(\beta))$ is acyclic.*

PROOF   Let T be visible to T_0 in β. The proof demonstrates that $SG(serial(\beta), T)$ is acyclic by showing that both $conflict(serial(\beta))$ and $precedes(serial(\beta))$ are subrelations of the partial order $completion\text{-}order(\beta)$.[2]

Suppose $(T, T') \in precedes(serial(\beta))$. Then a report event for T and a **REQUEST_CREATE**(T') occur in $serial(\beta)$, in that order. But there must be a completion event for T preceding the report event; moreover, any completion event for T' must follow the **REQUEST_CREATE**(T'). It follows that $(T, T') \in completion\text{-}order(\beta)$.

Now suppose that $(T, T') \in conflict(serial(\beta))$. Then there are events ϕ and ϕ' in $visible(\beta, T_0)$ such that $\phi = $ **REQUEST_COMMIT**(U, v) where U is a descendant of T, $\phi' = $ **REQUEST_COMMIT**(U', v') where U' is a descendant of T', U conflicts with U', and ϕ precedes ϕ' in $visible(\beta, T_0)$. Since U and U' conflict, there is some

---

[2]Recall from Section 6.2.1 that $(U, U') \in completion\text{-}order(\beta)$ if U and U' are siblings such that either β contains a completion event for U preceding a completion event for U' or else β contains a completion event for U and no completion event for U'.

object name X such that U and U' are both accesses to X. Then $\beta|UL(X)$ is a generic object well-formed behavior of $UL(X)$ that contains both ϕ and ϕ'. Since $U = transaction(\phi)$ is visible to T_0 in β, it follows that U is not a local orphan in $\beta|UL(X)$. Lemma 6.40 implies that U is locally visible to U' in the prefix of $\beta|UL(X)$ preceding ϕ'. Since $lca(U, U') = parent(T)$, see that β contains an **INFORM-_COMMIT_AT**(X)**OF**(T) event preceding ϕ', and thus, (since β is a generic behavior) that a **COMMIT**(T) event occurs in β preceding ϕ'. On the other hand, U' is live in the prefix of β ending in ϕ', and U' is not an orphan in β (since **REQUEST_COMMIT**(U', v') occurs in $visible(\beta, T_0)$). Therefore, T' is live in the prefix of β ending in ϕ' so any completion event for T' in β must follow ϕ' and thus, follow the completion event for T. That is, $(T, T') \in completion\text{-}order(\beta)$. $\square$

THEOREM 9.14 *Let S be a generic system where for each object name X, $UL(X)$ is used as the corresponding generic object automaton. Let β be a finite behavior of S. Then β is atomic for T_0.*

PROOF   Proposition 9.12 implies that $serial(\beta)$ has appropriate return values. Proposition 9.13 implies that the graph $SG(serial(\beta))$ is acyclic. Then Theorem 9.11 implies that β is atomic for T_0. $\square$

This theorem should be compared to the development in Chapter 6, which establishes a stronger result: Theorems 6.41, 6.20, and 6.13, imply that β is atomic for every nonorphan transaction name, not just for T_0.

9.6   Discussion

This chapter has presented a proof technique for a class of nested transaction systems. Using this technique, two properties must be demonstrated to show correctness: the return values for operations must be shown to be *appropriate*, and a *serialization graph* must be shown to be acyclic. The first property corresponds to an assumption that is made implicitly in the classical theory of concurrency control. The second property generalizes the serialization graphs of the classical theory to nested transactions.

The classical theory has been extended in a variety of ways; for example, to model concurrency control and recovery algorithms that use multiple versions, and to model replication algorithms. These extensions to the classical theory have typically required redefining the notion of correctness (e.g., introducing the notion of *1-copy serializability*). In contrast, the definition of correctness used in this work, namely that a system's behaviors must be atomic for T_0, is sufficiently general to apply directly to these and many other kinds of systems.

It should be possible to develop techniques based on the model presented in this chapter that parallel the techniques used in the classical theory for these other kinds of systems.

9.7 Bibliographic Notes

The classical theory is described and applied to a number of different algorithms in [12]. The use of serialization graphs dates to the earliest papers on concurrency control, including the original paper on two-phase locking by Eswaran *et al.* [30] (where the graph was presented as a *dependency set*.) Most of the classical theory assumes a single model for recovery techniques based on update-in-place. As a result, it is not general enough to model certain kinds of algorithms, such as those using deferred update (e.g., the general locking algorithm presented in Chapter 6). Bernstein *et al.* [12] present a number of extensions to the classical theory to handle multiversion algorithms, replication algorithms, and other techniques. The property of appropriate return values defined in this chapter captures the assumptions made implicitly in the model used in most of the classical theory.

The proof mechanisms developed in this chapter are similar to others proposed for nested transaction systems [10, 43]. Hadzilacos and Hadzilacos [43] introduce *inter-object* and *intra-object* synchronization, corresponding to the "precedes" and "conflict" edges in this chapter.

A preliminary version of this chapter appeared in [34].

9.8 Exercises

1. Prove Lemma 6.35 and Lemma 6.36.

2. Develop an algorithm using timestamps based on Reed's (presented in Section 7.4), but with an extra variable *maxwrite*, which keeps the highest *time* for any transaction in *domain(version)*, and with an extra precondition on each **REQUEST_COMMIT** action that the access involved have a timestamp greater than *maxwrite*. Use Theorem 9.6 to prove the correctness of a distributed pseudotime system in which this algorithm is used for each pseudotime object.

3. Use the techniques of this chapter to prove correctness of the "unidirectional" version of the undo logging object $UL(X)$ described in Exercise 9 of Chapter 6.

Hint: You will need to modify the definition of the conflict edges in the serialization graph in Section 9.5.

OPTIMISTIC ALGORITHMS

10.1 Introduction

The methods of maintaining atomicity that we have discussed so far all involve delaying accesses until they can be performed safely. For example, in the locking algorithms of Chapter 6, an operation must wait if a non-ancestor transaction holds a conflicting lock, while in Reed's algorithm of Chapter 7, a read access must wait if the write access whose value it would return is not visible to it. Several algorithms have been proposed that are *optimistic*, that is, they allow accesses to proceed without waiting to ensure they can be performed safely, and then perform a *validation check* before committing a transaction to ensure that the responses given by its accesses are correct. In our model, this amounts to removing parts of the precondition from **REQUEST-_COMMIT** events and adding corresponding parts to the precondition of **COMMIT** events. Because a nonorphan transaction may receive incorrect responses to its accesses, an optimistic system generally does not guarantee atomicity for all nonorphan transactions. However, since a transaction that receives incorrect responses will not satisfy the final check, it will not commit. In particular, the validation checks ensure that no inaccurate information is returned to T_0, and so our main correctness condition, atomicity for T_0, is guaranteed.

Validation Checks: There are many different kinds of optimistic transaction management systems. For example, there are optimistic variants of locking, timestamp, and hybrid algorithms. In addition to their inherent differences in serialization order, optimistic algorithms differ in two other ways: in the choice of transactions to undergo validation checks (which depend on compatibility among the responses to accesses), and in the choice of accesses to be examined for compatibility as part of each check. In order to guarantee atomicity for T_0, the choices of which transactions to check and which sets of accesses to examine for compatibility in each validation check must combine to ensure that any pair of accesses that become visible to T_0 are checked for compatibility at some time.

For example, validation checks might be performed for every transaction, and in each check, say for a transaction T, compatibility might only be verified between accesses that are descendants of T and accesses that are descendants of siblings of T. Alternatively, checks might only be performed for top-level transactions (children of T_0), and in each check for a transaction T, compatibility might be verified between accesses that are descendants of T and all other accesses (including other descendants of T).

In a validation check, it is possible to check for compatibility with accesses of currently active transactions, a process that is known as *forward validation*, or only with accesses of transactions that have already been validated (*backward validation*). Optimistic algorithms also differ in many other ways, for example, in what serialization order is used, and in what information about the order is provided to the objects.

Chapter Outline: In this chapter, we do not attempt to be comprehensive. Instead, we describe two specific optimistic algorithms that contain different choices on many of these issues.

First, we develop a system that is similar to the hybrid system in Chapter 8 in that timestamps are assigned to transactions at the end of their execution and communicated to the objects. In this algorithm, all transactions are validated, and in each check for a transaction T, each object involved in the processing of T checks for compatibility of descendants of T with descendants of validated siblings of T. The timestamps are used in this check to provide information about the serialization order, which is used in the test for compatibility.

In this system, the timestamp for each transaction is chosen after it has finished executing, but (because the timestamp is used in the validation check) before the transaction actually commits. Because of this, the timestamps are not assigned as part of the **COMMIT** actions, as they are in Chapter 8, and consequently do not necessarily reflect the completion order exactly, as they do for hybrid systems. To model the new discipline for assigning timestamps, we introduce a new system, which we call the *simple-timestamp* system, and which is analogous to the simple-pseudotime system of Chapter 7. We show that the sibling order appropriate for the simple-timestamp system is suitable, so that the Atomicity Theorem can be applied. We then introduce an *optimistic hybrid system* with separate objects and controller, and define *optimistic hybrid atomicity*, a correctness criterion analogous to dynamic atomicity, static atomicity, and hybrid atomicity. We prove that if every object in an optimistic hybrid system is optimistic hybrid atomic, then behaviors of the system are atomic for T_0. (In contrast to the results of previous chapters, atomicity is not guaranteed for all nonorphan transactions, but only for T_0.) Finally, we present a specific algorithm and show that its objects are optimistic hybrid atomic.

Second, we develop a system that is similar to the pseudotime systems described in Chapter 7. It uses pseudotime intervals assigned at the time of transaction creation to determine the serialization order. It allows objects to validate *accesses* at arbitrary times and performs validation checks for all transactions on a single *frontier* of the transaction tree; the validation check for each transaction on the frontier involves checking that all its descendant accesses have previously been validated. We define an *optimistic pseudotime system*, in which each object has an output action to announce the validation of each of its accesses. We define *optimistic static atomicity*, and prove that it is sufficient to insure atomicity for the transactions above the frontier (including T_0). Finally, we give an optimistic version of Reed's algorithm described in Chapter 7, and show that its objects are optimistic static atomic.

10.2 Optimistic Hybrid Systems

In this section, we present our first example, optimistic hybrid systems. We begin with a description of simple-timestamp systems that capture the generation of timestamps and their use in defining a serialization order. Then we define optimistic hybrid systems, consisting of transaction automata, a controller, and a collection of objects with appropriate interfaces. Finally, we define optimistic hybrid atomicity as a condition on a single object.

10.2.1 Simple-Timestamp Systems

This section describes the timestamp generation mechanism needed for optimistic hybrid systems. The timestamps are very similar to those used in hybrid systems in Chapter 8. The major difference is that a transaction's timestamp is assigned in a separate **ASSIGN_TIMESTAMP** event, between the **REQUEST_COMMIT** and the

COMMIT, rather than in the **COMMIT**. The serialization order is thus not exactly the same as the completion order. In order to reason about the serialization order, we introduce a system that exposes the timestamp generation mechanism, in the same way as the simple-pseudotime system in Chapter 7 exposed the generation of pseudotimes. Here, however, an individual timestamp is chosen for each transaction instead of a range of pseudotimes, and also the timestamp is assigned at a point between the **REQUEST_COMMIT** and **COMMIT** events instead of before the **CREATE** event. Unlike in the simple-pseudotime system, there is no connection between the timestamp assigned to a transaction and that of its parent. However, the mechanism guarantees that siblings are assigned timestamps in increasing order.

Simple-Timestamp Database

The **simple-timestamp database** for a given system type is a specific automaton which is very similar to the simple database automaton defined in Section 5.3.1. The simple-timestamp database has the same actions as the simple database, together with an extra class of output actions, **ASSIGN_TIMESTAMP**(T, p), where $T \neq T_0$ and p is a *timestamp* chosen from a totally ordered domain $\mathcal{P}$. A state s of the simple-timestamp database has the same components as a state of the simple database, together with an additional component $s.time$, which is a partial function from $\mathcal{T}$ to $\mathcal{P}$. In the start state of the simple-timestamp database, *time* is everywhere undefined; and all other components are as in the start state of the simple database.

The transition relation is the same as that for the simple database, except that the actions **COMMIT**(T) have the additional precondition $T \in domain(s'.time)$, and the additional **ASSIGN_TIMESTAMP** actions are defined as follows:

ASSIGN_TIMESTAMP(T, p)
    Precondition:
        $T \in s'.commit\_requested$
        $T \notin domain(s'.time)$
        $p > s'.time(T')$ for all T' in $siblings(T) \cap domain(s'.time)$
    Effect:
        $s.time(T) = p$

We have straightforward results analogous to Lemmas 5.5 and 5.6.

LEMMA 10.1 *If β is a finite schedule of the simple-timestamp database that can lead to state s, then the following conditions are true.*

1. *T is in $s.create\_requested$ if and only if $T = T_0$ or β contains a **REQUEST_CREATE**(T) event.*

2. *T is in $s.created$ if and only if β contains a **CREATE**(T) event.*

3. (T, v) is in *s.commit_requested* if and only if β contains a **REQUEST__COMMIT**(T, v) event.

4. T is in *s.committed* if and only if β contains a **COMMIT**(T) event.

5. T is in *s.aborted* if and only if β contains an **ABORT**(T) event.

6. T is in *s.reported* exactly if β contains a report event for T.

7. *s.committed* $\cap$ *s.aborted* $= \emptyset$.

8. *s.reported* $\subseteq$ *s.committed* $\cup$ *s.aborted*.

LEMMA 10.2 *Let β be a schedule of the simple-timestamp database. Then all of the following hold:*

1. *If an* **ASSIGN_TIMESTAMP**(T, p) *event appears in β for $T \neq T_0$, then a* **REQUEST_COMMIT** *event for T precedes it in β.*

2. *If a* **COMMIT**(T) *event appears in β then an* **ASSIGN_TIMESTAMP** *event for T precedes it in β.*

3. *At most one* **ASSIGN_TIMESTAMP** *event appears in β for each transaction.*

4. *If T and T' are sibling transactions, and* **ASSIGN_TIMESTAMP**(T, p) *precedes* **ASSIGN_TIMESTAMP**(T', p') *in β, then $p < p'$.*

5. *$T \in domain(s.time)$ exactly if an* **ASSIGN_TIMESTAMP** *event for T appears in β.*

Simple-Timestamp Systems, Executions, Schedules and Behaviors

A **simple-timestamp system** is the composition of a set of automata indexed by the set of non-access transaction names and the single name TD (for *simple-timestamp database*). Associated with each non-access transaction name T is a transaction automaton A_T for T. Also, associated with the name TD is the simple-timestamp database automaton for the given system type.

When the particular simple-timestamp system is understood from context, the terms **simple-timestamp actions**, **simple-timestamp executions**, **simple-timestamp schedules**, and **simple-timestamp behaviors** are used for the system's external actions, executions, schedules, and behaviors, respectively.

The following is immediate.

PROPOSITION 10.3 *If β is a simple-timestamp behavior, then serial(β) is a simple behavior and serial$(\beta)|T = \beta|T$ for all transaction names T.*

Timestamp Order

The purpose of the **ASSIGN_TIMESTAMP** actions is to construct, at run-time, a sibling order that specifies the apparent serial ordering of transactions. This order will be similar to, but not exactly the same as, the completion order used in Chapters 6 and 8. In essence, the order is that of the timestamps assigned to siblings, which is the same as the order in the sequence of the **ASSIGN_TIMESTAMP** events. A complication arises because it is possible for a transaction to abort and still continue running (as an orphan) and eventually to receive a timestamp greater than that of its siblings that were affected by its abort. Thus, the order is determined by the timestamps only for transactions that do not abort.

If β is a sequence of events, and T a transaction name, we say that an event π in β is the **determining event** for T in β if either $\pi = \textbf{ABORT}(T)$ or else $\textbf{ABORT}(T)$ does not occur in β and $\pi = \textbf{ASSIGN\_TIMESTAMP}(T, p)$ for some p. By Lemma 10.2, there is at most one determining event for T in β for each T. We then define the relation $timestamp\text{-}order(\beta)$ as follows. Say that $(T, T') \in timestamp\text{-}order(\beta)$ exactly if T and T' are siblings, and either the determining event for T precedes the determining event for T' in β, or else there is a determining event for T in β and no determining event for T'.

This timestamp order has the properties required for application of the Atomicity Theorem. The proof is left as Exercise 1.

LEMMA 10.4 *Let β be a simple-timestamp behavior and T a transaction name. Then $timestamp\text{-}order(\beta)$ is a sibling order that is suitable for $serial(\beta)$ and T_0.*

The following variant of Corollary 5.25 to the Atomicity Theorem applies to the special case where R is the timestamp order and the system is a simple-timestamp system.

PROPOSITION 10.5 *Let β be a finite simple-timestamp behavior, and let $R = timestamp\text{-}order(\beta)$. Suppose that for each object name X, $view(serial(\beta), T_0, R, X)$ is a finite behavior of $S(X)$. Then β is atomic for T_0.*

EXAMPLE 10.2.1   A Banking System

We illustrate the definitions by considering a system based on the banking database serial system of Example 3.1.1, using positive integers as timestamps.

Consider the sequence β

CREATE(T_0),
   REQUEST_CREATE(T_1),
   CREATE(T_1),
   REQUEST_COMMIT(T_1, "OK"),
   ASSIGN_TIMESTAMP(T_1, 1),
   COMMIT(T_1),
   REPORT_COMMIT(T_1, "OK"),
     REQUEST_CREATE(T_2),
       REQUEST_CREATE(T_3),
       CREATE(T_3),
         REQUEST_CREATE($T_{3.1}$),
         CREATE($T_{3.1}$),
         REQUEST_COMMIT($T_{3.1}$, \$0),
         ASSIGN_TIMESTAMP($T_{3.1}$, 1),
         COMMIT($T_{3.1}$),
     CREATE(T_2),
         REPORT_COMMIT($T_{3.1}$, \$0),
          REQUEST_CREATE($T_{3.3}$),
         CREATE($T_{3.3}$),
    REQUEST_COMMIT(T_2, "OK"),
           REQUEST_CREATE($T_{3.1003}$),
          CREATE($T_{3.1003}$),
           REQUEST_CREATE($T_{3.1003.1}$),
          CREATE($T_{3.1003.1}$),
         ABORT($T_{3.1003}$),
         REQUEST_COMMIT($T_{3.3}$, \$200),
         ASSIGN_TIMESTAMP($T_{3.3}$, 2),
         COMMIT($T_{3.3}$),
           REQUEST_CREATE($T_{3.1003.2}$),
          REQUEST_COMMIT($T_{3.1003.1}$, \$1000),
          ASSIGN_TIMESTAMP($T_{3.1003.1}$, 1),
           CREATE($T_{3.1003.2}$),
           REQUEST_COMMIT($T_{3.1003.2}$, "OK"),
           ASSIGN_TIMESTAMP($T_{3.1003.2}$, 2),
           COMMIT($T_{3.1003.2}$),
          COMMIT($T_{3.1003.1}$),
          REPORT_COMMIT($T_{3.1003.1}$, \$1000),
           REPORT_COMMIT($T_{3.1003.2}$, "OK"),
        REPORT_COMMIT($T_{3.3}$, \$200),
         REQUEST_COMMIT($T_{3.1003}$, "OK"),
         ASSIGN_TIMESTAMP($T_{3.1003}$, 3),

$$\textbf{REPORT\_ABORT}(T_{3.1003}),$$
$$\textbf{REQUEST\_COMMIT}(T_3, \$200),$$
$$\textbf{ASSIGN\_TIMESTAMP}(T_3, 2),$$
$$\textbf{ASSIGN\_TIMESTAMP}(T_2, 3),$$
$$\textbf{COMMIT}(T_2),$$
$$\textbf{COMMIT}(T_3),$$
$$\textbf{REPORT\_COMMIT}(T_2, ``OK").$$

We leave the reader to check that β is a simple-timestamp behavior. The relation *timestamp-order*(β) contains (among others) the pairs (T_1, T_3), (T_3, T_2), $(T_{3.1}, T_{3.3})$, and $(T_{3.1003}, T_{3.3})$. Particularly worth notice are two points: that T_2 completes before T_3 but follows it in timestamp order, and that while $T_{3.1003}$ is running as an orphan, it is assigned a timestamp greater than that assigned to $T_{3.3}$ (which nonetheless follows $T_{3.1003}$ in the sibling order defined).

10.2.2 Optimistic Hybrid Systems

This subsection defines the system decomposition appropriate for describing optimistic hybrid algorithms. The structure is closely parallel to that of generic systems, pseudotime systems, and hybrid systems. Specifically, we define *optimistic hybrid systems*, to be composed of transaction automata, *optimistic hybrid object automata*, and an *optimistic hybrid controller*.

Optimistic Hybrid Object Automata

An **optimistic hybrid object automaton** $OHY(\mathrm{X})$ for an object name X of a given system type is an automaton with the following external action signature.

Input:
    CREATE(T), for T an access to X
    INFORM_COMMIT_AT(X)**OF**(T), for $T \neq T_0$
    INFORM_ABORT_AT(X)**OF**(T), for $T \neq T_0$
    INFORM_TIME_AT(X)**OF**(T, p), for $T \neq T_0, p \in \mathcal{P}$
Output:
    VALIDATE_AT(X)**OF**(T), for $T \neq T_0$
    REQUEST_COMMIT(T, v), for T an access to X and v a value for T

In addition, $OHY(\mathrm{X})$ may have an arbitrary set of internal actions.

The signature of an optimistic hybrid object automaton $OHY(\mathrm{X})$ is similar to that of a generic object $G(\mathrm{X})$. It differs in having two extra classes of actions. The

INFORM_TIME action indicates to the object that a transaction has finished running, and the object should then perform a validation check. Explicit timestamp information is included in each **INFORM_TIME** action. The **VALIDATE** action is the object's response, announcing that its check has been completed and giving its permission for the transaction to commit. (We do not include an explicit negative response in our model; rather, if no positive response is given the transaction can never commit. In practice, a timeout would eventually lead to the transaction aborting.)

In terms of the choices described in Section 10.1, optimistic hybrid systems are constrained to perform validation checks for *every* transaction. However, this system structure does not constrain exactly what is checked during each particular validation check (other than to say that the checks must be done locally, at the individual objects).

We define *local visibility*, the *local completion order*, and *local orphan* exactly as in Chapter 8. That is, if $OHY(\mathrm{X})$ is an optimistic hybrid object automaton for object name X, and β is a sequence of external actions of $OHY(\mathrm{X})$, then T is **locally visible at** X to T' in β if β contains an **INFORM_COMMIT_AT(X)OF**(U,p) event for every U in $ancestors(T) - ancestors(T')$, and $local\text{-}completion\text{-}order(\beta)$ is the binary relation on accesses to X where $(U,U') \in local\text{-}completion\text{-}order(\beta)$ if and only if $U \neq U'$, β contains **REQUEST_COMMIT** events for both U and U', and U is locally visible at X to U' in β', where β' is the longest prefix of β not containing the given **REQUEST-_COMMIT** event for U'. Also, we define a transaction name T to be a **local orphan** in β provided that at least one of the following holds:

1. An **INFORM_ABORT** event occurs in β for some ancestor of T, or

2. there is some access T' to X such that T' is locally visible to T in β, β contains **CREATE**(T'), and also β contains an **INFORM_COMMIT** event for an ancestor of T' with no preceding **REQUEST_COMMIT** event for T'.

An optimistic hybrid object automaton $OHY(\mathrm{X})$ is required to preserve *optimistic hybrid object well-formedness*, defined as follows. A sequence β of actions π in the external signature of $OHY(\mathrm{X})$ is said to be **optimistic hybrid object well-formed** for X provided that the following conditions hold.

1. There is at most one **CREATE**(T) event in β for any access T.

2. There is at most one **REQUEST_COMMIT** event in β for any access T.

3. If there is a **REQUEST_COMMIT** event for an access T in β, then there is a preceding **CREATE**(T) event in β.

4. There is no transaction T for which there are two different timestamps, p and p', such that **INFORM_TIME_AT**(X)**OF**(T, p) and **INFORM_TIME_AT**(X)**OF**(T, p') both occur in β.

5. There is no timestamp p for which there are two different sibling transactions, T and T', such that **INFORM_TIME_AT**(X)**OF**(T, p) and **INFORM_TIME-_AT**(X)**OF**(T', p) both occur in β.

6. There is no transaction T for which both an **INFORM_COMMIT_AT**(X)**OF**(T) event and an **INFORM_ABORT_AT**(X)**OF**(T) event occur in β.

7. If an **INFORM_COMMIT_AT**(X)**OF**(T) event occurs in β and T is an access to X, then there is a preceding **REQUEST_COMMIT** event for T.

8. If there is a **VALIDATE** event for T in β, then there is a preceding **INFORM-_TIME** event for T in β.

9. If an **INFORM_COMMIT_AT**(X)**OF**(T) event π occurs in β, and β contains a **REQUEST_COMMIT** event ϕ for an access that is a descendant of T and is locally visible to T in β, then there is a **VALIDATE** event for T that follows ϕ and precedes π in β.

The first seven conditions are analogous to those in the definition of hybrid object well-formedness. The eighth condition says that validation of a transaction should not occur until after the transaction's timestamp is known. The final condition in this definition expresses the requirement that in order to commit, a transaction must be validated at any object where some activity took place on behalf of that transaction.

LEMMA 10.6 *Let β be an optimistic hybrid object well-formed sequence of actions of $OHY(X)$. Let T be a transaction name that is locally visible to T_0 in β. Then T is not a local orphan in β.*

Optimistic Hybrid Controller

There is a single optimistic hybrid controller for each system type. It behaves much the same as the generic controller of the same type. The main difference is that, after a transaction T has requested to commit but before the commit occurs, the controller assigns a timestamp to T, informs objects of that timestamp in **INFORM-_TIME** actions, and receives **VALIDATE** actions from objects. The commit of T is delayed until a **VALIDATE** action for T has been received from every object that is *included* in the processing of T, that is, every object at which an access that is a descendant of T and visible to T has run. Timestamps are assigned to siblings in increasing order.

The assignment of timestamps is exactly as in the simple-timestamp database of Section 10.2.1. It is also very similar to that done by the hybrid controller of Chapter 8; the main difference is that in the optimistic hybrid controller the order of siblings' timestamps need not exactly match the order in which they commit.

The optimistic hybrid controller has the following action signature.

Input:
   REQUEST_CREATE(T), $T \neq T_0$
   VALIDATE_AT(X)**OF**(T), $T \neq T_0$
   REQUEST_COMMIT(T, v), v a value for T
Output:
   CREATE(T)
   ASSIGN_TIMESTAMP(T, p), $T \neq T_0$, $p \in \mathcal{P}$
   COMMIT(T), $T \neq T_0$
   ABORT(T), $T \neq T_0$
   REPORT_COMMIT(T,v), $T \neq T_0$
   REPORT_ABORT(T), $T \neq T_0$
   INFORM_COMMIT_AT(X)**OF**(T), $T \neq T_0$
   INFORM_ABORT_AT(X)**OF**(T), $T \neq T_0$
   INFORM_TIME_AT(X)**OF**(T, p), $T \neq T_0$, $p \in \mathcal{P}$

Each state s of the optimistic hybrid controller consists of the same six components as in the generic controller: $s.create\_requested$, $s.created$, $s.commit\_requested$, $s.committed$, $s.aborted$, and $s.reported$, plus two additional components, $s.time$ and $s.valid$. The set $s.commit\_requested$ is a set of operations, $s.time$ is a partial function from $\mathcal{T}$ to $\mathcal{P}$, $s.valid$ is a total function from $\mathcal{T}$ to sets of object names, and the others are sets of transactions. In the start state, $valid(T)$ is empty for every T, the partial function $time$ is everywhere undefined, and the sets are empty except for $create\_requested$, which is $\{T_0\}$. The component $s.time$ records the timestamps associated to transactions, while $s.valid$ records which objects have validated each transaction. We introduce derived variables, writing $s.completed = s.committed \cup s.aborted$, and, for each T, we define $s.included(T)$ to be the set of object names X such that there is an access T' to X where T' is a descendant of T and also every element of $ancestors(T') - ancestors(T)$ is in $s.committed$. Thus, $s.included(T)$ is exactly the set of objects where T needs to be validated, since work has been done there on behalf of T.

The transitions for **REQUEST_CREATE**, **REQUEST_COMMIT**, **CREATE**, **ABORT**, **REPORT_COMMIT**, **REPORT_ABORT**, **INFORM_COMMIT**, and **INFORM_ABORT** actions are just as for the generic controller. The other actions' transitions are as follows.

VALIDATE_AT(X)**OF**(T)
  Effect:
    $s.valid(T) = s'.valid(T) \cup \{X\}$

COMMIT(T)
  Precondition:
    $(T, v) \in s'.commit\_requested$ for some v
    $T \in domain(s'.time)$
    $T \notin s'.completed$
    $s'.included(T) \subseteq s'.valid(T)$
  Effect:
    $s.committed = s'.committed \cup \{T\}$

ASSIGN_TIMESTAMP(T, p)
  Precondition:
    $T \in s'.commit\_requested$
    $T \notin domain(s'.time)$
    $p > s'.time(T')$
      for all T' in $siblings(T) \cap domain(s'.time)$
  Effect:
    $s.time(T) = p$

INFORM_TIME_AT(X)**OF**(T, p)
  Precondition:
    $s'.time(T) = p$

Note that the precondition of **COMMIT**(T) includes a test that T has been validated at every object where some descendant access (that has become visible to T) ran. The controller is coded to allow information about a transaction's timestamp to be given to objects where no descendant accesses ran; whether the transaction is validated at some (or all) of these objects has no effect on the possibility of the transaction committing. Indeed the information about the timestamp may be passed redundantly to objects even after the transaction has completed.

EXAMPLE 10.2.2   The Optimistic Hybrid Controller for a Banking System

Consider a system based on the banking database serial system of Example 3.1.1, using positive integers as timestamps.

Consider the sequence β

CREATE(T_0),
  REQUEST_CREATE(T_1),
  CREATE(T_1),
  REQUEST_COMMIT(T_1, "*OK*"),
  ASSIGN_TIMESTAMP($T_1, 1$),
  INFORM_TIME_AT(ACCT_SVNG)**OF**($T_1, 1$),
  VALIDATE_AT(ACCT_SVNG)**OF**(T_1),
  COMMIT(T_1),
  REPORT_COMMIT(T_1, "*OK*"),
    REQUEST_CREATE(T_2),
      REQUEST_CREATE(T_3),
      CREATE(T_3),
        REQUEST_CREATE($T_{3.1}$),
        CREATE($T_{3.1}$),

$$\text{REQUEST\_COMMIT}(T_{3.1}, \$0),$$
$$\text{ASSIGN\_TIMESTAMP}(T_{3.1}, 1),$$
$$\text{INFORM\_TIME\_AT}(\text{ACCT\_CHK})\text{OF}(T_{3.1}, 1),$$
$$\text{VALIDATE\_AT}(\text{ACCT\_CHK})\text{OF}(T_{3.1}),$$
$$\text{COMMIT}(T_{3.1}),$$
$$\text{INFORM\_COMMIT\_AT}(\text{ACCT\_CHK})\text{OF}(T_{3.1}),$$
$$\text{CREATE}(T_2),$$
$$\text{REPORT\_COMMIT}(T_{3.1}, \$0),$$
$$\text{REQUEST\_CREATE}(T_{3.3}),$$
$$\text{CREATE}(T_{3.3}),$$
$$\text{REQUEST\_COMMIT}(T_2, \text{``}OK\text{''}),$$
$$\text{REQUEST\_CREATE}(T_{3.1003}),$$
$$\text{CREATE}(T_{3.1003}),$$
$$\text{REQUEST\_CREATE}(T_{3.1003.1}),$$
$$\text{CREATE}(T_{3.1003.1}),$$
$$\text{ABORT}(T_{3.1003}),$$
$$\text{REQUEST\_COMMIT}(T_{3.3}, \$200),$$
$$\text{ASSIGN\_TIMESTAMP}(T_{3.3}, 2),$$
$$\text{INFORM\_TIME\_AT}(\text{ACCT\_SVNG})\text{OF}(T_{3.3}, 2),$$
$$\text{VALIDATE\_AT}(\text{ACCT\_SVNG})\text{OF}(T_{3.3}),$$
$$\text{COMMIT}(T_{3.3}),$$
$$\text{REQUEST\_CREATE}(T_{3.1003.2}),$$
$$\text{REQUEST\_COMMIT}(T_{3.1003.1}, \$1000),$$
$$\text{ASSIGN\_TIMESTAMP}(T_{3.1003.1}, 1),$$
$$\text{CREATE}(T_{3.1003.2}),$$
$$\text{REQUEST\_COMMIT}(T_{3.1003.2}, \text{``}OK\text{''}),$$
$$\text{ASSIGN\_TIMESTAMP}(T_{3.1003.2}, 2),$$
$$\text{INFORM\_TIME\_AT}(\text{ACCT\_CHK})\text{OF}(T_{3.1003.2}, 2),$$
$$\text{VALIDATE\_AT}(\text{ACCT\_CHK})\text{OF}(T_{3.1003.2}),$$
$$\text{COMMIT}(T_{3.1003.2}),$$
$$\text{INFORM\_TIME\_AT}(\text{ACCT\_SVNG})\text{OF}(T_{3.1003.1}, 1),$$
$$\text{VALIDATE\_AT}(\text{ACCT\_SVNG})\text{OF}(T_{3.1003.1}),$$
$$\text{COMMIT}(T_{3.1003.1}),$$
$$\text{REPORT\_COMMIT}(T_{3.1003.1}, \$1000),$$
$$\text{REPORT\_COMMIT}(T_{3.1003.2}, \text{``}OK\text{''}),$$
$$\text{REPORT\_COMMIT}(T_{3.3}, \$200),$$
$$\text{REQUEST\_COMMIT}(T_{3.1003}, \text{``}OK\text{''}),$$
$$\text{ASSIGN\_TIMESTAMP}(T_{3.1003}, 3),$$
$$\text{INFORM\_TIME\_AT}(\text{ACCT\_SVNG})\text{OF}(T_{3.1003}, 3),$$
$$\text{INFORM\_TIME\_AT}(\text{ACCT\_CHK})\text{OF}(T_{3.1003}, 3),$$
$$\text{VALIDATE\_AT}(\text{ACCT\_CHK})\text{OF}(T_{3.1003}),$$

REPORT_ABORT$(T_{3.1003})$,

REQUEST_COMMIT$(T_3, \$200)$,

ASSIGN_TIMESTAMP$(T_3, 2)$,

INFORM_TIME_AT(ACCT_CHK)**OF**$(T_3, 2)$,

INFORM_TIME_AT(ACCT_SVNG)**OF**$(T_3, 2)$,

VALIDATE_AT(ACCT_CHK)**OF**(T_3),

ASSIGN_TIMESTAMP$(T_2, 3)$,

INFORM_TIME_AT(ACCT_CHK)**OF**$(T_2, 3)$,

VALIDATE_AT(ACCT_CHK)**OF**(T_2),

COMMIT(T_2),

VALIDATE_AT(ACCT_SVNG)**OF**(T_3),

COMMIT(T_3),

INFORM_COMMIT_AT(ACCT_CHK)**OF**(T_2),

REPORT_COMMIT$(T_2, \text{``}OK\text{''})$.

This sequence is a behavior of the optimistic hybrid controller. Observe that the **COMMIT** of T_3 does not occur until after both **VALIDATE-_AT**(ACCT_CHK)**OF**(T_3) and **VALIDATE_AT**(ACCT_SVNG)**OF**(T_3), since descendants of T_3 ran at both objects. On the other hand, T_2 can commit after **VALIDATE_AT**(ACCT_CHK)**OF**(T_2); it does not need to be validated at ACCT_SVNG.

Optimistic Hybrid Systems

An **optimistic hybrid system** of a given system type is the composition of a compatible set of automata indexed by the union of the set of non-access transaction names, the set of object names, and the singleton set $\{OHC\}$ (for *optimistic hybrid controller*). Associated with each non-access transaction name T is a transaction automaton A_T for T, the same automaton as in the serial system. Associated with each object name X is an optimistic hybrid object automaton $OHY(\text{X})$ for X. Finally, associated with the name OHC is the optimistic hybrid controller automaton for the system type. We use the terms **optimistic hybrid actions**, **optimistic hybrid executions**, **optimistic hybrid schedules**, and **optimistic hybrid behaviors** to denote the external actions, executions, schedules, and behaviors of an optimistic hybrid system, respectively.

As in other chapters, we find that the system structure ensures that all behaviors have the appropriate well-formedness properties.

PROPOSITION 10.7 *If β is an optimistic hybrid behavior, then the following conditions hold.*

1. *For every transaction name* T, $\beta|T$ *is transaction well-formed for* T.

2. *For every object name* X, $\beta|OHY(\mathrm{X})$ *is optimistic hybrid object well-formed for* X.

We have a straightforward relationship between an optimistic hybrid system and a simple-timestamp system. If β is a sequence of optimistic hybrid actions, then define *time*(β) by removing from β all **INFORM** and **VALIDATE** actions (thus, leaving only the timestamp actions and serial actions).

PROPOSITION 10.8 *If β is an optimistic hybrid behavior, then time(β) is a simple-timestamp behavior and time$(\beta)|T = \beta|T$ for all transaction names T.*

10.2.3 Optimistic Hybrid Atomicity

Now *optimistic hybrid atomicity* is defined. The definition is analogous to the definition of dynamic atomicity or hybrid atomicity, but based on optimistic hybrid systems instead of generic systems or hybrid systems, and using the timestamp order rather than completion order. Also the definition only concerns the actions visible to T_0 rather than to arbitrary nonorphan transactions.

Let $OHY(\mathrm{X})$ be an optimistic hybrid object automaton for object name X. Say that $OHY(\mathrm{X})$ is **optimistic hybrid atomic** for a given system type if for all optimistic hybrid systems $\mathcal{S}$ of the given type in which $OHY(\mathrm{X})$ is associated with X, the following is true. Let β be a finite behavior of $\mathcal{S}$ and $R = timestamp\text{-}order(\beta)$. Then *view*$(serial(\beta), T_0, R, \mathrm{X})$ is a behavior of $S(\mathrm{X})$.

THEOREM 10.9 *(Optimistic Hybrid Atomicity Theorem) Let $\mathcal{S}$ be an optimistic hybrid system in which all optimistic hybrid objects are optimistic hybrid atomic. Let β be a finite behavior of $\mathcal{S}$. Then β is atomic for T_0.*

EXAMPLE 10.2.3   Optimistic Hybrid Atomicity in a Banking System

Consider the sequence β given in Example 10.2.2. We see that the accesses visible to T_0 in β are T_1, T_2, $T_{3.1}$, and $T_{3.3}$. Let $R = timestamp\text{-}order(\beta)$. Notice that *time*$(\beta)$ is the sequence discussed in Example 10.2.1, so we see that R contains the pairs (T_1, T_3), (T_3, T_2), and $(T_{3.1}, T_{3.3})$ as well as other pairs that are not needed for the following calculation.

Thus, *view*$(serial(\beta), T_0, R, \text{ACCT\_CHK})$ is *perform*$((T_{3.1}, \$0)(T_2, \text{``OK''}))$, which is a behavior of the serial object given in Example 3.5.2. Similarly, *view*$(serial(\beta), T_0, R, \text{ACCT\_SVNG})$ is *perform*$((T_1, \text{``OK''})(T_{3.3}, \$200))$, which is also a behavior of the savings account serial object.

10.2.4 Local Optimistic Hybrid Atomicity

We now give a local version of optimistic hybrid atomicity. The development is analogous to those for local dynamic atomicity and local hybrid atomicity, but is slightly simplified because only visibility to T_0 is considered. We begin by defining *transaction-respecting* exactly as in Chapter 8. That is, a sequence ξ of operations of X is **transaction-respecting** provided that for every transaction name T, all the operations for descendants of T appear consecutively in ξ.

We define another binary relation, *local-timestamp-order*(β), on accesses to X. Namely, $(T, T') \in$ *local-timestamp-order*(β) if and only if T and T' are distinct accesses to X, U and U' are sibling transactions that are ancestors of T and T', respectively, β contains an **INFORM_TIME_AT**(X)**OF**(U, p) event, and β contains an **INFORM_TIME_AT**(X)**OF**(U', p') event, where $p < p'$. Note the similarity between this definition and that of the local timestamp order in Chapter 8. The only difference is that the order in Chapter 8 is based on information provided by **INFORM_COMMIT** actions rather than **INFORM_TIME** actions. This is because the **INFORM_COMMIT** actions in Chapter 8 play the roles of both the **INFORM_COMMIT** and the **INFORM_TIME** actions here.[1]

LEMMA 10.10 *Suppose β is an optimistic hybrid object well-formed sequence of external actions of OHY(X). Then local-timestamp-order(β) is a partial order.*

The relationship between the local timestamp and the global timestamp orders in an optimistic hybrid system is as follows.

LEMMA 10.11 *Let β be a behavior of an optimistic hybrid system in which optimistic hybrid object automaton OHY(X) is associated with X, and let $R =$ timestamp-order(β). Let T and T' be accesses to X. If $(T, T') \in$ local-timestamp-order$(\beta|$ OHY(X)) and T and T' are visible to T_0 in β, then $(T, T') \in R_{trans}$.*

Now suppose that β is a finite optimistic hybrid object well-formed sequence of external actions of OHY(X). Let *local-views*(β) be the set of sequences defined as follows. Let Z be the set of operations occurring in β whose transactions are locally visible at X to T_0 in β. Then the elements of *local-views*(β) are the sequences of the form *perform*(ξ), where ξ is the result of reordering Z according to a transaction-respecting total ordering consistent with both the partial orders *local-completion-order*(β) and *local-timestamp-order*(β) on the transaction components. (Compare with the definitions of *local-views* in Chapters 6 and 8.)

---

[1]The development in the earlier chapter could also have split these roles into separate actions.

We say that optimistic hybrid object automaton $OHY(\mathrm{X})$ for object name X is **local optimistic hybrid atomic** if whenever β is a finite optimistic hybrid object well-formed behavior of $OHY(\mathrm{X})$ then every sequence in $local\text{-}views(\beta)$ is a behavior of $S(\mathrm{X})$.

The main result of this section, Theorem 10.12, says that local optimistic hybrid atomicity is a sufficient condition for optimistic hybrid atomicity. The proof of this theorem is left as Exercise 3, being analogous to that of Theorem 8.8, but this time based on Lemma 10.11.

THEOREM 10.12 *If $OHY(\mathrm{X})$ is an optimistic hybrid object automaton for object name X that is local optimistic hybrid atomic then $OHY(\mathrm{X})$ is optimistic hybrid atomic.*

10.3 An Optimistic Dependency-based Algorithm

This section presents an algorithm for concurrency control in an optimistic hybrid system. It is based on a serial dependency relation, as defined in Section 4.5. The algorithm is described as an optimistic hybrid object automaton.

10.3.1 Optimistic Dependency Objects

This subsection describes, for each object name X and binary relation C between operations of X, a local optimistic hybrid object automaton $OD(\mathrm{X}, C)$ (an *optimistic dependency object*). Later, we will show that a sufficient condition for $OD(\mathrm{X}, C)$ to be local optimistic hybrid atomic is that C be a serial dependency relation.

The state components of $OD(\mathrm{X}, C)$ are $s.created$, $s.commit\_requested$, $s.intset$, $s.valid$, $s.depend$, and $s.time$. Here, $s.created$, $s.commit\_requested$, and $s.valid$ are sets of transactions, all initially empty. Also, $s.intset$ is a function from transactions to sets of operations, initially mapping every transaction to the empty set $\emptyset$. Also, $s.depend$ is a partial function from accesses to sets of operations, and $s.time$ is a partial function from transactions to timestamps, all initially everywhere undefined.

We would like to define the derived variable $total(T)$, which serves the same purpose here as in Section 6.3, that is, it is a sequence of operations of $S(\mathrm{X})$, which when performed gives the effective state produced by a transaction T. We use a technique identical to that used in Section 8.3. That is, we identify three properties of those states reachable in optimistic hybrid object well-formed executions. First, there is at most one operation for each access transaction name in the union of all the intsets. Second, if $(T', v') \in s.intset(T)$, then T' is a descendant of T, and $s.time(T'')$ is defined

CREATE(T)
  Effect:
    $s.created = s'.created \cup \{T\}$

INFORM_COMMIT_AT(X)**OF**(T)
  Effect:
    $s.intset(T) = \emptyset$
    $s.intset(parent(T))$
       $= s'.intset(parent(T)) \cup$
          $s'.intset(T)$

INFORM_ABORT_AT(X)**OF**(T)
  Effect:
    $s.intset(U) = \emptyset$,
       for all $U \in descendants(T)$

INFORM_TIME_AT(X)**OF**(T, p)
  Effect:
    $s.time(T) = p$

REQUEST_COMMIT(T, v)
  Precondition:
    $T \in s'.created - s'.commit\_requested$
    $perform(s'.total(T)(T, v))$ is a behavior of $S(X)$
  Effect:
    $s.commit\_requested = s'.commit\_requested \cup \{T\}$
    $s.depend(T) = s'.totset(T)$
    $s.intset(T) = \{(T, v)\}$

VALIDATE_AT(X)**OF**(T)
  Precondition:
    $T \in domain(s'.time)$
    $T \notin s'.valid$
    there do not exist T', U, U', u and u' such that
       $T' \in siblings(T) \cap domain(s'.time) \cap s'.valid$,
       $(U, u) \in s'.occur$
       $(U', u') \in s.occur$
       $U \in descendants(T)$
       $U' \in descendants(T')$
       either $(s'.time(T) < s'.time(T')$
          and $((U, u), (U', u')) \in C$
          and $(U, u) \notin s'.depend(U'))$
       or $(s'.time(T') < s'.time(T)$
          and $((U', u'), (U, u)) \in C$
          and $(U', u') \notin s'.depend(U))$
  Effect:
    $s.valid = s'.valid \cup \{T\}$

Figure 10.1: Transition Relation for an Optimistic Dependency-based Algorithm

for all $T'' \in s.ancestors(T') - s.ancestors(T)$. Third, whenever U and U' are siblings such that $s.time(U)$ and $s.time(U')$ are both defined, then $s.time(U) \neq s.time(U')$.

In a state s that satisfies the properties, we define a derived variable $s.intentions$, which is a function from transaction names to sequences of operations. Namely, if T is any transaction name, then the operations in the sequence $s.intentions(T)$ are exactly those in $s.intset(T)$. The order in which these operations occur is that of increasing values of $s.time$ on the transaction component of each operation. Finally, we let $s.total(T)$ be the sequence of operations defined recursively as follows: $s.total(T_0) = s.intentions(T_0)$, and $s.total(T) = s.total(parent(T))s.intentions(T)$ for $T \neq T_0$.

We also define a derived variable $s.totset(T)$ to be the set of those operations that occur in the sequence $s.total(T)$. Finally, we define $s.occur$ to be the union of $s.intset(V)$ over all V.

The transition relation of $OD(X, C)$ is given in Figure 10.1.

This algorithm is very similar to the one in Section 8.3. An important difference is that, here, the precondition on the **REQUEST_COMMIT** action does not check for compatibility between the new operation and other operations. Instead, the precondition of the **VALIDATE_AT**(X)**OF**(T) action includes a check for compatibility between descendant accesses of T and descendant accesses of previously validated siblings of T. That is, we use backward validation between each transaction and its siblings. In this algorithm, the compatibility check is to ensure that no access is serialized after another on which it ought to depend (as captured in the relation C), unless its return value was actually calculated using the other access. The variable $depend(U)$ is used to remember which accesses are used in computing the return value for access U.

LEMMA 10.13 $OD(X, C)$ *is an optimistic hybrid object for* X.

EXAMPLE 10.3.1   A Bank Account Object

Consider the checking account object ACCT_CHK in the banking system of Example 3.1.1. The serial object automaton is given in Example 3.5.2. A serial dependency relation (which we will call $C1$) is described in Exercise 12 of Chapter 4.

Let us consider the optimistic hybrid object automaton $OD($ACCT_CHK$, C1)$ constructed using the algorithm of this section. The following sequence is a behavior of this automaton.

CREATE($T_{3.1}$),
REQUEST_COMMIT($T_{3.1}$, \$0),
INFORM_TIME_AT(ACCT_CHK)**OF**($T_{3.1}, 1$),
VALIDATE_AT(ACCT_CHK)**OF**($T_{3.1}$),
INFORM_COMMIT_AT(ACCT_CHK)**OF**($T_{3.1}$),
   CREATE(T_2),
   REQUEST_COMMIT(T_2, "*OK*"),
      CREATE($T_{3.1003.2}$),
      REQUEST_COMMIT($T_{3.1003.2}$, "*OK*"),
      INFORM_TIME_AT(ACCT_CHK)**OF**($T_{3.1003.2}, 2$),
      VALIDATE_AT(ACCT_CHK)**OF**($T_{3.1003.2}$),
      INFORM_TIME_AT(ACCT_CHK)**OF**($T_{3.1003}, 3$),
      VALIDATE_AT(ACCT_CHK)**OF**($T_{3.1003}$),
      INFORM_ABORT_AT(ACCT_CHK)**OF**($T_{3.1003}$),
         INFORM_TIME_AT(ACCT_CHK)**OF**($T_3, 2$),
         VALIDATE_AT(ACCT_CHK)**OF**(T_3),
   INFORM_TIME_AT(ACCT_CHK)**OF**($T_2, 3$),
   VALIDATE_AT(ACCT_CHK)**OF**(T_2),
   INFORM_COMMIT_AT(ACCT_CHK)**OF**(T_2).

The prefix of β up to and including the action **INFORM_TIME-_AT**(ACCT_CHK)**OF**($T_{3.1003}, 3$) can lead to a state s' where $s'.occur$ is the set $\{(T_{3.1}, \$0), (T_2, \text{"}OK\text{"}), (T_{3.1003.2}, \text{"}OK\text{"})\}$, and $s'.valid$ is $\{T_{3.1}, T_2, T_{3.1003.2}\}$. Also, $s'.depend(T_{3.1003.2})$ is $\{T_{3.1}\}$. Let us examine the precondition of **VALIDATE_AT**(ACCT_CHK)**OF**($T_{3.1003}$) in state s'. The only sibling of $T_{3.1003}$ in $s'.valid$ is $T_{3.1}$, and $s'.time(T_{3.1}) = 1$ is less than $s'.time(T_{3.1003}) = 3$. The only operations of descendant accesses of these two sibling transactions that are in $s'.occur$ are $(T_{3.1}, \$0)$ and $(T_{3.1003.2}, \text{"}OK\text{"})$, but the serial dependency relation $C1$ being used does not contain the pair $((T_{3.1}, \$0), (T_{3.1003.2}, \text{"}OK\text{"}))$, since $kind(T_{3.1}) = $ "$balance$" and $kind(T_{3.1003.2}) = $ "$deposit$". In essence, the operation being serialized later (the deposit) is not affected by the presence or absence of the balance.

Similarly, if we consider the prefix of β up to and including the action **INFORM_TIME_AT**(ACCT_CHK)**OF**($T_2, 3$), and consider the state s to which this prefix can lead, we can see that **VALIDATE_AT**(ACCT_CHK)**OF**(T_2) is enabled. The only sibling of T_2 in $s.valid$ is T_3, which has an earlier timestamp than T_2. The only operation of a descendant of T_3 in $s.occur$ is $(T_{3.1}, \$0)$ (since $(T_{3.1003.2}, \text{"}OK\text{"})$ is removed from $s.occur$ in the action **INFORM_ABORT_AT**(ACCT_CHK)**OF**($T_{3.1003}$)). Thus, the precondition of the **VALIDATE** action is satisfied, since $((T_{3.1}, \$0), (T_2, \text{"}OK\text{"}))$ is not in $C1$.

It is important to notice that the check for compatibility is only performed against operations that are descendants of validated siblings. For example, when T_3 is validated, T_2 is not yet validated. Thus, the precondition of **VALIDATE_AT**(ACCT_CHK)**OF**(T_3) is true, even though $occur$ contains a deposit operation $(T_2, \text{"}OK\text{"})$ that is related to $(T_{3.1}, \$0)$ by $C1$.

Let γ denote the sequence formed when β is altered so that the timestamp assigned to T_3 is 4 (instead of 2). Then γ is not a behavior of OD(ACCT_CHK, $C1$). The validation of T_3 is still enabled, for the same reason as in β; however, let us denote by t the state in which the sequence up to and including **INFORM_TIME_AT**(ACCT_CHK)**OF**($T_2, 3$), then in t the precondition of the action **VALIDATE_AT**(ACCT_CHK)**OF**(T_2) is false. This is because there is the previously validated sibling T_3 with a higher timestamp, and there are operations $(T_2, \text{"}OK\text{"})$ and $(T_{3.1}, \$0)$ that are in $t.occur$, with $((T_2, \text{"}OK\text{"}), (T_{3.1}, \$0)) \in C1$ and $(T_2, \text{"}OK\text{"}) \notin t.depend(T_{3.1})$. In essence, the validation of T_2 is prevented because it would interfere with the return value calculated for $T_{3.1}$.

10.3.2 Correctness Proof

The correctness proof roughly follows the corresponding one in Chapter 8. We define **lock visible** and the **lock completion order** just as in Section 6.3. These definitions are also similar to those of Section 8.3.2, except that here there is no timestamp in an **INFORM_COMMIT** action. That is, we say that T is **lock visible** at X to T' in β if β contains a subsequence β' consisting of an **INFORM_COMMIT_AT**(X)**OF**(U) event for every $U \in ancestors(T) - ancestors(T')$, arranged in ascending order (so the **INFORM_COMMIT** for $parent(U)$ is preceded by that for U). Also, we say that $(U, U') \in lock\text{-}completion\text{-}order(\beta)$ if and only if $U \neq U'$, β contains **REQUEST_COMMIT** events for both U and U', and U is lock visible to U' at X in β', where β' is the longest prefix of β not containing the given **REQUEST_COMMIT** event for U'.

We have basic lemmas similar to those of Section 8.3.2.

LEMMA 10.14 *Let β be an optimistic hybrid object well-formed sequence of actions of $OD(X, C)$. Then $lock\text{-}completion\text{-}order(\beta)$ is a partial order.*

LEMMA 10.15 *Let β be a sequence of actions of $OD(X, C)$ and T and T' transaction names. If T is lock visible at X to T' in β, then T is locally visible at X to T' in β. Also $lock\text{-}completion\text{-}order(\beta)$ is a subrelation of $local\text{-}completion\text{-}order(\beta)$.*

LEMMA 10.16 *Let β be a finite optimistic hybrid object well-formed behavior of $OD(X, C)$. Suppose that β can lead $OD(X, C)$ to state s. If $(T, v) \in s.intset(T')$, then T is a descendant of T', **REQUEST_COMMIT**(T, v) occurs in β, and T' is the highest ancestor of T to which T is lock visible at X in β.*

LEMMA 10.17 *Let β be a finite optimistic hybrid object well-formed behavior of $OD(X, C)$, and suppose that a **REQUEST_COMMIT**(T, v) event π occurs in β, where T is not a local orphan at X in β. Let β' be the prefix of β ending with π, and let s be the (unique) state to which β' can lead $OD(X, C)$. Then the following are true.*

1. *The operations in $s.total(T)$ are exactly (T, v) plus the operations (T', v') that occur in β such that $(T', T) \in lock\text{-}completion\text{-}order(\beta)$.*

2. *$perform(s.total(T))$ is a finite behavior of $S(X)$.*

We have a straightforward lemma relating the values of the *depend* component of the state to the lock completion order.

LEMMA 10.18 *Let β be a finite optimistic hybrid object well-formed behavior of $OD(X, C)$, and suppose that a **REQUEST_COMMIT**(T, v) event π occurs in β, where T is not a local orphan at X in β. Let s be the (unique) state to which β can lead $OD(X, C)$. Then $s.depend(T)$ is exactly the set of operations (T', v') that occur in β such that $(T', T) \in lock\text{-}completion\text{-}order(\beta)$.*

The key lemma is next, which shows that certain sequences of actions, extracted from an optimistic hybrid object well-formed behavior of $OD(\mathrm{X}, C)$, are behaviors of $S(\mathrm{X})$. This lemma is similar to Lemma 8.14, but note that here a specific set Z of operations is used, rather than an arbitrary *allowable* set. This simplification is possible because we are only interested in the view of transaction T_0.

LEMMA 10.19 *Suppose that C is a serial dependency relation. Let β be a finite optimistic hybrid object well-formed behavior of $OD(\mathrm{X}, C)$, and let Z be the set of those operations that occur in β and are locally visible to T_0. If ξ is a transaction-respecting total ordering of Z that is consistent with both lock-completion-order(β) and local-timestamp-order(β) on the transaction components, then perform(ξ) is a behavior of $S(\mathrm{X})$.*

PROOF   We use the definition of a serial dependency relation. Since no two operations in Z have the same transaction name, ξ is a serial object well-formed sequence of operations of $S(\mathrm{X})$. Let (T, v) be any operation in ξ. We will produce a C-closed subsequence η of ξ containing (T, v) such that $perform(\eta)$ is a behavior of $S(\mathrm{X})$. Since C is a serial dependency relation, it will follow that $perform(\xi)$ is a behavior of $S(\mathrm{X})$, as needed.

Let β' be the prefix of β ending in **REQUEST_COMMIT**(T, v) and let s' be the state resulting from β'; let η be the sequence $s'.total(T)$, and let Z' be the set of operations occurring in η. By Lemma 10.17, $perform(\eta)$ is a behavior of $S(\mathrm{X})$.

We show that η is a subsequence of ξ. First, we show that $Z' \subseteq Z$. By Lemma 10.17, Z' consists exactly of (T, v), together with the set of operations (T', v') occurring in β such that $(T', T) \in$ lock-completion-order(β). By assumption, $(T, v) \in Z$. If (T', v') is any other operation in Z', then (T', v') occurs in β and $(T', T) \in$ lock-completion-order(β). Thus, T' is lock visible to T in β, and so by Lemma 10.15 T' is locally visible to T in β. By the transitivity of local visibility T' is locally visible to T_0 in β. This shows that $(T', v') \in Z$. Therefore, $Z' \subseteq Z$.

Now we show that the order of operations in η is the same as that in ξ. Suppose (T_1, v_1) and (T_2, v_2) are two distinct operations in η, where (T_1, v_1) precedes (T_2, v_2) in η. We show that (T_1, v_1) precedes (T_2, v_2) in ξ. There are two cases to consider. (These are exhaustive.)

1 . (T_1, v_1) precedes (T_2, v_2) in $s'.intentions(U)$ for the same transaction U.

Lemma 10.16 implies that T_1 and T_2 are both descendants of U and are *lock visible* to U in β. Then both are locally visible to U in β', by Lemma 10.15. Let U_1 and U_2 be the children of $lca(T_1, T_2)$ that are ancestors of T_1 and T_2, respectively. By definition of local visibility, it must be that **INFORM_COMMIT** events occur in β for both U_1 and U_2. By the definition of optimistic hybrid object well-formedness, **VALIDATE** (and hence **INFORM_TIME**) actions for U_1 and U_2 must occur in β'. That is, U_1 and U_2 are both in the domain of $s'.time$, and by optimistic hybrid object well-formedness the values of $s'.time(U_1)$ and $s'.time(U_2)$ are not equal. Since (T_1, v_1) precedes (T_2, v_2) in $s'.intentions(U)$, it must be that $s'.time(U_1) < s'.time(U_2)$. By definition of the *local-timestamp-order* relation, it follows that $(T_1, T_2) \in local\text{-}timestamp\text{-}order(\beta)$. Since ξ is consistent with *local-timestamp-order*, it follows that (T_1, v_1) precedes (T_2, v_2) in ξ.

2. $(T_1, v_1) \in s'.intset(U)$ and $(T_2, v_2) \in s'.intset(V)$, for some transactions U and V, where U is a proper ancestor of V.

   Then let U' be the ancestor of V that is a child of U. Then T and T_2 are both descendants of V, and hence of U'. However, we claim that T_1 is not a descendant of U'. Suppose it is; then there must be an **INFORM_COMMIT** event for U' in β_1, which implies that T is a local orphan in β. But by Lemma 10.6 this contradicts the fact that T is locally visible to T_0 in β.

   Also, $(T_1, T) \in lock\text{-}completion\text{-}order(\beta)$, by the characterization of Z' given above. (Note that (T_1, v_1) is not (T, v), because (T_1, v_1) appears in $s'.intset(U)$ and U is not an access.) Since ξ is consistent with $lock\text{-}completion\text{-}order(\beta)$, it must be that (T_1, v_1) precedes (T, v) in β. Since ξ is transaction-respecting, it must be that (T_1, v_1) precedes (T_2, v_2) in ξ.

Thus, in either case, (T_1, v_1) precedes (T_2, v_2) in ξ, which implies that η is a subsequence of ξ.

Now we show that η is C-closed in ξ. Suppose that (T_1, v_1) appears in η, (T_2, v_2) precedes (T_1, v_1) in ξ, and $((T_2, v_2), (T_1, v_1)) \in C$. We must show that (T_2, v_2) appears in η.

Let U_1 and U_2 be the children of $lca(T_1, T_2)$ that are ancestors of T_1 and T_2, respectively. Since (T_1, v_1) appears in ξ, T_1 is locally visible to T_0 in β, and hence β contains an **INFORM_COMMIT** event for U_1. By optimistic hybrid object well-formedness, β includes a **VALIDATE_AT**(X)**OF**(U_1) action following **REQUEST_COMMIT**(T_1, v_1). Optimistic hybrid object well-formedness also shows that an **INFORM_TIME** action for U_1 precedes the **VALIDATE** for U_1. Similarly β includes a **VALIDATE_AT**(X)**OF**(U_2) action following **REQUEST_COMMIT**(T_2, v_2), and an **INFORM_TIME** action for U_2 preceding the **VALIDATE**. By optimistic hybrid object well-formedness, the timestamps in the **INFORM_TIME** actions for U_1 and U_2 are different, and since (T_2, v_2) precedes (T_1, v_1) in the sequence ξ whose order is compatible with $local\text{-}timestamp\text{-}order(\beta)$, we deduce that β contains **INFORM_TIME_AT**(X)**OF**(U_1, p_1) and **INFORM_TIME_AT**(X)**OF**(U_2, p_2) where $p_2 < p_1$.

There are two cases.

1. **VALIDATE_AT**(X)**OF**(U_2) precedes **VALIDATE_AT**(X)**OF**(U_1) in β.

   Let β_1 be the prefix of β ending with **VALIDATE_AT**(X)**OF**(U_1), and s_1 be the state after β_1. Since **REQUEST_COMMIT**(T_1, v_1) precedes **VALIDATE-**

_AT(X)OF(U_1) in β, (T_1, v_1) must be a member of $s_1.occur$. Since **REQUEST-_COMMIT**(T_2, v_2) precedes **VALIDATE_AT**(X)**OF**(U_2), it precedes **VALIDATE-_AT**(X)**OF**(U_1), so also (T_2, v_2) is in $s_1.occur$. Since **INFORM_TIME** actions for U_1 and U_2 both occur in β_1, we have that $s_1.time(U_1)$ and $s_1.time(U_2)$ are both defined, and $s_1.time(U_2) < s_1.time(U_1)$. Since the **VALIDATE** action for U_2 occurs in β_1, $U_2 \in s_1.valid$. Then since $((T_2, v_2),(T_1, v_1)) \in C$ the precondition of **VALIDATE_AT**(X)**OF**(T_1) implies that $(T_2, v_2) \in s_1.depend(T_1)$. Then, by Lemma 10.18, $(T_2, T_1) \in lock\text{-}completion\text{-}order(\beta)$.

Since (T_1, v_1) is in η, either $(T_1, v_1) = (T, v)$ or $(T_1, T) \in lock\text{-}completion\text{-}order(\beta)$, by the characterization of Z'. Then transitivity of $lock\text{-}completion\text{-}order(\beta)$ (Lemma 6.24) implies that $(T_2, T) \in lock\text{-}completion\text{-}order(\beta)$. The characterization of Z' then implies that (T_2, v_2) appears in η.

2. **VALIDATE_AT**(X)**OF**(T_1) precedes **VALIDATE_AT**(X)**OF**(T_2) in β.

This case is symmetric to the previous one.

Thus, we have shown that (T_2, v_2) appears in η, which implies that η is C-closed in ξ. The definition of a serial dependency relation then implies that $perform(\xi)$ is a behavior of $S(X)$, as needed to complete the proof of the lemma.　　□

Now one can prove that the objects $OD(X, C)$ are locally optimistic hybrid atomic.

PROPOSITION 10.20 *If C is a serial dependency relation, then $OD(X, C)$ is local optimistic hybrid atomic.*

PROOF　　Let β be a finite optimistic hybrid object well-formed behavior of $OD(X, C)$. We must show that each sequence in $local\text{-}views(\beta)$ is a behavior of $S(X)$. So let Z be the set of operations occurring in β whose transactions are locally visible to T_0 at X in β. Let ξ be a transaction-respecting total ordering of Z consistent with $local\text{-}completion\text{-}order(\beta)$ and $local\text{-}timestamp\text{-}order(\beta)$ on the transaction components. The proof must show that $perform(\xi)$ is a behavior of $S(X)$.

We argue that the ordering of ξ is consistent with $lock\text{-}completion\text{-}order(\beta)$ on the transaction components. This is because the ordering of ξ is consistent with $local\text{-}completion\text{-}order(\beta)$, and Lemma 10.15 implies that $lock\text{-}completion\text{-}order(\beta)$ is a subrelation of $local\text{-}completion\text{-}order(\beta)$.

Lemma 10.19 then implies that $perform(\xi)$ is a behavior of $S(X)$, as needed.　　□

Finally, one can show the main result of this section.

THEOREM 10.21 *If C is a serial dependency relation, then $OD(X, C)$ is optimistic hybrid atomic.*

PROOF　　By Proposition 10.20 and Theorem 10.12.　　□

An immediate consequence of Theorem 10.21 and the Optimistic Hybrid Atomicity Theorem is that if $\mathcal{S}$ is an optimistic hybrid system in which each optimistic hybrid object is an implementation of an object of the form $OD(\mathrm{X}, C)$, where C is a serial dependency relation, then every finite behavior of $\mathcal{S}$ is atomic for T_0.

10.4 Optimistic Pseudotime Systems

Now we present our second example, optimistic pseudotime systems. In this case, the serialization order is determined by pseudotime intervals generated at transaction creation time, just as in Chapter 7.

We fix $\mathcal{V}$, an arbitrary nonempty subset of the non-access transaction names with the property that for any T in $\mathcal{V}$, $parent(T) \in \mathcal{V}$; thus, T_0 is in $\mathcal{V}$. Optimistic pseudotime systems are designed to guarantee atomicity for nonorphan transactions in $\mathcal{V}$. Accesses are permitted to run optimistically, which can cause violations of atomicity for transactions not in $\mathcal{V}$. In order to ensure correctness for the nonorphans in $\mathcal{V}$, before any transaction on the frontier (that is, not in $\mathcal{V}$ but its parent is in $\mathcal{V}$) commits, the results of its descendant accesses are validated. Since every access is not in $\mathcal{V}$, and T_0 is in $\mathcal{V}$, we see that any access has exactly one ancestor that is on the frontier. One obvious choice for $\mathcal{V}$ is the set consisting only of T_0; in this case the frontier consists of all the children of T_0.

We first define a class of systems, the *optimistic pseudotime systems*. These are like the pseudotime systems of Chapter 7, except that they have an extra class of validation actions between the objects and the controller, and an extra clause in the precondition on some **COMMIT** events in the controller. We then define *optimistic static atomicity*, a condition on the optimistic pseudotime objects. This is sufficient to insure atomicity for the nonorphan transactions in $\mathcal{V}$. We also define *local optimistic static atomicity*, a sufficient condition for proving optimistic static atomicity. Because the development is similar to that in Chapter 7, we omit most of the proofs.

10.4.1 Optimistic Pseudotime Systems

An optimistic pseudotime system is composed of the transaction automata, optimistic pseudotime object automata, and an optimistic pseudotime controller.

Optimistic Pseudotime Objects

For each object name X, we define the **optimistic pseudotime object automata** for X to be those automata with the following external action signature that preserve the well-formedness condition given below. We use $OP(\mathrm{X})$ to denote an arbitrary optimistic pseudotime object automaton for X.

Input:
    CREATE(T), T an access to X
    INFORM_COMMIT_AT(X)**OF**(T)
    INFORM_ABORT_AT(X)**OF**(T)
    INFORM_TIME_AT(X)**OF**(T, p), $T \in accesses(\text{X}), p \in \mathcal{P}$
Output:
    REQUEST_COMMIT(T, v), $T \in accesses(\text{X})$
    VALID(T), $T \in accesses(\text{X})$

A sequence β of external actions of $OP(\text{X})$ is **optimistic pseudotime object well-formed** for X if it satisfies the following conditions.

1. There is at most one **CREATE**(T) event in β for any transaction T.

2. There is at most one **REQUEST_COMMIT** event in β for any transaction T.

3. If there is a **REQUEST_COMMIT** event for T in β, then there is a preceding **CREATE**(T) in β and also a preceding **INFORM_TIME_AT**(X)**OF**(T, p) for some p.

4. There is no transaction T for which there are two different pseudotimes, p and p', such that **INFORM_TIME_AT**(X)**OF**(T, p) and **INFORM_TIME_AT**(X)**OF**(T, p') both occur in β.

5. There is no pseudotime p for which there are two different transactions, T and T', such that **INFORM_TIME_AT**(X)**OF**(T, p) and **INFORM_TIME_AT**(X)**OF**(T', p) both occur in β.

6. There is no transaction T for which both an **INFORM_COMMIT_AT**(X)**OF**(T) and an **INFORM_ABORT_AT**(X)**OF**(T) event occur in β.

7. If an **INFORM_COMMIT_AT**(X)**OF**(T) event occurs in β and T is an access to X, then there is a preceding **REQUEST_COMMIT** event for T.

8. If a **VALID**(T) event occurs in β, then there is a **REQUEST_COMMIT** for T in β.

9. If an **INFORM_COMMIT_AT**(X)**OF**(T) event π occurs in β where $T \notin \mathcal{V}$ and $parent(T) \in \mathcal{V}$, and β contains a **REQUEST_COMMIT** event ϕ for an access T' where T' is a descendant of T and is locally visible to T in β, then there is a **VALID**(T') event that follows ϕ and precedes π in β.

These conditions are the same as those comprising the definition of pseudotime object well-formedness, with the addition of the last two conditions for the **VALID** actions. We require optimistic pseudotime objects to preserve optimistic pseudotime object well-formedness.

Optimistic Pseudotime Controller

The *optimistic pseudotime controller* has the following action signature.

Input:
    REQUEST_CREATE(T), $T \neq T_0$
    REQUEST_COMMIT(T, v)
    VALID(T) $T \in accesses$
Output:
    ASSIGN_PSEUDOTIME(T, P), P a pseudotime interval, $T \neq T_0$
    CREATE(T)
    COMMIT(T), $T \neq T_0$
    ABORT(T), $T \neq T_0$
    REPORT_COMMIT(T,v), $T \neq T_0$
    REPORT_ABORT(T), $T \neq T_0$
    INFORM_COMMIT_AT(X)**OF**(T), $T \neq T_0$
    INFORM_ABORT_AT(X)**OF**(T), $T \neq T_0$
    INFORM_TIME_AT(X)**OF**(T,p), T an access to X

A state s of the optimistic pseudotime controller has the same components and initialization as that of the pseudotime controller of Section 7.3.2, with the addition of a component $s.valid$, which is a set of accesses, initially empty. We introduce the abbreviations $s.nonorphans$ for $\{T \in \mathcal{T} : ancestors(T) \cap s.aborted = \emptyset\}$, and $s.vis(T)$ for the set of transaction names T' such that every element of $ancestors(T') - ancestors(T)$ is in $s.committed$. The steps of the optimistic pseudotime controller are the same as the corresponding actions of the pseudotime controller, except for those **COMMIT**(T) actions where $T \notin \mathcal{V}$ and $parent(T) \in \mathcal{V}$, and for the **VALID** actions. For these actions, the transition relation is as follows.

VALID(T)
    Effect:
        $s.valid = s'.valid \cup \{T\}$

COMMIT(T), $T \notin \mathcal{V}$ and $parent(T) \in \mathcal{V}$
    Precondition:
        $(T, v) \in s'.commit\_requested$
        $T \notin s'.completed$
        $s'.vis(T) \cap descendants(T) \subseteq s'.valid$
    Effect:
        $s.committed = s'.committed \cup \{T\}$

Thus, the optimistic pseudotime controller is the same as the pseudotime controller, except that there are actions that record the validation of accesses, and there is an extra clause in the precondition on the **COMMIT** of a transaction T on the frontier, to check that all the nonorphan accesses of descendants of T have been validated.

Next we give an obvious invariant of the algorithm. (In addition, the properties of the pseudotime controller enumerated in Lemma 7.12 remain true.)

LEMMA 10.22 *Let β be a finite schedule of the optimistic pseudotime controller, and suppose that β can lead to state s. Then T is in $s.valid$ exactly if **VALID**(T) occurs in β.*

Optimistic Pseudotime Systems

An *optimistic pseudotime system* is the composition of a set of automata indexed by the union of the set of non-access transaction names, the collection of object names, and the single name OPC (for *optimistic pseudotime controller*). Associated with each non-access transaction name T is the transaction automaton $A(T)$ for T. Associated with each object name X is an optimistic pseudotime object automaton $OP(\text{X})$. Also, associated with the name OPC is the optimistic pseudotime controller for the given system type. When the particular optimistic pseudotime system is understood from context, we use the terms *optimistic pseudotime schedules* and *optimistic pseudotime behaviors*, respectively, for the system's schedules and behaviors.

PROPOSITION 10.23 *If β is an optimistic pseudotime behavior, then the following conditions hold.*

1. *For every transaction name T, $\beta|T$ is transaction well-formed for T.*

2. *For every object name X, $\beta|OP(\text{X})$ is optimistic pseudotime object well-formed for X.*

If β is a sequence of external actions of an optimistic pseudotime system, then define $pseudo(\beta)$ by removing from β all **INFORM** and **VALID** actions.

LEMMA 10.24 *If β is an optimistic pseudotime behavior, then $pseudo(\beta)$ is a pseudotime behavior, and $pseudo(\beta)|T = \beta|T$ for all transaction names T.*

10.4.2 Optimistic Static Atomicity

Let $OP(\text{X})$ be an optimistic pseudotime object automaton for object name X. We say that $OP(\text{X})$ is *optimistic static atomic* for a given system type if for all optimistic pseudotime systems $\mathcal{S}$ of the given type in which $OP(\text{X})$ is associated with X, the following is true. Let β be a finite behavior of $\mathcal{S}$, $R = pseudotime\text{-}order(pseudo(\beta))$, and T a transaction name that is in $\mathcal{V}$ and is not an orphan in β. Then $view(serial(\beta), T, R, \text{X})$ is a behavior of $S(\text{X})$.

THEOREM 10.25 *(Optimistic Static Atomicity Theorem) Let $\mathcal{S}$ be an optimistic pseudotime system in which all optimistic pseudotime objects are optimistic static* *atomic. Let β be a finite behavior of S. Then β is atomic for every nonorphan trans-action name in V.*

Let β be a sequence of external actions of the optimistic pseudotime system, and T an access transaction. We say T is *valid* in β if **VALID**(T) occurs in β.

The following is the fundamental lemma, which shows that to ensure that all accesses visible to any transaction in V are valid, it is enough to check the relevant accesses before allowing the commit of a transaction T at the frontier of V, as is done in the optimistic pseudotime controller.

LEMMA 10.26 *Let β be an optimistic pseudotime behavior and T a transaction that is in V and is not an orphan in β. Let T′ be an access such that a **REQUEST_COMMIT** action for T′ occurs in β and T′ is visible to T in β. Then T′ is valid in β.*

PROOF Since T' is an access, $T' \notin V$. Let U be the highest ancestor of T' such that $U \notin V$. Since T is in V and V includes the parent (and hence any ancestor) of any of its elements, U is not an ancestor of T.

Since T' is visible to T in β, **COMMIT**(U) must occur in β. Let α be an execution of the optimistic pseudotime system with behavior β, and let s be the state of the optimistic pseudotime controller immediately before **COMMIT**(U) in α. Since **COMMIT**(U) must be preceded by **CREATE**(T'), $T' \in s.created$. Since T is not an orphan in β, T' is not an orphan in β, so $T' \in s.nonorphans$. By the precondition of **COMMIT**(U), T' is in $s.valid$. Thus, **VALID**(T') occurs in β, so that T' is valid in β. □

10.4.3 Local Optimistic Static Atomicity

In this subsection, we provide a sufficient condition for showing that an optimistic pseudotime object automaton $OP(\mathrm{X})$ is optimistic static atomic. The condition, called *local optimistic static atomicity*, depends only on the behaviors of $OP(\mathrm{X})$, and does not require reasoning about the context in which $OP(\mathrm{X})$ is placed. First we define **local visibility**, **local orphan**, **local-pseudotime-order**, and **local-view** as in Chapter 7.

We say that optimistic pseudotime object automaton $OP(\mathrm{X})$ is **local optimistic static atomic** if whenever β is a finite optimistic pseudotime object well-formed behavior of $OP(\mathrm{X})$ and T is a transaction name in V that is not a local orphan at X in β, then *local-view*(β, T) is a behavior of $S(\mathrm{X})$.

The main result of this subsection is that local optimistic static atomicity is a sufficient condition for optimistic static atomicity. The proof is immediate.

THEOREM 10.27 *If $OP(X)$ is an optimistic pseudotime object automaton that is local optimistic static atomic then $OP(X)$ is optimistic static atomic.*

10.5 An Optimistic Version of Reed's Algorithm

In this section we describe an optimistic extension of Reed's multiversion timestamp algorithm, which was presented in Chapter 7.

Suppose X is an object name such that $S(X)$ is a read/write serial object automaton for X, as defined in Example 3.5.3. We describe a particular optimistic pseudotime object automaton, $OR(X)$, (the *optimistic Reed object*) for X.

Each state s of $OR(X)$ has the same components (with the same initial values) as $R(X)$, the Reed object of Section 7.4.1, plus an additional component, $s.valid$, which is a set of accesses to X, initially empty. We introduce some derived variables. Given a state s, we define $s.nonorphans$ as the set of names T for which $ancestors(T) \cap s.aborted = \emptyset$. Also, if T_1 and T_2 are accesses of X, we say T_1 is *visible in s* to T_2 if either $T_1 = T_X$, or $ancestors(T_1) - ancestors(T_2) \subseteq s.committed$.

The actions of $OR(X)$ are identical to those of $R(X)$ except for the **REQUEST_COMMIT**(T, v) and, of course, the **VALID**(T) actions. These are given in Figure 10.2:

The algorithm allows any write access to create a version, and allows a read access to return the value associated with any previously written version. We allow backward validation of an access to be performed at arbitrary time. When a read access is validated, the region of pseudotime from the writer's timestamp to the reader's timestamp is (conceptually) assigned to the version involved, and a check is made in the **VALID** action to ensure that the interval is available, that is, no nonorphan validated writer has a version blocking the interval. The **VALID** action also is delayed until the writer is locally visible to the reader. Similarly, the **VALID** for a write access checks that the version that was written is not interrupting a region of pseudotime assigned to another validated nonorphan writer.

Realistic implementations would restrict the nondeterminism of this algorithm. For example, a write access might not be performed if its pseudotime was within an interval assigned to a validated version. For read accesses, there is an obvious choice for the version to return: the version written by the nonorphan access with closest lower timestamp. This is appropriate if aborts are rare, and the reader may be validated after the writer of that version becomes visible to it. However, other choices are possible, and by proving static atomicity for our nondeterministic algorithm, we allow the correctness of many implementations to be consequences of our result.

REQUEST_COMMIT$(T, \text{``}OK\text{''})$,
 for $kind(T) = \text{``}write\text{''}$
 Precondition:
   $T \in s'.created$
   $T \notin s'.commit\_requested$
   $T \in domain(s'.time)$
 Effect:
   $s.commit\_requested$
     $= s'.commit\_requested \cup \{T\}$
   $s.version(T) = data(T)$
   $s.reads\text{-}from(T) = \emptyset$

VALID(T),
 for $kind(T) = \text{``}write\text{''}$
 Precondition:
   $T \notin s'.valid$
   $T \in s'.commit\_requested$
   $T \in domain(s'.time)$
   there do not exist T' and T'' such that
     $T' \in domain(s'.time)$
     $T'' \in domain(s'.time)$
     $T'' \in s'.reads\text{-}from(T')$
     $T'' \in s'.nonorphans \cap s'.valid$
     $s'.time(T') < s'.time(T) < s'.time(T'')$
 Effect:
   $s.valid = s'.valid \cup \{T\}$

REQUEST_COMMIT(T, v),
 for $kind(T) = \text{``}read\text{''}$
 Precondition:
   $T \in s'.created$
   $T \notin s'.commit\_requested$
   $T \in domain(s'.time)$
   $T' \in domain(s'.version)$
   $v = s'.version(T')$
 Effect:
   $s.commit\_requested =$
     $s'.commit\_requested \cup \{T\}$
   $s.reads\text{-}from(T') = s'.reads\text{-}from(T') \cup \{T\}$

VALID(T),
  for $kind(T) = \text{``}read\text{''}$
 Precondition:
   $T \notin s'.valid$
   $T \in s'.commit\_requested$
   $T \in domain(s'.time)$
   $T \in s'.reads\text{-}from(T')$
   $T' \in domain(s'.time)$
   $s'.time(T') < s'.time(T)$
   there does not exist T'' such that
     $T'' \in domain(s'.version)$
     $T'' \in s'.nonorphans \cap s'.valid$
     $T'' \in domain(s'.time)$
     $s'.time(T') < s'.time(T'') < s'.time(T)$
   either $T' = T_X$ or
     T' is visible to T in s'
       and $T' \in s'.valid$
 Effect:
   $s.valid = s'.valid \cup \{T\}$

Figure 10.2: Transition Relation for an Optimistic Version of Reed's Algorithm

EXAMPLE 10.5.1   An Optimistic Reed Object in a Message Queue System

Consider the message queue system of Example 3.5.7. This system contains a read/write serial object COPY_A, which is accessed by transaction names $T_{Rj.Ax}$, the value recorders (with $kind(T_{Rj.Ax}) = \text{``}write\text{''}$ and $data(T_{Rj.Ax}) = x$) and $T_{Vk.A}$, the viewers (with $kind(T_{Vk.A}) = \text{``}read\text{''}$). When we use the set of finite sequences of positive integers, ordered lexicographically, as pseudotimes, and the set $\{T_0\}$ as $\mathcal{V}$, we can construct the optimistic pseudotime object automaton $OR(\text{COPY\_A})$ using the algorithm of this section. The following sequence β is a schedule of $OR(\text{COPY\_A})$.

INFORM_TIME_AT(COPY_A)OF($T_{R1.A3}, 2, 2$),
CREATE($T_{R1.A3}$),
   CREATE($T_{V1.A}$),
REQUEST_COMMIT($T_{R1.A3}$, "OK"),
INFORM_COMMIT_AT(COPY_A)OF($T_{R1.A3}$),
   INFORM_TIME_AT(COPY_A)OF($T_{V1.A}, 8, 3$),
      CREATE($T_{V3.A}$),
      INFORM_TIME_AT(COPY_A)OF($T_{V3.A}, 3, 5$),
   REQUEST_COMMIT($T_{V1.A}, 3$),
         INFORM_TIME_AT(COPY_A)OF($T_{R2.A1}, 5, 2$),
         CREATE($T_{R2.A1}$),
         REQUEST_COMMIT($T_{R2.A1}$, "OK"),
      REQUEST_COMMIT($T_{V3.A}, 3$),
VALID_OF($T_{R1.A3}$),
INFORM_COMMIT_AT(COPY_A)OF(T_{R1}),
   VALID_OF($T_{V3.A}$),
   VALID_OF($T_{V1.A}$),
      INFORM_COMMIT_AT(COPY_A)OF($T_{V3.A}$).

Let s be the state to which β can lead $OR(\text{COPY\_A})$. In s the action **VALID**($T_{R2.A1}$) is not enabled, since the pseudotime of $T_{R2.A1}$ is $5, 2$, which lies in the interval between the pseudotime of $T_{R1.A3}$ and the pseudotime of $T_{V1.A}$, which has been validated after reading the version produced by $T_{R1.A3}$.

We see that the different transactions are able to run concurrently at this object. For example, the response to $T_{V1.A}$ is generated before $T_{R1.A3}$ is visible to it. This is in contrast to the Reed object without optimism, as shown in Example 7.4.1. However, the **VALID** actions for $T_{V3.A}$ and $T_{V1.A}$ could not occur earlier in β than they do: they must wait until after $T_{R1.A3}$ is visible to T_0.

10.5.1 Correctness Proof

First we give the basic invariants of the algorithm.

LEMMA 10.28 *Let β be a finite optimistic pseudotime object well-formed schedule of $OR(\text{X})$. Suppose that β can lead to a state s from the start state. Then the following conditions hold.*

1. *$T \in s.created$ if and only if **CREATE**(T) appears in β.*

2. $T \in s.committed$ if and only if $\textbf{\textit{INFORM\_COMMIT\_AT}}(X)\textbf{\textit{OF}}$(T) appears in β.

3. $T \in s.aborted$ if and only if $\textbf{\textit{INFORM\_ABORT\_AT}}(X)\textbf{\textit{OF}}$(T) appears in β.

4. $s.time(T) = p$ if and only if either $T = T_\text{X}$ and $p = -\infty$ or else $\textbf{\textit{INFORM\_TIME-}}$ $\textbf{\textit{\_AT}}$(X)$\textbf{\textit{OF}}$(T,p) appears in β.

5. $T \in s.commit\_requested$ if and only if a $\textbf{\textit{REQUEST\_COMMIT}}$ for T appears in β.

6. $T \in s.valid$ if and only if $\textbf{\textit{VALID}}$(T) appears in β.

Of these properties, only 6 does not appear in the corresponding Lemma 7.25.

LEMMA 10.29 $OR(\text{X})$ *is an optimistic pseudotime object for* X.

LEMMA 10.30 *Let β be a finite optimistic pseudotime object well-formed schedule of $OR(\text{X})$. Suppose that β can lead to a state s from the start state. Then the following conditions hold.*

1. *If $s.time(T) = s.time(T')$, then $T = T'$.*

2. *$s.commit\_requested \subseteq domain(s.time)$.*

3. *$T_\text{X} \in domain(s.version)$ and $s.version(T_\text{X}) = d_0$.*

4. *If $T \in domain(s.version)$ and $T \neq T_\text{X}$, then*

   (a) T is a write access to X and

   (b) $\textbf{\textit{REQUEST\_COMMIT}}(T, OK)$ occurs in β and $s.version(T) = data(T)$.

5. *If T is a write access to X and $T \in s.commit\_requested$, then $T \in domain(s.version)$.*

6. *$domain(s.reads\text{-}from) = domain(s.version)$.*

7. *If $T \in s.reads\text{-}from(T')$, then*

   (a) T is a read access,

   (b) $\textbf{\textit{REQUEST\_COMMIT}}(T, v)$ occurs in β where $v = s.version(T')$.

8. *Suppose T is a read access to X and $T \in s.commit\_requested$. Then $T \in s.reads\text{-}from(T')$ for some T'.*

9. *Suppose T and T' are write accesses to X in $s.commit\_requested$. Then $s.reads\text{-}from(T) \cap s.reads\text{-}from(T') = \emptyset$.*

Note that Lemma 10.30 is slightly weaker than the corresponding Lemma 7.26; specifically, Part 7 of the earlier lemma is now weaker, and Part 10 is no longer true. Properties analogous to these now require an extra hypothesis about validation, as follows. The proof is left as Exercise 7.

LEMMA 10.31 *Let β be an optimistic pseudotime object well-formed schedule of $OR(\text{X})$ that can lead $OR(\text{X})$ to state s. Suppose $T \in s.reads\text{-}from(T')$ and $T \in s.valid$. Then the following conditions hold.*

1. *Either $T' = T_{\text{X}}$ or T' is visible to T in s.*

2. *Either $T' = T_{\text{X}}$ or $T' \in s.valid$.*

3. *T and T' are both in $domain(s.time)$ and $s.time(T') < s.time(T)$.*

4. *If $T'' \in domain(s.version)$, $T \in s.nonorphans$, and $s.time(T') < s.time(T'') < s.time(T)$, then $T'' \notin s.nonorphans \cap s.valid$.*

5. *If $T \in s.nonorphans$, then either $T' = T_{\text{X}}$ or $T' \in s.nonorphans$.*

We now proceed to the main lemma that we use to show the correctness of this algorithm. We need some preliminary definitions.

The value of variable $s.time$ can be used to define a derived partial order $s.timeorder$ on accesses to X, exactly as in Chapter 7. That is, if T and T' are distinct accesses to X, $s.time(T)$ and $s.time(T')$ are both defined, and $s.time(T) < s.time(T')$, then (T, T') is included in $s.timeorder$.

Also, if s is a state of $OR(\text{X})$, then define $\mathcal{U}$ to be an **allowable** set of accesses to X for s provided that the following conditions hold.

■ All accesses in $\mathcal{U}$ are in $s.valid \cap s.nonorphans$.

■ All accesses in $\mathcal{U}$ are in $s.commit\_requested$.

■ If $T' \in s.reads\text{-}from(T)$ and $T' \in \mathcal{U}$, then either $T = T_{\text{X}}$ or $T \in \mathcal{U}$.

The only difference between this and the corresponding definition in Chapter 7 is the addition of the requirement for the accesses to be valid.

The following lemma corresponds exactly to Lemma 7.28, but uses the new definition of "allowable". The proof also corresponds, and is left as Exercise 8.

LEMMA 10.32 *Let β be any finite schedule of $OR(\text{X})$ that is optimistic pseudotime object well-formed for X, and suppose β can lead to state s. Let $\mathcal{U}$ be an allowable set of accesses to X for s. Let Z be the set of operations occurring in β whose transaction components are in $\mathcal{U}$. Let ξ be the sequence that results when Z is arranged in an order consistent with that determined by $s.timeorder$ on the transaction components. Let $\gamma = perform(\xi)$. Then γ is a behavior of $S(\text{X})$.*

Now we can prove that a data object is local optimistic static atomic if it is implemented using the algorithm described in this section.

PROPOSITION 10.33 $OR(X)$ *is local optimistic static atomic.*

PROOF   Let β be a finite optimistic pseudotime object well-formed behavior of $OR(X)$, and T a transaction name in $\mathcal{V}$ that is not a local orphan at X in β. Let Z be the set of operations occurring in β whose transactions are locally visible to T at X in β. Then $local\text{-}view(\beta, T) = perform(\xi)$, where ξ is the result of ordering Z according to the order $R = local\text{-}pseudotime\text{-}order(\beta)$ on the transaction components. The proof must show that $local\text{-}view(\beta, T)$ is a behavior of $S(X)$.

Since $OR(X)$ has no internal actions, β is also a schedule of $OR(X)$. Choose state s of $OR(X)$ such that β can lead to s. Let $\mathcal{U}$ be the set of first components of operations in Z. The proof shows that $\mathcal{U}$ is an allowable set of accesses to X for s.

Let T' be an access in $\mathcal{U}$.

Since T' is an access, $T' \notin \mathcal{V}$; we will denote by U the highest ancestor of T' such that $U \notin \mathcal{V}$. Since $lca(T', T)$ is an ancestor of T, and $\mathcal{V}$ contains the parent of any of its elements, $lca(T', T) \in \mathcal{V}$. Thus, $lca(T', T)$ is an ancestor of $parent(U)$. Since T' is locally visible to T in β, the action **INFORM_COMMIT_AT**(X)**OF**(U) must occur in β. Since $U \notin \mathcal{V}$, $parent(U) \in \mathcal{V}$, and T' is a descendant of U that is locally visible to U in β, optimistic pseudotime object well-formedness implies that **VALID**(T') occurs in β. Thus, T' is in $s.valid$. Also. T is not a local orphan at X in β and T' is locally visible to T at X in β, so (by the analog of Lemma 7.19) T' is not a local orphan in β. Thus, $T' \in s.nonorphans$.

Since a **REQUEST_COMMIT** for T' occurs in β, $T' \in s.commit\_requested$.

Now suppose $T' \in s.reads\text{-}from(T'')$. We must show that either $T'' = T_X$ or else $T'' \in \mathcal{U}$. Suppose $T'' \neq T_X$. Since $T' \in s.valid$, Lemma 10.31 implies that T'' is visible to T' in s, so that T'' is locally visible to T' at X in β. Since T' is locally visible to T at X in β, the analog of Lemma 7.18 implies that T'' is locally visible to T in β. Also by Lemma 10.30, because $T' \in s.reads\text{-}from(T'')$ and $T'' \neq T_X$, there is a **REQUEST_COMMIT** for T'' in β. Since T'' is locally visible to T in β, $T'' \in \mathcal{U}$, as required.

It follows that $\mathcal{U}$ is an allowable set of accesses to X for s.

Now let $Z' = \{(T', v')$: **REQUEST_COMMIT**(T', v') occurs in β and $T' \in \mathcal{U}\}$. Let ξ' be the result of ordering Z' using $s.timeorder$ on the transaction components. Let $\gamma' = perform(\xi')$. Then Lemma 10.32 implies that γ' is a behavior of $S(X)$.

However, we observe that optimistic pseudotime object well-formedness implies that each access in $\mathcal{U}$ has at most one **REQUEST_COMMIT** in β. Thus, $Z = Z'$. Furthermore, $local\text{-}pseudotime\text{-}order(\beta)$ is the same as $s.timeorder$. Therefore, $\xi = \xi'$, and hence $\gamma = \gamma'$. Therefore, γ is a behavior of $S(X)$ as required. $\square$

10.6   Discussion

This chapter uses the theory of Chapter 5 to show two ways of building systems in which accesses are allowed to proceed optimistically, and in which later checks ensure atomicity. In each case we obtain a local condition, so objects may be implemented independently.

There are many other ways of incorporating optimism into a system, varying in the timing and location of validation and the information provided to the objects. It would be an interesting extension of these ideas to model and verify algorithms for such systems. The following section lists some references from the literature.

10.7   Bibliographic   Notes

The idea of optimistic concurrency control was introduced (for a system without nesting) by Kung and Robinson [61]. An important simulation study of the performance of optimistic algorithms has been done by Agrawal *et al.* [4]. This study and most other work assumes that a transaction is restarted after being aborted (because it fails to validate). An algorithm that prevents repeated aborts for the same transaction is given by Thomasian and Rahm [111]. Algorithms using optimistic concurrency control for abstract data types were given in [50].

Closely related to the systems described here are algorithms that allow objects to delay transaction commit until atomicity is guaranteed. These methods are discussed by Agrawal and El Abbadi [1] and Badrinath and Ramamrithan [7].

10.8   Exercises

1. Prove Lemma 10.4.

2. Prove Lemma 10.6.

3. Prove Theorem 10.12.

4. Prove the following: If β is an optimistic hybrid object well-formed sequence of external actions of $OHY(\mathrm{X})$, then *local-timestamp-order*(β) is a total order on accesses to X having **REQUEST_COMMIT** actions in β and locally visible at X to T_0 in β. Conclude that *local-views*(β) contains at most one sequence.

5. The algorithm $OD(\mathrm{X}, C)$ removes operations from *intset* (and thus, from *occur*) when informed of the abort of an ancestor. However, if an operation runs (as an orphan) after the information of the ancestor's abort, it will remain in *occur* unless the information is repeated. Thus, the check in the precondition of the **VALIDATE** action may prevent some validation unnecessarily. Design an optimistic hybrid object that is similar to $OD(X, C)$, but even more abstract, and that validates in these cases.

The object should maintain information about the entire behavior. In the precondition for a **VALIDATE** action, it should check for compatibility between descendants of the validating transaction and descendants of its validated siblings, but it need not check any operation of an access that can be deduced to be an orphan. Prove that the object you have given is locally optimistic hybrid atomic.

6. The algorithm presented as $OD(X, C)$ in this chapter is very abstract, and must maintain a large amount of information in the $depend(T)$ variables. Here is a more concrete algorithm, $OD1(X, C)$, that maintains instead a timestamp $start(T)$ for transaction T, recording the highest timestamp of a sibling of T that is known to have committed when activity starts on behalf of T. When T validates, checks for incompatible operations need not be made against siblings with timestamps less than $start(T)$. In order to keep optimistic hybrid atomicity, the algorithm greatly restricts the flexibility of validation. We say a transaction is **dubious** during the period from validation until information is received about the completion. We require validation to be *serial* for each set of siblings, in that at most one may be dubious at any time. Also validation of siblings must be *monotonic*, so the order of occurrence of **VALIDATE** events must match the order of the timestamp values. Finally, a transaction T may not be validated until every descendant access that has run at the object is either lock visible to the T (and thus, in $intset(T)$) or deleted from the collection of $intset$ values by an **INFORM_ABORT**. An extra restriction is that a response to an access is not given if any ancestor of the access has already validated.[2]

The state components of $OD1(X, C)$ are $s.created$, $s.commit\_requested$, $s.intset$, $s.valid$, $s.start$, $s.known$, and $s.time$. Here, $s.created$, $s.commit\_requested$, $s.valid$, and $s.known$ are sets of transactions, all initially empty. Also $s.intset$ is a function from transactions to sets of operations, initially mapping every transaction to the empty set $\emptyset$. The components $s.start$ and $s.time$ are partial functions from transactions to timestamps, both initially everywhere undefined.

The value of variable $s.time$ can be used to define a derived partial order $s.time\text{-}order$ on accesses to X, as for $OD(X, C)$. We then define derived variables $s.in\text{-}$

---

[2]This last constraint is not needed for correctness, but it is needed for a system containing $OD1(X, C)$ to be an implementation of the same system with $OD(X, C)$ substituted for $OD1(X, C)$.

CREATE(T)
    Effect:
        $s.created = s'.created \cup \{T\}$

INFORM_COMMIT_AT(X)**OF**(T)
    Effect:
        $s.known = s'.known \cup \{T\}$
        $s.intset(T) = \emptyset$
        $s.intset(parent(T))$
            $= s'.intset(parent(T)) \cup s'.intset(T)$

INFORM_ABORT_AT(X)**OF**(T)
    Effect:
        $s.known = s'.known \cup \{T\}$
        $s.intset(U) = \emptyset,$
           for all $U \in descendants(T)$

INFORM_TIME_AT(X)**OF**(T, p)
    Effect:
        $s.time(T) = p$

REQUEST_COMMIT(T, v)
    Precondition:
        $T \in s'.created - s'.commit\_requested$
        $ancestors(T) \cap s'.valid = \emptyset$
        $perform(s'.total(T)(T, v))$
           is a behavior of $S(X)$
    Effect:
        $s.commit\_requested =$
          $s'.commit\_requested \cup \{T\}$
        $s.start(U) = max(s'.time(U') :$
          $U' \in siblings(U)$
             $\cap s'.known \cap domain(s'.time))$
          for all $U \in ancestors(T)$
            $- domain(s'.start)$
        $s.intset(T) = \{(T, v)\}$

VALIDATE_AT(X)**OF**(T)
    Precondition:
        $T \in domain(s'.time)$
        $T \notin s'.valid$
        $T' \notin s'.dubious$
          for all $T' \in siblings(T)$
        $s'.time(T') < s'.time(T)$
          for all $T' \in siblings(T) \cap s'.valid$
        there do not exist U, V, u such that
          $(U, u) \in s'.intset(V),$
          $U \in descendants(T),$
          and $V \in ancestors(T)$
        there do not exist T', U, U', u, u' such that
          $T' \in siblings(T) \cap s'.valid,$
          (U, u) in $s'.occur,$
          (U', u') in $s'.occur$
          $U \in descendants(T)$
          $U' \in descendants(T')$
          $(((U', u'), (U, u)) \in C)$
          $s'.start(T) < s'.time(T')$
    Effect:
        $s.dubious = s'.dubious \cup \{T\}$
        $s.valid = s'.valid \cup \{T\}$

Figure 10.3: Transition Relation for a Compressed Optimistic Algorithm

tentions, *s.total*, and *s.occur* as for $OD(X, C)$. In addition we define *s.dubious* to be $s.valid - s.known$.

The transition relation of $OD1(X, C)$ is given in Figure 10.3.

Prove that if C is a serial dependency relation, then $OD1(X, C)$ is local optimistic hybrid atomic.

7. Prove Lemma 10.31.

8. Prove Lemma 10.32.

9. Develop an optimistic pseudotime object based on Herlihy's algorithm from Chapter 7. Prove that the object is local optimistic static atomic.

10. Develop a version of an optimistic pseudotime system that is more flexible than the one given in the chapter, in that it allows the decision between optimistic and non-optimistic concurrency control to be made separately for each access. For accesses that are not optimistic, the **REQUEST_COMMIT** action performs the work of the **VALID** as well as its own work.

11. Develop an alternative optimistic system structure based on hybrid atomicity, where validation is done only for children of T_0, rather than for all transactions as in the optimistic hybrid system of this chapter. Develop a local atomicity condition for the system, and present an algorithm that ensures this condition. Hint: The validation of a child of T_0 at an object should check for compatibility between pairs of descendants of the validating transaction, as well as between these descendants and the descendants of other children of T_0.

11
ORPHAN MANAGEMENT ALGORITHMS

11.1 Introduction

In distributed systems, various factors, including node crashes and network delays, can result in orphan transactions—descendants of aborted transactions—continuing to run even though their results can no longer be used. For example, in the Argus system developed at MIT [75], a transaction T making a remote request for access to data at another node does so by issuing a local subtransaction T_1 to handle the access. The calling transaction T may give up because a network partition or some other problem prevents it from communicating with the other node; it does this by aborting the local subtransaction T_1. This may leave a transaction T_2 at the called node, running as a descendant of T_1; this descendant transaction T_2 is an orphan.

Since the Argus system is atomic for nonorphan transactions, the orphan T_2 does not have any permanent effects on the observed state of the shared data. However, even if a system is designed to prevent orphans from permanently affecting shared data, orphans are still undesirable, for two reasons. First, they waste resources: they use processor cycles, and may also hold locks, causing other computations to be delayed.

Second, they may see inconsistent states of the shared data. For example, in a locking-based generic system, a transaction might read data at two nodes, with some invariant relating the values of the different data objects. If the transaction reads data at one of the nodes and then becomes an orphan, another transaction could change the data at both nodes before the orphan reads the data at the second node. This could happen, for example, because the first node learns that the transaction has aborted and releases its locks. While the inconsistencies seen by an orphan should not have any permanent effect on the shared data in the system, they can cause strange behavior if the orphan interacts with the external world; this can make programs difficult to design and debug.

EXAMPLE 11.1.1   Orphans Can See Inconsistent States

The following example illustrates another way in which an orphan can see an inconsistent state in a locking-based generic system. Suppose that T is a transaction with children T_1 and T_2, both of which are accesses to an object X. Consider the following scenario: T first accesses X through its child T_1. T then requests the creation of T_2, which will access X again. Furthermore, assume that T_2 is requested only if T_1 completes successfully, and that T_1 modifies X. Now suppose that T aborts before T_2 starts running at X, and X learns of the abort via an **INFORM_ABORT_AT**(X)**OF**(T) event. If T_1's modification of X is undone when X learns that T aborted (as is done, for example, in the general locking algorithm described in Chapter 6), then T_2 will not see the value for X that it expects, since T_2 only runs if T_1 has modified X successfully. This scenario is captured more precisely by the following fragment of a generic schedule.

CREATE(T),
    REQUEST_CREATE(T_1),
    CREATE(T_1),
    REQUEST_COMMIT(T_1, v_1),
    COMMIT(T_1),
    REPORT_COMMIT(T_1, v_1),
        REQUEST_CREATE(T_2),
ABORT(T),
INFORM_ABORT_AT(X)**OF**(T),
        CREATE(T_2),
        REQUEST_COMMIT(T_2, v_2),

   . . .

Two Algorithms: Several algorithms have been proposed to prevent orphans from seeing inconsistent information. Some are designed to cope with orphans created by explicit aborts of transactions that leave running descendants, as described above, whereas others are designed to cope in addition with orphans created by node crashes in which the contents of volatile memory are destroyed. The goal of all of these algorithms is to detect and eliminate orphan transactions before they can see inconsistent information.

In this chapter we give formal descriptions and correctness proofs for two orphan management algorithms appearing in the literature, (i.e., the "piggyback algorithm" used in the Argus system, and the "clock algorithm" developed at Carnegie-Mellon University). Our analysis covers only orphans resulting from explicit transaction aborts; there is another component of the Argus algorithm that handles orphans that result from node crashes, but we leave its analysis as a research exercise. Although the piggyback algorithm and the clock algorithm appear to be quite different, our proofs show that the fundamental concepts underlying them are very similar; in fact, each can be regarded as an implementation of the same high-level algorithm.

Our results relate the behavior of a system, S', containing an orphan management algorithm to that of a corresponding system, S, having no orphan management; namely, S' "simulates" S in the sense that each transaction in S' sees a view of the system that it could see in an execution of S in which it is not an orphan. (A transaction's "view" of the system is the projection of the system's execution on that transaction.) Thus, when system S includes a concurrency control algorithm that ensures that nonorphans see consistent views, our results imply that in S', *all* transactions, orphans as well as nonorphans, see consistent views. Note the modularity of our treatment of concurrency control and orphan management: the same orphan management algorithms work correctly with any system S incorporating a correct concurrency control algorithm (provided that it is describable within the given framework).

Chapter Outline: The remainder of the chapter is organized as follows. Section 11.2 describes the orphan management problem formally, in terms of converting a system that guarantees atomicity for nonorphans into one that guarantees atomicity for all transactions. Section 11.3 contains some definitions and results about the dependencies among different events in a generic system; these concepts underlie the results in the rest of the chapter.

Sections 11.4 through 11.7 contain the principal contributions of this chapter, in which we prove the correctness of the two orphan management algorithms, the piggyback algorithm and the clock algorithm. Our proofs have an interesting structure. We first define a simple abstract algorithm that uses global information about the history of the system, and show that it ensures that orphans see consistent views.

We then formalize the piggyback algorithm and the clock algorithm in a way that requires the use of purely local information, and show that each simulates the more abstract algorithm. The simulation proofs are quite simple and do not require re-proving the properties already proved for the abstract algorithm. The correctness of the piggyback and clock algorithms then follows directly from the correctness of the abstract algorithm.

Each orphan management algorithm is described as a system obtained by transforming an arbitrary generic system without orphan management. Each of these systems contains the same transactions as the given generic system, but each manages orphans using a different transaction-processing algorithm. The abstract algorithm is modeled by the *filtered database*, which maintains information about the global history of the system and uses tests based on this history information to prevent orphans from learning that they are orphans. The *piggyback database* models the behavior of the Argus orphan management algorithm; it manages orphans using tests based on local information about direct dependencies among system events. The *strictly filtered database* models another abstract algorithm, introduced to simplify the proof of the correctness of the clock algorithm; it also uses tests based on global history information and is even more restrictive than the filtered database. Finally, the *clock database* models a different orphan management algorithm; it manages orphans using information about logical clocks. Each of these four databases is described as the result of a transformation of the generic database (i.e., the combination of the generic controller and the generic objects).

We prove that the *filtered system* (the system consisting of the transactions and the filtered database) "simulates" the generic system in the sense that each transaction, including orphans, sees a "view" that it could see in the generic system, in an execution in which it is not an orphan. It follows that if the generic system ensures atomicity for nonorphan transactions, then the filtered system ensures atomicity for all transactions. We also prove that the *piggyback system* implements the filtered system, and so inherits the same correctness property. Similarly, we prove that the *clock system* implements the *strictly filtered system*, which in turn implements the filtered system, thus showing that the clock system has the same correctness property as the filtered system.

11.2 The Orphan Management Problem

For the sake of concreteness, we work in terms of generic systems only in this chapter; the ideas generalize to other types of systems such as pseudotime systems and hybrid systems, and we leave the extensions to such systems as exercises. Thus, for the remainder of the chapter, we fix a particular generic system. For each non-access transaction name T, let A_T be the transaction automaton for T in this generic system, and for each object name X, let $G(X)$ be the generic object automaton for X.

We consider two of the notions of correctness for generic systems defined earlier, in Chapter 3. The first and stronger notion is that the system be *atomic for all transaction names*. This is the correctness condition that we would like to try to achieve. Without orphan management, however, systems will typically not meet this strong requirement. Therefore, we consider the second and weaker notion of correctness, namely, that *each of the system's finite behaviors β be atomic for all transaction names that are not orphans in β*. This condition says that nonorphan transactions see serial views (whereas orphans can see arbitrary views). This is the correctness condition guaranteed, for example, by generic systems in which all objects are dynamic atomic. In this section, we will abbreviate this latter condition by saying that the system is *atomic for nonorphans*.

The orphan management algorithms of this chapter ensure that the systems that use them are atomic for all transaction names. To ensure this, the orphan management algorithms rely on the generic objects to ensure atomicity for nonorphans; in fact, the algorithms work with any generic objects that ensure atomicity for nonorphans. In this sense, the orphan management algorithms and the concurrency control algorithms are independent. We prove a result of the following sort for each orphan management algorithm: if β is a behavior of the system with orphan management and T is a transaction name, then there exists a behavior γ of the underlying generic system such that $\gamma|T = \beta|T$ and T is not an orphan in γ. In other words, the orphan management algorithms prevent transactions from "knowing" that they are orphans—everything a transaction sees is consistent with what it could see in the underlying generic system, in some execution in which it is not an orphan. These results imply that if the generic system is atomic for nonorphans, then the corresponding system with orphan management is atomic for all transactions.

11.3 An Affects Relation

We begin by defining a partial order, *GS-affects*(β), which models the information flow between events in behaviors of a generic system: if an event ϕ does not GS-affect an event π in a behavior β, then π cannot "know" that ϕ occurred, in the sense that there is a "possible world" in which π occurs but ϕ does not. The algorithms described later in this chapter ensure that no event of a transaction is affected by the abort of an ancestor; thus, no event of a transaction ever knows that the transaction is an orphan.

We first define a subrelation *directly-GS-affects*(β), which captures the direct dependencies between actions, and then take the transitive closure. For a sequence β of generic actions, define the relation *directly-GS-affects*(β) to be the relation containing the pairs (ϕ, π) of events such that ϕ occurs before π in β, and at least one of the following holds:

■ $transaction(\phi) = transaction(\pi)$ and π is an output event of the transaction,

■ $object(\phi) = object(\pi)$ and π is an output event of the object,

■ ϕ is a **REQUEST_CREATE**(T) and π a **CREATE**(T) event,

■ ϕ is a **REQUEST_COMMIT**(T, v) and π a **COMMIT**(T) event,

■ ϕ is a **REQUEST_CREATE**(T) and π an **ABORT**(T) event,

■ ϕ is a **COMMIT**(T) and π a **REPORT_COMMIT**(T,v) event,

■ ϕ is an **ABORT**(T) and π a **REPORT_ABORT**(T) event,

■ ϕ is a **COMMIT**(T) and π an **INFORM_COMMIT_AT**(X)**OF**(T) event, or

■ ϕ is an **ABORT**(T) and π an **INFORM_ABORT_AT**(X)**OF**(T) event.

(We also say that ϕ **directly GS-affects** π in β when $(\phi, \pi) \in$ *directly-GS-affects*(β).)

Now define the relation *GS-affects*(β) to be the transitive closure of *directly-GS-affects*(β). It is easy to see that *GS-affects*(β) is a partial order.

The idea is that ϕ directly affects π if they both occur at the same transaction or object and π is an output of the transaction or object, or if they involve different transactions or objects but the generic system will require ϕ to occur before π can occur. This notion of one event affecting another is "safe," in the sense that ϕ affects π if there is any way that the precondition for π could require ϕ to have occurred. If the events involve different transactions or objects, the precondition for π in the generic controller require ϕ to occur if ϕ directly affects π. If the events occur at the same transaction or object, however, it might be that ϕ happens to occur before π, yet that the particular transaction or object does not require ϕ to occur before π. In the absence of more information about the particular transactions or objects used in a system, however, it is difficult to say more about the ways in which one event can affect another. Thus, we make the "safe" choice of assuming an effect whenever one could occur. Fortunately, the orphan management algorithms described in this chapter are essentially independent of the particular transactions and objects used in a system, and do not rely on more information about them.

When no confusion seems likely, we will often say "ϕ affects π in β", or just "ϕ affects π", to mean that $(\phi, \pi) \in$ *GS-affects*(β). Likewise, we will say "ϕ directly affects π in β" or "ϕ directly affects π" to mean that $(\phi, \pi) \in$ *directly-GS-affects*(β).

Note the relationship between the *GS-affects* relation and the *affects* relation defined in Chapter 5. Namely, the *GS-affects* relation includes dependencies at the objects as well as at the controller and the transactions. Also, the dependencies at the transactions are slightly weaker here because they only describe the dependencies for transaction output events.

The following lemma describes a sense in which the relation $GS\text{-}affects(\beta)$ captures all the dependency relationships between events. The condition implies that if π is not affected by ϕ in some behavior β, then π cannot "know" that ϕ occurred, since π could also have occurred in a different behavior in which ϕ did not occur. This lemma uses the definition of an R-closed subsequence of a sequence, given in the Appendix.

LEMMA 11.1 *If β is a finite generic behavior and γ is a $GS\text{-}affects(\beta)$-closed subsequence of β, then γ is a generic behavior.*

PROOF By Proposition 2.5, it suffices to show that $\gamma|T$ is a behavior of A_T for all non-access transaction names T, that $\gamma|G(\mathrm{X})$ is a behavior of $G(\mathrm{X})$ for all object names X, and that γ is a behavior of the generic controller. We show these in turn.

First, suppose that T is a non-access transaction name. If $\gamma|T$ contains no output events of A_T, then the input-enabling property implies that $\gamma|T$ is a behavior of A_T. So assume that there is at least one output event of A_T in $\gamma|T$, and let π be the last such event. Let γ' be the prefix of γ ending with π. Since γ is closed in β, it follows from the definition of $GS\text{-}affects(\beta)$ that γ contains all events of T that precede π in β. Thus, $\gamma'|T$ is a prefix of $\beta|T$ and so is a behavior of A_T. Since $\gamma|T$ differs from $\gamma'|T$ only by the possible inclusion of some final input events of A_T, the input-enabling property implies that $\gamma|T$ is a behavior of A_T.

A similar argument shows that if X is an object name, then $\gamma|G(\mathrm{X})$ is a behavior of $G(\mathrm{X})$.

Now we show that γ is a behavior of the generic controller. Note that the generic controller is deterministic in the sense that for a given state s' and action π, there is at most one state s such that (s', π, s) is a step of the generic controller. We proceed by induction on the lengths of prefixes δ of γ. The basis, where the length of δ is 0, is obvious. So suppose that $\delta = \delta'\pi$, where π is a single event. Let $\beta'\pi$ be the prefix of β ending with π. Let s' be the state of the generic controller after δ'. We consider cases, showing in each case that π is enabled in s'.

1. $\pi = \mathbf{CREATE}(T)$

Then basic properties of generic systems imply that $\mathbf{REQUEST\_CREATE}(T)$ occurs in β', and no $\mathbf{CREATE}(T)$ occurs in β'. Since γ is $GS\text{-}affects(\beta)$-closed in β, $\mathbf{REQUEST\_CREATE}(T)$ also occurs in δ'. Also, δ' is a subsequence of β', so no $\mathbf{CREATE}(T)$ occurs in δ'. If follows that π is enabled in s'.

2. $\pi = \mathbf{COMMIT}(T)$

Then basic properties of generic systems imply that β' contains $\mathbf{REQUEST\_COMMIT}(T, v)$ and contains no completion events for T. Since γ is $GS\text{-}affects(\beta)$-closed in β, δ' contains $\mathbf{REQUEST\_COMMIT}(T, v)$ and does not contain a completion event for T. It follows that π is enabled in s'.

3. $\pi = \textbf{ABORT}(T)$

Then β' contains **REQUEST_CREATE**(T) and contains no completion events for T, so δ' contains **REQUEST_CREATE**(T) and no completion events for T. Thus, π is enabled in s'.

4. $\pi = \textbf{REPORT\_COMMIT}(T,v)$

Then β' contains **COMMIT**(T) and **REQUEST_COMMIT**(T,v) and contains no report events for T. Therefore, the same is true of δ', so π is enabled in s'.

5. $\pi = \textbf{REPORT\_ABORT}(T)$

Similar to the preceding arguments.

6. $\pi = \textbf{INFORM\_COMMIT\_AT}(X)\textbf{OF}(T)$

Similar to the preceding arguments.

7. $\pi = \textbf{INFORM\_ABORT\_AT}(X)\textbf{OF}(T)$

Similar to the preceding arguments.   □

The following lemma gives a technical condition that describes certain limitations on the pattern of information flow. It says that whenever an **ABORT**(T) event ϕ affects an event π of any of certain types, there is a specific type of intervening event ψ that is also affected by ϕ.

LEMMA 11.2 *Suppose that β is a generic behavior and $(\phi, \pi) \in$ GS-affects(β), where ϕ is an **ABORT**(T') event and π is a **CREATE**, **COMMIT ABORT**, or **REPORT-COMMIT** event, a **REPORT_ABORT**(T) event for $T \neq T'$, an output of a non-access transaction, or an output of an object. Then there is an event ψ strictly between ϕ and π in β such that $(\phi, \psi) \in$ GS-affects(β) and $(\psi, \pi) \in$ directly-GS-affects(β), where ψ is related to π as follows:*

1. *If $\pi = $ **CREATE**(T) then $\psi = $ **REQUEST_CREATE**(T).*

2. *If $\pi = $ **COMMIT**(T) then $\psi = $ **REQUEST_COMMIT**(T,v).*

3. *If $\pi = $ **ABORT**(T) then $\psi = $ **REQUEST_CREATE**(T).*

4. *If $\pi = $ **REPORT_COMMIT**(T,v) then $\psi = $ **COMMIT**(T).*

5. *If $\pi = $ **REPORT_ABORT**(T) then $\psi = $ **ABORT**(T).*

6. *If π is an output of non-access transaction T, then ψ is an event of transaction T.*

7. *If π is an output of object* X, *then ψ is an event of object* X.[1]

PROOF By the definition of *directly-GS-affects*, each designated type of event π is only directly affected by earlier events that satisfy the indicated restrictions on ψ. Thus, if π is affected by ϕ, it must be so affected by the transitive closure over a chain of directly affects relationships in which an event ψ of the appropriate type occurs. $\square$

The intuitive idea behind the orphan management algorithms described in this chapter is that they ensure that an event of a transaction T is never affected by the abort of an ancestor of T. Then we can show that every transaction gets a view it could get in a behavior in which it is not an orphan: we simply take the subsequence of the original behavior containing all events of T and all events that affect them in that behavior. The resulting sequence is a generic behavior, by Lemma 11.1, and does not contain an abort for an ancestor of T, by construction.

EXAMPLE 11.3.1 **Preventing Orphans From Seeing Inconsistent States**

In Example 11.1.1 above, recall that a difficulty arises when the object X is informed about the abort of T, via an **INFORM_ABORT_AT**(X)**OF**(T) event. The definition of *GS-affects* ensures that the **ABORT**(T) event affects the **INFORM_ABORT_AT**(X)**OF**(T) event, and that the **REQUEST_COMMIT** event for T_2 is affected by all prior events at the object. By preventing T_2 from running when its **REQUEST_COMMIT** would be affected by the abort of an ancestor, we can prevent T_2 from learning that it is an orphan and hence from seeing an inconsistent view.

11.4 Filtered Systems

In the remainder of this chapter, we describe and analyze two orphan management algorithms, the piggyback algorithm and the clock algorithm. The two algorithms use quite different techniques. However, each can be proved correct by showing that it implements a common abstract algorithm. This abstract algorithm is captured by *filtered systems*, which we describe in this section.

---

[1]Note that ψ can be either a serial or a non-serial (**INFORM_COMMIT** or **INFORM_ABORT**) event.

One way of ensuring that actions of a transaction T are never affected by the abort of an ancestor of T is simply to strengthen the preconditions of all the actions of the generic system to permit actions of T to occur only if they would not be affected in this way. It turns out, however, that this approach checks for orphans much more frequently than necessary. Since checking for orphans can be expensive, and since the algorithms studied later in this chapter check for orphans less frequently than this, we define filtered systems so that they check for orphans only when **REQUEST_COMMIT** events occur for access transactions. We then show that this is sufficient to ensure that transactions are never affected by the aborts of ancestors.

We construct a filtered system based on the given generic system. The filtered system consists of the given transaction automata A_T and a *filtered database automaton*. The filtered database automaton is obtained by slightly modifying the generic controller and generic object automata; it "filters" **REQUEST_COMMIT** events of access transactions so that any transaction, orphan or not, sees a view it could see as a nonorphan in the generic system.

1 1 . 4 . 1   T h e   F i l t e r e d   D a t a b a s e

We begin by defining the **generic database** for the given generic system to be the composition of the generic controller and the generic object automata from that system. The filtered database is obtained via a simple transformation from the generic database. The only difference between the behaviors of the two databases is that the new database only allows a **REQUEST_COMMIT** of an access to occur if it is not affected by the abort of an ancestor.

Notice that the filtered database is not obtained from the generic database by composing it with other automata. Rather, we define the signature, set of states and start states, and transitions of the filtered database in terms of the generic database. More specifically, the filtered database has the same signature as the generic database. The state of the filtered database has two components, *basic-state* and *history*, where *basic-state* is a state of the generic database and *history* is a sequence of generic actions. Start states of the filtered database are those with *basic-state* equal to a start state of the generic database and *history* equal to the empty sequence.

A triple (s', π, s) is a step of the filtered database if and only if the following conditions hold.

1 . $(s'.basic\text{-}state, \pi, s.basic\text{-}state)$ is a step of the generic database.

2 . $s.history = s'.history\pi$ if π is a generic action and $s.history = s'.history$ otherwise.[2]

---

[2]Recall that internal actions of the generic objects are not classified as generic actions.

3. If $\pi = \textbf{REQUEST\_COMMIT}(T, v)$ where T is an access to object X, and if T' is an ancestor of T, then no $\textbf{ABORT}(T')$ event affects an event ψ with $object(\psi) = $ X in $s'.history$.

Thus, at the point where the **REQUEST_COMMIT** of an access is about to occur, an explicit test is performed to verify that no preceding event at the same object is affected by the abort of any ancestor of the access. The following obvious lemma says that the *history* state component keeps track of the system behavior.

LEMMA 11.3 *Let β be a finite schedule of the filtered database that can lead the filtered database to state s. Then $s.history = beh(\beta)$.*

11.4.2 The Filtered System

The **filtered system** is the composition of the transaction automata A_T and the filtered database automaton. We call its executions, schedules, and behaviors the **filtered executions**, **filtered schedules**, and **filtered behaviors**, respectively.

LEMMA 11.4 *The filtered system implements the generic system.*

PROOF The mapping f that assigns to each state s of the filtered system the singleton set $f(s)$ consisting of $s.basic\text{-}state$ is easily seen to be a possibilities mapping. Theorem 2.10 implies the result. $\square$

As described above, the filtered database performs an explicit test to ensure that the **REQUEST_COMMIT** of an access is not affected by the abort of any ancestor. The following key lemma shows that this test actually guarantees more: that a similar property holds for all events.

LEMMA 11.5 *Let β be a filtered behavior and let T be any transaction name. Let ρ be an event in β such that $transaction(\rho) = T$. Then there is no $\textbf{ABORT}(T')$ event ϕ such that $(\phi, \rho) \in GS\text{-}affects(\beta)$ and T' is an ancestor of T.*

PROOF The proof of the lemma is by induction on the length of β. If β is empty, the result clearly holds. Suppose $\beta = \beta'\pi$, and that the lemma holds for β'. By the definition of the affects relation, $GS\text{-}affects(\beta) \subseteq GS\text{-}affects(\beta') \cup \{(\phi, \pi) | \phi$ is an action in $\beta'\}$. Thus, by induction, it suffices to show that the lemma holds when $\rho = \pi$.

Suppose that the lemma does not hold, that is, that $\phi = \textbf{ABORT}(T')$ affects π in β, where $transaction(\pi) = T$ and T' is an ancestor of T. We derive a contradiction. We consider cases.

1. T is a non-access and π is an output action of T.

Then by Lemma 11.2, there is an event ψ of T between ϕ and π such that ϕ affects ψ in β'. This contradicts the inductive hypothesis.

2. T is an access to object X and π is a **REQUEST_COMMIT** for T.

Then by Lemma 11.2, there is an event ψ of object X between ϕ and π in β' such that ϕ affects ψ in β'. Then the precondition for π in the filtered database is violated, a contradiction.

3. $\pi = $ **CREATE**(T).

Then by Lemma 11.2, there is a **REQUEST_CREATE**(T) event ψ between ϕ and π such that ϕ affects ψ in β'. Since **REQUEST_CREATE**(T) is an action of $parent(T)$, the inductive hypothesis implies that T' is not an ancestor of $parent(T)$. The only possibility is that $T' = T$, which implies that **ABORT**(T) precedes **REQUEST_CREATE**(T) in β. But this contradicts the definition of the generic controller.

4. T is a non-access and π is **REPORT_COMMIT**(T'',v), where T'' is a child of T.

Then T' is an ancestor of T''. By Lemma 11.2 applied twice, there is a **REQUEST_COMMIT**(T'',v) event ψ between ϕ and π such that ϕ affects ψ in β'. Since $transaction(\psi) = T''$, this contradicts the inductive hypothesis.

5. T is a non-access and π is **REPORT_ABORT**(T''), where T'' is a child of T.

By Lemma 11.2, there is a **REQUEST_CREATE**(T'')v event ψ between ϕ and π such that ϕ affects ψ in β'. Since $transaction(\psi) = T$, this contradicts the inductive hypothesis.

6. π is an **INFORM_COMMIT** or **INFORM_ABORT** action.

Then $transaction(\pi)$ is undefined, a contradiction. $\qquad\qquad\square$

11.4.3 Simulation of the Generic System by the Filtered System

The following theorem is the key result of this chapter. It shows that the filtered system ensures that every transaction gets a view it could get in the generic system when it is not an orphan. (Formally, a transaction T's "view" in a behavior β is its local behavior, $\beta|T$.) In other words, an orphan cannot discover that it is an orphan, since the view it sees is consistent with it not being an orphan.

THEOREM 11.6 *Let β be a filtered behavior and let T be a transaction name. Then there exists a generic behavior γ such that T is not an orphan in γ and $\gamma|T = \beta|T$.*

PROOF   Let γ be the subsequence of β containing all actions π such that *transaction*$(\pi) = T$, and all other actions ϕ that affect, in β, some action whose transaction is T. Since *GS-affects*(β) is a transitive relation, γ is *GS-affects*(β)-closed in β. Lemma 11.1 then implies that γ is a generic behavior. It suffices to show that there is no ancestor T' of T for which **ABORT**(T') occurs in γ. Suppose not; that is, there exists an ancestor T' of T for which **ABORT**(T') occurs in γ. Then by the construction of γ, β contains an event π of T such that an **ABORT**(T') event ϕ affects π in β. By Lemma 11.5, this is impossible.   □

We obtain an important corollary of Theorem 11.6.

COROLLARY 11.7 *If the generic system is atomic for nonorphans, then the filtered system is atomic for all transaction names.*

PROOF   Let β be a filtered behavior and let T be any transaction name. Theorem 11.6 yields a generic behavior δ such that T is not an orphan in δ and $\delta|T = \beta|T$. Since the generic system is atomic for nonorphans, there is a serial behavior γ with $\gamma|T = \delta|T$; this is equal to $\beta|T$, as needed.   □

At first it might seem somewhat surprising that it is enough to prevent the **REQUEST_COMMIT** events of orphan accesses to ensure atomicity for all orphans. The reason it is not necessary to filter other actions is because of the dependencies described in Lemma 11.2. Essentially, this lemma indicates that an event, say **CREATE**(T), cannot "know" about an **ABORT**(T') event unless some earlier event, in this case **REQUEST_CREATE**(T), already "knows" about the **ABORT**(T'). (Lemma 11.1 implies that if π is not affected by ϕ, π cannot know that ϕ has occurred, since there is a behavior of the system in which π occurs and ϕ does not.) If we assume inductively that **REQUEST_CREATE**(T) does not know about the abort of an ancestor of T, then Lemma 11.2 guarantees that **CREATE**(T) will not know about it either.

The restrictions on information flow derive from the restricted communication patterns in typical systems: a non-access transaction receives information from its parent when it is created, and from its children when they report, but not from any other source. Access transactions may receive information from other accesses (e.g., accesses to the same object share state), but can only affect non-accesses through **REPORT_COMMIT** events, which must be preceded by corresponding **REQUEST_COMMIT** events. As long as T does not receive reports from any accesses that "know" that its ancestor has aborted, T cannot observe a state that depends on the abort. In effect, by preventing **REQUEST_COMMIT** actions for orphan accesses, we isolate orphan transactions from the objects, ensuring that an orphan transaction never sees that it is an orphan.

11.5 Piggyback Systems

In this section we analyze the orphan management algorithm used in the Argus system. We present the algorithm by defining a *piggyback database* that describes the Argus algorithm in formal terms. As with the filtered database, the piggyback database is obtained from the generic database via a simple construction. We then define the piggyback system, which is composed of the transaction automata A_T and the piggyback database, and show that the piggyback system implements the filtered system. Thus, if the filtered system is atomic for all transaction names, so is the corresponding piggyback system.

11.5.1 The Piggyback Database

The filtered database uses global knowledge of the entire history of actions to filter the **REQUEST_COMMIT** events of access transactions. This kind of global knowledge is not practical in a distributed system. Thus, the piggyback algorithm makes use of local knowledge about the aborts that have occurred. To ensure that the **REQUEST-_COMMIT** of an access is not affected by the abort of an ancestor, the piggyback algorithm keeps track of the aborts "known" by each event that occurs and propagates this knowledge from an event to any later events that it affects.

In the actual Argus system, knowledge about aborts is propagated in messages sent over the network; we model this formally by propagating knowledge from an event to every event that it directly GS-affects. If one event ϕ directly affects another event π only if the two events occur at the same site, or if a message is sent from ϕ's site to π's after ϕ occurs and before π occurs, then it is straightforward to implement the algorithm in a distributed system using information available locally at each site, by transmitting the information about aborted transactions on messages sent between sites.

The piggyback database has the same signature as the generic database. The state of the piggyback database has three components: *basic-state*, *history*, and *known-aborts*, where *basic-state* is a state of the generic database, *history* is a sequence of generic actions, and *known-aborts* is a partial function from generic events to sets of transactions. This component records the transactions whose aborts affect each event that has occurred. The set *known-aborts*(π) may actually include more transactions than those whose aborts affect π. By adding more aborted transactions to this set, an implementation would restrict the behavior of orphans further than is strictly necessary to ensure the correctness conditions. In Argus, for example, each event occurs at some physical node of the network, and each node manages a single set of aborted transactions for the entire set of events that occur at that node. In this case, *known-aborts*(π) includes at least the transactions whose aborts affect π, as well as those transactions whose aborts affect any other event that has occurred at the same physical node as π.

Start states of the piggyback database are those with *basic-state* equal to a start state of the generic database, *history* equal to the empty sequence, and *known-aborts* everywhere undefined. A triple (s', π, s) is a step of the piggyback database if and only if the following conditions hold.

1. $(s'.basic\text{-}state, \pi, s.basic\text{-}state)$ is a step of the generic database.

2. $s.history = s'.history\pi$ if π is a generic action, and $s.history = s'.history$ otherwise.

3. If π is a generic action and $(\phi, \pi) \in directly\text{-}GS\text{-}affects(s.history)$ then $s'.known\text{-}aborts(\phi) \subseteq s.known\text{-}aborts(\pi)$.

4. If $\phi \neq \pi$, then $s.known\text{-}aborts(\phi) = s'.known\text{-}aborts(\phi)$.

5. If π is a generic action and ϕ is an **ABORT**(T) event in $s'.history$ such that $(\phi, \pi) \in directly\text{-}GS\text{-}affects(s'.history)$ then $T \in s.known\text{-}aborts(\pi)$.

6. If π is a **REQUEST_COMMIT**(T, v) action for an access T to object X, then there is no ancestor of T in $s'.known\text{-}aborts(\phi)$, for any event ϕ of object X in $s'.history$.

There are two significant differences between the piggyback database and the generic database. First, the effect for each action π in the piggyback database requires $s.known\text{-}aborts(\pi)$ to include $s'.known\text{-}aborts(\phi)$ for each ϕ that directly affects π. In addition, an event π that is directly affected by **ABORT**(T) requires T to be in $known\text{-}aborts(\pi)$. As Lemma 11.12 below shows, these constraints are enough to ensure that $s.known\text{-}aborts(\pi)$ contains T whenever **ABORT**(T) affects π.

Second, the precondition for the **REQUEST_COMMIT** of an access to X permits the event to occur only if the access does not "know about" the abort of an ancestor, that is, no ancestor is in $s'.known\text{-}aborts(\phi)$ for any event ϕ of object X in $s'.history$. As Lemma 11.13 below shows, this is enough to ensure that every piggyback behavior is a filtered behavior.

The *known-aborts* component models the distributed information maintained by the piggyback algorithm to keep track of actions that abort. However, rather than modeling nodes directly and keeping the information on a per-node basis as is done in the actual algorithm, we maintain the information for each event, propagating it whenever one event directly affects another.

The *known-aborts* component is managed so as to ensure that at least the minimum amount of necessary information is propagated at each step. An implementation is permitted to propagate more than the minimum; for instance, an implementation might keep track of the known-aborts information at a coarser granularity. (By maintaining the *known-aborts* partial function on a per-node basis, the implementation of the piggyback algorithm in the current Argus prototype follows this strategy.) In describing the algorithm, we have tried to focus on the behavior necessary for correctness and to avoid constraining an implementation any more than necessary.

Notice also that the piggyback database does not put any upper limit on what goes into the *known-aborts* component. For example, it is permissible for *known-aborts*(π) to contain a transaction that has not aborted. This might cause nonorphans to block but will otherwise not result in incorrect behavior. It would be easy (and intuitively appealing) to add a requirement that *known-aborts*(π) only includes aborted transactions, but this is not necessary to prove that the algorithm prevents all orphans from seeing inconsistent views. To prove other properties, such as that the algorithm only detects real orphans, we would need to add additional requirements such as the one just mentioned. We will not attempt to state or prove such properties in this chapter; the property just described is a special case of more general liveness properties, which are an appropriate subject of further research.

Finally, while the piggyback database is distinguished from the filtered database by maintaining information about **ABORT** actions on a more local basis, we have kept the state component *s.history*, which maintains global knowledge of the past behavior of the system. A practical implementation of this algorithm would maintain less voluminous history information in a distributed fashion. Examination of the stronger precondition imposed by the piggyback database on any action π reveals that *s.history* is used to determine the events ϕ that directly affect π, and when π is a **REQUEST_COMMIT**(T, v) action for an access T to object X, to determine the events that precede π at X. The details of efficient maintenance of sufficient history information are dependent on the particular generic database and distribution scheme and are not addressed further in this chapter.

EXAMPLE 11.5.1   Explicit Description of Piggyback Database

The definition given above for the steps of the piggyback system uses the *directly-GS-affects* relation. Here, we describe the steps of the piggyback system explicitly, in terms of the various cases in the definition of *directly-GS-affects*. Namely, a triple (s', π, s) is a step of the piggyback database if and only if the following conditions hold.

1. $(s'.basic\text{-}state, \pi, s.basic\text{-}state)$ is a step of the generic database.

2. $s.history = s'.history\pi$ if π is a generic action, otherwise $s.history = s'.history$.

3. If $\phi \neq \pi$, then $s.known\text{-}aborts(\phi) = s'.known\text{-}aborts(\phi)$.

4. If π is a **REQUEST_CREATE**(T) action, then $s'.known\text{-}aborts(\phi) \subseteq s.known\text{-}aborts(\pi)$ for all ϕ in $s'.history$ such that $transaction(\phi) = parent(T)$.

5. If π is a **REQUEST_COMMIT**(T, v) action, where T is a non-access transaction name, then $s'.known\text{-}aborts(\phi) \subseteq s.known\text{-}aborts(\pi)$ for all ϕ in $s'.history$ such that $transaction(\phi) = T$.

6. If π is a **REQUEST_COMMIT**(T, v) action, where T is an access transaction name, then $s'.known\text{-}aborts(\phi) \subseteq s.known\text{-}aborts(\pi)$ for all ϕ in $s'.history$ such that $object(\phi) = object(T)$.

7. If π is a **CREATE**(T) action, then $s'.known\text{-}aborts(\phi) \subseteq s.known\text{-}aborts(\pi)$ for all **REQUEST_CREATE**(T) events ϕ in $s'.history$.

8. If π is a **COMMIT**(T) action, then $s'.known\text{-}aborts(\phi) \subseteq s.known\text{-}aborts(\pi)$ for all **REQUEST_COMMIT**(T, v) events ϕ in $s'.history$.

9. If π is an **ABORT**(T) action, then $s'.known\text{-}aborts(\phi) \subseteq s.known\text{-}aborts(\pi)$ for all **REQUEST_CREATE**(T) events ϕ in $s'.history$.

10. If π is a **REPORT_COMMIT**(T,v) action, then $s'.known\text{-}aborts(\phi) \subseteq s.known\text{-}aborts(\pi)$ for all **COMMIT**(T) events ϕ in $s'.history$.

11. If π is a **REPORT_ABORT**(T) action, then $s'.known\text{-}aborts(\phi) \subseteq s.known\text{-}aborts(\pi)$ for all **ABORT**(T) events ϕ in $s'.history$, and T in $s.known\text{-}aborts(\pi)$.

12. If π is an **INFORM_COMMIT_AT**(X)**OF**(T) action, then $s'.known\text{-}aborts(\phi) \subseteq s.known\text{-}aborts(\pi)$ for all **COMMIT**(T) events ϕ in $s'.history$.

13. If π is an **INFORM_ABORT_AT**(X)**OF**(T) action, then $s'.known\text{-}aborts(\phi) \subseteq s.known\text{-}aborts(\pi)$ for all **ABORT**(T) events ϕ in $s'.history$, and T in $s.known\text{-}aborts(\pi)$.

14. If π is a **REQUEST_COMMIT**(T, v) action for an access T to object X, then there is no ancestor of T in $s'.known\text{-}aborts(\phi)$, for any event ϕ of object X in $s'.history$.

The *known-aborts* set for a **REQUEST_CREATE**(T) action is obtained from the *known-aborts* sets for all preceding events at *parent*(T). Since **REQUEST_CREATE**(T) is generated by *parent*(T), the *known-aborts* set for it can easily be computed with information available locally at *parent*(T) when the **REQUEST_CREATE**(T) action occurs. A similar situation arises with **REQUEST_COMMIT** actions, which are outputs of transactions and objects. The other actions, which are outputs of the generic controller, are directly affected by exactly one preceding event each. Thus, the *known-aborts* set for one of these actions can easily be computed from the *known-aborts* set for the single event that precedes it. For instance, the *known-aborts* set for a **CREATE**(T) event can be obtained directly from the *known-aborts* set for the preceding **REQUEST_CREATE**(T) event. If the two events occur at the same site in a network, this information would be available locally; if they occur at different sites, it could be sent in the message used to transmit the **REQUEST_CREATE** event to the site that performs the **CREATE** event.

11.5.2 The Piggyback System

The **piggyback system** is the composition of transaction automata and the piggyback database. Executions, schedules, and behaviors of the piggyback system are called **piggyback executions**, **piggyback schedules**, and **piggyback behaviors**, respectively.

LEMMA 11.8 *The piggyback system implements the generic system.*

LEMMA 11.9 *Let β be a finite piggyback behavior that can lead the piggyback database to state s. Then $s.known\text{-}aborts(\pi)$ is defined if and only if π is an event in β.*

The following lemma says that each *known-aborts* set is defined at most once during a piggyback execution.

LEMMA 11.10 *Let $\beta'\beta$ be a finite piggyback schedule, where β' can lead the piggyback database to state s' and (s', β, s) is an extended step of the piggyback database. If $s'.known\text{-}aborts(\pi)$ is defined, then $s'.known\text{-}aborts(\pi) = s.known\text{-}aborts(\pi)$.*

The next lemma says that the *known-aborts* set for an event π includes the *known-aborts* sets for each event that directly affects π, and that the *known-aborts* set for π includes T if π is directly affected by an **ABORT**(T) event.

LEMMA 11.11 *Let β be a finite piggyback behavior that can lead the piggyback database to state s.*

1. *If ϕ and π are events in β such that ϕ directly affects π in β, then $s.known\text{-}aborts(\phi) \subseteq s.known\text{-}aborts(\pi)$.*

2. *If π is directly affected by an **ABORT**(T) event in β, then $T \in s.known\text{-}aborts(\pi)$.*

PROOF   Immediate by the definition of the piggyback database steps and Lemmas 11.9 and 11.10. $\square$

The next lemma is the key to the proof of correctness for the piggyback system: it says that the *known-aborts* set for an event π includes all transactions T such that an **ABORT**(T) event affects π. In other words, the piggyback database propagates enough information about aborts so that every event π "knows about" (stores in $s.known\text{-}aborts(\pi)$) every abort that affects it.

LEMMA 11.12 *Let β be a finite piggyback behavior that can lead the piggyback database to state s. If ϕ and π are events in β such that ϕ affects π in β and ϕ is an* **ABORT***(T) event, then $T \in s.known\text{-}aborts(\pi)$.*

PROOF   The proof proceeds by induction on the length of the chain in the directly affects relation by which ϕ affects π in β. If the length of the chain is 1, then ϕ directly affects π in β. Then Lemma 11.11 implies that $T \in s.known\text{-}aborts(\pi)$.

Now suppose that the length of the chain is $k + 1$, where $k \geq 1$. Then there is an event ψ in β such that ϕ affects ψ in β by a chain of length at most k and ψ directly affects π in β. By inductive hypothesis, $T \in s.known\text{-}aborts(\psi)$. Lemma 11.11 implies that $s.known\text{-}aborts(\psi) \subseteq s.known\text{-}aborts(\pi)$, so that $T \in s.known\text{-}aborts(\pi)$.   □

11.5.3 Simulation of the Generic System by the Piggyback System

The following lemma shows that the information in *known-aborts*, combined with the precondition on **REQUEST_COMMIT** actions for accesses, is enough to ensure that the piggyback system implements the filtered system.

LEMMA 11.13 *The piggyback system implements the filtered system.*

PROOF   We define a mapping f that assigns to each state s of the piggyback system the singleton set $f(s)$ consisting of the state of the filtered system that is the same except for the omission of the $s.known\text{-}aborts$ component of the piggyback database state. We must show that f is a possibilities mapping. Condition 1 is easy to check. For Condition 2, suppose that s' is a reachable state of the piggyback system, $t' \in f(s')$ is a reachable state of the filtered system, and (s', π, s) is a step of the piggyback system. The only interesting case to check is when $\pi = $ **REQUEST_COMMIT**(T, v), where T is an access to an object X. In this case, we claim that (t', π, t) is a step of the filtered system, where t is the single element of $f(s)$.

To show that (t', π, t) is a step of the filtered system, we must show the three conditions defining these steps. The first two are immediate from the definition of the steps of the piggyback database. To see the third, suppose that T' is an ancestor of T. We must show that no **ABORT**(T') event affects an event of object X in $t'.history$. Suppose the contrary, that an **ABORT**(T') event ϕ affects an event ψ of object X in $t'.history$. Then ϕ also affects ψ in $s'.history$. By Lemma 11.12, $T' \in s.known\text{-}aborts(\psi)$. But this violates the precondition for π in the piggyback database. Therefore, π is enabled in t', which suffices. $\square$

The following theorem shows that piggyback systems, like filtered systems, ensure that every non-access transaction gets a view it could get in an execution in which it is not an orphan.

THEOREM   11.14 *Let β be a piggyback behavior and let T be a transaction name. Then there exists a generic behavior γ such that T is not an orphan in γ and $\gamma|T = \beta|T$.*

PROOF   Immediate by Lemma 11.13 and Theorem 11.6. $\square$

As for the filtered system, we obtain an important corollary about atomicity.

COROLLARY   11.15 *If the generic system is atomic for nonorphans, then the piggyback system is atomic for all transaction names.*

11.6   Strictly   Filtered   Systems

The orphan management algorithm described by Herlihy and McKendry in [51] actually ensures a stronger property than does the piggyback algorithm. It ensures that **REQUEST_COMMIT** *can never occur* for an orphan access, whereas the piggyback algorithm merely ensures that no such **REQUEST_COMMIT** can occur if the access can "observe" that it is an orphan. In this section we define the "strictly filtered database," which allows a **REQUEST_COMMIT** to occur for an access only if no ancestor has aborted. (Compare this to the filtered database, which allows an access to **REQUEST_COMMIT** if an ancestor has aborted as long as the access is not affected by the abort.) We then define the strictly filtered system, which is composed of transaction automata and the strictly filtered database, and show that the strictly filtered system implements the filtered system. In the next section we will describe formally the clock algorithm of Herlihy and McKendry [51] and show that it implements the strictly filtered system.

11.6.1   The   Strictly   Filtered   Database

The strictly filtered database is similar to the filtered database; it has the same actions and the same states. A triple (s', π, s) is a step of the strictly filtered database if and only if the following conditions hold.

1. $(s'.basic\text{-}state, \pi, s.basic\text{-}state)$ is a step of the generic database.

2. $s.history = s'.history\pi$ if π is a generic action, otherwise $s.history = s'.history$.

3. If $\pi = \textbf{REQUEST\_COMMIT}(T, v)$ where T is an access and T' is an ancestor of T, then no $\textbf{ABORT}(T')$ event occurs in $s'.history$.

Thus, at the point where the **REQUEST_COMMIT** of an access is about to occur, an explicit test is performed to verify that there is no preceding abort of any ancestor of the access.

11.6.2 The Strictly Filtered System

The **strictly filtered system** is the composition of transaction automata and the strictly filtered database. Executions, schedules, and behaviors of the strictly filtered system are **strictly filtered executions**, **schedules**, and **behaviors**, respectively.

LEMMA 11.16 *The strictly filtered system implements the generic system.*

11.6.3 Simulation of the Generic System by the Strictly Filtered System

LEMMA 11.17 *The strictly filtered system implements the filtered system.*

PROOF We define a mapping f that assigns to each state s of the strictly filtered system the singleton set $f(s)$ that consists of the same state. We must show that f is a possibilities mapping. Condition 1 is easy to check. For Condition 2, suppose that s' is a reachable state of the strictly filtered system, $t' \in f(s')$ is a reachable state of the filtered system, and (s', π, s) is a step of the strictly filtered system. As before, the only interesting case to check is when $\pi = \textbf{REQUEST\_COMMIT}(T, v)$, where T is an access to an object X. In this case, we claim that (t', π, t) is a step of the filtered system, where t is the unique element of $f(s)$.

To show that (t', π, t) is a step of the filtered system, we must show the three conditions defining these steps. The first two are immediate from the definition of the steps of the strictly filtered database. To see the third, suppose that T' is an ancestor of T. We must show that no $\textbf{ABORT}(T')$ event affects an event of object X in $t'.history$. But $t'.history = s'.history$, and by the precondition for π in the strictly filtered database, no $\textbf{ABORT}(T')$ event occurs in $s'.history$. Therefore, no $\textbf{ABORT}(T')$ event affects an event of object X in $t'.history$. Thus, π is enabled in t', which suffices. $\qquad\qquad\square$

Strictly filtered systems, like filtered systems and piggyback systems, prevent orphans from discovering that they are orphans.

THEOREM 11.18 *Let β be a strictly filtered behavior and let T be a transaction name. Then there exists a generic behavior γ such that T is not an orphan in γ and $\gamma|T = \beta|T$.*

PROOF   Immediate by Lemma 11.17 and Theorem 11.6.   □

COROLLARY 11.19 *If the generic system is atomic for nonorphans, then the strictly filtered system is atomic for all transaction names.*

11.7 Clock Systems

In this section we describe the clock algorithm formally. We do this by defining the "clock database", which uses a global clock to ensure that transactions do not abort until all their descendant accesses have stopped running. We then define the clock system, which is composed of transaction automata and the clock database. Finally, we show that the clock system implements the strictly filtered system and thus simulates the generic system in the same way as the previously mentioned systems do.

11.7.1 The Clock Database

The clock database maintains a *quiesce time* for each access transaction and a *release time* for every transaction. A **REQUEST_COMMIT** event is only permitted to occur for an access T provided that T's quiesce time has not been reached. Release times are chosen so that once a transaction's release time is reached, all its descendant accesses have quiesced. A transaction is allowed to abort only if its release time has passed. This ensures that, after a transaction aborts, none of its descendant accesses will request to commit.

If quiesce and release times are fixed in advance, some transactions may be forced to abort unnecessarily as their quiesce times expire, and aborts may need to be delayed until release times are reached. It is possible to obtain extra flexibility by providing actions in the clock database for adjusting quiesce and release times.

The action signature of the clock database is the same as that of the generic database, except that the clock database has three additional kinds of internal actions. The new actions are:

Internal:
TICK
ADJUST_QUIESCE(T), T an access
ADJUST_RELEASE(T), T any transaction

The **TICK** action advances the clock, while the two **ADJUST** actions adjust quiesce and release times. By adjusting the quiesce time for a transaction to be later than its current value, we can extend the time during which a transaction is allowed to run. Similarly, by adjusting the release time for a transaction to be earlier than its current value, we can allow a transaction to abort without waiting as long as would otherwise be necessary.

The state of the clock database consists of components *basic-state*, *aborted*, *clock*, *quiesce*, and *release*. Here, *basic-state* is a state of the generic database, initialized at a start state of the generic database. The component *aborted* is a set of transactions, initially empty. The component *clock* is a real number, initialized arbitrarily. The component *quiesce* is a function from access transaction names to real numbers, and the component *release* is a function from all transaction names to real numbers. The initial values of quiesce and release are arbitrary, subject to the following condition: for all transaction names T and T', where T is an access and T' is an ancestor of T, $quiesce(T) \leq release(T')$.

A triple (s', π, s) is a step of the clock database if and only if the following conditions hold.

1. If π is an action of the generic system, then $(s'.basic\text{-}state, \pi, s.basic\text{-}state)$ is a step of the generic database.

2. If π is a **TICK**, **ADJUST_QUIESCE**, or **ADJUST_RELEASE** action, then $s.basic\text{-}state = s'.basic\text{-}state$.

3. If $\pi = \textbf{ABORT}(T)$, then

    (a) $s.aborted = s'.aborted \cup T$.

    (b) $s'.release(T) \leq s'.clock$.

4. If π is not an **ABORT** action, then $s.aborted = s'.aborted$.

5. If $\pi = \textbf{REQUEST\_COMMIT}(T, v)$ where T is an access, then $s'.clock < s'.quiesce(T)$.

6. If $\pi = \textbf{TICK}$, then $s'.clock < s.clock$.

7. If π is not a **TICK** action, then $s.clock = s'.clock$.

8. If $\pi = \textbf{ADJUST\_RELEASE}(T)$, then

    (a) if $T \in s'.aborted$, then $s.release(T) \leq s'.clock$,

    (b) $s'.quiesce(T') \leq s.release(T)$ for all $T' \in descendants(T) \cap accesses$, and

    (c) $s.release(T') = s'.release(T')$ for all $T' \neq T$.

9. If π is not an **ADJUST_RELEASE** action, then $s.release = s'.release$.

1 0 . If $\pi = $ **ADJUST_QUIESCE**(T), then

    (a) $s.quiesce(T) \leq s'.release(T')$ for all $T' \in ancestors(T)$, and

    (b) $s.quiesce(T') = s'.quiesce(T')$ for all $T' \neq T$.

1 1 . If π is not an **ADJUST_QUIESCE** action, then $s.quiesce = s'.quiesce$.

LEMMA 11.20 *Let β be a finite schedule of the clock database that can lead the clock database to state s.*

    1 . *If $T \in s.aborted$, then $s.release(T) \leq s.clock$.*

    2 . *For all accesses T and all ancestors T' of T, $s.quiesce(T) \leq s.release(T')$.*

PROOF   Straightforward by induction. $\square$

11.7.2 The Clock System

The **clock system** is the composition of transaction automata and the clock database. External actions of the clock system are called **clock actions**. Executions, schedules, and behaviors of a clock system are called **clock executions**, **clock schedules**, and **clock behaviors**.

LEMMA 11.21 *The clock system implements the generic system.*

11.7.3 Simulation of the Generic System by the Clock System

LEMMA 11.22 *The clock system implements the strictly filtered system.*

PROOF   We define a mapping f that assigns to each state s of the clock system the set $f(s)$ of states t of the strictly filtered system such that $t.basic\text{-}state = s.basic\text{-}state$ and $t.history$ is a sequence of generic actions in which the set of transaction names T for which **ABORT**(T) occurs in $t.history$ is exactly $s.aborted$. We must show that f is a possibilities mapping. Condition 1 is easy to check. For Condition 2, suppose that s' is a reachable state of the clock system, $t' \in f(s')$ is a reachable state of the strictly filtered system, and (s', π, s) is a step of the clock system.

    There are two interesting cases to check: where $\pi = $ **ABORT**(T) and where $\pi = $ **REQUEST_COMMIT**(T, v) for an access T. In either case, we claim that (t', π, t) is a step of the strictly filtered system, where t is the state of the strictly filtered system in which $t.basic\text{-}state = s.basic\text{-}state$ and $t.history = t'.history\pi$, and we also claim that $t \in f(s)$.

If $\pi = \textbf{ABORT}(T)$, it is easy to see that (t', π, t) is a step of the strictly filtered system. To show that $t \in f(s)$, note that since $t' \in f(s')$, the set of transaction names U for which $\textbf{ABORT}(U)$ occurs in $t'.history$ is exactly $s'.aborted$. Then the set of transaction names with aborts in $t.history$ is exactly $s'.aborted \cup T$, which is equal to $s.aborted$. Thus, $t \in f(s)$.

If $\pi = \textbf{REQUEST\_COMMIT}(T, v)$, where T is an access, then it is easy to see the first three conditions of the definition of strictly filtered database steps. For the fourth condition, we must show that if T' is an ancestor of T, then no $\textbf{ABORT}(T')$ event occurs in $t'.history$. So suppose the contrary, that T' is an ancestor of T and $\textbf{ABORT}(T')$ occurs in $t'.history$. Since $t' \in f(s')$, we have $T' \in s'.aborted$. Since π is enabled in s', $s'.clock < s'.quiesce(T)$. Lemma 11.20 implies that $s'.release(T') \leq s'.clock$ and also that $s'.quiesce(T) \leq s'.release(T')$. Thus, $s'.quiesce(T) \leq s'.clock$, a contradiction. It follows that (t', π, t) is a step of the strictly filtered system.

Since $t' \in f(s')$, the set of transaction names U for which $\textbf{ABORT}(U)$ occurs in $t'.history$ is exactly $s'.aborted$. Then the set of transaction names with aborts in $t.history$ is exactly $s'.aborted = s.aborted$. Thus, $t \in f(s)$. □

THEOREM 11.23 *Let β be a clock behavior and let T be a transaction name. Then there exists a generic behavior γ such that T is not an orphan in γ and $\gamma|T = \beta|T$.*

PROOF By Lemma 11.22 and Theorem 11.18. □

COROLLARY 11.24 *If the generic system is atomic for nonorphans, then the clock system is atomic for all transaction names.*

11.8 Discussion

This chapter shows how different aspects of transaction management can be modeled separately. This allows proofs of correctness to be divided into simpler pieces. We show how orphans can be detected and eliminated by algorithms that are not influenced by the choice of concurrency control mechanism used in each object. In the Argus nested transaction system, orphans can be produced both by explicit aborts and by node crashes. Interesting algorithms have also been developed for detecting and eliminating orphans arising from crashes. These algorithms seem more complicated than the algorithms for handling aborts. An open question is whether the known algorithms for handling crash orphans can be analyzed using techniques similar to those in this chapter.

1 1 . 9   B i b l i o g r a p h i c   N o t e s

Early work on the orphan management problem appears in [93], which describes algorithms for detecting and eliminating orphans that arise because of node crashes. Nelson's work did not assume an underlying transaction mechanism, so it is difficult in his setting to assign simple semantics to abandoned computations. In a nested transaction system, abandoned computation does not have any permanent effect on the state of the data.

The problem of orphans in Argus is described by Liskov *et al.* [77] and Walker [112], where the piggyback algorithm of this chapter is presented. The clock algorithm of this chapter is from Herlihy and McKendry [51]. These papers deal with orphans from explicit aborts and node crashes.

The piggyback algorithm described in this chapter needs further optimization to be practical, since the *known-aborts* set grows without bound. Two approaches are suggested in [77, 112], one based on timeouts to delete old information and the other based on using a logically centralized server to store the information. These two algorithms have been implemented as part of the prototype Argus implementation. Preliminary performance experiments [85, 94] indicate that maintaining the *known-aborts* information imposes substantial overhead. Unfortunately, comparable experiments have not been done for the clock algorithm.

Earlier work on verifying the Argus orphan management algorithm appears in [39]. The presentation in that paper is somewhat more complex than the one presented in this chapter, mainly because the treatments of concurrency control and orphan management are intermingled, whereas here we separate the two.

A more general treatment of the results of this chapter, including extensions to other types of systems besides generic systems (such as the pseudotime systems of Chapter 7), appears in [46].

1 1 . 1 0   E x e r c i s e s

1. Carry out a development similar to the one in this chapter for pseudotime systems rather than generic systems. That is, define a relation *PS-affects* to describe the dependencies among operations in a pseudotime database. Using this relation, show how to transform an arbitrary pseudotime system into a filtered system, a piggyback system, a strictly filtered system and a clock system, and state and prove the appropriate simulation results for these systems.

2. Carry out a development similar to the one in this chapter for hybrid systems rather than generic systems.

3. The clock algorithm described in this chapter uses a single physical clock to

detect and eliminate orphans. Adapt the algorithm to work with distributed, loosely synchronized physical clocks, or with logical clocks (e.g., see [65]). Describe and analyze the adapted algorithms in a manner similar to that used for the piggyback algorithm.

4. (Research) Carry out a formal treatment of the algorithms in [51, 77] designed for handling orphans produced by node crashes that lose volatile information. This will involve, among other things, establishing a model for nodes that includes stable and volatile memory components, where the stable component gets reset to a default state when a node crash occurs. It would be especially desirable to find a general modular presentation, allowing these crash-orphan algorithms to be understood independently of concurrency control protocols and abort-orphan algorithms.

REPLICATION

12.1 Introduction

In distributed database systems, data are often *replicated* in order to improve availability, reliability and performance. Whenever replication is used, a *replication algorithm* is required in order to ensure that replication is transparent to the user programs. In understanding replication algorithms, it is convenient to think of each *logical object* as being implemented by a collection of *replicas* and *logical access programs*. The replicas retain state information, and the collective state of the replicas defines the current state of the logical object. The user programs invoke logical access programs in order to read or write the logical object; the logical accesses accomplish this by accessing some subset of the replicas. Example 3.7.1 described a simple example of a replication algorithm.

Quorum Consensus: One of the best known replication algorithms is the *quorum consensus* algorithm. In the quorum consensus algorithm, each replica is assigned a certain number of *votes* and keeps as part of its state a data *value* with an associated *version number*. Each logical object X has an associated *configuration* consisting of two integers, called *read-quorum* and *write-quorum*. If k is the total number of votes assigned to replicas of X, then the configuration for X is constrained so that *read-quorum* + *write-quorum* > *k*. To read X, a logical access program collects the version numbers and values from enough replicas so that it has at least *read-quorum* votes; then it returns the value associated with the highest version number. To write X, a logical access program first collects the version numbers from enough replicas so that it has at least *read-quorum* votes; then it writes its value with a higher version number to a collection of replicas with at least *write-quorum* votes. This method generalizes both the read-one/write-all algorithm of Example 3.7.1 and the simple strategy of reading and writing a majority of the replicas.

In this chapter, we describe quorum consensus replication algorithms. We use a replication strategy that is slightly more general than the one described above: a configuration consists of a set of read quorums and a set of write quorums. Each quorum is a set of replica names; thus, the voting strategy above corresponds to the special case where any set of replicas is a read quorum if and only if the total votes among its members exceeds the threshold *read-quorum*. To read a logical object, a logical access program accesses all the replicas in some read quorum and chooses the value with the highest version number. To write a logical object, a logical access program first discovers the highest version number written so far by accessing all the replicas in some read quorum; then the logical access increments that version number by one and writes the new value and version number to all the replicas in some write quorum. In this generalization, the constraint on the sum of the *read-quorum* and *write-quorum* numbers becomes that every read quorum must have a nonempty intersection with every write quorum. This ensures that each read of the logical object reads at least one of the replicas written by the most recent logical write.

Two Algorithms: Two principal algorithms are described in this chapter. The first is the simpler of the two, and is based on a *fixed* configuration. The second includes a mechanism for changing the configuration dynamically. This capability, known as *reconfiguration*, is useful for coping with site or link failures.

As are the rest of the algorithms in this book, the quorum consensus algorithms are presented in the setting of nested transactions. Thus, users are permitted to invoke accesses to logical objects using arbitrary nested transactions. However, not only is transaction nesting useful for describing user programs, but it also provides a natural way to write and understand the replication algorithms themselves. This is because the logical access programs may be written as subtransactions of the user transactions, and the different tasks performed by a logical access may be written as subtransactions of the logical access transactions.

Modularity of Reasoning: The presentation separates the treatment of replication entirely from the treatment of concurrency control and recovery. That is, we consider the replication issues solely in the context of serial systems. We prove that a system that includes the new replication algorithm and that is serial at the level of the individual data copies looks the same, to the user transactions, as a system that is serial at the level of the logical objects. The fact that both systems involved in this simulation are serial systems helps to simplify the reasoning.

Of course, systems that are truly serial at the level of the data copies are of little practical interest. However, previous chapters of this book have described many interesting algorithms that guarantee that a system looks to the user like a serial system. Combining any of these algorithms (defined for a system having the replicas among its objects) with either of the replication algorithms we present yields a combined algorithm that appears both serial and unreplicated. In fact, our results show that the replication algorithm can be combined with *any* algorithm that guarantees atomicity at the copy level, to yield a system that is atomic at the logical object level.

Chapter Outline: The remainder of the chapter is organized as follows. In Section 12.2, we give a formal definition of configurations. In Section 12.3, we describe the algorithm for a fixed configuration. In Section 12.4, we give the reconfigurable algorithm. In Section 12.5, we show that the correctness of interesting concurrent replicated systems follows directly from these results.

12.2 Configurations

We begin with a definition that will be used throughout this chapter. If S is an arbitrary set, we define a *configuration* c of S to be any pair, $(c.read, c.write)$, where each of $c.read$ and $c.write$ is a nonempty collection of subsets of S, and where every element of $c.read$ has a nonempty intersection with every element of $c.write$. (We will sometimes refer to $c.read$ and $c.write$ as the sets of *read quorums* and *write quorums*, respectively, of configuration c.) We write $configs(S)$ for the set of all configurations of S.

EXAMPLE 12.2.1 Three Replicas

If the set S consists of three elements X, Y, and Z, then one configuration c has $c.read = \{\{X\}, \{Y\}, \{Z\}\}$ and $c.write = \{\{X, Y, Z\}\}$. This configuration corresponds to the read-one/write-all replication strategy. Another configuration has $c.read = \{\{X, Y\}, \{X, Z\}, \{Y, Z\}\}$ and $c.write = \{\{X, Y\}, \{X, Z\}, \{Y, Z\}\}$, corresponding to a read-majority/write-majority strategy.

12.3 Fixed Configuration Quorum Consensus

In this section, we present and prove the correctness of a fixed configuration quorum consensus algorithm. For simplicity, we carry out the formal development in this chapter for the replication of a single object, which we call X. Repeated use of the ideas in this chapter will allow treatment of an arbitrary finite number of objects.

First, Section 12.3.1 defines system $\mathcal{A}$, a serial system that has X as one of its object names. In system $\mathcal{A}$, the object automaton associated with X is a read/write serial object automaton $S(X)$, representing the logical object to be replicated. System $\mathcal{A}$ is used in order to define system correctness.

Then Section 12.3.2 defines the replicated serial system $\mathcal{B}$. System $\mathcal{B}$ is identical to $\mathcal{A}$ except that logical object $S(X)$ is implemented as a collection, $S(Y), Y \in \mathcal{Y}$, of serial read/write objects that we call *replica objects*, and each logical read (or write) of X is implemented as a subtransaction that performs multiple read and write accesses to some subset of the replicas according to the quorum consensus algorithm.

Section 12.3.3 shows that the algorithm is correct by demonstrating a relationship between $\mathcal{B}$ and $\mathcal{A}$; this proof is easy because both systems are serial.

12.3.1 System $\mathcal{A}$, the Unreplicated Serial System

We begin by defining the unreplicated serial system $\mathcal{A}$. System $\mathcal{A}$ is defined to be an arbitrary serial system having a distinguished object name X, and in which the object automaton $S(X)$ associated with X is a read/write serial object with domain D and initial value d_0, as defined in Example 3.5.3. This is the same type of system used in Example 3.7.1; the simple replicated data algorithm described in that example can be thought of as a special case of the ones considered in this chapter, and we suggest you review that example at this point.

We define la_r and la_w to be the sets whose elements are the respective names of the read and write accesses to X, in $\mathcal{A}$, and define $la = la_r \cup la_w$. (Here, la stands for "logical access".)

Since each transaction name $T \in la_r$ is a read access to $S(X)$, the definition of a read/write serial object says that $kind(T) = read$ for each such T. Also, each transaction name $T \in la_w$ has $kind(T) = write$, as well as an associated value, $data(T) \in D$.

12.3.2 System $\mathcal{B}$, the Fixed Configuration Quorum Consensus Algorithm

In this subsection, we describe system $\mathcal{B}$, which represents the quorum consensus algorithm with a fixed configuration.

System $\mathcal{B}$ is a serial system in which object $S(\mathrm{X})$ is replicated; that is, it is implemented as several serial objects (replicas), $S(\mathrm{Y}), \mathrm{Y} \in \mathcal{Y}$, rather than just one. The accesses to X are implemented as subtransaction automata called *logical access automata* (LA's). The LA's use the quorum consensus algorithm to manage the replicas.

System $\mathcal{B}$ generalizes the strategy in Example 3.7.1, in which logical reads need only access a single replica, but logical writes must access all replicas. Here, we allow arbitrary quorums, as long as each read quorum has a nonempty intersection with every write quorum. In order to read the logical object, a read-LA accesses all the replicas in some read quorum, while in order to write the logical object, a write-LA writes to all the replicas in some write quorum. The intersection property guarantees that each read-LA receives at least one copy of the latest logical data value.

Note that, in the algorithm of Example 3.7.1, it is sufficient for each replica to maintain and return data values only, since there is only one possible data value that might be returned to any particular read-LA. However, in the present case, reads of different replicas could return different data values. A mechanism is required to identify, among several different data values, which is the most up-to-date. Thus, each replica in the quorum consensus algorithm maintains a nonnegative integer *version-number* in addition to its data value. Successive write-LA's use successively larger version numbers, and a read-LA selects the data value associated with the largest version number it receives. This strategy requires each write-LA to learn what version number it is supposed to write, which in turn requires it to learn the largest version number previously used. In order to learn this number, each write-LA first does a preliminary read of a read quorum of the replicas.

Since both the read-LA and the write-LA programs must perform reads of a read quorum of the replicas, it is helpful to have a subtransaction that performs such a read. This subroutine can be invoked by a read-LA to perform nearly all of its work, and can also be invoked by a write-LA to perform its preliminary read. We can describe such a subroutine in the nested transaction framework by introducing *two* extra levels of nesting (rather than just one, as in Example 3.7.1). Thus, read-LA and write-LA transactions will have children known as *read-coordinator* transactions, which will be responsible for reading from a read quorum of replicas. Write-LA transactions will also have children known as *write-coordinator* transactions, which will be responsible for writing to a write quorum of replicas. Read-coordinators and write-coordinators will, in turn, have children that are individual read and write accesses to the replicas.

We begin by defining the type of $\mathcal{B}$, and then give the new automata that appear in $\mathcal{B}$ but not in $\mathcal{A}$. The new automata are the replica objects, and the coordinator and LA transaction automata. We define these automata "bottom up," starting with the replicas and the configuration automata.

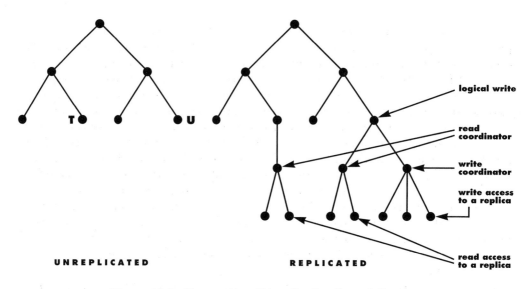

Figure 12.1: Transaction Trees for Replicated Systems

System Type

The type of system $\mathcal{B}$ is defined to be the same as that of $\mathcal{A}$, with the following modifications. First, the object name X is now replaced by a new set of object names $\mathcal{Y}$, representing the replicas. (The replicas will store both a value and a version number.) There are some new transaction names, co_r and co_w, representing read and write-coordinators, respectively, and acc_r and acc_w, which are the read and write accesses to the replicas, respectively. We let $co = co_r \cup co_w$ and $acc = acc_r \cup acc_w$.

The transaction names in la are accesses in $\mathcal{A}$, but in $\mathcal{B}$ they are not; each transaction name in la_r now has children that are in co_r, while each transaction name in la_w now has children in co_r and children in co_w. Also, each transaction name in co_r has children in acc_r, and each transaction name in co_w has children in acc_w. These are the only changes to the system type—for example, no transaction names other than those indicated are parents of the new transaction names. This is illustrated in Figure 12.1, which shows a transaction tree containing a read access T and a write access U, and also shows the extended transaction tree suitable once the object is replicated. The diagram only shows one coordinator of each type for each logical access; in general, there can be multiple coordinators.

In system $\mathcal{A}$, some information is associated with some of the transaction names; for example, each T in la (that is, each access to X) has $kind(T)$ indicating whether the access reads or writes, and write accesses have $data(T)$ indicating the value to be written. In $\mathcal{B}$, we keep all such associated information from $\mathcal{A}$ and add more information as follows. First, every transaction name $T \in co_w$ has an associated value $data(T) \in D$ and an associated version number $version\text{-}number(T) \in N$. These denote, respectively, the value for X and the associated version number to be written by the write-coordinator in the quorum consensus algorithm. Second, we associate some information with the accesses to the replicas. Namely, we assume that every transaction name $T \in acc_r$ has $kind(T) = read$ and that every transaction name $T \in acc_w$ has $kind(T) = write$ and $data(T) \in N \times D$, the version number and value to be written.[1]

Throughout the rest of this section, we let c denote a fixed configuration of $\mathcal{Y}$.

Replica Automata

A *replica automaton* is defined for each object name $Y \in \mathcal{Y}$. Each replica is a read/write serial object that keeps a version number and a value for X. More formally, the object automaton for each $Y \in \mathcal{Y}$ in system $\mathcal{B}$ is a read/write serial object for Y with domain $N \times D$ and initial value $(0, d_0)$. For $v \in N \times D$, we use the record notation $v.version\text{-}number$ and $v.value$ to refer to the components of v.

Coordinators

In this section, we define the coordinator automata in $\mathcal{B}$, the transaction automata, which are invoked by the LA's and access the replicas. We first define read-coordinators. The purpose of a read-coordinator is to determine the latest version number and value of X, on the basis of the data returned by the read accesses it invokes. A read-coordinator for transaction name $T \in co_r$ has state components *awake*, *value*, *version-number*, *requested*, *reported*, and *read*, where *awake* is a Boolean variable, initially *false*; *value* $\in D$, initially d_0; *version-number* $\in N$, initially 0; *requested* and *reported* are subsets of *children*(T), initially empty; and *read* is a subset of $\mathcal{Y}$, initially empty. The set of return values V_T is equal to $N \times D$.

The transition relation for read-coordinators is shown in Figure 12.2. Recall that c is a fixed configuration. This is used to determine when the coordinator has collected enough information to be sure of having seen the most recent value of X. A read-coordinator collects data from replicas for object names in $\mathcal{Y}$, and keeps track of the value from the replica with the highest version number seen so far. Whenever the read-coordinator reaches a state in which (1) some read quorum, according to c, is a subset of the replicas it has seen (i.e., those in $s'.read$) and (2) it has learned of

---

[1]The transaction names in acc_w name accesses to read/write objects. Hence, to agree with the definition in Example 3.5.3, the version number and data value are combined into a single *data* attribute.

CREATE(T)
  Effect:
    $s.awake = true$

REQUEST_CREATE(T')
  Precondition:
    $s'.awake = true$
    $T' \notin s'.requested$
  Effect:
    $s.requested = s'.requested \cup \{T'\}$

REPORT_COMMIT(T',v)
  Effect:
    $s.reported = s'.reported \cup \{T'\}$
    $s.read = s'.read \cup \{object(T')\}$
    if $v.version\text{-}number > s'.version\text{-}number$
    then $s.version\text{-}number = v.version\text{-}number$
      $s.value = v.value$

REPORT_ABORT(T')
  Effect:
    $s.reported = s'.reported \cup \{T'\}$

REQUEST_COMMIT(T, v)
  Precondition:
    $s'.awake = true$
    $s'.requested = s'.reported$
    $\mathcal{R} \in c.read$
    $\mathcal{R} \subseteq s'.read$
    $v = (s'.version\text{-}number, s'.value)$
  Effect:
    $s.awake = false$

Figure 12.2: Transition Relation for Read-Coordinators

the fates (i.e., commit or abort) of all of its requested child transactions, then the read-coordinator may request to commit and return its data.

We have written the read-coordinator with a high degree of nondeterminism. It may request any number of accesses to replicas, at any time while it is active. In practice, you would probably start at most one access to each replica at a time, and then request another one only after the failure of an earlier access to that replica. There is also a natural trade-off in practice between two methods of choosing which replicas to access at first: you could request initially only enough accesses to complete one read quorum, and then request others if these fail to commit in reasonable time, or else you could request accesses to all replicas concurrently. The first method minimizes communication cost in the best case (when all accesses complete successfully) and the second reduces latency in the bad case where some accesses fail. Each of these possibilities, and many others, could be modeled as an implementation of the automaton given here, obtained by restricting nondeterminism.

We next define write-coordinators. The purpose of a write-coordinator is to write a given value to a write quorum of replicas for object names in $\mathcal{Y}$. A write-coordinator for transaction name $T \in co_w$ has state components *awake*, *requested*, *reported*, and *written*, where *awake* is a Boolean variable, initially *false*; *requested* and *reported* are subsets of *children*(T), initially empty; and *written* is a subset of $\mathcal{Y}$, initially empty. The set of return values V_T is equal to $\{\text{"OK"}\}$.

The transition relation for a write-coordinator named $T \in co_w$ is shown in Fig-

CREATE(*T*)
   Effect:
      $s.awake = true$

REQUEST_CREATE(*T'*)
   Precondition:
      $s'.awake = true$
      $T' \notin s'.requested$
      $data(T') = (version\text{-}number(T), data(T))$
   Effect:
      $s.requested = s'.requested \cup \{T'\}$

REPORT_COMMIT(*T'*,*v*)
   Effect:
      $s.reported = s'.reported \cup \{T'\}$
      $s.written = s'.written \cup \{object(T')\}$

REPORT_ABORT(*T'*)
   Effect:
      $s.reported = s'.reported \cup \{T'\}$

REQUEST_COMMIT(*T*, *v*)
   Precondition:
      $s'.awake = true$
      $s'.requested = s'.reported$
      $W \in c.write$
      $W \subseteq s'.written$
      $v = \text{``OK''}$
   Effect:
      $s.awake = false$

Figure 12.3: Transition Relation for Write-Coordinators

ure 12.3. When created, a write-coordinator begins invoking write accesses to replicas for object names in $\mathcal{Y}$, overwriting the version numbers and values at the replicas with its own (*version-number*(*T*) and *data*(*T*), respectively). After writing to a write quorum, the write-coordinator may request to commit.

Logical Access Automata

Now we define logical access automata, beginning with read-LA's. The purpose of a read-LA for a transaction name $T \in la_r$ is to perform a logical read access to X. A read-LA has state components *awake*, *value*, *requested*, *reported*, and *value-read*, where *awake* and *value-read* are Boolean variables, initially *false*; *value* $\in D \cup \{nil\}$, initially *nil*; and *requested* and *reported* are subsets of *children*(*T*), initially empty. The set of return values V_T is equal to D.

The transition relation for read-LA's is shown in Figure 12.4. The read-LA invokes any number of read-coordinators. After receiving a **REPORT_COMMIT** from at least one of these coordinators, and receiving reports of the completion of all that were invoked, the read-LA may request to commit, returning the value component of the data produced by the first read-coordinator.

We next define write-LA's. The purpose of a write-LA for a transaction name in la_w is to perform a logical write access to X on behalf of a user transaction. A write-LA has state components *awake*, *value-read*, *value-written*, *version-number*, *requested*, and *reported*, where *awake*, *value-read*, and *value-written* are Booleans, initially *false*;

CREATE(T)
  Effect:
    $s.awake = true$

REQUEST_CREATE(T')
  Precondition:
    $s'.awake = true$
    $T' \notin s'.requested$
  Effect:
    $s.requested = s'.requested \cup \{T'\}$

REPORT_COMMIT(T',v)
  Effect:
    $s.reported = s'.reported \cup \{T'\}$
    if $s'.value\text{-}read = false$
    then $s.value = v.value$
        $s.value\text{-}read = true$

REPORT_ABORT(T')
  Effect:
    $s.reported = s'.reported \cup \{T'\}$

REQUEST_COMMIT(T, v)
  Precondition:
    $s'.awake = true$
    $s'.requested = s'.reported$
    $s'.value\text{-}read = true$
    $v = s'.value$
  Effect:
    $s.awake = false$

Figure 12.4: Transition Relation for Read LA's

version-number $\in N \cup \{nil\}$, initially *nil*; and *requested* and *reported* are subsets of *children*(T), initially empty. The set of return values V_T is equal to $\{$ "*OK*" $\}$.

The transition relation for write-LA's is shown in Figure 12.5. A write-LA invokes any number of read-coordinators. After receiving a **REPORT_COMMIT** from one of the read-coordinators, the write-LA remembers the version number returned. The write-LA then invokes any number of write-coordinators, using a version number one greater than that returned with the first **REPORT_COMMIT** of a read-coordinator, along with its particular data value. In order for the write-LA to request to commit, it must receive at least one **REPORT_COMMIT** of a write-coordinator.

12.3.3 Correctness Proof

In this section, we prove the correctness of the quorum consensus algorithm given above as system $\mathcal{B}$. That is, we show that $\mathcal{B}$ is indistinguishable from $\mathcal{A}$, to the transactions and objects the two systems have in common. We begin by stating some definitions that are useful for reasoning about the sequence of logical accesses in an execution of $\mathcal{B}$. In each definition, β is a sequence of actions of $\mathcal{B}$.

First, the *logical access sequence* of β, denoted *logical-sequence*(β), is defined to be the subsequence of β containing the **CREATE**(T) and **REQUEST_COMMIT**(T, v) events, where $T \in la$. That is, the logical access sequence is the sequence of requests and responses for the logical accesses to X.

Next, if β is finite, then *logical-value*(β) is defined to be either *data*(T) if **REQUEST-**

CREATE(T)
    Effect:
        $s.awake = true$

REQUEST_CREATE(T'), $T' \in co_r$
    Precondition:
        $s'.awake = true$
        $T' \notin s'.requested$
    Effect:
        $s.requested = s'.requested \cup \{T'\}$

REPORT_COMMIT(T',v), $T' \in co_r$
    Effect:
        $s.reported = s'.reported \cup \{T'\}$
        if $s'.value\text{-}read = false$
        then $s.version\text{-}number = v.version\text{-}number$
            $s.value\text{-}read = true$

REQUEST_CREATE(T'), $T' \in co_w$
    Precondition:
        $s'.awake = true$
        $s'.value\text{-}read = true$
        $data(T') = data(T)$
        $version\text{-}number(T') = s'.version\text{-}number + 1$
        $T' \notin s'.requested$
    Effect:
        $s.requested = s'.requested \cup \{T'\}$

REPORT_COMMIT(T',v), $T' \in co_w$
    Effect:
        $s.reported = s'.reported \cup \{T'\}$
        $s'.value\text{-}written = true$

REPORT_ABORT(T')
    Effect:
        $s.reported = s'.reported \cup \{T'\}$

REQUEST_COMMIT(T, v)
    Precondition:
        $s'.awake = true$
        $s'.requested = s'.reported$
        $s'.value\text{-}written = true$
        $v = \text{``}OK\text{''}$
    Effect:
        $s.awake = false$

Figure 12.5: Transition Relation for Write LA's

_COMMIT(T, v) is the last **REQUEST_COMMIT** event for a transaction name in la_w that occurs in *logical-sequence*(β), or d_0 if no such **REQUEST_COMMIT** event occurs in *logical-sequence*(β). In other words, the logical value is the value of the last logical write (or the initial value of the logical object if no such write occurs).

Finally, if β is finite, then *current-vn*(β) is defined to be the highest *version-number* among the states of all replica automata in the global state led to by β.

The next lemma is the key to the proof of Theorem 12.7, the main correctness theorem. Condition 1 of the lemma, which enumerates some simple properties on the state led to by particular schedules of $\mathcal{B}$, is only needed for carrying out the inductive argument. These properties say that (a) there is a write quorum in which every replica has the current version number, and (b) any replica with the current version number also has the logical value as its data. The more important part of the lemma is Condition 2, which says that each read-LA returns the value associated with the previous logical write. (That is, each read-LA returns the *logical-value* of the logical object.) The schedules of $\mathcal{B}$ that we consider are those in which no logical access to X is active.[2] The fact that $\mathcal{B}$ is a serial system makes the reasoning simple (though detailed).

LEMMA   12.1 *Let β be a finite schedule of $\mathcal{B}$ such that no logical access to X is active in β.*

   1. *The following properties hold in any global state led to by β:*

  (a) There exists a write quorum $\mathcal{W} \in c.write$ such that for any replica $S(Y)$ with object name $Y \in \mathcal{W}$, if v is the data component of $S(Y)$, then $v.version\text{-}number = current\text{-}vn(\beta)$.

  (b) For any replica $S(Y)$, if v is the data component of $S(Y)$ and $v.version\text{-}number = current\text{-}vn(\beta)$, then $v.value = logical\text{-}value(\beta)$.

   2. *If β ends in $\mathbf{REQUEST\_COMMIT}(T, v)$ with $T \in la_r$, then $v = logical\text{-}value(\beta)$.*

PROOF   Since $\mathcal{B}$ is a serial system, Lemma 3.13 shows that *logical-sequence*(β) consists of a sequence of pairs, each of the form $\mathbf{CREATE}(T)$ $\mathbf{REQUEST\_COMMIT}(T, v)$, where $T \in la$. We proceed by induction on the number of such pairs. For the basis, suppose *logical-sequence*(β) contains no such pairs. Then *logical-value*$(\beta) = d_0$. Since β contains no $\mathbf{CREATE}(T)$ events for $T \in la$, it contains no $\mathbf{REQUEST\_COMMIT}$ events for accesses in *acc*; therefore, since all replicas initially have *version-number* = 0 and *value* = d_0, this is also the case in any global state led to by β. It follows that *current-vn*$(\beta) = 0$. This implies Condition 1, and Condition 2 holds vacuously.

For the inductive step, suppose that *logical-sequence*(β) contains $k \geq 1$ pairs and assume that the lemma holds for sequences with $k - 1$ pairs. That is, let $\beta = \beta'\gamma$, where *logical-sequence*(γ) begins with the last $\mathbf{CREATE}$ event in *logical-sequence*(β), and assume that the lemma holds for β'. (Note that Lemma 3.13 shows that no logical access to X is live in β'.) So, *logical-sequence*$(\gamma) = \mathbf{CREATE}(T_f)\mathbf{REQUEST\text{-}}$
$\mathbf{\_COMMIT}(T_f, v_f)$ for some $T_f \in la$ and v_f of the appropriate type. The following observation enables us to argue only in terms of the transaction subtree rooted at T_f.

  CLAIM   12.2 *Any access or coordinator for which a $\mathbf{CREATE}$ or $\mathbf{REQUEST}$-$\mathbf{\_COMMIT}$ action appears in γ is a descendant of T_f.*

  PROOF   This follows since $\mathcal{B}$ is a serial system.   □

Now, since T_f has a $\mathbf{REQUEST\_COMMIT}$ in γ, we know by the definition of T_f that there is at least one $\mathbf{REPORT\_COMMIT}$ event for a transaction name in co_r in

---

[2]Recall that a transaction name is active in a sequence if the sequence contains a $\mathbf{CREATE}$ action but no $\mathbf{REQUEST\_COMMIT}$ action for that transaction.

γ. Let T' be the read-coordinator in co_r with the first **REPORT_COMMIT** in γ; by Claim 12.2 $T' \in children(T_f)$. Let γ' be the portion of γ up to and including the **REPORT_COMMIT** event for T'. If T_f is in la_r, then the system type shows that it invokes no write-coordinator, while if T_f is in la_w, the code shows that T_f invokes no write-coordinator before receiving a **REPORT_COMMIT** for a read-coordinator. Thus, no actions of any write-coordinator or its descendants appear in γ'. Therefore, there are no **REPORT_COMMIT** events in γ' for descendants of T_f that are write accesses. We now give two claims about the states of the automata for T_f and T'.

CLAIM 12.3 *Let s be the state of the transaction automaton associated with T' in any global state led to by any extension δ of β' that is a prefix of $\beta'\gamma'$. Then s.version-number and s.value contain the highest version-number and associated value among the states led to by β' of the replicas whose names are in s.value-read.*

PROOF This claim holds because T' retains the maximum *version-number* reported by a read access, together with its associated *value* upon each **REPORT_COMMIT** of a read access. Again, since no write accesses occur in γ', the *version-number* and *value* components of all replicas observed by T' must be the same during γ' as in the state led to by β'. □

CLAIM 12.4 *Let s be the state of the automaton associated with T_f in any global state led to by any extension δ of $\beta'\gamma'$ that is a prefix of β. Then s.version-number = current-vn(β') and s.value = logical-value(β').*

PROOF Let s' be the state of T' just before it issues its **REQUEST_COMMIT** event in γ'. By the definition of a read-coordinator, $s'.read$ must contain a read quorum $\mathcal{R} \in c.read$. By 1(a) of the inductive hypothesis, there is some write quorum $\mathcal{W} \in c.write$ such that the states of all replicas for object names in $\mathcal{W}$ in any global state led to by β' have *version-number* $= current\text{-}vn(\beta')$. Since c is a configuration, $\mathcal{R}$ and $\mathcal{W}$ have a nonempty intersection. So $s'.read$ must contain at least one object name in $\mathcal{W}$. So, by Claim 12.3, $s'.version\text{-}number = current\text{-}vn(\beta')$. Therefore, by 1(b) of the inductive hypothesis, $s'.value = logical\text{-}value(\beta')$.

When T' reports its commit to T_f, the *version-number* and *value* components of T_f are set equal to $s'.version\text{-}number$ and $s'.value$, respectively. By definition of T_f, these components are never again modified. Therefore, Claim 12.4 is proved. □

We now return to the main proof, and we consider the two possible cases for T_f.

1. $T_f \in la_r$.

Then $logical\text{-}value(\beta) = logical\text{-}value(\beta')$ by definition. Also, since T_f invokes only read-coordinators, which in turn invoke only read accesses, the *version-number* and *value* components of the states of the replicas in any global state led to by β are the same as in any global state led to by β', and so $current\text{-}vn(\beta) = current\text{-}vn(\beta')$. Therefore, Condition 1 holds for β.

By definition, T_f cannot request to commit until at least one of its read-coordinators commits. Since T' is the first read-coordinator child that reports its commit, the **REQUEST_COMMIT** for T_f must occur at some point after $\beta'\gamma'$. When T_f requests to commit, it returns the *value* component of its state. By Claim 12.4, this value is *logical-value*(β') = *logical-value*(β). Thus, Condition 2 holds for β.

2. $T_f \in la_w$.

Then *logical-value*$(\beta) = data(T_f)$. We first give two claims about the information associated with the descendants of T_f invoked during γ.

> **CLAIM 12.5** *If T is a write-coordinator invoked by T_f then version-number*$(T) = current\text{-}vn(\beta') + 1$ *and* $data(T) = data(T_f)$.
>
> **PROOF**   Let s be the state of T_f just before the **REQUEST_CREATE**(T) event that occurs in γ. By definition, *version-number*$(T) = s.version\text{-}number +$ 1 and $data(T) = data(T_f)$. Also by definition, T_f cannot invoke a write-coordinator until at least one of its read-coordinators reports its commit. So, all **REQUEST_CREATE** events for write-coordinators in γ occur after $\beta'\gamma'$. By Claim 12.4, *s.version-number* = *current-vn*(β'). Thus, Claim 12.5 holds.   □
>
> **CLAIM 12.6** *If T is a write access for an object in $\mathcal{Y}$ invoked in γ, then* $data(T) = (current\text{-}vn(\beta') + 1, data(T_f))$.
>
> **PROOF**   The type of $\mathcal{B}$ is constrained so that T is invoked by some write-coordinator. The result follows from Claim 12.5 and the definition of a write-coordinator.   □

By definition, T_f cannot request to commit until it receives a **REPORT_COMMIT** from at least one of its write-coordinators. Let T_w be the write-coordinator child of T_f that has the first **COMMIT** event in γ, and let δ be the portion of γ up to and including **COMMIT**(T_w). By definition, T_w cannot request to commit until it has received **REPORT_COMMIT** events for write accesses to a write quorum of replicas. Therefore, by Claim 12.6, it follows that *current-vn*$(\beta'\delta) =$ *current-vn*$(\beta') + 1$ so Condition 1 holds in any global state led to by $\beta'\delta$.

We now show that Condition 1 still holds in any global state led to by β. By Claim 12.6, any write-coordinators that may execute in γ after δ merely propagate the new value and version number. Any read-coordinators that may execute in γ after δ cannot change the values at the replicas, since they do not invoke write accesses. Therefore, Condition 1 holds after β.

Since T_f does not name a read-LA, Condition 2 holds vacuously.

Thus, in both cases, the lemma holds.   □

Now we prove that $\mathcal{B}$ is correct by showing that transactions cannot distinguish between replicated serial system $\mathcal{B}$ and unreplicated serial system $\mathcal{A}$. Here, let $\mathcal{T}_A$ and $\mathcal{X}_A$ denote the transaction and object names of $\mathcal{A}$, respectively.

THEOREM 12.7 *Let β be a finite schedule of $\mathcal{B}$. Then there exists a schedule γ of $\mathcal{A}$ such that the following two conditions hold.*

1. $\gamma|T = \beta|T$ *for each transaction name $T \in \mathcal{T}_A - la$, and*

2. $\gamma|Y = \beta|Y$ *for each object name $Y \in \mathcal{X}_A$.*

PROOF (Note first that the second condition includes $\gamma|X$, even though X is not a component of $\mathcal{B}$. Recall that $\gamma|X$ is a shorthand for $\gamma|acts(X)$, so that this projection is well-defined.)

We construct γ by removing from β all **REQUEST_CREATE**(T), **CREATE**(T), **REQUEST_COMMIT**(T, v), **COMMIT**(T), **ABORT**(T), **REPORT_COMMIT**(T,v) and **REPORT_ABORT**(T) events for all transaction names T in $co \cup acc$. Clearly, the two conditions in the statement of the theorem hold. It remains to show that γ is a schedule of $\mathcal{A}$. By Lemma 2.4 it suffices to show that γ projects to yield a schedule of each component of $\mathcal{A}$. It is easy to see that, for each non-access transaction name T of $\mathcal{A}$, $\gamma|T$ is a schedule of the transaction automaton for T, and for each object name $Y \in \mathcal{X}_A - \{X\}$, $\gamma|Y$ is a schedule of the object automaton for Y. Since we construct γ by removing all the actions associated with a specific set of transactions, and since none of these transactions have children with actions in γ, the fact that β is a schedule of the serial scheduler implies that γ is as well.

It remains to consider the automaton for object name X: we must show that $\gamma|X$ is a schedule of $S(X)$, where $S(X)$ is the serial object associated with X in $\mathcal{A}$. We proceed by induction on the length of β. The basis, where β is of length 0, is trivial. Suppose that $\beta = \beta'\pi$, where π is a single event and the result is true for β'. The only case that is not immediate is the case where π is a **REQUEST_COMMIT** event for a transaction name in la. So suppose that $\pi = $ **REQUEST_COMMIT**(T, v), where $T \in la$. Let $\gamma = \gamma'\pi$; by the inductive hypothesis, $\gamma'|X$ is a schedule of $S(X)$. Let s' be the state of $S(X)$ led to by $\gamma'|X$.

One precondition for **REQUEST_COMMIT**(T, v) as an output of $S(X)$ is that $T \in s'.created$. By transaction well-formedness of β, **CREATE**(T) occurs in β'. By the construction, **CREATE**(T) occurs in γ', so that this precondition is satisfied. We consider the two possible cases for T in order to show that the remaining clauses of the precondition for **REQUEST_COMMIT**(T, v) are satisfied.

1. $T \in la_w$.

Then the definition of a write-LA implies that $v = $ *"OK"*, which satisfies the remaining precondition.

2. $T \in la_r$.

Then by the construction, $\gamma'|\mathrm{X} = logical\text{-}sequence(\beta')$. If there is a **REQUEST-_COMMIT** for a write access to $S(\mathrm{X})$ in γ', let T' be the last such write access. Then $s'.data$ is equal to $data(T')$. By the construction, we know that T' is also the name of the logical write access in $\mathcal{B}$ having the last **REQUEST_COMMIT** in β'. Therefore, $data(T') = logical\text{-}value(\beta')$. So the $data$ component of the state of $S(\mathrm{X})$ led to by γ' is $logical\text{-}value(\beta')$.

On the other hand, if there is no **REQUEST_COMMIT** for a write access to $S(\mathrm{X})$ in γ', then $s'.data$ is d_0, which is $logical\text{-}value(\beta')$. Therefore, the $data$ component of the state of $S(\mathrm{X})$ led to by γ' is again $logical\text{-}value(\beta')$.

Thus, in either case, $logical\text{-}value(\beta')$ is the $data$ component of the state of $S(\mathrm{X})$ in any global state led to by γ'. By Lemma 12.1, we know that the return value $v = logical\text{-}value(\beta')$. Thus, v is the $data$ component of the state, s', of $S(\mathrm{X})$ led to by γ', which implies that the remaining precondition for **REQUEST-_COMMIT**(T,v) in $S(\mathrm{X})$ is satisfied.

Therefore, γ is a schedule of $\mathcal{A}$. $\square$

12.4 Reconfigurable Quorum Consensus

Now we present the algorithm with reconfiguration. For the concurrent implementations that are our ultimate goal, we need to have the activity of changing the configuration interact correctly with reading the configuration during processing of a logical access. Thus, each reconfiguration needs to take its place as a transaction in the transaction nesting structure, accessing a configuration object that holds the current configuration. This might be done with reconfiguration transactions as children of T_0; however, the correctness arguments work equally well no matter which existing transaction is taken as parent of each reconfiguration transaction. Thus, we allow each reconfiguration to occur at an arbitrary location in the transaction tree.

The presentation and proof are carried out in stages. First, in Section 12.4.1, we define system $\mathcal{A}$, a serial system that has X as one of its object names[3] and that also has another special object name Z. As in Section 12.3, the object automaton $S(\mathrm{X})$ associated with X is a read/write serial object automaton. The object automaton $S(\mathrm{Z})$ associated with Z is a special *dummy* object, which simply receives requests from transactions to change the current configuration and responds to them with a trivial acknowledgement. As before, system $\mathcal{A}$ is used to define correctness.

---

[3]In this section, we redefine certain notations from Section 12.3, such as the system names $\mathcal{A}$ and $\mathcal{B}$.

Then in Section 12.4.2, we define replicated serial system $\mathcal{B}$. System $\mathcal{B}$ is identical to $\mathcal{A}$, except that logical object $S(\mathrm{X})$ is replicated as in system $\mathcal{B}$ of Section 12.3, and also dummy object $S(\mathrm{Z})$ is replaced by a *configuration object automaton* $S(\bar{\mathrm{X}})$, which is a read/write object containing the current configuration of replicas of X. In $\mathcal{B}$, reconfiguration requests involve a single write of object $S(\bar{\mathrm{X}})$. In the course of performing each logical read or write access to X, the configuration object $S(\bar{\mathrm{X}})$ is read to determine the current configuration. In Section 12.4.3, we show that the new algorithm is correct by demonstrating a relationship between $\mathcal{B}$ and $\mathcal{A}$. The proof is analogous to that in Section 12.3.3; the changes involve the handling of the new configuration object.

Next, in Section 12.4.4, we define serial system $\mathcal{C}$, which is the same as $\mathcal{B}$ except that the configuration object is replicated. That is, the configuration object $S(\bar{\mathrm{X}})$ from $\mathcal{B}$ is replaced in $\mathcal{C}$ by a collection of serial read/write objects that we call *configuration replica objects*, and each access to a configuration object is implemented by a subtransaction that performs accesses to a subset of the configuration replicas. The configuration replica management is based in an interesting way on the data replica management scheme. Finally, in Section 12.4.5, we prove a simulation relationship between $\mathcal{C}$ and $\mathcal{B}$, which in turn implies a similar connection between $\mathcal{C}$ and $\mathcal{A}$.

12.4.1 System $\mathcal{A}$, the Unreplicated Serial System with Dummy Reconfiguration

We begin by defining unreplicated serial system $\mathcal{A}$. System $\mathcal{A}$ is an arbitrary serial system having two distinguished object names, X and Z, in which the object automaton $S(\mathrm{X})$ associated with X is a read/write serial object with domain D and initial value d_0, and in which the object automaton $S(\mathrm{Z})$ associated with Z is a special *dummy* object automaton, defined below.

As before, we define la_r and la_w to be the respective names of the read and write accesses to X. Now we also define la_{rec} to be the set of names of accesses to the dummy object Z. We define $la = la_r \cup la_w \cup la_{rec}$.[4] As before, each transaction name $T \in la_r$ has $kind(T) = read$, and each transaction name $T \in la_w$ has $kind(T) = write$ and also has an associated value, $data(T) \in D$.

Recall that system $\mathcal{A}$ is used to define correctness, and that correctness is defined at the transaction boundary. Thus, it is desirable that we use the same transaction interfaces in $\mathcal{A}$ as we do in the later systems, $\mathcal{B}$ and $\mathcal{C}$. Since those systems will permit arbitrary transaction automata to invoke reconfiguration operations, we also allow

---

[4]Note this is different from the definition in Section 12.3, where la was just defined to be the union of la_r and la_w.

CREATE(T)
    Effect:
        $s.active = T$

REQUEST_COMMIT(T, v)
    Precondition:
        $T = s'.active$
        $v = \text{``}OK\text{''}$
    Effect:
        $s.active = nil$

Figure 12.6: Dummy Object Automaton

them to do so in $\mathcal{A}$. However, since X is not replicated in $\mathcal{A}$, these operations will not do anything interesting in $\mathcal{A}$. We simply make them operations on the dummy object, which merely responds "OK" in all cases.[5]

Dummy Object Automata

More precisely, we define a single *dummy object automaton* $S(Z)$, which is a serial object automaton having a single state component, $active \in accesses(Z) \cup \{nil\}$, initially *nil*. The set of return values V_T for accesses to Z is equal to $\{\text{``}OK\text{''}\}$. The (trivial) transition relation for $S(Z)$ is shown in Figure 12.6.

12.4.2 System $\mathcal{B}$, the Reconfigurable Quorum Consensus Algorithm with a Centralized Configuration

In this section, we define replicated serial system $\mathcal{B}$. This is similar to system $\mathcal{B}$ of Section 12.3 in that object $S(X)$ is implemented by replicas $S(Y)$, $Y \in \mathcal{Y}$, and the accesses to X are implemented as subtransaction automata called read-LA's and write-LA's, using the same basic strategy as in the fixed configuration algorithm. In addition, in the new $\mathcal{B}$, the dummy object $S(Z)$ is implemented by a *configuration object* $S(\bar{X})$, which is a read/write serial object that maintains a configuration, and the accesses to Z are implemented as subtransactions called *reconfigure-LA's* that invoke

---

[5] It may seem artificial to place the invocations of the reconfiguration transactions in the transaction automaton interface in $\mathcal{A}$; an alternative approach would be to make these reconfigurations invisible to users and application programmers by *not* having them appear explicitly in $\mathcal{A}$. In this approach, $\mathcal{A}$ would be defined just as it is in Section 12.3. An auxiliary system $\mathcal{A}'$ would be defined, which would represent an augmentation of $\mathcal{A}$ with added reconfiguration operations, where the augmentation is presumably made by programmers of the database system rather than application programmers. We leave the details of this approach as an exercise, and settle instead in this chapter for the simpler alternative of including reconfiguration requests in $\mathcal{A}$.

accesses to $S(\bar{X})$. (In $\mathcal{C}$, the configuration objects themselves will be replicated, and the reconfigure-LA's will invoke coordinator subtransactions to read and write them.)

We first define the type of $\mathcal{B}$, and then give the new automata that appear in $\mathcal{B}$ but not in $\mathcal{A}$. The new automata are the replica objects, the configuration object, and the coordinator and LA transaction automata. We again define these automata "bottom up".

System Type

The type of system $\mathcal{B}$ is defined to be the same as that of $\mathcal{A}$, with the following modifications. As in Section 12.3, the object name X is now replaced by a new set of object names $\mathcal{Y}$, and there are new transaction names, co_r and co_w, representing read and write-coordinators, respectively, and acc_r and acc_w, which are the read and write accesses to the replicas, respectively. In addition, object name Z is now replaced by a new object name $\bar{X}$, and there are new transaction names co_{rc} and co_{wc}, which are the read and write accesses to object $\bar{X}$, respectively. (We denote the configuration accesses in this way because, in $\mathcal{C}$, they will be replaced by coordinator automata.) We let $co = co_r \cup co_w \cup co_{rc} \cup co_{wc}$.

The transaction names in la are accesses in $\mathcal{A}$, but in $\mathcal{B}$ they are not; each transaction name in la_r now has children that are in co_{rc} and co_r, each transaction name in la_w now has children in co_{rc}, co_r, and co_w, and each transaction name in la_{rec} now has children in co_{rc}, co_{wc}, co_r, and co_w. Also, as in Section 12.3, each transaction name in co_r has children in acc_r, and each transaction name in co_w has children in acc_w. These are the only changes to the system type—for example, no transaction names other than those indicated are parents of the new transaction names.

In defining $\mathcal{A}$, we associated information with some of the transaction names. In $\mathcal{B}$, we keep all such information from $\mathcal{A}$ and add more information as follows. First, to denote the new configuration for each logical reconfigure access, we associate with every transaction name $T \in la_{rec}$ a configuration $config(T)$ in $configs(\mathcal{Y})$, the set of all configurations of $\mathcal{Y}$.

Second, to denote the configuration that is used by each read-coordinator, we assume that every transaction name $T \in co_r$ has an associated configuration $config(T) \in configs(\mathcal{Y})$. Similarly, every transaction name $T \in co_w$ has an associated value $data(T) \in D$, an associated version number $version\text{-}number(T) \in N$, and an associated configuration $config(T) \in configs(\mathcal{Y})$. These denote the value for X written by the write-coordinator, the associated version number in the quorum consensus algorithm, and the configuration to be used for writing the new value and version number.

Third, we associate some information with the accesses to both the configuration objects and the replicas. We assume that every transaction name $T \in co_{rc}$ has $kind(T) = read$, and that every transaction name $T \in co_{wc}$ has $kind(T) = write$ and $data(T) \in configs(\mathcal{Y})$, representing the new configuration. Also, as before, we assume that every transaction name $T \in acc_r$ has $kind(T) = read$ and that every transaction name $T \in acc_w$ has $kind(T) = write$ and $data(T) \in N \times D$.

Replica and Configuration Automata

As in Section 12.3, we define a *replica automaton* for each object name $Y \in \mathcal{Y}$. This is a read/write serial object for Y with domain $N \times D$ and initial value $(0, d_0)$. As before, for $v \in N \times D$, we write $v.version\text{-}number$ and $v.value$ to refer to the components of v.

For the rest of this chapter, let $C = configs(\mathcal{Y})$ and let $c_0 \in C$ be a distinguished *initial configuration*. The *configuration automaton* is defined to be a read/write serial object for $\bar{X}$, with domain C and initial value c_0. (Recall that its read accesses are the elements of co_{rc} and its write accesses are the elements of co_{wc}.)

Coordinators

In this section, we define the coordinator automata in $\mathcal{B}$. These transaction automata are invoked by the LA's and access the replicas. We first define read-coordinators; these are the same as those in Section 12.3, except that instead of using the fixed configuration, the new read-coordinator uses its own associated configuration. A read-coordinator for transaction name $T \in co_r$ has state components *awake*, *value*, *version-number*, *requested*, *reported*, and *read*, where *awake* is a Boolean variable, initially *false*; *value* is an element of D, initially d_0; *version-number* is a non-negative integer, initially 0; *requested* and *reported* are subsets of $children(T)$, initially empty; and *read* is a subset of $\mathcal{Y}$, initially empty. The set of return values V_T is equal to $N \times D$.

The transition relation for read-coordinators is shown in Figure 12.7. This code is identical to that in Figure 12.2, except that $config(T)$ is used to determine when the coordinator has collected enough information to be assured of having seen the most recent value of X.

We next define write-coordinators. Again, these are the same as those in Section 12.3, except that instead of using the fixed configuration, the new write-coordinator uses its own associated configuration. A write-coordinator for transaction name $T \in co_w$ has state components *awake*, *requested*, *reported*, and *written*, where *awake* is a Boolean variable, initially *false*; *requested* and *reported* are subsets of $children(T)$, initially empty; and *written* is a subset of $\mathcal{Y}$, initially empty. The set of return values V_T is equal to $\{\text{"OK"}\}$.

The transition relation for a write-coordinator named $T \in co_w$ is shown in Figure 12.8. Again, this code is identical to that in Figure 12.3, except that $config(T)$ is used to determine when the coordinator has written to enough replicas.

CREATE(T)
    Effect:
        $s.awake = true$

REQUEST_CREATE(T')
    Precondition:
        $s'.awake = true$
        $T' \notin s'.requested$
    Effect:
        $s.requested = s'.requested \cup \{T'\}$

REPORT_COMMIT(T',v)
    Effect:
        $s.reported = s'.reported \cup \{T'\}$
        $s.read = s'.read \cup \{object(T')\}$
        if $v.version\text{-}number > s'.version\text{-}number$
        then $s.version\text{-}number = v.version\text{-}number$
            $s.value = v.value$

REPORT_ABORT(T')
    Effect:
        $s.reported = s'.reported \cup \{T'\}$

REQUEST_COMMIT(T, v)
    Precondition:
        $s'.awake = true$
        $s'.requested = s'.reported$
        $\mathcal{R} \in config(T).read$
        $\mathcal{R} \subseteq s'.read$
        $v = (s'.version\text{-}number, s'.value)$
    Effect:
        $s.awake = false$

Figure 12.7: Transition Relation for Read-Coordinators

CREATE(T)
    Effect:
        $s.awake = true$

REQUEST_CREATE(T')
    Precondition:
        $s'.awake = true$
        $T' \notin s'.requested$
        $data(T') = (version\text{-}number(T), data(T))$
    Effect:
        $s.requested = s'.requested \cup \{T'\}$

REPORT_COMMIT(T',v)
    Effect:
        $s.reported = s'.reported \cup \{T'\}$
        $s.written = s'.written \cup \{object(T')\}$

REPORT_ABORT(T')
    Effect:
        $s.reported = s'.reported \cup \{T'\}$

REQUEST_COMMIT(T, v)
    Precondition:
        $s'.awake = true$
        $s'.requested = s'.reported$
        $\mathcal{W} \in config(T).write$
        $\mathcal{W} \subseteq s'.written$
        $v = "OK"$
    Effect:
        $s.awake = false$

Figure 12.8: Transition Relation for Write-Coordinators

CREATE(T)
 Effect:
  $s.awake = true$

REQUEST_CREATE(T'), $T' \in co_{rc}$
 Precondition:
  $s'.awake = true$
  $T' \notin s'.requested$
 Effect:
  $s.requested = s'.requested \cup \{T'\}$

REPORT_COMMIT(T',v), $T' \in co_{rc}$
 Effect:
  $s.reported = s'.reported \cup \{T'\}$
  if $s'.config$-$read = false$
  then $s.config = v$
   $s.config$-$read = true$

REQUEST_CREATE(T'), $T' \in co_r$
 Precondition:
  $s'.awake = true$
  $s'.config$-$read = true$
  $config(T') = s'.config$
  $T' \notin s'.requested$
 Effect:
  $s.requested = s'.requested \cup \{T'\}$

REPORT_COMMIT(T',v), $T' \in co_r$
 Effect:
  $s.reported = s'.reported \cup \{T'\}$
  if $s'.value$-$read = false$
  then $s.value = v.value$
   $s.value$-$read = true$

REPORT_ABORT(T')
 Effect:
  $s.reported = s'.reported \cup \{T'\}$

REQUEST_COMMIT(T, v)
 Precondition:
  $s'.awake = true$
  $s'.requested = s'.reported$
  $s'.value$-$read = true$
  $v = s'.value$
 Effect:
  $s.awake = false$

Figure 12.9: Transition Relation for Read LA's

Logical Access Automata

Now we define logical access automata, beginning with read-LA's. These are the same as those in Section 12.3, except that the new read-LA first invokes a read-configuration-coordinator in order to determine the current configuration. It then invokes only read-coordinators whose associated configuration is the same as the determined current configuration.

A read-LA has state components *awake*, *config*, *value*, *requested*, *reported*, *value-read*, and *config-read*, where *awake*, *value-read*, and *config-read* are Boolean variables, initially *false*; *config* is an element of $C \cup \{nil\}$, initially *nil*; *value* is an element of $D \cup \{nil\}$, initially *nil*; and *requested* and *reported* are subsets of *children*(T), initially empty. The set of return values V_T is equal to D.

The transition relation for read-LA's is shown in Figure 12.9. The changes to the code in Figure 12.4 are as follows. First, there are additional **REQUEST_CREATE** and **REPORT_COMMIT** actions for invoking and obtaining responses from the configuration-coordinators. There are two additional state components, *config*, which keeps track of the configuration returned, and *config-read*, a flag that records that a configuration has been read. Also, there are extra clauses in the precondition for the **REQUEST_CREATE** events for read-coordinators, which ensure that only read-coordinators with the current configuration are invoked.

We next define write-LA's. These are the same as those in Section 12.3, except that the new write-LA first invokes a read-configuration-coordinator in order to determine the current configuration, and then invokes only read-coordinators and write-coordinators having the proper associated configuration. A write-LA has state components *awake, config, config-read, value-read, value-written, version-number, requested*, and *reported*, where *awake, config-read, value-read*, and *value-written* are Booleans, initially *false*; *config* is an element of $C \cup \{nil\}$, initially *nil*; *version-number* is in $N \cup \{nil\}$, initially *nil*; and *requested* and *reported* are subsets of *children*(T), initially empty. The set of return values V_T is equal to $\{ "OK" \}$.

The transition relation for write-LA's is shown in Figure 12.10. The changes to the code in Figure 12.5 are as follows. First, there are additional **REQUEST_CREATE** and **REPORT_COMMIT** actions for invoking and obtaining responses from the configuration-coordinators, and associated state components for keeping track of the results. There are also extra clauses in the precondition for the **REQUEST_CREATE** events for read-coordinators and write-coordinators, ensuring that only coordinators with the current configuration are invoked.

Finally, we define reconfigure-LA's. The purpose of a reconfigure-LA is to change the current configuration to a given target configuration. The main thing it does in order to accomplish this change is to invoke a write access to the configuration object. However, this alone is not enough; the reconfigure-LA transaction must also maintain the crucial property that *all the members of some write quorum, according to the current configuration, must have the latest version number and data value.* (The importance of this property can be seen in the proof of Lemma 12.1.) An arbitrary configuration change might cause this property to become violated.

Thus, extra activity is required on the part of the reconfigure-LA to ensure that the latest data gets propagated to some write quorum of the new configuration. In particular, the reconfigure-LA must obtain this latest data, which requires that it first obtain the value of the old configuration from a read-configuration-coordinator and then the latest data value from a read-coordinator with the *old* configuration. Once it has the latest data, the reconfigure-LA must cause this data to be written to some write quorum, according to the *new* configuration. It accomplishes this by invoking write-coordinators whose corresponding configuration is the new configuration. (Note that the reconfigure-LA can *invoke* the write-coordinators and the write accesses to the configuration object concurrently, even though in the serial systems considered here, the subtransactions themselves will be run serially. This concurrent invocation

CREATE(T)
  Effect:
    $s.awake = true$

REQUEST_CREATE(T'), $T' \in co_{rc}$
  Precondition:
    $s'.awake = true$
    $T' \notin s'.requested$

  Effect:
    $s.requested = s'.requested \cup \{T'\}$

REPORT_COMMIT(T',v), $T' \in co_{rc}$
  Effect:
    $s.reported = s'.reported \cup \{T'\}$
    if $s'.config\text{-}read = false$
    then $s.config = v$
      $s.config\text{-}read = true$

REQUEST_CREATE(T'), $T' \in co_r$
  Precondition:
    $s'.awake = true$
    $s'.config\text{-}read = true$
    $config(T') = s'.config$
    $T' \notin s'.requested$
  Effect:
    $s.requested = s'.requested \cup \{T'\}$

REPORT_COMMIT(T',v), $T' \in co_r$
  Effect:
    $s.reported = s'.reported \cup \{T'\}$
    if $s'.value\text{-}read = false$
    then $s.version\text{-}number = v.version\text{-}number$
      $s.value\text{-}read = true$

REQUEST_CREATE(T'), $T' \in co_w$
  Precondition:
    $s'.awake = true$
    $s'.value\text{-}read = true$
    $config(T') = s'.config$
    $data(T') = data(T)$
    $version\text{-}number(T') = s'.version\text{-}number + 1$
    $T' \notin s'.requested$
  Effect:
    $s.requested = s'.requested \cup \{T'\}$

REPORT_COMMIT(T',v), $T' \in co_w$
  Effect:
    $s.reported = s'.reported \cup \{T'\}$
    $s'.value\text{-}written = true$

REPORT_ABORT(T')
  Effect:
    $s.reported = s'.reported \cup \{T'\}$

REQUEST_COMMIT(T, v)
  Precondition:
    $s'.awake = true$
    $s'.requested = s'.reported$
    $s'.value\text{-}written = true$
    $v = \text{``}OK\text{''}$
  Effect:
    $s.awake = false$

Figure 12.10: Transition Relation for Write LA's

will be useful in the concurrent systems we study later, where these activities can run in parallel to reduce latency.)

A reconfigure-LA for transaction name $T \in la_{rec}$ has state components *awake, config, value, version-number, requested, reported, config-read, value-read, value-written,* and *config-written,* where *awake, config-read, value-read, value-written,* and *config-written* are Boolean variables, initially *false; config* is in $C \cup \{nil\}$, initially *nil; value* is in $D \cup \{nil\}$, initially *nil; version-number* is in $N \cup \{nil\}$, initially *nil;* and *requested* and *reported* are subsets of *children*(T), initially empty. The set of return values V_T is equal to $\{\text{"}OK\text{"}\}$.

The transition relation for reconfigure LA's is shown in Figure 12.11. Just as for the read- and write-LA's, a reconfigure-LA first determines the current configuration with a read access to the configuration object. Then the reconfigure-LA invokes read-coordinators using that configuration; when the first read-coordinator reports its commit, the reconfigure-LA remembers the value and version number returned. Then the reconfigure-LA may invoke any number of write-coordinators, using its new configuration, along with the value and version number returned by the read-coordinator. This propagates the current value to every replica in a write quorum of the new configuration, as needed. Concurrently, the LA invokes at least one write access to the configuration object in order to record the new configuration. In order to request to commit, the reconfigure-LA must receive **REPORT_COMMIT** responses for at least one write-coordinator and at least one write access to X̄.

12.4.3 Correctness Proof

In this section, we prove the correctness of system $\mathcal{B}$. As in Section 12.3, we begin with some definitions. In each definition, β is a sequence of actions of $\mathcal{B}$. First, the *logical access sequence* of β, *logical-sequence*(β), is defined exactly as in Section 12.3 to be the subsequence of β containing the **CREATE**(T) and **REQUEST_COMMIT**(T, v) events, where $T \in la$. (But now this definition is based on the new definition of *la*, which includes the names in la_{rec}). Also, if β is finite, then *logical-value*(β) and *current-vn*(β) are defined, as before, to be the value of the last logical write (or the initial value of the logical object if no such write occurs), and the highest *version-number* among the local states of all replica automata in any global state led to by β, respectively.

We require one new definition, analogous to *logical-value*(β). Namely, if β is finite, then *logical-config*(β) is defined to be either *config*(T) if **REQUEST_COMMIT**(T, v) is the last **REQUEST_COMMIT** event for a transaction name in la_{rec} that occurs in *logical-sequence*(β), or c_0 if no such **REQUEST_COMMIT** event occurs. In other words, the logical configuration is the value of the last logical reconfigure access (or the initial configuration if no such reconfigure access occurs).

The next lemma is the key to the proof of Theorem 12.9, the main correctness theorem. As in Lemma 12.1, Condition 1 is only needed for the inductive argument. Parts (a) and (b) of Condition 1 are as before, and Part (c) says that the configuration object holds the logical configuration. As before, the important part of the lemma is Condition 2, which tells us that each read-LA returns the value associated with the previous logical write. The proof is left to the reader, as Exercise 1.

CREATE(T)
    Effect:
        $s'.awake = true$

REQUEST_CREATE(T'), $T' \in co_{rc}$
    Precondition:
        $s'.awake = true$
        $T' \notin s'.requested$

    Effect:
        $s.requested = s'.requested \cup \{T'\}$

REPORT_COMMIT(T',v), $T' \in co_{rc}$
    Effect:
        $s.reported = s'.reported \cup \{T'\}$
        if $s'.config\text{-}read = false$
        then $s.config = v$
            $s.config\text{-}read = true$

REQUEST_CREATE(T'), $T' \in co_r$
    Precondition:
        $s'.awake = true$
        $s'.config\text{-}read = true$
        $config(T') = s'.config$
        $T' \notin s'.requested$
    Effect:
        $s.requested = s'.requested \cup \{T'\}$

REPORT_COMMIT(T',v), $T' \in co_r$
    Effect:
        $s.reported = s'.reported \cup \{T'\}$
        if $s'.value\text{-}read = false$
        then $s.value = v.value$
            $s.version\text{-}number = v.version\text{-}number$
            $s.value\text{-}read = true$

REQUEST_CREATE(T'), $T' \in co_w$
    Precondition:
        $s'.awake = true$
        $s'.value\text{-}read = true$
        $data(T') = s'.value$
        $version\text{-}number(T') = s'.version\text{-}number$
        $config(T') = config(T)$
        $T' \notin s'.requested$
    Effect:
        $s.requested = s'.requested \cup \{T'\}$

REPORT_COMMIT(T',v), $T' \in co_w$
    Effect:
        $s.reported = s'.reported \cup \{T'\}$
        $s'.value\text{-}written = true$

REQUEST_CREATE(T'), $T' \in co_{wc}$
    Precondition:
        $s'.awake = true$
        $s'.value\text{-}read = true$
        $data(T') = config(T)$
        $T' \notin s'.requested$
    Effect:
        $s.requested = s'.requested \cup \{T'\}$

REPORT_COMMIT(T',v), $T' \in co_{wc}$
    Effect:
        $s.reported = s'.reported \cup \{T'\}$
        $s.config\text{-}written = true$

REPORT_ABORT(T')
    Effect:
        $s.reported = s'.reported \cup \{T'\}$

REQUEST_COMMIT(T,v)
    Precondition:
        $s'.awake = true$
        $s'.requested = s'.reported$
        $s'.value\text{-}written = true$
        $s'.config\text{-}written = true$
        $v = \text{``OK''}$
    Effect:
        $s.awake = false$

Figure 12.11: Transition Relation for Reconfigure LA's

LEMMA 12.8 *Let β be a finite schedule of $\mathcal{B}$ such that no logical access to X is active in β.*

1. *The following properties hold in any global state led to by β:*

    (a) There exists a write quorum $\mathcal{W} \in$ logical-config(β).write such that for any replica $S(\mathrm{Y})$ for an object name $\mathrm{Y} \in \mathcal{W}$, if v is the data component of $S(\mathrm{Y})$, then v.version-number = current-vn(β).

    (b) For any replica $S(\mathrm{Y})$, if v is the data component of $S(\mathrm{Y})$ and v.version-number = current-vn(β), then v.value = logical-value(β).

    (c) The data component of the configuration object is logical-config(β).

2. *If β ends in $\mathbf{REQUEST\_COMMIT}(T,v)$ with $T \in la_r$, then $v =$ logical-value(β).*

Now we give the main correctness theorem for $\mathcal{B}$. Again, let $\mathcal{T}_A$ and $\mathcal{X}_A$ denote the transaction names and object names of $\mathcal{A}$, respectively.

THEOREM 12.9 *Let β be a finite schedule of $\mathcal{B}$. Then there exists a schedule γ of $\mathcal{A}$ such that the following two conditions hold.*

1. *$\gamma|T = \beta|T$ for each transaction name $T \in \mathcal{T}_A - la$, and*

2. *$\gamma|\mathrm{Y} = \beta|\mathrm{Y}$ for each object name $\mathrm{Y} \in \mathcal{X}_A$.*

PROOF The proof is analogous to that for Theorem 12.7. We construct γ by removing from β all $\mathbf{REQUEST\_CREATE}(T)$, $\mathbf{CREATE}(T)$, $\mathbf{REQUEST\_COMMIT}(T,v)$, $\mathbf{COMMIT}(T)$, $\mathbf{ABORT}(T)$, $\mathbf{REPORT\_COMMIT}(T,v)$, and $\mathbf{REPORT\_ABORT}(T)$ events for all transaction names T in $co \cup acc_r \cup acc_w$. Clearly, the two conditions hold. It remains to show that γ is a schedule of $\mathcal{A}$; to do this, it suffices to show that γ projects to yield a schedule of each component of $\mathcal{A}$. It is easy to see that, for each non-access transaction name T of $\mathcal{A}$, $\gamma|T$ is a schedule of the transaction automaton for T, and for each object name $\mathrm{Y} \in \mathcal{X}_A - \{\mathrm{X}, \mathrm{Z}\}$, $\gamma|\mathrm{Y}$ is a schedule of the object automaton for Y. The sequence $\gamma|\mathrm{Z}$ is exactly the sequence of $\mathbf{CREATE}(T)$ and $\mathbf{REQUEST\_COMMIT}(T,v)$ actions in γ for $T \in la_{rec}$. Since reconfigure-LA's preserve transaction well-formedness and always return value $v = $ "*OK*", $\gamma|\mathrm{Z}$ is a schedule of the dummy object automaton. Also, as before, γ is a schedule of the serial scheduler.

It remains to show that $\gamma|\mathrm{X}$ is a schedule of $S(\mathrm{X})$. The proof is by induction on the length of β. The basis, when β is of length 0, is trivial. Suppose that $\beta = \beta'\pi$, where π is a single event and the result is true for β'. The only case that is not immediate is the case where π is a $\mathbf{REQUEST\_COMMIT}$ event for a transaction name in $la_r \cup la_w$, so suppose that $\pi = \mathbf{REQUEST\_COMMIT}(T,v)$, where $T \in la_r \cup la_w$. The proof that the precondition of π in $S(\mathrm{X})$ is satisfied is as in Theorem 12.7, but this time using Lemma 12.8 in place of Lemma 12.1. Therefore, γ is a schedule of $\mathcal{A}$. $\qquad\square$

12.4.4   System $\mathcal{C}$, the Reconfigurable Quorum Consensus Algorithm with Replicated Configurations

It is possible to manage configurations in a centralized fashion, directly implementing the algorithm described by system $\mathcal{B}$ above. However, it is also interesting to consider replicating the configuration information. This may avoid the risk of the configuration storage becoming a bottleneck or single point of vulnerability in the system. One way of doing this is using the fixed quorum consensus algorithm: define a fixed *meta-configuration* that describes read quorums and write quorums of replicas of the configuration. A *read-configuration-coordinator* reads a read quorum of configuration replicas and returns both the latest configuration and a *generation number*, which is analogous to a version number. A *write-configuration-coordinator* writes the new configuration to a write quorum of configuration replicas; it does this using the generation number obtained from a read-configuration-coordinator. Except for the need to manage the generation-number information, the LA's are the same in this algorithm as in $\mathcal{B}$. It is also possible to manage the configuration replicas using changing meta-configurations, that is, to reconfigure the configuration replicas! But then similar issues arise for the implementation of meta-configurations.

All of this could continue for any number of steps. However, in order to avoid an infinite regress, we must stop at some point and use an implementation that does not require further reconfiguration. Such a stopping point might be either a centralized implementation or a fixed quorum algorithm. (Note that a centralized implementation is just a special case of using fixed quorums, where there is only one replica.)

There is another interesting alternative, however, in which there is a one-to-one correspondence between the replicas at the last two stages and the same configurations are used for both stages. That is, at the last two stages, the same configurations are used to manage the data replicas and the copies of the configurations themselves. This means that the read-configuration-coordinators will need to read a set of replicas of the configuration objects that form a read quorum, without first knowing what the current read quorum is! It turns out that they can simply start reading configuration replicas and use the generation numbers and configurations stored in them to determine when a read quorum for the current configuration has been read.

In this subsection, we will describe this strategy. For simplicity, we consider the special case in which there are only two kinds of replicas—of logical objects and configurations—and both are managed using the same configurations.

The system we define is called $\mathcal{C}$. We first define the type of $\mathcal{C}$, and then give the new automata that appear in $\mathcal{C}$ but not in $\mathcal{B}$. The new automata are the configuration replica objects and the read-configuration-coordinator and write-configuration-coordinator transaction automata. Also, the LA's are slightly modified from those of $\mathcal{B}$.

System Type

The type of system $\mathcal{C}$ is defined to be the same as that of $\mathcal{B}$, with the following modifications. The object name $\bar{X}$ is now replaced by a new set of object names, $\bar{\mathcal{Y}}$, representing the configuration replicas. We assume that there is a bijective function i, from the names in $\bar{\mathcal{Y}}$ to those in $\mathcal{Y}$. There are new transaction names, acc_{rc} and acc_{wc}, which are the read and write accesses to the configuration replicas, respectively. We let $acc = acc_r \cup acc_w \cup acc_{rc} \cup acc_{wc}$. The transaction names in co_{rc} and co_{wc} are accesses in $\mathcal{B}$, but in $\mathcal{C}$ they are not; each transaction name in co_{rc} now has children in acc_{rc}, and each transaction name in co_{wc} has children in acc_{wc}. These are the only changes to the system type—for example, no transaction names other than those indicated are parents of the new transaction names.

In defining $\mathcal{B}$, we associated information with some of the transaction names. In $\mathcal{C}$, we keep all such information from $\mathcal{B}$ and add more information as follows. We now assume that every transaction name $T \in co_{wc}$ has associated values $old\text{-}config(T) \in C$ and $generation\text{-}number(T) \in N$, in addition to $data(T)$ as before. Also, we assume that every transaction name $T \in acc_{rc}$ has $kind(T) = read$ and that every transaction name $T \in acc_{wc}$ has $kind(T) = write$ and also $data(T) \in N \times C$.[6]

Configuration Replica Automata

We define a *configuration replica automaton* for each object name $Y \in \bar{\mathcal{Y}}$. This is a read/write serial object for Y with domain $N \times C$ and initial value $(0, c_0)$. For $v \in N \times C$, we write $v.generation\text{-}number$ and $v.config$ to refer to the components of v.

Coordinators

In this section, we define the coordinator automata in $\mathcal{C}$. The read- and write-coordinators are as in $\mathcal{B}$, so we need only define the read-configuration-coordinators and write-configuration-coordinators. We first define read-configuration-coordinators. The purpose of a read-configuration-coordinator is to determine the latest generation-number and configuration, on the basis of the data returned by the read accesses it invokes on configuration replica objects.

A read-configuration-coordinator for transaction name $T \in co_{rc}$ has state components *awake*, *config*, *generation-number*, *requested*, *reported*, and *read*, where *awake* is a Boolean variable, initially *false*; *config* is an element of C, initially c_0;

---

[6] As with the transaction names in acc_w, since the transaction names in acc_{wc} name accesses to read/write objects, agreement with that definition compels the combination of the generation number and configuration into a single *data* attribute.

CREATE(T)
 Effect:
  $s.awake = true$

REQUEST_CREATE(T')
 Precondition:
  $s'.awake = true$
  $T' \notin s'.requested$
 Effect:
  $s.requested = s'.requested \cup \{T'\}$

REPORT_COMMIT(T',v)
 Effect:
  $s.reported = s'.reported \cup \{T'\}$
  $s.read = s'.read \cup \{object(T')\}$
  if $v.generation\text{-}number > s'.generation\text{-}number$
  then $s.generation\text{-}number = v.generation\text{-}number$
   $s.config = v.config$

REPORT_ABORT(T')
 Effect:
  $s.reported = s'.reported \cup \{T'\}$

REQUEST_COMMIT(T, v)
 Precondition:
  $s'.awake = true$
  $s'.requested = s'.reported$
  $i(\mathcal{R}) \in s'.config.read$
  $\mathcal{R} \subseteq s'.read$
  $v = (s'.generation\text{-}number, s'.config)$
 Effect:
  $s.awake = false$

Figure 12.12: Transition Relation for Read-Configuration-Coordinators

$generation\text{-}number$ is a non-negative integer, initially 0; $requested$ and $reported$ are subsets of $children(T)$, initially empty; and $read$ is a subset of $\bar{\mathcal{Y}}$, initially empty. The set of return values V_T is equal to $N \times C$.

The transition relation for read-configuration-coordinators is shown in Figure 12.12. A read-configuration-coordinator invokes accesses to configuration replicas. On receiving a **REPORT_COMMIT**, the coordinator compares the returned generation number with the $generation\text{-}number$ component of its own state. If the returned generation number is larger, the coordinator updates its own $generation\text{-}number$ and $configuration$ components to the returned values. The interesting part of a read-configuration-coordinator is its precondition for the **REQUEST_COMMIT** action. When the coordinator reaches a state s' in which $s'.read$ contains a set of configuration replica names that corresponds (using the correspondence i between $\bar{\mathcal{Y}}$ and $\mathcal{Y}$) to a read quorum, according to $s'.config$, then it may request to commit, returning the highest generation number it has seen, along with the associated configuration. One should note the similarity of the read-configuration-coordinators and the read-coordinators in the way the most current configuration and generation number are obtained, and also the seemingly "circular" use of replicated configuration data in order to keep track of the current configuration of the configuration replicas themselves.

Of course, it remains to show that this method of determining the current configuration is correct. The key intuition is that the write-configuration-coordinators,

CREATE(T)
   Effect:
      $s.awake = true$

REQUEST_CREATE(T')
   Precondition:
      $s'.awake = true$
      $T' \notin s'.requested$
      $data(T') = (generation\text{-}number(T), data(T))$
   Effect:
      $s.requested = s'.requested \cup \{T'\}$

REPORT_COMMIT(T',v)
   Effect:
      $s.reported = s'.reported \cup \{T'\}$
      $s.written = s'.written \cup \{object(T')\}$

REPORT_ABORT(T')
   Effect:
      $s.reported = s'.reported \cup \{T'\}$

REQUEST_COMMIT(T, v)
   Precondition:
      $s'.awake = true$
      $s'.requested = s'.reported$
      $i(\mathcal{W}) \in old\text{-}config(T).write$
      $\mathcal{W} \subseteq s'.written$
      $v = \text{``}OK\text{''}$
   Effect:
      $s.awake = false$

Figure 12.13: Transition Relation for Write-Configuration-Coordinators

defined next and as in system $\mathcal{B}$, write the new configuration and generation number to a write quorum of the old configuration, which of course will intersect all read quorums of the old configuration. Hence, if a configuration replica's generation number is the largest found in reading a quorum according to that replica's configuration, then no such write has occurred and the given configuration is the current one.

As promised, we next define write-configuration-coordinators. A write-configuration-coordinator for transaction name $T \in co_{WC}$ has state components *awake*, *requested*, *reported* and *written*, where *awake* is a Boolean variable, initially *false*; *requested* and *reported* are subsets of *children*(T), initially empty; and *written* is a subset of $\bar{\mathcal{Y}}$, initially empty. The set of return values V_T is equal to $\{\text{``}OK\text{''}\}$.

The transition relation for write-configuration-coordinators is shown in Figure 12.13. Recall that a write-configuration-coordinator T has an associated old configuration, *old-config*(T), and a new configuration, *data*(T), as well as a generation number, *generation-number*(T). The purpose of a write-configuration-coordinator is to write its generation number and new configuration to a write quorum in its old configuration. It does this by invoking write accesses to the configuration replicas and can only request to commit after receiving **REPORT_COMMIT** actions for accesses to all configuration replicas in some set corresponding to a write quorum, according to *old-config*(T).

Logical Access Automata

A read-LA in $\mathcal{C}$ is identical to a read-LA in $\mathcal{B}$, except for the **REPORT_COMMIT** input action for children that are read-configuration-coordinators. The only difference is that the read-configuration-coordinator returns not only a configuration, but a pair consisting of a generation number and a configuration. The read-LA simply ignores the generation number. Formally, we have:

REPORT_COMMIT(T',v), $T' \in co_{rc}$
    Effect:
        $s.reported = s'.reported \cup \{T'\}$
        if $s'.config\text{-}read = false$
        then $s.config = v.config$
            $s.config\text{-}read = true$

A write-LA in $\mathcal{C}$ is identical to a write-LA in $\mathcal{B}$, except for the same change described above for read-LA's.

Unlike the read- and write-LA's, the reconfigure-LA's of $\mathcal{C}$ make use of the generation numbers returned by the read-configuration-coordinator, to manage the configuration replicas. Thus, the reconfigure-LA's of $\mathcal{C}$ differ more from those of $\mathcal{B}$ than do the read- and write-LA's. Here, a read-configuration-coordinator returns a pair consisting of a generation number and a configuration, both of which are saved by the reconfigure-LA. These are used to determine, for the write-configuration-coordinators T' invoked by the LA, the allowable values for $old\text{-}config(T')$ and $generation\text{-}number(T')$.

A reconfigure-LA for transaction name $T \in la_{rec}$ has the same state components as it does in $\mathcal{B}$, except for the addition of the component $generation\text{-}number$, which takes on values in $N \cup \{nil\}$ and has initial value nil. The signature is the same, except that the type of the return values for read-configuration-coordinators is now $N \times C$. The actions that change are:

REPORT_COMMIT(T',v), $T' \in co_{rc}$
    Effect:
        $s.reported = s'.reported \cup \{T'\}$
        if $s'.config\text{-}read = false$
        then $s.config = v.config$
            $s.generation\text{-}number$
                $= v.generation\text{-}number$
            $s.config\text{-}read = true$

REQUEST_CREATE(T'), $T' \in co_{wc}$
    Precondition:
        $s'.awake = true$
        $s'.value\text{-}read = true$
        $data(T') = config(T)$
        $old\text{-}config(T') = s'.config$
        $generation\text{-}number(T')$
            $= s'.generation\text{-}number + 1$
        $T' \notin s'.requested$
    Effect:
        $s.requested = s'.requested \cup \{T'\}$

12.4.5 Correctness Proof

In this section, we prove the correctness of system $\mathcal{C}$. Once again, we begin with definitions, this time for a sequence β of actions of $\mathcal{C}$. Specifically, we extend the definitions of *logical-sequence*(β) and *logical-config*(β) to apply to sequences of actions of $\mathcal{C}$. We also require one new definition, analogous to *current-vn*(β). Namely, if β is finite, then *current-gn*(β) is defined to be the highest *generation-number* among the states of all configuration replica automata in any global state led to by β.

We prove correctness of $\mathcal{C}$ by means of a correspondence between $\mathcal{C}$ and $\mathcal{B}$. If β is a sequence of actions of $\mathcal{C}$, then we define $f(\beta)$ to be the sequence of actions of $\mathcal{B}$ that results from

1. removing all **REQUEST_CREATE**(T), **CREATE**(T), **REQUEST_COMMIT**(T,v), **COMMIT**(T), **ABORT**(T), **REPORT_COMMIT**(T,v), and **REPORT_ABORT**(T) events for all transaction names $T \in acc_{rc} \cup acc_{wc}$, and

2. replacing all **REQUEST_COMMIT**(T,v) and **REPORT_COMMIT**(T,v) where $T \in co_{rc}$, with **REQUEST_COMMIT**$(T, v.config)$ and **REPORT_COMMIT**$(T, v.config)$, respectively.

The following lemma is the key to the proof of Theorem 12.15, the main correctness theorem for $\mathcal{C}$. As in Lemma 12.8, Condition 1 is only needed for the inductive argument. Part (a) says that any configuration replica $S(\bar{Y})$ either has the current generation number, or has a configuration such that all configuration replicas in some write quorum of that configuration hold generation numbers higher than the one held by $S(\bar{Y})$. Part (b) says that every configuration replica holding the current generation number also holds the logical configuration. Condition 2, the important part of the lemma, says that our construction yields a schedule of $\mathcal{B}$.

LEMMA 12.10 *Let β be a finite schedule of $\mathcal{C}$ such that no logical access is active in β.*

1. *The following properties hold in any global state led to by β.*

   (a) *For any configuration replica automaton $S(\bar{Y})$, if v is the data component of $S(\bar{Y})$ and $v.generation\text{-}number < current\text{-}gn(\beta)$, then there exists a write quorum $\mathcal{W} \in v.config.write$ with the following property. For any configuration replica $S(\bar{Y})$ for an object name $\bar{Y}$ such that $i(\bar{Y}) \in \mathcal{W}$, if v' is the data component of $S(\bar{Y})$, then $v'.generation\text{-}number > v.generation\text{-}number$.*

   (b) *For any configuration replica $S(\bar{Y})$, if v is the data component of $S(\bar{Y})$ and $v.generation\text{-}number = current\text{-}gn(\beta)$, then $v.config = logical\text{-}config(\beta)$.*

2. *The sequence $f(\beta)$ is a schedule of $\mathcal{B}$.*

PROOF We proceed by induction on the number of pairs of the form **CREATE**(T) **REQUEST_COMMIT**(T, v) in *logical-sequence*(β). For the basis, suppose *logical-sequence*(β) contains no such pairs. Then *logical-config*$(\beta) = c_0$. Since all configuration replicas initially have *generation-number* $= 0$ and *config* $= c_0$, the same is true in any global state led to by β. Thus, *current-gn*$(\beta) = 0$. This implies Condition 1, and Condition 2 holds because the two systems behave identically if no LA's are invoked.

For the inductive step, let $\beta = \beta'\gamma$, where *logical-sequence*(γ) begins with the last **CREATE** event in *logical-sequence*(β), and assume that the lemma holds for β'. Then *logical-sequence*$(\gamma) = $ **CREATE**(T_f)**REQUEST_COMMIT**(T_f, v_f) for some $T_f \in la$ and v_f of the appropriate type. As before, the fact that the system is serial shows that we can restrict attention to T_f and its descendants.

For any LA to issue a **REQUEST_COMMIT**, it must first receive a **REPORT_COMMIT** for a read-configuration-coordinator and a read-coordinator. Let T' be the read-coordinator in co_r with the first **REPORT_COMMIT** in γ, and let γ' be the portion of γ up to and including the given **REPORT_COMMIT** event. Also, let T'' be the read-configuration-coordinator in co_{rc} with the first **REPORT_COMMIT** in γ, and let γ'' be the portion of γ up to and including this **REPORT_COMMIT** event. We give a claim about the return value of T''; the proof of the claim is left to the reader as Exercise 2.

> **CLAIM 12.11** *If* *REQUEST_COMMIT*(T'', v) *occurs in* γ*, then* $v = $ (*current-gn*(β'), *logical-config*(β')).

Now we consider three cases.

1. $T_f \in la_r$.

It is easy to see that Condition 1 is preserved, since no descendants of T_f are write accesses to configuration replicas. Claim 12.11 implies that the value returned by T'' in γ has as its configuration component the value *logical-config*(β'). By the definition of *logical-config*, this is the same value that would be returned by the configuration automaton in $\mathcal{B}$. Also, the automaton associated with T_f in $\mathcal{C}$ behaves identically to that associated with T_f in $\mathcal{B}$ except that, in $\mathcal{C}$, it receives and ignores the *generation-number* component of the return value of T'', exactly as the correspondence f requires. Since β is a schedule of $\mathcal{C}$, it follows that $f(\beta)$ is a schedule of $\mathcal{B}$, which shows Condition 2.

2. $T_f \in la_w$.

The argument is similar to the one for the previous case.

3. $T_f \in la_{rec}$.

We first give several claims about the state of T_f and the information associated with the descendants it invokes.

CLAIM 12.12 *If s is a state of T_f in a global state led to by some prefix of β that extends $\beta'\gamma''$, then $s.generation\text{-}number = current\text{-}gn(\beta')$ and $s.config = logical\text{-}config(\beta')$.*

CLAIM 12.13 *If T is a write-configuration-coordinator invoked by T_f in γ, then $data(T) = config(T_f)$, $generation\text{-}number(T) = current\text{-}gn(\beta') + 1$, and $old\text{-}config(T) = logical\text{-}config(\beta')$.*

CLAIM 12.14 *If T is a write access in acc_{wc} invoked by a write-configuration-coordinator in γ, then $data(T) = (current\text{-}gn(\beta') + 1, config(T_f))$.*

By definition, T_f cannot request to commit until at least one of its write-configuration-coordinators has committed; let T_w be any write-configuration-coordinator child of T_f that has a **COMMIT** event in γ. Moreover, at least one write access to a configuration replica must commit before a write-configuration-coordinator can request to commit. From Claim 12.14, we know that any write configuration access T that is a descendant of T_f has $data(T) = (current\text{-}gn(\beta')+1, config(T_f))$. Therefore, $current\text{-}gn(\beta) = current\text{-}gn(\beta') + 1$. Furthermore, by the definition of $logical\text{-}config$, $config(T_f) = logical\text{-}config(\beta)$. So, all write accesses T in acc_{wc} invoked by a write-configuration-coordinator in γ have $data(T) = (current\text{-}gn(\beta), logical\text{-}config(\beta))$.

To show that 1(a) of the inductive hypothesis holds for β, we consider three cases for each configuration replica $\bar{Y}$ with data v, in any global state led to by β; by the preceding arguments, these cases are exhaustive.

(a) $v.generation\text{-}number < current\text{-}gn(\beta')$.

Then $\bar{Y}$ is not updated by any descendant of T_f in β. That is, v is the data in $\bar{Y}$ in any global state led to by β'. Therefore, it follows immediately from 1(a) of the inductive hypothesis that there exists a set $\mathcal{W}$ with $i(\mathcal{W}) \in v.config.write$ such that for any configuration replica $S(\bar{Y}')$ for an object name $\bar{Y}' \in \mathcal{W}$, if v' is the *data* component of $S(\bar{Y}')$ in any global state led to by β' then $v'.generation\text{-}number > v.generation\text{-}number$. During γ, either the *generation-number* in the data held in $S(\bar{Y}')$ is unchanged, or else it is set to $current\text{-}generation(\beta)$ (which is greater than $v.generation\text{-}number$) by a descendant of T_f. In either case, 1(a) holds for β.

(b) $v.generation\text{-}number = current\text{-}gn(\beta')$.

Then by 1(b) of the inductive hypothesis, we know that $v.config = logical\text{-}config(\beta')$. By definition of a write-configuration-coordinator, just prior to the **REQUEST_COMMIT** for T_w in γ, there must be a set $\mathcal{W}$ with $i(\mathcal{W}) \in old\text{-}config(T_w).write$ such that write accesses to all configuration replicas for object names in $\mathcal{W}$ have committed, so by our arguments above, all of these configuration replicas have $generation\text{-}number = current\text{-}gn(\beta)$ in any global state led to by β. By Claim 12.13, $old\text{-}config(T_w) = logical\text{-}config(\beta')$. Therefore, $\mathcal{W}$ satisfies $i(\mathcal{W}) \in v.config.write$ and all configuration replicas for object names in $\mathcal{W}$ have *generation-number* = *current-gn*(β) > *v.generation-number* in any global state led to by β. Therefore, 1(a) holds.

(c) *v.generation-number* = *current-gn*(β).
Then 1(a) is trivial.

So, in all three cases, 1(a) holds for β.

We now show 1(b). By the definition of *current-gn*, we know that if v' is the data component of the state of a configuration replica $S(Y)$ in any global state led to by β', then $v'.generation\text{-}number \le current\text{-}gn(\beta')$. Therefore, any configuration replica that has, in any global state led to by β, a generation number equal to *current-gn*(β) (and so larger than *current-gn*(β')), must be written after β'. The writer of such a configuration replica must be a descendent of T_f, and therefore must be a child of some write-configuration-coordinator $T_{w'}$ invoked by T_f. Since all such $T_{w'}$ have $data(T_{w'}) = config(T_f)$, which by definition is *logical-config*(β), 1(b) holds.

Condition 2 is straightforward, as for Case 1.

$\square$

The lemma above immediately yields a relationship between $\mathcal{C}$ and $\mathcal{B}$. Let $\mathcal{T}_B$ and $\mathcal{X}_B$ denote the transaction names and object names of $\mathcal{B}$, respectively.

THEOREM 12.15 *Let β be a finite schedule of $\mathcal{C}$. Then there exists a schedule γ of $\mathcal{B}$ such that the following two conditions hold.*

1. $\gamma|T = \beta|T$ *for each transaction name $T \in \mathcal{T}_B - (co_{rc} \cup co_{wc})$, and*

2. $\gamma|Y = \beta|Y$ *for each object name $Y \in \mathcal{X}_B$.*

Now we can combine Theorems 12.9 and 12.15 to prove a relationship between $\mathcal{C}$ and $\mathcal{A}$. Let $\mathcal{T}_A$ and $\mathcal{X}_A$ denote the transaction names and object names of $\mathcal{A}$, respectively.

THEOREM 12.16 *Let β be a finite schedule of $\mathcal{C}$. Then there exists a schedule γ of $\mathcal{A}$ such that the following two conditions hold.*

1. $\gamma|T = \beta|T$ *for each transaction name $T \in \mathcal{T}_A - la$, and*

2. $\gamma|Y = \beta|Y$ *for each object name $Y \in \mathcal{X}_A$.*

12.5 Concurrent Replicated Systems

So far, this chapter has dealt exclusively with serial systems. Now we present some immediate corollaries of the theorems in the previous sections that may be used to show the correctness of *concurrent* replicated systems. These corollaries show that any correct concurrency control algorithm can be combined with any of our replication algorithms to yield a correct system. These corollaries allow us to treat issues of concurrency control and recovery separately from issues of replication.

We require one minor extension to a previous definition. In Chapter 3, the definition of atomicity is made with respect to a particular, implicitly understood serial system. Now that we are considering several different serial systems at once, we restate the definition to include explicit mention of the serial system. Thus, let $\mathcal{S}$ be a serial system, and let β be a sequence of actions. We say that β is *atomic with respect to $\mathcal{S}$ for transaction T* provided that $\beta|T = \gamma|T$ for some schedule γ of $\mathcal{S}$.

In this section, we let $\mathcal{A}$ and $\mathcal{C}$ denote the systems defined in Section 12.4.

COROLLARY 12.17 *Let β be a sequence of actions that is atomic with respect to $\mathcal{C}$, for transaction name $T \in \mathcal{T}_A - la$. Then β is also atomic with respect to $\mathcal{A}$ for T.*

PROOF By Theorem 12.16. □

As an immediate consequence of the preceding corollary, we can obtain a corollary about generic systems:

COROLLARY 12.18 *Let $\mathcal{S}$ be any generic system. Assume that all behaviors of $\mathcal{S}$ are atomic with respect to $\mathcal{C}$ for all nonorphan transaction names in $\mathcal{T}_A - la$. Then all behaviors of $\mathcal{S}$ are atomic with respect to $\mathcal{A}$ for all nonorphan transaction names in $\mathcal{T}_A - la$.*

Thus, for example, we consider a generic system $\mathcal{D}$ that has the same system type as $\mathcal{C}$, as well as the same transaction automata. Suppose that the object associated with each object name Y of $\mathcal{D}$ is dynamic atomic, with respect to the serial object $S(Y)$ associated with Y in $\mathcal{C}$. (For instance, this object could implement the general commutativity-based locking algorithm for object $S(Y)$, as described in Chapter 6.) The results of Section 6.3 imply that all behaviors of $\mathcal{D}$ are atomic with respect to $\mathcal{C}$, for all nonorphan transaction names, in particular, for all nonorphan transaction names in $\mathcal{T}_A - la$. Then Corollary 12.18 implies that all behaviors of $\mathcal{D}$ are atomic with respect to $\mathcal{A}$ for all nonorphan transaction names in $\mathcal{T}_A - la$. This says that system $\mathcal{D}$, which combines concurrency control techniques for achieving dynamic atomicity with the replication strategies of this chapter, looks the same as the serial, unreplicated system $\mathcal{A}$, to the nonorphan transaction names in $\mathcal{T}_A - la$ (in particular, to T_0).

Similar conclusions can be drawn for pseudotime systems such as those described in Chapter 7, or for hybrid systems such as those described in Chapter 8. Also, similar conclusions can be drawn when $\mathcal{C}$ is replaced by system $\mathcal{B}$ of Section 12.4, or by $\mathcal{B}$ of Section 12.3. In general, any concurrency control algorithm that provides atomicity at the level of the replicas may be combined with any of our replication algorithms to produce a correct system.

Finally, we note that our techniques allow combination of algorithms for orphan management (as described in Chapter 11) with algorithms for concurrency control and for replication. For example, consider the generic system $\mathcal{D}$ described just above, and let $\mathcal{E}$ be another system that is constructed from $\mathcal{D}$ by adding one of the orphan management algorithms of Chapter 11. The results of Chapter 11 imply that $\mathcal{E}$ is atomic with respect to $\mathcal{C}$, for *all* transaction names (including orphans), in particular, for all transaction names in $\mathcal{T}_A - la$. Then Corollary 12.17 implies that $\mathcal{E}$ is atomic with respect to $\mathcal{A}$ for all transaction names in $\mathcal{T}_A - la$. Thus, system $\mathcal{E}$, which combines concurrency control techniques from Chapter 6 and orphan management techniques from Chapter 11 with the replication strategies of this chapter, looks like $\mathcal{A}$ to all the transaction names in $\mathcal{T}_A - la$, and in particular, to T_0.

1 2 . 6   D i s c u s s i o n

This chapter demonstrates one way in which disparate aspects of a transaction processing method may be considered separately. We show how replication can be managed, replacing logical accesses with subtransactions accessing multiple replicas. This can be done without regard for concurrency, if concurrency control is provided on the copies as if they were unconnected data items.

There are many other replication algorithms, some of which are described in the bibliographic notes below. It would be interesting to see whether the techniques of this chapter can be extended to verify them. One difficulty is that some algorithms deal with partitions of the database into separate components that cannot communicate with one another. Often these algorithms allow transactions in different components to observe serialization orders that are not consistent with the order in which the transactions actually run. (A read may miss a preceding write in another component.) Such executions are not atomic, and a weaker correctness condition, similar to sequential consistency [66], is appropriate. Because these algorithms exhibit different external behavior (at least when partitions occur), we feel a distinct correctness definition is appropriate.

12.7 Bibliographic Notes

The quorum consensus algorithm was originally developed by Gifford [37], based on an earlier majority-voting algorithm by Thomas [110]. Gifford's paper does not include transaction nesting, but rather permits the user to access the logical objects using single-level transactions. The ideas of Gifford's algorithm underlie many more recent and sophisticated replication techniques (see, e.g., [2, 24, 25, 26, 47, 48]).

There are also other approaches to replication besides quorum consensus. One of the most important is based on the idea of a *primary copy*. Early algorithms did not ensure atomicity in all situations. More recently, Oki developed a primary copy method for a nested transaction system that ensures atomicity despite both site crashes and partitions [95, 96]. To improve availability, some researchers have also explored the use of "loosely consistent" replication methods, in which the replicated object does not give the appearance of a single copy (see, e.g., [14]).

The modularity achieved in this chapter by treating replication in the context of serial systems and separating it from concurrency control and recovery cannot be achieved for all replication algorithms. For example, Herlihy [48] also describes algorithms in which replication and concurrency control are integrated; these algorithms can achieve higher availability and higher concurrency than can algorithms in which the two are separated.

The generalized configuration strategy presented in this chapter, using intersecting quorums rather than votes, is justified by Garcia-Molina and Barbara in [35]. The reconfiguration mechanism described here is based on a brief description given in [37].

There have been some previous attempts at rigorous presentation and proof of replicated data algorithms. Most notable among these is the presentation and proof given by Bernstein, Hadzilacos, and Goodman [12] of Gifford's basic algorithm; this work is based on classical serializability theory. Their approach, however, does not appear to generalize easily to the case where nesting and failures are allowed. Also, Herlihy [47] extends Gifford's algorithm to accommodate abstract data types and offers a correctness proof. Again, nesting is not considered.

A preliminary version of the results of this chapter appeared in [38].

12.8 Exercises

1. Prove Lemma 12.8.

2. Complete the proof of Lemma 12.10 by proving each Claim.

3. This question presents some ideas for optimizing the algorithms for reconfigurable quorum consensus.

(a) In the special case that each new write quorum is contained in a current write quorum, the logical reconfiguration transaction need not read and write the data replicas. Explain.

(b) Find a similar condition on read quorums. Does one imply the other?

(c) Give code and correctness claims and proofs for an alternative strategy implementing these optimizations.

4. Work out the details of the alternative strategy for modeling reconfiguration invocations described in Footnote 5. That is, some of the transaction automata of $\mathcal{A}'$ would be compositions of correspondingly named automata of $\mathcal{A}$ with certain auxiliary automata. For example, the transaction automaton for T in $\mathcal{A}'$ might be constructed as the original transaction automaton A_T from $\mathcal{A}$, composed with a new transaction automaton B_T that only invokes reconfiguration requests, composed with another *coordinator* automaton. The job of the coordinator is to convert a **CREATE**(T) event into two **CREATE** events, one for each of A_T and B_T, and to convert two **REQUEST_COMMIT** actions, one for each of A_T and B_T, into a single **REQUEST_COMMIT** event for T. (Some renaming of actions is needed in order to avoid name conflicts.)

The constructions in the rest of this chapter, of systems $\mathcal{B}$ and $\mathcal{C}$, would then be based on $\mathcal{A}'$ rather than on $\mathcal{A}$. The resulting theorems would say that executions of $\mathcal{B}$ and $\mathcal{C}$ look like executions of $\mathcal{A}'$ to the transaction automata. But then projecting the executions onto the subautomata representing the original A_T shows that they also look the same to these transactions.

5. Give code and correctness claims and proofs for the alternative strategy for replicated configuration management, involving a fixed meta-configuration, suggested at the beginning of Section 12.4.4.

6. Design and prove correct a reconfigurable replication algorithm in which both the configurations and the data are replicated, and in which the accesses to data replicas may run concurrently with accesses to configuration replicas. That is, the algorithms in this chapter first read the current configuration and then initiate reads of data replicas. However, a different system architecture would allow the logical read and logical write transactions to request concurrent reads of the configuration objects and of the data replicas, and use the configuration returned to determine when enough data replicas have been read. (Why doesn't the current architecture allow this concurrency?)

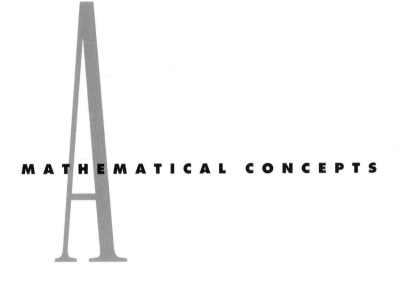

MATHEMATICAL CONCEPTS

A.1 Introduction

This appendix contains some basic definitions that will be used as part of the foundation for the material in the rest of the book. All the definitions are of basic set-theoretic concepts involving partial orders, sequences, and so on. These concepts are used throughout discrete mathematics; unfortunately, the details of definitions vary among different sources. You should use this appendix as a reference for the precise choices we have made. If you are not comfortable with any of the concepts, you should consult a textbook of discrete mathematics such as [5].

A.2 Sets

The basic construct used to express all mathematical ideas in this book is the **set**. If A is a set and a is an **element** of the set we write $a \in A$; otherwise, we write $a \notin A$. A set can be described in several ways: by listing its elements explicitly (for example $A = \{1, 3, 5\}$); by abstraction, that is, by giving a condition that characterizes the members precisely (for example $A = \{i : 0 < i < 6 \text{ and } i \text{ is odd }\}$); or by comprehension, that is, by giving an expression all of whose values form the membership of the set (for example, $A = \{2k + 1 \text{ where } k \in \{0, 1, 2\}\}$). Notice that the same set can have many different descriptions. One important set is the **empty set** (written $\emptyset$), which has no elements.

We say that A is a **subset** of B if every element of A is an element of B, and we write $A \subseteq B$. To say A is a **proper subset** of B means that both $A \subseteq B$ and $A \neq B$. The fundamental operations on sets are **union, intersection**, and **difference**. One can define these by $A \cup B = \{x : x \in A \text{ or } x \in B\}$ $A \cap B = \{x : x \in A \text{ and } x \in B\}$ $A - B = \{x : x \in A \text{ and } x \notin B\}$. For example, when $A = \{1, 2, 3\}$ and $B = \{1, 3, 5\}$, we have $A \cup B = \{1, 2, 3, 5\}$, $A \cap B = \{1, 3\}$, and $A - B = \{2\}$. We say that A is **disjoint** from B when $A \cap B = \emptyset$. We say an indexed collection of sets A_i is **pairwise-disjoint** when $i \neq j$ implies A_i disjoint from A_j.

We give the name **power set** of A to the set whose elements are the subsets of A.

A.3   Tuples

A **tuple** is an ordered list of **components**. When there are only two or three components, we use the terms **pair**—ii and **triple**, respectively. We denote by $A \times B$ the set of all the pairs where the first component is an element of A and the second component is an element of B.

It is common to use names to distinguish the components, rather than the position in a list. For example, one can consider a set of pairs of integers, where each pair has a component called *high* and another component called *low*. More generally, suppose I is a set of names (an **index set**), and for each $i \in I$ a set A_i is given. We denote by $\Pi_{i \in I} A_i$ the set consisting of every tuple where for each i the component called i is an element of the set A_i. This set is called the **Cartesian product** of the sets A_i.

A.4   Relations

A **relation** is a set of tuples, all with the same names for their components. That is, a relation is a subset of a Cartesian product. We refer to a subset of $A \times A$ as a **binary relation** on A.

We next define some properties that binary relations may have. We say that a binary relation R on A is **reflexive** if for every a in A, $(a, a) \in R$. We say R is **irreflexive** if for every a in A, $(a, a) \notin R$. We say R is **symmetric** if for every a and a' in A, $(a, a') \in R$ implies $(a', a) \in R$. We say R is **antisymmetric** if for every a and a' in A, $(a, a') \in R$ and $(a', a) \in R$ imply $a = a'$. We say R is **transitive** if for every a, a', and a'' in A, $(a, a') \in R$ and $(a', a'') \in R$ imply $(a, a'') \in R$. We say R is **total** if for every a and a' in A, at least one of the following is true: $a = a'$, $(a, a') \in R$, or $(a', a) \in R$.

We say that a binary relation is an **equivalence relation** if it is reflexive, symmetric, and transitive. We say that R is a **partial order** if it is irreflexive, antisymmetric, and transitive. We say that it is a **total order** if it is a partial order and also total.

If R is a binary relation on A, we define the **transitive closure** of R to be the binary relation that is the intersection of all the transitive binary relations on A of which R is a subset. It can be shown that the transitive closure of R is itself transitive, and R is a subset of it. It can also be shown that (a, a') is an element of the transitive closure of R if and only if there exists a finite chain of elements $a_0, a_1, \ldots, a_k$ such that $a_0 = a$, $a_k = a'$, and for all i, $(a_i, a_{i+1}) \in R$.

We say that a binary relation R is **acyclic** when the transitive closure of R is irreflexive. Notice that any partial order is acyclic, and that the transitive closure of any acyclic relation is a partial order. If R is an acyclic relation, then a **topological sort** of R is any total order R' such that R is a subset of R'. Every acyclic relation has a topological sort.

If R and R' are two partial orders on the same set A, we say that R and R' are **consistent** provided that the union $R \cup R'$ is acyclic. This is equivalent to the existence of a partial order R'' of which both R and R' are subsets.

One can represent a binary relation on A pictorially, by a **graph**. Each **node** of the graph corresponds to an element of A. There is an **edge** from the node representing a to the node representing a' if and only if $(a, a') \in R$.

A.5 Functions and Partial Functions

A **function** f from A to B is a subset of $A \times B$ with the property that for each a in A, there is exactly one b so that $(a, b) \in f$. Usually we use functional notation, and say "f maps a to b (written $f(a) = b$) in this situation, calling b the **value** of f on the **argument** a. The set A is called the **domain** of f, written $domain(f)$. We can indicate that f is a function from A to B by writing $f : A \to B$.

We next define some properties that functions may have. We say that a function f from A to B is **injective** when for every b in B there is at most one argument a so that $f(a) = b$ (equivalently, f is injective when $f(a) = f(a')$ implies $a = a'$). We say f is **surjective** when for every b in B there is at least one argument a so that $f(a) = b$. We say that f is **bijective** when it is both injective and surjective. If f is a function from a subset of the integers to a (possibly different) subset of the integers, we say that f is **monotone increasing** when $i < j$ implies $f(i) < f(j)$. Notice that a monotone increasing function is injective.

Sometimes we want to associate values in B to arguments in A, but find that no value seems sensible for some argument a in A. We could deal with this by considering a function from a subset of A to B; however, a common alternative is to use a **partial function** from A to B, which is a subset f of $A \times B$ with the property that for each a in A, there is at most b so that $(a, b) \in f$. Thus, despite the way the terms are named, every function is a partial function, but not every partial function is a function. The set of a for which there is exactly one b with $(a, b) \in f$ is called the **domain** of f, written $domain(f)$. We continue to use functional notation and write $f(a) = b$ when $(a, b) \in f$; we say that f is **undefined** (written $f(a) = $ "*undefined*") when $a \notin domain(f)$.

A.6   Trees

A **tree** is a set A together with a distinguished element r of A (called the **root**) and a function $parent$ from $A - \{r\}$ to A, with the property that for every a there is a finite chain $a_0, a_1, a_2 \ldots, a_k$ such that $a_0 = a$, $a_k = r$, and for every i, $parent(a_i) = a_{i+1}$. If we regard $parent$ as a binary relation R on A instead of a function on a subset of A, this property is that for every a, (a, r) is in the transitive closure of R. If a and a' are elements of A, and $parent(a') = a$, then we say a is the **parent** of a' and that a' is a **child** of a. We denote the set $\{a' : parent(a') = a\}$ as $children(a)$. We use other terms, some from genealogy and some from botany: a is an **ancestor** of a' (equivalently, a' is a **descendant** of a) when $a = a'$ or (a', a) is in the transitive closure of $parent$; a is a **sibling** of a' when $a \neq a'$ and $parent(a) = parent(a')$; a is a **leaf** when it has no children. Particularly important is the least common ancestor (**lca**) of two elements: $lca(a, a')$ denotes the element b with the properties that b is an ancestor of a, b is an ancestor of a', and whenever b' is an ancestor of both a and a', then b' is an ancestor of b. The lca of two elements always exists; also, if neither a nor a' is an ancestor of the other then there are two siblings b and b' that are children of $lca(a, a')$ with the property that b is an ancestor of a, and b' is an ancestor of a'.

A tree is often represented pictorially as a graph, with an edge from each node to its parent. However, the direction is not explicitly marked; instead, the parent is shown higher on the page—thus the root node is at the top of the picture.

A.7   Sequences

Formally, a **sequence** β of elements of A is a function from D to A, where D is either the set of positive integers or else a set consisting of all positive integers less than or equal to n, for some integer n. However, this book usually does not use functional notation for a sequence. Instead, it generally describes the sequence by listing the images of successive integers under the mapping, writing $\beta = \beta(1)\beta(2)\beta(3)\ldots$. The **length** of β is the size of the domain of the function. This domain might be empty, in which case β is the **empty sequence** (written λ), which has length zero. At the other extreme, the domain could include all the positive integers, in which case β is an **infinite sequence**. Any sequence that is not infinite is called a **finite** sequence.

If β γ are sequences where β has finite length k, then the **concatenation** of β and γ, written as $\beta\gamma$, is the sequence δ where $\delta(i) = \beta(i)$ if $i \leq k$, and $\delta(i) = \gamma(i - k)$ if $i > k$ and $i - k \leq length(\gamma)$. We say that β is a **prefix** of δ when there exists a sequence γ so that $\delta = \beta\gamma$ (equivalently, when $\beta(i) = \delta(i)$ for all i in $domain(\beta)$). (Note that the empty sequence is a prefix of every sequence, and that every sequence is a prefix of itself.)

It is possible for the same value to appear more than once in a sequence; in this case, it is sometimes convenient to distinguish the different occurrences. Thus, a particular occurrence of an action in a sequence is referred to as an "event". Formally, an **event** in a sequence $\beta = \beta_1\beta_2\ldots$ is an ordered pair (i, a), where i is a positive integer and $a = \beta_i$, the ith element in the sequence. We say that the event (i, β_i) **precedes** (j, β_j) in β when $i < j$. Usually we abuse notation and write β_i for the event; we naturally extend this abuse to all concepts defined for values (for example, if R is a binary relation on elements of A, we say that R relates the event (i, β_i) to the event (j, β_j) provided $(\beta_i, \beta_j) \in R$).

Suppose β and γ are both sequences of elements of A. We say that γ is a **subsequence** of β if there exists a function f from $domain(\gamma)$ to $domain(\beta)$ such that f is monotone increasing and $\beta(f(i)) = \gamma(i)$ for all i in $domain(\gamma)$. We abuse notation and identify[1] the event $(i, \gamma(i))$ of γ with the event $(f(i), \beta(f(i)))$ of β; for example, we say that γ contains the event $(f(i), \beta(f(i)))$ from β. Notice that any prefix of β is a subsequence of β. Also notice that the definition of subsequence does not require $f(i + 1) = f(i) + 1$; in other words, the subsequence need not consist of contiguous (adjacent) events from β.

If R is a binary relation on the events of β and γ is a subsequence of β, we say that γ is R-**closed** in β provided that whenever γ contains an event β_j from β, it also contains every event β_i of β such that β_i precedes β_j in β and $(\beta_i, \beta_j) \in R$.

If β is a sequence of elements of A, and Φ is a subset of A, we define the **projection** of β on A (written $\beta|\Phi$) to be the subsequence of β containing exactly the occurrences in β of events that are in Φ. Formally, $\beta|\Phi$ is the sequence γ, where the domain of γ is the number of positive integers k such that $\beta(k) \in \Phi$, and for any i in this domain $\gamma(i) = \beta(j)$ for the unique integer j such that $\beta(j) \in \Phi$ and i is equal to the number of positive integers k such that $k \leq j$ and $\beta(k) \in \Phi$. It is a simple fact that there is a unique function f that can be used in showing that $\beta|\Phi$ is a subsequence of β.

We say that γ is a **reordering** of β if there exists a function f from $domain(\gamma)$ to

---

[1] Notice that technically, this identification depends on the choice of the function f. Where we use this concept, there will be an obvious or unique choice, as for example, when γ is a projection of β.

$domain(\beta)$ such that f is bijective and $\beta(f(i)) = \gamma(i)$ for all i in $domain(\gamma)$. In this case we must have $domain(\beta) = domain(\gamma)$. Again, we abuse notation by identifying the event $(i, \gamma(i))$ of γ with the event $(f(i), \beta(f(i)))$ of β.

If R is a total order on the events of β, then there exists a unique sequence γ (and a unique f) such that f shows γ to be a reordering of β and the identification given by f converts the *precedes* order on events in γ into the order R on the events in β. We describe this unique β as obtained by **ordering β according to** R. If R is a partial order on the events in β, we say that γ is a **reordering of β consistent with** R if it is obtained by ordering β according to some topological sort of R.

A property P of sequences of elements of A is said to be a **safety property** provided the following conditions hold: there exists some sequence β satisfying P; whenever β satisfies P and γ is a prefix of β, then γ satisfies P; and whenever β is an infinite sequence such that every finite prefix of β satisfies P, then β itself satisfies P. It follows that the empty sequence must satisfy P.

BIBLIOGRAPHY

[1] D. Agrawal and A. El Abbadi. Locks with constrained sharing. In *Proceedings of 9th ACM Symposium on Principles of Database Systems*, pages 85–93, April 1990.

[2] D. Agrawal and A. El Abbadi. The tree quorum protocol: An efficient approach for managing replicated data. In *Proceedings of 16th International Conference on Very Large Data Bases*, pages 243–254, August 1990.

[3] D. Agrawal and S. Sengupta. Modular synchronization in multiversion databases. In *Proceedings of the 1989 ACM SIGMOD International Conference on the Management of Data*, pages 408–417, May 1989.

[4] R. Agrawal, M. Carey, and M. Livny. Concurrency control modeling: Alternatives and implications. *Transactions on Database Systems*, 12(4):609–654, December 1987.

[5] A. Aho and J. Ullman. *Foundations of Computer Science*. Computer Science Press, New York, NY, 1992.

[6] J. Aspnes, A. Fekete, N. Lynch, M. Merritt, and W. E. Weihl. A theory of timestamp-based concurrency control for nested transactions. In *Proceedings of 14th International Conference on Very Large Data Bases*, pages 431–444, August 1988.

[7] B. Badrinath and K. Ramamritham. Semantics-based concurrency control: Beyond commutativity. *Transactions on Database Systems*, 17(1):163–199, March 1992.

[8] J. Baeten and W. Weijland. *Process Algebra*. Cambridge University Press, Cambridge, UK, 1990.

[9] R. Bayer and M. Schkolnick. Concurrency of operations on B-trees. *Acta Informatica*, 9:1–21, 1977.

[10] C. Beeri, P. A. Bernstein, and N. Goodman. A model for concurrency in nested transaction systems. *Journal of the ACM*, 36(2):230–269, April 1989.

[11] C. Beeri, P. A. Bernstein, N. Goodman, M. Lai, and D. Shasha. A concurrency control theory for nested transactions. In *Proceedings of 2nd ACM Symposium on Principles of Distributed Computing*, pages 45–62, August 1983.

[12] P. A. Bernstein, V. Hadzilacos, and N. Goodman. *Concurrency Control and Recovery in Database Systems*. Addison-Wesley, Reading, MA, 1987.

[13] P. A. Bernstein, D. Shipman, and J. Rothnie. Concurrency control in a system for distributed databases (SDD-1). *Transactions on Database Systems*, 5(1):18–51, March 1980.

[14] A. Birrel, R. Levin, R. Needham, and M. Schroeder. Grapevine: An excercise in distributed computing. *Communications of the ACM*, 25(4):260–274, April 1982.

[15] T. Bolognesi and E. Brinksma. Introduction to the ISO specification language LOTOS. *Computer Networks and ISDN Systems*, 14(1):25–59, 1987.

[16] M. Broy. Algebraic and functional specification of an interactive serializable database interface. *Distributed Computing*, 6(1):5–18, July 1992.

[17] S. Budkowski and P. Dembinski. An introduction to Estelle: A specification language for distributed systems. *Computer Networks and ISDN Systems*, 14(1):3–23, 1987.

[18] K. M. Chandy and J. Misra. *Parallel Program Design: A Foundation*. Addison-Wesley, Reading, MA, 1988.

[19] C. Chou and E. Gafni. Understanding and verifying distributed algorithms using stratified decomposition. In *Proceedings of 7th ACM Symposium on Principles of Distributed Computing*, pages 44–65, August 1988.

[20] P. Chrysanthis, S. Raghuram, and K. Ramamrithan. Extracting concurrency from objects. In *Proceedings of the 1992 ACM SIGMOD International Conference on the Management of Data*, pages 108–117, June 1991.

[21] C. T. Davies. Recovery semantics for DB/DC system. In *Proceedings of 28th ACM National Conference*, pages 136–141, August 1973.

[22] J. deBakker. *Stepwise Refinement of Distributed Systems: Lecture Notes in Computer Science 430*. Springer-Verlag, Berlin, Germany, 1990.

[23] D. L. Detlefs, M. P. Herlihy, and J. M. Wing. Inheritance of synchronization and recovery properties in Avalon/C++. *IEEE Computer*, 12(12):57–69, December 1988.

[24] D. Eager and K. Sevcik. Robustness in distributed database systems. *Transactions on Database Systems*, 8(3):354–381, September 1983.

[25] A. El Abaddi and S. Toueg. Maintaining availability in partitioned replicated databases. *Transactions on Database Systems*, 14(2):264–290, June 1989.

[26] A. El Abbadi, D. Skeen, and F. Cristian. An efficient fault-tolerant protocol for replicated data management. In *Proceedings of 4th ACM Symposium on Principles of Database Systems*, pages 215–229, March 1985.

[27] C. Ellis. Concurrency in linear hashing. *Transactions on Database Systems*, 12(2):195–217, June 1987.

[28] A. Elmagarmid. *Database Transaction Models*. Morgan Kaufmann, San Mateo, CA, 1991.

[29] J. Eppinger, L. Mummert, and A. Spector. *Camelot and Avalon: A Distributed Transaction Facility*. Morgan Kaufmann, San Mateo, CA, 1991.

[30] K. P. Eswaran, J. N. Gray, R. A. Lorie, and I. L. Traiger. The notions of consistency and predicate locks in a database system. *Communications of the ACM*, 19(11):624–633, November 1976.

[31] A. Farrag and M. Ozsu. Using semantic knowledge of transactions to increase concurrency. *Transactions on Database Systems*, 14(4):503–525, December 1989.

[32] A. Fekete, N. Lynch, M. Merritt, and W. E. Weihl. Nested transactions and read/write locking. In *Proceedings of 6th ACM Symposium on Principles of Database Systems*, pages 97–111, March 1987. Expanded version available as Technical Memo MIT/LCS/TM-324, Laboratory for Computer Science, Massachusetts Institute of Technology, Cambridge, MA, April 1987.

[33] A. Fekete, N. Lynch, M. Merritt, and W. E. Weihl. Commutativity-based locking for nested transactions. *Journal of Computer and System Sciences*, 41(1):65–156, August 1990.

[34] A. Fekete, N. Lynch, and W. E. Weihl. A serialization graph for nested transactions. In *Proceedings of 9th ACM Symposium on Principles of Database Systems*, pages 94–105, April 1990.

[35] H. Garcia-Molina and D. Barbara. How to assign votes in a distributed system. *Journal of the ACM*, 32(4):841–860, October 1985.

[36] D. Gawlick. Processing "hot spots" in high performance systems. In *Proceedings of 30th IEEE Computer Society International Conference (COMPCON'85)*, pages 249–251, February 1985.

[37] D. Gifford. Weighted voting for replicated data. In *Proceedings of 7th ACM Symposium on Operating System Principles*, pages 150–162, December 1979.

[38] K. Goldman and N. Lynch. Nested transactions and quorum consensus. In *Proceedings of 6th ACM Symposium on Principles of Distributed Computation*, pages 27–41, August 1987. Expanded version is available as Technical Memo MIT/LCS/TM-390, Laboratory for Computer Science, Massachusetts Institute of Technology, Cambridge, MA, May 1987.

[39] J. A. Goree. Internal consistency of a distributed transaction system with orphan detection. Master's thesis, Massachusetts Institute of Technology, Cambridge, MA, January 1983. Also, Technical Report MIT/LCS/TR-286, Laboratory for Computer Science, Massachusetts Institute of Technology, Cambridge, MA, January, 1983.

[40] J. Gray, R. Lorie, A. Putzulo, and J. Traiger. Granularity of locks and degrees of consistency in a shared database. Technical Report RJ1654, IBM, San Jose, CA, September 1975.

[41] J. Gray, R. Lorie, A. Putzulo, and J. Traiger. The recovery manager of the System R database manager. *ACM Computing Surveys*, 13(2):223–242, June 1981.

[42] J. Gray and A. Reuter. *Transaction Processing: Techniques and Concepts*. Morgan Kaufmann, San Mateo, CA, 1992.

[43] T. Hadzilacos and V. Hadzilacos. Transaction synchronization in object bases. *Journal of Computer and System Sciences*, 43(1):2–24, August 1991.

[44] I. Hayes. *Specification Case Studies*. Prentice-Hall International, Englewood Cliffs, NJ, 1987.

[45] M. Hennessy. *Algebraic Theory of Processes*. MIT Press, Cambridge, MA, 1988.

[46] M. Herlihy, N. Lynch, M. Merritt, and W. Weihl. On the correctness of orphan elimination algorithms. *Journal of the ACM*, 39(4):881–930, October 1992. Also appeared in *Proc. of 17th IEEE Symp. on Fault-Tolerant Computing*, pages 8–13, July 1987.

[47] M. P. Herlihy. *Replication Methods for Abstract Data Types*. PhD thesis, Massachusetts Institute of Technology, Cambridge, MA, May 1984. Also, Technical Report MIT/LCS/TR-319, Laboratory for Computer Science, Massachusetts Institute of Technology, Cambridge, MA, May 1984.

[48] M. P. Herlihy. A quorum-consensus replication method for abstract data types. *ACM Transactions on Computer Systems*, 4(1):32–53, February 1986.

[49] M. P. Herlihy. Extending multiversion time-stamping protocols to exploit type information. *IEEE Transactions On Computers*, C-36(4), April 1987.

[50] M. P. Herlihy. Apologizing versus asking permission: Optimistic concurrency control for abstract data types. *ACM Transactions on Database Systems*, 15(1):96–124, March 1990.

[51] M. P. Herlihy and M. McKendry. Timestamp-based orphan elimination. *IEEE Transactions on Software Engineering*, 15(7):825–831, July 1989.

[52] M. P. Herlihy and W. E. Weihl. Hybrid concurrency control for abstract data types. *Journal of Computer and System Sciences*, 43(1):25–61, August 1991.

[53] M. P. Herlihy and J. M. Wing. Linearizability: A correctness condition for concurrent objects. *ACM Transactions on Programming Languages and Systems*, 12(3):463–492, July 1990.

[54] C. A. R. Hoare. *Communicating Sequential Processes*. Prentice-Hall International, Englewood Cliffs, NJ, 1985.

[55] G. Holzmann. *Design and Validation of Computer Protocols*. Prentice-Hall Software Series, Englewood Cliffs, NJ, 1991.

[56] J. Hopcroft and J. Ullman. *Introduction to Automata Theory, Languages and Computation*. Addison-Wesley, Reading, MA, 1979.

[57] B. Jonsson. *Compositional Verification of Distributed Systems*. PhD thesis, Uppsala University, Uppsala, Sweden, 1987.

[58] H. F. Korth. Locking primitives in a database system. *Journal of the ACM*, 30(1), January 1983.

[59] H. F. Korth, E. Levy, and A. Silberschatz. A formal approach to recovery by compensating transactions. In *Proceedings of 16th International Conference on Very Large Data Bases*, pages 95–106, August 1990.

[60] H. F. Korth and G. D. Speegle. Formal model of correctness without serializability. In *Proceedings of the 1988 ACM SIGMOD International Conference on the Management of Data*, pages 379–386, June 1988.

[61] H. Kung and J. Robinson. On optimistic methods for concurrency control. *ACM Transactions on Database Systems*, 6(2):213–226, June 1981.

[62] R. Kurki-Suonio. Operational specification with joint actions: serializable databases. *Distributed Computing*, 6(1):19–38, July 1992.

[63] S. S. Lam and A. U. Shankar. A relational notation for state transition systems. *IEEE Transactions on Software Engineering*, 16(7):755–775, July 1990.

[64] S. S. Lam and A. U. Shankar. Specifying modules to satisfy interfaces: a state transition system approach. *Distributed Computing*, 6(1):39–64, July 1992.

[65] L. Lamport. Time, clocks and the ordering of events in a distributed system. *Communications of the ACM*, 21(7):558–565, July 1978.

[66] L. Lamport. How to make a multiprocessor that correctly executes multiprocess programs. *IEEE Transactions on Computers*, C-28(9):690–691, September 1979.

[67] L. Lamport. On interprocess communication, parts I and II. *Distributed Computing*, 1(1):77–101, 1986.

[68] L. Lamport. A simple approach to specifying concurrent systems. *Communications of the ACM*, 32(1):32–45, January 1989.

[69] L. Lamport. Critique of the Lake Arrowhead three. *Distributed Computing*, 6(1):65–71, July 1992.

[70] B. Lampson, M. Paul, and H. Seigert. *Distributed Systems: Architecture and Implementation (An Advanced Course)*. Springer-Verlag, New York, NY, 1981.

[71] J. Lee and A. Fekete. Multi-granularity locking for nested transactions. In *Proceedings of 3rd Biannual Symposium on Mathematical Fundamentals of Database and Knowledge Base Systems: Lecture Notes in Computer Science 495*, pages 160–172. Springer-Verlag, New York, NY, May 1991.

[72] J. Lee and A. Fekete. Proof of a concurrency control algorithm using a possibilities mapping. In *Proceedings of 1st Australian Database Research Conference*, pages 185–194, February 1990.

[73] J. Lee and A. Fekete. Predicate locking for nested transaction systems. In *Proceedings of 3rd Australian Database Research Conference*, pages 217–231, February 1992.

[74] W. Lin and J. Nolte. Basic timestamp, multiple version timestamp and two-phase locking. In *Proceedings of 9th International Conference on Very Large Data Bases*, pages 109–119, August 1983.

[75] B. Liskov. Distributed computing in Argus. *Communications of ACM*, 31(3):300–312, March 1988.

[76] B. Liskov, D. Curtis, P. Johnson, and R. Scheifler. Implementation of Argus. In *Proceedings of 11th ACM Symposium on Operating Systems Principles*, pages 111–122, November 1987.

[77] B. Liskov, R. Scheifler, E. F. Walker, and W. E. Weihl. Orphan detection. In *Proceedings of 17th International Symposium on Fault-Tolerant Computing*, pages 2–7. IEEE, July 1987.

[78] D. Lomet. MLR: A recovery method for multi-level systems. In *Proceedings of the 1992 ACM SIGMOD International Conference on the Management of Data*, pages 185–194, June 1992.

[79] N. Lynch. Concurrency control for resilient nested transactions. In P. C. Kanellakis and F. P. Preparata, editors, *Advances in Computing Research: A Research Annual*, volume 3, pages 335–373. JAI Press, Greenwich, CT, 1986.

[80] N. Lynch and M. Merritt. Introduction to the theory of nested transactions. *Theoretical Computer Science*, 62:123–185, December 1988. Also, in *International Conference on Database Theory*, pages 278–305, September 1986; expanded version in MIT/LCS/TR-367, Laboratory for Computer Science, Massachusetts Institute of Technology, Cambridge, MA, July 1986.

[81] N. Lynch, M. Merritt, W. E. Weihl, and A. Fekete. A theory of atomic transactions. In *Proceedings of 2nd International Conference on Database Theory: Lecture Notes in Computer Science 326*, pages 41–71. Springer-Verlag, Berlin, Germany, 1988.

[82] N. Lynch and M. Tuttle. Hierarchical correctness proofs for distributed algorithms. In *Proceedings of 6th ACM Symposium on Principles of Distributed Computation*, pages 137–151, August 1987. Expanded version available as Technical Report MIT/LCS/TR-387, Laboratory for Computer Science, Massachusetts Institute of Technology, Cambridge, MA, April 1987.

[83] N. Lynch and M. Tuttle. An introduction to input/output automata. *CWI-Quarterly*, 2(3):219–246, September 1989. Also, in Technical Memo MIT/LCS/TM-373, Laboratory for Computer Science, Massachusetts Institute of Technology, Cambridge, MA, November 1988.

[84] Z. Manna and A. Pnueli. *The Temporal Logic of Reactive Systems*. Springer-Verlag, New York, NY, 1991.

[85] S. Markowitz. Central-server based orphan detection for Argus. Technical Report MIT/LCS/TR-485, Laboratory for Computer Science, Massachusetts Institute of Technology, Cambridge, MA, May 1990.

[86] S. Mehrota, R. Rastogi, Y. Breitbart, H. F. Korth, and A. Silberschatz. The concurrency control problem in multidatabases: Characteristics and solutions. In *Proceedings of the 1992 ACM SIGMOD International Conference on the Management of Data*, pages 288–297, June 1992.

[87] R. Milner. *Communication and Concurrency*. Prentice-Hall International, Englewood Cliffs, NJ, 1989.

[88] C. Mohan and Levine F. ARIES/IM: An efficient and high-concurrency index management method using write-ahead logging. In *Proceedings of the 1992 ACM SIGMOD International Conference on the Management of Data*, pages 371–380, June 1992.

[89] C. Mohan, D. Haderle, B. Lindsay, H. Pirahesh, and P. Schwarz. ARIES: A transaction recovery method supporting fine-grained locking and partial rollbacks using write-ahead logging. *Transactions on Database Systems*, 17(1):94–162, March 1992.

[90] C. Mohan, H. Pirahesh, and R. Lorie. Efficient and flexible methods for transient versioning of records to avoid locking by read-only transactions. In *Proceedings of the 1992 ACM SIGMOD International Conference on the Management of Data*, pages 124–133, June 1992.

[91] J. E. B. Moss. *Nested Transactions: An Approach to Reliable Distributed Computing*. PhD thesis, Massachusetts Institute of Technology, Cambridge, MA, 1981. Also, Technical Report MIT/LCS/TR-260, Laboratory for Computer Science, Massachusetts Institute of Technology, Cambridge, MA, April 1981. Also, published by MIT Press, Cambridge, MA, March 1985.

[92] J. E. B. Moss, N. Griffeth, and M. Graham. Abstraction in concurrency control and recovery management(revised). Technical report, University of Massachusetts at Amherst, May 1986. COINS Technical Report 86-20.

[93] B. J. Nelson. *Remote procedure call*. PhD thesis, Carnegie-Mellon University Department of Computer Science, Pittsburgh, PA, May 1981. Also, Technical Report CMU-CS-81-119.

[94] T. Nguyen. Performance measurements of orphan detection in the Argus system. Master's thesis, Massachusetts Institute of Technology, Cambridge, MA, June 1988.

[95] B. Oki. Viewstamped replication: A general primary copy method to support highly available distributed systems. In *Proceedings of ACM Symposium on Principles of Distributed Computing*, pages 8–17, August 1988.

[96] B. Oki. *Viewstamped Replication for Highly Available Distributed Systems.* PhD thesis, Massachusetts Institute of Technology, Cambridge, MA, 1988. Also, Technical Report MIT/LCS/TR-423, Laboratory for Computer Science, Massachusetts Institute of Technology, Cambridge, MA, August 1988.

[97] P. E. O'Neil. The escrow transactional method. *ACM Transactions on Database Systems*, 11(4):405–430, December 1986.

[98] C. H. Papadimitriou. The serializability of concurrent database updates. *Journal of the ACM*, 26(4):631–653, October 1979.

[99] C. H. Papadimitriou. *The Theory of Concurrency Control.* Computer Science Press, New York, NY, 1986.

[100] S. Perl. *Distributed Commit Protocols for Nested Atomic Actions.* PhD thesis, Massachusetts Institute of Technology, Cambridge, MA, November 1988. Also, Technical Report MIT/LCS/TR-431, Laboratory for Computer Science, Massachusetts Institute of Technology, Cambridge, MA, November 1988.

[101] C. Pu. Superdatabases for composition of heterogenous databases. In *Proceedings of 4th International Conference on Data Engineering*, pages 548–555, February 1988.

[102] D. Reed. Implementing atomic actions on decentralized data. *ACM Transactions on Computer Systems*, 1(1):3–23, February 1983.

[103] D. P. Reed. *Naming and Synchronization in a Decentralized Computer System.* PhD thesis, Massachusetts Institute of Technology, 1978. Also, Technical Report MIT/LCS/TR-205, Laboratory for Computer Science, Massachusetts Institute of Technology, Cambridge, MA, October 1978.

[104] D. J. Rosenkrantz, P. M. Lewis, and R. E. Stearns. System level concurrency control for distributed database systems. *ACM Transactions on Database Systems*, 3(2):178–198, June 1978.

[105] Y. Sagiv. Concurrent operations on B*-trees with overtaking. *Journal of Computer and System Sciences*, 33(2):275–296, October 1986.

[106] P. Schwarz and A. Z. Spector. Synchronizing shared abstract types. *ACM Transactions on Computer Systems*, 2(3):223–250, August 1984.

[107] D. Shasha and N. Goodman. Concurrent search structures. *Transactions on Database Systems*, 13(1):53–90, March 1988.

[108] M. Stonebraker (ed). *Readings in Database Systems*. Morgan Kaufmann, San Mateo, CA, 1988.

[109] Y. Tay, N. Goodman, and R. Suri. Locking performance in centralized databases. *Transactions on Database Systems*, 10(4):415–462, December 1985.

[110] R. Thomas. A majority consensus apprach to concurrency control for multiple copy databases. *ACM Transactions on Database Systems*, 4(2):180–209, June 1979.

[111] A. Thomasian and E. Rahm. A new distributed optimistic concurrency control algorithm and a comparison of its performance with two-phase locking. In *Proceedings of 10th International Conference on Distributed Computing Systems*, pages 294–301, May 1990.

[112] E. Walker. Orphan detection in the Argus system. Technical Report MIT/LCS/TR-326, Laboratory for Computer Science, Massachusetts Institute of Technology, Cambridge, MA, May 1984.

[113] W. E. Weihl. *Specification and Implementation of Atomic Data Types*. PhD thesis, Massachusetts Institute of Technology, Cambridge, MA, 1984. Also, Technical Report MIT/LCS/TR-314, Laboratory for Computer Science, Massachusetts Institute of Technology, Cambridge, MA, March 1984.

[114] W. E. Weihl. Distributed version management for read-only actions. *IEEE Transactions on Software Engineering*, SE-13(1):55–64, January 1987.

[115] W. E. Weihl. Commutativity-based concurrency control for abstract data types. *IEEE Transactions on Computers*, 37(12):1488–1505, December 1988.

[116] W. E. Weihl. The impact of recovery on concurrency control. In *Proceedings of 8th ACM Symposium on Principles of Database Systems*, pages 259–269, March 1989.

[117] W. E. Weihl. Local atomicity properties: modular concurrency control for abstract data types. *ACM Transactions on Programming Languages and Systems*, 11(2):249–282, April 1989.

[118] G. Weikum. A theoretical foundation of multi-level concurrency control. In *Proceedings of 5th ACM Symposium on Principles of Database Systems*, pages 31–42, March 1986.

[119] G. Weikum. Principles and realization strategies of multi-level transaction management. *Transactions on Database Systems*, 16(1):132–180, March 1991.

[120] J. Welch, L. Lamport, and N. Lynch. A lattice-structured proof of a minimum spanning tree algorithm. In *Proceedings of 7th ACM Symposium on Principles of Distributed Computation*, pages 28–43, August 1988.

[121] M. Yannakakis. Serializability by locking. *Journal of the ACM*, 31(2):227–244, April 1984.

INDEX